Junot Díaz and the De

Junot Díaz

and the Decolonial Imagination

MONICA HANNA,
JENNIFER HARFORD VARGAS,
and JOSÉ DAVID SALDÍVAR, Editors

DUKE UNIVERSITY PRESS . . . DURHAM AND LONDON . . . 2016

© 2016 Duke University Press
All rights reserved
Printed and bound by CPI Group (UK) Ltd, Croydon, CR0 4YY
Designed by Natalie F. Smith
Typeset in Quadraat Pro by Westchester Publishing Services

Library of Congress Cataloging-in-Publication Data
Junot Díaz and the decolonial imagination / edited by Monica Hanna,
Jennifer Harford Vargas, and José David Saldívar.
pages cm
Includes bibliographical references and index.
ISBN 978-0-8223-6024-7 (hardcover : alk. paper)
ISBN 978-0-8223-6033-9 (pbk. : alk. paper)
ISBN 978-0-8223-7476-3 (e-book)
1. Díaz, Junot, [date]—Criticism and interpretation. 2. Decolonization
in literature. I. Hanna, Monica, editor. II. Harford Vargas, Jennifer,
[date] editor. III. Saldívar, José David, editor.
PS3554.I259Z975 2016
813'.54—dc23
2015026284

Cover art: Line drawing of Junot Díaz by Jaime Hernandez. Illustration coloring and background art by Andrew H. Leung.

Portions of Chapter 6 were published in *Neocolonialism and Cultural Memory: Narrative in Chicana/o and Latina/o Fiction*. Used with permission of the University of Illinois Press. Chapter 8 was published in an earlier form in MELUS: *Multi-Ethnic Literature of the United States* 39, no. 3 (fall 2014): 8–30. Chapter 9 was published, in a slightly modified version, in *The Social Imperative: Race, Close Reading, and Contemporary Literary Criticism* by Paula Moya, © 2016 by the Board of Trustees of the Leland Stanford Jr. University. All Rights reserved. Used with the permission of Stanford University Press; www.sup .org. Chapter 15 was originally published in *The Boston Review*, June 26, 2012. Reprinted with permission.

Contents

Acknowledgments

The intellectual framework for this book had its genesis in "Junot Díaz: A Symposium," which we hosted at Stanford University on May 18 and 19, 2012. We are very thankful for the broad support we received from the Stanford community. Specifically we would like to thank the following centers, departments, and programs for their contributions: African and African American Studies; American Studies; Anthropology; Asian American Studies; Center for Comparative Studies in Race and Ethnicity; Center for Latin American Studies; El Centro Chicano; Chicano/a Studies; The Clayman Institute for Gender Research; Comparative Literature; Creative Writing; Division of Literatures, Cultures, and Languages; English; French and Italian; German; Iberian and Latin American Cultures; Sociology; Modern Thought and Literature; Native American Studies; Stanford Humanities Center; and Taube Center for Jewish Studies. We would also like to thank the Anne and Loren Kieve Endowment for its support in sponsoring Junot Díaz's Distinguished Kieve Lecture at our symposium, as well as the Offices of the Provost and the Vice Provost for Graduate Education for their support. We are particularly grateful to Guadalupe Carrillo, Edrik López, Elena Machado Sáez, Enmanuel Martínez, Ernesto Javier Martínez, and John "Rio" Riofrio for their intellectual contributions to this project. We would also like to express our appreciation to Sarah Gamino, Teresa Jimenez, and

Kyle Williams for their logistical assistance with the symposium. Finally, we are deeply indebted to Ken Wissoker and the editorial staff at Duke University Press who made publishing this book a wonderful experience, and to the anonymous reviewers who read the manuscript with great care and offered many important suggestions for revision.

Introduction.
Junot Díaz and the Decolonial Imagination From Island to Empire

Monica Hanna, Jennifer Harford Vargas, and José David Saldívar

Junot Díaz's work reflects a turn in American letters toward a hemispheric and planetary literature and culture. Furthermore, the immense acclaim Díaz has achieved marks a dramatic change in the larger cultural sphere around the place of Latinos/as in the literary canons of the United States, the Caribbean, and Latin America. This book offers the first collective reading of Junot Díaz for our time and does so by analyzing his texts through a wide range of lenses, including narrative, queer, racial, gender, disability, and decolonial theory. The authors attend equally to the power of Díaz's mesmerizing prose and to current theoretical debates that call our planet's coloniality of power into question. Drawing on Latino/a literary, cultural, and critical theory, the combined labor of the chapters uncovers how Junot Díaz's twinned American worlds of New Jersey and the Dominican Republic are constituted by a set of reciprocating colonial complicities between the United States and the Greater Antilles in the world-system. Although Díaz's first three books have already led to his being canonized as a master of contemporary literature, the creative and critical project of what we call "becoming Junot Díaz" is still taking place.

Becoming Junot Díaz

Every *historia* has a beginning, and this is Junot Díaz's. He was born in Santo Domingo, Dominican Republic, on December 31, 1968, and was raised there until he was six years old. He, his mother Virtudes, and his siblings emigrated from the Dominican Republic in 1974 to Parlin, New Jersey. Joining Díaz's father, Ramón, who had moved to New Jersey years before, the diasporic family settled in a working-class neighborhood. His mother worked on an assembly line and his father drove a forklift. Shifting worlds from an island in the Global South to the empire of the Global North was akin to living out a science fiction time travelling text, a cultural and linguistic shock of truly fantastical dimensions. As a young, poor Afro-Dominican, Díaz's only access to the world outside his Parlin neighborhood was through television, film, and literature. He attended Madison Park Elementary School and became an inveterate reader of such popular writers as Ray Bradbury, Tom Swift, J. R. R. Tolkien, and later Stephen King. Aptly, he learned to read in English by poring over a novel of colonial revenge, the children's illustrated version of Sir Arthur Conan Doyle's *The Sign of the Four*. At eleven, Díaz started working his first job, a paper route in Parlin, so that he could pay for tickets to Hollywood movies, which became his "first narrative love."[1] From 1974 to 1989, Díaz and his family lived in Parlin's London Terrace apartments, an industrial red-orange-brick building complex. New Jersey's mean streets, its malls, and monumental garbage and toxic landfills were Díaz's first glimpse into the underside of Nuestra América.

The American cities from the Global South and Global North in which Díaz grew up, Santo Domingo and Parlin, shaped his worldview and his decolonial imagination. As early as the 1990s, when he was an unpublished graduate student at Cornell University, he conceived that his unfolding fictions would come together in the American cosmos of New Jersey and the Dominican Republic. The majority of his fiction is set in the working-class suburbs of New Jersey, with the island as a haunting background presence; several of the stories from *Drown* (1996) and *This Is How You Lose Her* (2012), as well as half of his first novel, *The Brief Wondrous Life of Oscar Wao* (2007), take place on the island of the Dominican Republic. Furthermore, his language testifies to the presence of these dual locations; his creative work is marked by a creolized vernacular, equal parts urban and island slang, that moves seamlessly between English and Spanish.

After graduating from Cedar Ridge High School in Old Bridge, New Jersey, in 1987, Díaz attended Kean College in Union, New Jersey, for a year before transferring to Rutgers, the State University of New Jersey, where he completed his BA degree in English and History in 1992. At Rutgers, Díaz read for the first time the two feminist writers of color who inspired him to become a writer: Toni Morrison and Sandra Cisneros. Díaz confessed to Toni Morrison while interviewing her that when he read her novel *Song of Solomon* his first semester at Rutgers, "the axis of [his] world shifted and it has never returned."[2] These women of color gave him a formative education in the aesthetics of decolonization.

Díaz went on to pursue a Master of Fine Arts in creative writing at Cornell University, where he fashioned a thesis titled "Negocios" (1995), developed an activist consciousness, and began crafting a racialized (decolonial) aesthetic. "Negocios" is a gritty realist and postminimalist work comprising seven stories equally set in Santo Domingo and Parlin that introduces his central character and principal narrator, Yunior de las Casas, who has appeared in all of his subsequent work.[3] While writing his MFA thesis, Díaz published his first story, "Ysrael" (1995), in *Story* magazine. Another short story, "How to Date a Brown Girl (Black Girl, White Girl, or Halfie)" (1995), was published in *The New Yorker* under the editorship of Bill Buford, which paved the way for Díaz to acquire his literary agent, Julie Grau, and to publish his first book, *Drown* (1996). These interconnected stories center on the experiences of diasporic Dominicano characters and are relayed in powerful, creatively wrought Dominican and Afro-Latino vernaculars. *Drown* introduced some of Díaz's enduring preoccupations with Afro-Latinidad, hypermasculinity, and the ravages of internalized racism and transnational poverty on individuals, families, and communities.[4] Published to critical acclaim, this was a stunning beginning for an Afro-Dominican writer in his midtwenties.

Ten years passed before Díaz's second book and first novel, *The Brief Wondrous Life of Oscar Wao* (2007), was published. After winning a Guggenheim Fellowship in 1999, Díaz spent a year living in Mexico City trying to write a novel and to improve his Spanish. He lived next door to his Guatemalan American friend and fellow novelist Francisco Goldman. One night after carousing through the streets of Mexico City with Goldman, Díaz picked up a copy of Oscar Wilde's *The Importance of Being Earnest* and said Oscar Wilde's name in "Dominican": Oscar Wao. It was a "quick joke," Díaz notes, but he suddenly had a "vision of a poor, doomed ghetto nerd" and, inspired by this Mexico City epiphany, he quickly dashed off the first part of what would become the novel.[5]

The Brief Wondrous Life of Oscar Wao interweaves urban American vernaculars and idiolects with references to speculative realism, science fiction, fantasy, comic books, role-playing games, the anarchy of imperial histories, and Caribbean literary and cultural theory. Díaz strategically transculturates Anglo-American, Latino/a, and Latin American discourses to narrate the traumas of coloniality, dictatorship, and diaspora, all while rendering the heartbreaking beauty of Afro-Latinidad. The novel won the Pulitzer Prize in 2008, along with many other awards. One can count on two hands the number of first-time novelists like Junot Díaz who have won the coveted prize, and Díaz was only the second Latino to win a Pulitzer Prize for Fiction. In 2007, Díaz was also named to the "Bogotá 39"—a list of the top thirty-nine contemporary Latin American authors under the age of thirty-nine. Díaz thus entered the broader public consciousness, giving Latino/a fiction an unprecedented visibility in the Américas and across the planet. In other words, when Junot Díaz's The Brief Wondrous Life of Oscar Wao was published in 2007, the landscapes of American literature and culture changed forever.[6]

Five years later he published a new short story cycle, This Is How You Lose Her (2012), as well as a section of a new novel in progress in The New Yorker, a racial apocalyptic zombie story set in the Dominican Republic and Haiti entitled "Monstro" (2012). This Is How You Lose Her generated incredible buzz, garnering a National Book Award shortlisting, and Díaz won the prestigious MacArthur Fellowship that same year. With this most recent book, Díaz again transformed the genre of the short story cycle by mixing the locus of enunciation between first-, second-, and third-person narratological perspectives, generating a complex and sustained critique of the negative impact of racism, white supremacy, machismo, and poverty on intimacy, affect, and love, in order to decolonize not only the mind but also the heart.

While Díaz has transformed the field of American letters, he has also established himself as a prominent Latino public intellectual. The Rudge and Nancy Allen Professor of Writing at MIT, Díaz is a dynamic public speaker and pedagogue. He has given countless interviews and readings, and has been invited to lecture in diverse venues around the world, ranging from prestigious universities, conferences, and major urban centers to local bookstores and cultural community centers. He has been featured in a wide range of magazines, news media, and blogs. Díaz's presence in the popular and cultural spheres has given Latino fiction unparalleled exposure. Moreover, Díaz uses the media attention to help shape a much-needed popular critical discourse about coloniality and the intersections of race, class, heteropatriarchy, and imperialism. At the same time, he is activist-oriented and committed to using his privilege to help marginalized communities and people of color access education. For example, he is a cofounder of Voices of Our Nation Arts Foundation, which is dedicated to training emerging writers of color. He is a member of the board of advisers for Freedom University, which is dedicated to providing college courses to undocumented students. He is the honorary Chairman of the DREAM Project, which is dedicated to increasing educational access in the Dominican Republic. Junot Díaz is a politically engaged public intellectual and scholarly creative writer in the tradition of other major U.S. and Latin American writer-scholars of color like Toni Morrison and Gabriel García Márquez. Like his predecessors, Díaz draws upon his local and transnational literary and historical inheritances but designs his fiction with lineaments of his own shaping.

Tracing the becoming of Junot Díaz, the chapters in this book take us from Díaz's activist years at Cornell in the 1990s to his rapid success with the publications of Drown, The Brief Wondrous Life of Oscar Wao, This Is How You Lose Her, and "Monstro," alongside his current activism. Employing a range of disciplinary field-imaginaries, the chapters situate and examine Díaz's work by addressing the significance of his literary output as well as his politically engaged public intellectual work, challenging us to see them as mutually imbricated. In other words, these chapters reveal that what makes Díaz such a crucial figure in our contemporary moment is his commitment to aesthetic projects that are deeply political in the most expansive sense of the word. The scholars whose work is included in this book are established and emerging figures in the field of U.S. Latino/a studies, coming from both the east and west coasts of the United States. With backgrounds in literary studies and the social sciences, their scholarship has been shaped by the field-imaginaries of Caribbean studies, Chicano/a studies, African diaspora studies, border studies, cultural studies, gender studies, queer studies, and disability studies. As each chapter in this book unpacks from a different angle Díaz's intersectional critique of hierarchies of power, we see what is at the center of his fiction and his work as a public intellectual. The collective achievement of the chapters thereby reveals the multiple axes of Díaz's decolonial aesthetic and activist projects, while at the same time providing a window onto the critical terrain of contemporary Latino/a cultural politics.

Junot Díaz's Decolonial Turn

The chapters in this book collectively sketch out the contours of what we call the decolonial imagination. We use the decolonial imagination as a framework for studying the literary, cultural, and political work that Junot Díaz's fictional, intellectual, and activist projects accomplish. As part of what the Puerto Rican scholar Nelson Maldonado-Torres has called the "decolonial turn," our book contributes to the emergent scholarship on de-colonial formations and to the cross-genealogical, multidisciplinary, and transnational mappings of that turn.[7] More specifically, it is dedicated to conceptualizing the decolonial imagination as a critical tool for examining, challenging, and countering the lasting effects of colonial domination in the New World Américas.

Díaz's decolonial imagination entails a critique of the coloniality of power matrix that the Iberians and Admiral Columbus brought with them when they first landed on Hispaniola (now Haiti and the Dominican Republic) and helped institute the oldest colonial system of domination in the West. Objects of literary and cultural study that once called for a postcolonial frame of analyses—studies that chiefly focused on nineteenth-century and twentieth-century colonization and decolonization practices in Asia, Africa, and the Middle East—now demand a focus on colonization and decolonization in the New World Américas, which originated centuries earlier in the transoceanic adventures of the Spanish colonialists from which Junot Díaz's concept of the fukú americanus (or "the Curse and Doom of the New World") and Aníbal Quijano's theory of coloniality were born. It is, of course, not easy to explore the idea of Díaz's island of the Dominican Republic outside of the celebratory rhetoric of Columbus's "discovery" and the subsequent arrival of modernity in the Américas, and to fully enter into the logic of the coloniality of power that his novel rigorously unravels and deconstructs. Díaz's fiction works through the four interlinked domains of the human experience that the Peruvian sociologist Aníbal Quijano theorized as the coloniality of power matrix in the New World Américas: the appropriation of land, the exploitation of labor, and the control of finance by the Iberians; the control of authority; the control of gender, ethnicity, and race through the Iberian classification and reclassification of the planet's population; and the control of subjectivity and knowledge through an epistemological perspective from which the Iberians articulated the meaning and profile of the matrix of power that placed them at the top of the hierarchy and indigenous and African subjectivities and epistemologies at the very bottom. This logic of coloniality—or the conflictual logic, sensibilities, and beliefs of what Díaz dubs in his novel the fukú americanus—is the key historical chronotope where the coloniality of power in the Américas can be located and from which it can be dismantled. While the fukú's origins are in 1492, the fukú was spectacularly visible under the U.S.-supported Trujillo dictatorship from the 1930s to the 1960s, it was ever-present in the haunting afterlife of the Trujillato on the island and in the 1980s Reagan-era United States of Oscar's and Lola's youth, and it still persists today. To enter into the logic of the coloniality of power matrix from the decolonial imagination in Díaz's texts means to think from the perspective of his subjugated de León and Cabral characters and their own traumatic personal and transgenerational memories of rape, torture, violence, and domination that his novel renders visible and central.[8] In other words, when we consider Díaz's New World Américas from the perspectives of his characters and let their decolonial perspectives take center stage, another historia becomes powerfully apparent in his text.[9]

In a cogent précis of the novel's decolonial scale that he outlined to Paula M. L. Moya (see "Junot Díaz's Search for Decolonial Aesthetics and Love," chapter 12 in this book), Díaz adopts the key theoretical assumptions from Quijano's work on the coloniality of power matrix: "In *Oscar Wao* we have a family that has fled, half-destroyed, from one of the rape incubators of the New World, and they are trying to find love. . . . The kind of love I was interested in, that my characters long for intuitively, is the only kind of love that could liberate them from the horrible legacy of colonial violence." Díaz is not making an exceptionalist claim about the coloniality of power in the New World Américas in his novel but rather is attempting to set the stage for his artistic crafting of the decolonial imagination in order to critique the colonial difference and the "horrible legacy of colonial violence" in the Dominican Republic and the New World Américas. Díaz himself has explained (and we elaborate more later) that Quijano's work on the coloniality of power matrix allowed him to see the "secret, animating force that gives all things in fantasy life," which, in turn, helped Díaz to conjure the matrix of coloniality as "the subconscious of the speculative genres" he evokes throughout *The Brief Wondrous Life of Oscar Wao*. Moreover, we suggest, along with many of the chapters in this book, that engaging with Díaz's decolonial imagination entails a critique of the epistemic history of the violence of Eurocentrism and a critique of the type of knowledge that contributed to the legitimation of Spain's colonial domination and pretenses of universal validation, at the same time that it strives to imagine another world, another way of being, another way of loving.

Díaz's fiction, thus envisaged, is a forerunner in creating, articulating, and shaping the decolonial imagination in contemporary American literature. He gives all of his fictional texts a projected futurity for a decolonial world beyond his texts. Since the colonization of the New World Américas consisted in the first place, as Quijano has demonstrated, of a colonization of "the imaginary of dominated people" and coloniality acted "within that very imaginary," the coloniality of power imposed itself on all of the "ways of knowing, producing knowledge, images, and system of images, symbols [and] modes of signification" in the New World Américas.[10] As Díaz's novel makes clear, particularly through the concept of the fukú americanus, the uninterrupted practice of colonialism in the Dominican Republic and the Américas not only entailed the subjugation of the inhabitants of the island from the conquest, through the U.S.-supported Trujillo dictatorship, into the contemporary lives of diasporic Dominicans; it also changed their knowledge of their world and forced them to adopt the mystified cognitive horizon of coloniality as their worldview. The decolonial imagination is a productive force through which Díaz's characters manage, evaluate, and challenge the colonial difference.[11] The process of decolonization thus compels us to grapple with literary aesthetics as a conceptual problem because dismantling ingrained modern and colonial structures of thought and modes of being must occur at the creative and cultural level of the imagination.

The decolonial imagination in Díaz's texts, we suggest, is as an act of social and cultural criticism, since it is through his imagination as a creative writer that he is able to envision and articulate alternatives to the logics of coloniality. Our use of the term *decolonial imagination* has been influenced by a range of scholars and activists who have variously invoked the imagination—through concepts such as the social imagination, the radical imagination, and the diasporic imagination—as a critical faculty for envisioning into existence alternative worlds that have not yet been recognized or conjured. With the anthropologist Arjun Appadurai, we are interested in "the work of the imagination" and how it can serve as "a space of contestation in which individuals and groups seek to annex the global into their own practices of the modern" and, we would add, into their own practices of decolonization.[12] The imagination in this context engenders new possibilities for political praxis and social movements. For Appadurai, there is a "projective sense" of the imagination—"the sense of being a prelude to some sort of expression, whether aesthetic or otherwise"—and this enables it to function as a "staging ground for action."[13] The central feature of the decolonial imagination is its projective power, because it is oriented toward transformation, collective action, and the restless invocation of new futurities. The decolonial imagination envisions a radically different world, a world not structured through dominance but through solidarity. The creative faculty of the decolonial imagination thus conceptualizes a society decolonized of hierarchies of racist and heteronormative gender oppression and subalternization. Díaz's decolonial imagination is real and central to the aspirational politics of his literature and to our collective literary and cultural criticism of it throughout this book.

Díaz's decolonial work illuminates the creative faculty of the imagination, highlighting its powerful and generative capacities both for cultural production and for activist work. Díaz's work as a decolonial writer, cultural critic, and theorist places him in a long tradition of anticolonial Latino/a and Latin American radical intellectuals including the Cuban revolutionary and writer José Martí. In his keynote speech at the "Facing Race" conference in Baltimore on November 29, 2011, for example, Junot Díaz applied Martí's vision of "Nuestra América" to our twenty-first century. He explained: "You need to cultivate the Martí mind—the Martí mind is simply that as much love as I have for my own group I have for every other group. To take possessive investment in each other's struggle, where whatever is happening to the gay community is happening to us, whatever is happening in the Asian community, that's us. Instead of possessive commodified investments in our identities we need to take possessive investments in our other community's struggles."[14] Counter to what the historian George Lipsitz has famously critiqued as the "possessive investment in whiteness" undergirding white supremacy in the United States, Díaz envisions what we call a possessive investment in decolonizing the lives and imaginations of all minority peoples and communities.

It is precisely the duty of the Martí mind to continually expose the distance between idealized perceptions of the United States—as the supposed bastion of freedom, democracy, diversity, and the American Dream of up-ward mobility—and the realities of injustice, inequality, and racial violence within the nation. The literary critic Michael Hames-García illumes how Martí's decolonial vision can guide our scholarly work: "What Martí's essay ['The Truth about the United States'] suggests to us is that, instead of a one-sided, celebratory vision of the rise of the nation or a distortion of the reality of diverse cultures in unequal conflict, cultural critics should base the study of 'American literature' on a more accurate, less celebratory vision. Martí's perspective on U.S. society enabled him to eventually come to see the na-tion as first and foremost a site of violence, discord, and social struggle."[15] According to this vision, then, those critics studying "American literature" and those cultural producers working in the Martí mode have a duty to pres-ent an accurate vision of the United States and not to be an accomplice to silence or, worse, unfounded celebration. As Díaz commented to Bill Moyers after the reelection of Barack Obama in 2012, "there is an enormous gap between the way the country presents itself and imagines itself and projects itself and the reality of this country. . . . And listen, this is a country that doesn't like talking about race. I loved how we jumped from, 'we haven't ever talked about race,' to 'now we're postracial.'"[16] Díaz's fiction and his work as a public activist and intellectual intervene in this discourse, expos-ing how the postrace era is a fantasy, given the enduring reality of structural racism in the United States.

Díaz's injunctions about needing to acknowledge and challenge white supremacy in our age of Obama are not merely epistemological pursuits—they are also contingent on engaging in solidarity work, which is particularly relevant in the realm of educational and social justice. For example, when Díaz's book Drown was part of the banned curriculum of Mexican American studies in public high schools in Tucson, Arizona, in 2012, he did not shy away from attacking what he described as "the real beast" looming in the xenophobic mainstream U.S. culture and society. Díaz expounded: "This is covert white supremacy in the guise of educational standard-keeping—nothing more, nothing less. Given the sharp increase of anti-Latino rheto-ric, policies, and crimes in Arizona and the rest of the country, one should not be surprised by this madness and yet one is. The removal of those books before those students' very eyes makes it brutally clear how vulnerable com-munities of color and our children are to this latest eruption of cruel, divi-sive, irrational, fearful, and yes racist politics. Truly infuriating. And more reason to continue to fight for a just society."[17] Díaz challenges us not only to speak out against state-sanctioned racism and educational repression but also, crucially, to actively work to decolonize these structures of power.

In an interview with Stephen Colbert on *The Colbert Report* on March 25, 2013, Díaz brought national attention to Freedom University, an institution of higher education established in Georgia in 2011 by University of Georgia professors after the state barred undocumented youth from attending the top five public universities in Georgia. Extending the work of liberation done by the freedom schools during Civil Rights, which gave alternative, free access to education for African Americans in the South, Freedom University carries the decolonial legacy of civil rights struggles for educational equality into the contemporary moment by providing free college classes regardless of immigration status. As a member of the board of advisers, Díaz describes Freedom University to Colbert, who quips, in typical neoconservative fashion so characteristic of his political satire, that undocumented students are "taking American thoughts and ideas—that's American knowledge." Díaz reframes the discussion:

> Every single immigrant we have, undocumented or documented, is a future American. . . . Every generation of Americans has to answer what we call the Superman question. Superman comes, lands in America, he's illegal. He's one of these kids. He's wrapped up in a red bullfighter's cape, and you've got to decide what we're going to do with Superman. Are we going to give him the boot and say you know what, you're an illegal, you're not an American. Or are we gonna have compassion and say listen, this kid was brought here before he knew; this kid was brought here and he didn't have a say whether he was going to come. But he's living in this country, and I think he is an American. . . . When it comes down to it, we as a country are going to have to decide what we do with the reality on the ground. . . . We've got to extend the franchise, and we've got to start thinking of the country in a way of how do we pull folks together, not how we do attack them and afflict them.[18]

Echoing his comments about how to have a Martí mind, Díaz challenges us to reimagine our community of the nation in a way that enfranchises rather than disenfranchises migrants. Linking up with migrant rights artists who use the images of superheroes—such as Dulce Pinzón's "Superheroes" photograph collection, featuring migrants dressed in superhero costumes while laboring, or Neil Rivas's "Illegal Superheroes" posters, which feature comic book superheroes as "ILLEGAL" and tell the viewer to report them to ICE—Junot Díaz's "Superman question" shifts the discourse around whom we imagine as a citizen.[19]

Crucially, Díaz's critique of our imagined community is not limited to the U.S. nation-state but instead encompasses a hemispheric notion of America. Again insisting on speaking truth to power, Díaz was criticized by Dominican officials after he condemned the Dominican government in the wake of the Constitutional Court's decision to "denationalize" Dominicans of Haitian descent, stripping them of citizenship in the country of their birth. Generating a promigrant, antiracist imagination, Díaz, in collection with other migrant rights and civil rights activist-artists, extends the struggle for social justice in Our America into our contemporary moment.

Díaz's pursuit of a radical educational model is a career-long project; in 1999 he cofounded Voices of Our Nation Arts Foundation (VONA), along with Elmaz Abinader, Victor Díaz, and Diem Jones, in order to offer MFA-quality workshops for writers of color, taught by writers of color. Díaz defines the central problem of our program era as the "MFA vs POC," and the model of VONA differs dramatically from traditional MFA programs like the one at Cornell University that Díaz attended.[20] In bearing witness to his experience, Díaz reveals with honesty the painful alienation he felt in his MFA program because, as he puts it with characteristic bluntness, "That shit was too white."[21] Reinforcing literary historian Mark McGurl's argument that U.S. English departments in general and creative writing programs in particular have exercised a decisive (programmed) influence on postwar U.S. literary production, Díaz explains that in most MFA programs race is not considered a proper subject of "True Literature."[22] Yet, the presumed universality of literature is contingent on a normalized white, straight, able-bodied, male subject position—in other words, notions of universal aesthetics are deeply colonial. Feeling intensely marginalized by the near total silence around race, Díaz almost dropped out of his MFA program because of the "unbearable too-whiteness of [his] workshop," which smothered him and the few other fellow "Calibans" in his workshop.[23] Díaz persisted, however, and found solidarity in the Latino/a student movement on campus—a movement that succeeded in getting the first MFA faculty of color in fiction, the eminent feminist Chicana Helena María Viramontes, hired at Cornell. Though twenty years have passed, unfortunately, little has changed in MFA programs, so Díaz continues to labor to fill this void through VONA's decolonial writing workshops, which have trained over two thousand writers of color. By "creat[ing] in the present a fix to a past that can never be altered"—a past where talented writers of color who were not as lucky as Díaz and did not make it through their MFAs or find publishing outlets and whose words have been lost to the abyss—VONA opens a new futurity for writers of color.[24] Junot Díaz's decolonial imagination exists both in the pages of his fiction as well as in his rallying dictum for more political work in the arts and humanities by and for people of color.

The Corpus of a Writer

The chapters in this book, which individually and collectively unpack Junot Díaz's decolonial activist and aesthetic practice, began to take shape in May 2012, when we organized a two-day scholarly and cultural event, "Junot Díaz: A Symposium," at Stanford University. We designed the symposium around four roundtables, a format we intended to foster the intersubjective process of collaborative knowledge production over the model of panels with individual scholars presenting their expertise. These roundtables were structured to create a critical conversation on Díaz's oeuvre with a great deal of time devoted to group conversation between panelists and the audience. It was an exceptional opportunity, especially since it is rare to have an academic gathering devoted to an individual Latino/a writer.

As part of the two-day symposium, we invited Junot Díaz to give Stanford's Center for Comparative Studies in Race and Ethnicity's annual Anne and Loren Kieve Distinguished Lecture. Stepping away from the podium and speaking without any written notes, Díaz surprised everyone by announcing at the outset, "Guess what? No fucking lecture."[25] Walking to the front of the packed auditorium filled with "lit heads," undergraduates, graduate students, faculty, and scholars attending the symposium, Díaz delivered a brilliant off the cuff discussion on our planetary racial imagination entitled "Dark America." The talk was peppered with references that ranged from the literary and the pop cultural to the political and the theoretical, all imbued with Díaz's unique bilanguaging skills that move between English and Spanish with some occasional Elvish thrown into the mix. Díaz's talk was a performance of his decolonial imagination at work as he unpacked white supremacy and the logic of coloniality in J. R. R. Tolkien's *The Lord of the Rings*, providing a glimpse into the theoretical underpinnings of his aesthetic and activist formation.

In the first half of his dialogic, audience-interactive talk, he rejected the notion that we live in a postrace society in the age of Obama with our first president of color. Rather, we live in a moment when race is not openly acknowledged or discussed, which the literary theorist Stephanie Li calls "signifying without specifying."[26] Díaz implored that we discuss honestly the reality of race and in particular of white supremacy in the United States (and Latin America). His aspiration as a writer is to "figure out a way to represent more honestly the way people variously talk about race, its discourses, its silences, its logics, its reality—that is, figure out a way that the actual material did not endorse that reality—that one could actually represent our insane racial logic without endorsing that insane logic." Unlike J. K. Rowling's witches and wizards (including Harry Potter), he wants us to "not be afraid of saying Voldemort's name." Instead of using implicitly race-free or race-neutral epithets such as "universalism," "colorblindness," and "postrace," Díaz explicitly declared, "I write about race. By extension, I write about white supremacy." "How many books published about racism do not have the term 'white supremacy' in their indexes?" he asked. "The real beast," he added, "is still off the page—invisible, silenced—no one wants to touch it." Díaz, in contrast, continually and explicitly names racism and white supremacy in all of his fiction, interviews, and lectures, and his Kieve lecture at Stanford was no exception. Díaz called out how the hegemonic idea of the United States as a postracial society and culture is a "happy delusion," because "we are as hyper-racial today as we were two hundred years ago," and describing oneself as somehow "beyond race" is as delusional as a man's saying he is not sexist. The coloniality of race and the coloniality of gender's privilege continue to structure and overdetermine our social world, which is why the decolonial imagination is such a necessary critical tool. We must all, people of color as well as white people, work to dismantle white supremacy and internalized racism in order to become more human selves.

In the second half of his talk, Díaz demonstrated how he is a creative intellectual steeped in theory, using the paradigm of the coloniality of power to analyze the intertextual books that loom behind *The Brief Wondrous Life of Oscar Wao*—in particular J. R. R. Tolkien's *The Lord of the Rings*, Richard Wagner's *Das Rheingold*, H. P. Lovecraft's gothic fantasies, and J. K. Rowling's *Harry Potter*. Ever since he was a young, immigrant Afro-Latino boy growing up in the impoverished barrioscapes of New Jersey, Díaz has read Tolkien's *The Lord of the Rings* as primarily centered on race, power, and magic. Díaz is interested in speculative genres because this "nerd stuff" has had an immense significance on our planet's cultural unconscious, building his reading of Tolkien on Victoria Nelson's argument in *The Secret Life of Puppets* that the Enlightenment displaced our impulses for wonder and magic.[27] In the West, the Enlightenment "knocked the shit out of wonder," Díaz explained, and then these very impulses "began to express" themselves in and "find a home" in "our sub-zeitgeist—that is, in all the pop cultural crap that exists in our culture's comics books, role playing games, and movies." By combining Nelson's philosophical ideas about the Enlightenment with the Peruvian historical sociologist Aníbal Quijano's iconic insights about the coloniality of power's planetary genesis in 1492, Díaz theorized that "Quijano's coloniality of power is the secret, animating force that gives all things [power] in fantasy life."

According to Díaz, Tolkien's achievement, "when one thinks about the curses" in his work, "is the totalizing thematization of slavery" and the fact that he took coloniality seriously. The ring in Richard Wagner's opera *Das Rheingold*, Díaz pointed out, "operates like objects in many fairy tales do: they exacerbate whatever your vice is and thus Wagner's *Rheingold* greed exacerbates people's greed." In contradistinction to Wagner's ring "just making stuff go bad for you," in Tolkien's innovative work "the ring produces slavery" and functions, Díaz argued, "racially." Díaz analyzed Tolkien's work in this way: "The fear that everyone has in Middle Earth is not that he is going to be conquered; rather, it is that Lord Sauron is going to enslave him—'a slavery without limits,' Tolkien writes." At the heart of what Díaz called "classic heroic fantasy" is what, after Aníbal Quijano, he called "the coloniality of power." Coloniality—as theorized by Quijano and explained by Díaz in terms of the world of Middle Earth—is "the rendering of the world into races, and in Tolkien, we see that the fantasy world was rendered into races. . . . We certainly know that the terror Tolkien places at the very heart of *The Lord of the Rings* is the terror at the heart of gothic fantasies—all of the forms of repressed and forced enslavement." Explaining the intersection between Tolkien's imaginative work and Quijano's theories, Díaz revealed how decolonial theory shaped his writing of *The Brief Wondrous Life of Oscar Wao*: "For me, what I attempted to do in *Oscar Wao* was to align the nerd stuff with the Dominican coloniality of power because I saw them sharing a discourse or vocabulary." It is Oscar de León's familiarity and his fluency in "nerdishness that allows him to begin to see the stark operations of the coloniality of power working in his mundane and deracinated life in New Jersey."

Inherent in our discussion of Díaz's work and our explication of his "Dark America" Kieve lecture is the premise that writers and other cultural producers can productively participate in the generation of scholarship and the dissemination of knowledge. At all of the symposium roundtables, leaning casually against the wall at the back of the Terrace Room in Stanford's Margaret Jacks Hall, Díaz watched and listened as the panelists analyzed and debated his imaginative work. When the roundtables evolved into animated discussions about the role of humor, jokes, and the racial and political unconscious in his books, Díaz eagerly became an active participant in the symposium, recounting stories about how an idea developed or suggesting theoretical texts to expand our conversations. It is rare indeed to have a living, thinking, and feeling writer in the space of a symposium where panelists are deconstructing and reconstructing his fiction. Thus, having Junot Díaz participate in the event was energizing and memorable for the panelists and the audience. Most importantly, it reflected our collective commitment, Díaz's included, to knowledge production and community building.

While New Criticism had valid reasons for being skeptical of biographical criticism and justifiably warned literary critics against intentional fallacy since authors cannot know all the layers of meaning in their texts, we put together the symposium and this book under the premise that we can productively cultivate decolonial imaginations alongside contemporary creative writers and public intellectuals such as Junot Díaz. Díaz's biography is not something external to the literary and cultural exegesis of his fiction. In our program era, we cannot simply consider a writer's imaginative work without engaging with the writer's biography and intellectual or institutional formation. The philosopher Jacques Derrida once playfully asked: "What was Heidegger's life?" Well, he quipped, "he was born, he thought, and he died."[28] Refuting the privileging of the text to the exclusion of an author's life, we invited Díaz to attend every session of the symposium and engage with us as a writer and scholar. He thus joined us in advocating for the invention of a new literary and cultural approach to the biographical in general and of the biography of the living, thinking, feeling writer in particular. That is, we need to rigorously rethink the borderlines between "corpus" and the "body" (carne, corps), especially when it comes to writers of color.

Shortly after the publication of The Brief Wondrous Life of Oscar Wao, Díaz spelled out the nuanced etymological relationships between carne and carnality in his fiction: "What I do think is very present in the book is the root of the word 'carnality,' which is carne. Bodies are extremely present in this book. Because there is no Caribbean-African diasporic experience that doesn't in some ways revolve around the question of these bodies—these bodies that guaranteed us for a certain period of time that we were going to be slaves, that we were going to breed. And the problematics around those bodies, how those bodies work. Given the history of the Caribbean and the Américas, if you're a person of African descent, that kind of discussion of what role the body plays not only in organizing identity, but in organizing a quest for home—it just couldn't be avoided."[29] We likewise refuse to deny people of color and writers of color the agency to recover their bodies and to use their bodies to engage in decolonial love and to use their pens (or laptops) to craft decolonial aesthetics. These chapters reflect our possessive investment in decolonization in dialogue with the embodied and textual corpus of Junot Díaz.

Contestaciones

We have divided this book into four dialogic sections. The chapters address the separate but interrelated themes explored at the symposium: the place of Díaz's transamerican fiction and essays in twenty-first-century American literatures and cultures; the planetary forces animating his texts; his decolonial aesthetics and the concept of decolonial love; and the resurgent significance of race, Afro-Latinidad, gender, sexuality, ability, poverty, and the coloniality of power as analytic and experiential categories in his fiction and essays. Our aim is for the book's chapters to proceed less as a series of monologues on Díaz's fiction and activism and more as a series of dialogues, debates, and *contestaciones*. To contest is to answer but also to dispute and to imagine alternatives. We thus conceive of our book as engaged in a series of contestaciones, that is, in a series of analyses that draw on both the Spanish and English senses of the interlingual pun.[30]

The chapters collectively, though differently, assess how Díaz's short fiction, novel, essays, interviews, and activist work are changing the landscapes of our American and planetary imaginaries. This book lays out a series of robust analyses of Junot Díaz's work and theoretical articulations of the critical vibrancy of contemporary Latino/a cultural politics. While Latino/a studies has traditionally been divided by West and East Coast scholars focusing, respectively, on the cultural production of Chicanos/as versus the cultural production of Puerto Ricans, Dominican Americans, and Cuban Americans, Junot Díaz's fiction also provides a groundbreaking opportunity for us to bring together scholars from various subsets in Latino/a literary and cultural studies, including Chicano/a, Afro-Latino/a, Caribbean American, and U.S. Central American studies. We have fashioned a book that models how to bring together a trans-Latino/a range of scholars to focus on a single Latino author, and we hope that other writers—such as Sandra Cisneros, Oscar Hijuelos, or Francisco Goldman—will be the focus of other edited books with a similar sustained critical Latino/a studies focus. Moreover, by using Junot Díaz's work as the occasion of analysis, this book uniquely brings together three fields that are seldom engaged in contestaciones and thereby generate what we consider to be a necessary foundational dialogue between Latino/a, Latin American, and American critical studies.

Many of the chapters are transdisciplinary and crosscut field-imaginaries as they address related questions. As a result, the chapters might have been placed in several possible locations and in various ordering configurations. Like Julio Cortázar's novel *Rayuela* (*Hopscotch*), we invite readers to read traditionally, following the chapters in sequential order as we will lay out below, or to read like a *rayuelero* (hopscotcher), skipping between chapters and following the threads of our various intellectual contestaciones.

Part I: Activist Aesthetics

The first section of the book examines the connections between Díaz's literary production and activism. The chapters in this section consider the ways Díaz's accomplishments within the literary sphere relate to his commitment to social justice. This section opens with the anthropologist Arlene Dávila's "Against the 'Discursive Latino': On the Politics and Praxis of Junot Díaz's Latinidad," in which she provides a heretofore unknown genealogy of Díaz's political activism, in particular as a graduate student at Cornell University. The chapter examines two elements that are central to Díaz's interventions into Latino/a cultural politics. The first is Díaz's critical and assertive engagement with Latinidad and how this position impacts his work as well as his political involvements and activism. The second is Díaz's consistent critique of capitalism, which is best appreciated as a critique to the simultaneity of global racism and capitalism. These two strands are informed by Díaz's keen ethnographically realist eye, as both a social observer and active participant of contemporary Latino/a cultural politics. Dávila argues that Díaz has thus crafted a praxis-oriented and antidiscursive Latino/a political project, a project that puts him in conversation with ethnic studies scholars, activists, and grassroots cultural workers, as well as with anyone who is actively involved in creating a progressive political (decolonial) imagination. Dávila's chapter lays the contextual biographical groundwork for many of the other chapters in the book that examine decolonial aesthetics and racial politics in Díaz's fiction.

Dávila's chapter is followed by "The Decolonizer's Guide to Disability," contributed by the literary scholar Julie Avril Minich, in which she argues that the decolonization of disability is a central, though often overlooked, concern in Díaz's work. His characters' bodies show the effects of poor nutrition, addiction, overwork, inadequate housing, and cancer. The stories "Ysrael" and "No Face," from Drown, depict a young boy, Ysrael, in the Dominican Republic, whose face is disfigured after a pig attacks him when he is a baby. Meanwhile, the stories "Nilda," "Miss Lora," and "The Pura Principle," from his later collection This Is How You Lose Her, show Rafa de las Casas dying of cancer and the emotionally complicated aftermath of his death. Minich demonstrates how disability and disease are linked to the unstable boundaries between narrative forms and the legacies of the conquest of the Américas and the transatlantic slave trade. Minich thus demonstrates how a critical disability perspective on Díaz's fiction offers new theoretical insights not only on one writer's work but also more broadly on the aesthetics of decolonization.

The literary scholar and novelist Lyn Di Iorio's chapter, entitled "Laughing through a Broken Mouth," examines theories of laughter, suggesting that the Western intellectual tradition's attitude toward laughter up until the twentieth century can be encapsulated by a phrase from Thomas Hobbes's Leviathan: "sudden glory." According to Hobbes, Di Iorio argues, we laugh at other people or situations because we feel superior to them. Mikhail Bakhtin famously expanded the Western literary tradition's approach to laughter when he underscored how carnivalesque laughter resists the political status quo. Díaz's novel, Di Iorio contends, structures a fascinating interplay between Hobbesian "sudden glory" and the carnivalesque laughter of the oppressed. Relative to this dynamic, it is important to notice who laughs in the book and when. Although the hyperintellectual Yunior de las Casas's laughter of dominance starts off the book, Oscar de León's more tempered and textured laughter "through his broken mouth" ends it. Di Iorio's examination of laughter in The Brief Wondrous Life of Oscar Wao reveals the significant contrapuntal interplay between oppressors and oppressed and traces a trajectory for Latino/a literature that both comments on and remakes the American literary tradition.

Closing this first section, the literary scholar Monica Hanna's chapter, "A Portrait of the Artist as a Young Cannibalist: Reading Yunior (Writing) in *The Brief Wondrous Life of Oscar Wao*," addresses the identity of the mysterious narrator of *The Brief Wondrous Life of Oscar Wao*. Hanna traces Yunior de las Casas's artistic coming of age, his *Künstlerroman*, arguing that what emerges in his narrative is an aesthetics of artistic consumption, which reflects Díaz's vision of the development of the model writer-activist. Yunior, as a budding writer and intellectual not yet sure of his own place in the world but desperate to try to narrate the story of the de León and Cabral family, consumes and embodies their stories as a way to write Dominican Americans into history. According to Hanna, the bodies that are traditionally rejected because of their blackness, fatness, foreignness, or femaleness are, in Yunior's loving consumption, transformed and "sung" into a sacred and central position. The novel's narrative form, via its aesthetics of consumption, creates a literary space for Dominican American identity through an artistic cannibalism, drawing on the artistic vision provided by "Cannibalist Manifesto," written by the Brazilian modernist Oswald de Andrade. Díaz's cannibalism, Hanna demonstrates, utilizes a dense referentiality that encompasses traditions from the United States and the Caribbean, recombining them in a way to forge an artistic identity for Dominicans.

Part II: Mapping Literary Geographies

The second section of the book situates Díaz's literary production within a transamerican context. The four chapters in the section consider Díaz's overlapping incorporations of national and transnational identities and the effects of diaspora and dictatorship on his fictional subjects. In the first chapter, "Artistry, Ancestry, and Americanness in the Works of Junot Díaz," the literary scholar Silvio Torres-Saillant takes up the Greater Antillean routes in Díaz's work to unveil how a central site of the modern era's most intense mobility of people as point of departure and destination, the Caribbean, has given rise to diasporic formations. Torres-Saillant's chapter places Díaz in relation to his celebrated peers in the wider spectrum of Caribbean diaspora writers, stressing the figuration of Dominicanness in his fiction, the political implications of Díaz's manner of representing his national origins, and the significance of the image of Dominican society evoked by his works in contrast to the normative stature that American society attains in the cosmos of his fiction. The chapter closes with a consideration of the ways writers of the Caribbean diaspora have altered the geography of the literary imagination of the metropolises where they operate while wielding an unequal power to represent the Caribbean experience vis-à-vis writers operating in the societies located in the Caribbean region.

In the following chapter, "This Is How You Lose It: Navigating Dominicanidad in Junot Díaz's Drown," the literary scholar Ylce Irizarry analyzes Díaz's work through his critique of U.S. neocolonialism. His attention to classism, intraethnic racism, and internalized racism illustrates Drown's effectiveness as what Irizarry terms a "narrative of loss." Díaz's text grapples with the immediate, measurable losses associated with immigration: loss of a physical home, loss of family, loss of language. His principal narrator, Yunior de las Casas, illustrates the psychocultural migration intrinsic to people who are stuck in the "narrative of loss." The stories in Drown, Irizarry argues, are striking examples of contemporary Dominican immigrant narratives where characters must navigate the riptides of cultural identity. Because identity construction in Anglo and Latino/a America is deceptively narrow, Yunior illustrates how one must swim entirely out of them or drown between them.

The next chapter in this section examines the complex ways literature is "raced" and "Latined" in Díaz's work. In "Latino/a Deracination and the New Latin American Novel," contributed by the literary scholar Claudia Milian, she explores the links that bind The Brief Wondrous Life of Oscar Wao to larger Latin American literary practices. Milian begins her chapter by engaging the claim, made by Sergio Ramírez, the Nicaraguan writer and former vice president of the country, that the new Latin American novel is currently being written in English by Latino/as. Ramírez's understanding of new Latin American cultural practices, as taken up by Latino/as, places their oeuvres in a new regional context that is also navigating mass migrations, transnational communities, cultural alterations, and millennial transitions. Milian thus frames the broader level of "Latined" signification in Díaz's work as it resonates in the North's Global South as well as the Global South's peripheries, querying ways that Díaz's literary forms unsettle U.S. and Latin American literary conventions. Mindful of the different histories and trajectories, emergence, and institutionalization of Latino/a and Latin American literature in the United States, the chapter looks toward the interpretive possibilities of global Latino/a literary practices. In so doing, Milian's work advances a rereading of the literary practices of Latino/as in the twenty-first century as one of deracination that exceeds a simple, insular connection to ideological Americanness.

The final chapter in this section situates Díaz's work within the history of a foundational literary form in the Global South: the dictatorship novel. The literary scholar Jennifer Harford Vargas provides a cultural history and literary exegesis of Díaz's rewriting of the Global South's dictatorship novel in "Dictating a Zafa: The Power of Narrative Form as Ruin-Reading." Harford Vargas's chapter argues that Junot Díaz's *The Brief Wondrous Life of Oscar Wao* is a central text in an emerging set of dictatorship novels written by Latinos/as. The chapter contends that *The Brief Wondrous Life of Oscar Wao* performs and enacts its broader critique of dictatorial relations through the form in which the story is told. It first demonstrates how the novel marginalizes and parodies the dictator Trujillo in the overall narrative structure, reallocates responsibility for structures of domination, and centralizes nonnormative characters to challenge authoritarian power and hegemonic discourses. It then shows how the novel's various structuring devices—specifically its hearsay, footnotes, and silences—mimic and formally critique the dissemination and repression of information under conditions of domination. Considering the tradition of the dictatorship novel within a broader hemispheric framework reveals that Díaz and his contemporaries are generating what Harford Vargas terms a "Latina/o counter-dictatorial imaginary" that reconceptualizes dictatorial power by constructing intersectional analyses of authoritarianism, racial domination, heteropatriarchy, and imperialism in the hemisphere.

Part III: Doing Race in Spanglish

The third section of the book tackles Díaz's engagement with the intersectional oppressions of race, gender, class, and language. The chapters in this section analyze how Díaz's creolized short stories and novel expose the entrenched effects of white supremacy, heteropatriarchy, and capitalist exploitation on both the individual and society. The chapter "Dismantling the Master's House: The Decolonial Literary Imaginations of Audre Lorde and Junot Díaz," contributed by Paula M. L. Moya, is rooted in her theorization of race as a "doing"—meaning race is a sociohistorical construct and institutionalized category and that both whites and people of color participate in the complex process of racialization—articulating how Díaz's fiction skillfully represents the process of doing race. Moya opens by critically reading Díaz's fiction alongside the black lesbian poet Audre Lorde to highlight Díaz's concern with race, class, gender, and sexuality as mutually constituting and consequential aspects of identity. She then addresses those features of his work that place him in a genealogy of activist writers that includes women of color writers, such as Lorde. Moya ends with a close and rigorous reading of the story "How to Date a Browngirl, Blackgirl, Whitegirl, or Halfie," in *Drown*, as a way of highlighting his fictional exploration of the corrosive effects of the racial self-hatred that remains a notable legacy of European colonialism for people of color in the Américas. She thus illuminates that, for all their temporal, generic, stylistic, gender, and sexual differences, Díaz and Lorde are engaged in complementary critical projects.

The literary scholar Glenda R. Carpio continues this section with "Now Check It: Junot Díaz's Wondrous Spanglish," a black Atlantic reading of Díaz's diasporic craft as a novelist, in particular his sharp-witted eloquence in representing the complexities of Afro-Latinidad and black-brown alliances. Carpio argues that Díaz breaks away from the conventions set in place by earlier U.S. immigrant classics such as Henry Roth's *Call It Sleep* and builds on the work of other Afro-Latinos such as Piri Thomas's *Down These Mean Streets*, producing an Afro-Latino literature that takes race as a given and instead shifts narrative attention to language. The focus of *Drown* and *The Brief Wondrous Life of Oscar Wao* is on what Carpio calls "craft, and the art of showing, *in language*, what it means to be black, Latino, and immigrant in the United States." Díaz's Spanglish is expertly rendered in narrative form, which, as Carpio points out, is important, given that most Latino writers have used the form of poetry to render and experiment with black and Latino street slang. This is not to say that Díaz dispenses with historical context; to the contrary, she reads Díaz as firmly rooted in the specificities of Dominican history and legacies of survival. Carpio expertly shows the ways the African Diaspora, U.S. imperialism, and the exodus of Dominicans to the United States are interrelated in Díaz's work through his wondrous use of language.

This section closes with "A Planetary Warning?: The Multilayered Caribbean Zombie in Junot Díaz's 'Monstro,'" in which the literary scholar Sarah Quesada investigates the significance of the apocalyptic landscape and zombie figure in Díaz's short story "Monstro." Quesada focuses on the zombie within the Caribbean context to suggest that this particular incarnation "mirrors the historical progression of capital-based societies, insofar as they inherit westernized structures of power and have now entered an unsustainable era of production." Reading the zombies of the story as symbols related to dominant economic, racial, and power structures, Quesada suggests that "these paradigms, reused in the literary imaginary, culminate in a decolonial reading which conveys that the zombie may be a mere illusion meant to be morally and futuristically cautionary." Quesada's chapter thus ruminates not only on the figure of the zombie but also more generally on the ways the genres of horror and science fiction, seemingly removed from literary realism, can adeptly effect social critiques of colonialism and its legacies.

Part IV: Desiring Decolonization

The final section of the book reveals how Díaz's fiction challenges us to decolonize our imaginations at the level of both ideology and affect. Decolonization entails not just decolonizing the mind but also the heart, for only then can we be our most human selves individually and collectively. This section opens with "Junot Díaz's Search for Decolonial Aesthetics and Love," contributed by the literary scholar José David Saldívar, which unpacks aesthetics, dispossession, trauma, and decolonial love in Díaz's fiction. Saldívar begins by demonstrating why Junot Díaz is "a new kind of U.S. Latino/a writer, one whose fearless projection of a new America releases new creative possibilities and changes the terms of the cultural conversation in which the dissident racial and gender politics of literary expression are articulated." He then goes on to unpack a footnote from *The Brief Wondrous Life of Oscar Wao* in which Yunior de las Casas critically reflects on his neighborhood friend's "spectacularly closeted" reading of science fiction and fantasy books and the effects Oscar's reading in the closet has on Oscar's mother, community friends, and Yunior himself. The whole point of Yunior's observation and incomparable allegory of Oscar's reading in the closet, Saldívar suggests, is for readers to start thinking critically about what happens to "immigrant rising" barrio kids when they read imaginative literature, and, more importantly, what goes on in their complex inner lives. Saldívar concludes by focusing in the chapter's last section on Yunior's fulsome search for decolonial love in "The Cheater's Guide to Love," the concluding story of *This Is How You Lose Her*. Now a fully professionalized creative writing assistant professor, Yunior de las Casas offers readers much more than a low brow "guide." Saldívar reads Díaz's texts as extended exercises in dissident antihomophobic inquiry and racial hermeneutics which have had important effects on the author's provocative theories about the coloniality of power and gender, identity, sexuality, and their interrelation.

In the penultimate chapter of this section entitled "Sucia Love: Losing, Lying, and Leaving in Junot Diaz's *This Is How You Lose Her*," the sociologist Deborah R. Vargas focuses on the racialized, classed politics of *lo sucio*: the unclean, the filthy, the imperfect. In her analysis, lo sucio operates as an analytic for explaining the constructions of racialized, classed masculinities and femininities. Moreover, Vargas considers the various ways lo sucio operates as a structural metonym for nonnormative constructions of intimacy, sexual desire, and kinship. In other words, the *sucias* and *sucios* of Díaz's book inhabit racialized genders and sexualities that represent the "deficit citizenry" of institutional regimes of normative love and intimacy, including marriage, monogamy, biological reproduction, fidelity, and commitment. Vargas considers how the Latina characters, including Magdalena, Pura, and Yasmin, love aggressively and cynically with no commitments to a life promised by the American dream. These sucias are brown, diasporic, working class, Spanglish-speaking, gendered subjects who are persistently seen as having to be cleaned up by projects of neoliberal capitalism as well as by white, middle-class feminism. Vargas's chapter is a consideration of nonnormative and offensive modes of intimacy in *This Is How You Lose Her*, which reveal the ways love and desire are never delinked from the structural underpinnings of power and thus are never pure or redeemable.

This section concludes with "'Chiste Apocalyptus': Prospero in the Caribbean and the Art of Power," written by the literary scholar Ramón Saldívar. In this chapter, Saldívar suggests that there are many links between Shakespeare's monster Caliban in *The Tempest* and Abelard Cabral's story in *The Brief Wondrous Life of Oscar Wao*: ideas concerning human monsters, education, language, political power, and the magical agency of books. This final chapter considers the relationship between political power and aesthetics, especially the aesthetic form of knowledge in books, using examples from both Díaz's novel and Shakespeare's play to demonstrate how politics is itself an aesthetic practice. It is a human endeavor that is rooted, Saldívar suggests, in individuals' desire to impose their imprint upon particular situations and things. In order to shape their world, individuals must use means to represent ideas, sometimes misrepresent motives, carefully imitate past deeds and actors, and mobilize people through the rhetorical manipulation of emotional reactions. All this, Saldívar contends, for the grand aim of giving lasting form to a particular state, political struggle, or to shape the course of a movement.

We close the book with an interview of Junot Díaz in conversation with Paula M. L. Moya, entitled "The Search for Decolonial Love." After the first day of the Junot Díaz Symposium at Stanford University, Moya met with Díaz over breakfast. Both were attending the two-day symposium, and the private meal provided Moya and Díaz the happy opportunity to renew their friendship, which began when they were both graduate students in the English department at Cornell University in the early 1990s. The resulting interview, first published in *The Boston Review*, touches on Díaz's concern with race, his debt to the writings of women of color, and his fictional explorations of psychic and emotional decolonization. Since then, the interview has helped to reshape the discourse regarding Díaz's work, especially in relation to gender and sexuality.

A final collaboration echoed in the presentation of this book is its cover, which contains a drawing of Junot Díaz by the Chicano artist Jaime Hernandez, coauthor and illustrator of the groundbreaking *Love and Rockets* comic book series. Along with being an important influence on Junot Díaz's storytelling, Hernandez also collaborated with Díaz on an illustrated deluxe version of *This Is How You Lose Her*, published in 2013. Hernandez's drawing of Junot Díaz is projected onto an *Akira*-inspired postapocalyptic background created by the film concept designer Andrew H. Leung, an artistic collaboration that highlights Díaz's critically revelatory imagination. As Díaz so eloquently argues in "Apocalypse: What Disasters Reveal," apocalypses illuminate the heretofore unseen or ignored underlying hierarchies of power and forms of inequality and oppression. The many conversations, collaborations, and contestaciones in this book illuminate how Díaz's activism, work as a public intellectual, and writing craft a decolonial imagination, unveiling a transformative, radically egalitarian vision of social life in the Américas.

Notes

1. Giancarlo DiTrapano, "A Brief History of Junot Díaz," *Playboy Magazine*, September 2013, 100–102 and 130.

2. See Junot Díaz's opening remarks for his conversation with Toni Morrison at the New York Public Library on December 13, 2013, accessed April 22, 2015, http://www.nypl.org/events/programs/2013/12/12/toni-morrison-junot-diaz.

3. The only story from Junot Díaz's 1995 MFA thesis, "Negocios," that did not appear in *Drown* was the splendid text entitled "London Terrace." It appeared under the new title "Invierno" in *This Is How You Lose Her*.

4. For a lucid history of the arrival of Spanish-speaking Africans and the emergence of Afro-Latinos/as in the United States, see Miriam Jiménez Román and Juan Flores, eds., *The Afro-Latin@ Reader: History and Culture in the United States* (Durham, NC: Duke University Press, 2010).

5. Junot Díaz, "Q&A," Penguin, accessed April 22, 2015, http://www.penguin.com /author/junot-diaz/1000039301.

6. In his iconic essay on Richard Wright, "Black Boys and Native Sons" (1963), Irving Howe claimed that "the day *Native Son* appeared American culture was changed forever" (100). In much the same way that Howe envisioned Wright's text reinvigorated African American, Anglo-American, and modernist traditions, thereby integrally connecting the U.S. black experience to the experience of other cultures, we believe that the day Junot Díaz's *The Brief Wondrous Life of Oscar Wao* appeared likewise significantly changed American culture by broadening and deepening the interconnectedness of Afro-Latino/a, Anglo-American, Greater Antillean, Latin American experiences and transmodernist literary traditions at the dawn of the twenty-first century. See Howe's essay in *A World More Attractive: A View of Modern Literature and Politics* (New York: Horizon, 1963).

7. See Nelson Maldonado-Torres, *Against War: Views from the Underside of Modernity* (Durham, NC: Duke University Press, 2008). According to Maldonado-Torres, "the decolonial turn [advanced through the ethico-political works of Emmanuel Levinas, Frantz Fanon, and Enrique Dussel] is a simultaneous response to the crisis of Europe and the condition of racialized and colonized subjects in modernity" (7). See other scholarship that is part of this decolonial turn, including, among others, the work of Maria Lugones, Walter Mignolo, Emma Pérez, Aníbal Quijano, Chela Sandoval, and Sylvia Winter as well as the anthologies *Coloniality at Large: Latin America and the Postcolonial Debate* and *Latin@s in the World-System: Decolonization Struggles in the 21st Century U.S. Empire*.

8. For a formalist analysis of how the novel structurally centers the de Leon and Cabral characters and crafts a decolonial zafa or countercurse to the fukú americanus and Trujillo's dictatorship, see Jennifer Harford Vargas, "Dictating a Zafa: The Power of Narrative Form in *The Brief Wondrous Life of Oscar Wao*," MELUS 39, no. 3 (fall 2014): 8–30.

9. For an articulation of how the novel crafts an alternative historiography from the perspective of the diasporic Dominican characters, see Monica Hanna, "'Reassembling the Fragments': Battling Historiographies, Caribbean Discourse, and Nerd Genres in Junot Díaz's *The Brief Wondrous Life of Oscar Wao*," *Callaloo* 33, no. 2 (2010): 498–520.

10. See Aníbal Quijano, "Colonialidad y modernidad/racionalidad," in Robin Blackburn and Horacio Bonilla, eds., *Los Conquistadores: 1492 y la población indígena de las Américas* (Bogota: Tercer Mundo Editores, 1992), 438.

11. For an elaboration of the ways that Díaz manages, crafts, and evaluates the colonial difference in his novel, see José David Saldívar, "Conjectures on 'Americanity'

and Junot Díaz's 'Fukú Americanus' in *The Brief Wondrous Life of Oscar Wao*," *Global South* 5, no. 1 (2011): 120–36.

12. Arjun Appadurai, *Modernity at Large: Cultural Dimensions of Globalization* (Minneapolis: University of Minnesota Press, 1996), 4.

13. Appadurai, *Modernity at Large*, 7.

14. Junot Díaz, keynote address at the "Facing Race" conference in Baltimore on November 16, 2011, accessed April 22, 2015, https://facingrace.raceforward.org/archive /2012/sessions/keynote-event-junot-diaz.

15. Michael Hames-García, "Which America Is Ours?: Martí's 'Truth' and the Foundations of 'American Literature,'" *Modern Fiction Studies* 49, no. 1 (spring 2003): 22–23.

16. Junot Díaz, interview by Bill Moyers, "Junot Díaz on Rewriting the Story of America," Moyers and Company, December 28, 2012, accessed April 22, 2015, http:// billmoyers.com/episode/full-show-rewriting-the-story-of-america/.

17. Posted by TAMARA on January 26, 2012, *The Progressive*, accessed April 22, 2015, http://www.progressive.org/junot-diaz. As part of the state-mandated termination of its Mexican American studies program that went into effect on January 1, 2012, the Tucson Unified School District released a list of books to be banned from its schools. The books were cleared from all classrooms, boxed up, and sent to the Textbook Depository for storage. The ruling board of Tucson, Arizona's largest school district, officially abolished the thirteen-year-old Mexican American studies program in an attempt to come into compliance with the racist Arizona state ban on the teaching of critical ethnic studies. In addition to Díaz's *Drown* being banned from being taught and read by Tucson high school students, the list included books by other Chicano/a writers such as Rodolfo Acuña's iconic *Occupied America: A History of Chicanos*; Rudolfo Anaya's *Bless Me, Ultima*; Gloria Anzaldúa's *Borderlands/La Frontera*; Sandra Cisneros's best-selling novel *The House on Mango Street*; Luis Alberto Urrea's *Into the Beautiful North*; and Luis Valdez's *Zoot Suit and Other Plays*; among other texts. Even Shakespeare's last play, *The Tempest*, was removed from the Mexican American studies classrooms in Tucson's public schools, presumably because Europe's Other, Caliban (Shakespeare's anagram for cannibal), curses and talks back to his white master, Prospero.

18. Junot Díaz, interview by Stephen Colbert, *The Colbert Report*, March 25, 2013, accessed April 22, 2015, http://thecolbertreport.cc.com/videos/bwz16t/junot-diaz.

19. For Pinzón's work, see http://www.dulcepinzon.com/en_projects_superhero.htm; for Rivas's work, see http://neilrivas.com/section/360995_Illegal_Superheroes.html.

20. Junot Díaz, "MFA v. POC," *The New Yorker*, April 30, 2014. "POC" refers to people of color.

21. Introduction to *Dismantle: An Anthology of Writing from the VONA/Voices Writing Workshop*, edited by Marissa Johnson-Valenzuela (Philadelphia: Thread Makes Blanket Press, 2014), 2.

22. See Mark McGurl's *The Program Era* (Cambridge, MA: Harvard University Press, 2010). Pointing to the proliferation of degree-granting "creative writing programs" in U.S. universities during the postwar era of the twentieth-century, McGurl requires

we take into account the institution of the university and the processes of the democratization of higher education in the United States to fully understand the nature of postcontemporary literature in the postwar period.

23. McGurl, The Program Era, 2.

24. McGurl, The Program Era, 8.

25. Junot Díaz, "Dark America," Anne and Loren Kieve Lecture, Stanford University, May 16, 2012. Subsequent quotations attributed to Díaz in this section all come from this address.

26. See Stephanie Li, Signifying without Specifying: Racial Discourse in the Age of Obama (New Brunswick, NJ: Rutgers University Press, 2011).

27. See Victoria Nelson, The Secret Life of Puppets (Cambridge, MA: Harvard University Press, 2003).

28. Benoit Peeters, Derrida: A Biography, trans. Andrew Brown (Cambridge: Polity, 2013), 1.

29. Junot Díaz, interview by Matt Okie, "Mil Máscaras: An Interview with Pulitzer-Winner Junot Díaz (The Brief Wondrous Life of Oscar Wao)," Identity Theory, September 2, 2008, accessed April 22, 2015, http://www.identitytheory.com/interview-pulitzer-winner-junot-diaz-wondrous-life-oscar-wao/.

30. We owe this interlingual deconstruction of the pun contestación (contestation) to the U.S. Latino literary scholars Gustavo Pérez Firmat and José David Saldívar. See their introduction to "Toward a Theory of Latino Literature," Dispositio 16, no. 41 (1991): iii–iv.

Part I

Activist Aesthetics

1. Against the "Discursive Latino"
The Politics and Praxis of Junot Díaz's Latinidad
Arlene Dávila

I was in Puerto Rico when El *Nuevo Día* published an interview with Junot Díaz during his visit to the Festival de la Palabra in 2011, the same trip he had vividly recalled during one of our coffee get-togethers in New York City. True to the Junot Díaz I know, his recollection was not about what happened at the festival or about any literary gossip. Instead, it was about the rapid capitalism and colonialism that had colored his visit to the island. He marveled at how sanitized Puerto Rico had felt to him, at how he had only hung out with intellectuals, remarking on the social segregation he experienced, which he attributed to the island's devastating colonialism and capitalism. The interview was titled "La rebeldía de leer," after Díaz's statements in defense of books and of reading as antidote. As he put it, "It is impossible to compete when you're reading, when you're focused on a novel or a poetry book . . . All those vices that capitalism promotes to keep us 'full' in the market, art helps us lessen a bit" (or, in his words, "el arte nos ayuda a cortar un chín").[1]

When I began to write about Junot Díaz, a literary powerhouse but also a dear friend and colleague, I hesitated, imagining that others would certainly do a better job of giving Díaz's literary work its due. Then I realized that I could write about the Díaz that many people do not know about, not only because they have not had him as a colleague or shared quotidian coffee get-togethers with the author, but also because interviews and exposés of Junot Díaz have seldom seized on Díaz as the critical participant-observer and ethnographer or as the political activist and passionate Latino advocate that I know him to be. These are qualities that are seldom explored in the many literary exposés and interviews with the author that have tended instead to focus on more traditionally personal topics such as his immigrant past, his upbringing, the provenance of his characters, or more specific aspects of his writing. Among them, Díaz's use of history, his mixing of genres and references from science fiction to comic books, and his inventive mixing of Spanish, street vernaculars, Dominican slangs, and English are especially prominent themes. Still, his political positions and drives, while always palpable, are seldom probed. In fact, when Díaz the political commentator and activist comes out, it seems to always create uproar and surprise, as if these positions were not already evident in his body of work. Recent examples include Díaz's bold criticism of the Dominican Republic's decision to strip Dominicans of Haitian descent of their Dominican citizenship, and his statements against Israeli policies toward Palestinians. In both cases, critics responded by raising questions about his "Dominicaness" or by accusing him of "hating Jews," as if Díaz's critical exposés of these instances of racial discrimination, white supremacy, and global empire represented major betrayals, rather than long-time concerns of his work. Díaz's vehement critique of the Dominican government's 2013 ruling to expel Haitian immigrants and strip Haitian-descended Dominicans of citizenship is even more significant in light of the relative silence that characterized the Latino/a media and the mainstream activist community on the issue until days before the ruling began to be executed in the summer of 2015. Throughout, Junot's Facebook page served as the source of information, news, and commentary exposing the racist foundations of the ruling, and strengthening the larger diaspora-led activism of groups like "We Are All Dominican" to fuel a larger #BlackLivesMatter Everywhere movement linking the Dominican immigration debacle to a rising tide of anti-black racism.

Of course, Díaz's pride in his Dominican, Caribbean, and Latino background and his assertive and perceptive critiques of the larger social ills affecting Latinos/as and people of color more generally are well known to anyone who has met the author or attended one of his readings. How could they not? The point is that when Díaz is discussed by the literati, his political opinions are somehow lessened through more formalist treatment of his work, as if to fit him into dominant artistic requirements for art and its creators as "universal"—above and beyond particular politics. In particular, his vehement activist stance and critique of racism and white supremacy, which at the Stanford symposium he described as key elements of his work, are repeatedly missed. Thus, in what follows, I want to delve deeper into two elements that I consider central to his interventions into contemporary Latino/a cultural politics and to what he informally refers to as "our Latino/a project" or "movimiento," thereby providing some additional texture to appreciate his literary work. First is his critical and assertive engagement with Latinidad and how this position impacts his work as well as his political involvements and activism, which both engage with but also extend beyond any ethnic, specific, or nationalist defined boundary. Second is Díaz's consistent critique of capitalism, which is best appreciated as a critique of the simultaneity of global racism and capitalism (akin to Aníbal Quijano's coloniality of power) that touches on all aspects of contemporary society, as well as Latinos' position in it. I suggest that these two strands are informed by Díaz's keen ethnographic eye, as both a social observer and active participant in contemporary Latino/a cultural politics, and that they come together in what I describe as Díaz's praxis-oriented and antidiscursive Latino/a political project. This project puts him in conversation with ethnic studies scholars, activists, and grassroots cultural workers, as well as with anyone who is actively involved in creating progressive political imaginaries more readily than with other writers or literary figures.

I want to start with a formative moment in his trajectory: his student activism over ethnic studies and more specifically over the strengthening of Latino/a Studies at Cornell University during the historic strike and takeover of Day Hall in 1993. Indeed, the occupation at Cornell was the first event Díaz mentioned when I shared with him my ideas for this chapter, and I soon learned why. Díaz was one of the students who took over the administration building to protest the vandalizing of an artwork by a Chicano, a piece that was part of a group of site-specific installations by Latino artists on campus. The students charged that the university administration had not protected the artwork, which was vandalized repeatedly with anti-Latino slurs, and that the university had contributed to the hostile racial climate that enabled the racist incident. The students' four-day occupation of Day Hall was accompanied by numerous demands, including the hiring of more

Latino/a faculty and the diversification of the curriculum, demands that led to the establishment of a Latino Living Center and to the strengthening of Cornell University's Latino/a Studies Program through additional hires.[2]

For Díaz, the experience at Cornell was "the moment where everything came together." This is how he put it:

> I was in Cornell, completely alienated from the white students in my MFA program, and from all undergraduate students of color, and with no space to get to know anybody. But then Latino studies brought this incredible artist Daniel Martínez, who made that extraordinary piece in the front of the quad, and for a budding artist, to see this Latino and his work at the center of the university, in a way that it had never been. When this piece went up the world and Cornell had to deal with Latino artists—the whole university had to stop.

Díaz described this experience as a germinal moment in his understanding of how art connects to politics and to communities, as well as a formative lesson about the political potential of a really progressive work of art. Martínez's installation became especially charged after it was stamped with anti-Latino graffiti, which became the crystallizing moment expressing the active racism that until then had remained largely invisible. Once vandalized, the political potential of the piece was maximized and racism was finally made visible in a way that validated Díaz's sentiments and those of other students who experienced racism on a daily basis, both implicitly and explicitly. Most important, the artwork's reception and the Latino/a students' response became the catalyst for demands that transcended the immediacy of the event to touch on the position of Latinos/as within the university and society at large. Junot had experienced student activism at Rutgers, primarily Afrocentric and feminist activism. Cornell, however, represented his first Latino-centered movement, a pivotal event that, as he described, "activated, charged and energized his Latinoness," more than any other place or event he had experienced.

Almost twenty years later, the battle over Latino/a and ethnic studies continues; these programs are increasingly affected by the growing postracialism and anti-immigrant xenophobia that envelops our society, which have surfaced as especially contested battlegrounds in states like Arizona, where Mexican American studies was recently banned from the curriculum. In fact Díaz was in good company in Arizona; his books were banned alongside Rodolfo Acuña's *Occupied America*, Shakespeare's *The Tempest*, and

Pedro Freire's *Pedagogy of the Oppressed*, among other key texts in critical race theory and Mexican American history and literature that were all deemed guilty of "promot[ing] resentment toward a race or class of people" and "advocat[ing] ethnic solidarity instead of the treatment of pupils as individuals." Such a move of course ignored how the racist curriculum, centered on Euroamerican and Anglo-American culture, does exactly that against people of color. Indeed, ample research by education scholars has documented the dominance of Euroamerican perspectives in mainstream curricula and how the overwhelming dominance of Euroamerican perspectives contributes to minority students' disengagement from academic learning. In sum, Latino/a and minority students learn better and more, and have overall higher graduation rates, when they learn through inclusive curricula that resonate with their experiences. Something transformative and empowering occurs when students in my Latino/a studies classes in New York first learn about the history of Mexican Americans in the Southwest, about the legacy of the Spanish-American War, and about the first *colonias hispanas* in New York City. And it is obvious that leaders in Arizona are very afraid of the possibility of having more educated and unafraid Latinos/as in their state. For now, the ban has brought renewed attention to issues of education, empowerment, and race, fueling a much needed revalorization of ethnic studies, which may challenge our distancing from the social struggles that made these programs possible, as more of us become savvy in the antiracism talk but less willing to take the definite positions necessary to defend the integrity of these hard-won spaces in the postracial academy.[3]

Díaz, however, has never wavered from the need to defend spaces where Latinos/as can shine, strive, and build community. He remains an active supporter of ethnic studies and of Latino-led organizations, as well as of a variety of progressive Latino/a groups, just as he was when we first met almost fifteen years ago as junior faculty members at Syracuse University. Except his support now extends to other grassroots community organizations and groups that many Latino/a and ethnic studies intellectuals would be quick to dismiss as too populist, too ghetto, too "identitarian," or too contradictory. In this regard much has been said about Junot's community activism. After graduating from Cornell, Díaz became actively involved with ProLibertad, in support of Puerto Rican political prisoners, the Dominican Workers Party, and organizations like the Committee Against Anti-Asian Violence (CAAAV) and the Asian American Writers Workshops, which paved the way for his work with Dominicans 2000, the grassroots group behind the first national conference for the Dominican diaspora. However, less is known about his involvement in the more contradictory realm of Latino/a electoral politics that grew out of this same community activism. In fact, Dominicans 2000 launched the political career of Ydanis Rodriguez, the first Dominican candidate for city council for District 10, Washington Heights, in 2001 and 2003. He lost both races but was finally elected in 2009. More recently, Díaz endorsed the Dominican and Latino candidates Angel Tavera, who ran in Rhode Island's gubernatorial race (defeated), and Dennis Benzan, the first Latino elected to Cambridge City Council and the first Latino vice mayor. Díaz is not blind to the limits of institutional politics as a realm for representation and progressive change, but the choice to remain "above politics" has never been an option whenever there is an opportunity to bring about incremental change. This to me is a valuable lesson of Junot's activism and one that often remains under the radar of his academic persona: his struggle against political paralysis. In other words, despite being fully aware of how power operates through racial and ethnic categories, Díaz does not remain paralyzed by the many theoretical contradictions and difficulties of threading spaces that may be associated with identitarian politics. Díaz's Latino/a movimiento involves rescuing the political imaginaries contained in grassroots politics, but also the real, material alternatives that can be embodied by progressive choices.

In East Harlem, Díaz has been a vehement supporter of La Casa Azul Bookstore, the first independent Latino/a bookstore in this community and the city's only Latino/a bookstore, which opened in 2012. Casa Azul has become a catalyst for Latino/a writers, artists, visitors, and residents to meet and to learn about each others' work, providing the type of social, artistic, and community platform that is rare to find within mainstream literary and artistic circuits. Artists, scholars, and activists do not strive in isolation; we are nurtured by each other's work, and Díaz has never lost sight of the importance of forging spaces where Latino/a scholars and activists of color can overcome their isolation and reach out into a larger community of stakeholders who would otherwise remain ignorant of each other's work or become lost in the majority-white spaces in which many of us work or have to maneuver. The Junot Díaz I know craves these spaces, both the ones that are socially and temporarily created through Latino/a specific events, as well as the ones that are more physically grounded in place, such as the community of Washington Heights or La Casa Azul Bookstore.

In other words, Díaz's cultural politics revolve around the assertion and reevaluation of a progressive anti-marketable Latinidad that challenges the whitening impulse of most mainstream Latino pundits and marketers. Foremost, his reevaluation of Latinidad is forged in direct response, and as a challenge to the dominant, Eurocentric, evaluative structures and ideologies that he and many people of color grow up with and that are constantly honed by dominant institutions and the media. He described the reaction of some upper-class Dominican kids traveling as tourists that visiting or dwelling in a primarily Dominican space like Washington Heights, or any Latino-specific space or event, represents the "equivalent of sticking their feet into a pile of mojon [pile of shit]." Díaz recalls, "I grew up with that same ideology in the air: that all things Latino were bad, that all things Dominican were bad, and that the farther away from Dominicanness you could get the better. Dominicanness in my mind was directly connected to the Dominican community in the States and even Santo Domingo, which was predominantly poor and of color and in their mind predominantly backward. And I grew up with such an avalanche ideology, this constant drumbeat like a cacophony that never went away."

It is not surprising that island-based Dominicans are exposed to the same cacophony that Díaz heard in New Jersey; they are the product of the same imperial veil that Latinos/as and Latin Americans have historically faced, whether as racial minorities in the United States or as imperial subjects in Latin America. Nationality may buffer Dominicans and other Latin Americans' exposure to these dynamics while Latinos/as in the United States are left to contend with what is primarily a minority racial subjectivity as "Latino," but neither experience is left untouched. Beliefs in Anglo-American supremacy were especially rampant during my own upbringing in Puerto Rico, where these views were expounded by the island's colonial condition. There, local culture was not only debased on accounts of its supposedly faulty and lesser nature, but also because it was considered subversive and, even worse, "anti-American," as was any pretense of national pride in one's Puerto Ricanness.[4] Decades later, Puerto Rican and Latino/a culture continues to be devalued even when it is commonly appropriated and celebrated to fit the demands of mainstream culture. As a result, the shame in Latinidad continues apace alongside its celebrations and public visibility in the realm of media and popular culture, rendering critical positions like Díaz's more necessary than ever.

It is in response to this dominant devaluation of Latinidad that Díaz's work is best seen and the author's purposeful embrace of his Dominican,

Afro-Caribbean, and Latino identity is most fruitfully appreciated. Foremost, these identities are appreciated in mutual articulation, not in opposition to each other, as many critical scholars pose these identities by drawing strict antagonisms between Latinidad and Afro-Caribbeanness or between nationalist identifiers such as Dominican and Mexican. In fact, this open stance to Latinidad is a position that distances Díaz from many Latino/a writers who resist their identification and "pigeonholing" as Latinos in favor of more "universalist" artistic positionings. Díaz is especially keen to reject this dominant presentation, and his position is especially powerful given that he is one of the few Latinos who has in fact reached and inhabited the supposedly "superior" spaces that minority artists, and all artists, are taught to most value: the white spaces, where Latino culture is erased or sanitized or kept in check. His many awards, from recognized entities such as the Guggenheim and MacArthur fellowships, his work as fiction editor at the *Boston Review*, his endowed professorship at MIT, his Pulitzer Prize for Fiction, and his appointment as the first Latino to serve on the Pulitzer board of jurors have assuredly opened doors to these spaces. Privileged as they are, however, these spaces have never proved to be the safest and most productive for Díaz. As he put it, "I have been offered the position of being a discursive Latino versus one that had any type of praxis in the community, and I ran as fast as I could." In other words, Díaz's position and his critique of the exotification of Latino/a authors and artists is voiced from a position that is fully informed by the hierarchies of evaluations that affect all artists, and by the added pressures to find and identify "discursive Latinos" to fit the literary market's demands for Latino/a writers and Latino/a literature as a niche market. This is a context wherein the market plays a central role in the production, consumption, and circulation of all cultural texts and where Latino/a authors surface as "discursive" objects to be discussed, sold, referenced, or analyzed as embodiments of Latinidad, rather than as active agents that have involvements with particular communities and political positions of their own.[5] As he described during his magnificent lecture at the Stanford symposium, he came of age at a moment when his generation of writers found opportunities but where the trend was to write about their communities without offending or without touching on race. "Signifying without specifying" was the order of the day, but nothing he wanted to be part of. On this note, he spoke at length to describe how he did not want to be one of those writers who writes about race in ways that people at the short end of the stick cannot identify with—that is, without delving into the actual material realities of race. He had been told not to be political or specific, exactly the recommendations that could have destroyed him as a writer.

In particular, Díaz has been uncompromising at never shunning or lessening his ethnic and racial identity to project a more "universal" artistic presence. This positioning is not about ignoring dominant othering practices that reduce minority writers to narrow identity markers and treat them and their work as always representative of particularized communities. Instead, it is about challenging the implicit erasure and disdain for ethnicity contained in the view that adopting universalist positions is the unequivocal answer—not that this strategy has ever been fully successful when deployed by people of color. As he has stated in numerous interviews, he has no interest in simply being a writer cut off from any community connections. Or as he told an interviewer for Slate:

> I try to battle the forces that seek to "other" people of color and promote white supremacy. But I also have no interest in being a "writer," either, shorn from all my connections and communities. I'm a Dominican writer, a writer of African descent, whether or not anyone else wants to admit it. I know also that Stephen King and Jonathan Franzen are white writers. The problem isn't in labeling writers by their color or their ethnic group; the problem is that one group organizes things so that everyone else gets these labels but not it. No, not it.[6]

"It" is obviously white supremacy, which is the main reason why for Díaz the problem and the solution for whatever societal problem we face are not primarily about the discourse and labels we use; they involve the larger politics, structures, and practices that shape, inform, and help mobilize these categories. Unlike many minority artists, Díaz embraces his background to expose and explore the complexities of Latinidad, but also uses it as the medium through which to expose the skillful operations of race and racism in the literary world. Junot elaborated his position when I raised this issue with him: "For me, there is no postmodern acrobatics that is going to alter the fact that from within my community I'm being told to hate my community and from without my community I've been told to avoid my community and to hate it. And to me any solution that has born any fruit and any productive and positive emotional outcome, any positive intellectual outcome, has been to ignore both of these messages and all these toxic ideas around our communities."

I find Junot's ideas addressing the identity conundrum that frames the work of Latino/a artists and writers politically important and invigorating. I especially appreciate his stance because it echoes some of the lessons that have come out of my own research on the commodification of Latino/a culture: that eschewing categories and representations is never enough. We need to first foreground and address the larger context that frames these categories, representations, and politics—the very racial politics that further whiteness and cultural hierarchies.

In this spirit, Díaz seldom loses an opportunity to highlight the whiteness of the literary world, akin to the whiteness of the academic world he once fought, except Díaz's claims now wrest a lot more cultural capital than they did when he was a graduate student, though he has never reveled in this capital or taken it too seriously. Instead, Díaz has systematically drawn on his newly found privileged position as an award-winning writer to attack this very privilege and to expose its racist linings. Junot has questioned his embrace by the literary establishment—"they're so happy to claim me as literature because it makes them look better."[7] He has also openly criticized the "supposedly liberal" National Book Award for failing to nominate people of color. Not one to mince words, he attributed their nomination of all-white books at the very same time that minorities have become a numerical majority to the jury's "unthinking white reflex" and incredible disconnect from larger society.[8] Díaz has lessened the role that merit and talent play in comparison to luck in attaining success, even downgrading his own achievements and being unabashed in his embrace of low popular culture genres like science fiction, fantasy, comic books, or "junk" literature. He self-deprecatingly admits that he is as capable of writing a disappointing work as the next guy.

Díaz has also resisted being used as an example of an immigrant success story or of upward mobility by consistently connecting his fate to a larger community whose bulk remains dispossessed and marginalized. On his Pulitzer win, he insists that it not be interpreted as a coming of age for Latinos/as, or used to silence discussion of the societal conditions they face: "The real question is not what happens at the individual level. The real question always to me is what happens at the collective level."[9]

This self-reflexivity about the spuriousness of evaluative structures, this concern with exposing the power of gatekeepers and with lessening his own individual talents and achievements is an extremely uncommon stance within the high art, literary, and academic circles Díaz treads. After all, these are spaces whose existence and survival have been historically predicated on the maintenance and reproduction of judgments of quality and merit that can be easily consumed as "apolitical" or "unraced" and that can be linked to a single individual "genius." In this context, Díaz's stance about his work, his persona, and the literary establishment is not only rare but also extremely powerful and politically significant. Díaz's critical self-reflexivity disturbs dominant evaluative structures and turns them on their head with context and social conditions. Even luck trumps individual talent and merit as the definite source of artistic success. In this way, Díaz pokes holes in the dominant evaluative narratives of the literary and artistic establishment, without ever compromising rigor and quality. Junot is also well known as an acerbic critic of good writing and as a widely read thinker who can distinguish a recycled idea as quickly as he can produce a sarcastic rejoinder when needed. The point is that Díaz's criticism is always anchored in his politics, in his ethnic, racial, and working-class background and in his "activist" stance, making him far less concerned with dominant artistic evaluative standards than with the real, substantive goal of furthering a progressive Latino/a political project. Yet this is not the type of project that is predicated on what elsewhere I have called "marketable" Latinidad. Instead, I identify it as an expansive project that is critical of all the spurious views that support capitalism's evaluative structures: the dominant literary canon, Eurocentrism, upward mobility myths, meritocracy, "discursive literary figures," etc. But, foremost, it is a project where Latinos/as and people of color are placed at the forefront, a project that imagines a world of possibilities if "our people" could be unencumbered and given the opportunities, the education, and the privileges that nonracialized groups grow up taking for granted. Foremost, it is an expansive project where Latinos/as make bold progressive strides toward the elimination of racism, empire, and colonialism, wherever they are manifested.

In Díaz's political imaginary, Latinos' political, intellectual, and social aspirations are realized, and they are no longer robbed of their history and dignity but are positioned at an equal starting point in their quest for humanness. Díaz's statements in an interview for a special issue on literature of the Dominican diaspora evoke this vision: "Imagine having institutional, intellectual, all the historical ancestry that you and me have now, but imagine that and being a Puerto Rican in 1950s Manhattan. Being on the ground floor, but with all the intellectual institutional apparatus we've managed to accumulate after long years of struggles—it's a wonderful opportunity and it certainly draws all my energies, both intellectual, artistic, and in some ways even spiritual."[10]

Díaz's political project is to shorten the distance Latinos/as have to travel to get to the starting line; it involves addressing social conditions and poverty, as well as vindicating Latinos' history, demanding this history to be part of the center, not marginalized, and therefore "counted" as cultural capital. Foremost this project involves and requires visibility, not only that Latinos/as are made visible, but that we ourselves address how we consistently "un-see"—in short, that we *see* clearly.

Indeed, visibility and rendering visible all that remains powerfully hidden is a central concern for Díaz. Powerfully invisible elements of Latino and diaspora culture that are consistently tackled by Díaz include the region's colonial legacy, as well as issues of racism, classism, and nationalism that create rifts among Latinos living in the states and in the diaspora. He attends as well to the pull of history and how these forces, while invisible, continue to vividly affect us. Díaz traced these concerns to one of his earliest memories, recalled when I prompted him about moments that had most contributed to his politicization. This is the instance when his father, who worked as a military police officer and whose visit Díaz so anticipated and craved, took him not to the malecón or to the movies but to visit a military cell. Junot was four or five years old when he was left alone in the cell, surrounded by feces and rotten food:

> And I'm thinking that I would be left there. This is the point zero and the seed where that tree of my art came out, 'cause all the things that interest me, questions of power, dictatorship, the human experience of how people survive in those conditions, all those interests started there. Maybe it's the mythology I constructed after the fact . . . but there's not a month I do not think of that event. When I have to build a personal story it starts with that memory. Being exposed so young to one of the most hidden institutions of society, these spaces that are supposed to be outside of public discourse, it was useful as an artist to have such an exposure to this space, and it came early and gave me a different panorama to experience the physical institution, which is hard to conjure otherwise.

Díaz considers himself a realist observer, and his apocalyptic vision and his fascination with visibility colors his critical and assertive engagement with Latinidad. His characters have always been contradictory, flawed, and often at the borders of dominant definitions of Dominicanness and Latinidad. What greater contrast to the Dominican *tíguere* than Oscar the virgin nerd. His exploration of the terrors of dictatorship and the hold of history on generations are all part of this critical position that is assertive of Latinos/as and their need to expose their histories, but through stories that are often messy and that deal equally with the terrors of dictatorship as with those of dominant definitions of masculinity and that do not shy away from confronting the most difficult questions of race and racism. Some may argue that Díaz's vision is highly critical and hopeless, but the author thinks otherwise. As he explained in an interview: "I always think that true optimism is demonstrating that even though there is a crack, that the bottle still has value, still is beautiful. True optimism isn't un-seeing that crack in the bottle and saying the bottle's wonderful. . . . Real positivity is seeing how fucked-up and crazy things are and still thinking that we're worthy of all the things human beings should be worthy of: justice and fuckin' fairness and peace and well-being."

One area where Díaz is especially careful to avoid any optimism is in regard to Latinos' engagement with racism. Given how pervasively nationalism has been used to trump any discussions of race and racism throughout Latin America, Díaz is especially keen not to fall into the false, optimistic view that Latin Americans are not racist, or that our racism is lesser or more benign than North American racism. Díaz refers to the Dominican Republic's racism as a "standard apartheid" and has ample evidence to back up his view. In 2004, on the eve of Leonel Fernández's election as president, Díaz was denied entrance to a club, solely on the basis of his race. Díaz was accompanied by a group of Dominicans of all hues, but the club's doormen made it explicitly clear that only he and another dark-skinned friend could not come in. "Tu sabes bien porque tu no puedes entrar [You know full well why it is that you can't come in]," the guard kept telling him. Ironically, the very guard denying them entrance was also dark-skinned, or as Díaz recalled, a "dark big Sammy Sosa type before the whitening, a big morenote." Díaz was perplexed at the lack of solidarity he witnessed, as white Dominicans went in and out without stopping or showing surprise or outrage at what was transpiring right in front of their eyes. The event came to public light thanks to Díaz's contacts and those of the Boston-based Dominican activist Hector Piña, who, as part of the group, had witnessed the incident. It was covered in the media and spurred a suit that led nowhere, as the Dominican legal system lacks legislation to protect against racism. As he recalled, the legal system "took our complaint, wiped their ass with it, and we did not even get a hearing." Most poignant for Díaz was meeting President Fernández at a Dominican event in Boston, and hearing him deny that something like that could ever happen in the Dominican Republic: "Eso no puede ser, tu sabes que en Santo Domingo no hay racismo. [That is impossible; you know that there is no racism in Santo Domingo.]" Díaz was appalled. Fernández has always cast himself as more progressive on social and racial issues because of the time he lived in the United States, or in Díaz's words, because of his "exposure to the metropolis's evolutionary light," but his denial revealed that he was stuck in the same racist thinking.

I want to return to this idea of the "discursive Latino" and how running away from the pressure to conform to this "ideal" has shaped Díaz's praxis and politics. So who is this "discursive Latino"—someone palatable to the mainstream, a good writer who dresses pretty, looks white, and avoids swear words and politics? Junot elaborated as follows:

I have detected a peculiar but pervasive centripetal force in our society that welcomes a certain expression of Latinidad—the Salsa Level. Which is to say you can talk about music and food and other charming Latino cultural simplifications that an outsider can connect with and consume ahistorically but that simultaneously discourages any practical Latinidad that recognizes and engages with progressive political projects, with immigration reform, with the country's oppressive social realities, with activism, with the neocolonial umbra that define in large part the Latino reality.

Our economic marginalization, the dismal educational opportunities of Latino youth, the ruptures and amnesias inflicted on us by our many traumas—familial, national, immigrant—often abets in moving Latinos towards an apolitical, dehistoricized, consumerist, pseudo-nationalist Latinidad open to every oppression the larger society wishes to unleash upon it yet decoupled from all the histories and resources which could make necessary resistance possible.

If it weren't for the cultural organizations, the churches, the community groups, the activists, the artists, the committed professionals and academics, the political clubs, the students, shit would even be much worse. This is the Movimiento that I come out of and am committed to.

Junot went on to describe the numerous times he had been asked to join the boards of various mainstream literary publications that have no Latino/a representation and where he would be in an "honorary'" position that would only help cover their biases, and how for him the only sensible re-action had been to explain the biases and run. You would think that Díaz would always be running, given the political moment when so many of us are interpellated into this dominant "apolitical, dehistoricized, consumer-ist, pseudo-nationalist Latinidad" that he so neatly described. But thank-fully this is not the case.

At the Stanford symposium, it was especially touching to see him repeat the powerful and optimistic message that he has so generously shared with me throughout the years, which is to focus and attack what you can right now to achieve a more "human self" and to ensure that our art, our writing, our work is part of a praxis to achieve that better and more humane world. Others will follow. And this was especially evident at the symposium, which bore testament to a living Latino/a politics and praxis, beyond all the in-sightful readings and literary criticism that were also at play. This is the praxis of a growing Chicano-Caribbean connection in scholarship and lit-erature, evidenced in the very organization of a symposium in Díaz's honor at Stanford University, a literary program based on the West coast and at-tended by a growing cadre of young and diverse Latino and Latina schol-ars who gave many moving glimpses of what reading Díaz meant not only for themselves—as young people, as students, and emerging scholars—but also for many other Latinos/as who were not at the symposium but who ev-eryone recognized had found a voice through Díaz: the ghetto nerds, the self-destructive, the oppressed, the angry, the youth, the queer, the suburban, the immigrant, the "unfit" for not speaking "proper" Spanish or Spanglish or English, or for not dancing *bachata* or for dancing it too well. In sum, the most powerful lesson of the day was displayed right there and then. It con-sisted not only in the multiple readings of Díaz's work but in the powerful community that his work helps make possible by keeping it *very* real.

Notes

1. Carmen Graciela Díaz, "La rebeldía de leer," El Nuevo Día, July 24, 2011.

2. See "Hispanic Students at Cornell University Protest Vandalism of Art Work," New York Times, November 20, 1993; and Max Schindler, "Students Gather, Recount La-tino Day Hall Takeover," Cornell Daily Sun, November 23, 2010.

3. Arlene Dávila, "A Fix for Ignorance and Exclusion," New York Times, April 27, 2011.

4. Ramón Bosque-Pérez and José Javier Colón Morera, Las carpetas: Persecucion política y derechos civiles en Puerto Rico (San Juan: Centro para la Investigación y Promoción de los Derechos Civiles, 1997).

5. Elena Machado Sáez and Raphael Dalleo, *The Latino/a Canon and the Emergence of Post-Sixties Literature* (New York: Palgrave Macmillan, 2007).

6. Meghan O'Rourke, "Questions for Junot Díaz: An Interview with the Pulitzer Prize–winning Author," *Slate*, 2008, accessed April 22, 2015, http://www.slate.com/id /2188494/.

7. Diógenes Céspedes and Silvio Torres-Saillant, "Fiction Is the Poor Man's Cinema: An Interview with Junot Díaz," *Callaloo* 23, no. 3 (2000): 905.

8. Matt Okie, "Mil Máscaras: An Interview with Pulitzer-Winner Junot Díaz (*The Brief Wondrous Life of Oscar Wao*)," *Identity Theory*, 2008, http://www.identitytheory.com /interviews/okie_Díaz.php.

9. Katherine Miranda, "Junot Díaz, Diaspora and Redemption: Creating Progressive Imaginaries," *Sargasso* 2 (2008–9): 31.

10. Miranda, "Junot Díaz, 24.

2. The Decolonizer's Guide to Disability

Julie Avril Minich

In *Black Skin, White Masks,* Frantz Fanon writes bitterly against a white-supremacist logic that correlates blackness to bodily defect. Rejecting "the humility of the cripple," Fanon exposes how disability is used to naturalize domination when colonized people are associated with physical or cognitive impairments.[1] Yet his own linking of disability and humility (perhaps even humiliation) opens him to criticism from disability scholars. Rosemarie Garland-Thomson accuses Fanon of depicting "disability as the true mark of physical inadequacy from which he wishes to differentiate racial marking" and of implying that "racial difference does not make one inferior, but disability does."[2] She reminds readers that oppressed peoples' efforts to undo the stigma of disability association can inadvertently reinforce disability oppression. Her critique exemplifies what Susan Antebi identifies as an "encounter between two general modalities of reading corporeal difference," one that exploits disability "for the proliferation of meanings and the generation of collective identities-as-alterities" and another "construed through emphasis on the specificity of material bodies and their individual histories."[3] This chapter will probe the boundary between these two modes, arguing that the work of the Dominican writer Junot Díaz can help us to understand disability as an embodied experience—one that is often misrepresented and misappropriated—while also attending to its discursive function in both the subjugation and the liberation of colonized people.

As Garland-Thomson charges, Fanon reduces disability to a textual device representing the alterity of the colonized subject. At the same time, his work also indirectly reveals how colonialism creates disability—promoting global inequities in wealth, nutrition, health care, housing, and working conditions, and fostering direct violence like military interventions, hate crimes, and police brutality.[4] As Ato Quayson notes, colonized people are more likely to become disabled, since "certain impairments can be directly linked to social systems."[5] When he refuses "the humility of the cripple," Fanon does not merely employ a politically fraught metaphor (although he does precisely that); he also makes an embodied political critique. As a result, Garland-Thomson's reading of Fanon calls to mind an argument Paula M. L. Moya has made for approaching problems from different social positions: "Divergent perspectives can lead to the sparking of a productive dialectic that might lead to . . . advancement in knowledge."[6] In other words, reading Fanon and Garland-Thomson together forces us to confront the theoretical and ethical complexity of undoing the discursive links between disability and colonialism.

The decolonization of disability is a central (but overlooked) problem in Díaz's fiction. His characters' bodies are affected by inadequate housing and nutrition, addiction, overwork, and cancer. The stories "Ysrael" and "No Face," from his debut short story collection *Drown* (1996), depict a young boy in the Dominican Republic (Ysrael) whose face is disfigured after a pig attacks him when he is a baby. Meanwhile, the stories "Nilda," "Miss Lora," and "The Pura Principle," from the collection's sequel, *This Is How You Lose Her* (2012), show a young man (Rafa) dying of cancer. "The Cheater's Guide to Love" also deals with the effects of physical labor. Uniting these stories is Yunior, Rafa's younger brother and Díaz's best-known character, who (along with Rafa) bullies Ysrael in *Drown* and who later grieves Rafa's death in *This Is How You Lose Her*.[7] In both collections, disability and disease are linked to two of the primary concerns of Díaz's fiction: the unstable boundaries between narrative modes and the legacies of the conquest of the Americas and the transatlantic slave trade. Indeed, as Anne Garland Mahler points out, these issues are themselves connected, for Díaz offers an "overarching political critique regarding the role of the written word in maintaining colonial relations of power" and a search for "writing that does not repress its own inherent violence but rather exposes it in order to disarm tyrannical power."[8] By linking disability to these concerns, I reveal how a critical disability perspective on Díaz's work offers new insights not only about one writer but also, more broadly, about the aesthetics of decolonization.

Examining Díaz's work through a disability studies framework requires critical engagement with both the metaphorical (even fantastical) treatment of disability in some parts of his work and the concrete depiction of disability as an embodied experience in others. Taking seriously both modes of representation, in turn, requires departing somewhat from the emphasis on science fiction, fantasy, and magical realism that tends to dominate Díaz criticism without falling into the emphasis on autobiography that often surfaces in media interviews with Díaz and popular reviews of his work. This chapter builds on the work of literary critic Ulka Anjaria, who credits realist writers with producing "an aesthetics adequate for representing the instabilities of modern life" and whose reading of the Indian novel of the late colonial period "places social realism alongside, rather than opposed to, other modes of realist innovation, such as magical realism."[9] I argue that by paying attention to the realist aspects of Díaz's fiction—particularly in his depictions of disability—we might reevaluate the opposition between disability critique and postcolonial critique that Garland-Thomson's critique of Fanon suggests.

Behind Ysrael's Mask

A remarkably compelling character, Ysrael appears prominently in much of the scholarship on Drown. The first of Ysrael's stories, titled with his name, depicts the book's narrator and protagonist Yunior and his older brother Rafa forcibly removing Ysrael's mask in order to see his face; the second, "No Face," describes Ysrael's efforts to fend off attackers like Yunior and Rafa. As Tobin Siebers describes him, Ysrael "literally runs through the book" to escape his bullies.[10] Critics—who, with the exception of Siebers, have not used a disability studies framework—often read his facial disfigurement as a metaphor. As Anne Connor puts it, "Ysrael's monstrous face expresses the experience of being a minority, of not fitting in a given culture, and even worse, of suffering complete rejection by the dominant culture."[11] Mahler's reading is more sophisticated, avoiding language that equates minority identity with abjection: "Ysrael's mask appears . . . as a metaphor for the false promises of the First World, or the illusion of power and autonomy that covers Ysrael's fundamental vulnerability and exploitation at the bottom of the social hierarchy."[12] Yet while from a disability studies perspective it is preferable to see Ysrael's mask—and not the character himself—as a metaphor for coloniality, this reading still reduces his disability to metaphor, neglecting to investigate what *Drown* teaches us about life with a disability in the Global South. I argue that Ysrael's condition also pushes us to acknowledge the materiality of persistent poverty in the Dominican Republic and the stark inequities that separate the Global South and the Global North, conditions that place young children in dangerous situations (for instance, being forced to live in close proximity to livestock) and deny them medical care when they are harmed. It furthermore demands that we attend to the ways poverty magnifies disability oppression. In other words, Ysrael's condition has metaphorical significance but is never fully reducible to a metaphor.

Although Ysrael appears only in *Drown*, he is a crucial figure for Díaz, bridging this book with the Pulitzer Prize–winning novel *The Brief Wondrous Life of Oscar Wao* (2007), as he functions as a precursor to the protagonist Oscar de León.[13] Like the fat Oscar, Ysrael is an avid reader with a socially devalued body. Ysrael's stories also represent an early foray into the generic innovation of *The Brief Wondrous Life of Oscar Wao*, which Ramón Saldívar elegantly describes as "a hybrid amalgam of realism, magical realism, metafiction, and genre fictions such as science fiction, graphic narrative, and fantasy proper."[14] While other stories in *Drown* employ a realist narrative style, "No Face" shows Díaz experimenting with the departures from realism and the incorporation of other literary genres that are a trademark of *The Brief Wondrous Life of Oscar Wao*, including a moment when Ysrael escapes a bully by uttering the word strength.[15]

Beyond his place in Díaz's fiction overall, Ysrael is also vital to the narrative momentum of *Drown* as a collection. The story "Ysrael," in which Yunior describes bullying Ysrael, is the book's first story; the story "No Face," in which Ysrael's story is (apparently) told by an omniscient third-person narrator, is its second to last. The importance of Ysrael's position in *Drown* is evident when we compare it to that of Papi, Yunior's father. "Fiesta 1980," in which Yunior describes his father's violence, is the second story in the collection, while "Negocios," in which Yunior compassionately tells his father's story, ends the collection. In other words, the first and penultimate stories describe Yunior's acts of abuse and the perspective of the person he abuses; the second and final stories describe Yunior's experience of abuse and the perspective of the man who abuses him. Ysrael is therefore central to Yunior's character development. As John Riofrio points out, a major problem in *Drown* is the "very real possibility that Yunior . . . may someday turn out to be just like his father."[16] Ysrael represents compelling evidence of a different possibility, for the boys' interactions reveal Yunior's "profound and growing sense of empathic connection" with Ysrael, even as the story itself depicts Rafa's mentoring Yunior in how to brutalize people who are more vulnerable.[17]

The theme of empathy in *Drown* is both liberating and troubling. Empathy is frequently invoked in disability scholarship as a counterpoint to pity. Garland-Thomson writes: "Pity is . . . repugnance refined into genteel condescension. Empathy, in contrast, bonds in a mutual recognition of shared humanity."[18] Yunior's empathy with Ysrael, his recognition of their shared humanity, ultimately makes it possible for him to understand his father—an understanding that may allow him to avoid his father's destructive behaviors. *Drown* suggests that Yunior, unlike Rafa, might find a different masculinity. The Cuban postcolonial theorist Roberto Fernández Retamar also invokes empathy as an element of decolonization, emphasizing the need for members of the privileged classes to make "common cause with the oppressed."[19] Yunior's capacity for empathy, then, influences not only his character but also the political interventions of Díaz's fiction.

Emphasizing Ysrael's role in helping Yunior develop empathy has some unsettling implications, however. After all, this emphasis reduces the disabled character (Ysrael) to a narrative device employed in the development of the central, nondisabled character (Yunior). This, in turn, opens up the possibility that Ysrael's second story, "No Face," is not, as readers and critics generally assume (and as I hinted above), narrated by an omniscient third-person narrator. Perhaps "No Face" is actually narrated by Yunior, imagining life from the perspective of the child he has tormented. Monica Hanna paves the way for this hypothesis in her analysis of *The Brief Wondrous Life of Oscar Wao*, which also includes one section narrated not by Yunior but by Oscar's older sister (and Yunior's ex-lover) Lola: "Is this really Lola speaking? . . . Is Yunior simply reconstructing Lola's voice, writing her voice himself, as a way to regain a connection to her? If this last possibility is the case, does Yunior in a small way fall into the Trujillan model of narrative, as characters . . . are not allowed to speak for themselves?"[20] Hanna's queries, applied to *Drown*, force us to ask whether Ysrael functions as what David Mitchell and Sharon Snyder call a narrative prosthesis—an exploitive use of disability to make a sociopolitical intervention that is not about disability.[21] Because the narrative prosthesis is not a literary device embraced by disability critics, a disability analysis of Drown requires addressing the possibility that Ysrael fills this function.

For the critic—like me—who is both enamored with Drown and invested in the political commitments of disability critique, this dilemma might inspire an attempt to rescue Ysrael from the status of narrative prosthesis. (This is what I set out to do in my first draft of this piece.) Instead, I wonder whether the stories might contribute to disability theory even if Ysrael's story is controlled by the imperatives of Yunior's character development. My analysis will therefore proceed from the assumption that Ysrael does not narrate for himself, that Yunior drives both of Ysrael's stories.[22] This places Ysrael into a dilemma similar to one that Retamar, in his famous essay on Caliban, identifies as that of the Latin American colonial subject: "While other colonials . . . speak among themselves in their own language, we Latin Americans continue to use the languages of our colonizers. . . . Right now as we are discussing, as I am discussing with these colonizers, how else can I do it except in one of their languages, which is now also our language, and with so many of their conceptual tools, which are now also our conceptual tools?"[23] Ysrael is doubly caught within an unjust system of representation: on the level of the author-character relationship, he is a disabled character invented by a writer who does not identify as disabled, while on the level of the narrative, he is a Spanish-speaking Dominican child whose story is told in English, in the United States, by his oppressor (Yunior). What makes Retamar essential for understanding this dilemma is his insistence on using the colonizer's language against the colonial enterprise. Retamar asserts, in other words, Caliban's capacity to use Prospero's language to curse him. In this way, he helps us contemplate how Ysrael, a character created with ableist and colonizing conceptual tools, might use those conceptual tools against themselves.

Garland-Thomson's work on staring as a "complex and compelling social exchange in which we all participate" is helpful here.[24] She emphasizes the agency of starees, who manage staring encounters in ways that recast them as "subjects not objects."[25] Her work resonates with that of Fanon, who is also concerned with staring or gazing: "The white gaze, the only valid one, is already dissecting me. I am fixed. . . . I sense, I see in this white gaze that it's the arrival not of a new man, but of a new type of man, a new species. A Negro, in fact!"[26] Despite her critique of him, Garland-Thomson shares with Fanon a theoretical aim: to understand, and thus to curtail, the power of the dominating gaze. It is significant, then, that the short story "Ysrael" is about the gaze—about the desire of Yunior and Rafa to see Ysrael's facial disfigurement. "Ysrael" describes how Yunior and Rafa are sent to stay with relatives in the countryside every summer because their mother "worked long hours at the chocolate factory and didn't have the time or energy to look after [them] during the months school was out."[27] These summers are excruciating: "In the campo there was nothing to do, no one to see."[28] The boys seek out Ysrael to cope: "I was nine that summer, but my brother was twelve, and he was the one who wanted to see Ysrael."[29] Rafa's desire to see Ysrael calls to mind how Garland-Thomson and Fanon theorize the gaze as "a dominance display."[30] As Garland-Thomson puts it, "A stare can communicate social status, conferring subordination on a staree and ascendancy on a starer."[31] Fanon, for his part, emphasizes that a stare can create a subordinated class of people—"A Negro, in fact!"[32]

The boys' encounter with Ysrael, however, reinforces Garland-Thomson's observation that the stare's "capacity to create meaning is unstable and open-ended." A stare can "evoke emotion, increase involvement, and stimulate reaction."[33] Yunior at first sees only Ysrael's disfigurement: "You couldn't help but see the scar tissue that circled his left eye, a red waxy crescent, and the saliva that trickled down his neck."[34] Yet when he mentions wrestling (a sport he knows Ysrael likes), he notices that "something rippled under the mask."[35] When the mask twitches again, Yunior realizes that Ysrael is smiling. At this moment, Rafa initiates the attack, a connection that Díaz emphasizes by placing Ysrael's smile and Rafa's violence in a single run-on sentence: "I realized he was smiling and then my brother brought his arm around and smashed the bottle on top of his head."[36] Although he does not avoid violence, Ysrael uses his smile to force Yunior to recognize his humanity. This smile changes Yunior's relationship to his older brother. Although he goes with Rafa to see Ysrael because he loves and looks up to Rafa, by the time they are adults this admiration is gone. In *This Is How You Lose Her*, an older Yunior describes his brother in unrelentingly pejorative terms as "a monster" and a "motherfucker."[37] Ysrael, then, does not have narrative control, but he does convert the stare from a one-way assertion of dominance to a shared encounter that leaves Yunior transformed.

The story "No Face" depicts Ysrael as a critical reader, thus offering a more direct image of his using his colonizer's conceptual tools for subversive ends. At Stanford University's Kieve Distinguished Speaker Lecture, in

2012, Díaz argued that despite the well-documented racism of both H. P. Lovecraft and J. R. R. Tolkien, it is possible to read their novels as analyses of white supremacy. Both writers manifest a fear of the return of ancient, dormant evils (Lovecraft's *Great Old Ones* and Tolkien's *One Ring*). Díaz sees in this fear a reflection of the dominant culture's struggle to repress the legacy of its own old evils (slavery and colonialism). Here it is instructive to recall Fanon's critique of comic books "written by white men for white children."[38] For Fanon, these comics are invariably harmful to nonwhite children: "Since one always identifies with the good guys, the little black child, just like the little white child, becomes an explorer, an adventurer, and a missionary 'who is in danger of being eaten by the wicked Negroes.'"[39] For Díaz, these stories are also harmful, but it is possible for nonwhite children (like himself and Ysrael) to find alternative meanings in them. In "No Face," he depicts Ysrael engaged in such a practice of resistant reading, since each "week Padre Lou lets him buy a comic book."[40] The comic Ysrael selects is Kalimán, featuring the Mexican comic book hero who "takes no shit."[41] "No Face" describes Kalimán as a valuable but imperfect hero: "If his face were covered he'd be perfect."[42] Ysrael—like the young Díaz reading Tolkien and Lovecraft—uses his oppressor's conceptual tools while acknowledging their flaws. Furthermore, these flaws center on disability, as it is Kalimán's lack of a mask that Ysrael critiques.

Despite their imperfections, Ysrael's comics empower him, enabling him to imagine himself with secret superpowers that help him navigate a hostile social environment. These are written, comic-book-style, in capital letters: "invisibility," "flight," and "strength."[43] Ysrael's superpowers simultaneously make possible fantastic occurrences (as when he utters the word *strength* and repels his bullies) and reflect his social reality. Ysrael's powers of strength result from living in fear of violence; the story "No Face" begins with a description of his average morning: "He goes to the guanábana tree and does his pull-ups, nearly fifty now, and then he picks up the café dehuller and holds it to his chest for a forty count. His arms, chest, and neck bulge and the skin around his temple draws tight, about to split."[44] This passage depicts Ysrael's rigorous strength-training routine (necessary for self-defense) and shows his body as marked by the same geopolitical forces that shape those of everyone around him. The guanábana tree, native to the Caribbean, constitutes one source of his strength, as does the coffee dehuller, a reference to the dependence of the Dominican economy on a luxury export crop originally cultivated and harvested by African slaves.

Ysrael's power of invisibility, meanwhile, invokes health care inequities between the Global North and the Global South, as his medical advocate, Padre Lou, is brushed off after inquiring at the local clinic when Ysrael will go to Canada for treatment: "We'll get him there eventually."[45] That Ysrael remains invisible within the health care system parallels the relationship between the nations of the Global North and those of the Global South.

Finally, Ysrael's power of flight exemplifies my argument that, even if his disability is not devoid of troubling metaphorical uses, Díaz also treats disability as concrete experience. In "Ysrael," Yunior recalls watching Ysrael run while he and his friends throw rocks at him: "He's faster than a mongoose, someone said, but in truth he was even faster than that."[46] The mongoose is an important figure for Díaz, appearing as a guardian during crucial moments in *The Brief Wondrous Life of Oscar Wao*. Díaz explains in an interview with Marisel Moreno, conducted in 2010: "For me there's no animal more representative of the Caribbean experience than the mongoose, our little scrappy, transplanted survivor . . . put to a task that it refused to do; brought over to catch snakes and kill rats, and rebelled."[47] Ysrael, then, shares more with the mongoose than just his speed. Brought to the text to perform a certain kind of work (develop Yunior's character), he exceeds his job, forcing critical scrutiny of the relationship between coloniality and disability.

Rafa the Super Asshole

This Is How You Lose Her reads like a sequel to *Drown*, taking place after Yunior's move to the United States and following him into adulthood: Rafa dies of cancer while Yunior is still a teenager. It might be tempting to read Rafa's disablement and death either as a tragic redemption of his character or as a punishment for his childhood cruelty. However, unlike Ysrael's stories, Rafa's stories seem to refuse metaphorical significance; he appears as the opposite of a narrative prosthesis. His story draws directly from Díaz's life: after migrating to New Jersey, Díaz's family lived less than a mile from one of the state's largest landfills, and several years later, one of his brothers was diagnosed with leukemia. Where critics are tempted to read Ysrael for his metaphorical function alone rather than for the stark social realities he makes visible, we might be similarly tempted to read Rafa for his realistic (even autobiographical) function. By reading social realist novels not only for their mimetic function but also for their aesthetic engagements—in other words, by insisting that "social realism is significant not only for the radical content of its forms but also for the forms of its content"—Anjaria offers a model for reading Rafa's illness as a larger meditation on different responses to social injustice.[48] Attending, once again, to both the metaphorical and the material helps us to read Rafa as a much more complex character than he appears to be in *Drown*, for here he becomes, like Ysrael, both a literary device that develops Yunior's character as well as a reflection of social reality.

Rafa's disease initially manifests as a change in skin color and, as a result, is racialized from the beginning. In the story "Nilda," Yunior recalls: "Rafa was tired all the time and pale: this had happened in a matter of days. I used to say, Look at you, whiteboy, and he used to say, Look at you, you black ugly nigger."[49] This exchange reminds us that Rafa's lighter skin is a source of tension between the brothers, as Yunior reveals in *Drown*: "Rafa . . . had about five hundred routines he liked to lay on me. Most of them had to do with my complexion, my hair, the size of my lips."[50] Rafa's illness thus takes on a particular meaning—and certain symptoms become salient—because of what white supremacy has taught them about the social meaning of skin color variations. When Rafa's color becomes a symptom instead of a prized feature, its meaning is complicated but not totally subverted: Yunior refers to Rafa as "whiteboy," which is pejorative but nonetheless lacks the legacy of racialized violence contained in Rafa's retort of "black ugly nigger." The two insults, in other words, are not equivalent.

The intersection of Rafa's social location and his disease intensifies when he goes to the doctor and is diagnosed with anemia despite the fact that he clearly has a much more serious condition, a misdiagnosis that reflects racism and classism in the health-care system. Yet the racialized aspects of Rafa's illness do not merely reflect medical inequity; they also provide the opportunity to evaluate the different ways Yunior and Rafa confront their social world. Yunior is encouraged by his brother's initial diagnosis ("Anemic ain't bad"), just as in *Drown* he tries to convince himself that Ysrael will be fine ("they're going to fix him").[51] In response to Yunior's reassurances, Rafa is unmoved: "Yeah, Rafa said, laughing bitterly. God bless Medicaid." This echoes his reply to Yunior's hopeful assessment of Ysrael's situation in *Drown*: "Yunior, he said tiredly. They aren't going to do shit to him."[52] These parallel conversations reveal a fundamental difference between Yunior and Rafa. As Yunior confides in the first story of *This Is How You Lose Her*, "Deep down, where my boys don't know me, I'm an optimist."[53] Yunior believes in the possibility of a just society in which doctors tell the truth, in which access to adequate health care is not systemically denied to the racialized poor. Rafa does not. Rafa is never likable, but the experience of cancer reveals an element of his character that is much less discernible in *Drown*: his behavior results from his astute reading of his unjust social world. As the Chicana feminist Cherríe Moraga has observed in a very different context, "Oppression. Let's be clear about this. Oppression doesn't make for hearts as big as all outdoors. Oppression makes us big and small. Expressive and silenced."[54] Rafa's resignation to his cancer as well as to Ysrael's situation, then, reveals the consequences of living in oppressive conditions without any belief in the possibility for social change. His heart is not as big as all outdoors; he compensates for his smallness in the world by making himself big to those he can intimidate (including Yunior, Ysrael, his mother, and women in general), and he teaches Yunior to do the same. Yet it is also Rafa who gives Yunior some of his most important lessons about injustice. Ultimately, for social change to be possible, both Rafa's accurate understanding of the way things are and Yunior's vision for the way things should be are necessary.

The story "The Pura Principle" describes Rafa's behavior in the final months of his life. Much of this behavior is erratic and mean: "Dead now a year and you still feel a fulgurating sadness over it even though he really was a super asshole at the end."[55] In this story, Rafa realizes he is dying and struggles against it, first by taking a job at a local crafts store called the Yarn Barn and then by marrying an undocumented Dominican single mother (Pura) he meets there. Throughout, he treats his family terribly, stealing from his mother and taking violent revenge on Yunior for intervening. Disability critics have long pointed out the destructive stereotypical representation of the person who acquires a disability and then becomes angry at life, and a superficial reading of Rafa might interpret his behavior as angry acting out. It is important to remember, however, that Rafa is not a "super asshole" because he has a terminal illness; he simply is a "super asshole" and has been all along. In this sense, Rafa's cancer is an extension of the things he is already angry about (poverty and racism), both because poverty and racism exacerbate his disease and make his death more painful, and because he approaches cancer with the same resignation with which he approaches poverty and racism.

Finally, "Miss Lora" describes the adolescent Yunior's affair with an older neighbor. Although its plot is focused on Yunior's teenage infatuation with Miss Lora (including detailed descriptions of their very intimate sexual encounters), the story's opening invokes Rafa as its motivation: "Years later you would wonder if it hadn't been for your brother would you have done it? You remember how all the other guys had hated on her—how skinny she was, no culo, no titties, como un palito but your brother didn't care. I'd fuck her."[56] This opening hints that what will draw Yunior to Miss Lora is competitive desire for a woman Rafa wanted and never possessed, but as the story progresses it becomes clear that Yunior's desire is actually to understand his brother, his father, and himself: "Both your father and your brother were sucios. . . . Sucios of the worst kind and now it's official: you are one, too."[57] Despite not wanting to be like his brother, Yunior is compelled by a desire to understand him. This is, then, a version of the desire that causes him to bully Ysrael with Rafa when they are children, but in *This Is How You Lose Her* this desire is also a recognition that Rafa, for all of his horrible flaws, has something to teach Yunior. For Yunior's optimism to become an effective force for social change, he must acquire some of Rafa's cynicism; he needs Rafa's ability to see and recognize the most sucio aspects of life. From a feminist perspective, of course, his use of a woman to work through his conflict with his brother is flawed—a fact that Yunior himself must confront by the end of the collection and one that I will address in the final section of this analysis.

I have argued here that Rafa's cancer functions not only as a concrete representation of health-care inequity but also as a textual device that contributes to Yunior's character development, making visible the inefficacy of his optimism as a force for social change unless he can also accept the truth of Rafa's brutal view of the world. However, although I posit Rafa's disease as a textual device, I also wish to vehemently dispute that it functions as a facile metaphor for the failure of masculinity. This reading is tempting because (as its title indicates) *This Is How You Lose Her* is about Yunior's learning to relate differently to women, and so reading Rafa's death as the death of a particularly destructive form of masculinity seems to align with this focus.[58] Here it is important, however, to remember that the story "Miss Lora" specifically reveals that Rafa's misogyny continues after his death, as Yunior becomes a "sucio" just like Rafa and just like their (now absent) father. Indeed, Yunior's name itself implies the inheritance of a masculine legacy that he must confront after realizing that he, too, is a sucio: "You had hoped the gene missed you, skipped a generation, but clearly you were kidding yourself. The blood always shows."[59] As the final section of my analysis will demonstrate, disability is implicated in Yunior's struggle to find a different masculinity but not through a simplistic metaphorical rendering of bodily decline as the decline of misogyny.

Yunior's Transformation

This Is How You Lose Her concludes with "The Cheater's Guide to Love," which depicts the five-year aftermath of Yunior's most traumatic heartbreak. As his heart deteriorates, so does his body; he develops plantar fasciitis, a ruptured disc, and finally spinal stenosis. As with both Ysrael and Rafa, the weakening of Yunior's body contains both metaphorical significance (his life is falling apart!) and a concrete, embodied history. Yunior performs extensive manual labor during early adulthood, including a job with the Raritan River Steel Company and another delivering pool tables, and this labor causes his body to age rapidly as he enters his third decade. His doctor, "impressed" and confounded by the decline of Yunior's body, confirms hard physical labor as the cause: "That would do it."[60] Yet Yunior's corporeal degeneration appears as an aside to the real plot of the story: Yunior's heartbreak and recognition of his own misogyny. Díaz himself privileges this feminist interpretation in recent interviews. For instance, in a conversation with Moya published in *Boston Review* two months before the release of *This Is How You Lose Her*, he states: "Yunior's desire for communion with self and with other is finally undermined by his inability, his unwillingness, to see the women in his life as fully human."[61] He echoed this language in an interview with National Public Radio's Steve Inskeep on the day of the book's release: "I think that a lot of guys, part of our journey is wrestling with, coming to face, our limited imagina[tion] and growing in a way that allows us not only to imagine women as fully human, but to imagine the things that we do to women . . . as actually deeply troubling and as hurting another human being."[62]

What fascinates me as a disability critic, however—and what Díaz has not, to date, addressed—is that Yunior's bodily deterioration is linked to his struggle with misogyny. His physical decline is neither an insignificant element of the text nor a mere autobiographical detail, Díaz's recent forthrightness about his health problems notwithstanding.[63] Furthermore, Yunior is not even the only character in the story to experience bodily damage while learning to see women as "fully human." His friend Elvis undergoes a parallel struggle: "Four years earlier Elvis had a Humvee blow up on him on a highway outside of Baghdad. The burning wreckage pinned him for what felt like a week, so he knows a little about pain. His back and buttocks and right arm so scarred up that even you, Mr. Hard Nose, can't look at them."[64] Elvis, too, devalues women, cheating on his wife and longing for a son instead of a daughter. One of Elvis's lovers, an impoverished woman in the Dominican Republic, has a boy whom he believes to be his son and whom he showers with baseball-themed clothing and toys. However, when Elvis finds out that the child is not his (after taking him for a paternity test at Yunior's prompting), he cuts off contact with her and accuses her of betrayal. Only later, as Yunior begins to recognize the magnitude of his crimes against women, does Elvis also come to see his actions as the more serious betrayal.

To elucidate the significance of Yunior's bodily decline, I emphasize the repetition of the phrase fully human in both of the interviews cited above. In fact, the precise meaning of human is a long-standing preoccupation in Díaz's work; in his interview with Moreno (which precedes the others by two years), he states: "All the books I care about are an attempt to make us more human and to give us narratives that lead to 'the human.'"[65] His focus on the human calls to mind a claim that Siebers has made about the function of disability in modern art: "Disability acquires aesthetic value because it represents for makers of art a critical resource for thinking about what a human being is."[66] My claim, then, is that the struggle of Yunior's character arc is, in fact, to discover what it means to be human in a world in which access to human status remains tightly guarded, a world in which he himself—a poor, immigrant man of African descent—is not consistently recognized as human. If, as Díaz claims in his interview with Moya, there is a fundamental link between Yunior's capacity for recognizing his own humanity and his capacity for recognizing the humanity of women, then I would add to this insight that it is only through the experience of corporeal failure that Yunior is able to achieve this fundamental recognition. Disability comes to function in This Is How You Lose Her as what Mitchell and Snyder call "a mode of experience-based knowledge," for it is through a bodily experience that Yunior experiences as dehumanizing—losing his ability to exercise, living with extreme pain, gaining weight, growing old—that he is able to recognize how he has dehumanized others.[67] It is, in fact, the deterioration of Yunior's body that prompts the decolonization of his consciousness.

This returns me to the question that began this chapter: the relationship between decolonization and disability. The exchange between Fanon and Garland-Thomson appears to pit two struggles over the meaning of human status against one another. Because colonization operates in part by discursively aligning colonized people with corporeal and mental defects, Fanon's anticolonial project seeks to undo this link. Yet Garland-Thomson's critique of Fanon reminds us that attending to only one form of dehumanization can mean restoring humanity to one group by further dehumanizing another. Her critique, however, also fails to explore fully how colonization and disability work together; the link is not purely discursive, as it also contains a material component, for disability can result from longstanding structural inequality. Throughout this chapter, I have argued that the link between disability and colonization is both discursive and material. In other words, I have sought to expand on the necessity for critical attention to what Anjaria calls "innovations on traditional mimesis" within decolonial writing, arguing that Díaz's use of disability—which is neither purely mimetic nor purely metaphorical—provides a better means of undoing the relationship between coloniality and disability than simply rejecting disability (as in Fanon) or the discursive uses of disability (as in Garland-Thomson).[68]

In *Drown* and *This Is How You Lose Her*, Díaz reveals how the restoration of humanity for one group is linked to the restoration of humanity for others. His public statements about his work reveal him to be primarily concerned with white supremacy and misogyny, in particular with the ways men who experience white-supremacist dehumanization often fail to connect this experience with the ways they perpetuate the misogynist dehumanization of women. Examining this question has turned out to be an incredibly complex endeavor for Díaz, spanning three books written decades apart. And, significantly, it is also intimately bound up with disability and, more precisely, with the ways the regulation of human status takes the form of rigid enforcements of bodily norms. What Díaz calls "leading to the human" is an incredibly fraught and difficult endeavor. To decolonize—to contest the denial of one's humanity—requires attention to all of the discursive and material elements that go into that denial. To decolonize requires a rigorous understanding of disability oppression.

Notes

1. Frantz Fanon, *Black Skin, White Masks*, trans. Richard Philcox (New York: Grove Press, [1952] 2008), 119.

2. Rosemarie Garland-Thomson, *Staring: How We Look* (Oxford: Oxford University Press, 2009), 42.

3. Susan Antebi, *Carnal Enscriptions: Spanish American Narratives of Corporeal Difference and Disability* (New York: Palgrave Macmillan, 2009), 4.

4. The passage Garland-Thomson critiques examines the film *Home of the Brave* (1949), which depicts a black soldier injured during the Second World War and alludes to the disproportionate risk to men of color in combat; in this way, the passage comments on the disabling effects of racism.

5. Ato Quayson, *Aesthetic Nervousness: Disability and the Crisis of Representation* (New York: Columbia University Press, 2007), 3.

6. Paula M. L. Moya, "Who We Are and from Where We Speak," *Transmodernity* 1, no. 2 (fall 2011): 79–94.

7. Yunior is the principal narrator in all three of Díaz's published books; he also shares some biographical details with Díaz himself.

8. Anne Garland Mahler, "The Writer as Superhero: Fighting the Colonial Curse in Junot Díaz's *The Brief Wondrous Life of Oscar Wao*," *Journal of Latin American Cultural Studies: Travesía* 19, no. 2 (2010): 119, 120.

9. Ulka Anjaria, "Staging Realism and the Ambivalence of Nationalism in the Colonial Novel," *Novel: A Forum on Fiction* 44, no. 2 (2011): 186, 188.

10. Tobin Siebers, *Disability Aesthetics* (Ann Arbor: University of Michigan Press, 2010), 130. Siebers offers an excellent analysis of how Ysrael reveals the strategies of visual reading to apply to literary texts in his wonderful book *Disability Aesthetics*, which I do not cite extensively here only because my focus is quite different.

11. Anne Connor, "Desenmascarando a Ysrael: The Disfigured Face as Symbol of Identity in Three Latino Texts," *Cincinnati Romance Review* 21 (2002): 153.

12. Garland Mahler, "The Writer as Superhero," 125.

13. Junot Díaz, *The Brief Wondrous Life of Oscar Wao* (New York: Riverhead Books, 2007).

14. Ramón Saldívar, "Historical Fantasy, Speculative Realism, and Postrace Aesthetics in Contemporary American Fiction," *American Literary History* 23, no. 3 (2011): 585.

15. Junot Díaz, *Drown* (New York: Riverhead Books, 1996), 156.

16. John Riofrio, "Situating Latin American Masculinity: Immigration, Empathy and Emasculation in Junot Díaz's *Drown*," *Atenea* 28, no. 1 (June 2008): 34.

17. Riofrio, "Situating Latin American Masculinity," 30.

18. Garland-Thomson, *Staring*, 93.

19. Roberto Fernández Retamar, *Caliban and Other Essays*, trans. Edward Baker (Minneapolis: University of Minnesota Press, 1989), 27.

20. Monica Hanna, "'Reassembling the Fragments': Battling Historiographies, Caribbean Discourse, and Nerd Genres in Junot Díaz's *The Brief Wondrous Life of Oscar Wao*," *Callaloo* 33, no. 2 (2010): 509.

21. David Mitchell and Sharon Snyder, *Narrative Prosthesis: Disability and the Dependencies of Discourse* (Ann Arbor: University of Michigan Press, 2000).

22. One inconsistency between the two stories provides evidence that it is, in fact, Yunior who narrates both. In "Ysrael," Ysrael tells Yunior that his father lives in Nueva York. In "No Face," however, Ysrael lives with his father, and his father (like Yunior's Papi) is a threatening presence. Ysrael's mother finds him outside their home in the

morning without his mask; she gives him his mask and says, "Go . . . Before your father comes out," a command Ysrael obeys because he "knows what happens when his father comes out." That Yunior, after moving to the United States to live with his father, might look back empathetically on the circumstances of the boy he once bullied and imagine a threatening father figure for him would make sense, given that Yunior himself comes to live with a threatening father figure. Díaz, *Drown*, 160.

23. Retamar, *Caliban and Other Essays*, 5.

24. Garland-Thomson, *Staring*, 11.

25. Garland-Thomson, *Staring*, 11.

26. Fanon, *Black Skin, White Masks*, 95.

27. Díaz, *Drown*, 3.

28. Díaz, *Drown*, 4.

29. Díaz, *Drown*, 3.

30. Garland-Thomson, *Staring*, 41.

31. Garland-Thomson, *Staring*, 40.

32. Fanon, *Black Skin, White Masks*, 95.

33. Garland-Thomson, *Staring*, 39.

34. Díaz, *Drown*, 15.

35. Díaz, *Drown*, 17.

36. Díaz, *Drown*, 18.

37. Junot Díaz, *This Is How You Lose Her* (New York: Riverhead Books, 2012), 33, 94.

38. Fanon, *Black Skin, White Masks*, 124.

39. Fanon, *Black Skin, White Masks*, 125.

40. Díaz, *Drown*, 155.

41. Díaz, *Drown*, 155.

42. Díaz, *Drown*, 155.

43. Díaz, *Drown*, 155, 153, 156.

44. Díaz, *Drown*, 153.

45. Díaz, *Drown*, 159.

46. Díaz, *Drown*, 15.

47. Marisel Moreno, "'The Important Things Hide in Plain Sight': A Conversation with Junot Díaz," *Latino Studies* 8, no. 4 (2010): 541.

48. Anjaria, "Staging Realism," 186.

49. Díaz, *This Is How You Lose Her*, 35.

50. Díaz, *Drown*, 5.

51. Díaz, *This Is How You Lose Her*, 37; Díaz, *Drown*, 19.

52. Díaz, *This Is How You Lose Her*, 37; Díaz, *Drown*, 19.

53. Díaz, *This Is How You Lose Her*, 8. Here it appears that Yunior is talking about love, not social justice, but in fact love and social justice are not so clearly separable in Díaz's work, as a recent interview with Moya makes clear. Here Díaz foregrounds the "inequality of love" as a concern of his work, identifying as explicitly political his novel-in-progress, *Monstro*, because of its willingness to confront a "girl's search for—yes—love in a world that has made it its solemn duty to guarantee that poor raced 'conventionally

unattractive' girls like her are never loved." Paula M. L. Moya, "The Search for Decolonial Love, Part II: An Interview with Junot Díaz," *Boston Review*, June 27, 2012, accessed October 6, 2012, http://www.bostonreview.net/BR37.4/junot_diaz_paula_moya_2_oscar _wao_monstro_race.php).

54. Cherríe L. Moraga, *Loving in the War Years: Lo que nunca pasó por sus labios*, 2nd ed. (Cambridge, MA: South End, 2000), 125.

55. This quote actually comes from a different story ("Miss Lora"). Perhaps because Rafa's actions in "The Pura Principle" are so disturbing that such a description is unnecessary, there is no description that is quite so perfectly forthright within the story itself. Díaz, *This Is How You Lose Her*, 149.

56. Díaz, *This Is How You Lose Her*, 149.

57. Díaz, *This Is How You Lose Her*, 161.

58. As Díaz states in an interview with Steve Inskeep of National Public Radio: "The progress of the character is . . . really interesting because, you know, when you encounter Yunior at the beginning, he thinks that, you know, all he has to do is sort of 'fix the relationship.' . . . And I think that by the end of the book we see a Yunior that's completely different. The crime, the pain he has caused, the betrayal of a relationship [with] this woman, he can't escape [it]. . . . And it's a very, very different character at the end as far as his compassion than who we're introduced to at the beginning." NPR staff, "Fidelity in Fiction: Junot Díaz Deconstructs a Cheater," NPR Books, September 11, 2012, accessed October 6, 2012, http://www.npr.org/2012/09/11/160252399 /fidelity-in-fiction-junot-diaz-deconstructs-a-cheater.

59. Díaz, *This Is How You Lose Her*, 161.

60. Díaz, *This Is How You Lose Her*, 209.

61. Paula M. L. Moya, "The Search for Decolonial Love, Part I: An Interview with Junot Díaz," *Boston Review*, June 26, 2012, accessed October 6, 2012, http://www .bostonreview.net/BR37.4/junot_diaz_paula_moya_drown_race.php.

62. NPR staff, "Fidelity in Fiction."

63. During "Junot Díaz: A Symposium," at Stanford University, Díaz was open about his physical deterioration, talking about the pain he feels when he sits still for too long and moving around during scholarly presentations in ways that demanded public acknowledgment of human bodily limitations. Although he has not, as of this writing, identified publicly as a writer with a disability, and although it is beyond the scope of this paper to analyze Díaz's public persona, I see his actions in line with those of disability activists who demand public accommodation for their bodies instead of subjecting their bodies to unnecessary pain in order to comply with professional convention. Based on his willingness to draw attention to his own embodiment and to critique the ableist behavioral norms of academic gatherings, I would say that Díaz was engaged in a kind of disability activism at that symposium. He also calls attention to his bodily limits in interviews; for instance, telling Moya: "Ever since my life exploded five years ago, I've learned a bunch of things and now, with the body failing, it makes you a little bit more humble." Moya, "The Search for Decolonial Love, Part II."

64. Díaz, *This Is How You Lose Her*, 180.
65. Moreno, "'The Important Things Hide in Plain Sight,'" 542.
66. Siebers, *Disability Aesthetics*, 3.
67. Mitchell and Snyder, *Narrative Prosthesis*, 61.
68. Anjaria, "Staging Realism," 188.

3. Laughing through a Broken Mouth in *The Brief Wondrous Life of Oscar Wao*
Lyn Di Iorio

Junot Díaz's Pulitzer Prize–winning *The Brief Wondrous Life of Oscar Wao* has received numerous accolades and an enraptured critical reception. But there has been a dearth of commentary on an important aspect of the book: its laughter. This is a book in which instances of laughter abound, some of them uproarious. Not all the laughter in Díaz's book, however, is related to humor. Laughter is a bodily event, which includes the expulsion of air from the lungs and can involve the whole body, as when one shakes with laughter. Humor, according to the online Oxford dictionary is "the quality of being amusing or comic."[1] Laughter can be tied to humor, but it can also be unrelated to it, as when a baby laughs upon seeing her mother.[2] Here the baby laughs not because mom is funny to look at, but with joy and love. It is therefore important to discuss the different aspects of laughter, particularly the one that opens up a space of freedom in the face of a traumatic and oppressive past and present for Oscar Wao, Latinos living in the United States, and anyone struggling to emerge from an oppressive past or present. Lastly, the many accolades of Díaz emphasize his unique voice. My view is that laughter informs the rhythms of this voice. This laughter not only explains why Díaz's work is important but also posits an important turning point in U.S. Latino/a literary expression, one between narratives that largely explore the transition from Back There to Over Here to narratives that are concerned with showing that identity is fluid and multilayered, filled with experiences that elevate and destroy, and that Latino/a literature is ready to acknowledge the complexity of the many traditions and experiences that form U.S. Latino/a subjectivity.[3] U.S. Latino/a literary expression may be more than a hundred years strong, but the U.S. Latino/a writers that make us laugh are, relatively speaking, few and far between. Sandra Cisneros does it in *Caramelo* (2003) and Roberto G. Fernández does it in *Raining Backwards* (1997), and I do it a bit in my novella *Outside the Bones* (2011), but there are few U.S. Latino/a writers besides Díaz who so consistently have unleashed a multiperspectival laughter in such a successful and profound way. By "multiperspectival laughter" I mean that in Díaz's first novel different characters laugh differently, reflecting their varied perspectives: power (or lack thereof), social standing, and psychology. Sometimes they laugh in counterhegemonic protest, sometimes from a stance of superiority over those less powerful whom they find ridiculous, sometimes from a wretchedly sadistic jokesterism, and once toward the book's end, which is certainly not often enough, from joy and self-affirmation.

Before discussing some instances of laughter in *The Brief Wondrous Life of Oscar Wao*, I need to briefly examine a few of the philosophical stances that inform laughter as a concept, because philosophy's rather snooty attitude toward laughter paradoxically helps explain laughter's power. There is a long history of the philosophy of laughter, and this of itself might generate at least a wry smile. At least four main philosophical strands are easily discernible.[4] First, the so-called superiority strand, first discussed by Plato, marks the attitude of Greek philosophy toward laughter. Second, the "incongruity" strand flows from Kant, Schopenhauer, and Kierkegaard, among others. Third is a strand that critics call "relief theory," tied to Freud's book on jokes. Then there is Nietzsche's position where laughter provides momentum for his notorious Overman's creativity and self-affirmation. Although some critics say that the laughter of Nietzsche's Overman fits the superiority theory, I find that it is Nietzsche's notion that the creator's laughter destabilizes rigid formulations about moral values, thereby carving out a space of freedom for individuals who disagree with dominant values. A fifth strand is Mikhail Bakhtin's well-known notion about the power of "carnivalesque" laughter, which allows the working class to critique those in power. Also flowing from this fifth strand is the idea that there is a "laughter of the oppressed," put forth by the contemporary theologian Jacqueline Bussie, which allows oppressed and minority populations to construct a space of freedom through laughter and allows them to tell their stories.

Philosophers' Takes on Laughter Warped Western Culture

Of little surprise, considering the likes of Plato, Greek philosophy did not approve of laughter. Plato's view was simply that we laugh at vice, weakness, or ignorance in other people who are not as powerful as we are. For Plato, our laughter is a kind of malice, and it is also a lapse of rationality. For both these reasons, Plato thought that the Greeks should be wary of laughter and humor. Violent laughter in particular could provoke a violent reaction and so, in a sense, Plato suggests a relationship between laughter and violence. "And surely we don't want our guardians to be too fond of laughter, either. Indulgence in violent laughter commonly invites a violent reaction."[5] We may read this nowadays and smile, or laugh outright, at the idea that having a good bellyache of risus is dangerous; nonetheless, this notion has powerfully influenced and colonized our world. This, then, is the superiority theory and suggests that those who laugh do so from a position of perceived social dominance. Aristotle and Cicero continue in this vein, and it is ultimately reflected, centuries thereafter, in Thomas Hobbes's notion that laughter strikes its subject with a sense of "Sudden Glory" in the superiority of his position over the object of laughter.[6]

The incongruity theory of laughter is associated with Immanuel Kant, Arthur Schopenhauer, Soren Kierkegaard, and others. In the *Critique of Judgement* Kant says, "In everything that is to excite a lively convulsive laugh there must be something absurd (in which the understanding, therefore, can find no satisfaction)."[7] Kant, like Plato, sees irrationality in laughter, and he notes that it stems from the incongruity between our expectations and their negation. Schopenhauer adds to Kant's position and highlights the importance of paradox in laughter: "The source of the ludicrous is always the paradoxical . . . Accordingly, the phenomenon of laughter always signifies the sudden apprehension of an incongruity between . . . a conception and . . . [its] . . . object . . . thus between the abstract and concrete object of perception." Schopenhauer's addition underlines the incongruity between what is abstract and concrete in humor and what is ideal and real. Kierkegaard expands by noting that laughter springs from contradiction, "for wherever there is life, there is contradiction, and wherever there is contradiction the comical is present."[8]

Freud, differently from these philosophers, argues that jokes are much deeper than just mere comedy and entertainment. The "tendentious joke," he notes, is subversive in nature. Freud says: "By making our enemy small, inferior, despicable or comic, we achieve in a roundabout way the enjoyment of overcoming him."[9] Freud's contribution is important in two ways. First, he notes that in jokes repressed feelings and drives find indirect expression. This explains why so many jokes have sexual, hostile, or indeed sexually aggressive tones, as in homophobic jokes often made by those who fear their own homosexual inclinations. Second, and perhaps more importantly, he points out the potential for social critique in the joke. By making a joke, the powerless can launch an attack on the high and mighty, and despite the humor, there is a note of seriousness. On the other hand, in his paper on humor, which Freud wrote more than twenty years later, he made a distinction between humor and jokes, pointing out that humor is qualitatively better than jokes, which are so often the product of unanalyzed feelings welling up from the unconscious (hence the aforementioned homophobic, as well as ethnophobic and misogynistic jokes). Humor, according to Freud, is more self-reflective, and I will address Freud's notion of humor a little later.

Nietzsche, in contradistinction to the above philosophers, underlines the physicality of laughter, turning it into a metaphor for lightness of spirit in *Thus Spoke Zarathustra*, wherein he has Zarathustra (the product of Nietzsche's own laughter at the notion of Christ as a religious paragon) note that those who are too serious and weighted by absolute and rigid concepts such as God and morality will be unable to laugh. The Overman, who has freed himself from absolute notions, can laugh at others and himself. Laughter for Nietzsche thus suggests flexibility, spontaneity, self-reflection, and, above all, joy in life and in the body. Although Freud and, later, Bakhtin spelled out some of Nietzsche's insights in more detail, Nietzsche brought a revolutionary focus on the self as a body, not an abstraction, spirit, or mental construct. Dancing, as well as laughing, in *Thus Spoke Zarathustra* underline both the joy that can come from being a body and its contingent, ephemeral nature.[10]

Mikhail Bakhtin follows up on the Nietzschean emphasis on the relationship between laughter and the body in his now classic study *Rabelais and His World* (1965, 1968). Here he shows us how carnivalesque laughter allows a momentary taking on of the roles of those in power and a celebratory resistance to the everyday order of things. Bakhtin's idea of resistance focuses on the body, its sexuality and its emissions, and reads this working-class body as filled with a vitality that encompasses the life cycle from birth to death. Bakhtin's ideas about carnivalesque laughter are crucial because they focus on the agency of those who are either disempowered or less powerful. Strongly influenced by Bakhtin, Jacqueline Bussie, in her book *The Laughter of the Oppressed* (2007), discusses laughter as a kind of resistance practiced by the oppressed and notes in particular that laughter can combine with tragedy, which expands Bakhtin's ideas and counters those of most of the philosophers (with the exception of Nietzsche). For Bussie, laughter opens up a terrain of freedom for those experiencing intense oppression.

But let us momentarily leave the philosophers of laughter. With the possible exception of Bakhtin, philosophers might be the least funny people that we can think of. Let us instead look at some instances of laughter in Díaz's book.

The Neocolonized Strike Back Laughing

The first unmistakable example is the instance of the *fukú*. This is the Dominican colloquial word for a magical spell that is, precisely speaking, a curse. What is funny about the fukú? Well, to begin with, Fuck You. The language differentiality between Spanish and English is the immediate cause of laughter with the fukú. You do not even have to be a Spanish speaker to laugh, since the "Fuck You" joke is funny in the Schopenhauerian vein, underlining the incongruity between what appears to be an apparently exotic, foreign, or unintelligible word and the quotidian curse that an English-language reader immediately hears and that has colonized the world.

Incongruity also marks our laughter at the wonderfully lofty history that Díaz creates for the fukú. The little word, hitherto known only in the Caribbean, designates a widespread blight in the Americas: "the Curse and the Doom of the New World" and *Fukú americanus*.[11] Ultimately it is a worldwide phenomenon, since "the arrival of Europeans on Hispaniola" unleashes it "and we've all been in the shit ever since."[12] Some might find Díaz's critique of Columbus to be de rigueur political correctness. Indeed, an examination of a few of the more than 1,000 reader reviews of *The Brief Wondrous Life of Oscar Wao* on Amazon.com shows that conservative reviewers sometimes view the book this way. But what those reviewers might call "politically correct" is actually rendered funny by Díaz's use of the mild expletive "in the shit." The use of the expletive itself is often very funny on its own terms—as naming a body emission to describe a state of being is funny because body emissions bring us down to earth and the earth that is in our bodies, as Bakhtin showed to marvelous effect in his discussion of Rabelais's work.

It is also particularly funny to think of Columbus's discovery of the New World through this expletive. Until quite recently the discovery of the New World has been celebrated with exalted language and rather dull stone statues of the admiral, in the major cities of the Americas as well as Madrid. It is the incongruity between what we normally associate with the name of Columbus (whether it exalts or excoriates, as in the truly politically correct) and what Díaz's narrative underlines: not glory or infamy but muck, feces, and the heaviness it brings to bodies (and minds) that need to labor to get out of the shithole that Columbus dug for us. The hilarity of the *fukú* in this sense is not far from hysteria. It is a counterattack that starts in the unconscious, working its way up to the surface through this word with complex origins, similar to one of the colloquial words used in Puerto Rico, my own originary *sitio*, for the magic spell *fufú*, a word rooted in Afro-Caribbean religion and sorcery, practices which in themselves were resistant to colonization and which frequently in the Caribbean accompanied outright rebellion, as in the case of Haiti. So a *fufú* can be a spell that helps you resist or control a powerful enemy. Additionally, in places where people believe in magic and *brujería* (or witchcraft), such as the Caribbean, where brujería still has more of a pull on even supposedly well-educated people, a fufú or fukú is a spell that, as Díaz indicates, is often used to explain why things have gone wrong. It is because your enemies put something on you, a *trabajito*, a fufú, a fukú.

But Díaz does not refer to the word's Afro-Caribbean origins in much detail; instead he exposes the *revulú* and cultural hysteria that ensue when misfortunes are attributed to magical curses. The laughter might come from what Plato cautioned us is a misplaced feeling of superiority—we laugh because as readers we feel superior to the people who believe in fukús or fufús (it has been "real baaad" to laugh since Plato). But what is particularly brilliant about the fukú, the way that Díaz writes it, is that even as readers we laugh with anxiety. Smartly, the narrator recognizes this when he says: "It's perfectly fine if you don't believe in these 'superstitions' . . . Because no matter what you believe, fukú believes in you."[13] The narrator's comic yet also threatening tone underlines the type of anxiety and hysteria that the fukú entails. Although it may be a Dominican or Latino/a "thing," the anxiety about having "bad shit" put on you by a brujo or voodoo doctor has had a way of seeping into the culture of the Americas in general. Witness to this is the general interest in things like astrology and the Tarot, Afro-Caribbean magic in and out of horror flicks, and, generally speaking, doomsday fears about current and approaching political and natural catastrophes of our own making. Many of us partially or fully repress acknowledgment of these things, thereby often increasing our sense of anxiety. As well, the threatening tone of the narrator's voice, softened by laughter, makes the point that populations that used to practice fukús on their little islands, far from the metropolis, are now not just residents of the metropolis but, by virtue of Díaz's seductive voice, a part of "you," that is, the reader.

If fukú, or Fuck You, is a hilarious critique of Europe's conquest of the Americas, the U.S. military presence in the Caribbean and the Third World is not left untouched or rather un-fukúed: "What do you think these soldiers, technicians, and spooks carried with them, in their rucks, in their suitcases, in their shirt pockets, on the hair inside their nostrils, caked up around their shoes? Just a little gift from my people to America, as small repayment for an unjust war. That's right folks. Fukú."[14] It is hilarious, by way of incongruity, to imagine the Dominican curse attaching to the all-mighty American military forces. Freud's relief theory helps us get that the joke is coming from the apparently powerless Dominicans, connecting their guerrilla humor with other more lethal guerrilla tactics. Bakhtin's notion that carnivalesque laughter creates, if only for a moment, an opening for the beginnings of social change is also helpful here, as this is one of the first passages in which Díaz's social critique of the imperialistic militarism of the United States in particular is facilitated by the laughter.

Finally, when it comes to the fukú, the narrator introduces both the particularity of the terrain he wishes to cover as well as its relevance to very recent history: "But in those elder days, fukú had it good; it even had a hypeman of sorts, a high priest, you could say. Our then dictator-for-life Rafael Leonidas Trujillo Molina."[15] What a real fuck you, I mean fukú. Classical Greek literature makes out comedy to be one of the lowest of the literary forms, and most theorists of laughter to this day hold that, as we discuss above, there can be no fear or even other emotions associated with laughter. Bakhtin disagrees with this, and so does Díaz, introducing a serious and even ominous note with the mention of Trujillo, but still retaining the note of laughter by calling Trujillo the "hypeman" or "high priest" of the fukú.

Incongruity still causes the laughter, but anger is also seeping into it as when the narrator calls the leader who thought of himself as Napoleonic "fuckface." However, one of the book's most creative renditions of incongruity happens in the way that Trujillo gets turned into a Dungeons and Dragons evil villain: "He was our Sauron, our Arawn, our Darkseid, our Once and Future Dictator, a personaje so outlandish, so perverse, so dreadful that not even a sci-fi writer could have made his ass up."[16] Thinking of Trujillo as a character in the Dungeons and Dragons fantasy role-playing game is an amazingly lucid step in two ways. First, it provides a distancing mechanism from the tragedy and fear that Trujillo visited on the Dominican Republic, Haiti, and even other countries (as his powerful fukú extended to Cuba, Venezuela, and even stateside). And distance allows not just for humor but for an increased ability to understand the situation, both in its terror and absurdity. Second, reading Trujillo as a "dark lord" is an excellent way of introducing a reader to the history of the Dominican Republic, a history not a lot of Americans have cared about, probably up to the publication of Díaz's novel, a lack of interest the narrator and author recognize wryly at the beginning of the footnote. Avid science fiction fans can now try to find other correspondences between the literature they love and this historically inflected novel. In the detailing of Trujillo's many outlandish crimes in the footnote, we also see a bit of what Jacqueline Bussie terms the mixing of tragedy with laughter in the work of those writing about oppressed populations. Nonetheless, in these early pages, and even when the narration veers to the darkness of the Trujillo regime, laughter still emanates from humor.

Although the book is often hilariously funny, humor-related laughter does not permeate its tapestry evenly. We need to ask ourselves, I think, who (besides the reader) laughs in this book and when? And also at what point does the book's laughter start to reveal a texture different than that of humor tinged with anger, cruelty, or a sense of superiority?

Yunior Laughs First but Not Last

I would like to suggest that Yunior is laughing as he tells the story, especially when he tells us about Oscar's beginnings. Here the superiority theory of laughter applies because Yunior's relationship with Oscar is frequently marked by Yunior's feeling of superiority. After all, from the beginning of the book, Yunior finds Oscar laughable from the perspective of Dominicans who believe masculinity is based on hypersexuality and the serial seduction of women, and we later learn that Yunior thinks of himself as fulfilling this stereotype of Latino Lover. However, by focusing on how much of an opposite Oscar is to the stereotype of Latino hypermasculinity, Yunior opens up a space of reflection on how Latino males can move beyond the stereotype.[17] Since Yunior feels guilty about his constant and compulsive womanizing, and especially guilty in hindsight about cheating on Lola, who is depicted as being as noble and kind as she is beautiful, Oscar, Lola's brother, becomes an opposite image, a kind of alter ego or double that allows Yunior to contemplate their differences—his hypermasculinity and Oscar's tenderness and softness—and try to consider whether change is possible. Since Oscar does change over the course of the book, as I will examine shortly, the possibility of Yunior's transformation is broached as well, even though we can see in Díaz's latest book, *This Is How You Lose Her* (2012), that Yunior's compulsive philandering continues unabated. But it is ultimately Yunior who looks back on the story of Oscar as one that must be told, so in this sense we can posit the idea that their relationship is one that challenges Yunior to reexamine his conceptions about tenderness as a characteristic of masculinity and about what it means to be a Latino male either Back There or Over Here.

Attendant to the recognition that Oscar awakens in Yunior is the sense in hindsight that Oscar was not as easy to dominate as Yunior at first assumed and turned out to be stronger in character in the end than Yunior. In this sense the laughter that attends the earlier parts of the book in Yunior's account of Oscar's early experiences gives way to a self-deprecating kind of humor as Yunior becomes more conscious of how wrong he was about Oscar: "But I wasn't as old-school as I am now, just real fucking dumb, assumed keeping an eye on somebody like Oscar wouldn't be no Herculean chore. I mean, shit, I was a weight lifter, picked up bigger fucking piles than him every damn day. You can start the laugh track any time you want."[18] Yunior judges Oscar at first as someone whose physical deviation from the norm renders him easily handled. And Yunior seems to think that fat people have the sentience of barbells. But later Yunior regards this mistake with rue and so, interestingly, instructs the reader to start the laugh track, assuming that for his own stupidity he is the one who should now be laughed at, thereby underlining how strong the Platonic to Hobbesian line on laughter as superiority is in Western-inflected literary texts, since Yunior, who once laughed at Oscar, is now conscious that he is the one somebody, God or reader, should laugh at.

Yunior as narrator is very aware of the observer-reader's readiness to laugh at him in yet another moment when he promises Lola he will not lie to her and he tells the reader, "Don't laugh. My intentions were pure."[19] Yunior shows in these moments that he understands that the stereotype of the Latino Don Juan is less sexy than it is laughable, not just to observers but even to the Don Juans themselves. And that is partly what he is learning in his exploration of his relationship with Oscar. Oscar seemed like the buffoon early on in the book, but the more we progress, the more we find that it is really Yunior whose behavior can seem ludicrous, even to himself. We also start to see that as Yunior seems more ridiculous and Oscar more noble, as in fact they lose their distinctiveness and become each other's doubles, the notions of individualism and Platonic hierarchy are put more and more in question.

Green Martian Laughter

After I gave an early version of this article at "Junot Díaz: A Symposium," at Stanford, the author noted in conversation, and later in an e-mail exchange, that there were some lines having to do with laughter that were cut from an early draft of the book. "Oscar's mother, Belicia, was supposed to laugh at Oscar when he came home crying after he loses Maritza. But I decided to go in a different direction," Díaz told me by e-mail. The line that was cut was "His mother laughed like a Green Martian. Which is to say when she laughed, you cried."[20] By calling it "Green Martian laughter," Díaz highlights how alienating and strange it is for a mother to laugh at her child's sadness. The line may not have made it to the final version of Oscar Wao, but it certainly throws light on the psychological profile of Oscar's small family unit. Belicia has experienced a life of hardship and trauma back on the island, one which her children know very little about, and it has endowed her with a cruelty that affects her relationship with her children, particularly her daughter, who notes that her mother always seems to be screaming at her and Oscar. Because what happened to Belicia to deform her psyche is part of the social drama and traumatic history of the Dominican Republic, and since Oscar's murder shows that this history is ongoing, it is not just Plato's and Hobbes's superiority theory that explains her attitude but an understanding that Belicia is reenacting the trauma she has suffered and is also unconsciously perhaps trying to toughen up her children so that they will not suffer as she has.

Díaz thus shows how traumatic history repeats on the individual level—since Beli's cruelty may be said to be a belated and wounded response to her past—and also on the communal level, when Oscar is beaten to near death, just as his mother was many years before. Thus, even though he does not know much at all about his mother's beating or her past, Oscar's death could be attributed to the ongoing structure of a communal trauma. As Kai Erickson notes, sometimes the tissues of community can be damaged in much the same way as the tissues of an individual mind and body. Traumatic wounds inflicted on individuals can combine to create a mood, a group ethos, different from the sum of the private wounds that make up that community.[21] Also, clearly, Beli received very little love when she was growing up, except from her grandmother La Inca, and she does not know how to really give her children love. Her laughter in the excised quote and her harshness and cruelty in instances throughout the final version of the book can be explained by her own traumatic story, and also that of the larger Dominican community, on the island and in the United States. If the community as a whole cannot attempt to correct behavior patterns, the book suggests, the traumatic wounds will continue to repeat into the future.

A Joke Can Spell Death, but Death Is No Joke

Interestingly, the murder of Oscar the second time he is taken to the cane fields by the *Capitán* and his goons is also the product of this kind of cruel laughter: "Listen, we'll let you go if you tell us what fuego means in English." To this Oscar responds, "Fire."[22] The henchmen, we know from what happens later, kill him, and Yunior's narration does not describe the actual moment. In fact, the death scene ends with this literally terminal joke. So the nasty joke not only highlights the henchmen's sense of superiority, but actually is part of the murder, which also shows how paternalism back on the island of origin marries a cruel, and obviously unethical, jokesterism with derision of U.S. Latinos. Freud's understanding of hostile jokes as releases for feelings the jokester has repressed informs an understanding of this moment. The henchmen are laughing at Oscar's innocence, and perhaps chalking it up to the fact that he is a U.S. Latino.

While the henchmen are envious of U.S. Latinos, cannot honestly articulate this envy, and thus have to partially transform it into a joke, I do not completely want to let Oscar off the hook, for while Oscar is noble, given his family's warnings and his knowledge of the violence of Dominican history, he is blind, to say the least. Oscar sees what he wants to see and, in a sense, one wonders if he prefers a brief romance punctuated by death to reality, because he does not believe that he could have a relationship with someone less psychically compromised than Ybón, whose status as a sex dancer is less the issue than is her role as the monstrous Capitán's steady mistress. If one were to follow, for example, René Girard's theory that triangular relationships reveal not the desire, lust, or love for one object but, rather, the subject's desire to be somehow like the model, then Oscar's desire for Ybón is indeed revealing.[23] There is homoeroticism here, but I will leave that strand for queer theorists to untangle. What is most interesting to me is Oscar's fascination with patriarchal male figures who also stand in for the origin. After all, the Capitán's violent persona is a near replica of Trujillo's. Oscar's self-destructive desire for the mistress of a killer may show that what he is after is a confrontation with the archetype of violent Latino manhood.

A Joke Started It All

Another important part of the narrative that is shaped by a joke is the origin of the traumatic history of the Cabral family. This is brought to light late in the book, in the "Chiste Apocalyptus," or "Apocalyptic Joke," section. Here we learn of the unease, and mounting anxiety, that follows Dr. Abelard Cabral's refusal to take his beautiful daughter Jacquelyn to meet Trujillo at a party, despite the fact that the dictator had mandated it. A few weeks afterward, Abelard is cornered by some men who invite him for a few drinks at a local men's club. Abelard gets very drunk, driven by his anxiety about what might happen to him and his family for having disobeyed Trujillo's implicit order to, essentially, present and offer up his daughter to the dictator. He asks the men to assist him in putting a piece of furniture that was strapped on top of his car into the trunk and when he does so he makes a joke.

> I hope there aren't any bodies in here. That he made the foregoing remark is not debated. Abelard conceded as much in his "confession." This trunk-joke in itself caused discomfort among the "boys," who were all too aware of the shadow that the Packard automobile casts on Dominican history . . . During the Hurricane of 1931 the Jefe's henchmen often drove their Packards to the bonfires where the volunteers were burning the dead, and out of their trunks they would pull out "victims of the hur-

ricane." All of whom looked strangely dry and were often clutching opposition party materials. The wind, the henchmen would joke, drove a bullet straight through the head of this one. Har-har![24]

We have here of course the interesting contrast in humor of oppressors and oppressed. The oppressors, the henchmen, can be said to be laughing from the position of Sudden Glory, finding their victims, whose protests have led to their deaths, ridiculous and themselves superior as a consequence. Abelard's humor is more complex, and a direct result of the terribly anxious state in which he finds himself after defying Trujillo, knowing that if he stays on the island, he may be punished, tortured, and executed and his beloved daughter Jacquelyn will be kidnapped by Trujillo, who was notorious for raping hundreds of Dominican women he found attractive.

In his essay "Humour," published in 1927, almost twenty years after the book on jokes, Freud makes a distinction between jokes, the comic, and humor, which may throw light on the difference between the henchmen's joke and Abelard's comment. Whereas Freud's book on jokes holds that jokes are the contribution of the unconscious to the comic, humor, on the other hand, according to Freud, stems from the superego's observing the ego and finding its concerns to be somewhat trivial. Jokesters, tellingly, according to this later essay, laugh at others the way the henchmen do in the example above, find them ridiculous and themselves superior. Such jokes can tell us a great deal about the unconscious motives of the jokesters. And, of course, what the henchmen's jokes tell us is that they murdered the victims of the hurricane. Although this is hardly "unconscious" knowledge for the henchmen themselves, it certainly is knowledge that the regime represses from direct discussion or confrontation, so one could say that the knowledge that the protestors of Trujillo have been murdered lurks in the unconscious of the country at this time, since it is so constantly repressed from discussion and many citizens do not want to believe it. And even today, older Dominicans in New York will blithely discuss how great the Trujillo regime was, still arguably repressing from consciousness its darkness.

Unlike jokes, humor, on the other hand, according to Freud, emanates from the split in the psyche between superego and ego, in which part of the self (the superego) laughs at itself (the ego) and finds itself ridiculous in a way that contributes to its self-knowledge: "Like jokes and the comic, humour has something liberating about it; but it also has something of grandeur and elevation, which is lacking in the other two ways of obtaining pleasure from intellectual activity . . . The ego . . . insists that it cannot be affected by the traumas of the external world. It shows, in fact, that such traumas are no more than occasions for it to gain pleasure."[25] Humor, in effect, according to Freud, is a kind of defense against trauma, and of course this fits Abelard's comment very well, as its black humor is a defense against Trujillo's attempt to control him and rape his daughter. Although I wouldn't go as far as saying that Abelard derives pleasure from the trauma of his situation, he certainly evinces a great deal of self-knowledge through humor. I actually disagree to a certain extent with Freud's notion that the ego learns from the superego that the traumatic situation is no more than an occasion for it to gain pleasure. It seems to me that much of the wisdom of this remark of Abelard's also stems from a realization that hitherto he and all who have chosen not to protest against the Trujillo regime are complicit to a certain extent and thus they are all, in some sense, carrying the bodies in the trunks of their Packards. Of course, one of the "hidden witnesses" against Abelard later lyingly turns the latter's humorous and oblique critique into an obvious condemnation of Trujillo by adding the sentence, "Trujillo must have cleaned them out for me," which clarifies Abelard's oblique humor, making it easier to accuse him of trying to subvert the Trujillo regime.[26] It is clear, however, that the latter sentence is an interpretation of the remark.

Another interesting trait of Abelard's actual remark is its melancholy. Simon Critchley, in discussing Freud's essay "On Mourning and Melancholia" in his book on humor, says that in melancholia the subject becomes an "abject object." He is referring to Freud's well-known proposal that conscience is produced by the split between the ego and the critical agency of the superego, in which instead of mourning the loss of a concrete, real-world person or thing, which is usually a finite process, the subject instead introjects the lost object, thereby internalizing the sense of loss into melancholia, which, unlike mourning, never ends.[27] Abelard's melancholic humor is nascent with the threat to his daughter and his family and to some extent helps him traverse the horror of his situation by allowing him to recognize in himself a Dominican everyman. When Abelard's mistress wants him to leave the island with her, and send for his family later, and Abelard turns her down, one wonders why Abelard does not instead act to get his family out of the island before the looming disaster. This reader thinks it would have been better to have menos chistes tristes y más acción. But the feeling that one cannot take action because the consequences may be even more horrific is what increases the melancholic humor.

After All, Oscar Has the Last Laugh

Oscar himself does not do a great deal of outright laughing in the book, but he does evince a deep and rich, if quiet, sense of humor, whereby he shows great self-knowledge even as he gently pokes fun at others. For example, when he first meets Yunior, he says, "Hail, Dog of God," riffing on both the Latin roots of "Dominican" and on nationality in wordplay that Yunior initially does not understand but eventually figures out.[28] But Yunior does not seem to figure out that Oscar is also referring to Yunior's reputation as a womanizer and is subtly calling him out on it, double playing with "dog," which is also a slang term for a hypersexual and untrustworthy man. In this sense he is also a jokester in the Freudian sense, obliquely critiquing those who are more powerful.

In his early history, Oscar was a victim of ridicule and laughter and emphasized this by weeping copiously, starting with his rejection by Maritza as a little kid, as mentioned before. Oscar's first experience in the Dominican Republic, by virtue of not killing him right away, makes him strong enough to face death when it comes, as he had courted it in his courting of Ybón. In fact, any laughter linked with humor almost completely dries up when Oscar weeps the first time he is beaten up in the cane fields in the Dominican Republic. Whereas Yunior narrated the child Oscar's humiliation in a way that made readers complicit with Yunior's laughter at Oscar, he narrates the last segment of Oscar's life with tenderness, showing how he and his double have matured by this point in the story: "This time Oscar didn't cry when they drove him back to the cane fields . . . The smell of the ripening cane was unforgettable, and there was a moon, a beautiful full moon, and Clive begged the men to spare Oscar, but they laughed."[29] The military men (those who because of their status and power in society should behave ethically but do not, and thus are filled with malice of the soul according to Plato) express their feelings of superiority in their laughter.

So, Díaz's text is enriched by different kinds of laughter. We have the laughter of those who laugh at others and feel superior to them, such as all the henchmen of the Trujillo regime, whose cruel jokes reveal the fears they attempt to kill in their killings; Beli's laughter in the sentence excised from the book (although her schadenfreude appears in other episodes, too); and Yunior at the start of the book, as he distances himself from Oscar. However, Yunior's and Beli's laughter is not as lethal as the henchmen's. Then we have the ribald laughter that attaches to the whole notion of the fukú, both as a word and as a wonderful counterhegemonic reading of the colonial history that Columbus's discovery spurred. And we have Oscar obliquely laughing and critiquing Yunior.

Lastly, we have a laughter that is somewhat new for the book, and that is Oscar's laughter right before his death: "You should be worrying, Grod said, about yourself. Oscar laughed a little too through his broken mouth. Don't worry, Clive, he said. They're too late."[30] One of the many triumphs of the book is that in the face of those who laugh through their sense of dominance and privilege, Oscar, who has suffered disenfranchisement of all kinds—economic, racial, sexual, and psychic—learns to laugh from a stance that transcends superiority, since it needs no object to deride and ridicule in order to affirm itself. For Oscar, instead of detaching (and protecting) himself with irony, as he did when he called Yunior a Dog of God, now laughs, clear that he has finally achieved what he wanted, even if the price is death. He in fact is filled with openness, calmness, and courage. The laughter here comes close to the laughter of Nietzsche's Overman, a being whose creativity and joy in it elevates him, according to Zarathustra. I compare him to the Overman inasmuch as Oscar finally creates his life and death. He has never felt complete joy in his writing, because his life diverged too much from his projected creations. His final letter to Yunior, in which he revels in the fact that he and Ybón have had sex and notes in wonder that she "tastes like Heineken," shows that he is finally finding joy in what is bodily, also something that characterizes Nietzsche's Overman.[31]

Once he has even the brief experience of heightened vitality that his dogged (Dominicanus) love for Ybón brings, he is able to plunge into life and to challenge the particularly brutish hypermales who will kill him. He was able to see through them before and to obliquely critique them through humor, but now he speaks back to them directly in his long speech, describing how they are wrong to kill him and how he will haunt them when they are close to death:

> He told them about Ybón and the way he loved her and how much they had risked and that they'd started to dream the same dreams and say the same words. He . . . told them if they killed him they would probably feel nothing . . . not until they were old and weak . . . and then they would sense him waiting for them on the other side and over there he wouldn't be no fatboy or dork or kid no girl had ever loved; over there he'd be a hero, an avenger. Because anything you can dream (he put his hand up) you can be.[32]

The last sentimental sentence here shows how inexperienced Oscar is at speaking truth to evil. It's also possible to read the passage as escapist, as Oscar seems to be saying that he will fulfill his dream of being a hero only in death. In a provocative article on laughter in Kafka's work, Chris Danta extends Deleuze and Guattari's observation that all of Kafka's work leads to laughter, rather than tragedy, by suggesting that Kafkaesque laughter allows neither heroic status for his protagonists nor the satisfaction of tragic catharsis for his readers.[33] Tragedy typically consoles us, Danta says, by presenting us with the interiority of the hero, a figure of honor and solitude. But Kafka's heroes are allowed no interiority—Danta poses the example of Josef K.—and are subject to humiliation. In Kafka, laughter tinged with humor wipes away the consolation that true tragedy would offer readers; instead it unsettles them.[34] René Girard further illuminates differences and similarities between comedy and tragedy by noting that both stage conflicts among characters who are opposites and doubles. But whereas tragedy tends to focus on the tragic hero as unique, comedy shows us that this individualism is lost amid mimetic struggles in which the contestants become more similar to each other through their mimetic desires.[35] Something similar happens in this instance. Oscar speaks soulfully of being an avenger after his death. But the heroic interiority and individualism this speech proffers is then denied Oscar by the Capitán's henchmen, who pretend that they are moved by the speech and will let Oscar go, but then pull the "How do you say fuego in English?" joke. By answering the question, Oscar turns from potential tragic hero to fool, and Díaz unsettles us with this joke, the cruelest of jokes, indeed, in that it is an execution.

However, even as Oscar is divested of both interiority and heroic status by the joke that is reality, his laughter through his broken mouth also shows that he has nonetheless been transformed through his efforts to create his own fate, however dark. The theologian Jacqueline Bussie's idea of "the laughter of the oppressed" is helpful here as she underlines laughter as not so much a response to humor and comedy as an expression of self-affirmation that happens in moments of affliction, torture, and death, an acknowledgment of the reality of human suffering. So, for example, Bussie points to several moments of laughter that occur in Toni Morrison's *Beloved* (1987), the strangest of which is the slave Sixo's laughter as he is burned on a pyre by white men. He laughs in joy at the knowledge that his love, the Seven Mile Woman, has escaped to freedom and is carrying his child. Bussie notes, "If Sixo, or any member of the African American community for that matter, had waited around for someone to offer him an alternative consciousness rather than creatively constructing one, Morrison implies that he would have died moaning rather than laughing."[36] Just so with Oscar. In the past, Oscar's weeping tried to stave off suffering and, in doing so, he negated himself and was floored by the ridicule of others. Oscar's laughter "through a broken mouth" allows him for the first time to feel "through," in an acknowledgment of his present heightened life experience and beyond that to his death. With a newfound sense of freedom and joy, he laughs, preempting and countering the soulless laughter of the jokesters of death. In this most important instance, the sovereignty of either disappears, and laughter is like tears.[37]

Notes

1. *Oxford Online Dictionaries*, accessed April 22, 2015, http://oxforddictionaries.com/definition/english/humour.

2. John Morreall discusses the distinction between laughter and humor with great clarity in his wonderfully well-edited anthology, *The Philosophy of Laughter and Humor* (Albany: SUNY Press, 1987), 4–5.

3. I owe this locution to Alejo Carpentier, who uses it to explore the disjunct between Africa as an origin and New World reality in his seminal magical realist work, *The Kingdom of This World* (1949), trans. Harriet de Onís (New York: Farrar, Straus and Giroux, 1957), 14–15.

4. I owe the first three delineations, the Superiority Theory, the Incongruity Theory, and the Relief Theory, to John Morreall's discussion in *The Philosophy of Laughter and Humor*, 5–7.

5. Plato, *The Republic*, trans. Desmond Lee, 2nd ed. (New York: Penguin Books, 2003), 59.

6. Thomas Hobbes, *The Leviathan* [1651] (Buffalo, NY: Broadview Books, 2011), 73.

7. Immanuel Kant, *Critique of Judgement* [1790] (New York: Cosimo Classics, 2007), 133.

8. Arthur Schopenhauer, *The World as Will and Idea* [1818], vol. 2, trans. E. F. J. Payne (Mineola, NY: Dover, 1966), 91; Søren Kierkegaard, *Concluding Unscientific Postscript to Philosophical Crumbs*, ed. Alastair Hannay (Cambridge: Cambridge University Press, 2009), 459.

9. Sigmund Freud, *Jokes and Their Relation to the Unconscious* [1905], trans. James Strachey (New York: W. W. Norton, 1990), 122.

10. See Walter Kaufmann, *The Portable Nietzsche* (New York: Penguin, 1959), 103–439.

11. Junot Díaz, *The Brief Wondrous Life of Oscar Wao* (New York: Riverhead Books, 2007), 1.

12. Díaz, *Oscar Wao*, 1.

13. Díaz, *Oscar Wao*, 5.

14. Díaz, *Oscar Wao*, 4.

15. Díaz, Oscar Wao, 2.

16. Díaz, Oscar Wao, 2.

17. I make a similar point in a very brief analysis of the eponymous short story, which gave rise to Díaz's first novel, in my first academic book Killing Spanish: Literary Essays on Ambivalent U.S. Latino/a Identity (New York: Palgrave Macmillan, 2004, 2009).

18. Díaz, Oscar Wao, 171.

19. Díaz, Oscar Wao, 199.

20. It seems appropriate to observe in a note that the aforementioned excised line had a footnote attached to it, a quote from Edgar Rice Burroughs's A Princess of Mars (1917) as described by Díaz: "But I was to learn that the Martian smile is merely perfunctory, and that the Martian laugh is a thing to cause strong men to blanch in horror. The ideas of humor among the green men of Mars are widely at variance with our conceptions of incitants to merriment. The death agonies of a fellow being are, to these strange creatures provocative of the wildest hilarity, while their chief form of commonest amusement is to inflict death on their prisoners of war in various ingenious and horrible ways."

21. See Kai Erickson's groundbreaking article, "Notes on Trauma and Community," in Trauma: Explorations in Memory, ed. Cathy Caruth (Baltimore: Johns Hopkins University Press, 1995), 183–99.

22. Díaz, Oscar Wao, 322.

23. See René Girard, Deceit, Desire, and the Novel: Self and Other in Literary Structure (Baltimore: Johns Hopkins University Press, 1976).

24. Díaz, Oscar Wao, 234.

25. Sigmund Freud, "Humour," trans. Joan Riviere, International Journal of Psychoanalysis 9, no. 1 (1927): 1–6, 163.

26. Díaz, Oscar Wao, 235.

27. Simon Critchley, On Humour (London: Routledge, 2002), 97.

28. Díaz, Oscar Wao, 171.

29. Díaz, Oscar Wao, 320.

30. Díaz, Oscar Wao, 320.

31. Díaz, Oscar Wao, 334. Let us not forget, though, that Nietzsche himself fell far short of the Overman's joy in the body, and may have been more like the pre-Ybón Oscar.

32. Díaz, Oscar Wao, 322.

33. See Gilles Deleuze and Felix Guattari, Kafka: Toward a Minor Literature (1975); (Minneapolis: University of Minnesota Press, 1986).

34. Chris Danta, "Sarah's Laughter: Kafka's Abraham," Modernism/modernity 15, no. 2 (2008): 343–59.

35. See Girard's brilliant discussion on how laughter involves both mastery and its failure in "Perilous Balance: A Comic Hypothesis" in René Girard, To Double Business Bound (Baltimore: Johns Hopkins University Press, 1978), 124–25.

36. Jacqueline Bussie, The Laughter of the Oppressed: Ethical and Theological Resistance in Wiesel, Morrison, and Endo (New York: T and T Clark, 2007), 186.

37. With this formulation, I am clearly indebted to Girard's essay on comedy.

4. A Portrait of the Artist as a Young Cannibalist
Reading Yunior (Writing) in *The Brief Wondrous Life of Oscar Wao*
Monica Hanna

> I would devour this race to sing it,
> this race that according to Emerson
> managed to preserve to a hair
> for three or four thousand years
> the ugliest features in the world.
> I would eat these features, eat
> the last three or four thousand years, every hair.
> And I would eat Emerson, his transparent soul, his
> soporific transcendence.
> —Li-Young Lee, "The Cleaving"

As a *Künstlerroman*, an "artist's novel" that tracks the artistic formation of a protagonist, Junot Díaz's novel *The Brief Wondrous Life of Oscar Wao* (2007) draws on a tradition that includes diverse European works such as Goethe's *Wilhelm Meister's Apprenticeship* (1795) and James Joyce's *A Portrait of the Artist as a Young Man* (1916), but also works in the U.S. Latino/a literary canon, like José Antonio Villareal's *Pocho* (1959) and Sandra Cisneros's *The House on*

Mango Street (1984). Unlike many *Künstlerromane*, Díaz's novel tracks the formation of not one but two artists: Oscar, the presumed protagonist, and Yunior, the narrator. The latter, Yunior, is a narrator and character appearing throughout much of Díaz's writing to date with some variations. The Yunior in this novel reveals much less about his personal life and family than in the stories in *Drown* (1996) and *This Is How You Lose Her* (2012). While he does disclose some information about his relationships with Lola and Oscar, the main areas of the narrator's self-revelations relate to his development as a writer and intellectual, from his college experiments in genre to his maturation into a productive writer-historian and creative writing instructor at a college in New Jersey. These revelations run parallel to his depiction of Oscar's development as a prolific writer of science fiction and fantasy. Reading *Oscar Wao* as a Künstlerroman allows for an investigation into the aesthetic project that Díaz theorizes in the novel. This chapter traces the novel's vision of the power available to the engaged Dominican American writer and intellectual, and also the warnings that it sounds. This vision is inextricably linked to the imagination of the artist not as a singular heroic figure but rather one deeply rooted in his community and motivated to create art in part by a desire to embody that greater community beyond himself.

The novel privileges what I term an aesthetic of artistic and cultural consumption. Whereas in *Drown* one of the central motifs is that of Yunior's constant vomiting, indicating a rejection of his father and the violence and insecurity that surround him daily, in *The Brief Wondrous Life of Oscar Wao*, we have instead the motif of a Yunior who is constantly trying to consume the story agents in order to narrate. Consuming Oscar's experience metaphorically, he becomes the filter through which the story is told. His path as a budding writer mirrors Oscar's: he is, in a sense, Oscar's apprentice in college, though his role morphs after Oscar's death when he becomes the caretaker of Oscar's literary oeuvre. This apprenticeship goes beyond the literary, however, as Yunior conflates elements of Oscar's biography with his own. By the end of the novel, Yunior oversees Oscar's literary legacy by appointing himself as his friend's executor, storing Oscar's surviving journals and artistic production in four refrigerators in Yunior's basement. Reflecting this consumption is the storage of Oscar's papers in refrigerators (normally a storage site for food) and the references to "eating toto" in relation to Lola, another character consumed and then told by Yunior as he experiments with giving her a narrative voice in the novel. Metaphorically consuming these characters and even going so far as to speak for them, and thus in a sense embodying them, allows Yunior to forge a connection and create an affiliation with this family through his writing. Writing and narrative consumption become ways of forging community.

Yunior as a writer might be in part motivated by a desire for control or power, but he is primarily motivated by a love that allows him to consume these historically discarded figures, figures who are historically unloved and unintegrated into the Dominican national story, especially as members of the diaspora. Consumption becomes a transformative experience, a loving gesture that imagines figures deemed ugly and irrelevant into a position of significance as a source of nourishment. In Díaz's work, this gesture is a response to the anti-Dominican, and especially antiblack, racism of the Dominican Republic and the United States, both of which violently exclude, reject, and elide these figures from official national histories. In this novel we see the emergence of the trope of writing as a healing process.[1] The bodies that are so rejected because of their blackness or fatness or foreignness or femaleness are in Yunior's loving consumption transformed and "sung" into a sacred and central position, to use the imagery of the poem by Li-Young Lee, "The Cleaving," cited in the epigraph of this chapter. In *The Brief Wondrous Life of Oscar Wao*, Yunior's heroic singing contrasts with the condemnatory representation of intellectuals, like Abelard, who in Yunior's estimation fail to save their world because they remain silent too long as they are motivated primarily by fear rather than heroic love.

Yunior consumes and embodies the stories of Oscar, Lola, Belicia, and Abelard as a way to write Dominican Americans into history. And in order to narrate that story, he consumes not just their individual stories, but also a wide range of literary traditions and models from the Americas, including U.S. popular and high literature, along with literature and scholarship from the Caribbean. This ties Díaz's work into a tradition of scholars throughout the Americas concerned with the cultural inheritances of colonization; indeed, he names key scholars whose work focuses on this inheritance, such as Fernando Ortiz, the Cuban ethnographer whose concept of transculturation describes the novel's literary and cultural modes of representation.

An American continental model of transculturation that I would like to insert into this discussion is that of the *antropofagia* movement from the early twentieth century in Brazil, which theorized an aesthetic that adopted indigenous models while also cannibalizing the European artistic inheritance. Oswald de Andrade's "Cannibalist Manifesto," published in

1928, is a useful lens for considering Yunior's developing aesthetic, which I will consider at greater length in the final section of this chapter. As part of the antropofagia movement, Andrade insisted that Brazilian art should consume and cannibalize not just European traditions but also indigenous ones to create something new through that digestion. This reference to cannibalism evokes violence (one cannot eat the flesh of another without first killing that Other) and also its often-disputed relationship to native peoples throughout the Americas. At the same time, Andrade's vision of cannibalism is one that involves not just violence but also the integration of the Other into the self, which is thus a transformative experience and a type of renewal through the hybridization of already existing elements. The narrative form of Díaz's novel reflects this aesthetic of consumption, creating a literary space for Dominican American identity through a dense referentiality that incorporates traditions from the United States and the Caribbean, recombining them and transforming them as a way to forge an artistic identity for Dominicans.[2] Through the portrayal of Yunior and his developing aesthetic in the novel, Díaz presents a version of this cannibalizing aesthetic on the levels of both content and form.

"What Is It with Dictators and Writers Anyway?": Yunior as Author, Yunior as Authoritarian

One of the questions that haunts Junot Díaz's The Brief Wondrous Life of Oscar Wao is Who is Yunior? This question seems almost simplistic, but the narrator's identity and his role in the novel constitute one of the central puzzles that the text sets before the reader. Implicit in this question is a consideration of the narrator's stake in the novel and, by extension, the power of authorship. In The Brief Wondrous Life of Oscar Wao, Yunior presents himself as simultaneously a minor character in the story of the de León and Cabral family and the real controlling force behind that story as the supremely powerful (a power of which he reminds his readers often) and potentially nefarious narrator. While leaving bread crumbs for the reader to follow, he studiously deflects attention from his own story, not even revealing his name until almost halfway into the novel. Moreover, the only part of the narrator's name revealed in the novel is "Yunior." The text does not divulge a last name, and of course "Yunior" is just a nickname or suffix, a Hispanicization of junior, and readers are never given the name this suffix references in The Brief Wondrous Life of Oscar Wao. Even while ostensibly revealing himself by speaking his name, he hides his identity. Yunior reveals only minor details about his personal life, some of which seem like outright lies, like the lies he admits to telling in his relationship with Lola.

Díaz has suggested that there are two ways to read Yunior—as either a hero or a villain. Yunior does indeed take on two roles in the novel: first, as a narrator of the lives of the de León and Cabral family, a "watcher," as he calls himself, which is a rather neutral term, attesting to his role as a type of archivist or historian, a mediator or translator, but maybe also as a "parigüayo," in the sense that he can only look on while the events unfold.[3] Second, as a character within the novel he sometimes functions as a nemesis: Oscar's false friend and Lola's unfaithful lover. As the narrator, Yunior often dissimulates regarding the true power that he holds, luring the reader in by revealing just enough of his writerly manipulations to make the reader feel complicit, while still insisting on the overall truthfulness of his story. Examples of this kind of gesture include the various moments at which Yunior explicitly admits purposeful anachronisms, such as a reference to Oscar's dancing the perrito or the use of imagination to fill in the many blanks of the story, as when he admits his substitution of cities as the setting for Belicia's and the Gangster's love nest. In a footnote, the narrator admits: "In my first draft, Samaná was actually Jarabacoa, but then my girl Leonie, resident expert in all things Domo, pointed out that there are no beaches in Jarabacoa. Beautiful rivers but no beaches. Leonie was also the one who informed me that the perrito (see first paragraphs of chapter one, 'GhettoNerd at the End of the World') wasn't popularized until the late eighties, early nineties, but that was one detail I couldn't change, just liked the image too much. Forgive me, historians of popular dance, forgive me!"[4] This footnote reveals one inaccuracy in the author's writing that is subsequently corrected, as well as one purposeful change that the author makes to the past in the name of his art.

Two moments in Junot Díaz's *The Brief Wondrous Life of Oscar Wao* help to further elucidate the difficulty of reading the novel's narrator, illuminating the ways he embeds himself in the text and manipulates Oscar's story. In an early footnote about Oscar's nerdiness, Yunior considers Oscar's love of what he calls "genre" (referring to science fiction and fantasy), speculating as follows: "It might have been a consequence of being Antillean (who more sci-fi than us?) or of living in the DR for the first couple of years of his life and then abruptly wrenchingly relocating to New Jersey—a single green card shifting not only worlds (from Third to First) but centuries (from almost no TV or electricity to plenty of both). After a transition like that I'm guessing only the most extreme scenarios could have satisfied."[5] This footnote draws a critical connection between Oscar's experiences as an immigrant and the experiences of the outsiders, "freaks," and aliens often featured in the comics and novels that Oscar devours. However, this footnote also represents a logical lapse in the story. Belicia boards a plane from Santo Domingo shortly after her near fatal beating in the cane fields and "never again live[s] in Santo Domingo."[6] Thus, the reader can assume that Lola and Oscar are born and grow up in the United States and only return to the Dominican Republic for short trips, with the narrative disclosing Oscar's summer stays in La Inca's home and Lola's sojourns with her grandmother following her stint as a runaway on the Jersey Shore. If Oscar and Lola are born in the United States, what sense does this footnote make? Part of the answer lies in the fact that Yunior later reveals in another footnote that he was born in the Dominican Republic and moved to the United States as a nine-year-old child.[7]

A second authorial intervention that might complicate the reader's understanding of Yunior's role as narrator is the scene of Yunior at the end of the novel, now a more-or-less-happily-married creative writing professor, and the four refrigerators filled with Oscar's writing that occupy his basement. Just as the note mentioned above, which constitutes a slippage in Yunior's storytelling, blurs the line between the narrator and his subject, the image of Yunior's four refrigerators calls into question Yunior's motives. While Yunior claims that Oscar's work is stored in the refrigerators for safekeeping, could his real reasons be more nefarious? Is this his way of silencing his subject? Is the narrator really invested in giving "a true account of the Brief Wondrous Life of Oscar Wao," or is Oscar merely a screen onto which Yunior can project some of the elements of his own intellectual and artistic development while flexing his growing writing skills?[8] In the novel, the narrator details the changes that occur in his aesthetic over time and his professionalization as a creative writing professor. He eventually acknowledges his indebtedness to Oscar, especially in terms of his work ethic and commitment to his writing. While he is giving voice to his dead friend, then, he is simultaneously silencing Oscar, taking over his story and keeping a firm grip on the narrative despite his gestures at multivocality. In a sense, then, Oscar is a mentor, but also a rival. While Yunior focuses so much attention on Oscar's writing throughout the story, he reveals none of Oscar's actual writing, instead locking away Oscar's surviving work in four refrigerators in his basement. He is a cannibal because he gets rid of the physical traces of his friend, locking away his work in a refrigerator, which is meant to hold food, but he is also a cannibalist—a practitioner of the antropofagia aesthetic—because he integrates Oscar's work into his own and creates a new artistic expression meant to reflect the communion of the two writers' work and thought.

His use of narrative bread crumbs that hint at a more negative reading of Yunior can also be read as a playful gesture, like the "plums" that Nabokov embedded in his novel *Pale Fire* (1962), which could lead readers to a variety of alternative interpretations of the text. These gestures are also very much in line with the interactive kinds of texts over which Oscar obsesses, such as fantasy and choose-your-own-adventure, the latter forming a major part of the novel's structure. However, these bread crumbs also force readers to look more critically at the connection between narrative control and political power. Still, this line of investigation eventually leads to the question of Yunior's right to write Oscar's story, especially in the way that he does.

Yunior invites the reader to consider him as a possible villain, a Trujillo-style tyrant, by drawing parallels between authorship and authoritarianism.[9] He consistently describes Trujillo as a self-appointed author of the Dominican nation, while also alerting the reader to all Dominicans' inheritance of the dictatorial legacy along with writers' particular propensity for Trujillan behavior.[10] And all along he draws attention to his manipulations of facts and people. Yunior thus implicitly implores readers to question his authority in taking over the narration of the lives of Oscar and his family members. I have argued elsewhere that Díaz's novel stages a historiographic battle royale between Trujillo and Yunior, suggesting that Yunior sees his narrative as being in competition with modern Dominican history as dominated and shaped by Trujillo; Yunior seeks to replace a Trujillan historical mode founded on silences with one based on recovered, multiple "ordinary" voices.[11] While the novel does indeed function as a form of historical recovery, it does not validate the narrator himself as an unquestionable hero. Indeed, the novel pushes us to consider what exactly we mean by the term *hero* in the first place, especially because Díaz's novel so explicitly references the superhero genre of comics and especially those works like *Fantastic Four* and *Watchmen* that complicate readers' understandings of heroes and heroism.

Yunior suggests the dictatorial possibility of writing in another footnote: "What is it with Dictators and Writers, anyway? Since before the infamous

Caesar-Ovid war they've had beef. . . . Rushdie claims that tyrants and scribblers are natural antagonists, but I think that's too simple; it lets writers off pretty easy. Dictators, in my opinion, just know competition when they see it. Same with writers. Like, *after all, recognizes like.*"[12] Yunior alerts the reader to this similarity, almost forcing the reader to suspect him, as a writer figure, of bearing many of the marks of the figure of the dictator. He seems to insist that we not let him off too easily. He urges readers not to be lulled into seeing him as a hero but rather to consider him a powerful character with the capacity for evil. While Trujillo changes "ALL THE NAMES of ALL THE LANDMARKS in the Dominican Republic to honor himself," Yunior does a similar thing through a seemingly opposite tactic.[13] He remakes Oscar, partially in his own image; he hides behind Oscar, onto whom he projects his "otakuness" as a kind of shield against the backlash that this nerdiness would elicit from his peers.[14] Even Oscar, the other writer character in the novel, is not completely able to escape his likeness to the dictator; Yunior imagines Oscar's death scene as one in which Oscar places a multigenerational curse on his murderers, reminding the reader of the fact that Abelard is said to have received a fukú from the dictator. The power differential here is fairly clear: Oscar is using words while faced with firearms but unlike a dictator he now has the power to use state violence to enforce such a fukú. Nonetheless, Yunior's imagination of Oscar's final moments in this way echoes the historical cycle represented in the novel as the curse of the Americas. This relates to one of the most memorable phrases of the novel, in which Lola insists that the entire Dominican pueblo, not just writers, resemble the dictatorial figure: "Ten million Trujillos is all we are."[15]

Yunior's desire for control manifests itself both in his interpersonal relationships and in his narrative. He seems to harbor a consuming admiration for Oscar that he shrouds in controlling, and sometimes violent, behavior. While Oscar is alive, Yunior embarks on his project to "fix Oscar's life," which ends in Yunior's shoving Oscar against a wall after Oscar mimics Melville's Bartleby and decides he would "rather not" stick to Yunior's prescriptive exercise regimen.[16] After Oscar's death, Yunior consumes Oscar narratively, reshaping the story of his family to fit his narrative aesthetic. One bread crumb that might lead the reader to realize just how much Yunior has actively reshaped the narrative, over and against the narrative vision of Oscar and his family, comes in a footnote in the chapter devoted to Abelard. Chapter 5 begins with the sentence "When the family talks about [the fukú] at all—which is like never—they always begin in the same place: with Abelard and the Bad Thing he said about Trujillo."[17] This statement is footnoted as follows: "There are other beginnings certainly, better ones, to be sure—if you ask me I would have started when the Spaniards 'discovered' the New World—or when the U.S. invaded Santo Domingo in 1916—but if this was the opening that the de Leóns chose for themselves, then who am I to question their historiography?"[18] In this footnote, Yunior once again calls attention to his handiwork. The joke of the footnote is that Yunior suggests rhetorically that he has no right to alter the family's version of its history while, if the reader looks at the shape of the novel in her hands, that is exactly what Yunior has done. The novel indeed starts not with the history of the family but rather with a history of the fukú, whose origin Yunior traces to the first encounters between Europeans, the indigenous peoples of the Americas, specifically mentioning the Tainos, and enslaved Africans. This draws attention to the fact that Yunior is not just battling Trujillo; he also battles Oscar's family for the right to narrate its story with his own interpretive slant. He ostensibly uses the family's narrative structure, at least in this chapter, while negating it in both the footnotes and the novel's overall structure. The footnote here reinforces the narrator's power while calling attention to it, winking at readers while making them accomplices in the consumption of the de León and Cabral family story. In the end, like a choose-your-own-adventure, the book supplies no conclusive answer to the appropriate way of reading Yunior. Instead, it forces the reader to participate in the narration by deciding how to navigate the novel and choose among the variety of narrative frameworks and interpretations offered by its ambiguous narrator.

A Writerly Education: From Dictator to Hero

While Yunior often questions his own motivations and morality as a character, what emerges with clarity is the novel's overarching vision of the poetics and politics of the committed diasporic artist. The novel vindicates writer-intellectuals who are involved in working toward positive political change, while excoriating writer-intellectuals who lack the courage to act against evil. Throughout the novel Yunior traces a history and trajectory of both the heroic figures of historical writers and scholars like Jesús de Galíndez and Orlando Martínez, with whom the narrator allies himself, as well as those he deems failed intellectuals, like the character of Oscar's grandfather,

Abelard. Yunior might be a morally ambiguous character because of his tendencies toward dictatorial action and narration, but ultimately he acts against the narratives of true dictatorship, inspired by a large pantheon of writer-intellectuals from the Caribbean and the greater Americas. Over the course of the novel, readers follow the development of Yunior's aesthetic; he goes from a "genre" writer like Oscar ("genre" in this case refers to popular literary styles such as science fiction, fantasy, crime fiction, and thrillers) to a more "literary" writer who, in telling Oscar's story, develops an alternative hybrid aesthetic. While he grapples with anxiety regarding his authenticity and his right to write, he reconciles this anxiety through the development of an aesthetic focused on reference and recovery, which also serves as a political act. His actions seek to remedy the inaction of Abelard that Oscar begins to address at the end of his life.

Yunior frequently describes the writing process not as an art but rather as a craft, using the language of labor. This language already hints at Yunior's anxiety regarding the shift in class position that attends his professional-ization as a writer. Starting in Chapter 4, "A Sentimental Education, 1988–1992," while Oscar is toiling away in obscurity on his fan fiction and fantasy masterpieces, we learn about Yunior's development as a writer in college and into the present of the novel as a creative writing professor at Middlesex Community College, using the work ethic he learned from Oscar, writing "from can't see in the morning to can't see at night," a description more in line with language related to labor (Yunior clocks in and out in a sense, noting the hours spent at his work) rather than the language of rev-elation and epiphanies often associated with literary production.[19] This language points to one of the reasons behind Yunior's forcing the reader to recognize his own stake in the story as its writer, and even his potential for narrative abuse: his anxiety related to his shift in class as a result of his writing, especially as this relates to questions of ethnic and national authenticity.

Drawing on Bakhtin's essay on the bildungsroman, Franco Moretti notes that this type of novel is "the great bourgeois form," in that it signals the protagonist's assimilation into the values of the bourgeoisie.[20] Through his development as a writer, Yunior does indeed join the middle class. Yunior's shifting aesthetic marks this passage toward institutional accep-tance as well. He notes that his early writings share an affinity with Oscar's in that both work in specific subgenres not recognized as high literature: "[Oscar's writing w]asn't my cup of tea—*Drop the phaser, Arthurus Prime!*—

but even I could tell he had chops. Could write dialogue, crack snappy exposition, keep the narrative moving. Showed him some of my fiction too, all robberies and drug deals and *Fuck you, Nando,* and BLAU! BLAU! BLAU! He gave me four pages of comments for an eight-page story."[21] While this early writing shows that both writers work in genres considered subliterary, Yunior displays his sense of inferiority in relation to Oscar, as he recognizes that Oscar "ha[s] chops," while Oscar seems to find more to critique in Yunior's writing, as evidenced by the quantity of his pages of commentary.

Then Yunior reports a shift in his artistic development. He makes the switch from his crime stories to ones about his native land, earning himself recognition from a representative of the literary establishment, a professor. He explains: "That winter I even managed to sit in my dorm room long enough to write a story that wasn't too bad, about the woman who used to live in the patio behind my house in the DR, a woman everybody said was a prostitute but who used to watch me and my brother while my mom and my abuelo were at work. My professor couldn't believe it. I'm impressed. Not a single shooting or stabbing in the whole story. Not that it helped any. I didn't win any of the creative-writing prizes that year. I kinda had been hoping."[22] His professor approves of his development. The professor is impressed because Yunior has left behind the world of crime fiction to enter the more accepted role for the contemporary writer of color in the United States: that of realism, especially "authentic" representations that focus on the homeland.[23] Despite the professor's appreciation, though, the writing does not earn top honors, which perhaps functions as a commentary on the literary world outside the novel, pointing to the lack of respect and recognition for writers of color.[24]

Eventually, the reader sees Yunior's professionalization, first hinted at when he references the Modern Language Association annual conference and later in the section titled "As for Me" when he informs the reader about his current station:[25]

These days I live in Perth Amboy, New Jersey, teach composition and creative writing at Middlesex Community College, and even own a house at the top of Elm Street, not far from the steel mill. Not one of the big ones that the bodega owners buy with their earnings, but not too shabby, either. Most of my colleagues think Perth Amboy is a dump, but I beg to differ. . . . When I'm not teaching or coaching baseball or going to the gym or hanging out with the wifey I'm at home, writing. These days I write a lot. From can't see in the morning to can't see at night. Learned that from Oscar. I'm a new man, you see, a new man, a new man.[26]

This short section outlines the material gains that he has made as a result of his writing. Yunior has attained all of the trappings of a new member of the middle class: a stable and prestigious job, a house, and a family. He is thus "a new man" in relation to his earlier economic status as well as in relation to his personal development. While Yunior receives much as a result of his encounters with Oscar, gaining position and also a type of rebirth (becoming "a new man" through the process of narration), he does so in part by telling the story of Oscar, whose own storytelling Yunior only obliquely reveals. This summary of Yunior's accomplishments also suggests Yunior's anxiety about his achieved position. Yunior's depiction of his home at first suggests a pride in his achieved position ("even own a house at the top of Elm Street") but then a demotion of that status by explaining that the house is near a steel mill (a fixture of working-class life), that it's "not one of the big ones" that he associates with the merchant class, and that his colleagues see his town as a "dump." Just as Yunior calls into question the authenticity of historical representations, he also calls into question the notion of authenticity as it relates to creative writers who take up the subject of communities of ethnic minorities. The writer of color seems to face a crisis in regard to the possibility of ever being able to represent his community, because, in becoming a professional writer, the writer seems to have forfeited the "authenticity" associated with working-class realities often linked to the "true" roots of ethnic identity, especially in U.S. Latino/a literature.

Like other Künstlerromane, Díaz's novel includes a flight from the location of the artist's childhood. As a homeowner in Perth Amboy, Yunior is physically dislocated from his origins. Various novels of artistic formation suggest that becoming an artist requires the artist's physical movement away from the spaces of one's youth, and that this distance is what allows the writer to return narratively to these original sites. Such is the case, for example, with Stephen Dedalus's Icarian flight from Ireland, the "old sow that eats her farrow," in A Portrait of the Artist as a Young Man.[27] The end of the novel has Stephen imagining his departure and projecting his personal goals as they relate to larger collectives: "I go to encounter for the millionth time the reality of experience and to forge in the smithy of my soul the uncreated conscience of my race."[28] Although The House on Mango Street is geographically and temporally removed from Joyce's work, it also explores a protagonist's longing to escape from the circumstances of her youth. Cisneros's protagonist, Esperanza, imagines an escape from her Chicago neighborhood in "Mango Says Goodbye Sometimes" that will nonetheless allow her to maintain her ties to her community by writing on their behalf: "Friends and neighbors will say, What happened to that Esperanza? Where did she go with all those books and paper? Why did she march so far away? They will not know I have gone away to come back. For the ones I left behind. For the ones who cannot out."[29] These novels figure the exiled writer narratively returning to the landscape of her or his youth, perhaps to atone for the perception of betrayal of a writer whose escape appears aimed at accomplishing self-fulfillment rather than directly working in and for the community. In the case of Esperanza, Cisneros presents a silent answer to the questions that the community will ask of the budding working-class artist of color, suggesting that she will return artistically for "the ones who cannot out," using her privilege not just to help herself but to help her community. Both Joyce's and Cisneros's works suggest an ethical impulse in the writer's development.

Unlike these novels, *The Brief Wondrous Life of Oscar Wao* does not end on this parting note; it represents the artist after his physical departure from his original community and once he is already a working writer. The novel portrays the narrator at a temporal remove from the subject of his youth. He is now the artist at work refining his craft. Cisneros's novel has a protagonist that envisions a future return to the milieu of her current youth, while Díaz's novel presents a grown writer grappling with the process of representing his community. The content and form of the novel display Yunior's desire to recuperate figures and experiences actively forgotten by history. At the same time, Yunior continues to manifest anxiety about the possibility of representing this community truthfully and fairly. He attempts to resolve this problem by invoking others and allying himself with the genealogy of artist-intellectuals that he creates via intertextual reference and direct citation. Giving up on the attempt to represent an authentic reality of the family, the nation, or the diaspora, Yunior instead seeks to represent an ever multiplying reality or at least acknowledge and gesture toward that multiple reality.

Despite the failures and potential dictatorial moves on Yunior's part, his actions in attempting to recover and re-create the de León and Cabral family's story are meant to contrast with the inaction of Abelard, the model of the failed intellectual in the novel. This way of understanding Abelard—as a failed intellectual—is certainly not the only one available to readers. Indeed, Yunior does seem to evoke some sympathy for Abelard's refusal to bring his daughter Jackie to a party with Trujillo, whose regime Yunior describes as a "culocracy" because of the notoriety of the dictator's sexual appetite and its seemingly inextricable connection to the violence that marked his power over the Dominican Republic. However, the great majority of Yunior's representations of Abelard focus not on his actions in relation to the threat posed by Trujillo's party invitations, which explicitly name his eldest daughter, but rather on his inaction. Many of the pages in the section devoted to Abelard detail his paralysis as well as a long list of actions available to him of which he does not avail himself. One example comes after Abelard receives the party invitation in the mail that specifically requests the attendance of Jackie. Yunior speculates: "Maybe if the doctor had immediately grabbed his daughters and wife and smuggled them all aboard a boat in Puerto Plata, or if he'd stolen with them across the border into Haiti, they might have had a chance. The Plátano Curtain was strong but it wasn't that strong. But alas, instead of making his move Abelard fretted and temporized and despaired."[30] While Yunior acknowledges the many obstacles to action in the Dominican Republic, he ultimately makes statements that highlight Abelard's lack of courage in comparison to others in his position in the Dominican Republic and abroad. This inability to act on issues of vital importance to his family members is aligned in the book with his use of his academic intelligence as a type of screen: rather than using his credibility as an intellectual to denounce the regime, he instead writes on obscure scientific issues in specialized journals. Nonetheless, ultimately Abelard does resist, at least insofar as he does not deliver his daughter into the hands of a rapist, a decision which leads to years of torture and ultimately death. Furthermore, Yunior reports on rumors that Abelard had written a book (lost, of course, like many other books referenced in the novel) about Trujillo's otherworldly power and its possible origin. This seems to align him with other resistant writers, and yet Yunior's ultimate assessment of Abelard as an intellectual model is overwhelmingly negative. Could it be that Abelard, as an "advocate of outlandish abstractions" represents a type of intellectualism that Yunior fears he might fall prey to once he becomes part of academe?[31]

For Yunior, Abelard's intellectualism is a failure because it is one that is devoid of ethics until far too late, as suggested by the Latin phrase that Abelard's eldest daughter, Jackie, writes every morning before focusing on her studies: "*Tarde venientibus ossa*," or "To the latecomers are left the bones."[32]

This phrase is repeated several times in the chapter about Abelard as a type of indictment of the lateness of his actions; he does not speak out on the evils of the dictatorship, even those that he witnesses personally, until his family faces a direct threat. While Yunior goes to pains to describe the ways resistance is violently quashed under Trujillo's rule, filling the footnotes with the names of writers and political figures killed, at the same time he asserts often that the possibility of political action still exists: "But let's not go completely overboard: Trujillo was certainly formidable, and the regime was like a Caribbean Mordor in many ways, but there were plenty of people who despised El Jefe, who communicated in less-than-veiled ways their contempt, who *resisted*. But Abelard was simply not one of them."[33]

Yunior makes distinctions between Abelard and his Mexican colleagues as well as juxtaposing his activities with those of the long lists of resisters collected in the footnotes. Yunior frames Abelard's denial as one that shapes what he is willing to articulate and the narratives that he is willing to entertain. Although there are rumors of a book written by Abelard about Trujillo, in response to stories of Trujillo's atrocities, "Abelard listened to these horrors tensely, and then after an awkward silence would change the subject. He simply didn't wish to dwell on the fates of Unfortunate People, on the goings-on in Peaksville. *He didn't want those stories in his house.*"[34] The narrator characterizes Abelard's willful ignorance of the realities outside of his home as a rejection of those stories within his home. Abelard replicates the power structures of the state by imposing a gag rule in his home. While viewing his silence as one that enables his intellectual pursuits to continue, Abelard in fact makes those very pursuits meaningless. Abelard, whom Yunior describes as "a Brain," is eventually reduced to a "vegetable" (another food reference that marks Abelard as a figure to be consumed) in Nigüa prison after he survives "La Corona," a torture device applied to the head, before eventually dying in prison. The safety that he sought in silence is nowhere on the island, and that silence marks his lack of courage and his death as well. The novel, in contrast, enacts an aesthetic that opposes Abelard's desire to keep the stories out of his house. Specifically, it broadens the central family story to include the story of the Trujillato, its origins in the earliest history of contact in the Americas, and its afterlife in the present. In this way, the novel brings stories of the political world into the home and it reiterates this choice aesthetically in a structure that can include a variety of stories at once, particularly through the structural element of the extensive footnotes.

Within the de León and Cabral family, Oscar seems to follow in the silencing footsteps of Abelard and Belicia. Oscar appears out of touch with the historical recurrences that become clear over the course of the novel, as when he proclaims to Yunior that the fukú is "our parents' shit."[35] This attitude shifts, however, when he returns to the Dominican Republic. This difference registers on the syntactic level; in the section of chapter 6 titled "Oscar Goes Native," there is a three-page-long sentence with myriad clauses, many of which begin with "after," marking a temporal shift for Oscar that signals the breaking of the cycle of historical ignorance. He establishes a legacy in those last twenty-seven days of his life, in which he focuses on the Dominican Republic in his research and writing. Oscar begins to search for the "full story" in his final days, even though "it's not certain whether he found it."[36] The search, though, marks an important break with the tradition of ignoring the past, and it is a search that Yunior takes up after Oscar's passing. Perhaps Oscar becomes "an amateur ethnographer in the Fernando Ortíz mode" like his grandfather, but unlike his grandfather, he searches for the truth about his family's past in relation to the fukú.[37] This search eventually leads to the action of directly confronting the "Capitán," who figures as a remnant of the corrupt dictatorial legacy on the island. It is important to note that Oscar's courage is motivated by his romantic love for Ybón; courage and romantic desire are often twinned in the novel. According to the narrator, "For twenty-seven days he did two things: he researched-wrote and he chased her."[38]

When Oscar dies in the process of his familial and historical research and his pursuit of Ybón, and his writing from this period is lost, Yunior sums up the courage to take up the charge to write. While not explicitly mentioned in *The Brief Wondrous Life of Oscar Wao*, Yunior's last name in *Drown* is de las Casas. This name recalls Bartolomé de las Casas, another chronicler, the Spanish priest who condemned the encomienda system of the Americas in the *Brevísima relación de la destrucción de las Indias*. This links Yunior to the ethical imperative of condemning abuses of power. Yunior attempts to continue Oscar's legacy through this activity. Yunior functions as a type of surrogate for Oscar; Yunior's consumption of Oscar allows the dead writer to continue to speak. He cannibalizes Oscar's work, consuming it and others to forge a story to encompass the multiple Dominican and Dominican American identities denied by the totalizing narrative of dictatorship. Just like the *accumulatio* of the three-page sentence in "Oscar Goes Native," which lists the diversity of Oscar's experiences in the Dominican

Republic, Yunior in the novel rejects the push to choose anyone (even himself) as a singular, authentic, ethnic representative, instead embodying and representing a wider swath of experiences. He gains sustenance and courage from these narratives, which are stored in the refrigerator like food and which he envisions will one day be consumed by Isis, the rightful heir who is tasked with taking on the role of researcher and writer along with putting an end to the "fukú story," as Yunior calls it.[39] Envisioning Isis's visits, he hypothesizes, "And maybe, just maybe, if she's as smart and as brave as I'm expecting she'll be, she'll take all we've done and all we've learned and add her own insights and she'll put an end to it."[40] This is a vision of continuous consumption as a type of inheritance, a creation that is communal and requires the input of various generations. The novel does not provide a full endorsement of Yunior as an individual author, in fact quite the contrary because of the problematic nature of Yunior as a character. Nonetheless, the novel does present a vindication of the ability of writers as a community to confront the evils of corrupt powers.

An Aesthetic of Consumption

The culmination of Yunior's writerly education is the development of his aesthetic, an aesthetic of consumption that attempts to forge community through the artistic process. This aesthetic allows for a move away from a paralyzing focus on the subject of representative authenticity toward one of heterogeneity. This aesthetic of consumption functions as a reconciliatory model of hybridization, in that it signals the acceptance of the Other and the embodiment of that Other within oneself. The narrator presents a Dominican diasporic aesthetic that incorporates a variety of inheritances, privileges "low" discourses as well as "high," and creates new literary and intellectual genealogies.

Here I would like to reflect a bit more on the ways "Cannibalist Manifesto" ("Manifesto antropófago"), by the Brazilian writer Oswald de Andrade, might aid in understanding Yunior's theorization and employment of this alternative consumptive aesthetic. Andrade's manifesto of the antropofagia literary movement, published in 1928, is known for a variety of equally piercing and playful statements, such as "Tupi or not Tupi, that is the question," an invocation of *Hamlet* that suggests a reclamation of indigenous Brazilian heritage at the same time it acknowledges and reframes the Western canon.[41] Andrade claims the figure of the indigenous cannibal as an aesthetic metaphor for the "absorption of the sacred enemy," a phrase that displays reverence for the Other in representing the use of European traditions along with a desire for the native, creating a particularly Brazilian mixture.[42] This is a model of hybridity that emphasizes the incorporation of the other and a mixture at the corporeal level as a metaphor for aesthetic and cultural concerns.

The literary scholar Luis Madureira explains that the revolutionary aspect of Andrade's manifesto comes not from a real invocation of the native culture of the Tupi, but instead from the poetic form suggested by Andrade:

> For the adherents of the 1928–29 *antropofagia* movement . . . it is in the recovery and resignification of the most emblematic and infamous ritual [cannibalism] associated with the Tupi—the "first peoples" of Brazil—that the possibility of reclaiming a genuine national culture resides. Yet, having been effectively eradicated by the early seventeenth century, these "original Brazilians" had long been tragically unavailable as "native informants." They linger only as distorted and unreliable traces in the very colonial archive in which their utter destruction is not only recorded but all too often justified, even celebrated. *Antropofagia*'s metaphoric return to Brazil's authentic "cannibalistic" roots, then, cannot but assume the form of a treacherous detour through inauthentic and unstable textual regions.[43]

Madureira suggests that antropofagia's recovery of Tupi culture through the invocation of cannibalism is only a rhetorical recovery, that it is "inauthentic." This rhetorical recovery serves primarily in the development of an aesthetic that imagines the use of European forms and language with a resistant difference. Madureira explains further: "Its reclamation of the 'anthropophagus' is invariably reduced to the structures (and strictures) of speculative reason—in other words, the future *antropofagia* sets out to construct adheres in large measure to the familiar contours of western discourses of emancipation. On the other hand, however, *antropofagia*'s attempt to convert the Tupi's alleged craving for the heterogeneous into an ethical and political imperative seems to indicate a new historical direction: a future that is at least imaginatively distinct from the one enforced by European models of modernization."[44] While rejecting antropofagia's claim to an authentic Brazilian indigeneity in "reclaiming a genuine national culture," Madureira nonetheless suggests that the move toward a "craving for the heterogeneous" as "an ethical and political imperative" marks the real innovation of Andrade's work. Similarly, I suggest that Yunior's self-consciously incomplete and problematized recovery of Oscar is nonetheless attempted via a hybrid aesthetic that aims to achieve a heterogeneous representational mode rather than to set down a definitive narrative. The most striking features of the work remain the freshness of its language, the variety of its literary and cultural reference points, and the overlaying of aesthetic traditions from throughout the Americas and Europe that lead to a new and engaging voice that emerges from the subtle but compelling fusion of Oscar and Yunior, along with a greater web of "old" reference points.

The resonance of the cannibalist aesthetic model of transculturation via formal incorporation is most evident in the various references of the novel (to high literary and popular literary sources as well as historical references from throughout the Americas). However, there are echoes of that model of hybridity via consumption also on the level of narration. The two writers in the novel—Oscar and Yunior—are both represented in the novel as consumers. Oscar is a voracious eater, as suggested by his physical form—"The fat! The miles of stretch marks! The tumescent horribleness of his proportions!"[45] Yunior also describes Oscar's love of literature using the language of eating. Oscar "gorg[es] himself on a steady stream of Lovecraft, Wells, Burroughs, Howard, . . . Asimov [and other science fiction writers], moving hungrily from book to book, author to author, age to age."[46] Like Oscar, Yunior is also a consuming artist in this novel. Unlike in Drown, wherein Yunior is portrayed as vomiting and rejecting the traditions to which he is heir, in The Brief Wondrous Life of Oscar Wao, Yunior is often portrayed as embracing and embodying a variety of traditions in telling the story of the family. Yunior consumes some of the same literary fare as Oscar, but along with the sci-fi and fantasy, he also incorporates writers from the Caribbean, with references to Walcott, Ortiz, Glissant, and others who theorize and employ transculturated traditions.

Yunior consumes and embodies Oscar after his death. He takes over Oscar's story in a variety of senses—taking possession of his writings, narrating his life story, keeping his work in refrigerators in his basement to then become Oscar's self-appointed literary executor after his death. But it goes even further than this: there are various moments in the text when Yunior's and Oscar's lives blur. One is the conflation in footnote number 6, as mentioned in the first section of this chapter. There is also that small exchange with Isis, Lola's daughter, at the end, when the little girl at first calls Yunior *tío* before being corrected and told that he was "*tío's friend*."[47] These moments suggest that Yunior sometimes superimposes his life on Oscar's, embodying his former "friend" while also maintaining control of the narrative throughout. This iron grip on the narrative is partially obscured by Yunior's narrative self-reflexivity. Yunior critiques Trujillo for presenting himself as the embodiment of the Dominican nation by renaming geographical locales after himself, and yet in a move reminiscent of this renaming impulse, Yunior imprints himself onto the characters he attempts to narrate.[48]

This embodiment of the other characters and taking over of their stories may seem in part a dictatorial move, taking narrative control of other people's lives. However, as I have argued, the artistic model posited by the novel is one informed by an intense love and a desire to recover the figures who are historically unloved. In Li-Young Lee's poem, "The Cleaving," cited in the epigraph of this chapter, eating is a transformative experience, a loving gesture, that transforms into significance as nourishment figures historically and literarily deemed ugly.[49] In the poem, the speaker imagines a confrontation with the anti-Chinese racism of Emerson, while Díaz's novel presents a response to the anti-Dominican (and especially antiblack) racism of both the Dominican Republic and the United States, both of which work through exclusion, rejection, and elision. This ideal of loving consumption is also a model for the engaged artist. The novel's aesthetic of consumption seeks to establish a literary and cultural genealogy for Dominican American identity through a dense referentiality encompassing U.S. and Caribbean traditions. The consumption in the novel is a loving gesture that valorizes the role of the artist and intellectual. The artist here has the ability to reconfigure the bodies rejected for their blackness or fatness or foreignness or femaleness into bodies whose lived experiences gain a sacred and central position.

Notes

Epigraph: Li-Young Lee, "The Cleaving," *The City in which I Love You* (Rochester, NY: BOA Editions, 1990), 83.

1. This trope is also present in *This Is How You Lose Her.*
2. This position links Díaz's work to the model of engaged scholarship and authorship by U.S. writers of color, including African diasporic writers, along with those in the Latin American and Caribbean canons.

3. In the Marvel universe, the Watchers are a race of extraterrestrials that are displaced from their home planet and function as observers with unclear intentions.

4. Junot Díaz, *The Brief Wondrous Life of Oscar Wao* (New York: Riverhead Books, 2007), 132.

5. Díaz, *Oscar Wao*, 21.

6. Díaz, *Oscar Wao*, 164.

7. Díaz, *Oscar Wao*, 253.

8. Díaz, *Oscar Wao*, 285.

9. Jennifer Harford Vargas provides a useful, in-depth analysis of ties between contemporary U.S. Latino/a literature and the Latin American tradition of the dictatorship novel, as in her piece included in this collection, which considers that connection in Junot Díaz's work. See also her article "Dictating a Zafa: The Power of Narrative Form in Junot Díaz's *The Brief Wondrous Life of Oscar Wao*," MELUS 39, no. 3 (fall 2014): 8–30.

10. In attempting to harness the power of written language, writers also engage in a discursive practice historically used as a repressive tool. Aníbal González traces this recurrent concern in Latin American literature: a postcolonial "graphophobia" resulting from the violence that has been signaled by the colonizers' use of the written word. See his *Killer Books: Writing, Violence, and Ethics in Modern Spanish American Narrative* (Austin: University of Texas Press, 2001).

11. See my article "'Reassembling the Fragments': Battling Historiographies, Caribbean Discourse, and Nerd Genres in Junot Díaz's *The Brief Wondrous Life of Oscar Wao*," *Callaloo* 33, no. 2 (2010): 498–520.

12. Díaz, *Oscar Wao*, 97.

13. Díaz, *Oscar Wao*, 2.

14. Díaz, *Oscar Wao*, 21.

15. Díaz, *Oscar Wao*, 324.

16. Díaz, *Oscar Wao*, 175, 178.

17. Díaz, *Oscar Wao*, 211.

18. Díaz, *Oscar Wao*, 211.

19. Díaz, *Oscar Wao*, 326.

20. Franco Moretti, *The Way of the World: The Bildungsroman in European Culture* (London: Verso, 1986), ix.

21. Díaz, *Oscar Wao*, 173.

22. Díaz, *Oscar Wao*, 196.

23. The reader might note that Yunior's story centers on a prostitute from his own past, much like the latter part of the novel focuses on Oscar's relationship with Ybón, a prostitute as well. This could be another conflation or narrative appropriation on Yunior's part. In different senses, both writers get closer to their homelands via prostitutes—Yunior via his short story, and Oscar via his love for Ybón, which causes him to return to the Dominican Republic and remain there despite his first beating in the cane fields.

24. This trend has been slowly shifting in the last couple of decades, especially if one examines the spate of awards earned by Junot Díaz following the publication of *Oscar Wao*, from the Pulitzer to a MacArthur "Genius Grant."

25. Yunior compares Oscar's first beating in the cane fields to the dreaded early morning time slots of the annual national convention for literary scholars: "It was like one of those nightmare eight-a.m. MLA panels: endless" (Díaz, *Oscar Wao*, 299).

26. Díaz, *Oscar Wao*, 326.

27. James Joyce, *A Portrait of the Artist as a Young Man* (New York: Penguin, 2003), 220.

28. Joyce, *Portrait*, 275–76.

29. Sandra Cisneros, *The House on Mango Street* (New York: Vintage, 1984), 110.

30. Díaz, *Oscar Wao*, 231.

31. Díaz, *Oscar Wao*, 213.

32. Díaz, *Oscar Wao*, 219.

33. Díaz, *Oscar Wao*, 226.

34. Díaz, *Oscar Wao*, 227 (my emphasis).

35. Díaz, *Oscar Wao*, 194.

36. Díaz, *Oscar Wao*, 243.

37. Díaz, *Oscar Wao*, 213.

38. Díaz, *Oscar Wao*, 317.

39. Díaz, *Oscar Wao*, 6.

40. Díaz, *Oscar Wao*, 330–31.

41. Oswald de Andrade, "Cannibalist Manifesto," trans. Leslie Bary, *Latin American Literary Review* 19, no. 38 (July–December 1991): 38.

42. De Andrade, "Cannibalist Manifesto," 43. This aesthetic relates to other American (continental) theories by Andrade's contemporaries regarding racial identities, such as José Vasconcelos's visions of the role of "mestizaje" in the creation of what he termed "the cosmic race" in his work published in 1925.

43. Luis Madureira, *Cannibal Modernities: Postcoloniality and the Avant-garde in Caribbean and Brazilian Literature* (Charlottesville: University of Virginia Press, 2005), 13.

44. Madureira, *Cannibal Modernities*, 13.

45. Díaz, *Oscar Wao*, 29.

46. Díaz, *Oscar Wao*, 21.

47. Díaz, *Oscar Wao*, 327.

48. There are many instances in which Oscar's story becomes conflated with Yunior's. However, there is another conflation in chapter 2, which for the most part is ostensibly narrated by Lola, but resembles Yunior's narrative voice and linguistic tics too much to read as credibly narrated in her own voice, reading instead as Yunior's imagination of Lola or Lola's admissions as filtered by Yunior. This might help to explain the strange structure of chapter 2, which moves from second to third person, as if Yunior is breathing life into his representation of Lola's voice.

49. Jeffrey Partridge's article "The Politics of Ethnic Authorship: Li-Young Lee, Emerson, and Whitman at the Banquet Table" provides some analysis of the "big eating hero" as employed by Lee, which I found helpful in considering the role of eating and

consumption in Díaz's novel. Partridge cites Sau-ling Cynthia Wong on the figure of the big eating hero in Asian American literature: a character that is able to derive sustenance and even pleasure from seemingly unpalatable or even inedible fare, which functions as a metaphor for the ability of Asian Americans to survive and thrive despite racial persecution. Jeffrey Partridge, "The Politics of Ethnic Authorship: Li-Young Lee, Emerson, and Whitman at the Banquet Table," *Studies in the Literary Imagination* 37, no. 1 (spring 2004): 108–9.

Part II

Mapping Literary Geographies

5. Artistry, Ancestry, and Americanness in the Works of Junot Díaz

Silvio Torres-Saillant

American Preamble

These pages hope to locate the trajectory of fiction writer Junot Díaz, an author from the present, in its proper genealogies. I place the works of this still young storyteller in their American context by tracing his literary training, aesthetic creed, artistic praxis, cultural worldview, accomplishments, and reception by the reading public. I pay particular attention to the intersections between the critical discourse generated by Díaz's published fiction and the writer's own formulations about art, history, the literary craft, and the rapport among genres and forms. Díaz entered the republic of letters during the 1990s in a manner that seems uniquely auspicious for an American literary artist from a racialized, minority segment of the country's population. He did not elicit the reception typically accorded to voices from groups perceived as newcomers onto the ethnic tapestry of the nation. It did not happen in his case as in that of Piri Thomas, a New York–born Puerto Rican author from El Barrio (Spanish Harlem), whom Díaz acknowledges as an important influence. The novelist Daniel Stern, writing in *The New York Times Book Review*, did not extol the "literary quality" of

Thomas's *Down These Mean Streets* (1967), but he ascribed to it "an undeniable power that I think comes from the fact that it is a report from the guts and the heart of a submerged population group, itself submerged in the guts and heart of our cities. It claims our attention and our emotional response because of the honesty and pain of a life led in outlaw, fringe status, where the dream is always to escape."[1]

Conversely, the critical comments that welcomed the work of Díaz did not focus primarily on what his texts offered in terms of awareness about the lives of people in a little known community in New Jersey, their relatives in New York, or their origins in Santo Domingo, Dominican Republic. Rather, they mostly saluted the author's entry onto the American literary scene as a remarkable new presence in contemporary fiction. The very first short fiction text that Díaz published in 1995, "Ysrael," ended up being included in the following year's edition of *Best American Short Stories*. A piece entitled "Fiesta, 1980," which appeared in the winter 1996 issue of *Story*, earned him similar inclusion in the next edition of *Best American Short Stories* (1997), a distinction that he went on to receive several times in subsequent years. Lois Rosenthal, editor of *Story*, a magazine boasting the distinction of having first published John O'Hara and Carson McCullers, recalled that "Junot just leaped out of the mail pile," his voice "so incredibly fresh and so powerful."[2] Similarly, "Edison, New Jersey," which appeared originally in *The Paris Review*, now rubs elbows with many of the classics of the country's fiction within the pages of the second edition of *The Oxford Book of American Short Stories*, edited by Joyce Carol Oates.[3]

The release in 1996 of *Drown*, Díaz's debut collection of stories, enjoyed unrestrained acclaim, the string of accolades, awards, and honors growing progressively in the years that followed, including the author's induction into the rising pantheon of "the twenty writers for the 21st century," as proclaimed in the summer of 1999 by the *New Yorker* in its "summer fiction issue."[4] The highbrow weekly magazine responsible for announcing this new cohort of "great writers for the new millennium" included, in addition to Díaz, the likes of Sherman Alexie, Michael Chabon, Edwidge Danticat, Jhumpa Lahiri, George Saunders, and David Foster Wallace. Bill Buford closed his salute to the writers identified in the issue as "the best fiction writers in America today" by asking, "What is the future of American fiction?" and then providing his own answer: "We can't know. But the Polaroid of this generation, snapped as the century turns, offers a satisfying picture of a highly accomplished group of writers robustly taking on the stories of their Americanness."[5] Starting in 2001, the prestigious *New Yorker* went on to grant Díaz a "First Look Contract." Reviewers of *Drown* identified in the author a superior command of his craft as well as his infusing the stories therein with a mature worldview. Praise included such characteristics as the "controlled lyricism" of the author's prose as well as a terseness of diction "spare and supple . . . stark and startling" that invites comparison with "the working class simplicity of Raymond Carver and the visceral, tropical-urban mania of Piri Thomas," no less than with "the irreverence of the young Henry Miller."[6] The reviewer for the *Village Voice* ventured to affirm that, "in truth *Drown* lacks clearly identifiable precedents."[7]

Without articulating it explicitly, commentators no doubt zeroed in on the features that most seemed to distinguish the author's craft as deployed in his inaugural collection: namely, a verbal economy reminiscent of the stark concision in the poetry of Emily Dickinson and a pervasively metaphorical stance in the handling of dramatic situations or emotional states among his characters. The successful marriage of the human experience evoked in the texts and the studied artistry of the author's choice of style made it difficult for reviewers to extricate the content from the form, isolating the elements of setting and storyline to speak about the texts in the collection as constituent parts of an immigrant narrative. *Drown* may even operate as an antithesis to the immigrant narrative, a point noted by Ylce Irizarry, who finds in the collection the articulation of "a new ethics of immigration," inviting us to consider whether coming to the United States from the Caribbean may be deemed invariably good.[8] The critics could not, in other words, celebrate the book as a means to know Dominicans as immigrants seeking a second chance at life in the proverbial land of American promise.

People of Dominican ancestry in the United States have risen to visibility over the last two decades. Witness as graphic illustration the stardom of the Hollywood actress Zoe Saldaña, the Passaic-born daughter of the Dominican immigrant Aridio Saldaña; the spectacular feat of third baseman Alex Rodríguez, the New York–born child of Dominican parents whose contract signed in 2007 with the New York Yankees made him the highest-paid player in baseball history; the choice of the Dominican neighborhood of Washington Heights by the Puerto Rican composer and performer Lin-Manuel Miranda for his Tony-award-winning musical *In the Heights* (2007); and the launch by MTV of the "docu-reality" television series *Washington Heights*, following the lives of nine primarily Dominican young adults in the spring of 2013.[9] The increased presence of Dominicans in the media corresponds also to their rise in politics, with many holding elected office in municipal and state legislatures, apart from the recent confirmation of Buffalo-born Thomas Perez as U.S. Secretary of Labor. In light of this background, the triumph of Díaz as celebrated best-selling author of *Drown*, winner of the Pulitzer Prize for Fiction in 2008 for his novel *The Brief Wondrous Life of Oscar Wao* (2007), and recipient of the MacArthur "Genius" Award in 2012, can hardly escape drawing attention to the implications specifically for Dominicans of his remarkable literary career.

Predictably, many scholars and commentators on his fiction have felt compelled to search for any light that his novel and stories might shed on the intricacies of the Dominican experience.

A scholar reads Díaz's novel, for instance, as using the topos of hair to explore the complexities of racial relations and racial knowledge among Dominicans in the Dominican Republic and the United States.[10] Another finds that, in dramatizing the "not quite successful assimilation" of Dominicans in the United States, the novel "stretches the boundaries of post-colonial and immigrant discourses."[11] The Belgian scholar Rita de Maeseneer reads Díaz comparatively with writers from the Dominican Republic to show him free of the nostalgic gaze at the ancestral homeland, escaping the temptation to romanticize the rural landscape as edenic habitat.[12] Referring specifically to *The Brief Wondrous Life of Oscar Wao*, de Maeseneer finds Díaz contending with the authoritarian tradition in multiple ways: secluding himself in the fantastic world of science fiction, away from the rigidity of autocratic history, lessening the presence of masculine power in his texts, and creating an unreliable narrator who subverts his own epistemic authority.[13] Tim Lanzerdörfer, for his part, places great emphasis on the novel's intent to awaken diasporic Dominicans as to their marvelous history, affirming that it "offers a uniquely Dominican American fantasy perspective that enables Dominicans to recover in the diaspora a sense of how to relate to their history, even as that history remains out of reach."[14] Similarly, Juanita Heredia offers a sound reading of the novel with a focus on race, an element that the critic contends Díaz insists in highlighting as a key facet of each character's overall profile both in the Dominican Republic and in the United States.[15] The Cuban American novelist Achy Obejas, who translated *The Brief Wondrous Life of Oscar Wao* into Spanish for the Alfaguara and Vintage Español editions, has attested to how much the book taught her about the Dominican Republic and about the Trujillo regime: "The book gives a very concise story of what the dictatorship was."[16] By the same token, the literary scholar Efrain Barradas stresses the identity of Díaz as a "profoundly Dominican" writer, the novel as a "Dominican cultural product," and the language and overall cosmos of the text as delimited by knowledge of things Dominican.[17] Barradas cites moments in the text that, in his view, "only a reader who is familiar with Dominican Spanish and with the history of that country can understand."[18] While addressing its implications for the ethnicity that the novel names, but without circumscribing the sphere of its signification, a well-informed essay by Elena Machado Sáez reads *The Brief Wondrous Life of Oscar Wao* as a corrective to the critical reception of *Drown* and the definitions of authentic representation that emerged in commentaries about the author's writing. The essay persuasively construes the novel's narrator, Yunior, as heir of the sins of the Dominican nation and offers the overall project of the novel as that of mocking the naiveté of readers intent on expecting happy resolutions to dramas born of tragic histories of colonial barbarity.[19]

While the foregoing readings, focusing on a Dominican métier, point to something objectively discernible in Díaz's writings, one can similarly find much else, indeed much more, that speaks to non-Dominican systems of significance and larger sites of knowledge of the human experience. The greater bulk of the signifying that the author engages in, especially in *Oscar Wao*, addresses questions of Americanness and the place of the artist in society. We can verify this assertion by attending to three areas of emphasis that in my view have received insufficient critical consideration. One involves Díaz's artistic identity, his manner of inhabiting the republic of letters as a major voice in contemporary American literature and culture. Another corresponds to the author's layered identity as a metropolitan writer linked to the Caribbean diaspora, his engaging with the memory of a history elsewhere that shapes his manner of belonging within the contours of Americanness. The third deals with Díaz's particular manner of deploying his Dominican ancestry, the heritage that provides a great deal of his métier. As I hope will become clear in the pages ahead, the American writer Junot Díaz, his imagination deeply rooted in the world of fiction, speaks from an artistic identity that envelops and organizes his Caribbean diasporic selfhood, a composite selfhood that in turn shapes the performance of his Dominican ancestry in his writings. Díaz has spoken of his college years, at Rutgers University, as a moment when his layered identity cohered in his mind: he came to see himself "as a Dominican, an American, and a writer."[20]

Perhaps recognizing the centrality of the Caribbean to the core structure of the Dominican experience, Díaz owns his regional descent in a manner that makes him into a kind of American to whom the Antillean world matters at the level of existential immediacy.

The Dominican references in his texts should lead to no confusion as to Díaz's standing as an American writer and as a voice of the American public sphere, just as the Chinese characters in Pearl Buck's *The Good Earth* (1931) or the Cuban protagonist in Ernest Hemingway's *The Old Man and the Sea* (1951) raise no question as to the Americanness of the works involved. Díaz has described the years of his creative stagnation, when the novel that would become *The Brief Wondrous Life of Oscar Wao* seemed to evade him, referring mockingly to what many take to be the timeless aspiration of every writer in the United States, namely to write the great American novel. "Five years of my life and the dream that I had of myself, all down the tubes because I couldn't pull off something that other people seemed to pull off with relative ease: a novel," he says, adding that by then he had already given up on "a Great American Novel. I would have been elated with the eminently forgettable New Jersey novel."[21] Even in jest it would not occur to him to think of it as the great or forgettable "Dominican" or "Azua" novel. Indeed, when PBS's Bill Moyers, an institution of American journalism and conscientious social commentary, asked Díaz what advice he would give President Barack Obama, he seemed to harbor no doubt about the legitimacy of the writer's American credentials.[22] Nor did the interviewee's Americanness quiver in his response as he pleaded for more honesty from "our" national leaders regarding the severity of "our" present troubles as a country. "When was the last time we were asked to sacrifice?" asked Díaz rhetorically. The writer went on to seize the authority to speak eloquently as a legitimate voice of the country's national community, urging the commander-in-chief to consider carefully the implications of the kinds of story we choose to tell to the population, just as he called on all of us, the nationwide viewing public, to overcome the temptation to listen only to the stories conveyed to us through "the biggest megaphones," which concern themselves solely with the "person on the top," the "hero or the winner," urging us instead to pay attention to "the little megaphones" that tell us about the librarian in the library, people going to a church basement "to help folks out," people coming to a home to read to the elderly. "There are all these little megaphones that are telling you, whispering, that this is beauty, this is humanity, this is America."[23]

Significantly, Ben Railton, a scholar of American literature, has looked at *The Brief Wondrous Life of Oscar Wao* and Philip Roth's novel *American Pastoral* (1997) as texts that illustrate a "new mimesis" in the manner in which their narrators Yunior and Nathan Zuckerman, who are themselves writers, wrestle with the lure of the American Dream.[24] The two texts evolve as "(meta-) realistic chronicles" that connect to influential predecessors, the character of Jim in Willa Cather's *My Ántonia* (1918) and that of Nick in F. Scott Fitzgerald's *The Great Gatsby* (1925). All four novels, Railton argues, dramatize the power of teleological aspiration, which proves ongoing when the characters form part of "a family's multigenerational story and Dream," as in *The Brief Wondrous Life of Oscar Wao*, in which Lola's daughter Isis remains as "the family's future and its legacy."[25] Railton contends that "at all levels of American society, national narratives such as the American Dream—and literary equivalents such as the Great American Novel—contribute greatly to the identities and experiences of both individuals and communities."[26] Similarly, Brannon Costello, an American literature scholar with an interest in comics and graphic novels, invites us to consider *A Visitation of Spirits* (1989), the novel by the African American author Randall Kenan, as a precursor to Díaz's *The Brief Wondrous Life of Oscar Wao*, insofar as both rely heavily on "metaphors and allusions drawn from comic books, science fiction, and role-playing games" in their search for a language suitable for articulating the protagonist's onerous plight.[27]

A consequence of his inhabiting the republic of letters as a prominent artistic voice in American fiction and a spokesperson for the national community in the public sphere is that Díaz has reached the point of commanding the discursive power necessary to alter the literary tradition from which he writes. He attests to the dynamic impact of the individual talent on the structure of the tradition, which T. S. Eliot viewed as "organic wholes" in relation to which individual works of literary art have their significance.[28] One could argue that, with *The Brief Wondrous Life of Oscar Wao*, Díaz effectuates a more intimate rapport between literature proper and the kind of storytelling found in science fiction, fantasy, horror, and comic books than any other American literary artist before him. Similarly, the cross-national setting of the novel may be said to expand the physical territory that the country's literary imagination can cover to encompass genealogies, places, histories, and people in sites located elsewhere. Consequently, through the effective intervention of writers with the profile of Díaz, American readers now may encounter the city of Salcedo, a character named Joaquín Balaguer, and an instance of *perejiling* ethnic others within a menu of signifieds that they can no longer misrecognize as foreign. One can credit Díaz, along with the cadre of diasporic Caribbean writers of which he is part, with having contributed significantly to expanding the geography of the American literary imagination.

Artistic Identity

Much that stands out in the numerous interviews that Junot Díaz has granted throughout his celebrated and continuously ascendant career reads like a *biographia literaria* in the sense Samuel Taylor Coleridge used the phrase as title of his *Biographia Literaria; or, Biographical Sketches of My Literary Life and Opinions*, published in 1817. Certainly, Díaz speaks much about poverty in his childhood and youth, especially after his father left the house, the disarray of his life at Old Bridge High School, and about roguish adolescence in Perth Amboy, an area of affective isolation that did not seem to provide the benefit of a supportive social network to the family to help alleviate the consequences of economic disempowerment. He recalls illness, desolation, and death. Yet, seldom do those recollections come unaccompanied by equally memorable references to his engagement with books, literary expression, and the world that writers and graphic storytellers assemble in various sorts of figurations. At age nineteen, during senior year in high school, his life offering no sign of a future, he did "nothing but stare at the walls and read Stephen King books."[29] On rainy days, he says, he would troop "down to the Sayreville library" to poke around the stacks, therein discovering, among other items he would come to cherish, Doris Lessing's *Canopus in Argos: Archives*, the five-novel science fiction series set in "future history" that shows a number of societies undergoing accelerated evolution.[30] If Díaz's description of his first arrival in New York City from Santo Domingo as a child does justice to the memory of the self he was, by then he must have already had at his disposal a wealth of fantasy and imagined worlds to help structure his perception of reality. New York for him "went from the Oz I dreamed about in the Dominican Republic to the distant sight of the Verrazano Bridge," and when he first came into contact with the city, the name of a literary tradition seemed best suited to encapsulate his impression: "The city looked like science fiction."[31]

An "inveterate reader," as a child Díaz consumed a menu of texts that included works by Isaac Asimov, Benjamin Williams Bova, Arthur C. Clarke,

Robert A. Heinlein, and Roger Zelazny.[32] The day after Ray Bradbury's death, Díaz posted a moving tribute that credits the renowned fantasy and science fiction author with having shown him the way to life as a writer. Díaz reminisces about encountering Bradbury as a youth and following him "to Mars, to the veldt, to the future, to the past, to the heart of America, I rode with him on the Pequod, and on the rockets."[33] Calling Bradbury one of his "first literary obsessions," Díaz tells about the dramatically transformative impact that the story "All Summer in a Day," by the author of *Fahrenheit 451* (1953), had on him. "In a few short pages, Bradbury gave me back to myself," not only offering him his "first real taste of the power of fiction," but also putting him squarely "on the path to my calling."[34] Díaz has similarly lavished much praise on Ursula K. Le Guin's "The Ones Who Walk Away from Omelas," a story that he read the same year of his encounter with Bradbury's work. One can get a glimpse of his admiration for Le Guin by observing that few of the photographs of Díaz accessible via the Internet show him exuding as much unadulterated happiness as when he appears hugging the author of *The Wizard of Earthsea* (1968) at the PEN/Malamud Award ceremony in 2002.

An artist first and foremost, Díaz has thought much about literature, language, imagination, and the relations among the various differentiated expressive forms. Díaz's introduction to the choice of texts he selected for inclusion in *The Beacon's Best of 2001*, pointing as it does to issues of artistry, can serve as prolegomena to his literary creed. Díaz's selections for *Beacon's Best* included prominent fiction writers and poets of the caliber of Edwidge Danticat, Louise Erdrich, Cornelius Eddy, Rhina P. Espaillat, Chang-Rae Lee, and Zadie Smith, but he also found space for "one of the finest 'undiscovered' writers working in the United States," Terrence E. Holt, his former teacher at Rutgers University. Speaking generally of the texts that went into the *Beacon* anthology, Díaz articulates what reads like an explicit *ars poetica*:

> It is the gap between the Real Story and the Official Story that interests me. It is inside this gap that the best writers, or at least the writers I admire the most, often reside. You don't, despite what you might think, have to be a radical or a revolutionary to be a resident of the gap. You don't have to write about dictators, or the slave trade, or "issues." You don't even have to write about twenty-first century earth (hello, Octavia Butler!). Simply present a vision of the world that is complex, multivocal, and contradictory, that does not seek to simplify, that does not

succumb to what Bruce Lee called "fearful formulas," and you will find yourself with a new address, no questions asked. All the writers gathered in this anthology have, in their own way, made a home of the gap.[35]

During an interview on *Maria Hinojosa: One on One*, Díaz diplomatically and gracefully counterbalanced the interviewer's stress on the lessons that Dominicans can derive from the history that the novelist unearths in *The Brief Wondrous Life of Oscar Wao*.[36] The writer politely asserted that he is an artist, not a historian, and that he uses "history as a tool" for his literary project, which he described as one that acknowledges "the need to be in conversation with the dead." "Literature," he says, "is about encountering the human experience," and history can play a role in that quest the way it did for Herman Melville and William Faulkner. The more specifically the interviewer wished to prod into the valence of the novel for understanding the drama of Haitian-Dominican relations or the locality of the Trujillo dictatorship, the more the novelist veered away from accepting a role as historian of the Dominican experience, insisting that a prime mover in his work is his sense of amazement about "how illusory and contradictory life is."[37] The answers given by the writer, against the grain of the questions asked by the interviewer, would seem to invite a cautious reading of the history one finds in *The Brief Wondrous Life of Oscar Wao* lest one should read in it a more stable truth claim than in the fantasy to which it is inextricably linked.

Trujillo in *The Brief Wondrous Life of Oscar Wao* is not just Trujillo but also a Sauron ruling a nation as his own private Mordor. The life of Oscar, from his early beginnings as a baby Porfirio Rubirosa to his final demise at the hands of El Capitán's henchmen, could fit the pattern of life as a quest, a classic theme of the fantasy world, a world, ultimately, made up "of antinomies."[38] Especially in *The Brief Wondrous Life of Oscar Wao*, Díaz presents the reader with a narrative scheme that constantly exposes the narrator's tension between the competing desires to exercise epistemic authority and to challenge it. Witness the footnote that explains the narrator's reticence to fix his anachronistic reference to the *perrito* dance. The footnote in question glosses the narrator's evocation of the stunning beauty of Samaná, the Gangster's "old haunts" where he takes Beli on a memorable vacation. Deploying a technique akin to Brecht's *Verfremdungseffekt*, devised to remind the reader of the artifice at hand, the narrator confesses that in his "first draft" he had extolled the beauty of Jarabacoa instead, but, as he learned from his friend Leonie, "resident expert on all things Domo," this city lacks the "flawless resortless beaches" required for the landscape of his plot. While crediting Leonie with helping him avoid this error of Dominican geography, he opts out of correcting his erroneous chronology for the perrito: "That was one detail I couldn't change, just liked the image too much. Forgive me, historians of popular dance, forgive me!"[39]

The narrator displays a no less mocking treatment of documentary accuracy in an earlier footnote ascribing a key role to the Dominican Republic (via Trujillo and fukú) in the so-called Kennedy curse and the mighty U.S. army's failure to capture Vietnam after years of horrific warfare. Addressing readers as "conspiracy-minded fools," Yunior intimates that "on the night" of the plane crash that killed President Kennedy's elder son "John-John" along with his wife and his sister-in-law, the late president's "favorite domestic, Providencia Paredes, dominicana, was in Martha's Vineyard cooking up for John-John his favorite dish: chicharrón de pollo."[40] Inquisitive readers may certainly verify a Dominican woman of that name within the Kennedy family. Indeed, Paredes began her association with the family in 1957, as personal assistant to Senator John F. Kennedy's wife Jacqueline Bouvier, a job that she retained when the senator became president and relocated to the White House. While maintaining contact with the family, figuring among a select few at the burial of the former First Lady in 1994, Paredes served the Kennedys for a dozen years. The 1970s found her on the staff of the United States Postal Service until retirement in 1992.[41] When JFK Jr.'s Piper Saratoga dived fatally into the Atlantic Ocean in July 1999, the seventy-five-year-old Paredes had long left the environs of the Kennedy family. She appears cooking chicharrón de pollo in Martha's Vinyard then merely because that's when the plotline of The Brief Wondrous Life of Oscar Wao needs her there, not when documentary accuracy would warrant.

The science fiction scholar T. S. Miller insightfully points to the function of the footnotes in The Brief Wondrous Life of Oscar Wao "to turn the novel into a sort of self-annihilated, self-undermining text," insofar as they serve the historiographical impulses of the narrator to speak of a secret history that he tells "from the margins and in the margins."[42] Though such maneuvers show up in the footnotes the narrator leaves hardly any room for doubting that he controls the logic of time, space, and overall verisimilitude in his tale. He will assert ultimate authority over the cosmos of his story not only in relation to history but also to the world of literary fantasy. He on occasion speaks irreverently about genre books, saying, for instance, "Negro, please—this ain't a fucking comic book," a negative comparison that he extends even to the world created by the revered Tolkien when he asserts, "You know exactly what kind of world we live in. It ain't no fucking Middle-earth."[43] Garland Mahler makes a relevant point about narrative power when looking at the novel's political argument, namely the political significance of *zafa* (counterspell to the evil forces of fukú, the curse brought to the Caribbean region by the agents of empire and colonial domination). She observes that, armed with words and the power of the imagination, the writer uses zafa as a hero's lance to speak truth to power even as he acknowledges his own involvement with the structures employed in sustaining the status quo.[44]

At the level of language and invention, Díaz has long recognized himself using language as a tool of artifice. In a brief essay published in 2002 on the experience of seeing his work appear in translation, he made clear that even the small portion of Spanish words found in *Drown* did not consist all of "Dominicanisms."[45] At the time he did not see himself much influenced by the international scene, claiming "I am very US-situated," but even within the country's landscape, he found a wealth of linguistic resources: "There is plenty of 'urban' language, youth language, hip hop language, and a lot of intellectual language."[46] He revealed his increasing appetite for linguistic options: "I am becoming more voracious at mixing varieties of languages and registers. This is nothing new, but just a specific variety coming out of the Dominican diasporic experience. . . . where before I'd stick to Latino and black slang, I find myself now using South African slang because it sounds right."[47] Subsequently, speaking about the experience of translating *The Brief Wondrous Life of Oscar Wao* into Spanish, Achy Obejas would attest to Díaz's voracity by recalling a time when she needed to consult the author on a seemingly Dominican word that she had found hard to identify, and he disabused her by revealing that he had actually taken the word from Urdu.[48]

The trope of the lost book recurs pervasively in *Oscar Wao*. We find it associated with Maria Montez, with Oscar, and especially with Abelard. José David Saldívar has noted that in "bringing forth atrocities and memories of the Trujillo regime, Dr. Abelard Cabral's book became a kind of Antillean textbook of magic or grimoire."[49] But whether lost, found, in-progress, or enigmatically written, the motif of the book pervades the text. Witness the death of Jesús de Galíndez over a book on the Trujillo regime, the memoir with a blank page written by the demonically crafty Balaguer, and the text of the life of Oscar whose pages we read as narrated by Yunior. Nor can one fail to notice the proliferation of bibliography and bookish details sprinkled across the pages of the novel, including those used to name particular subsections of the text. A selective list of titles could include L. Frank Baum's The Wizard of Oz, Octavia Butler's Clay's Ark, Frank Herbert's Dune, Ayn Rand's The Fountainhead, Julia Alvarez's In the Time of the Butterflies, Mario Vargas Llosa's The Feast of the Goat, Herman Melville's Moby Dick, and Aimé Césaire's Cahier d'un retour au pays natal.[50] The narrator, for instance, tells about the immediate sense of total familiarity that the phrase "the moronic inferno" evoked to Oscar when he first heard it.[51] The phrase in question names the title of the collection of essays written by Martin Amis on various aspects of American life, published in 1986. Amis took the title from a phrase he had found in a text by Saul Bellow, who in turn may have gotten it from Wyndham Lewis. Amis says he used the phrase primarily as "a metaphor, a metaphor for human infamy: mass, gross, distracting human infamy. One of the many things I do not understand about Americans is this: what is it like to be a citizen of a superpower, to maintain democratically the means of planetary extinction."[52] If, as readers, we care to look for more meaning in the phrase than we can glean from its straightforward denotative resonance, an awareness of Amis's intended metaphorical use would no doubt serve to increase in our minds the sense of things uncanny that dominates the ordinary life of Oscar.

Ultimately, however, it matters just the same that the phrase names a book, among many of the books that the novel names or to which it alludes. The abundant references or allusions to texts, from "literature proper" as well as from science fiction, fantasy, and comic books, renders the story of Oscar into a rumble of texts, forms, genres, languages, and traditions reminiscent of the "Battle of the Books" that Jonathan Swift narrated satirically in 1704. The discursive tapestry that Díaz designs in The Brief Wondrous Life of Oscar Wao levels the playing field among utterances, allowing for books, authors, works, and forms irrespective of time (ancient or modern) or prestige (literary or low brow) to contribute what they might to the narrative of Oscar's life. Oscar imagines himself becoming the Dominican Stephen King, the Dominican James Joyce, and the Dominican Tolkien. Heartbroken over the failure to materialize a romantic liaison with Ana Obregón, Oscar attempts suicide. When, through a lucky happenstance, he survives, the narrator, tongue in cheek, salutes the good tidings by musing about the blow that Oscar's death would have dealt to "the future of American letters."[53] It is against the backdrop of this confluence of written and other expressive forms that one can see the applicability of Ramón Saldívar's nomenclature to characterize the novel thus: the "story of the disposed takes the form of what I call 'historical fantasy' and 'speculative realism' to signify the odd amalgam of historical novel, bildungsroman, post-magical realism, sci-fi, fantasy, and super-hero comic romance that structures the story of *The Brief Wondrous Life of Oscar Wao*."[54]

Science fiction, fantasy, or "the more speculative genres," in the words of Oscar de León, have a special place in the education of Díaz's literary sensibility. The novelist contends that those "bizarre American imports," from France as well as from England, which this country then "somehow perfected in a bizarre form," stand, along with the comic book and the blues, as the most original indigenous forms of the United States.[55] Though he finds that those expressive forms have suffered marginalization, he regards them as "an important part of what we would call the North American narrative, what we would call the formative literary experience," and in his own aesthetic practice he finds science fiction, fantasy, and comic books ideally suited to talk about the "extreme, ludicrous transformations" that people undergo in conditions of oppression and coerced migration from the Caribbean to the United States.[56]

The author's fascination with the imaginative ambience of fantasy and science fiction dates back to his debut collection, *Drown*. It makes a modest appearance in the title story, "Drown," at one of the narrator's most tender moments of communication with his mother. He looks caringly at her in her silence and unobtrusive presence and dulcifies her using language that could easily have come from Tolkien even as it gestures to Akira Kurosawa's *Kagemusha* (1980). He approaches her and whispers: "You have travelled to the East and learned many secret things," adding, "You are like a shadow warrior."[57] Describing the terminality of a young man's resolve to leave his girlfriend, the voyeuristic narrator in the story "Boyfriend" says that the lover simply had gotten "a little escape velocity going," referring to the speed necessary to break free from the gravitational attraction of a massive body without further propulsion.[58] Similarly, fantasy appears in "No Face," a story that takes us back to the character who, as an infant, had his face eaten by a pig. We meet him first in the opening story "Ysrael," but in "No Face" we have occasion to look deeply into the personal drama of the young man. There we gather that he relies on fantasy to cope with the animosity he encounters in everyday life. A reader of Kaliman, the Mexican comic book hero made popular in the 1960s, he imagines himself invincible. He says "FLIGHT and jumps up and his shadow knifes over the tops of the trees."[59] In the face of harassment from passersby who yell all manner of disparagements, he wills "INVISIBILITY" into being.[60] He calls forth "STRENGTH" to loosen himself from the grip of four aggressive bullies who have ambushed him, vowing to make him "a girl," and he manages to escape to safety.[61] This unlucky young man has no doubt discovered a world of the imagination where he can enjoy access to the resources necessary for his own protection from the cruelty of others. He imagines himself in possession of some of the extraordinary gifts of the superheroes: the ability to move about unencumbered by the force of gravity, to remain undetected while physically in close proximity to others, and to lift objects of limitless weight and dimension.

Science fiction, fantasy, comic books, and role-playing rise to visibility graphically, assertively, reiteratively in *The Brief Wondrous Life of Oscar Wao* as the titular character and the interventionist narrator avidly consume the "speculative genres." What has seemed less evident to critics of the novel is not only that the genre books have afforded Díaz a framework for approaching the strange history of the Dominican Republic, but that the author superimposes the tenor and the texture of the fantasy world on the historical milieu that he sets out to evoke in the novel. In a certain way, Díaz erects the foundations of his Dominican cosmos by means of imaginative resources that resemble in principle those used by Tolkien in the creation of Middle-earth. Although he presents us with characters from Dominican history like Balaguer and Rubirosa or with places from the verifiable geography of the country such as Azua and Santo Domingo, as artificer of the cosmos of his novel, Díaz engages no less emphatically than Tolkien in the practice of what science fiction and fantasy scholars refer to as "world building."[62] The extraordinary quality of magnification that stands out in the evocation of Trujillo, "the dictatingest dictator who ever dictated," the Dominican Sauron, Darkseid, the alpha and the omega, corresponds to the novel's design to invent rather than remember the Dominican tyrant. A "Mobutu before Mobutu was Mobutu," Díaz's Trujillo possesses boundless carnal energy paired with an insatiable sexual appetite. He dwarfs the great lechers of history from King Solomon to Silvio Berlusconi as the mate of "thousands upon thousands of women" and arguably builder of the "world's first culocracy."[63] The tyrant oversees an insuperable surveillance system which keeps him informed of the words and deeds of every single member of the country's population, which ensured that if you said something about him at 8:40 AM, by 10:00 AM you would find yourself in jail enduring unspeakable torture.[64]

The hypertrophic augmentation of reality, which students of science fiction and fantasy call "enlargement," extends to the oversized penises of the men associated with the Trujillo regime.[65] Witness the "enormous phallus" that gave the cosmopolitan playboy Porfirio Rubirosa his successes in the erotic arena internationally and the supremely endowed Jack Pujols, the inaugural love interest of Beli at El Redentor who boasted "a Shiva-sized lingam, a destroyer of worlds."[66] Enlargement dominates much of the description having to do with Beli's birth, life, and sorrows, especially for the scenes whose action takes place in the Dominican Republic. The offspring of phenotypically white parents, she comes out of the womb not just black, but "black black—kongoblack, shangoblack, kaliblack, zapoteblack, rekhablack."[67] An orphan shortly after her birth, she becomes a child of scorn, despised by kith and kin on account of her phenotype. She endures all manner of maltreatment when a family takes her in to reduce her to servitude. Among other misfortunes, she suffers burns "extending from the back of her neck to the base of her spine," which leave a scar that resembles a "bomb crater" and gives her the appearance of the "hibakusha," the people bearing the impact of the atomic blast in Hiroshima and Nagasaki.[68] Surviving the horror thanks to La Inca's intervention and sustained nursing, Beli grows into adolescence, "hit[ting] the biochemical jackpot," transforming into "an underage stunner" with a body so "berserk that only a pornographer or a comic book artist could have designed it with a clear conscience."[69] In the pectoral area, she possessed "globes so implausibly titanic they made generous souls pity their bearer and drove every straight male in their vicinity to reevaluate his sorry life," but her gluteus muscles reached no less spectacular dimensions, "supersonic" buttocks "that could tear words right out of niggers' mouths" and "pull windows" out of "their frames," all manner of extremities that in the magnifying eyes of the narrator made her a "babe."[70]

Ethnicity and Craft

I have periodically taught Drown to classes made up of students representing varying demographic make ups in keeping with their distinct campus locations, once each as a visiting professor at the City College of New York, Amherst College, and Harvard University, and at least ten times at Syracuse University, my home institution. Seldom have I begun the discussion of the collection without wondering how students will engage with the geographical or cultural references in the stories, such as Ocoa, short for the province of San José de Ocoa, where the boys Yunior and Rafa go from the capital city of Santo Domingo to stay with relatives when their mother, Virtudes, has trouble making ends meet, or Tunti, for a street in the neighborhood of Villa Consuelo called Calle Tunti Cáceres, which memorializes a national hero who died plotting against the murderous Trujillo. I have wondered thus because most of the times when I have covered the book I have not had a significant portion of Dominican or even Latino students in the class. I have seldom been able to assume the students' familiarity with the geography, society, or culture that the characters inhabit in the stories. The empirical observation I have culled from the classroom over these years suggests that non-Latino students do not generally experience the setting of the plots as an impediment to their engagement with the lives of the characters. Drawing on the tentative findings of my classroom experience, I have arrived at the understanding that this successful communication of the texts with their readers beyond familiarity with the ethnicity of the characters or the particulars of their setting lies at the core of the uniquely auspicious sort of reception accorded to Drown by reviewers and critics. We might invoke here the testimony of the Ghanaian writer Nii Ayikwei Parkes, an avid reader of what he calls "migration narratives." Parkes recalls that as a young man he read the novel The Lonely Londoners (1957), a story by the Guyanese writer Samuel Selvon "on the Caribbean coming to 'lime' in London," mostly to find out what made his father "laugh so hard." With Selvon's book setting the standard as his "blueprint migration narrative," Parkes muses that if his daughter wanted to hear him now laugh the way his father did then, "I would probably have to be reading Junot Díaz's Drown."[71]

The stories in Drown, along with their humor, exhibit a keen intellectual sensibility that delves piercingly into the lives of characters whose humanity the author renders tangible through an effective representation of their putative Dominicanness. I would speculate that readers appreciate the relative novelty of the ethnic specificity involved as it brings into view an added site of the human fauna, expanding the imaginative landscape and ethnology of American fiction. Set in a discrete history and geography—following the characters' whereabouts from the homeland in Santo Domingo through their immigrant odyssey in New Jersey and New York—the stories in the collection unveil a contemporary yarn of misery, uprooting, and endurance. Irrespective of the narrator's frequent invocation of the Dominican specificity of the characters, captured mockingly in a snide observation about the group's questionable taste in interior decoration, "Contemporary Dominican Tacky," the manner of representation at play does not impede their recognition as just people.[72] To a caring reader, they simply stand for those self-absorbed beings who inhabit the earth, harboring the greatness, the baseness, the good, the evil, the beauty, the ugliness, the brilliance, and the mediocrity of their species.

The recognition, for instance, that young Yunior's inability to keep his food down in "Fiesta, 1980" has its source in some psychosomatic expression of a strained relationship with his authoritative father, exacerbated by the boy's inarticulate discomfort about his unintended complicity with his father's marital infidelity, outweighs any unfamiliarity that readers may have with gender inequity or social relations within families one might identify as Dominican. Probably with that interethnic power of signification in mind, more than one scholar has assumed a comparative glance to look at *Drown*. Lizabeth Paravisini-Gebert, for instance, has drawn useful parallels between *Down These Mean Streets* by Piri Thomas and the debut collection by Díaz.[73] Similarly, Richard Perez has launched a comparative analysis of face-related events in a passage from the well-known memoir by Piri Thomas and the story "Ysrael," from *Drown*, so as to search for clues to a discernible relationship between the figuration of the face, "the fleshy threshold to the extreme limits of being," and the affirmation of Latino personhood, finding that Thomas and Díaz both "narrate the difficult emergence of a Latino I."[74]

Reading "Aurora" in the classroom, I have found my students hard put to demonstrate, upon my injunction, in what fundamental ways the story by Díaz differs in essence from the idyll of Romeo and Juliet once we get over the desolation of the setting in contrast to the aristocratic Verona where William Shakespeare chooses to place his characters. Shakespeare tells the story to its fatal end, and Díaz leaves it in medias res, but one would find it hard to envision in what way Aurora and Lucero, the former a junkie frequently in juvenile detention and the latter a drug dealer, are less "star-crossed" than the two youths from Verona or less fated for an unfortunate end. By the same token, Ana María Manzanas-Calvo has advanced a reading of "Aurora" that probes into the semantic reach of the title to explicate the story as another iteration of the treatment of the myth of Eos, the rosy-fingered goddess of dawn who hastens every morning from her home at the edge of Oceanus to bring light to mortals and immortals. Manzanas-Calvo thus places the story by Díaz in an august lineage of writers, especially poets, from Homer, to Ovid, to Petrarch, to Sir Philip Sidney who have evoked the Aurora, or Eos, myth with varying degrees of resignification.[75]

Drown consists of ten stories in which we see aptly rehearsed a well-crafted elliptical style that for the most part dispenses with the documentary details of historical reality. Ellipsis has the potential for enabling readers to decode the human problem on the page by filling in documentary details from their own historical reality. Because of how much it conveys elliptically and metaphorically, the collection can afford, for instance, to have characters speak Spanish without translation, italics, or any other editorial assistance for the Anglophone reader, who can bear the minor loss of data without forfeiting access to meaning. Critics have often stressed the author's adroit engagement with words, his knack for language ultimately enabling him to achieve a visual richness by conferring a sort of tangibility to emotions and sensations. As the narrator's older brother, Rafa, walks away upset, we read: "He turned away from me. His feet crackling through the weeds, breaking stems."[76] Subsequently, as the two of them ride the bus back home, Yunior observes his brother: "Rafa crossed his arms and watched the fields and roadside shacks scroll past, the dust and smoke and people almost frozen by our speed."[77] In the story called "Drown," the son is vexed over his gullible mother's torment, caused by the sly absentee father who sweet-talks her on the telephone from Florida to strip her of some money. "His words coil inside her, wrecking her sleep for days," says a protective son.[78] In "Negocios," as the sense of obligation to his original family begins to exert pressure on Ramon's conscience after he has formed a parallel family in his immigrant abode, the deceit and contradiction send him on an unbearable moral pirouette: "He listened to his heart beating, and began to sense its slick contours."[79] Ramon cannot continue the pretense for long thereafter, and the inevitable draws near: "The couple began to fight on a regular schedule. Locks were changed, doors were broken, slaps were exchanged."[80] Pervasively spangled with concrete images and vivid scenes that effectively translate feelings and states of mind, the writing draws on the robust lexical fund at the author's disposal to sculpt, to paint, and to physically imprint the internal and external reality of his characters. Although readers may indeed recognize the human drama that afflicts literary characters via prior knowledge of the social, cultural, or historical setting in which a particular plot evolves, they may no less efficaciously achieve a comparable recognition by means of what the text makes presently available to their senses.

Not surprisingly, *Drown* has provoked both readings that privilege ethnicity and those that dispense with it. Stressing ethnic specificity, Marisel Moreno has offered a fine exegesis of "How to Date a Browngirl, Blackgirl, Whitegirl, or Halfie," one of the most intriguing stories in *Drown*, by first looking at the rise of the author as an indication that Dominicans in the United States may well be on the way to overcoming the invisibility that plagued them when literary works by U.S. Dominicans could be said to exist "on the periphery of the margins."[81] For the critic the various areas of conflict that emerge in the story in the realms of class, race, ethnicity, sexuality, and culture all provide fertile ground for sensing a reconfiguration of the Dominican diaspora that substantially breaks from the corresponding legacies of the ancestral homeland. Similarly, Jason Frydman reads the stories in *Drown* in a resolutely literalist way with an eye on exploring the "crisis of masculinity" that plagues the characters, standing as a more "direct obstacle to upward mobility for the diasporic Dominican subject" than any impediment attributable to "oppressive socioeconomic conditions."[82] Interpreting such a pathology as an operative factor throughout the book, Frydman points to a self-generated "crisis" that results in a cohort of male characters "compulsively repeating a frustrated lumpen adolescence."[83]

In contrast, however, the novelist David Gates, appraising *Drown* for the *New York Times Book Review*, felt comfortable placing the book "smack-dab in the middle" of the American literary tradition. This the reviewer believes despite the narrator's scrutinizing glances at contemporary Dominican society, evocation of the drama of new immigrants, emphasis on cross-cultural dynamics, and gestures to a poetics of difference via Spanish-language phrases or dialogue utterances throughout the collection.[84] Obsessed "with outsiders," Gates argues, American literature's "Hucks and Holdens are forever duking it out with the King's English, and writers as different as Ezra Pound, Zora Neale Hurston and Donald Barthelme have delighted in defiling the pure well with highbrow imports, nonstandard vernacular and Rube Goldberg coinages."[85] I also find it significant, for instance, that the Paris-based firm that released the French version of *Drown* described it as having been "traduit de l'américain" (translated from the American), as if wishing to highlight the peculiarly American fabric of the language of the text. Similarly, the foreign-language translations of the book that I have perused, as well as the British edition put out in London by Faber and Faber, carry a glossary of the Spanish words that seems designed to give non-U.S. readers access to an ethnically differentiated segment of American slang.

On the whole, the texture of the pieces produced by Díaz in *Drown* display a capacity for engaging us, at the level of language and characterization, with an elliptical style that dominates the narration and a pervasive metaphorical stance that together enable communication. More than teaching us about a particular group we may not have known before, the book's success seems to lie in its ability to supply us with opportunities for delving deeper into the psychopathology of the people we already knew. The reception accorded by reviewers to *Drown* as a welcome contribution to American letters reveals a critical appreciation of the author's success at the literary craft more than any sort of valuation of the knowledge about Dominicans that he may have made available to readers. This acclaim perhaps confirms the intuition voiced by the fourteenth-century Arab scholar Ibn Khaldûn in his compendium *The Muqaddimah*. He says, "Poetry and prose work with words, and not with ideas. The ideas are secondary to the words. The words are basic."[86]

Those with privileged access to Díaz prior to the successful publication of *Drown* knew of the young author's engagement with varied literary forms, including the production of a parallel oeuvre in fantasy books yet unpublished. Now the author himself feels comfortable speaking publically about his dissatisfaction with his three unpublished science fiction novels: *Shadow of the Adept*, *The Shadow of the Torturer*, and *Dark America*, which have long languished under contract, failing to meet his own standards.[87] Perhaps his agreeing to publish "Monstro," an excerpt from the novel of the same name, in the first ever science fiction issue of the *New Yorker* (June 11, 2012), indicates a greater commitment to bringing this project into fruition as a completed novel than he has mustered with the previous ones. But, apart from his unpublished oeuvre, the greater bulk of the short fiction that appeared in print under his name following the acclaimed collection published in 1996 treaded territory already familiar to his readers. The author's reputation continued to grow on the strength of the narrative verve and the registers that had become as distinct as a trademark in his writing. However, with the novella "The Brief Wondrous Life of Oscar Wao," which appeared in the issue of the *New Yorker* published December 25, 2000, Díaz showed a clear resolve to venture into an appreciably different aesthetic domain. There the author essays a far more obtrusive combination of styles, introducing a narrator with a strident voice and a chip on his shoulder. To describe Oscar's experience as he endures "the beating to end all beatings" from the henchmen of his nemesis the Capitán, the narrator displays a penchant for irreverent sarcasm: "The niggers kicked him in the nuts and perked him right up! It was like one of those nightmare 8 am MLA panels that you think will never, ever end."[88]

As Díaz endeavored to expand the novella into a full-fledged novel, he increased the textures of the speaking voices and enriched the cosmos inhabited by Oscar, whose story now became a dominating narrative frame enveloping the lives and times of other characters. These include mostly his mother Beli, his grandmother La Inca, his sister Lola, and his friend Yunior. Told primarily by Yunior, who functions as a first-person narrator boasting the power of omniscience, the story of the novel evolves as a quest for meaning. The more inquisitive characters prowl after any sense they could make of the heritage, history, and immigrant experience that seem to structure and over-determine their lives. Oscar and Lola are Dominican American siblings with tormentous ties to their ancestry who must come to terms with a curse that hovers over them from a staggered history of family (de León), nation (Dominican Republic), and region (the Caribbean), all connecting seamlessly to the arrival of Christopher Columbus on the shores of the western hemisphere in 1492, the historical event that unleashed the horrid drama of the New World and its microscopic expression in the de León household.

The metaphoric stance of Drown gives way to the proliferation of simile and enlargement in the text of The Brief Wondrous Life of Oscar Wao. The subtlety and understatement that Díaz cultivated in his debut collection of short fiction has now morphed into a predominantly hyperbolic tonality. Mood swings and epistemic self-sufficiency pervade the texture of the narrator's voice, which glides easily from analytical to meditative to irascible within the space of a few paragraphs. The narrative assembles an assortment of dictions, integrating a continuum of linguistic registers ranging from demotic, to urbane, to scientific, sprinkled with a dispassionate deployment of Spanish words, phrases, and dialogues. The narrator arrogates to himself the authority to launch social commentary about Dominican politics, U.S. imperial domination of the western hemisphere, white supremacy, negrophobia, and the moral structure of the Dominican mind, decking his composite discourse with a wealth of references and allusions to historical characters, events from the present or the past, cultural phenomena, writers, bibliographical citations, and literary genres.

Upon publication the novel received endorsement as one of the "best books of 2007" by the New York Times, San Francisco Chronicle, New York Magazine, *Boston Globe*, *Los Angeles Times*, *Washington Post*, and *Village Voice*, among many other major newspapers and magazines throughout the country. Then the string of distinctions followed in quick succession, with the Pulitzer Prize for Fiction, the National Book Critics Circle Award, and the John Sargent Sr. First Novel Prize, among many others, leading up to the accumulation of prestige that in 2012 made Díaz deserving of a MacArthur "Genius" Fellowship. The acclaim enjoyed by *This Is How You Lose Her* (2012), a second collection that assembles several of the stories Díaz had published since the release of *Drown*, along with a few new pieces, could actually have resulted from the lingering aftereffect of the powerful aesthetic impact exerted by *The Brief Wondrous Life of Oscar Wao*. The collection competed as a finalist for the National Book Award for fiction, and it received enthusiastic praise from reviewers, most memorably from the novelist Leah Hager Cohen, the author of *The Grief of Others* (2011), who describes Díaz's idiom as "so electrifying and distinct it's practically an act of aggression, at once alarming and enthralling, even erotic in its assertion of sudden intimacy" and who makes sense of the main character's compulsive sexual indiscretions by musing that maybe Yunior "is just a sucio? Or maybe Díaz means to suggest that it's human nature to be divided against ourselves, that we are all conflicted, displaced creatures, making our way within the diaspora of the human heart."[89]

With *The Brief Wondrous Life of Oscar Wao* Díaz succeeded in firmly establishing his artistic credentials, securing a position of prominence in the country's literary community, thereby inducing learned audiences to recognize the extent to which he invests himself in the mystery of the creative act. One would be hard put to think of a greater tribute to Díaz's craft than the *Sunday Times* EFG Private Bank Short Story Prize awarded to "Miss Lora," one of the stories in *This Is How You Lose Her*, in 2013. Not only did the distinction bring the highest monetary award granted to a single story in the world, thirty thousand pounds sterling as reported by *The Guardian*, but his text bested entries from such top British authors as Mark Haddon, Ali Smith, and Sarah Hall. The words of the British writer Andrew O'Hagan, a member of the panel of judges that selected "Miss Lora" as the winner, compellingly described Díaz "as a short story writer who gives everything its due. No words are wasted and his characters harbour both a sense of dignity and a wealth of surprise." O'Hagan called "Miss Lora" "a contemporary classic," adding that it stood out "with its precise, unflinching prose, and with its brilliant evocation of an immigrant world struggling with modernity."[90]

Diasporic Identity and Americanness

Efraín Barradas has ventured a provocative comparison between Yunior's prologue in *The Brief Wondrous Life of Oscar Wao* and Alejo Carpentier's prologue in his famous novel *El reino de este mundo* (1949), the ür-text of magical realism in Caribbean and Latin American literature. Confident that Díaz engages in conversation with Carpentier, Barradas points to the forwardness, cockiness, and irreverence of Yunior's narration to suggest that *The Brief Wondrous Life of Oscar Wao* relies more on comic effect than on science fiction and fantasy to fashion a new version of Carpentier's magical realism—reconfigured from the perspective of the diaspora—into comic realism.[91] Contrastingly, while Monica Hanna's study of *The Brief Wondrous Life of Oscar Wao* stresses magical realism and its Latin American literary context, it looks at the cosmos of the novel through a lens sufficiently wide as to realize that it "consciously engages Caribbean literary and historical discourses" along with "narrative structures and references particular to United States literature and popular culture in a language that crackles with vibrancy."[92] Hanna perceptively pairs the two epigraphs that usher in the story of Oscar, a poem by the Nobel Prize–winning poet from St. Lucia, Derek Walcott, and a rhetorical question from the comic book series *Fantastic Four*, as indicators of the existential loci that shape the reality of the characters, primarily Oscar and Yunior. The juxtaposition of a classic poem by a towering figure of Caribbean literature and a core text of American popular youth culture reveals from the outset the novel's investment in "creating a pastiche that attempts to capture the Caribbean diasporic experience."[93]

Hanna's identification of the way the novel negotiates the Caribbean background of the author invites further consideration here as it opens the possibility for understanding what Díaz does with ancestry as tackling what is in effect a problematic of Americanness. Far from encouraging readings that construe *The Brief Wondrous Life of Oscar Wao* as partaking of the magical realism practiced by an earlier generation of major Caribbean and Latin American writers, recognizing Díaz's diasporic identity would make patently clear his existential location in the United States and its implications. Díaz has consistently invoked the icons of American popular culture—Stephen King, television, comic books, hip hop, cinema in general, and Bruce Lee in particular—as sources that, along with his literary education, proved "crucial to his formation as an artist."[94] But, irrespective of what the author might declare, his texts recurrently dramatize the demeanor of the diasporic observer when confronted with persons or situations from the Antilles. Jacqueline Loss has suggestively offered a reading of "The Sun, the Moon, the Stars," a story by Díaz that appeared in the *New Yorker* in 1998, with an eye on the narrator's "diasporic anguish."[95] Enacting a pivotal moment in Yunior's relationship with his Cuban American girlfriend Magda, when they spend time in Santo Domingo, the story shows the Dominican narrator's distance from the local habitat, often in contrast to the welcome reception accorded to Magda by people there.[96]

Recalling the stories in *Drown*, one can, for instance, identify the gaze to which the narrator in "Edison, New Jersey" subjects the young domestic who works for Pruit as that of a diasporic observer looking on a recently arrived Dominican immigrant. He, the pool table delivery guy, and she, the maid with a possible crush on her boss, may share Dominican ancestry, but they differ radically at the level of cultural logic and social orientation. In "Negocios," the final story in *Drown*, we read the tale of a Dominican immigrant in the United States, his trials, tribulations, deception, and enigma. But, conceived as the story of the narrator's quest for knowledge, one must read it as the tale of an American of Dominican descent looking for answers to questions about his family history and personal destiny. As the story of Ramón de las Casas, it deals with the experience of an immigrant. As the story of Yunior, it addresses diasporic disquisitions. When in *The Brief Wondrous Life of Oscar Wao* Lola goes to the Dominican Republic, she does so as a foreigner, hence her difficulties to fit in as a "Dominican York" in the school she attends there.[97] As an outsider unfamiliar with working-class realities in the ancestral homeland, she finds the job that her boyfriend Max Sanchez does there intriguingly charming—his motorcycle shuttling between movie theaters, making it possible, by sheer speed, coordination, and precision, for two cinemas to screen the same film simultaneously by sharing the reels that he would transport from one site to the other as soon as they finished rolling.

Similarly, in going to Santo Domingo, Oscar travels to a world of difference, at least as we gather from the narrator's mediation of his perceptions there. The poverty, the traffic, the heat, the idiosyncrasies of the people, all strike him as features of an alien world: "People walking languidly with nothing to shade them from the sun and the buses that charged past so overflowing with passengers that from the outside they looked like they were making a rush delivery of spare limbs to some far off war and the general ruination of so many buildings as if Santo Domingo was the place that crumbled crippled concrete shells came to die."[98] Oscar "goes native" because he is not native. Otherwise he would not train his eyes so intensely on "the mind-boggling poverty, the snarl of streets and rusting zinc shacks that were the barrios populares . . . the skinny watchmen standing in front of stores with their brokedown shotguns, the music, the raunchy jokes heard on the streets, the mind-boggling poverty."[99] Oscar is a Don Bosco kid just as Lola is "a Jersey dominicana." Yunior and the de León siblings illustrate the diasporic, denormalizing gaze of the Western metropolitan youth experiencing for the first time as grown-ups the shocking strangeness of their ancestral Caribbean homeland. Nothing hits them more acutely than the realization that, by virtue of their U.S. socialization, education, and experience, they and their parents are simply not the same people. Lola captures the divide when she calls Beli "my Old World Dominican mother" and so does Yunior when he, in exultation of La Inca, valorizes "the Catholic devotion of our Viejas," often dismissed "as atavistic" by "[us] postmodern plátanos."[100] It takes a U.S. socialization, for instance, to develop the racial knowledge that enables Lola to divide the whole population into "we colored folks," who do not really care about children as we say we do, and "white people," who would move heaven and earth to secure the well-being even of the family dog.[101] Dominicans socialized in the Dominican Republic, even those living abroad as either immigrants or exiles, do not inhabit the same geography of knowledge as their diasporic coethnics.

Closing Thoughts

The foregoing pages have set out to contribute to contemporary literary history by locating the trajectory of Junot Díaz as a writer who has carved a space of recognition within the core of American fiction. As an author of Dominican descent, born in the Dominican Republic but educated, socialized, and trained as a literary artist in the United States, Díaz bears the ethnic markers of his ancestral homeland in the Caribbean and of the Latino panethnicity in the United States. I have sought to explore the uniqueness of his reception since his successful literary career began. I set out to examine the extent to which his investment in a particular way of practicing his craft may have enabled many in the reading public as well as among literary critics to refrain from reducing his texts to mere anthropological vehicles for the conveyance of knowledge about an ethnic minority. I have made the case that paying attention to the axes of identity one can discern from a reading of his works in combination with the body of discourse that has accumulated in his numerous interviews and nonfiction statements is useful in more than one way. Centering Díaz's artistry, his Americanness, his Caribbean diasporic negotiations, and his particular uses of Dominican ancestry sheds useful light on the complexity of his layered identity, making it discernible that the multiple parts of his composite selfhood go seamlessly together. Viewed thus, it would seem unwise for literary scholars to seek to extricate the parts by stressing, for instance, the author's Dominican heritage without attention to his standing as a prominent American fiction writer and a compelling voice of the public sphere in the United States. By the same token, viewing him as simply an American writer without the cultural and existential implications of his Caribbean background and ensuing diasporic identity may risk leaving crucial elements of his oeuvre unattended.

Nor can we read Díaz's work without engaging his commitment to artistry and, as a result, the profound symbolization to which he subjects his métier. The author makes it hard for an alert reader to ignore the movement from understatement to narratorial self-assertiveness, from metaphor to simile, from nearly clinical objective evocations of dramatic situations to willfully overt manipulation of people, time, and place. It behooves a learned reader of *The Brief Wondrous Life of Oscar Wao*, for instance, to make sense of enlargement, science fiction-induced world building, and the other manifestations of the author's active deployment of artistic narrative techniques. A Dominican reader of the novel might at first take issue with the adverse representation of the "community" in the text. There is the extreme machismo of all the men, the infidelity of all husbands, and the abusiveness imputed to mothers, to name only a few of the unflattering traits ascribed to males and females of Dominican ancestry. But, on closer inspection, the initial reaction must change once the reader recognizes discursive excess and consistent essentializing as narrative features that pervade the telling of the tale at hand. The book intentionally frustrates any aspiration on the part of the reader to use it as a document that represents or speaks for "the community." Díaz engages enthusiastically with his craft, and he seems to enjoy playing with techniques. He rehearses linguistic registers, learned vocabulary, profanity galore, and the game of putting erudition to work on the page, displaying a ludic sense reminiscent of the old *cento* poetry tradition. On the whole, with Junot Díaz we have a literary artist whose texts we cannot read strictly through the self-evident civil rights paradigms that abound in the criticism of much ethnic American literature. His writing will not let us find the politics unless we first commit to fumbling through the complexities of the art.

Notes

1. Daniel Stern, "One Who Got Away," review of *Down These Mean Streets*, by Piri Thomas, *New York Times Book Review*, May 21, 1967, 43.

2. Barbara Stewart, "Outsider with a Voice," *New York Times*, December 8, 1996.

3. Joyce Carol Oates, ed., *The Oxford Book of American Short Stories*, 2nd ed. (New York: Oxford University Press, 2013), 857–68.

4. *The New Yorker*, June 21 and 28, 1999.

5. Bill Buford, "Reading Ahead," *The New Yorker*, June 21 and 28, 1999, 68.

6. Ed Morales, "Junot What?" *Village Voice*, September 10, 1996.

7. Morales, "Junot What?," 66.

8. Ylce Irizarry, "Making It Home: A New Ethics of Immigration in Dominican Literature," in Vanessa Pérez, ed., *Hispanic Caribbean Literature of Migration: Narratives of Displacement* (New York: Palgrave Macmillan, 2010).

9. Silvio Torres-Saillant and Ramona Hernandez, "Dominicans: Community, Culture, and Collective Identity," in Nancy Foner, ed., *One Out of Three: Immigrant New York in the Twenty-First Century* (New York: Columbia University Press, 2013), 223.

10. Ashley Kunsa, "History, Hair, and Reimagining Racial Categories in Junot Díaz's *The Brief Wondrous Life of Oscar Wao*," *Critique: Studies in Contemporary Fiction* 54, no. 2 (2013): 211–24.

11. Brygida Gosztold, "A Dominican American Experience of Not Quite Successful Assimilation," in Jacek Fabiszak, Ewa Urbaniak-Rybicka, and Bartosaz Wolski, eds., *Crossroads in Literature and Culture: Second Language Learning and Teaching* (Berlin: Springer, 2012), 209.

12. Rita De Maeseneer, *Encuentros con la narrativa dominicana contemporánea* (Madrid: Iberoamericana/Vervuert, 2006).

13. Rita De Maeseneer, *Seis ensayos sobre narrativa dominicana contemporánea* (Santo Domingo: Colección del Banco Central de la República Dominicana, 2011), 98, 101–2.

14. Tim Lanzendörfer, "The Marvelous History of the Dominican Republic in Junot Díaz's *The Brief Wondrous Life of Oscar Wao*," MELUS 38, no. 2 (2013): 139.

15. Juanita Heredia, "The Dominican Diaspora Strikes Back: Cultural Archive and Race in Junot Díaz's *The Brief Wondrous Life of Oscar Wao*," in Vanessa Pérez Rosario, ed., *Hispanic Caribbean Literature of Migration: Narratives of Displacement* (New York: Palgrave Macmillan, 2010).

16. Achy Obejas, "A Conversation with Junot Díaz," *Review: Literature and Arts of the Americas* 42, no. 1 (2009): 45.

17. Efrain Barradas, "El realismo cómico de Junot Díaz: Notas sobre *The Brief Wondrous Life of Oscar Wao*," SECOLAS 53, no. 1 (2009): 99, 100, 101.

18. Barradas, "El realismo cómico de Junot Díaz," 101.

19. Elena Machado Sáez, "Dictating Desire, Dictating Diaspora: Junot Díaz's *The Brief Wondrous Life of Oscar Wao* as Foundational Romance," *Contemporary Literature* 52, no. 3 (2011): 522–55.

20. Stewart, "Outsider with a Voice."

21. Junot Díaz, "Becoming a Writer," *O, The Oprah Magazine*, November 2009, accessed April 22, 2015, http://www.oprah.com/spirit/Junot-Diaz-Talks-About-What-Made -Him-Become-a-Writer/2.

22. *Moyers and Company*, Public Broadcasting System, December 28, 2012.

23. *Moyers and Company*.

24. Ben Railton, "Novelist-Narrators of the American Dream: The (Meta-) Realistic Chronicles of Cather, Fitzgerald, Roth, and Díaz," *American Literary Realism* 43, no. 2 (2011): 136.

25. Railton, "Novelist-Narrators," 149.

26. Railton, "Novelist-Narrators," 150.

27. Brannon Costello, "Randall Kenan beyond the Final Frontier: Science Fiction, Superheroes, and the South in *A Visitation of Spirits*," *Southern Literary Journal* 43, no. 1 (2010): 129.

28. T. S. Eliot, *Selected Essays*, new ed. (New York: Harcourt, Brace, and World, 1950), 12–13.

29. Junot Díaz, "How (In a Time of Trouble) I Discovered My Mom and Learned to Live," in Esmeralda Santiago, ed., *Las Mamis: Favorite Latino Authors Remember Their Mothers* (New York: Vintage, 2000), 158.

30. Díaz, "How (In a Time of Trouble)," 158.

31. Junot Díaz, "New York: Science Fiction," in David S. Dunbar and Kenneth T. Jackson, eds., *Empire City: New York through the Centuries* (New York: Columbia University Press, 2002), 963, 964.

32. Geek's Guide to the Galaxy, "Junot Díaz Aims to Fulfill His Dream of Publishing Sci-Fi Novel with Monstro," Wired.com Geek's Guide to the Galaxy, episode 70, October 3, 2012, accessed April 22, 2015, http://www.wired.com/2012/10/geeks-guide -junot-diaz/.

33. Junot Díaz, "Loving Ray Bradbury," *The New Yorker*, June 6, 2012, accessed April 22, 2015, http://www.newyorker.com/online/blogs/books/2012/06/loving-ray -bradbury.html.

34. Díaz, "Loving Ray Bradbury."

35. Junot Díaz, introduction to *The Beacon Best of 2001: Great Writing by Women and Men of All Colors and Cultures*, ed. Junot Díaz (Boston: Beacon, 2001), ix.

36. *Maria Hinojosa: One on One*, WGBH, October 6, 2010.

37. *Maria Hinojosa*.

38. Albert Jordy Raboteau, "Conversation with Junot Díaz: (To the Woman in the Mountain Cabin)," *Callaloo* 31, no. 3 (2008): 921.

39. Junot Díaz, *The Brief Wondrous Life of Oscar Wao* (New York: Riverhead, 2007), 132.

40. Díaz, *Oscar Wao*, 4.

41. "Weddings: Gustavo Paredes, Elizabeth Alexander," *New York Times*, September 19, 1993; R. W. Apple Jr., "Death of a First Lady: The Overview; Jacqueline Kennedy Onassis Is Buried," *New York Times*, May 24, 1994; Cathy Horyn, "Jacqueline Kennedy's Smart Pink Suit, Preserved in Memory and Kept out of View," *New York Times*, November 14, 2013; Elizabeth Llorente, "John F. Kennedy's Legacy through the Eyes of the First Lady's Top Assistant," *Fox News Latino*, November 22, 2013; Thomas Sparrow, "La dominicana que conoció los secretos de los Kennedy," *BBC Mundo*, November 22, 2013.

42. T. S. Miller, "Preternatural Narration and the Lens of Genre Fiction in Junot Díaz's *The Brief Wondrous Life of Oscar Wao*," *Science Fiction Studies* 38, no. 1 (2011): 96.

43. Díaz, *Oscar Wao*, 138, 194.

44. Anne Garland Mahler, "The Writer as Superhero: Fighting the Colonial Curse in Junot Díaz's *The Brief Wondrous Life of Oscar Wao*," *Journal of Latin American Cultural Studies: Travesia* 19, no. 2 (2010): 119–40.

45. Junot Díaz, "Language, Violence, and Resistance," in Daniel Balderston and Marcy E. Schwartz, eds., *Voice-Overs: Translation and Latin American Literature* (Albany: State University of New York Press, 2002), 42.

46. Díaz, "Language, Violence, and Resistance," 43.

47. Díaz, "Language, Violence, and Resistance," 44.

48. Obejas, "A Conversation with Junot Díaz," 47.

49. José David Saldívar, "Conjectures on 'Americanity' and Junot Díaz's 'Fukú Americanus' in *The Brief Wondrous Life of Oscar Wao*," *Global South* 5, no. 1 (2011): 130.

50. Díaz, *Oscar Wao*, 6, 37, 39, 62, 83, 90, 95, 272.

51. Díaz, *Oscar Wao*, 19.

52. Martin Amis, *The Moronic Inferno and Other Visits to America* (New York: Viking, 1987), x–xi.

53. Díaz, *Oscar Wao*, 47.

54. Ramón Saldivar, "Historical Fantasy, Speculative Realism, and Postrace Aesthetics in Contemporary American Fiction," *American Literary History* 23, no. 3 (2011): 585.

55. Armando Celayo and David Shook, "In Darkness We Meet: A Conversation with Junot Díaz," *World Literature Today* 82, no. 2 (2008): 15.

56. Celayo and Shook, "In Darkness We Meet," 15.

57. Junot Díaz, *Drown* (New York: Riverhead, 1996), 94.

58. Díaz, *Drown*, 113.

59. Díaz, *Drown*, 153.

60. Díaz, *Drown*, 155.

61. Díaz, *Drown*, 156.

62. Gary Westfahl, ed., *The Greenwood Encyclopedia of Science Fiction and Fantasy: Themes, Works, and Wonders* (Westport, CT: Greenwood, 2005), 12–13.

63. Díaz, *Oscar Wao*, 2, 216–17.

64. Díaz, *Oscar Wao*, 226.

65. Westfahl, *Greenwood Encyclopedia*, 244–46.

66. Díaz, *Oscar Wao*, 12, 99.

67. Díaz, *Oscar Wao*, 248.

68. Díaz, *Oscar Wao*, 257.

69. Díaz, *Oscar Wao*, 92.

70. Díaz, *Oscar Wao*, 92.

71. Nii Ayikwei Parkes, "What to Read Now: Migration Narratives," *World Literature Today* 86, no. 4 (2012): 7.

72. Díaz, *Drown*, 32.

73. Lizabeth Paravisini-Gebert, "Junot Díaz's *Drown*: Revisiting 'Those Mean Streets,'" in Harold Augenbraum and Margarite Fernández Olmos, eds., *US Latino Literature: A Critical Guide for Students and Teachers* (Westport, CT: Greenwood, 2000).

74. Richard Pérez, "Racial Spills and Disfigured Faces in Piri Thomas's *Down These Mean Streets* and Junot Díaz's 'Ysrael,'" in Lyn Di Iorio Sandín and Richard Perez, eds., *Contemporary U.S. Latino/a Literary Criticism* (New York: Palgrave Macmillan, 2007), 93, 95.

75. Ana María Manzanas-Calvo, "Teaching Junot Díaz's 'Aurora,'" Salzburg Seminar 2010: American Literary History in a New Key, Salzburg, Austria, 2010.

76. Díaz, *Drown*, 14.

77. Díaz, *Drown*, 19.

78. Díaz, *Drown*, 101.

79. Díaz, *Drown*, 197.

80. Díaz, *Drown*, 200.

81. Marisel Moreno, "Debunking Myths, Destabilizing Identities: A Reading of Junot Díaz's 'How to Date a Browngirl, Blackgirl, Whitegirl, or Halfie,'" *Afro-Hispanic Review* 26, no. 2 (2007): 103–17.

82. Jason Frydman, "Violence, Masculinity, and Upward Mobility in the Dominican Diaspora: Junot Díaz, the Media, and *Drown*," in Harold Bloom, ed., *Bloom's Modern Critical Views: Hispanic American Writers* (New York: Infobase, 2009), 141.

83. Frydman, "Violence, Masculinity, and Upward Mobility," 141.

84. David Gates, "English Lessons," review of *Drown* by Junot Díaz, *New York Times*, September 29, 1996.

85. Gates, "English Lessons."

86. Ibn Khaldûn, *The Muqaddimah: An Introduction to History*, trans. Franz Rosenthal, abr. and ed. by N. J. Dawood (Princeton, NJ: Princeton University Press, 1967), 450.

87. Geek's Guide to the Galaxy.

88. Junot Díaz, "The Brief Wondrous Life of Oscar Wao," *The New Yorker*, December 25, 2000.

89. Leah Hager Cohen, "Love Stories: Review of *This Is How You Lose Her* by Junot Díaz," *New York Times Book Review*, September 23, 2012, 1, 16.

90. Alison Flood, "Junot Díaz Wins World's Richest Story Prize," *Guardian*, March 22, 2013; Dennis Abrams, "Junot Díaz Wrote a Short Story Worth a New Mercedes," *Publishing Perspectives*, March 26, 2013, accessed April 22, 2015, http://publishingperspectives .com/2013/03/junot-diaz-takes-30000-story-prize-from-the-brits/.

91. Barradas, "El realismo cómico de Junot Díaz," 105, 106, 108.

92. Monica Hanna, "Reassembling the Fragments: Battling Historiographies, Caribbean Discourse, and Nerd Genres in Junot Díaz's *The Brief Wondrous Life of Oscar Wao*," *Callaloo* 33, no. 2 (2010): 499.

93. Hanna, "Reassembling the Fragments," 500.

94. Jacqueline Loss, "Junot Díaz," in Alan West-Duran, ed., *Latino and Latina Writers*, vol. 2 (New York: Scribner, 2004), 804.

95. Loss, "Junot Díaz," 806.

96. Loss, "Junot Díaz," 806.

97. Díaz, *Oscar Wao*, 71.

98. Díaz, *Oscar Wao*, 273.

99. Díaz, *Oscar Wao*, 277.

100. Díaz, *Oscar Wao*, 55, 143.

101. Díaz, *Oscar Wao*, 35, 66.

6. This Is How You Lose It
Navigating Dominicanidad in Junot Díaz's *Drown*
Ylce Irizarry

Our money is always welcome in Santo Domingo,
but not our intellectual or cultural ideas . . .
Sometimes you have to get recognized from outsiders
before your own culture values what you are.
—Junot Díaz

The comment above is emblematic of the cultural ocean Junot Díaz navigates as a Dominican American writer. Díaz has noted his lack of recognition from Dominican literati, despite his international visibility. A few years after the publication of *Drown*, his first book, Díaz asserted, "I had to leave Santo Domingo to even have a chance to be acknowledged by elites. These are not people who would sit down at my grandfather's house in Villa Juana to have dinner with me."[1] Not all Dominican American writers have experienced such exclusion. The work of Julia Alvarez, whose affluent parents fled Trujillo's rule as political exiles, has not only been well received but has also catalyzed state-sponsored revision of public memorials of the Trujillato.[2] Díaz's parents, in contrast, were poor and fled post-Trujillo instability as economic immigrants. His work has not met with the critical success

Alvarez's has in their home nation. When discussing the success of *The Brief Wondrous Life of Oscar Wao*, Díaz returns to his indictment of Dominican classism, as illustrated in the epigraph above.[3] This disparity in reception is critical in reading Díaz's fiction. He is always concerned with how difference is used to maintain hierarchies. Differences internal to Dominicans—differences of class, race, and sexuality—structure Díaz's fictional world. The stories in *Drown* defy the perception that Dominican American literature is mainly concerned with assimilation to the Anglo American mainstream. Rather, these stories explore how class status, sexual orientation, and racial appearance determine one's *Dominicanidad*.[4]

Neocolonialism and Narrative

Dominicans are a rapidly growing immigrant population in cities such as Boston, Miami, New York, Orlando, and San Juan.[5] Unlike Puerto Ricans and Cubans, Dominicans—especially the second, economic wave of Dominican immigrants—have not significantly benefited from the United States' neocolonial, immigration, or asylum policies.[6] The characters of *Drown* represent these Dominican economic immigrants.[7] Díaz contextualizes their cyclical migrations as geographical but portrays them as psychocultural: his characters repeatedly assess their identity because of their continuous movement within the Hispanic diaspora. This chapter will illustrate how the stories of *Drown* theorize Dominican intranational migration and extranational immigration as experiences of poverty, disillusion, racism, and cultural loss within the Dominican diaspora.[8]

Immigration experiences vary significantly due to their historic, geographic, and racial context. Popularly, the immigrant experiences of early twentieth-century European immigrant groups such as the Germans, Italians, or Irish represent "the immigrant story," the one linking assimilation to the American Dream.[9] For those earlier groups, the phrase "we have arrived" meant economic success and public recognition of that improved social status. Such conceptions of *arrival*—that individuals or ethnic groups attain social mobility through the assimilation of three generations of immigrants—simplify contemporary immigrants' possibilities for integration.[10] This early notion of arrival was predicated on the desire to shed ethnic or national identity, enter the melting pot, and emerge an "American." For late twentieth-century Hispanic-descended immigrants, *arrival* means success without the loss of national or cultural specificity.

To arrive is to be recognized not only as American but also as Chicano/a or Latino/a.[11]

Thus defined, arrival has never been possible for Hispanic-descended immigrants. Individuals who are dark-skinned, working-class, recent immigrants, or retain their original linguistic practices face barriers to such acculturation. Because of this reality, Latino/a literatures often reject arrival as a narrative end. These economic, rather than political, immigrations are responses to conditions developed by U.S. neocolonialism. Starting around midcentury, the rejection of arrival becomes visible in narratives about economic immigrations. It is particularly clear in the narratives about Puerto Ricans following the island's designation as "Free Associated State" in 1952 and in fiction portraying Cuban and Dominican economic immigrants of the 1980s. The change in the signification of arrival occurs in the context of immigration catalyzed by U.S. neocolonialism. Literature depicting such immigration is distinct from literatures portraying exile: characters do not leave their country for political asylum and they do not believe they will "make it big" in America.[12] Rather, economic immigration is portrayed as a means through which individuals work extranationally until they can earn enough money to survive in their nations of origin.

The terms *imperialism*, *colonialism*, *internal colonization*, *postcolonialism*, and *neocolonialism* have all been used to describe political relationships between dominant and subordinate nations.[13] Neocolonialism best describes relationships between the United States and Latin American nations, which are defined by continual U.S. intervention in Latin American politics. In fact, the first recorded use of the term was in 1961, in a reference to the relationship between the United States and the Hispanic Caribbean.[14] U.S. neocolonialism is distinct from African, European, and Asian models of colonialism; the primary difference is that in neocolonialism the U.S. moves human resources into its own borders. This movement is not just encouraged by neocolonial conditions; it has been legislated, as in the case of Puerto Rico. I use the broad definition of neocolonialism stated in the *Oxford English Dictionary*: "The acquisition or retention of influence over other countries, especially one's former colonies, often by economic or political measures."[15] Whether or not Caribbean or Latin American immigrants come from a former U.S. colony is moot; they come from nations tremendously influenced by the economic, political, and military power of the United States. U.S. neocolonialism has been hemispheric: it has intervened in Latin America and the Caribbean Basin, especially in the nations of El Salvador, Guatemala, Haiti, and Nicaragua. The process of neocolonialism in the Caribbean has been rapid and traceable. That process involves the following: first, economic interests require political stability; next, political stability is obtained through military intervention or political manipulation; finally, political reorganization is enacted in order to maintain political stability.

The United States came to the Caribbean and began exporting its human resources for continued economic growth. Its occupations of the Dominican Republic (from 1916–24 and in 1965) and Cuba (from 1898–1902, 1906–9, and 1912–13) are directly related to the first exile waves of Dominican and Cuban emigration beginning in the 1960s.[16] Rafael Leónidas Trujillo rose to power after the United States had occupied the Dominican Republic for nearly a decade; when his brutal thirty-year reign ended, chaos erupted and Dominicans sought U.S. asylum. When Fidel Castro assumed power in 1959, he removed American influence over Cuba; those Cubans who rejected life under Castro similarly sought and were given U.S. asylum. Immigrants from the Caribbean, thus, have not simply come to the United States to begin a new life and forget their homeland. The neocolonial web of the United States is intricate and its long-lasting effects are the impetus for much of Latino/a literature.

Navigating Dominicanidad in *Drown*

Most prevalent among Latino/a immigration narratives is the trope of loss. The narrative of loss maps changes in geography, mourns disruptions in families, and explores the syncretism of cultures wrought by U.S. neocolonialism. In the work of Díaz in particular, the narrative of loss is primarily cultural. As narratives of loss, Díaz's stories engage various tropes of immigrant literature but ultimately reject most of them, especially the trope associated with acculturation: the trope of arrival. The title of Díaz's collection, Drown, is the dominant metaphor for the struggle characters experience. They drown—economically and culturally—and are well aware of their failure to arrive. The de Las Casas family must learn how to survive and re-create their culture in each new locale because they have no permanent physical home.[17]

In "Cultural Identity and Diaspora," Stuart Hall argues that cultural identity is "always constructed through memory, fantasy, narrative and myth. Cultural identities are the points of identification, the unstable points of identification or suture, which are made within the discourses of history and culture. Not an essence but a *positioning*. Hence, there is always a politics of identity, a politics of position, which has no absolute guarantee in an unproblematic, transcendental 'law of origin.'"[18] Hall's work is especially useful in reading Díaz's fiction within Latino/a discourses on culture and identity, where the "law of origin" is indeed complex and problematic. Hall's view of identity as a process occurring along a continuum is also key to understanding Díaz's authorial project: "We have now to reconceptualize identity as a *process of identification*, and that is a different matter. It is something that happens over time, that is never absolutely stable, that is subject to the play of history and the play of difference."[19] In the stories of *Drown*, the play of these differences becomes evident in the author's critique of both U.S. neocolonialism and Dominican hegemonic discourses on race, class, and sexuality. Díaz uses the narrative of loss to structure the challenges of self-positioning within the Dominican diaspora.

Because Díaz rejects arrival and foregrounds the narrative of loss, his immigration narrative differs significantly from those projected through the popular Anglo-American rhetoric of immigration. Though the dominant metaphor of the collection is aquatic, most of the narrative action in *Drown* occurs in landed, specifically Dominican, Latino, or Afro-Latino but not Anglo, spaces. The collection begins in *el campo*, the Dominican Republic's premigration rural spaces, where poverty is the norm, violence is unpunished, and sexual predation is concealed. The stories are alternatively set in *el barrio*, the postimmigration, urban, ethnic space in the United States that is contained by projects, elevated trains, and highways. The liminality of emigration leaves Díaz's characters always on the threshold of the immigrant wave: sometimes floating, sometimes treading, sometimes drowning in the spaces between el campo and el barrio. My analysis now turns to illustrating how this threshold develops from the struggle not to lose one's Dominicanidad.

The stories "Ysrael," "Aguantando," "Drown," and "How to Date a Browngirl, Blackgirl, Whitegirl, or Halfie" reveal how Dominican immigration creates a diaspora through class difference and internal migration. The characters are immigrants who might be described as first generation. Dominican immigrants are often perceived as not truly Dominican by island-living Dominicans because those who immigrated did not grow into adulthood on the island or, if adults, the immigrants somehow lost their innate Dominicanidad postmigration. All of the stories reveal how characters negotiate class, race, and national constructions of identity. The stories "Ysrael" and "Aguantando" particularly illustrate how children are disillusioned with the realities of immigration, as they try to reconcile family abandonment and expectation, before they emigrate. "Drown" portrays a young man's struggle with narrow constructions of masculinity and social mobility. The fruitless struggle for characters to become American and Dominican is the focus of "How to Date a Browngirl, Blackgirl, Whitegirl or Halfie."

"Ysrael" depicts an intranational pattern of migration between two arenas of Dominican life: urban poverty and rural poverty. Nowhere are there descriptions of an island paradise, even for the older generations; matter of fact assessments of a sustained but not luxurious past replace nostalgia. For example, the narrator, Yunior, recalls his grandfather's bemoaning a time when "a man could still make a living from his finca, when the United States wasn't something folks planned on."[20] This depicts America as a source of temporary employment, allowing the rural poor to return to their nation of origin without poverty.

Two brothers' contrasting experiences of this internal migration are portrayed in "Ysrael." For Yunior's older brother, Rafa, rural Ocoa is a nightmare: "In the campo there was nothing to do, no one to see. You didn't get television or electricity and Rafa, who was older and expected more, woke up every morning pissy and dissatisfied."[21] While Yunior has to be forced onto the bus to Ocoa every summer, he eventually grows accustomed to the conditions of rural poverty, asserting, "I didn't mind these summers, wouldn't forget them the way Rafa would."[22] Their different perceptions of Ocoa can be attributed to their relationship as brothers. Rural Ocoa offers Yunior a sense of importance as a city boy and as his brother's pal he is denied in Santo Domingo: "In the Capital Rafa and I fought so much that neighbors took to smashing broomsticks over us to break it up, but in the campo it wasn't like that. In the campo we were friends."[23] This is strongly contrasted in Santo Domingo, where Rafa asserts his dominance by using slurs that expose Dominican racism against Haitians: "Back in the Capital, he rarely said anything to me except Shut up, pendejo. Unless of course, he was mad and then he had about five hundred routines he liked to lay on me. Most of them had to do with my complexion, my hair, the size of my lips. It's the Haitian, he'd say to his buddies."[24] These taunts combine more typical childlike taunting with a racism intended to distinguish Haitians from Dominicans. The "routines" powerfully remap "the proper place" of Haitians—at work for, but not at home in, the country—encouraged by Trujillo.[25]

Yunior describes the lives he has in each place, giving the reader a sense of the disparities and disillusionment the image of the United States—generally referred to as North America or Nueva York—conjures in the boys' minds, before migration. Perhaps because so few Dominicans had arrived in the United States by the 1970s, Yunior and those around him are very suspicious of anything connected to America. Nueva York becomes a taunting imaginary: the children simultaneously long for and loathe what it offers. Objects from Nueva York mark those who possess them as traitorous. For example, Ysrael, the mutilated child whom Rafa and Yunior assault in Ocoa, is doubly marked. His face is horrifically disfigured; because he is a friendless victim of bullying, his father buys him clothes and toys from Nueva York, positioning him as an outsider in his own community.

These gifts provide Yunior a reason to hate the boy: "Ysrael's sandals were of stiff leather and his clothes were Northamerican. I looked over at Rafa, but my brother seemed unperturbed."[26] While Rafa isn't bothered by the boy's material possessions, such as his kite or clothes, he is bothered by Ysrael's belief in America, because it reminds him of his own disjointed relationship to it: "Where did you get that? I asked. Nueva York, he said. From my father. No shit! Our father's there too! I shouted. I looked at Rafa, who, for an instant, frowned. Our father only sent us letters and an occasional shirt or pair of jeans at Christmas."[27] Thus, Nueva York offers material and emotional comfort to very few. Rafa and Yunior's father has been away for years but his occasional letters and gifts revive the brothers' expectations and subsequent feelings of resignation about Nueva York. When Ysrael asserts that the American doctors are going to help him, Rafa attempts to dash the younger boy's hopes: "They're lying to you. They probably just felt sorry."[28] Rafa's unwillingness to believe in Nueva York is not a thinly masked jealousy. Rather, Nueva York is an ebb tide of lost family members and hopes. Here, Díaz engages the reader's and the characters' (Yunior's and Ysrael's) beliefs about migration. He challenges the notion that the United States is even accessible for emigrants. The perceptions of the United States by the wave of Dominicans immigrating in the years following Trujillo's assassination, in 1961, were starkly different from those of Puerto Ricans and Cubans immigrating during the same era. Significantly, even though Dominicans immigrate, they do not articulate the sense of hope about the United States that Puerto Ricans often do, nor the nostalgia for "old Havana" that the first wave of Cubans often express. The expectation of the second wave of Dominicans is to immigrate several times for the explicit purpose of surviving financially on the island. This is one of Díaz's earliest and most significant uses of the narrative of loss.

Aguantando means bearing or standing, in the sense of "putting up with" a situation. In this story, Yunior juxtaposes several kinds of aguantando: what his mother had to bear with a husband absent for five years, what Yunior had to bear as a son waiting endlessly for his father's return, and the poverty they all had to bear. The word is a nice play on the collection's title: non-Spanish speakers might recognize *agua* and suppose the story has something to do with water. "Aguantando" evokes the principal mode of immigration for Dominicans: travel by boat and swimming, which often lead to their deaths by shark attacks or drowning. "Aguantando" offers an even more radical critique of arrival than does "Ysrael": rather than drowning in cultural marginalization from Anglo America, characters drown in expectations of escaping poverty and reuniting as a nuclear family.

Yunior asserts that their poverty is so comprehensive, few are worse off: "We lived south of the Cementerio Nacional in a wood frame house with three rooms. We were poor. The only way we could have been poorer was to have lived in the campo or to be Haitian immigrants, and Mami regularly offered these as brutal consolation."[29] The story foregrounds the boys' repeated disappointment in Papi's failure to send for them or to return from Nueva York in grand style. Yunior notes, "The year Papi came for us, the year I was nine, we expected nothing. There were no signs to speak of."[30] Rafa cautions Yunior that even though they receive a letter, Papi might not come at all: "It ain't the first time he's made that promise."[31] In his adult narration, Yunior recognizes the distance between himself and his father, despite being his father's namesake: "He was pieces of my friends' fathers, of the domino players on the corner, pieces of Mami and Abuelo. I didn't know him at all."[32] Yunior ultimately decries his father's deferred literal arrival due to his failed metaphorical arrival. The adult Yunior is as bitter as the teenage Rafa: "I didn't know that he'd abandoned us. That this waiting for him was all a sham."[33]

The boy's father looms large in these stories but readers do not learn his full name or the details of his migration experience until the final story, "Negocios." The boys have become aware of their father's extramarital affair with a Puerto Rican woman as well as his presumably bigamous marriage to a Cuban woman. The ethnicity of these women is telling: Díaz is indicting some Dominican immigrants' desire to move higher up on the Caribbean social scale, even if that means abandoning their national identity. At a very practical level, it reflects the increasing population of Dominicans immigrating to Puerto Rico to marry and gain U.S. citizenship, rather than undergoing the expensive and lengthy process of obtaining a visa.[34] By the time Yunior enters high school, his father has left both of his families, only to continue his own cycle of migration between the two, calling or appearing every few months asking for money.

The only story in which Yunior's father is conspicuously absent—mentioned in flashback only—is in the titular story, "Drown." The story depicts Yunior's life in urban New Jersey. In patches of neighborhoods and people, he narrates cyclical migration within the United States. He, his brother, and his mother experience repeated economic migration within the Dominican Republic; in the barrios of New Jersey, their migration reflects not only economic but also emotional resignations. One of these resignations introduces an element appearing only one other time in the collection: homosexuality. Yunior describes the loss of his friendship with Beto, another young man who, like Ysrael, is doubly marked: he is gay and he leaves el barrio for college.

When his father is present, Papi is often berating Yunior for being weak or crying. Moreover, his brother, Rafa, is the metonym for their father before and after they migrate.[35] In "Ysrael," when Yunior exits the bus crying because a stranger molested and threatened him, Rafa asks him what happened, but Yunior remains silent. Rafa becomes their father: "If you can't stop crying, I'll leave you."[36] This dialogue exemplifies what Danny Méndez describes as the family's character in the story "Drown": "Punishment, repression, and orality are the surface elements that characterize Yunior's family in this story."[37] The tropes of crying and emasculation are ones Díaz repeats. Elena Machado Sáez makes a compelling argument about Díaz's very similar conflation of Dominican masculinity and heterosexuality in *The Brief Wondrous Life of Oscar Wao*. She presents a unique reading of the protagonist, Oscar, as inevitably homosexual in Dominican culture because he performs "feminine" acts such as crying and engages in nonphysical exercises of power: he is a nerd whose prowess is literary, not sexual.[38]

In "A How-to Guide to Building a Boy: Dominican Diasporic Subjectivities in Junot Díaz's *Drown*," Méndez similarly examines the collection as an explicit illustration of how one "becomes . . . a Dominican diasporic subject."[39] His analysis of the collection frames the stories through the metaphor of return as a moment of Freudian uncanniness. Méndez argues, "The uncanniness of return comes, in part, from the disparity between the image of return, which is mythically that of the moment of healing and wholeness, of 'reconciliation,' and the actuality, which is a simulacrum of repression."[40] Return is a credible threat, especially to the construct of Dominican masculinity. In the case of the de Las Casas family, Papi's return threatens the reinscription of a premigration Dominicanidad, one created and encouraged by Trujillo. Méndez explains that un tíguere "refers to the kind of cunning working-class urban male who, through his wits and cojones (testicles), understands the art of social mobility. This was the image of Trujillo that was projected by his propagandists, who in this way made even his vices—his corruption, his brutality, his lechery and sexism—into virtues."[41] A former soldier of Trujillo, Papi fails to be un tíguere on the island but is somewhat successful in using women in Nueva York to climb the social scale.

Yunior's friendship with Beto reveals another form of Dominican masculinity Yunior resists. Méndez usefully observes, "If, on one side, Yunior deals with (homo) sexuality in his New Jersey community through the signs produced within his own family, on the other side, the topic touches on latent emotional currents abroad in the diasporic experience that are unconsciously but collectively defined, as well as individually felt."[42] Readers can see this consciousness readily in the collection's first story, "Ysrael." While traveling to Ocoa with Rafa to torment the disfigured boy, a pedophile molests Yunior. Initially, he resists victimization, calling the man pato. Yunior continues his verbal counterassault, saying, "You low-down pinga-sucking pato."[43] The muscular pedophile threatens him in a manner clearly invoking Trujillo's punishment for talking about him negatively: "You should watch your mouth, he said."[44] Thus, before migration, Yunior had learned the homophobic discourse of tigueraje.

In "Drown," Yunior introduces Beto in a manner illustrating their past familial intimacy. Yunior's language suggests he completely identified with Beto: "He's a pato now but two years ago we were friends and he would walk into the apartment without knocking, his heavy voice rousing my mother from the Spanish of her room and drawing me up from the basement, a voice that cracked and made you think of uncles or grandfathers."[45] Since Yunior's father was more absent than present in his life, Yunior associates Beto with the only male family figures he has known. Papi's absence is painful but sanctioned; the father is the one who can leave. His emigration is necessary to create opportunities for his family; he must be el tíguere. Díaz implies, however, that Papi's absence makes Yunior vulnerable to homosexuality. Papi's über-heteronormative masculinity would have been a cultural barrier to Yunior's socialization with Beto; he would not be welcome in Yunior's house and Beto would not "belong" in his own neighborhood.[46]

In a recent analysis of the collection, Dorothy Stringer argues, "Díaz's fiction could easily be identified with the still-conventional, middlebrow immigrant narrative, arcing cleanly from individual Bildung to national inclusion."[47] While her close attention to inclusion and exclusion in relation to sexual citizenship is interesting, the analysis, as a whole, misses Díaz's consistent point: diasporic Dominicans are subject to racial stigmatization by Anglo Americans and by nondiasporic Dominicans alike. Stringer's thesis problematically elides Díaz's critiques of the intersections of internalized racism and homophobia originating in Dominican culture: "Díaz's work suggests that, although the invitation to pass for straight is ostensibly race-neutral, it actually reinforces spatial and psychological limits on his Dominican characters' citizenship."[48] This claim might be true of Yunior's character but it fails to account for Beto's defiance of the very same spatial limits within which Yunior chooses to remain.

Yunior describes his nights without Beto because his friend "would usually be at home or down by the swings, but other times he wouldn't be around at all. Out visiting other neighborhoods."[49] Yunior interprets Beto's movements as trying to get out of the economic poverty by which their community is trapped. He notes the poverty, filth, and decay Beto hates and explains that he begins associating with club hoppers—people who have the means to spend "money on platform shoes and leather backpacks."[50] Stringer applies Crystal Parikh's conceptualization of "ethnic betrayal" to Beto's movement, undermining her own argument regarding the limits on characters' spatial and psychological movements: "One of Beto's acts of treason, then, is simply that of the cosmopolitan against the national: he moves and becomes continually, rather than staying in one place and accepting its available roles."[51] These excursions are dual purposed; they reflect Beto's desire for social mobility and his homosexuality. Beto does not choose to leave only to become something. Rather, because the neighborhood denies him economic opportunity and performance of his true sexuality, he chooses to leave. Readers ought not ignore the numerous moments of hyper-heterosexuality and performance of masculinity by Yunior's father, brother, and friends in other stories. Beto would not be safe in his own neighborhood if he were "out." This is painfully clear when Yunior describes harassing homosexuals when out with his other friends.[52] Yunior's recollection of Beto's telling him, "You need to learn how to walk in the world . . . There's a lot out there," suggests Beto was inviting him out of el barrio.[53] Whether the invitation is economic or sexual, Yunior chooses not to accept the invitation—he chooses not to explore or accept other roles.

As "Drown" progresses, readers begin to question the closeness of the two boys. Yunior recalls when Beto was around the two would skip school and shoplift or go to their favorite spot, the community pool. The pool is the metaphor for his dialectical relationship with Beto, simultaneously empowering and threatening. Yunior's memories of the pool trigger his confessional of his sexual activity with Beto: "Twice. That's it."[54] The community pool is the one space youth of different ethnicities share without overt racism or violence. The pool differentiates people such as Beto, the ones who get out of el barrio, from people like Yunior, those who do not seem to even try to leave. While Beto comes and goes, Yunior visits the pool for so long that kids of his own age do not go there anymore: "Many of the kids here are the younger brothers of the people I used to go to school with. Two of them swim past, black and Latino, and they pause when they see me, recognize the guy who sells them their shitty dope."[55] The water, metaphor for their friendship, is an imperfect oasis: "While everything above is loud and bright, everything below is whispers. And always the risk of coming up to find the cops stabbing their search lights out across the water."[56] Any positive imagery the scene opens with is quickly undermined by the diction ("stabbing") implying police brutality, the Coast Guard interdiction and subsequent drowning of Dominican emigrants at sea, and foreshadowing a split between the friends.

The first time the young men meet at the pool, their conversation reveals the loss of equality between the two friends. When Yunior knows what the word "expectorating" means, Beto taunts Yunior and asserts his physical strength. Yunior explains: "He was wearing a cross and cutoff jeans. He was stronger than me and held me down until water flooded my nose and throat. Even then I didn't tell him; he thought I didn't read, not even dictionaries."[57] This scene unites Yunior's anxieties about his masculinity and his literacy. Despite the fact that Beto is literally drowning him, Yunior does not meet Beto's demand to tell how he knows what he knows. Díaz employs this aspect of Beto's character to contrast widely accepted stereotypes about homosexuals, particularly within Anglo American culture, that gay men are passive victims, incapable of violence. Díaz also suggests Beto is a hypocrite; since he is wearing a cross, his Christianity should prevent him from enacting such violence. More important, it should prevent him from acting on homoerotic desire. Many Dominicans are Catholic or Pentecostal; in both religions' doctrines, homosexuality remains defined as an abomination.

When they return to Beto's house to watch pornography, Beto starts to masturbate Yunior. He is surprised and afraid; he ejaculates quickly and leaves immediately afterward. What precisely Yunior fears becomes clear the next day: he is afraid he will "end up abnormal, a fucking pato."[58] Yunior's fear is rooted not just in the notion that having sex with a man defines you as gay, but in the more specific Latin American discourse on homosexuality that suggests the receiver of homosexual action is gay, not the giver. To be *pasivo*, the recipient of sexual penetration or another penetrative sex act, makes a man a pato.[59] Stringer discusses this pejorative term but argues, "The word pato, [is] an ordinary obscenity that ironically names Beto's most important betrayal. The friends are estranged because Beto performed sexual acts on the narrator."[60] To call *pato* an "ordinary obscenity" is to elide its intense negativity and underlying potential for contagion within homophobic discourse. Yunior is not afraid of patos; he is afraid of, as he notes, *becoming* a pato.[61] Moreover, one cannot be made a pato by someone else; in cases of consensual homosexual relations, a man who chooses or prefers to be pasivo is responsible for his performance as pato. Yunior's assertion that Beto changed from a friend to a pato reinforces these distinctions.

Yunior is cognizant Beto could initiate another sexual encounter when he returns to the pool the next evening. Beto offers Yunior two coded escapes. First, Beto puts his hand on Yunior's shoulder, and Yunior describes his response thus: "My pulse a code under his palm."[62] Reading that code, Beto says, "Let's go . . . Unless of course you're not feeling good."[63] Yunior provides Beto sexual consent when he says, "I'm feeling fine."[64] His anticipation and consent to their sexual activity negates the idea that Beto's performance of the sex act is the source of the friends' estrangement. Once they enter the apartment, Beto assumes the role of pasivo; by performing oral sex on Yunior, he makes himself the receiver of a penetrative sex act. Yunior assesses his sense of self and, at least temporarily, no longer seems to fear becoming what he perceives Beto to be, a pato. His active self-construction indicates he is *activo*: "After I was done, he laid his head in my lap. I wasn't asleep or awake, but caught somewhere in between, rocked slowly back and forth the way the surf holds junk against the shore, rolling it over and over."[65] Though Yunior might not fully understand the performance of sex roles, he no longer sees them in a simplistic binary.

The liminal aquatic metaphors perform two functions. Beto represents another part of Yunior's life he cannot control, one that leaves him feeling caught, like the junk, between the sexual pleasure he receives from women and men. More devastatingly, he is caught between his love for his friend and his culture's homophobic demands to disassociate himself from Beto. Méndez illustrates this deftly: "When Beto leaves for college, Yunior processes these experiences into terms he can deal with by regressing towards old patterns of *tíguere* masculinity, which require on their side an overtness and excess of masculine toughness in the streets."[66] Readers feel the tenuous line of emotion Yunior experiences; even though he is "terrified that I would end up abnormal, a fucking pato," he completes the sentence thus: "But he was my best friend and back then that mattered to me more than anything."[67] After their second encounter, Yunior does not use the term *pato* again in the story.

Ultimately, Beto is a catalyst to Yunior's realization of his economic drowning and loss of his incipient tigueraje. Though his mother can usually earn the rent and he can pay for utilities by selling pot, Yunior becomes painfully aware that he "wasn't like [Beto]. I had another year to go in high school, no promises elsewhere."[68] Beto's going to college leaves Yunior, literally, without a partner in crime; in their shoplifting, Beto was the one who remained calm and boldly dealt with security guards while in possession of stolen goods. Their last encounter ended with Yunior's crying; he describes Beto's "hand squeezing mine, the bones in our fingers pressing together."[69] Stringer suggests Yunior's sexual experience confines him to el barrio: "Sexual shame and homophobia, particularly the immediate unremarkable homophobia of quotidian homosociality, institutionalize 'self-hate and self-doubt' often in the specific form of passing-for-straight. They thereby help to perpetuate the racial ghetto."[70] Yunior clearly develops self-hate because of his sexual self-doubt; however, neither Beto nor the state ought to be blamed for Yunior's choice to remain in el barrio.

"Drown" ends with Yunior's recalling having thrown away the book, not even having read the inscription, that Beto had given him before leaving for college. The gift of the book is another element in this narrative of loss. Díaz suggests that Yunior chooses the loss: he throws away not only a friendship but also a potential guide out of el barrio. Both have equal access to education because they attended the same school, but Yunior does not use the resources Beto has accessed. Stringer similarly observes, "Beto, whom readers meet only in flashback, always represents possibilities that the narrator perversely refuses."[71] Indeed, earlier in the story, Yunior acknowledges two ways out of el barrio: education or military service, both of which he rejects. If Beto "betrays" Yunior in any way, he does so through the consequences of his movement, not in the perpetuation of a racial ghetto, as Stringer suggests.[72] Beto's social life outside el barrio has exposed him to the existence of different modes of Dominicanidad. Thus, while Yunior may be irritated by Beto's movements, he cannot accept their ultimate, painful consequence: Beto's permanent abandonment of el barrio. Beto's departure for college feels like the abandonment he experienced with his father and then his brother, who died from leukemia a few years earlier. Beto might have been trying to make up for belittling Yunior's literacy and could have been a mentor; however, Yunior is not willing to migrate again. He recalls, "You can't be anywhere forever, was what Beto used to say, what he said to me the day I went to see him off."[73] Because the story ends precisely where it began—with Yunior's watching TV with his mother—readers can only conclude Yunior will stay in el barrio forever. Díaz implies Yunior has realized Beto is more of a tíguere than he will ever be; this is a significantly more damaging betrayal than anything Beto has done. Yunior has betrayed himself.

By contrasting Yunior's stasis with Beto's mobility, Díaz criticizes individuals who are offered potential sources of empowerment but reject them without considering the consequences of their rejection. "Drown" distinguishes Yunior's experiences from those common in exile narratives, where adolescents are portrayed as victims of institutional discrimination. Díaz also forcefully challenges modernist depictions of immigrants as victims of a hostile urban environment or unjust industrial age by depicting characters that fail to choose or fail to act. The author expressed his concern about self-defeating actions in the interview with Céspedes and Torres-Saillant: "There's no state in the world that can facilitate all the ambitions of its underclass. So it throws up obstacles—plenty of intoxications, bad schools, aggressive cops, no jobs—and depends on us to do the rest. You don't know how many times I saw a person escape institutional discrimination only to knock themselves down with self-hate and self-doubt."[74] "Drown" begins a dénouement of sorts and the collection moves toward Yunior's ruminations about Papi's inability to arrive. Yunior meets Papi's other wife, Nilda, to learn how his father could have started a new family. Realizing he is never going to know why his father abandoned him, Yunior accepts the fact that Papi was not a great man whom Nueva York defeated. Yunior accepts that he was an ordinary man oppressed both by his own nation and the nation he thought would help him return home to a more privileged social position.

The plot concerning Yunior's father goes beyond established tropes of familial separation in modern immigrant and contemporary exilic fictions. Díaz revises the story of long-lost relatives and children into antinarratives on paternalism, nationalism, and neocolonialism. Yunior's obsession with his father is a subtle political narrative about Dominican national patriarchy. Toward the end of his reign, citizens who initially supported Trujillo realized he had become a brutal tyrant whose economic policies were ineffectual. Nonetheless, Trujillo's self-aggrandizement was so extensive that he required his picture to appear in every citizen's home. Yunior refers to the U.S. invasion in 1965 and efforts to control the populace throughout the collection. The "Yanquis" were not welcome; they dispersed protestors brutally with gas attacks and water hosing. The very presence of U.S. forces underscored Trujillo's failures. While Díaz was born in the Dominican Republic after Trujillo's death, the memories and legacies of the era remain with the nation's people. Readers ought to recall that the only image Yunior has of his father is one in which he wears military dress, while he is one of Trujillo's *guardia*. As a writer from a nation that does not care to discuss Trujillo with outsiders, Díaz breaks a profound silence on the failure of patriarchy as governance when he parallels the failures of the personal father with those of the national patriarch.

The final story from *Drown* I discuss here is "How to Date a Browngirl, Blackgirl, Whitegirl, or Halfie." This story appears, at first, to be a technical manual on interracial dating. Díaz's narrator, Yunior, has worked out a bitter and misogynist system for addressing the internalized racism that often travels with Dominicans. Díaz's attention to racism among people of color, despite their shared experiences of discrimination and second-class American citizenship, is critical. Of course, racism persists between Anglo Americans and ethnic minorities; however, it has also been prevalent among Hispanic-descended people. Institutional racism against darker-skinned Spaniards originated in post-Moorish and post-Judaic Spain, was legislated in the New World, and became commonplace in the Caribbean and the United States following the Cuban Spanish-American War (1896–98).[75]

In "The Tribulations of Blackness: Stages in Dominican Racial Identity," the Dominican studies scholar Silvio Torres-Saillant traces the development of Dominican racial identity. He argues, "A large part of the problem of racial identity among Dominicans stems from the fact that from its inception their country had to negotiate the racial paradigms of their North American and European overseers."[76] Torres-Saillant links Dominicans' occupation by Haiti and the United States to shifts in their racial self-conception. His work in this area supports my reading of the significant reinscription of racism in the context of U.S. neocolonialism: "One should look to the vigorous imperial expansion of the United States in the wake of the Spanish-American War of 1898 for the historical context wherein the widespread notion of a single Ibero-American race gained currency."[77] Rather than reading the overt racism and sexism within "How to Date a Browngirl, Blackgirl, White-girl, or Halfie" as racist misogyny, one should consider how effectively Díaz illustrates the process by which skin color supersedes nationality and facilitates internalized racism.

This story is the collection's exemplar of the perils of navigating Dominicanidad. In contrast to his point of view in other stories, here Yunior addresses the reader directly. Using a familiar second-person voice, he assumes a shared class background: urban, Latino, and poor. Make no mistake; this group has its own hierarchy. Yunior gives advice on how to deal with girls from particular neighborhoods, especially suggestions for hiding signs of poverty such as the "government cheese": "If the girl's from the Terrace stack the boxes behind the milk. If she's from the Park or Society Hill hide the cheese in the cabinet above the oven . . . Take down any embarrassing photos of your family in the campo, especially the one with the half-naked kids dragging a goat on a rope leash."[78] These instructions delineate the socioeconomic stratification among people of color; though many families in el barrio might be on welfare, the importance of concealing the government cheese varies by the girl's class status.

Díaz emphasizes the wide disparities among Dominicans through iconography as well. Yunior undermines the idea of a monolithic economic background of Dominicans by emphasizing his desired origins as urban, not rural. Leaving a picture of yourself in el campo, for example, signifies your class as rural poor. Because Mami sends the boys to Ocoa in the summer and other times of year when she has no money, Yunior is trapped in this geographic class binary as well. As Méndez notes, "Photographs throughout the collection figure as artifacts imbued with an aura of recollection, spatializing lost or forgotten lived experiences."[79] Often, photos he references spatialize experiences, people, or homes Yunior wants, urgently, to lose. For Dominican immigrants such as Yunior, there is no modernist shedding and self-reconstruction, there is no shield of Nuyorican second-class citizenship, and there is no acceptance as a temporary, exoticized Cuban exile.

On these dates, Yunior attempts to mask his linguistic losses as well. As a Dominican who immigrated as an adolescent, Yunior could retain or lose his Spanish and become English dominant, or become fluently bilingual. In "Drown," readers learned that when he left Santo Domingo at age nine, Yunior could not write his own name. Thus, speaking or writing in Spanish is just as much a class marker among Dominicans as is the government cheese. His illiteracy in Spanish directly affects whom he can impress and for whom he will make the most economic and cultural effort. He notes, "If the girl's from around the way, take her to El Cibao for dinner. Order everything in your busted-up Spanish. Let her correct you if she's Latina and amaze her if she's black. If she's not from around the way, Wendy's will do."[80] Redefining the linguistic retentions and losses often assumed about first-generation immigrants is especially important. Under a modern European or Asian immigration model, first-generation immigrants would have difficulty acquiring English. Yunior's poor education in the Dominican Republic switches this model, leaving him illiterate in his native language. This linguistic distance has significant consequences: Yunior cannot "smooth talk" women from his own nation or other parts of Latin America. His inability to speak Spanish, similar to his inability to reconcile queer pleasure and masculinity, is another fissure through which he loses his Dominicanidad.

Yunior's instructions provide the reader with an increasingly unflattering portrait of his racialized sexual hierarchy. He asserts, "If she's a white girl you know you'll at least get a hand job," then notes this about local, presumably ethnic women: "A local girl may have hips and a thick ass but she won't be quick about letting you touch."[81] Clearly, the object is to get as close to having sex as possible and this, ironically, becomes more difficult the closer the girl is to Yunior racially. In deft lines, the narrator sets up rules for dating conversation based on strategies of emotional distance, racial performance, and national masking: "A halfie will tell you that her parents met in the Movement, will say, Back then people thought it a radical thing to do . . . She will appreciate your interest . . . Black people, she will say, treat me real bad. That's why I don't like them. You'll wonder how she feels about Dominicans. Don't ask."[82] By indicting the perception of racial distances between racially mixed people and those who identify as black, Díaz illustrates the profound effect of black-on-black racism: Yunior assumes "the halfie" will not like him if she thinks he is more black than he is Latino. Racially, Dominicans have a higher percentage of dark-skinned people with African physiognomy than do Puerto Ricans or Cubans; however, all groups use a system of racial preference based on desirable physiognomy such as "good hair," "light skin," or "small lips." Each of these qualities is synonymous with more "whiteness."[83] Yunior believes his physiological characteristics prevent him from passing as Latino, superseding his nationality and marking him as black. The leading Caribbean sociologist Jorge Duany explains Dominicans' anti-Haitian sentiment and its effect on their racial self-perception in this way: "It is this sense of national pride and rejection of their own negritude that many Dominican migrants bring with them and must reevaluate when they confront the US model of racial stratification."[84] Such internalized racism is painfully clear when Yunior advises his listener thus: "Tell her that you love her hair, that you love her skin, her lips, because, in truth, you love them more than you love your own."[85] Close to the end of the story, this is Díaz's most powerful narrative of loss; it challenges the reader, especially a Latino/a reader, to question why Yunior is aware of such prescriptive constructions of Dominicanidad and yet persists in accepting them. In portraying explicit connections between racial perception and self-hate, Díaz is critiquing his own community for its perpetual internalization of racism.

Conclusion: Treading the Waters of Loss

Scholars in humanities fields have tended to study Cuban, Dominican, and Puerto Rican literatures in isolation; moreover, they have represented the groups as culturally homogeneous. Yet, as the philosopher Linda Martín Alcoff illustrates, "Latin America itself is undoubtedly the most diverse continent in the world, which in turn creates extreme racial and ethnic diversity within Latino communities."[86] The failure to consider the diversity within Latino/a communities is a continuing problem within literary studies, especially in analyses of Dominican American literature. Danny Méndez also discusses this problematic: "Identity processes begun in the Dominican Republic prefigure Dominican identities and the communities in the diaspora. Thus, it is a mistake to conflate hybridization as such with migration to the United States. Rather, it references a long-standing Hispanic Caribbean cultural pattern to which members of the diaspora gravitate as they (re) create it in their respective diaspora communities."[87] If we read Dominican

American literature in these contexts, immigrant self-identification becomes far more complex than has hitherto been conceptualized.

Díaz's narrative attentions to classism, migration, homophobia, and racism illustrate Drown's effectiveness as a narrative of loss. The stories portray measurable losses associated with immigration: loss of a physical home and loss of a native language. They also portray the immeasurable losses: loss of a family bond, loss of friendship, and loss of self-esteem. Díaz's principal narrator, Yunior, exhibits the psychocultural migration intrinsic to people who continually tell a narrative of loss. The stories in Drown are striking examples of contemporary Dominican immigrant characters who must navigate the riptides of cultural identity. Because identity construction in Anglo America and Latino/a America are deceptively narrow, Yunior illustrates that one must swim entirely out of them or drown between them.

Notes

Epigraph: Junot Díaz, "Junot Díaz, Diaspora, and Redemption: Creating Progressive Imaginaries." Interview, conducted by Katherine Miranda. Sargasso II (2008–9): 23–40.

1. Junot Díaz, Drown (New York: Riverhead Books, 1996); Diógenes Céspedes, Silvio Torres-Saillant, and Junot Díaz, "Fiction Is the Poor Man's Cinema: An Interview with Junot Díaz," Callaloo 23, no. 3 (2000): 893.

2. Following Julia Alvarez's novel In the Time of the Butterflies the government began a series of revisions of public memorials about the era. These included the repainting of Trujillo's Obelisk, issuing currency with the Mirabal Sisters' image, and the rededication of the Mirabal Sisters' Museum. In May 2012, on the fiftieth anniversary of his assassination, the first museum dedicated to the resistance to the Trujillato opened in Santo Domingo. For a discussion of the impact of In the Time of the Butterflies, see Ylce Irizarry, "When Art Remembers: Museum Exhibits as Testimonio del Trujillato," in Roy C. Boland Osegueda and Marta Caminero-Santangelo, eds., "Trujillo, Trauma, Testimony: Mario Vargas Llosa, Julia Alvarez, Edwidge Danticat, Junot Díaz and Other Writers on Hispaniola," special issue, Antipodas 20 (2009): 235–51.

3. Junot Díaz, The Brief Wondrous Life of Oscar Wao (New York: Riverhead Books, 2007).

4. Dominicanidad refers to one's Dominicanness or one's culturally authentic Dominican identity.

5. While Dominicans, particularly women, have begun to migrate to Spain and Puerto Rico in larger numbers, these migrations serve as a stepping-stone to the United States, with the final desired migration being the return to the Dominican Republic. For detailed analyses of Dominican immigration, see Jorge Duany, Blurred Borders: Transnational Migration between the Hispanic Caribbean and the United States (Chapel Hill: University of North Carolina Press, 2011).

6. Significant differences in the immigration patterns and degrees of acculturation exist among Cubans, Dominicans, and Puerto Ricans. These differences can be attributed to Puerto Rico's status as a "free associated state" (since 1952) and the immediate political asylum afforded to Cubans since the Cuban Refugee Adjustment Act (1966). Unlike both other groups, Dominicans have no special entrance to the United States; their visa process is long and complicated by their civil laws, making it very expensive and dangerous to immigrate.

7. Dominicans have emigrated in two waves: an initial exile wave escaping the dictatorship of Trujillo or the political instability immediately following his assassination in 1961 and a second wave following economic crisis in the 1980s. For a comprehensive study of Spanish Caribbean immigration and community establishment, see Daniel D. Arreola, *Hispanic Spaces, Latino Places: Community and Cultural Diversity in Contemporary America* (Austin: University of Texas Press, 2004).

8. The term *arrival* is important in Chicano/a and Latino/a literary history. This chapter represents an excerpted portion of a chapter from my book, *Chicano/a and Latino/a Fiction: The New Memory of Latinidad* (Champaign: University of Illinois Press, 2016), which compares Chicano/a (Mexican American) and Latino/a (Cuban, Dominican, and Puerto Rican American) literatures. The book illustrates that arrival has been rejected by authors since the civil rights movement. In the first chapter, I compare Tomás Rivera's novella . . . *And the Earth Did Not Devour Him* (Houston: Arte Público Press, 1987) with the stories of *Drown*, arguing that both foreground the narrative of loss. The remaining chapters offer comparative readings of fiction that I characterize as the "narrative of reclamation," "narrative of fracture," and the "narrative of new memory."

9. Terms used to describe cultural adaptation of minorities include *integration*, *assimilation*, and *acculturation*. Integration connotes a process of the colonizer. Assimilation and acculturation denote processes of the colonized. In the era of political correctness, *acculturation* replaced *assimilation*. From this point on, unless quoting, I will use the term *acculturation*.

10. For an extensive discussion of the three-generation model of immigrant acculturation, see Sollors, *Beyond Ethnicity: Consent and Descent in American Culture* (New York: Oxford University Press, 1986). In this essay, Sollors traces the three-generation model from Puritan authors such as Higginson and Mather to early twentieth-century Jewish immigration narratives and contemporary African American poetry and fiction.

11. A variety of terms have been used to describe people of Hispanic descent. In keeping with critical discussions and the authors' self-identification, I will use *Chicano/a* to describe authors of Mexican American heritage with a specific political and literary aesthetic developing since their civil rights movement, known as "El Movimiento." I use the term *Latino/a* very broadly, to describe Cubans, Dominicans, and Puerto Ricans. The o/a represents the gender inclusive politics that emerged in literary and cultural theory of the post–civil rights era. When describing the individual authors or the communities they write about, I use the appropriate specific national term: Cuban, Dominican, Mexican, or Puerto Rican American. The ending of each term (o/a) acknowledges the gender inclusive form of each word, which is generally preferred by scholars. These

terms are often debated within Latino/a literature; see Marta Caminero-Santangelo's introduction to *On Latinidad* for rigorous interrogation of the terms. For a nonliterary reference of the terms, see Allatson, *Key Terms in Latina/o Studies*.

12. I read the narratives as immigrant, not exile, in nature. Marisel Moreno makes a critical distinction between the narratives of Alvarez and Díaz, but she defines them both as exiles. See Marisel Moreno, "All the Important Things Hide in Plain Sight: A Conversation with Junot Díaz," *Latino Studies* 8, no. 4 (2010): 532–42.

13. For a discussion of postcolonialism, internal colonialism, and neocolonialism, see Lora Romero, "Nationalism and Internationalism: Domestic Differences in a Postcolonial World," *American Literature: A Journal of Literary History, Criticism, and Bibliography* 67, no. 4 (1995): 795–800. For discussion of postcolonialism and Latin American studies, see Santiago Colás, "Of Creole Symptoms, Cuban Fantasies, and Other Latin American Postcolonial Ideologies," PMLA 110, no. 3 (1995): 382–96. See also E. San Juan Jr., "The Poverty of Postcolonialism," *Pretexts: Literary and Cultural Studies* 11, no. 1 (2002): 57–74.

14. The *Oxford English Dictionary* cites the first appearance of this term in reference to the relationship between the United States and the Hispanic Caribbean. See Paul Johnson, "The Crisis in Central America," *New Statesman*, January 1961, 82–83.

15. *Oxford English Dictionary*, "neo-colonialism."

16. For an outline of the financial intervention undertaken by the United States in the Dominican Republic, which crippled its economy and led to its financial dependence on and debt to the United States, see Cyrus Veeser, "Inventing Dollar Diplomacy: The Gilded-Age Origins of the Roosevelt Corollary to the Monroe Doctrine," *Diplomatic History* 27, no. 3 (2003): 301–26.

17. Díaz's use of names is often intertextual: this is the surname of Bartolomé de las Casas, chronicler of the Spanish Conquest. A friar of the Dominican order, his narratives are known as one of the few to have criticized Spanish treatment of the indigenous. His advocacy garnered him an official status as "Protector of the Indians." Thus, when Yunior, the principal narrator in *Drown* reappears as the central narrator in *The Brief Wondrous Life of Oscar Wao*, readers should see that Yunior is patterned on Bartolomé. Even the title of Díaz's novel is a variation of the friar's most famous title, *Brevísima relación de la destrucción de las Indias* [A brief accounting of the destruction of the Indies].

18. Stuart Hall, "Cultural Identity and Diaspora," in Jonathan Rutherford and Padmini Mongia, eds., *Contemporary Postcolonial Theory: A Reader* (London: Arnold, 1996), 113, 110–21.

19. Stuart Hall, "Ethnicity: Identity and Difference," *Radical America* 23, no. 4 (1991): 15, 9–20.

20. Díaz, "Aguantando," 72.

21. Díaz, *Drown*, 4.

22. Díaz, *Drown*, 5.

23. Díaz, *Drown*, 5.

24. Díaz, *Drown*, 5.

25. For a discussion of Dominican-Haitian relations, see Michelle Wucker, *Why the Cocks Fight: Dominicans, Haitians, and the Struggle for Hispaniola* (New York: Macmillan,

2000). See also David Howard, "Development, Racism, and Discrimination in the Dominican Republic," *Development in Practice* 17, no. 6 (2007): 725–38.

26. Díaz, *Drown*, 15.

27. Díaz, *Drown*, 16.

28. Díaz, *Drown*, 17.

29. Díaz, *Drown*, 70.

30. Díaz, *Drown*, 77.

31. Díaz, *Drown*, 82.

32. Díaz, *Drown*, 70.

33. Díaz, *Drown*, 70.

34. For sociological research on Dominican migration, see Jorge Duany, "Transnational Migration from the Dominican Republic: The Cultural Redefinition of Racial Identity," *Caribbean Studies* 29, no. 2 (1996): 253–82. See also Jorge Duany, "Caribbean Migration to Puerto Rico: A Comparison of Cubans and Dominicans," *International Migration Review* 26, no. 1 (1992): 46–66.

35. I believe Díaz chose to name Yunior's brother Rafa, short for Rafael, to evoke his likeness to Trujillo. Without doubt, Rafa mirrors Trujillo's physical and linguistic terrorism of Yunior and women.

36. Díaz, *Drown*, 13.

37. Danny Méndez, *Narratives of Migration and Displacement in Dominican Literature* (New York: Routledge, 2012), 120.

38. See Elena Machado Sáez, "Dictating Desire, Dictating Diaspora: Junot Díaz's *The Brief Wondrous Life of Oscar Wao* as Foundational Romance," *Contemporary Literature* 52, no. 3 (2011): 522–55.

39. Méndez, *Narratives of Migration*, 117–18.

40. Méndez, *Narratives of Migration*, 121.

41. Méndez, *Narratives of Migration*, 127.

42. Méndez, *Narratives of Migration*, 128.

43. Díaz, "Ysrael," 12. *Pato* is a derogatory term for a homosexual; *pinga* is penis.

44. Díaz, "Ysrael," 12.

45. Díaz, *Drown*, 91.

46. The term *belong* has been used increasingly in the social and literary theorizations of Latino/a experience. For a sociological approach, see Suzanne Oboler, *Latinos and Citizenship: The Dilemma of Belonging* (New York: Palgrave Macmillan, 2006). For a literary theorization, see Maya Socolovsky, *Troubling Nationhood in U.S. Latina Literature: Explorations of Place and Belonging* (New Brunswick, NJ: Rutgers University Press, 2013).

47. Dorothy Stringer, "Passing and the State in Junot Díaz's *Drown*," MELUS: Multi-Ethnic Literature of the United States 38, no. 2 (2013): 111–26.

48. Stringer, "Passing and the State in Junot Díaz's *Drown*," 113.

49. Díaz, *Drown*, 102.

50. Díaz, *Drown*, 102.

51. Stringer, "Passing and the State in Junot Díaz's *Drown*," 120. Stringer applies the arguments of Crystal Parikh's monograph, *An Ethics of Betrayal: The Politics of Otherness in*

Emergent U.S. Literatures and Culture (New York: Fordham University Press, 2009). I find this especially problematic because while Parikh reads "betrayals as performances of social difference in the context of Asian American and Latina/o racial formation and literary and cultural production" the study offers readings of two Chicano authors and the case of Cuban exile, Elian González (quoted in Parikh, 1). The text does not include Dominican or Puerto Rican literatures in the study; the term *Dominican* does not appear in the index and none of Junot Díaz's or any other Dominican authors' work appears in bibliography or index.

52. Parikh, *An Ethics of Betrayal*, 103.

53. Díaz, *Drown*, 102.

54. Díaz, *Drown*, 103.

55. Díaz, *Drown*, 93.

56. Díaz, *Drown*, 93.

57. Díaz, *Drown*, 94.

58. Díaz, *Drown*, 104.

59. For discussions of homosexuality specific to Latin American culture, see David William Foster, *El Ambiente Nuestro: Chicano/Latino Homoerotic Writing* (Tempe: Bilingual Press, 2006), and Susana Chávez-Silverman, Librada Hernández, and Robert Richmond Ellis, *Reading and Writing the Ambiente: Queer Sexualities in Latino, Latin American, and Spanish Culture* (Madison: University of Wisconsin Press, 2000).

60. Stringer, "Passing and the State in Junot Díaz's *Drown*," 120.

61. Díaz, *Drown*, 95 (emphasis on "becoming" mine).

62. Díaz, *Drown*, 105.

63. Díaz, *Drown*, 96.

64. Díaz, *Drown*, 96.

65. Díaz, *Drown*, 105.

66. Méndez, *Narratives of Migration*, 143.

67. Díaz, *Drown*, 104.

68. Díaz, *Drown*, 92.

69. Díaz, *Drown*, 99.

70. Stringer, "Passing and the State in Junot Diaz's *Drown*," 119.

71. Stringer, "Passing and the State in Junot Díaz's *Drown*," 120.

72. The trope of leaving an ethnic enclave as "betrayal" is common in ethnic literatures depicting both rural and urban areas since the late nineteenth century.

73. Díaz, *Drown*, 107.

74. Díaz, quoted in Céspedes, Torres-Saillant, and Díaz, "Fiction Is the Poor Man's Cinema," 893.

75. Ramón A. Gutiérrez offers this stunning fact: "Mexico's eighteenth-century legal dictionaries contained as many as fifty different racial mixtures codified as the Regimen de Castas (Society of Casts). The Regimen was a code of legal color distinctions most of which were impossible to distinguish visually." See Ramón A. Gutiérrez, "Hispanic Diaspora and Chicano Identity in the United States," *South Atlantic Quarterly* 98, nos. 1–2 (1999): 205.

76. Torres-Saillant, "The Tribulations of Blackness: Stages in Dominican Racial Identity," *Latin American Perspectives* 25, no. 3 (1998): 126–46, 127.

77. Torres-Saillant, "The Tribulations of Blackness," 137.

78. Díaz, *Drown*, 143.

79. Méndez, *Narratives of Migration*, 136.

80. Díaz, *Drown*, 145.

81. Díaz, *Drown*, 147.

82. Díaz, *Drown*, 147.

83. For an extensive cultural studies discussion of preferred racial physiognomy in the Dominican Republic, see Ginetta Candelario, *Black behind the Ears: Dominican Racial Identity from Museums to Beauty Shops* (Durham, NC: Duke University Press, 2007). For a literary and historical discussion, see Silvio Torres-Saillant, "The Tribulations of Blackness."

84. Jorge Duany, "Reconstructing Racial Identity: Ethnicity, Color, and Class among Dominicans in the United States and Puerto Rico," *Latin American Perspectives* 25, no. 3 (1998): 147–72.

85. Díaz, *Drown*, 147.

86. Linda Martín Alcoff, "Philosophy in/and Latino and Afro-Caribbean Studies: Introduction," *Nepantla: Views from the South* 4, no. 1 (2003).

87. Méndez, *Narratives of Migration*, 5.

7. Latino/a Deracination and the New Latin American Novel

Claudia Milian

In 2008, the year that Junot Díaz was awarded the Pulitzer Prize for Fiction, Sergio Ramírez pontificated in a public reverie about the paths of the twenty-first-century Latin American novel. Ramírez—former vice president of Nicaragua (1984–1990) and winner of the Alfaguara Novel Prize in 1998, one of the most preeminent awards in the Hispanophone world—inquired in an op-ed whether the new Latin American fiction is being penned in English and produced in the United States. Ramírez identified Junot Díaz and Daniel Alarcón, a pair of "southerners in the north," as Jean and John L. Comaroff might designate them, as the two towering paragons chiseling out this innovative Latino and Latin American parity in literary states and modes of existence.[1] The Bogotá World Book Capital of 2007 concurred with Ramírez's encomium. There, Díaz and Alarcón shared the distinction of being the only U.S. Latinos who were named two of the most renowned thirty-nine authors under thirty-nine (or as pitched in Spanish, treinta y nueve escritores menores de treinta y nueve) in Bogotá.[2] Mexican novelist Jorge Volpi followed suit in 2009 with this oft-repeated equation of the Dominican American and Peruvian American littérateurs. Grouping together these same narrators as Latin Americans from the United States,

Díaz and Alarcón were the sole Latinos listed in a "brief inventory of works by Latin American authors born after 1960."[3] Through this valuation of Díaz and Alarcón gyrating across the Americas, the general trend of U.S. Latino history and its literary measure changes perspectives. Ramírez's "two dazzling stars" become regional: Latin American authors.[4]

Ramírez's remarks hold lasting merit at a moment when U.S. Latino literary identity is assigned worth through a seemingly copious stream of prizes. For the region's uninitiated, Ramírez familiarizes his readership with these writers' accomplishments, abridging their honors to Díaz's Pulitzer and his "harvested fame with his book of short stories, *Drown*." Since Ramírez's article, Díaz counts a 2012 MacArthur Fellowship, a 2013 *Sunday Times* Short Story Prize, and a 2013 Honorary Doctorate from Brown University, among other considerable tributes. Alarcón's eminence, at the time of Ramírez's column, includes his nomination in 2007 "as one of 21 best young novelists in the United States by *Granta* magazine" and his shaking of "the literary world with his novel, *Lost City Radio*."[5] Alarcón, to date, counts *At Night We Walk in Circles* (2013) as his latest novel, the 2009 International Literature Award from the House of World Cultures (Berlin), a 2007 John Simon Guggenheim Memorial Foundation Fellowship (an honor that Díaz and Ramírez also share, earning this distinction in 1999 and 2008, respectively), and a 2008 PEN USA Novel Award.

But as James F. English writes in *The Economy of Prestige*, "The cultural phenomenon of the prize cannot be understood strictly in terms of calculation and deal making: generosity, celebration, love, play, community are as real a part of the cultural prize as are marketing strategy and self-promotion."[6] The newfound literary communities that turn up from the rise of Díaz's Pulitzer success exposes the forging of reciprocal transnational—or, as Frances Aparicio might describe it, "trans-creative"—interests and associations under U.S. and Latin American transformation.[7] This millennial United States of America has grown into what Volpi appraises as los Estados Unidos de las Américas.[8] In this sinuous movement of Latin American representation and literary canon formation, Latin Americans size up the U.S. Latino north. U.S. Latinos intently gaze not just at the Global South. They also take in a United States that, in Alarcón's words, is "a Latin American country too."[9]

Still, there is concern for this U.S. Latin Americanization without the Latin American creative class. Volpi has recounted that "while Latinoness becomes fashionable around the world, Latin America is emptied of its content."[10] My entry point in this analytic and speculative gesture tracks this assumed Latin disintegration and its immediate ground, U.S. Latino texts. Affording Latinos—or Latin America's geographic "others"—with this critical genealogy heightens the two canonical directions and representations of Latin America in the hemisphere.[11] Yet Ramírez's suggestion, that U.S. Latino interlocutors are modeling and weathering these regional spaces of Latin American articulation, proves unusual. He punctuates, as Alarcón has determined in connection to Radio Ambulante—a Spanish-language radio program focusing on Latin America and U.S. human stories—that "there is a growing interest of Latin Americans in our own [U.S. Latino] reality."[12] But this nexus is not as straightforward as one imagines. Díaz claimed in El País, Spain's highest circulation daily, that Latino "minority" writers are deemed as lightweight, "second-class citizens in the republic of North American and Latin American letters."[13]

An integrated view of Latin America through Latinoness invites one to scrutinize the slippery discrepancies between these two Latin Americas and their suffused meanings. I will pause momentarily to clarify that my course is not to delineate, dwell on, or quibble about the institutionalization of Latino/a and Latin American literature through what has amounted to well-known disproportionate histories, disconnected trajectories, separate points of emergence, and uneven recognition in the U.S. academy. Rather than recapitulating and ruminating on Latino and Latin American writing as two antagonistic traditions circling around irreconcilable disciplinary orbits, we would do well to rethink the interpretive possibilities of global Latino literary modes and the sculpting of transnational discursive opportunities. Indulge me, as I advance a rereading of twenty-first-century Latino cultural expression as one of deracination. This deracination, molded here as a wide-reaching form of Latin unbelonging and "unhousability," cannot be fully housed or exclusively claimed in the U.S. literary sector. Díaz's American self in the continental sense fashions hermeneutic turns that disrupt literary conventions in Latin America as well as the United States. An alternative practice of allopatric Latinness emanates. The brevity of Ramírez's opinion piece—certainly briefer than Díaz's ambitious allocation of a "brief wondrous life" to the Latinized Oscar Wao—cannot fully flesh out what is at stake in this transplanting of Latin America within the Latino United States. Yet Ramírez's inquiry sets in motion just how U.S. Latinos become an active center of "real" and acceptable Latin American emergence as well as world consumption.

This chain of deracination, continental meaning making, and the negotiation of Latinos in the world immerse much that follows. I first delve into Ramírez's animating platform because his comments come from within the prominent writerly Latin American community—synthesized by Jill Robbins as "diplomats, human rights activists, news correspondents, [and] presidential candidates"—that frames humanistic dialogue and critique.[14] I proceed with a discussion of Díaz's *The Brief Wondrous Life of Oscar Wao* as a body of thought that reorients Ramírez's idea of Latin America. The Dominican American author's work hinges on a mingled gathering of Latinness that exceeds the "original" way of seeing and reading the region as well as "the" Latino. Díaz's Latin America is not a simple duplicate, as it relishes frequent displacements and other becomings. It is not just the Latin subject that is "oddly" positioned, but the Latin content of the Americas as well. Latin America and Latino America are a series of interrupted flows and processes. Can the entire American terrain be discursively covered in synonymous and overlapping ways? How, we should ask, are both the Latin American and Latino imaginaries being rewritten differently in light of discursive erasures? My essay offers a prolegomena to these timely questions.

Latin America's Reversal

Ramírez's op-ed gets to the very heart of Latinoness as cultural capital for Latin Americans. Unlike the final years of the twentieth century, when Alberto Fuguet and Sergio Gómez communicated in their coedited anthology, *McOndo*, that a cumbersome but indiscriminate "locura latina" was sweeping across the mass-mediated U.S. publishing industry, Ramírez emphasizes that Latin American belles-lettres have, at this juncture, taken on a different substantial shape.[15] U.S. Latinos, for the Central American novelist, are the distinct agents for understanding the region's creative imagination and the northward charting of a greater U.S.-based Latin America. "Today, literature in the English language from the beginning of this century," he opines, "is a literature of immigrants, where two worlds dispute with the author."[16] Ramírez's compass gears toward the delocalized world of a migratory Latin American literature as it is coming to be known. But Latino letters appear as a novelty, an unpolished amalgam that begins this century, and notably through the two aforementioned luminaries.

This standpoint drives one to question why Nilo Cruz's Pulitzer Prize in 2003 for *Anna in the Tropics* did not count for Ramírez (perhaps because it is a play), and why Oscar Hijuelos's Pulitzer triumph in 1990 with his novel *The Mambo Kings Play Songs of Love* was also slighted. Such elisions give rise to thorny queries: What would these Cuban American voices add, or detract, from Ramírez's U.S. Latin American house of culture? Could it be that an analysis of these Cuban American authors would touch on Cold War ideologies and a Cuban revolution that Ramírez may not want to revisit? Ramírez, after all, has retired from politics and is critical of Daniel Ortega's Sandinista policies. Is Dominican Americanness more linked to the signifying potential of a "CAFTA–DR reality," one where smaller geographies and economies regenerate cultural integration north and south? While I cite a free trade agreement signed in 2004 by the United States, Costa Rica, El Salvador, Guatemala, Honduras, Nicaragua, and the Dominican Republic, I underscore a political economy populated by Latinos who have not been symmetrically matched with the conventional triad of Mexican Americans, Puerto Ricans, and Cuban Americans. Ramírez does not draw this link. But its oversight makes one wonder if there are neglected reenactments and contextualizations that may satisfy his quest for the latest constitution of a Latin American reality. If so, how do "secondary" U.S. Latinos, with their particular disjunctions of ideas, invigorate this Latin America that is adrift regionally and through the casting of different groups that are articulating a new mode for Latinoness? Ramírez singularly locates *The Brief Wondrous Life of Oscar Wao* within the United States, given Díaz's Pulitzer, even as the novel's unhousable form hermeneutically rotates to other kinds of artistic sensibilities, historical "evidence," and debates.

But that being said, the consumption of an amalgamated global Latinness comes to the fore, as the distinction between the Latin American and the U.S. Latino becomes less fraught. Ramírez puts across the message that the region's symbolic value as well as its cultural livelihood are having a fresh start—or restart—through the production of Latino literature in English. If Díaz has penned a text riddled with so much epistemological portability and linguistic possibility, why, I ask, must Latin America be restrained to an essential divide unified by North-South and English-Spanish relations? The imaginative landscape of *The Brief Wondrous Life of Oscar Wao* uncovers, for Ramírez, an expanding Latin American reality that is enunciated through an English-specific form of literary expression germinating among U.S. Latinos. Ramírez's appraisal distinguishes, at first glance, a clear Latin American state of affairs that sprouts in Hispanophone Latin America and that is appended and equalized in the Anglophone United

States. This Latin American sociopolitical reality may smoothly glide between a dual directional Latino America and Latin America. In the Global North, this Latin America—los Estados Unidos de las Américas—deploys the simultaneity of Latino as a U.S. identity construction that coevally exists with amalgamated Latin American referents in the United States.

Ramírez bids that if a Latino "is the owner of two worlds," then this author is "also the owner of two languages, or, rather, of a broken language, alive and woken up."[17] This broken language is a migrant Latino's testing ground for English, striking "the narrative experience with its innovation and strangeness."[18] This motif of strangeness is taken up, as the reader may have gathered, throughout this piece. For now, let us sift through this commensurate possibility, as it somehow congeals to a Latin American definitive discourse. "The ghosts of the Latin American reality," Ramírez expounds, "cross U.S. borders like so many other clandestine ones, hidden in the genes, or in the luggage of immigrants who one day will be first-tier writers. Wet ghosts who do not allow themselves to get out of the way."[19] Contradicting his methodology and proclivity for American literary prizes and their expeditious tendering of Latin American prestige, Ramírez's aesthetic scale depreciates Latino writers by submitting that they have yet to acquire the moxie that will one day render them "first-tier writers." I am also not keen on this evocation of Latin American "wet ghosts." I tend to think such spirits would be indigenous, but the wetness of these literary or sociopolitical Latin American evanescent forms seems like an audacious conjuring of pejorative "wetbacks." The implication is that these Latin American ghosts wade and trespass the waters of the Rio Grande, like their migrant creators in the United States. And not dissimilar to the fictive depictions of their wet ghosts, the wet Latino author is conceivably second class—and with a tinge of lowbrow status—when it comes to the Latin American literary purview.

Ramírez manages to tally an official Latin American literature and sensibility reproduced in the United States. These Latino specters of Latin America are validated through the perceived American prize frenzy and close mainstream media attention devoted to Latinos. Not only this, but Ramírez infers that prizeless Latin Americans in Latin America seem to powerlessly watch the dawning twenty-first-century cultural economy of the region as its currency accrues more value elsewhere. If the new Latin American novel has become Latino, as Ramírez evaluates, equally forceful would be the awarding of accolades like the Rómulo Gallegos International Novel Prize and the Alfaguara Novel Prize to Latino and Latina writers. Will the borders of "referent[s] for quality literary awards," as the Alfaguara publishing house qualifies its prize, shift their geography of reason (to borrow the Caribbean Philosophical Association's maxim) and confer honors to Ramírez's English-speaking "wet ghosts"?[20] U.S. Latinos, as bearers of a "new geography of prestige," to take from English's study, exhibit the tensions in locating the new sites of Latin American epistemological transmission. And just as salient is this inference: that Latino prominence in Latin America could lead to what English calls a "deterritorialization of prestige" within the region, de-centering the symbolic power of Latin America in Latin America as its meanings "float" and become "offshore" through other communities.[21] Ramírez's intentional use of English and obvious sense of reality are markers not only of literary prestige but of a presumed cultural oneness for a Latin American diaspora that is "haunted by empire," as Ann Laura Stoler prompts.[22] Latino authors transmit the south-to-north and north-to-south condition of Latin American migrants in English, thereby "remigrating" it, in Spanish translation, back to Latin America from the United States (to invoke Juan Flores's phraseology).[23] In this production and circulation, Latinos make English bear witness to, as Ramírez has it, "the ghosts of the Latin American reality that persecutes us all."[24] Díaz's and Alarcón's narrative praxis deals with "public life, the horrors and hallucinations of the social and political reality, the one that comes from recent history, or from distant history."[25] They plot an experience of despair, vocalizing "the astounding excess of dictatorships, crime, torture, the disappeared. The Dominican Republic and Trujillo's dictatorship; Peru and the Shining Path. The old ghosts that come out of the basements of presidential palaces do not stop making the sound of the chains they are dragging."[26]

In this reviewing of the communal lines of a historical and political past, the viable versions of Latino writerly selfhoods are surrounded by an American "domestic and 'off-site' history," as Julie Greene puts it.[27] It admits, indeed ushers in, Latinos—an "ordinary" population that has been ideologically removed from "elite" Latin American discursive practices—as cocreators. Certain questions loom from this assembly of south-north Latin accretions: What kinds of tools do U.S. Latinos—who are generally surmised as "secondhand copies," as Frances Negrón-Muntaner pronounces in the context of Nuyoricans and Chicanos—have in the twenty-first century that allow for their present task as cohesive and influential framers of the public Latin American reality that has typically excluded them?[28] Who is now embodying and keeping the idea of Latin America alive? What kind of

Latin America are Latinos remembering? Finally, why is Ramírez's "high seriousness" preoccupied with the Global North's English, overlooking continual and sharp contrasts with Central America's English-speaking regions and indigenous literary workers? They, too, are surveyors of Latin American identities that shape this comparative pathway of Latin America's "reality," one that supersedes the particularities of its emergence and that is being delocalized and remapped through the Latin American narrative's northbound journeys.

Doubtlessly, Díaz is not an easy alibi to Ramírez's Latin America. Díaz critically and coetaneously engages with the Francophone and Anglophone Caribbean, while Ramírez proffers a changeless way of poring over Hispanophone Latin America through a Spanish-English dyad. It is as though Ramírez's expectations for the literary transmission of Latin America—in effect, the interpretive life of Latin America—is hardly ruptured in the U.S. retelling of the region. Volpi has written that "from where Latin America is narrated [it has] disappeared from the maps, like its dictators and guerrillas passed to a better life and took with them the horror and glory, like magical realism was buried in the jungle, and like this miraculous and torrid region becomes more diffuse, more boring, more normal every day."[29] Is the categorical quality of Latin America over for Latin Americans? If Latin America has discontinued in Latin America, as Volpi spurs, what is Ramírez's investment in the preservation and normalizing of literary Latin America through Latinos in the United States?

Arlene Dávila's attention to the "politics of value and worth" and the politics of cultural representation for a population that is considered as "de facto suspect citizen/subjects—as foreigners, newcomers, and not fully belonging to the US national body" should be kept in mind for making meaning of the placelessness—the deracination—of Latinos in the United States and Latin America.[30] Dávila's Culture Works examines the feasibility of building a National Museum of the American Latino (NMAL). She first takes note of the geographic uncertainties of such a project: whether it will be part of the Smithsonian Institution, built on the Mall located in Washington, D.C., or "in another state with more historical relevance for Latinos or else as a network of umbrella or satellite museums built throughout the nation."[31] The NMAL's challenge has been to widen the appeal and purpose of the ethnoracial population shaping the art and culture of the proposed American structure, making it a place "for the benefit of all Americans." This "strategic stance," she argues, is "intended to neutralize the project's perception as a balkanizing project that is only for and by Latinos."[32] In this production of an official American Latino culture that gives primacy to Americanness, the distinctions between Latin Americanness and Latinoness are blurred.[33] They are almost inoperative, to the extent that this version of American Latinoness is predicated on U.S.-centered narratives of absorption and success. Americanness must be ranked higher, particularly as we take in Blas Falconer and Lorraine M. López's assertion that "apart from some connection to Latin American culture, nothing defines Latino identity more in [U.S.] mainstream consciousness than the Spanish language."[34]

Ramírez's endorsement of a Latin Americanized U.S. Latino imagination parallels the tensions Dávila diagrams from a south-south panorama. The Latin American *becoming* of Latino—literarily speaking—does not mold an ontological U.S. Latino being. But what interests me in the politics of U.S. inclusion and representation is the approximation of thought and decolonial critique that Ramírez is trying to channel through the Latino as a needed appendix to Latin America. Following this logic, if Latinos are a site of Latin American struggle, at what point do Latin American intellectuals become, comparatively speaking, Latino? Will Latin American literary productions put to use significant crossover influences by Latinos?

Meanwhile, the Latin American literary space of appearance in the United States depends on the professionalization of future American authors publishing in Spanish. U.S. writing programs are now deeply entangled with the Spanish language, as recent fluxes demonstrate that some graduate programs are increasingly instructing students to hone their craft through the submission of manuscripts in Spanish. This American use of literary Spanish in creative writing classrooms is an obvious response to burgeoning Latino and Latina demographics, "one of the last identifiable and sizable market niches."[35] This latest approach to the social and marketable expectations of Spanish, as Dávila made us aware in *Latinos, Inc.*, reveals a "determinant influence in the global rendering of marketable identities."[36] Such consumption demands Latin consumers throughout the Americas and beyond.

The present-day politics and uses of the different registers of Spanish in the United States would almost make one lose sight of, as Kirsten Silva Gruesz heeds, how "the mainstream view of Spanish and its speakers has become profoundly, although not fully proletarianized."[37] Legislative efforts and campaigns to make English the nation's official language and to ban bilingual education from the classroom are the givens in racialized constructions and nativist policies that restrict the language and cultural rights of "the growing and diverse Spanish-speaking immigrant population."[38] Yet Spanish as a literary language is presumably on the same plane with English, practiced and perfected at high aesthetic levels, as certain Master of Fine Arts programs put forward. The University of Iowa, for instance, relayed not long ago that it has just instituted a Master of Fine Arts program in Spanish Creative Writing, joining other academic ventures at New York University, the City University of New York, and the University of Texas at El Paso.[39] Spring 2013 heralded the inaugural volume of *Iowa Literaria*. Published by Iowa's MFA in Spanish Creative Writing, the e-journal has been conceived as a "space to reflect on the art of creativity, to approach the complexities and challenges of creative writing, and to publish a variety of literary pieces."[40] And more: *Iowa Literaria*'s objective is to become "a link to the Spanish literary community in the USA and around the world, hosting the works of that community's writers."[41]

As of 2004, Mark McGurl fills us in, "there were more than 350 creative writing programs in the United States, all of them staffed by practicing writers, most of whom, by now, are themselves holders of an advanced degree in creative writing."[42] This is a staggering figure, if we recall that in the 1940s there were only a "handful" of creative writing programs, only to keep on flourishing as "by 1984 there were more than 150 graduate degree programs (offering the M.A., M.F.A., or Ph.D.)." McGurl's premise is that this acceleration, since the mid-1960s, marks a period he calls "the Program Era," or "the most original production of the postwar period."[43] These programs are "the most interesting and emblematic—and, yes, increasingly hegemonic—literary historical transformation." The institutionalization of writing programs provides a window into the making of literary production through apprenticeships in a literary trade, academicization, and commodification processes that clue us in on the "systematicity" of how Latinness is being created—or, put another way, as a system that also thinks through the acquired skills, techniques, and authorship behind the production of Latinness in U.S. institutions. For some, "'assembly-line' programs are blamed . . . for producing a standardized aesthetic, a corporate literary style that makes a writer identify as, say, an Iowa writer."[44] But McGurl insists that "what is needed now . . . are studies that take the rise and spread of the creative writing program not as an occasion for praise or lamentation but as an established fact in need of historical interpretation: how, why, and to what end has the writing program reorganized U.S. literary production in the postwar period?" (27). For our aims, we almost have to sit back and wait for the new literary networks and marketability of literary Latinness in this "Program Era" to unfold more pointedly in the context of postwar America and postwar Latin America. These developments illustrate the augmenting convergence and the two-sidedness of the Latino and Latin American novel. Ramírez may be correct in speculating that the great Latin American novel is being drafted in the United States. But there is an exception: this literature is being officially constituted in Spanish, too, and unsettling Ramírez's discursive Latin American community. The cultural and sociopolitical force attached to Latin America bypasses a regional categorization. It takes on new meanings, perhaps even an alterable identity production of Latinidad and Latinoamericanidad, considering that non-Latinos and non-Latin Americans participate in this communicative process of genre breaking and genre making.

Ramírez's special kind of attention rubber-stamps the role of U.S. Latinos in Latin America, despite this group's ethnoracial, national, and literary obscurity and ambiguity in the Americas. The typical class and linguistic asymmetries between U.S. Latino and Latin American intellectuals are sidestepped. Latinos are no longer outside observers of Latin America. In this discursive shift of Latin American alternatives, what happens to "foreign" Latin American readers, as they are brought to another "domestic" but competing version of the region? To my eyes, Ramírez's key premise, despite its shortcomings and disappointments, imparts a string of questions on the role of hemispherist Latino cultural workers in the twenty-first century. José Martí may have directed our attention to Hispanophone Pan-American thinking, but his comparative scope glossed over the "the borderlands of Greater Mexico," as José David Saldívar has incisively touched upon in *Trans-Americanity*.[45] Díaz's continental innovations simultaneously expose a trans-Americanness as well as a trans-Latin Americanness. Trans-Latin Americanness has yet to be conceptually charted. Néstor García Canclini's *Latinoamericanos buscando lugar en este siglo* (2002), however, cued us into Latin Americans trying to wrestle with the rearticulation and relocation of Latin American cultural and intellectual thought—their own take on "Latinidad"—outside the region. Whereas García Canclini is primarily concerned with the role of Latin Americans in the world, Ramírez's overall remarks furnish us with points of orientation about what this regional lens might involve through Latino participation.

Where does Díaz's "trans-ness" reside, in trans-America or trans-Latin America? There are different continental understandings of Díaz's works, as the American nation and the American hemisphere mark them. In effect, *The Brief Wondrous Life of Oscar Wao* is not purely (North or Latin) American, but an elective representation of a subject with multiple thresholds and continuous denationalizations. What might this signal for hemispherist Latino creative workers with many detours? And what of Latino translated writings, circulating in more and more globalized settings and linked to other "foreign" artistic and literary conventions?

Ramírez's proposition of a Latino "continental English," let us call it, evokes, in a different way, Latin America's modernista movement, whose roots took shape from 1888 to 1916.[46] For Hispanophone intellectuals, modernismo comprised, as Jean Franco has written, "a rebellion against a literary heritage [and] the invention of new forms of expression."[47] Modernistas attempted to revamp the Spanish language. Franco clarifies that "the conflict was not so much between pure Castilian and American Spanish as an ideological conflict between a language that had failed to develop with the modern world and their own spiritual and aesthetic experience."[48] Rubén Darío, the Nicaraguan poet generally regarded as the "Father of Modernismo," declared that Spanish "was walled in by tradition."[49] That is why it had to be updated with a "non-Spanish vocabulary" from the Americas.[50] Could this conception, in our contemporary moment, suggest that Latin American Spanish requires further modernization—rendered afresh—through the use of a Spanish that admits the English language, as penned by U.S. Latinos? But this is not just any lexicon. It may as well be the "weird English" that Evelyn Nien-Ming Ch'ien discusses in connection to "imaginative projections" of evolving, transitional selfhoods in the United States.[51] Continentally speaking, however, a ragbag of Latin American Spanish needs to utter the Latino "reality" in the United States, and claim its own reciprocal version of a weird Spanish.[52] This weird Spanish can be assessed through the different flows and directions in which Latino significations have spread to Latin America through stories of survival, mass deportations, return migrations, transnational citizenships, and family as well as "cultural remittances" (to draw from Flores).[53] Or, more broadly, Latin America's weird Spanish can be aligned with deracinations that, as Edward Said pegs, have "a precariousness of vision and a tentativeness of statement that renders the use of language something much more interesting and provisional than it would otherwise be."[54]

Díaz's uniqueness is not his weird English, or "strange" English, as Ramírez alluded to it earlier. It is the strange Latin America that Díaz brings to the fore. He takes us to the lived weirdness of bodies that are disregarded in normative America as well as Latin America. What types of consciousness and languages carry the weight of this continental American outsiderness? The fundamental issue is not this reordering of Latin America and its indeterminacy. Other matters to be asked are: How do we make forms of inter-American thinking by Latinos comprehensible? And how has Díaz changed the meaning of Latino, too?

Let us appreciate, then, Díaz's maneuvers in *The Brief Wondrous Life of Oscar Wao* and the manifestation of what seems "weirdly" out of place in the United States and Latin America. I have engaged with some of these "Latined" illustrations in my first monograph, *Latining America: Black-Brown Passages and the Coloring of Latino/a Studies* (2013). But I reintroduce them here, with emendations and elucidations, because they write in an amplified Latin language and milieu that speaks to the innovation of a bulkier Latined signifier and dispersal. In *Latining America*, I devise the idea of Latined to point to the instability of Latinos. I contend that the signifier *Latin* hosts a free flow of people that stirs with or without the easily assumed brown Latino subject in Latinidad. This referent often migrates and passes through black, brown, dark brown, and discursively parenthetical bodies. The Latin signifier travels through an array of geographies and populations, paving the way for a panoply of cultural and political liaisons. It grapples with the dispersal and multiplicity of the overlay of significations for Latin subjects—within and outside the United States—that may be regionally, culturally, or racially intangible.

Latinness at a Different Pace, Latinness in a Different Space

The Brief Wondrous Life of Oscar Wao outlines rich expressive sketches of Latining. The novel centers on Oscar de León, a nerdy, sci-fi-loving, pop culture aficionado, and his family's migration from the Dominican Republic to northern New Jersey. Whereas Latin America may have reached its limits, as conjectured earlier, the importance of *The Brief Wondrous Life of Oscar Wao* is its limitlessness and ever-evolving Latin anomalies. Another way to put it is that Díaz's Latino or Latin American outlook is one locus with many directions in the Americas. Díaz's moving odds and ends and timelines interweave Dominican and Dominican American life, the urban borderlands of New York and New Jersey, and the Greater Caribbean. These spacious realms map potential Latin genealogies. From one point of view, the quiddity of these millennial oddities, as Díaz limns them, are "the fat, the ugly, the smart, the poor, the dark, the black, the unpopular, the African, the Indian, the Arab, the immigrant, the strange, the femenino, the gay."[55] Díaz takes us to conceptual processes that are under flux in the Global North and Global South and that are productive to read from these geographies' margins. These margins require footnotes within the discursive practices of Latino/a and Latin American studies, as multiple sets of relations are going off their allotted space. It is a Latin semiotic and symbolic system that, to make use of Gruesz's keen insights on the canonization and periodization of Latino literature, has a "unique status as an institutional free radical."[56] These "leftovers" from North and South of the Americas seek to place and annotate the placelessness of this Latin amalgamation: the "Dominicanis," as Díaz alludes to them. Take note of one parenthetical but far from tangential footnoted comment that has the emerging peripheral subject indexing the self on scraps of paper, in composition books, and on the back of his hands.[57]

Deviations and discursive strategies are at work for these Dominicanis beginnings. A literary and epistemological archive from the Anglophone and Francophone Caribbean moves forward this Latined subject. Derek Walcott's poem, "The Schooner 'Flight,'" published in 1979, speaks to the rich cultural mixtures of the Caribbean, guides the reader through the protagonist's brief history of his life, and serves as the epigraph. The Brief Wondrous Life of Oscar Wao's first excerpt—"Of what import are brief, nameless lives . . . to Galactus??"—is attributed to Marvel Comics' fictional superhero team The Fantastic Four. Walcott's stanza follows this quote. Díaz was asked in an El País interview about this bridging of the "lowbrow" (superhero comics) and the "highbrow" (Nobel Laureate in Literature) and their specific connection to the Caribbean. He expounded:

> Stan Lee or Jack Kirby's characters are as far removed from the Caribbean reality like those of Homer, before Walcott recovered them. Walcott is very important. He cannibalizes the European colonial inheritance, perhaps the most distinguishing characteristic of the Caribbean culture. In the Caribbean we always have known to recycle the residues thrown by other cultures to the dump of history. One of my book's narrators takes advantage of the enormous amount of abandoned material, the literary

subgenres like horror stories and science-fiction, for two reasons. One is to demolish the prejudices that hierarchize the different forms of literature, and the other because there is no genre that best manifests the fear of otherness than science-fiction.[58]

The Brief Wondrous Life of Oscar Wao is a passport to this fantastic restructuring of the Caribbean, as a bibliophilic dumpster, an epistemological sea of ever-enlarging literary fusions. The brief but all too fantastic life of Oscar Wao, our superhero, is its own "thing" of relevant signification, coded with incredible—"weird"—powers, myths, symbols, marvels, and upcycled residue. Oscar's extreme differences allow him to stand for and signify a deracinated Latinness that moves and reshapes in different settings.

Díaz also references the Martinican intellectual Édouard Glissant, whose theorization of cultural interrelationships in the Caribbean through processes of creolization and conceptual terms like "relation," have served as puissant landmarks for diasporic studies and the relational links between the Caribbean and the Atlantic world.[59] And, as José David Saldívar puts forth, "Díaz superbly probes the Greater Antillean discourses of the Cuban social scientist Fernando Ortiz and the Martiniquean Aimé Césaire's négritude poetry."[60] But as Díaz's storyteller says, these citations are not mere "nerdery in circulation."[61] Analogous to Jorge Luis Borges, Díaz "conceives of writing as reading."[62] His narrative collaborations renew conceptual and cultural parameters for the interrelatedness of the Greater Antilles, especially since Díaz's recounter interrogates that "as a consequence of being Antillean (who more sci-fi than us?)."[63]

Not unlike Borges's proclivity for annotations—think back to his short story "The Garden of Forking Paths" (1941)—the value of Díaz's footnotes is not in their truthful accuracy, as Sandra Cisneros's Caramelo evinces. It lies, instead, in the craftiness and playfulness of the novel's "historiographer." The Brief Wondrous Life of Oscar Wao requires an autonomous sphere, "a self-contained realm of the imagination that the author [is] free to shape so long as he [can] persuade the reader to give it an appropriate degree of 'poetic faith.'"[64] The poetic faith of Díaz's explanatory notes—what José David Saldívar denominates as his "Greater Antillean and Global South poetics"—accounts for, embellishes, or disrupts his stories.[65] It pushes multiple points of view within the act of storytelling, taking to task, as Borges attempted, "the towering prestige of the novel" through "Gothic fantasy, tales of adventure, science fiction, and . . . detective stories."[66]

Díaz's writing and vernacular are incontestably Díazian. But what if we calibrate them to Borgesian *ficciones*, "metaphysical fantasies in which, for instance, the universe was compared to a well-ordered but limitless library that refused to disclose its overall design"?[67] Certainly the opening footnote to Díaz's novel alludes to the seemingly coherent Latin American reality that is unbound by categories of comprehension. The Dominican dictator Rafael Leónidas Trujillo Molina was "a personaje so outlandish, so perverse, so dreadful that not even a sci-fi writer could have made his ass up."[68] Footnoted *ficciones* become a constellation and frame of narration that step out of mediated understandings of a stern Latin American reality.

Díaz's novel creates fissures vis-à-vis the openness and multilayeredness of its form and language. *The Brief Wondrous Life of Oscar Wao* interrupts a linear English and Spanish—standard languages that have yet to catch up with the Latined being's existence. If Ramírez motions *The Brief Wondrous Life of Oscar Wao* to a trans-Latin Americanness, let us consider a central dynamic, or a not so bewildering intersection: how Díaz's endeavor falls under, in the United States, the category of a trans-American project that broadens the notion of the American canon. As the theoretically insightful works of Paula Moya, Ramón Saldívar, José David Saldívar, and Kirsten Silva Gruesz have brilliantly gauged, the trans-American imaginary focuses on the shifting articulations of American national identities and literatures. Paula Moya and Ramón Saldívar, for example, call for a body of thought in their special issue of *Modern Fiction Studies* that sees "American literature as heterogeneous and multiple"—requiring an alteration of the American corpus.[69] The influences of this representative body of writings exceed "nations other than England."[70] The trans-American hemispheric vantage point "yokes together North and South America instead of New England and England."[71] This literary form of geopolitical kinship "make[s] visible the centrality of Latinidad to the fictional discourses that continue to shape the American national imaginary."[72] Its theoretical contribution is a "chronotope, a contact zone that is both historical and geographical and that is populated by transnational persons whose lives form an experiential region within which singularly delineated notions of political, social, and cultural identity do not suffice."[73]

This renewed vision of American literature is opportune and valuable, for it seeks to extricate the recurring Americanness in normative domains that restrict a national American corpus. Emphatically dialoguing with trans-Americanness, I also want to disentangle the function of Latino literature outside the confines of the American geographic, national, cultural, and ethnoracial context. Both Latin America and Latino are reference points that have run out of their customary environments. At a time when, as Ed Morales urges, "there may be more styles and variations of being Latino than there are different Latin American countries," it seems as though an American novel (in the U.S. sense) is heralding a Latined perspective.[74] A Latined text could just as well reconstitute a "new" American self in the Americas. But it fashions a form of writing and engages with hermeneutic turns that integrate and disrupt literary conventions in Latin America and the United States—a grid that Díaz captures through both Gabriel García Márquez's fictional Macondo and Fuguet and Gómez's amended version of McOndo.[75]

The shadow of Trujillo's dictatorship follows Díaz's subjects. In their deeply meshed past and present, Oscar's family struggles with the effects of the inescapable new world curse, what José David Saldívar calls Díaz's "cultural theory" of Fukú americanus, "or more colloquially, fukú."[76] But the origins of Fukú americanus, which as speculatively written in the book's inaugural sentence, implying myth or hearsay—"they say it came first from Africa"—is hardly a punch line propitiously executed in Latin. It provokes thoughtful inquisitiveness on its sources and lineages, on what accounts for its presence, and what it means for the Latined diaspora of lowercase "americanus" to be conjoined by an interminable fukú. Díaz globalizes this emergent but fairly obfuscated subject, adjusting its "who-ness," "what-ness," and "how-ness," but not necessarily guaranteeing a clear Latino or even Latin American outcome. Let us bring back Oscar's capitalized outlier status, as conjured by Díaz: "Dude wore his nerdiness like a Jedi wore his light saber or a Lensman her lens. Couldn't have passed for Normal if he'd wanted to."[77] Given Oscar's corpulent body and his overall cultural "too-muchness," he does not, in the strict sense of the word, "fit in."

The types of americanus encountering the evenly spaced and distributed fukú—"because no matter what you believe, fukú believes in you"—eclipse Afro-Latinoness, Latinidad, and a formal nationality.[78] In one telling instance, Oscar de León, whose name appears to have an ironic alliteration with the Venezuelan salsa performer Oscar D'León, is recognized as an unknown species through the visionary greeting, "Hail, Dominicanis."[79] But this salutation is not so excessive, as the literary name de León and the musical D'León make this Dominicanis ordinary and quotidian. The acknowledgment gives prominence to the open conditions of Oscar's traveling Latinness. Under

Díaz's pen, this Latin subject is a revision of both Dominican and American subjectivity. It is a "God. Domini. Dog. Canis," and takes an "illegible" speciation depending on the geographic, physiological, and linguistic barriers at hand.[80] Oscar's Dominicanness—or his "Dominicanisness," even—is invoked rather awkwardly "over and over again," as though to stress and halt the authenticating importance of a Dominicanness's metamorphosing into Dominicanis.[81] At Rutgers University, in New Brunswick, Oscar insists somewhat robotically, "But I am. Soy dominicano. Dominicano soy."[82] A complementary scene takes place there as well, when Harold tells Oscar, "Tú no eres nada de dominicano, but Oscar would insist unhappily, I am Dominican, I am."[83] His reiterative persistence punctuates the need to hold this version of Dominicanis credible, for, as Díaz mentions, no one "had ever met a Domo like him."[84] Domo intones a similar alliance with "homo," reminding us of Oscar's queer significations.

In a similar vein to Oscar's Latinness, there is no fixed form or stable geography to Díaz's text, which like García Márquez's *One Hundred Years of Solitude*, was first conceived in Mexico City. Its multiple storylines, cultural vacillations, and interlacing linguistic styles admit a "Spanglish" marked by an urban vernacular, or a bigger language that carries the influences of literary and nonliterary texts and practices from the United States, the Caribbean, Latin America, and Europe. Lest we forget, Oscar Wao's mobile Dominicanis archive Latinizes Oscar Wilde (1856–1900), who is renowned for his contributions to English literature, not to count his great wit. The extravagant Wilde walks alongside the extravagant but radically ordinary— "eccentric" new world—Wao. This new pronunciation and subjectivity is affixed to Oscar: After being called "Wao" for a couple of weeks, "dude started *answering* to it."[85] Díaz's Wao rouses the exclamatory palindrome *wow*. This resignification of literary icons and situations, to extract from Díaz, cannibalizes European colonial inheritance.[86] Díaz's bursts of interconnections associate with other signs that alter, in this instance, the original literary signification of "Oscar Wilde." But this cannibalization of Wilde does not simply claim him, as was the quest of the canonical British alternative rock band, The Smiths, with the song "Cemetery Gates" (1986). In it, the lead singer and lyricist, Morrissey, vocalizes, "So let's go where we're wanted / And I meet you at the cemetery gates / Keats and Yeats are on your side / But you lose / 'Cause weird lover Wilde is on mine." Wilde shares his weird compatibility with Morrissey and Oscar Wao. The dissimilarity, however, is that new world Latin freakery is the well-oiled machine that keeps Díaz's Wao running wildly. If Oscar Wao looks so different and articulates his being so differently, how does he become such a straight continuum for Latin America, per Ramírez's gaze? Morrissey's Penguin Classic *Autobiography* appoints Wilde as "the world's first populist figure (first pop figure)" that "exploded with original wisdom, advocating freedom from heart and soul, *and for all*— regardless of how the soul swirled."[87] It could also be true that Wao has become the first Latino literary *pop* figure on an international scale, much like his creator, who transcends the novel. "Junot is Junot, and he is a rock star," decreed Rebecca Saletan, the editorial director of Díaz's publishing house, Riverhead Books, in the *Wall Street Journal*.[88] Wao, the literary pop star, pairs up with visual artist Keith Haring's resolutions that "thinking is cumulative" and that "people are afraid of being pop, but it's not easy to be simple."[89]

The open-ended resources of Díaz's novel exceed local, national, and regional circumstances. They are a source of explanation for the Latino and Latin American plenum, and how it has been read. Communicative Latinness north and south emerge through a Latined mode of rewriting, from the Dominicanis archive, the variable form and content of Latino and Latin American political memberships. Like Díaz's hero, the literary lineage of *The Brief Wondrous Life of Oscar Wao* moves across the boundaries of cultures, creating a Latined literary history that draws out, borrows from, and is steeped in a vast range of relationships and discourses that may, as a popular phrase goes, pop in—or pop out—anywhere. These textual relations bring into play questions about Latino cultural life, subjectivity, and interiority, especially pertaining to deracination. Deracinated Latin bodies exceed designations of identity and localization, as they live, travel, and move beyond unyielding labels and identifications. Oscar Wao revives the maladjusted—but traversing Latin body—footing Oscar Wilde's words, "if life be, as it surely is, a problem to me, I am no less a problem to life."[90]

Notes

1. Jean Comaroff and John L. Comaroff, *Theory from the South: Or, How Euro-America Is Evolving Toward Africa* (Boulder, CO: Paradigm, 2012), 4.

2. The rest of the "thirty-nine under thirty-nine" figures—selected by a jury comprising the Colombian novelists Piedad Bonnett, Hector Abad Faciolince, and Oscar Callazos—write primarily in Spanish and come from Latin America.

3. Jorge Volpi, *El insomnio de Bolívar: Cuatro consideraciones intempestivas sobre América Latina en el siglo XXI* (Mexico City: Debate, 2009), 205.

4. Sergio Ramírez, "La nueva novela latinoamericana," *La Insignia*, October 16, 2008, accessed April 22, 2015, http://www.lainsignia.org/2008/octubre/cul_002.htm (my translation).

5. Ramirez, "La nueva novela latinoamericana."

6. James F. English, *The Economy of Prestige: Prizes, Awards, and the Circulation of Cultural Value* (Cambridge, MA: Harvard University Press, 2005), 7.

7. Frances R. Aparicio, "On Sub-Versive Signifiers: U.S. Latina/o Writers Tropicalize English," *American Literature* 66, no. 4 (December 1994): 797.

8. Volpi, *El insomnio de Bolívar*, 209.

9. Claudio Iván Remeseira, "Authors Junot Díaz, Francisco Goldman Showcase Radio Program of Human Stories from Latin America," NBC *Latino*, February 4, 2013, accessed March 16, 2013, http://nbclatino.com/2013/02/04/authors-junot-diaz-francisco -goldman-showcase-a-radio-program-featuring-human-stories-from-latin-america/.

10. Volpi, *El insomnio de Bolívar*, 55.

11. The dual direction of Latino cultural expression spreads outside the novelistic form, as John Leguizamo's autobiographical one-man Broadway show, *Ghetto Klown*, indicated. The actor and playwright conducted the live, two-hour performance entirely in Spanish in preparation for Colombian audiences. Manhattan's Repertorio Español served as the testing ground for this sold-out show, days before Leguizamo took it to Colombia, his birthplace, on a three-city tour in Bogotá, Medellín, and Cali. Audiences in this South American country came to know *Ghetto Klown*, in translation, as *Pelado de barrio*. The *Daily News* reported that Leguizamo, who grew up in Queens speaking English and rebelled by always answering back in English to his Spanish-speaking parents, "prepared by taking grammar, pronunciation and vocabulary lessons, and even did tongue-twister exercises." Marcela Espíldora, "Leguizamo Makes Theater Debut in Spanish: Performs 'Ghetto Klown' en Español in NYC before Heading on Tour to Colombia," *New York Daily News*, January 25, 2012, accessed January 28, 2012, http://www.nydailynews .com/latino/john-leguizamo-speaking-article-1.1011313. Despite his efforts, a New York audience member, also Colombian, observed that Leguizamo did a "great job," but "he has more of a Puerto Rican accent." A "nationalist" Spanish is expected at this moment of authenticating "Colombianidad." The theatergoer ignores the enactments of a moving Colombianness that communicates—or, in Leguizamo's case, performs—a Colombian delocalization and denationalization that interact and mix with multiple "Spanishes" in U.S. settings. To put it more simply (though no less confoundingly): the Colombianness of Leguizamo's Colombianness has become Latino. Leguizamo, an Emmy Award winner, was called "the most famous Colombian in Hollywood" by the newspaper El *Tiempo*—ergo remaining a Colombian when he represents *Latin American* Colombianness in the United States. "John Leguizamo, el colombiano más famoso de Hollywood," El Tiempo, November 15, 2011, accessed on January 28, 2012, http://www.eltiempo.com /gente/john-leguizamo-el-colombiano-mas-famoso-de-hollywood_10767745-4. His "official" Colombianness was validated, too, when President Juan Manuel Santos designated the actor as Colombia's 2009 ambassador to the world of cinema. Also consult Leguizamo's PBS profile, *Tales from a Ghetto Klown* (2011).

12. Remeseira, "Authors Junot Díaz, Francisco Goldman Showcase Radio Program of Human Stories from Latin America"; consult Radio Ambulante's website, accessed April 22, 2015, http://radioambulante.org/en/.

13. Eduardo Lago, "'EE.UU. tiene pesadillas en español,'" El País, May 1, 2008 (my translation).

14. Jill Robbins, "Neocolonialism, Neoliberalism, and National Identities: The Spanish Publishing Crisis and the Marketing of Central America," Istmo 8 (January–June 2004), accessed April 22, 2015, http://istmo.denison.edu/n08/articulos/neocolonialism .html. Indubitably, Latino literature has entered numerous mainstreams and public spheres. The motley responses to this imaginative production across geographies warrant closer scrutiny. Raphael Dalleo and Elena Machado Sáez have carefully canvassed U.S. popular and critical reception to Latino writing by three paramount sectors, "reviewers, academics with a multiculturalist perspective, and academics with an anticolonial lens" (2). They submit that Latino cultural producers have entered the American "mainstream to an extent that previous work never could" (3). These texts' "remarkable market success" and their acceptance expose "how the circulation of Latino/a literature and its canonization are now also negotiated within the mainstream" (3). By challenging the tension between "marginal Latino/a culture and the American mainstream" (4), the two scholars give emphasis to a "double vision" that is heedful of processes of negotiation and "interaction of cultural producers and market forces" (10). Of great interest is how contemporary Latino/a authors proffer "a renewed political Latino/a literature" that is "able to speak confidently in the public sphere" (11). These problems of Latino visibility and inclusion in U.S. popular discourses are tied to how Latino literary production is imported wholesale into Latin America. Discursive power relations are at work, and in the quest for sociopolitical and cultural representation, which "Latin" (the one from los Estados Unidos de las Américas, or the one from an "authenticating" Latin America) voices and concretizes unity and coherence? Díaz gestures fluid identity formations that set up the present and future dispensations of Latin signifiers which may be outside the public sphere's grasp. Raphael Dalleo and Elena Machado Sáez, The Latino/a Canon and the Emergence of Post-Sixties Literature (New York: Palgrave Macmillan, 2007).

15. Alberto Fuguet and Sergio Gómez, "Presentación del país McOndo," in Alberto Fuguet and Sergio Gómez, eds., McOndo (Barcelona: Mondadori, 1996), 9–18. This "Latino craze" in the context of literature parallels the "Latin Invasion" or the "Latin Explosion" that bombarded U.S. popular culture in 1999 through such "Puerto Rican-American" performers as Ricky Martin, Marc Anthony, and Jennifer Lopez. Licia Fiol-Matta has analyzed these three top artists as "representatives of the new Latinidad" (28), a scripted "pop Latinidad" (29) that brings to the fore a "wholesale 'Latin identity'" (30). This Latinidad, premised on bilingualism as well as "two markets to rule over with their artistic productions," brings into view "Latino success in the global market" (30). But this globalized pop Latinidad erases "the everyday practices of the U.S. Latinos" (47) (Licia Fiol-Matta, "Pop Latinidad: Puerto Ricans in the Latin Explosion, 1999," Centro Journal 14, no. 1 [spring 2002]: 26–51). Fuguet and Gómez follow up on this consumer-oriented Latinidad from a literary vantage point. Suggesting

a literary pop Latinidad, they mention an incident with three young writers at the University of Iowa's International Writing Program. They "realize that without effort or contacts, they will be published in 'America' and in English. And just for being Latino, for writing in Spanish, for having been born in Latin America" (9, my translation). The reader nevertheless wonders where U.S. Latino writers fit in this literary schema. "The Latin is *hot* (as they say there) and both the Spanish Department [at the University of Iowa] and Yankee supplements are carried away with the theme," Fuguet and Gómez admit. "In the movies of the people, *Like Water for Chocolate* sweeps the box office. To say nothing of bookstore shelves, crammed with 'tasty' novels written by people whose Hispanic surnames are unmistakable, even though some write in English" (9, my translation). Latino and Latin American writers—the former writing in English, the latter in Spanish—become synonymous, and the overall U.S. message to these two dissimilar entities is "*Wellcome* [sic] *all Hispanics*" (10, italics in original). There is, as well, a blunt U.S. Latino and Latin American divide, although the *McOndo* editors advance an ethics on how to read Latin America. They tell us that "to sell a rural continent, when the truth of the matter is that it is urban (beyond that, their overcrowded cities are a chaos and do not work) seems aberrant, comfortable, and immoral" (16, my translation). Fuguet and Gómez hint at an interpretive cultural violence that is imposed in certain regions and populations. Social difference is imagined in a way that is problematic and dehumanizing. But while Fuguet and Gómez intimate that normative Americans should put themselves in the place of an "other," the Latin otherness of Latinos is foreclosed.

16. Ramírez, "La nueva novela latinoamericana."

17. Ramírez, "La nueva novela latinoamericana."

18. Ramírez, "La nueva novela latinoamericana."

19. Ramírez, "La nueva novela latinoamericana."

20. Alfaguara, "Premio Alfaguara de Novela," Alfaguara.com, n.d., accessed March 20, 2013, http://www.alfaguara.com/es/premio-alfaguara-de-novela/. Jill Robbins illuminates questions on how Latin America is currently marketed for a Spanish reading public. In her exegesis of the contemporary role of Spain's publishing houses, she writes that these outlets' changing structures are due to the New York and German acquisition of Spanish leading book companies. "Of all the Spanish-speaking regions in the world," she propounds, "Spain has the greatest reading public and thus constitutes the largest market for the winners of the Alfaguara." This publishing house "presents itself as the authentically pan-Hispanic globalizer of Spanish-language media products in Europe and the Americas" (Robbins). Alfaguara's goals, she adds, "are (1) to keep cultural Spanish people abreast of important writers in the former colonies; (2) to help Latin American texts circulate outside their countries of origins, and particularly in Spain; and (3) to create a unified Spanish-speaking cultural community, with its economic center in Madrid" (ibid.). She finds a rupture, however, between Spanish and Latin American Alfaguara prize winners from the late 1990s to the dawning of the twenty-first century. "In general terms," she observes, "the Spanish novels dealt with intimate and sentimental issues, rather than political ones, and they were

written in a classical, rather than avant-garde, style, whereas the Latin American novels were more concerned with the politics, history, and violence" (ibid.). Ramírez's Alfaguara prize in 1998 for *Margarita, está linda la mar* (Margarita, How Beautiful the Sea) "has it all . . . culture (Darío), politics (Somoza), and a kind of magical-realist exoticism, which includes 'personajes esperpénticos' [grotesque characters], wild twists of destiny, poetry, and delirium, all set, of course, in the far-off land on 'América en este siglo' [América in this century]" (ibid.).

21. English, *The Economy of Prestige*, 282.

22. Ann Laura Stoler, ed., *Haunted by Empire: Geographies of Intimacy in North American History* (Durham, NC: Duke University Press, 2006). Stoler elaborates that the parameters of being "haunted by empire," as the title of her edited anthology suggests, occasion "the familiar, strange, and unarticulated ways in which empire has appeared and disappeared from the intimate and public spaces of United States history; how relations of empire crash through and then recede from easy purview, sunder families, storm sequestered spaces, and indelibly permeate—or sometimes graze with only a scarred trace—in situations and the landscape of people's lives" (1). She explicates, "To haunt is 'to frequent, resort to, be familiar with,' to bear a threatening presence, to invisibly occupy, to take on a changing form. To be haunted is to reckon with such tactile powers and their intangibilities. To be haunted is to know that such forces are no less effective because of disagreement about their appropriate names" (ibid.). But as Díaz informed El País, his focus on the Trujillo dictatorship advances a counterhistory. Asked about this theme and how it has been "treated already by so many authors," Díaz had this to say: "It is true that it is a supersaturated subject. In the Dominican Republic, if you mention his name to a writer, she leaves running. Nobody wants another book on Trujillo. It seemed to me that after so much writing on the subject, something essential was missing. He is very strange. The problem is that the script that Trujillo's figure provides is so strong that if you write about him you inadvertently become his secretary. It even happened to [Mario] Vargas Llosa. As a novel, *The Feast of the Goat* is irreproachable, and still when I read it, it left a bad taste in my mouth, because I realized Trujillo would have loved it, because it perpetuates the myth. I try to interrupt the celebratory ritual. Trujillo's power is perpetuated in the histories that are written about him. My book tries to raise a counter-history" (Lago, "'EE.UU. tiene pesadillas en español,'" my translation).

23. Juan Flores, *The Diaspora Strikes Back: Caribeño Tales of Learning and Turning* (New York: Routledge, 2009). There are two points I wish to detail here. The first spells out Flores's use of "remigrants"; the second centers on translation and Latino narrators. For Flores, remigrants, or returning emigrant nationals from various countries, "bring cultural ideas and values acquired in diaspora settings to bear on their native lands or that of their forebears, often with boldly innovative and unsettling effect" (4). This "remigration" of Latino literary works—such as those by Sandra Cisneros, Nilo Cruz, and Díaz—in Spanish translation needs to be critically examined. How Latino difference is transmitted through a "fractured English" abridged to a standard Spanish that must be understood across national "Latin" borders must be scrutinized. How are Latino

and Latina urban and national alienation, sociopolitical, and cultural marginality, and multiracial coexistence conveyed in Spanish, particularly as these texts, written in English, mark the "perpetual foreignness" of certain ethnoracialized groups? Think about Díaz's *Drown*, whose translated title in Spanish became *Negocios* (1997). Gustavo Pérez Firmat's vital epigraph, which sets the stage for Díaz's short stories, has been omitted: "The fact that I / am writing to you / in English / already falsifies what I / wanted to tell you. / My subject: / how to explain to you that I / don't belong to English / though I belong nowhere else." Díaz's subjects linguistically dwell in English, even as this same language signals their U.S. "unbelongingness." This erasure reduces the national and cultural struggles that *Drown* communicates and simply houses *Negocios* in an "untroubled" Spanish. Curious about how Pérez Firmat's observations may read in Spanish, I translated this excerpt in the following manner: "El hecho de que / te estoy escribiendo / en inglés / ya falsifica lo que / quise decirte. / Mi asunto: / cómo explicarte que / no pertenezco al inglés / aunque no pertenezco a ninguna otra parte." The translation of these authors has implications for how Latinoness and Latinaness is understood in Latin America as well as Spain. Do these translations speak to recent migrations in a "Latinized" Spain? Might Latin American migrations in Spain engage with a "Latinidad" that may or may not have subaltern linkages with U.S. manifestations of Latinaness and Latinoness? Is there a cross-Atlantic Latinidad? And how can the complex ways that individuals respond to the said crises that heighten the sociopolitical identities and hierarchies that organize their being in relation to regional identity formations—often perceived, in the United States, across the North-South divide—be theorized from the perspective of Europe?

24. Ramírez, "La nueva novela latinoamericana."

25. Ramírez, "La nueva novela latinoamericana."

26. Ramírez, "La nueva novela latinoamericana."

27. Julie Greene, *The Canal Builders: Making America's Empire and the Panama Canal* (New York: Penguin Books, 2009), 7.

28. Frances Negrón-Muntaner, *Boricua Pop: Puerto Ricans and the Latinization of American Culture* (New York: New York University Press, 2004), 233.

29. Volpi, *El insomnio de Bolívar*, 27.

30. Arlene Dávila, *Culture Works: Space, Value, and Mobility across the Neoliberal Americas* (New York: New York University Press, 2012), 97.

31. Dávila, *Culture Works*, 95.

32. Dávila, *Culture Works*, 98, 99.

33. Dávila, *Culture Works*, 103.

34. Blas Falconer and Lorraine M. López, eds., *The Other Latin@: Writing Against a Singular Identity* (Tucson: University of Arizona Press, 2011), 3.

35. Arlene Dávila, *Latinos, Inc.: The Marketing and Making of a People* (Berkeley: University of California Press, 2001), 8.

36. Dávila, *Latinos, Inc.*, 6.

37. Kirsten Silva Gruesz, "Alien Speech, Incorporated: On the Cultural History of Spanish in the US," *American Literary History* 25, no. 1 (spring 2013): 19.

38. Antonia Darder, "The Politics of Language: An Introduction," *Latino Studies* 2 (2004): 233. Antonia Darder underscores that "the common practice of modern nation-states to racialize blatantly language minority populations within their own borders persists even today, particularly when such actions are judged by the dominant class to be in the interest of national security or economic well-being. More often than not, national assimilative policies to obtain and preserve cultural and class dominion over a nation's residents have relegated minority language speakers to a marginal existence. In order to insure that the 'Other' is kept in line with the system of production, racialized policies and practices have led to widespread deportation, incarceration, or extermination of immigrant and minority populations" (232). Consult Ana Celia Zentella for a rich perspective on "the fate and form of the languages spoken by US Latina/os" (26) and Latino/a unity. Ana Celia Zentella, "'Dime con quién hablas, y te dire quién eres': Linguistic (In)security and Latina/o Unity," in Juan Flores and Renato Rosaldo, eds., *A Companion to Latina/o Studies* (Malden, MA: Blackwell, 2007), 25–38.

39. "Iowa School to Offer Masters Degree in Creative Writing in Spanish," *Hispanically Speaking News*, November 9, 2011, accessed April 24, 2012, http://www.hispanically speakingnews.com/notitas-de-noticias/details/iowa-school-to-offer-masters-degree -in-creative-writing-in-spanish/11573.

40. Digital Humanities at the University of Iowa, "Iowa Literaria," n.d., accessed March 26, 2013, http://dsph.uiowa.edu/dhatiowa/node/56.

41. Digital Humanities at the University of Iowa, "Iowa Literaria."

42. Mark McGurl, *The Program Era: Postwar Fiction and the Rise of Creative Writing* (Cambridge, MA: Harvard University Press, 2009), 24.

43. McGurl, *The Program Era*, 31.

44. McGurl, *The Program Era*, 26.

45. José David Saldívar, *Trans-Americanity: Subaltern Modernities, Global Coloniality, and the Cultures of Greater Mexico* (Durham, NC: Duke University Press, 2012), 187. Saldívar elucidates: "I had always felt that Martí's comparative critiques of imperial América in the essays and chronicles of his *Escenas norteamericanas* (North American Scenes) were 'right on' and indispensable for any beginning attempt to theorize a new, critical reading of América. But as I also noted in my essay 'Las fronteras de Nuestra América,' a text superbly translated into Spanish and published in the *Revista Casa de las Américas* (1996), I often wonder why Martí's critical readings of 'Our América' and the 'America that is not ours' stopped, territorially, so prematurely and abruptly at the national borders between the Global North and the Global South. Why did he accept the political and cultural borders of the Treaty of Guadalupe Hidalgo of 1848, which had ended a US imperial war, this time with Mexico? What if Martí had thought of the borderlands of Greater Mexico—that is, both sides of the Rio Grande culturally going back to 1749, when parts of the US-Mexican border were first colonized by Spain?" (187).

46. Modernismo's timeline, 1888–1916, is debated broadly because it centers on the publication of Rubén Darío's *Azul* (1888) and ends with the year of his death (1916). This course does not mark modernismo per se, but what many have called "rubendarismo."

47. Jean Franco, *The Modern Culture of Latin America: Society and the Artist* (New York: Penguin, 1970), 26.

48. Franco, *The Modern Culture of Latin America*, 26.

49. Darío, *Azul*, 26.

50. Darío, *Azul*, 26.

51. Evelyn Nien-Ming Ch'ien, *Weird English* (Cambridge, MA: Harvard University Press, 2004), 15. Ch'ien indexes the following features as "instincts" that create weird English: "1. Weirding deprives English of its dominance and allows other languages to enjoy the same status; 2. Weird English expresses aesthetic adventurousness at the price of sacrificing rules; 3. Weird English is derived from nonnative English; 4. The rhythms and structure of orthodox English alone are not enough to express the diasporic cultures that speak it" (11). Restated: weird English is "the kind of language creation happening now—vernacular transcription that has a built-in self-consciousness of its political, social, and metaphorical implications, as well as aesthetic value" (18). Cultural producers of weird English "become conscious of language as a practice of their ethnicity" (20).

52. Achy Obejas, for example, has shared her first impressions on the monumental task that translating Díaz's *The Brief Wondrous Life of Oscar Wao* into Spanish would entail because of its "exuberant song to living on the hyphen, a mix of languages with a pop culture beat that references comics and science fiction, hip-hop and salsa, its characters possessed with a prodigious capacity for love." Achy Obejas, "Translating Junot: 'This Is How You Lose Her' by Junot Díaz," *Chicago Tribune*, September 14, 2012. That labor, she remarked, would prove challenging because the novel is "linguistically promiscuous: There are phrases in Creole, Japanese, even Urdu" (ibid.). Her immediate thought was "pity the poor sucker who has to translate that!" (ibid.). But she took up the job for *La breve y maravillosa vida de Óscar Wao*, telling readers that "the most daunting hurdle was the novel's herculean use of the F-word, that magical lexeme of profanity. Noun, verb, adjective—its versatility is unparalleled. And there's absolutely nothing that comes even close to it in Spanish. But thanks to Hollywood, most Latin Americans have not only heard the word but are quite familiar with its myriad meanings. I just had to make it sound like something that Junot's guys would say, and readers could relate to. Thus, 'fokin'" (ibid.).

53. Flores, *The Diaspora Strikes Back*.

54. Edward W. Said, *Reflections on Exile and Other Essays* (Cambridge, MA: Harvard University Press, 2000), xv.

55. Junot Díaz, *The Brief Wondrous Life of Oscar Wao* (New York: Riverhead Books, 2007), 264.

56. Kirsten Silva Gruesz, "What Was Latino Literature?" PMLA 127, no. 2 (March 2012): 339.

57. Díaz, *Oscar Wao*, 22.

58. Lago, "'EE.UU. tiene pesadillas en español'" (my translation).

59. Díaz, *Oscar Wao*, 92.

60. José David Saldívar, "Conjectures on 'Americanity' and Junot Díaz's 'Fukú Americanus' in *The Brief Wondrous Life of Oscar Wao*," *Global South* 5, no. 1 (spring 2011): 128.

61. Díaz, *Oscar Wao*, 21.

62. Beatriz Sarlo, *Jorge Luis Borges: A Writer on the Edge* (London: Verso, 1993), 6. She comments, "Placed on the limits between cultures, between literary genres, between languages, Borges is the writer of the *orillas*, a marginal in the centre, a cosmopolitan on the edge. He is someone who constructs his originality through quotations, copies and the rewritings of other texts, because from the outset he conceives of writing as reading, and from the outset distrusts any possibility of literary representation of reality" (6).

63. Díaz, *Oscar Wao*, 21.

64. Edwin Williamson, *Borges: A Life* (New York: Viking, 2004), viii.

65. Saldívar, "Conjectures on 'Americanity,'" 128.

66. Williamson, *Borges: A Life*, viii.

67. Williamson, *Borges: A Life*, viii.

68. Díaz, *Oscar Wao*, 2.

69. Paula M. L. Moya and Ramón Saldívar, "Fictions of the Trans-American Imaginary," *Modern Fiction Studies* 49, no. 1 (spring 2003): 2.

70. Moya and Saldívar, "Fictions of the Trans-American Imaginary," 2.

71. Moya and Saldívar, "Fictions of the Trans-American Imaginary," 2.

72. Moya and Saldívar, "Fictions of the Trans-American Imaginary," 5.

73. Moya and Saldívar, "Fictions of the Trans-American Imaginary," 2.

74. Ed Morales, *The Latin Beat: The Rhythms and Roots of Latin Music from Bossa Nova to Salsa and Beyond* (New York: Da Capo, 2003), xi.

75. Díaz, *Oscar Wao*, 7.

76. Saldívar, "Conjectures on 'Americanity,'" 121; Díaz, *Oscar Wao*, 1.

77. Díaz, *Oscar Wao*, 21.

78. Díaz, *Oscar Wao*, 5.

79. Díaz, *Oscar Wao*, 171.

80. Díaz, *Oscar Wao*, 171.

81. Díaz, *Oscar Wao*, 49.

82. Díaz, *Oscar Wao*, 49.

83. Díaz, *Oscar Wao*, 180.

84. Díaz, *Oscar Wao*, 180.

85. Díaz, *Oscar Wao*, 180.

86. Lago, "'EE.UU. tiene pesadillas en español.'" And this "wow," of course, brings about the literal incredulous interjection that was uttered by many upon Díaz's being awarded the Pulitzer. This wow underwent different forms across the Anglophone and Hispanophone worlds, as Ramírez's op-ed suggests and as Winston Manrique Saboga, an *El País* columnist, announced in the piece entitled "El alma hispana del inglés" ("The Hispanic Soul of English"). Manrique Sabogal's outlook contrasts with Ramírez's. For Manrique Sabogal, writers with "last names like Cisneros, Alarcón, Alvarez, Mestre, Sellers-García, Quiñonez, Hijuelos, Plascencia, Santiago, Manrique, Diaz, Jáuregui, and Goldman" craft a "narrative structure, sensitivities, and conception of life [that] is usually in Spanish." Winston Manrique Sabogal, "El alma hispana del ingles," *El País*,

June 7, 2008 (my translation). U.S. Latino writing is understood in linguistic terms of either/or. Most striking is the label that Manrique Sabogal exercises for this U.S. population. He christens Latinos as "latinogringos," in effect, as one subject. Claudio Iván Remeseira classifies Latinos somewhat similarly, but alters the category with a hyphen—"Latino-gringo"—a dualism that paradoxically accentuates foreignness more than U.S. Americanness. Remeseira's observation about Latinos vis-à-vis Alarcón's work reads thus: "A clear example of the Latino-gringo identity created by the immigration waves of the past decades, Daniel Alarcón is an ideal candidate to lead this project" (Remeseira).

87. Morrissey, *Autobiography* (New York: Putnam, 2013), 98.

88. Barbara Chai, "Junot Díaz Studies Heartbreak for 'This Is How You Lose Her,'" *Wall Street Journal*, May 29, 2012, accessed May 30, 2012, http://blogs.wsj.com/speakeasy /2012/05/29/junot-diaz-studies-heartbreak-for-new-book/. The cover of *Newsweek* from July 12, 1999, can be reintroduced in this equation. There, Díaz, alongside Colombian singer-songwriter Shakira and Oscar de la Hoya, the now retired professional Mexican American boxer, were featured on newsstands with the headline: "Latin U.S.A.: How Young Hispanics Are Changing America." Díaz donned a red *guayabera* for this mass media arrival of a U.S. Latino literary figure—bringing to mind a different and global celebration: Gabriel García Márquez's wearing of a traditional white guayabera when he accepted the 1982 Nobel Prize in Literature. The garb of choice imprints a Latin American and Latino literary identity. Marilyn Miller reveals that the guayabera "has arguably come to represent Latin American identity more thoroughly than any other garment in the American hemisphere." Marilyn Miller, "Guayaberismo and the Essence of Cool," *The Latin American Fashion Reader* (Oxford: Berg Publishers, 2005), 214. "The symbolic weight of the guayabera is surprising," she continues, "since it's just a shirt, after all. Nor is it an especially elaborate, technically complex, or exaggerated garment that takes weeks or even months to weave, sew, or construct, as is the case with Latin American fashion markers ranging from the indigenous *huipil* woven in highland Guatemala, to a Carmen Miranda hat" (ibid). But the guayabera "takes on special significance in its relationship to revolutionary struggles, an association that extends not only into the [Fidel] Castro years in Cuba, but also into socialist or left-leaning political struggles elsewhere in Latin America, to the extent that from the 1960s on, it was de rigueur to see other world leaders from the Americas appear at public events in a guayabera" (215). While there have been statements about the shirt's "status as *pasada de moda*" (217), its entry into these bookish ceremonies, with Díaz and García Márquez *enguayaberados*, gives prominence to key revolutionary moments bound by a Latin "literary style."

89. Keith Haring, *Keith Haring Journals* (New York: Penguin, 2010), 96.

90. Oscar Wilde, *De Profundis* (New York: Dover, 2011), 50.

8. Dictating a Zafa

The Power of Narrative Form as Ruin-Reading

Jennifer Harford Vargas

In his incisive *Boston Review* article, "Apocalypse: What Disasters Reveal," Junot Díaz meditates on the meaning of the earthquake that devastated Haiti in January 2010, deeming the earthquake an apocalypse. Explaining that *apocalypse* comes from the Greek word *apocalypsis*, which means "to uncover and unveil," Díaz argues that an apocalypse "is a disruptive event that provokes revelation."[1] As a revelatory event, an apocalypse uncovers the underlying hierarchies of power and forms of inequality and oppression that are too often veiled or disavowed. Catastrophe gives us the opportunity to be what Díaz calls "ruin-readers" or interpreters of the underlying structures and conditions that enable or bring about an apocalypse. "We must," he charges, "stare into the ruins—bravely, resolutely—and we must see. And then we must act." This chapter meditates on what it means to be a ruin-reader and how constructing critical narratives about apocalypses is a socially symbolic act that functions as a means of both seeing and acting. Dictatorship is a type of apocalypse, and Junot Díaz's novel *The Brief Wondrous Life of Oscar Wao* (2007) functions as a form of ruin-reading that reveals the abuses of Rafael Trujillo's authoritarian regime and its haunting afterlife. Yet, to effectively read (and write) the revelations in the ruins necessitates accounting for the problematic politics of narrative power and authority.

Reflecting creatively in 1967 on the production of his novel El señor presidente (1946), Miguel Ángel Asturias creates an imaginary scenario in which the dictator declares to the novelist that he, not the writer, is the real author of the novel because "toda dictadura es siempre una novela [every dictatorship is always a novel]."[2] With this self-authorizing claim, the dictator wrestles power from the author by declaring himself the supreme meaning maker. While the dictator—or, more accurately, the dictatorship—trumps the novelist in Asturias's text, a footnote in The Brief Wondrous Life of Oscar Wao expounds: "Rushdie claims that tyrants and scribblers are natural antagonists, but I think that's too simple; it lets writers off pretty easy. Dictators, in my opinion, just know competition when they see it. Same with writers. Like, after all, recognizes like."[3] Much as Asturias's dictator sees the novelist as his competitor, Díaz's footnote recognizes the slippery similarities between dictators and writers: they are both narrative makers and narrative controllers. The dictator and the novelist create metanarratives and produce meaning. They are fabulous inventors and can make the unbelievable believable. They also control subjects and exercise their authority through words to dictate their subjects' or characters' actions and thoughts.[4]

Establishing a similitude between writers and dictators, The Brief Wondrous Life of Oscar Wao grapples with how to circumnavigate authoritarianism—that is, the precarious link between authorship, authority, and authoritarianism. The novel plays on the tensions between the two definitions of "to dictate": on the one hand, to order or command authoritatively and absolutely and, on the other hand, to speak aloud words that are to be written down or transcribed. There are two types of competing dictators at the center of The Brief Wondrous Life of Oscar Wao: the political dictator (Rafael Trujillo) who rules over the subjects of his regime and the narrative dictator (Yunior) who retrospectively recounts the novel's events. As the primary narrator and storyteller, Yunior loosely functions as a dictator in both senses because he controls and orders representation and because he collects, writes down, and reshapes a plethora of oral stories that have been recounted to him.

Through the novel Yunior chronicles the life of Oscar de León, an obese Dominican American growing up as a social outcast in New Jersey from the mid-1970s to the mid-1990s. Oscar is obsessed with women and with what he calls the "more speculative Genres," meaning science fiction, fantasy, and comic books.[5] The book's middle sections center on the lives of Oscar's mother Hypatía Belicia Cabral ("Beli") and his grandfather Abelard Cabral in the Dominican Republic under the dictatorship of Rafael Trujillo. Yunior pieces together Abelard's, Beli's, and Oscar's lives through oral interviews, historical research, snooping in Oscar's journals, and a bit of imaginative re-creation. In doing so he recounts the family's sufferings under a transgenerational cycle of violence rife with references to apocalypse and disaster: Abelard is imprisoned and tortured purportedly for refusing to hand over his beautiful eldest daughter for Trujillo's sexual pleasure but more likely for his "Chiste Apocalyptus" that turns him into a victim of "The Fall"; Beli, the "Child of the Apocalypse," is beaten nearly to death in a cane field for having an affair with the Gangster, the husband of Trujillo's sister; and Oscar, the "Ghetto Nerd at the End of the World," is killed in a cane field for falling fatally in love with Ybón, a woman with "snarled, apocalyptic hair," who is the girlfriend of the capitán, a policeman in the post-Trujillato Dominican Republic.[6]

Yunior opens the book's preface by giving an apocalyptic origin story for the cursed fate of the de León and Cabral family:

> They say it came first from Africa, carried in the screams of the enslaved; that it was the death bane of the Tainos, uttered just as one world perished and another began; that it was a demon drawn into Creation through the nightmare door that was cracked open in the Antilles. Fukú americanus, or more colloquially, fukú—generally a curse or a doom of some kind; specifically the Curse and the Doom of the New World. . . . [I]t is believed that the arrival of the Europeans on Hispaniola unleashed the fukú on the world, and we've all been in the shit ever since. Santo Domingo might be the fukú's Kilometer Zero, its port of entry, but we are all of us its children, whether we know it or not.[7]

The fukú serves as a local folk hermeneutic for reading relations of domination in the Americas more generally and in the novel specifically. The result of colonization, slavery, and the eradication of indigenous peoples, the fukú "ain't just ancient history, a ghost story from the past with no power to scare," Yunior explains ominously.[8] Under the thirty-year reign of the "dictator-for-life Rafael Leónidas Trujillo Molina," the fukú "was real as shit" and to this day continues to haunt "its children" across the Dominican diaspora.[9] Interlocking Spanish colonialism, Trujillo's dictatorial regime, and Oscar's temporally and geographically distanced story, the fukú operates as a symbolic chronotope for the ruination of domination. The Trujillato is a crystallization of one violent epoch in a five-hundred-year apocalyptic saga of the New World whose modes of oppression are continually regenerating and transforming. The fukú—or the *fukú americanity*, as José David Saldívar appropriately terms it—thus generates an intersectional analysis of dictatorship that inserts it within the *longue durée* of the "coloniality of power" in the Americas.[10] The fukú foundational fiction that Yunior narrates establishes a trans-American community through an act of imagined identification across forms of domination, spaces of colonial and neocolonial violence, and histories of subalternization. It also offers an explanatory paradigm for the novel's events based on a folk history of coloniality and the hemispheric (the "Great American Doom") and personal apocalypses (the "Doom of the Cabrals") it engenders.[11]

Yunior imagines a way out of this Américan curse of violent domination via another folk belief in the ability to ward off a curse, positing resistance to the fukú as the novel's other central governing politic. He explains: "Anytime a fukú reared its many heads there was only one way to prevent disaster from coiling around you, only one surefire counterspell that would keep you and your family safe. Not surprisingly, it was a word. A simple word (followed usually by a vigorous crossing of index fingers). Zafa. . . . . Even now as I write these words I wonder if this book ain't a zafa of sorts. My very own counterspell."[12] Based on the Spanish verb *zafar*, meaning *soltar algo* ("to let go of" or "to release from") or *liberarse de un una molestia* ("to escape from" or "to liberate one's self from harm"), zafa is represented in the novel as a form of protection that enacts a liberatory function through the oral word combined with the physical action. Yunior transvaluates the power of the spoken word into the power of storytelling by envisioning the zafa as a speech act that occurs through his hand's narratorial act. That is, Yunior imagines that writing "this book," which is the text of the novel he narrates, is a zafa, a counterspell, a trans-American counter-dictatorial act.

Yunior takes a complex history of power hierarchies with dire structural, material, physical, and psychic effects and metaphorizes it as the fukú; by creating a narrative encapsulation of oppressive power, he creates a way to respond through another metaphor: the zafa. The novel thus stages a conflict between the fukú and the zafa—between dictating as a totalitarian act and dictating as a decolonial act. The two organizing symbolic principles embody the dual signification of dictating as dominating (the fukú) and dictating as recounting or writing back (the zafa). Yunior's self-proclaimed narrative zafa places him in competition with the novel's most salient incarnation of the fukú: the dictator Rafael Trujillo. Yunior's capacity to produce a narrative zafa is predicated on his ability to be a Janus-like narrator, since his challenge is to critique dictatorial power without reproducing it in his own text. Yet, due to "the decisive influence that the discourses of power have in constituting the discourses of resistance," Yunior is partially over-determined by what he is critiquing.[13] I argue that the novel mitigates this problematic formally. Examining the novel's narrative structure, I articulate how the text successfully negotiates between being complicit with and re-sisting authoritarian discourses and structures of power.

The zafa in *The Brief Wondrous Life of Oscar Wao*, then, is not Yunior's "book" per se but the narrative techniques and formal structures in the book that enact a mode of ruin-reading, which reveal the apocalypse of authoritarian power and interrogate repressive forms of power that dictate marginalization. In particular, the zafa functions through the character-system and through modes of narration. I first explicate how the novel structurally marginalizes and parodies the dictator and centralizes socially marginalized characters to challenge authoritarian power and hegemonic discourses. I subsequently demonstrate how the novel mobilizes underground storytelling modes—specifically hearsay, footnotes, and silences—to formally represent and con-test the dissemination and repression of information under dictatorship. I ultimately argue that the novel's so-called zafa against oppressive domination is performed and enacted through the counter-dictatorial form in which the story is told. I end by contextualizing *The Brief Wondrous Life of Oscar Wao* within a set of contemporary Latino/a novels that I contend narrate the apocalyptic ruins of dictatorships in the Americas. These novels collectively generate what I term a Latino/a counter-dictatorial imaginary that unveils various intersecting sociohistorical systems of domination in the hemisphere.

The Dictator as Minor Character

A fundamental component of the novel's zafa is the text's representation of Trujillo and his thirty-year dictatorship (1930–61) over the Dominican Re-public. In *The Brief Wondrous Life of Oscar Wao*, the historical subject with the most power, the dictator Trujillo, is a minor, flat character whose represen-tation is mediated by the narrator Yunior and the author Junot Díaz. The novel orders Trujillo as a minor character in the text's temporal and geo-graphic crisscrossing and prevents him from focalizing the narrative. A dic-tator who is a minor character and who is represented by other characters seems oxymoronic because a subordinate narrative position runs counter to the dominant position a dictator occupies in the political structure. In order to understand the importance of the subordination of Trujillo within the novel's narrative structure, I start with the premise that the narrative structures that allocate space and focalize perspective in a novel are structures of power. In other words, the uneven distribution of characters and perspectives in a novel can be analyzed as a system of power hierarchies.

The paradigm of dictatorship has its structural basis in the one dictator against the many subjects of the regime, making the novelistic tension between one protagonist and many minor characters particularly significant for a novel about dictatorship. In *The One vs. the Many: Minor Characters and the Space of the Protagonist in the Novel*, Alex Woloch cogently articulates the dialectics of narrative form and social power through an examination of the system of characterization. Woloch observes that novels are constructed around a "distributional matrix," meaning that "the discrete representation of any specific individual is intertwined with the narrative's continual apportioning of attention to different characters who jostle for limited space within the same fictive universe."[14] He terms "character-space" the relationship between an individual character's personality and that character's position within a narrative structure, while "character-system" is the various arrangements of these character-spaces in a narrative's overall structure. The asymmetrical configuration of major round characters and minor flat characters in a novel, Woloch argues, "reflects actual structures of inequitable distribution."[15] A social configuration of hierarchies of power is realized in narrative form, which for Woloch is evident in the unequal distribution of attention to and the distorted stylistic representation of characters.

If we consider Woloch's work in terms of other Latin American novels about dictatorship, we notice that the dictator's character-space dominates the character-system of seminal novels like Augusto Roa Bastos's *Yo el supremo* [*I the Supreme*] (1974) and Gabriel García Márquez's *El otoño del patriarca* [*The Autumn of the Patriarch*] (1975). These novels' fictional worlds are organized around the eponymous Supreme/Patriarch, and the narrative perspective and action are principally mediated through and constructed around the dictator who is both the primary protagonist and antagonist. This narrative structure centered on and through the dictator creates an inequitable distribution of power and voice similar to the hierarchy of power that exists under dictatorship. This argument does not assume that the dictator's position is stable or left uncontested within these narratives (it certainly is not), only that the dictator's positioning is important because different formal structures differently limit or enable particular kinds of interrogations of power.

The tension between major and minor characters, then, crystallizes a real world socioeconomic tension at the socioformal level of the novel in its organization and representation of characters. Yet, what happens when sociopolitical and socioeconomic "structures of inequitable distribution" are *not* reproduced structurally within the text to reflect their actual structuring in the real world? How do we understand power differentials in a novel like *The Brief Wondrous Life of Oscar Wao* that displaces the dictator from the center of the narrative and redistributes attention to those subjects at the bottom of the hierarchy or at the margins of power? By moving away from the presidential palace and outside of the dictator's head, *The Brief Wondrous Life of Oscar Wao* exchanges a dictator-centric character-system for a character-system centered on marginalized subjects. Díaz's novel thus alters the correlation in the character-system between character-space, socioeconomic status, and sociopolitical power. This modification of sociopolitical positions of power in the socioformal character-system of the novel enables *The Brief Wondrous Life of Oscar Wao* to interrogate the relations of domination enacted by the Trujillato.

Yunior's narratorial control over the dictator's representation and his manipulation of Trujillo's signification produce the text's critique of the Trujillato and its transnational, transgenerational specter in the present. Trujillo is an overwhelmingly absent presence, a kind of backstage character who is continually invoked and described but whose appearance on stage is extremely brief in relation to his overall manifestation in the narrative. In terms of the plot's fictional events (its story) Trujillo is a minor character who does not occupy much narrative space. Trujillo does not materialize as a character in the plot until page 221 of the 335-page novel; as a minor character, he only appears four brief times and in just two of these appearances does he actually speak. In contrast to his marginalization in the story and the character-system, Trujillo has a major and pervasive presence in the text's language, structure, and mode of narrating (its discourse). Less a fully realized fictional character, Trujillo is more of a symbol of dictatorial power and violence with an ominous, haunting presence. The omnipresent traces of the Trujillato that run through the novel imitate the inescapable dominance of the fukú while the text zafas Trujillo through its discursive representation of the dictator.

Trujillo's construction in the novel's discourse occurs principally through Yunior's multitudinous, vivid, and often iconoclastic characterizations of him. The real, historical Trujillo acquired over one hundred honorific titles during his reign. Title-granting was part of the regime's institutionalized pomp and its forging of a discourse of sanctified leadership, patriarchal protection, national unity, self-determination, and economic progress to legitimate itself.[16] Yunior signifies on these titles, creating an alternative set of titles for Trujillo. Yunior demeans him by calling him the "Failed Cattle Thief," "Fuckface," "Mr. Friday the Thirteenth," and the "Dictating-est Dictator who ever Dictated."[17] Putting him down and parodying him with praise, Yunior draws on preexisting epithets such as "Your Excellency" and "Your Enormity" and blasphemously employs Trujillo's nickname "El Jefe" throughout the novel. He satirically praises the Trujillato as "the first modern kleptocracy," gesturing toward the vast amounts of wealth and lives stolen from the Dominican people.[18] He even creates new and bilingually witty words to name Trujillo's abuses, deeming his regime, for example, "the world's first culocracy."[19] He hilariously mocks Trujillo as the "consummate culocrat," crowns him "Number-One Bellaco" for his infamously rogue playboy tactics, and scathingly condemns his sexual exploitation of women.[20] The epithets construct Trujillo as a figure who metonymically stands in for both dictatorship and heteropatriarchal power, satirically positioning him as the first and the best in a series of oppressive leaders in world history.

Overall, the accumulation of names and descriptions offer a set of alternative significations for the regime that highlight the regime's abuses instead of effacing them as Trujillo's historical epithets did. Yunior's *falta de respeto*, or lack of respect, for Trujillo deliberately breaks cultural and linguistic norms of respect for those in power at the same time that it fashions a resistant discursive repertoire vis-à-vis heteropatriarchal dictatorship. The humorously biting wordplay—alongside the footnoted historical references and the overlaid fantasy and science fiction allusions—fashions a discourse about the leader and his regime that is subversively humorous and linguistically capacious. The many *zafadas de lengua*, or zafa-like slips of the tongue, that Yunior uses freely and riotously throughout the novel destabilize rigidly controlled boundaries. Yunior's creative ability to signify on and talk back to power with parodic irony and with total sincerity shapes the book's style, which uses humor as a means of critical meaning-making and as a relief from the weight of oppressive relations.

Doubly made minor in the narrative hierarchy of power, Trujillo is relegated to the position of a minor character in the novel's plot at the same time that he is minoritized as a footnote in the novel's structure. Comparing his representation in the footnotes and the main text, Trujillo is referenced more frequently and described more elaborately and at greater length in the footnotes. In fact, Trujillo is initially introduced to the reader in the novel's first and quite lengthy footnote; and he, his "minions," and the violence of his regime appear in three-fourths of the novel's footnotes.[21] The positioning of Trujillo within the footnotes lowers Trujillo literally on the page. This structural move mirrors the way Yunior deflates Trujillo linguistically.

The overall structure of flatness and humorous minorness produces the novel's counter-dictatorial mode of narration. As a flat minor character, Trujillo is often the butt of the joke (he is, after all, a "culocrat") and the referent of Yunior's parody and expletives. Abstracting from this reveals that Trujillo is an object of reference in the narrative. Trujillo is not an omniscient narrator or a major character who directly produces meaning in the text. Meaning is mainly produced about him, not by him. This loss of narrative power runs counter to the definition the literary critic Juan Carlos García gives of dictators represented in the Latin American novel: the dictator is "él que da ordenes y él que crea. Esto lo aproxima a un ser entidad todopoderoso" [he who gives orders and he who creates. This approximates him to an all-powerful entity].[22] In The Brief Wondrous Life of Oscar Wao, Trujillo does not create and order like an omnipotent being; rather, he is created by and ordered through Yunior's descriptions.[23] Because he is not the origin of nor in control over the production of meaning and action in the text, Trujillo does not function as a dictator in the novel. Instead, he functions for the narrative discourse.[24] The novel formally counters, or zafas, Trujillo's power through its marginalization and functionalization of the dictator.

These narrative techniques also reinforce the novel's positioning of the dictatorship within various interlocking modes of domination. The novel suggests that the perpetration of violence is not caused solely by Trujillo's authoritarian political regime but by the five-hundred-year fukú americanus. This move first denies Trujillo the power of having a totalizing impact on the development of the story's events; second and more important, it turns Trujillo into a mediating figure of transhistorical modes of domination. Just as Trujillo is not an agent who directly produces meaning in the text, he is not the origin of oppression but one figure, though admittedly a very prominent and brutal one, whose rule upholds and extends the coloniality of power. A figure embedded in an entrenched structure of domination, the dictator is a crystallization of one violent epoch in a five-hundred-year trans-American saga. The novel thereby disavows the mistaken assumption that dictatorships are exceptional regimes and that subjects will be totally free once dictatorships are toppled.

Lola's condemnatory response to her brother's brutal murder over three decades after the death of Trujillo is perhaps the most telling and insightful analysis of power in the novel. "Ten million Trujillos is all we are," declares Lola.[25] Lola's denunciation implies that the responsibility for dictatorial relations of domination and social violence must be distributed more widely, that is, among the "ten million Trujillos" in the Dominican Republic and the United States. This allocation of accountability is reflected structurally in the novel's displacement of Trujillo within the overall character-system; its frequent denunciatory and exposé-like footnotes about high-ranking officials in the regime; its utilization of minor dictator characters like the Gangster, el capitán, and even Yunior; and its multigenerational, transnational narrative arc. Moreover, Lola's use of Trujillo's name as a communal proper noun highlights how subjects are complicit in the systems of power that govern them. Her use of the shared "we" not only implicates everyone, including Lola herself, for internalizing oppression and perpetuating marginality; it also asserts that collective responsibility must be assumed since a people—not a single figure of power—bears the blame for past and present acts of domination, whether they are perpetrated by political regimes or discursive regimes.

A Marginalized Hero

The Brief Wondrous Life of Oscar Wao frames its meditation on authoritarian power through Oscar de León, a marginalized and atypical Latino growing up in the United States after the Trujillo regime's official collapse. Tracing the fukú americanus through the de León and Cabral family, the novel's structure suggests that understanding Oscar's life requires a transgenerational family story and a trans-American history, just as understanding Trujillo's regime requires remembering the colonial past and recognizing contemporary dictatorial relations. Based on the lives of subjects who are traditionally deemed too insignificant as well as too temporally and spatially removed from "major" events, the novel positions Oscar's life at the social margins within a cyclical family history of violent subordination, making his marginalization a node through which various relations of domination overlap and are interrogated.

The cane field in which Beli nearly dies and Oscar does die serves as a chronotope for the family's experience of repression and as the time-space for the reenactment of intersecting oppressions. The cane field is a primal site where violence is perpetrated against black subjects: slaves, Haitian laborers, Dominican subjects (Beli), and transnational subjects (Oscar). "Plunged 180 years into rolling fields of cane," Beli is taken into the cane fields and "beat[en] . . . like she was a slave. Like she was a dog."[26] Beli's beating in 1962 establishes a similitude between physical repressions of black subjects across time and space. Going back 180 years positions the cane field in approximately the year 1782, during the time period of slavery and right before the beginning stirrings of the Haitian Revolution. Slaves were subject to the condition Orlando Patterson describes as "social death," which includes violent beatings, illiteracy, the lack of control over sexuality, and the denial of parental and filial birth ties in what he terms "natal alienation." It is not mere coincidence that Beli is a very dark-skinned Dominican woman who is nearly killed in a cane field for her romantic relationship or that she slips unconscious into "a loneliness that obliterated all memory, the loneliness of a childhood where she'd not even had her own name . . . alone, black, fea, scratching at the dust with a stick, pretending that the scribble was letters, words, names."[27] Moreover, the scar that covers Beli's back, the result of the burning she receives living parentless in Outer Azua, is "as vast and inconsolable as a sea," and with "her bra slung around her waist like a torn sail," it evokes a slave ship in the Middle Passage.[28] The novel does not imply that being subjected to slavery or economic servitude is the same as being subjected to dictatorship or heteropatriarchal domination, but it does establish intersectional resonances between the violence enacted upon Beli and Oscar and the slaves and laborers in the cane fields. Later, in 1995, when Oscar is beaten in the cane fields, the "world seemed strangely familiar to him; he had an overwhelming feeling that he'd been in this very place, a long time ago."[29] Ambiguous about precisely how long ago a "long time ago" is, the description evokes both his mother's experience and his enslaved ancestors' experiences.

The temporal ambiguity gestures toward the cyclical structure of events in the plot and the residual temporality of dictatorship. As Raymond Williams advises, "It is necessary at every point to recognize the complex interrelations between movements and tendencies both within and beyond a specific and effective dominance."[30] To understand a present hegemony, Williams maintains, we cannot focus solely on its features in the present but must look at its ever-changing contours through a dynamic process-oriented analysis. Díaz's novel enacts such a contextualized analysis vis-à-vis its characterization of Oscar's post-Trujillato death, which highlights what Williams would call the "residual" effects of slavery, colonialism, and dictatorship, because elements produced in the past continue their impact actively in the present. The "circumstances directly found, given, and transmitted from the past," to invoke Karl Marx, "weigh like a nightmare" on Oscar's life.[31] Oscar intuits this before his death, evident when in relation to his own suicide attempt he professes: "It was the curse that made me do it."[32] Disavowing Oscar's interpretation, Yunior exclaims, "I don't believe in that shit, Oscar. That's our parents' shit."[33] Undaunted, Oscar retorts, "It's ours too."[34] Inheriting his family's past and the bane of the fukú, Oscar astutely recognizes that his life is overdetermined by the long apocalyptic history of colonization, imperialism, and dictatorship in the Americas.

Oscar's claim on the curse and the effects of its inheritance on him are also revealing in relation to his own position in the novel's character-system. Given the novel's title and his status as the "hero," Oscar is surprisingly absent for most of the novel.[35] Oscar's absence, however, directly enables the presence of other family members—Lola, Beli, La Inca, and Abelard—who become major characters.[36] The partition of character-space among various main characters in the family reinforces on the level of the character-system the transgenerational vision undergirding Oscar's claim.

Not only does Oscar's "brief" life become part of a series of lives that together trace trans-American relations of domination, his "wondrous" life as a marginalized and atypical hero also becomes part and parcel of the novel's critique of dictatorial relations, be they political, social, or discursive. I suggest that the novel uses Oscar's abnormality and his nonnormative body to challenge authoritarian power and normative discourses and to draw a link between both forms of domination. The novel introduces Oscar as a kind of aberrant Dominican male and, thereby, an aberrant Dominican hero. The first chapter, "Ghetto Nerd at the End of the World," begins: "Our hero was not one of those Dominican cats everybody's always going on about—he wasn't no home-run hitter or a fly bachatero, not a playboy with a million hots on his jock. And except for one period early in his life, dude never had much luck with the females (how *very* un-Dominican of him)."[37] According to Yunior, as well as the conventions of Latino fiction, Oscar is not a typical

Dominican character or main protagonist. Oscar's overall characterization as un-Dominican in the novel is tied to four main characteristics: sexuality, body type, race, and culture. As a nerdy, overweight, dark-skinned Afro-Dominican fluent in the fantastic genres but illiterate in the game of sex, Oscar "couldn't have passed for Normal if he wanted to" as he fails to be a "Normal" (i.e., socially acceptable) Dominican male subject.[38] Establishing difference and anomaly over norms and stereotypes, the novel begins in the negative tense highlighting what Oscar is not, and maintains this technique of exaggerating differences throughout.

Oscar's nonnormativity serves as a vehicle for the novel's interrogation of the norms, discourses, and hierarchies of power that dictate marginalization and oppression. To mobilize Rosemarie Garland-Thomson's term, Oscar's "extraordinary body" is located at the bottom of what she characterizes as "accepted hierarchies of embodiment."[39] Black, Latino, fat, effeminate, poor, and a nerd, Oscar is multiply marginalized. Relegated to the social and economic margins, Oscar suffers ridicule and rejection throughout his life; yet, in stark contrast to his social ostracism, Oscar is the novel's titular hero and his life frames the novel. This privileged status calls into question both Oscar's social subalternization and the discourses that produce it.[40]

The novel centralizes the marginalized character of Oscar and marginalizes the dictator as a minor character. The demotion of the figure of power, Trujillo, and the elevation of the figure of marginality, Oscar, work contrapuntally in structuring a critique of dictatorial power and the dictates of heteropatriarchy and white supremacy. Trujillo is figured as the excessive embodiment of traditional Dominican masculinity, while Oscar is depicted as sorely inadequate according to these heteropatriarchal ideals. Trujillo is obsessed with whitening his skin, while Oscar is ridiculed for being a dark-skinned Afro-Dominican who does not corporeally embody the ideals of white supremacy. Using the latter extreme to interrogate the former extreme, the novel breaks down, or zafas, these hierarchies. Calling the dictatorial authority of the norm into question through the elevation and exaggeration of difference, Oscar's framing centrality is a key counter-dictatorial narrative strategy that works through characterization in the sense both of narrative description and distribution of attention.

Far from rejecting Oscar for being a "sci-fi-reading nerd," the novel places Oscar and his beloved genres, which are traditionally considered low cultural forms, at the very center of its narrative stylistics.[41] The novel harnesses the speculative and boundary-pushing genres of fantasy, science fiction, comic books, and marvelous realism to communicate the magnitude of dictatorial atrocities. The multigeneric modes of representation are epistemic as well as aesthetic, for they explore the hermeneutics used to comprehend absolute power. Each imaginative mode contributes one interpretive lens or set of critical references that differently decipher dictatorial political systems and authoritarian discourses in the Caribbean and the United States. Oscar's nonnormativity and reading list contribute to his life-long social marginalization but, when privileged within the novel, they serve instead as vehicles of critical interrogation.

Underground Storytelling

The Brief Wondrous Life of Oscar Wao also employs folk orality, paratextual footnotes, and blank pages to critique dictatorial relations. Subjects living under repressive regimes must either risk under-the-radar signifying and coded circumlocution or remain silent. Yunior mobilizes oral sources, footnotes, and silences to mimic the dissemination and repression of information under dictatorship and to dictate a story against dictatorship without being dictatorial.

Yunior recounts his story through a wide variety of named and unnamed oral sources, thereby forging an oral, hearsay hermeneutic that functions as a narrative structuring principle and as a means for reading dictatorial power. Yunior's style of narration frequently reflects this oral transcription, highlighting how sources have dictated their stories to him and how he has pieced his narrative together out of the stories he has gathered. The novel's narrative construction is situated in an oral chain of communication through which the anonymous folk of the Dominican community tell their fukú "tales," beginning on the novel's first page with what "they say" about the origin of their bane of domination.[42] A series of such phrases are interspersed throughout the text, signaling the narrative's embedment in orally circulating information. The novel's hearsay structure is subtle, most heavily signaled through phrases indicating the secondhand acquisition of information: it was said, it was believed, there are those alive who claim, it was rumored, legend has it, it was whispered, etc.[43] These and other phrases appear alongside occasionally specified sources of information such as Beli, La Inca, Lola, Yunior's mother, Yunior's girlfriend Leonie, etc. The anonymous sources of information predominate the novel's vernacular aesthetics and, importantly, references to these sources appear most often in the sections that recount life under the Trujillo dictatorship. Despite the fact that Yunior is not present throughout most of Oscar's life and, therefore, has learned much of Oscar's life story secondhand—the same way he hears about Beli's and Abelard's lives—the Oscar sections are rarely narrated in a manner that foregrounds Yunior's sources. In contrast, the sections set under the Trujillato rely on phrases that highlight that Yunior has acquired information secondhand and thirdhand. Though Yunior's style of narration generally has a first-person limited omniscient tone, his more frequent pauses to disclose the name of a source or signal an unnamed oral source in the sections of the novel set under the Trujillato imply that the events narrated about that time period are much more pieced together than those sections that deal with Oscar's brief life.

If, as James Scott has cogently demonstrated in *Domination and the Arts of Resistance*, "the process of domination generates a hegemonic public conduct and a backstage discourse consisting of what cannot be spoken in the face of power," then it is essential to take seriously the contextual significance of the anonymous storytellers.[44] I posit that this stylistic contrast is directly tied to the novel's representation of the effects of the conditions of dictatorship on the formal level of the text. Not by chance does Yunior keep the opinions, hearsay, and versions of events he gathers at the level of anonymity ("they say," for example) and indirection ("it is said," for instance). Such grammatical constructions, rendered in passive voice without a specific subject of the sentence, protect sources' identities at the same time that they register the dictatorship's effects on patterns of communication. Dominicans avoid direct speech and sometimes even speaking out at all because any dissent against or perceived discontent with the Trujillato could very quickly result in incarceration, torture, and even death. Yunior relates, "You could say a bad thing about El Jefe at eight-forty in the morning and before the clock struck ten you'd be in the Cuarenta having a cattleprod shoved up your ass . . . Mad folks went out in that manner, betrayed by those they considered their panas, by members of their own families, *by slips of the tongue*."[45] This description of the network of informants, and the resulting danger of verbally expressing discontentment, reveals how Dominicans had to resort to coded narratives. Below the surface of the phrases marking oral history, the anonymous speakers' experiences of negotiating domination under the Trujillato are present and continue to haunt their patterns of speech postdictatorship.

The paratextual apparatus of the footnotes also symbolically concretizes in narrative form covert styles of communicating. Thirty-three footnotes of varying length run throughout *The Brief Wondrous Life of Oscar Wao*.[46] The book's main text is double-spaced while all of the footnotes are single-spaced and written in smaller font. Though the footnotes run the length of the novel, thirty out of the thirty-three footnotes are found in the sections about Trujillo's regime.[47] As we saw with the references to a larger source community, the conglomeration of the footnotes in the sections set during the Trujillato takes on particular significance.

The footnotes are also important for our discussion of domination and narrative form because they play out power relations structurally within the text. As has been argued by critics who examine the paratext of the footnote in fictional novels, footnotes are, in their placement and form, "minor elements" that "are inherently marginal, not incorporated into the text but appended to it."[48] Footnotes are located literally at the bottom of the page and structurally at the bottom of the textual hierarchy, below the main text and peripheral to the primary or dominant storyline. While footnotes are at the "margin of the discourse," as Shari Benstock characterizes them, their secondary relationship is complicated in Díaz's novel because the subordinate footnotes are central to *The Brief Wondrous Life of Oscar Wao*.[49] The footnotes establish another set of commentaries and sequence of events that are below and subordinated to but also central to and constitutive of the main text.

Functioning as examples of what Scott calls "hidden transcripts" that enact "a critique of power spoken behind the back of the dominant," the footnotes evade the limitations imposed on narrative development much in the same way that a dissenting subject rhetorically evades and subverts power through indirection.[50] As marginalia, the footnotes appear below the main narrative, visually resembling forms of undercover storytelling. That is, the footnotes structurally mimic the ways subaltern agents navigate repressive power by communicating information indirectly, secretly, and below the radar of the repressive regime's gaze. The spatiality of the notational apparatus in *The Brief Wondrous Life of Oscar Wao* reproduces the asides and interruptions that constitute oral narrative, for oral narratives do not strictly follow one single line of thought, often veering into associative connections and tangential stories that build an interrelated network of details and substories around the primary story. Similarly, Díaz's footnotes contain digressions that provide important tangential information and generate other plot networks. This de-centers the main narrative, which does not follow a single, direct line but multiple ones instead. To borrow Kevin Jackson's captivating description, the footnotes "explode upwards into the soft black-and-white underbelly of the main text on contact with the reader's gaze."[51] The explosive and clandestine power of footnotes is heightened in a novel about dictatorship since dictatorship is intent on repressing subversive agency. The under-the-narrative footnotes in Díaz's novel function as underground oral storytelling modes to formally critique dictatorial relations and dictatorial narratives.

The single-spaced footnotes and double-spaced main text also cause the novel's structure to resemble that of an academic book. In traditional academic usage, footnotes establish authority, acting as the supportive and evidentiary structure. Yunior draws on the epistemic weight granted footnotes in scholarly convention to insert multiple kinds of sources into his fictional footnotes. The footnotes reference a report available in the JFK Presidential Library and cite historians, novelists, and even Yunior's girlfriend and mother, not to mention many science fiction and fantasy texts. The footnotes do not privilege academic sources over personal, let alone fictional, ones and instead gesture toward multiple perspectives on the Trujillato, which is especially important given the univocal, monological nature of dictatorship. Serving as a creative mode of chronicling the Trujillato's abuses and as a "critical appendage," many of the footnotes expose the dictatorship's atrocities as well as interject a more extensive vision of oppression in the Americas.[52] In the first footnote, Yunior gives a long list of the Trujillato's "outstanding accomplishments," designating the regime "one of the longest, most damaging US-backed dictatorships in the Western Hemisphere (and if we Latin types are skillful at anything it's tolerating US-backed dictators, so you know this was a hard earned victory, the chilenos and argentinos are still appealing)."[53] The comical discourse of victory belies a serious articulation of the violence of the Trujillato and the collusion of the United States in supporting authoritarian regimes in the hemisphere. The first of many such footnotes, the aside provides a metanarrative that connects Dominican history to the history of Latin America and the United States, which is especially important given the geopolitics of knowledge production in the United States that subalternizes, or footnotes, so to speak, Latino American histories. The footnotes write dictatorship back into Latino/a and Anglo-American historical and literary imaginaries, imparting a decolonial history of the violence caused by U.S. interventionism in the hemisphere.

Such a history, though, must account for how conditions of domination create erasures that can never be fully recuperated. The novel opens up the question of how to engage in historical recovery given the sometimes insurmountable challenges to recovering a violently repressed and disappeared past. *The Brief Wondrous Life of Oscar Wao* materializes these absences textually in its narrative form. The many gaps and silences in the novel create a multileveled portrayal of the effects of dictatorial power on information networks and oral histories. Most evident through the trope of the "páginas en blanco," Yunior cannot fill in these so-called blank pages due to a lack of complete information. Absent information in the novel is the result of several factors: it has simply not been recorded or spoken about; it has been repressed because people are afraid to speak or are silenced; it has been distorted because narratives about the past have been changed; it has been destroyed because the Trujillato burned the documents; and it has been lost because texts have disappeared. The novel generates a complex textual representation of silence through these various blank spaces in circulating and noncirculating information.

Working in conjunction with the text's oral and footnote structures, the silences give formal shape and thematic space to the habitus of people living under the pressures of dictatorship and what Yunior calls the "Chivato Nation."[54] The field of dictatorship conditions a subject's linguistic habitus. By describing the nation as a chivato, or snitch, the novel demonstrates that the Dominican people, functioning as a network of informants, enact and enforce the dictatorship. When Abelard, for example, talks with his best friend Marcus about his fear of following Trujillo's order for Abelard to bring Trujillo his daughter, he "waxed indignant to Marcus for nearly an hour about the injustice, about the hopelessness of it all (an amazing amount of circumlocution because he never once directly named who it was he was complaining about)."[55] Conditioned into silent deference to Trujillo, Abelard runs a grave risk with his under-the-radar signifying and coded circumlocution. This restrictive conditioning has long-term effects, evident in the "Source Wall" that prevents Yunior from acquiring accurate or complete information years later.[56] As Yunior explains, "Due partially to Beli's silence on the matter and to other folks' lingering unease when it comes to talking about the regime, info on the Gangster is fragmented."[57] Yunior's reliance on oral sources in the present is affected by the residual influence of the dictatorship on the production of contemporary oral stories. Impediment and fragmentation highlight how information has been distorted or erased and how the specter of dictatorship continues to shape the way survivors and their kin pass on oral histories.

In relation to what really causes Abelard's imprisonment and the subsequent vanishing of all of his books and papers, Yunior declares:

> So which was it? you ask. An accident, a conspiracy, or a fukú? The only answer I can give you is the least satisfying: you'll have to decide for yourself. What's certain is that *nothing's certain. We are trawling in silences here.* Trujillo and Company didn't leave a paper trail—they didn't share their German contemporaries' lust for documentation. And it's not like the fukú itself would leave a memoir or anything. The remaining Cabrals ain't much help, either; on all matters related to Abelard's imprisonment and to the subsequent destruction of the clan there is within the family *a silence that stands monument* to the generations, that *sphinxes all attempts at narrative reconstruction.* A whisper here and there but nothing more to say. Which is to say *if you're looking for a full story, I don't have it.*"[58]

In "trawling" the past for information, Yunior catches more silence than he does information. Full access to and knowledge of what truly occurred in the past is impossible because people have been silenced and information has been disappeared. Yunior explains that he relates "what I've managed to unearth and the rest you will have to wait for the day the páginas en blanco finally speak," keeping the integrity of the silences in his narrative.[59] Ironically, though, the blank pages do speak, for they "stand monument" to the abusive horrors of the dictatorship, functioning as testifying silences. The novel simultaneously foregrounds these absent presences and provides a narrative space in which repressed stories can be dictated and chronicled in the archive of fiction.

Moving beyond silence into speech and text is, for the oppressed, a liberatory act, but that act must also recognize the silence within its own production. Neither author nor narrator can produce a story that lays claim to full and complete meaning because doing so would produce a dictatorial story. Having a story but not "a full story," as Yunior implies, is the most accurate and effective story you can have under dictatorship and against dictatorship. Creating a counter-dictatorial narrative or a so-called zafa against domination, the novel suggests, necessitates a plurality of possibilities that are precisely impossible under dictatorship, for a dictatorship is univocal and does not allow multiple referents or traces of meaning to exist. It seeks to stabilize and control all meaning and action. In fact, Abelard is imprisoned when his darkly comical signifying "trunk-joke" about there being no bodies in the trunk of his car as he tries to put a bureau in his trunk is taken literally and distorted into a directly stated critique of Trujillo, as opposed to the indirect, implied reference it was.[60] The Trujillato cuts down the double-layered ambiguity of Abelard's statement, restricting what it signifies. In literary terms, dictatorships require an *authoritarian narrative*—that is, an authoritative narrative that is closed, controlled, and unitary, composed by an author whose word is sacrosanct and infallible.

Far from an objective observer in the positivist sense, from omniscient in the narratorial sense, and from panoptic in the disciplinarian sense, Yunior foregrounds the knowledge that is both available and unavailable from his social location as he constructs his narrative zafa. By keeping meaning multivalent and by continually interrogating narrative authority, Yunior dictates a narrative that is orally based but not authoritative. Yunior draws attention to the absent, partial, and sometimes inaccurate information on which his narrative is built, hence his comments about the silence that "sphinxes" his "attempts at narrative reconstruction" and his stated disregard for historical accuracy.[61] Yunior consistently foregrounds what he does not know, exclaiming "Who can say?" and "shit, who can keep track of what's true and what's false in a country as baká as ours," declaring to the reader "you'll have to decide for yourself."[62] Offering uncertainty, silence, self-referential critiques, and a bit of humor as antidotes to dictatorial fixity, the text pointedly disavows certainty and definitive closure. The novel's refusal to offer definitive explanations and its general destabilization of textual authority allow for multiple conclusions and generate multifarious readings as it refuses to fix interpretation or present an infallible account of events. Rife with ambiguity, the novel dictates without dictating; that is, it tells a story without fixing that story monologically.

The open-endedness of meaning, which subverts the dictatorial desire for total control and fixity, exists all the way through the last page of the novel. Deceptively, the novel's conclusion is not only in its last line—Oscar's affirmation, "The beauty!"—but also in the panel Oscar repeatedly circles from the graphic novel *The Watchmen*, which cautions, "Nothing ends, Adrian. Nothing ever ends."[63] Though the novel literally ends with the next and last chapter titled "The Final Letter," nothing is truly resolved, for the zafa against the familial and hemispheric fukú americanus remains unfinished.

The Latino/a Counter-Dictatorial Imaginary

Ultimately, Yunior's zafa fantasy of narrative justice does not offer a permanent resolution to the problem of dictatorship or to the curse of coloniality. It is just a fantasy, for violence and impunity continue to overdetermine lives all over the Americas. Yet, it is precisely the power of the imagination to express antiauthoritarian longings that makes the dictatorship novel an enduring and compelling form and an apt generic tradition for *The Brief Wondrous Life of Oscar Wao*.

The dictatorship novel is considered one of Latin America's oldest, most widely produced, and prominent genres.[64] Yet, to fully understand the dictatorship novel, I contend, we must look beyond the geopolitical boundaries of Latin America as well as the linguistic boundaries of Spanish and follow the genre's forking paths into the United States and the English language productions of Latino/a writers such as Junot Díaz. In the past two decades a new generation of U.S.-based Caribbean, Central American, South American, and Mexican American authors are producing a wide range of novels in English about authoritarian regimes in Latin America that are also rooted in U.S. experiences of Latinidad. We can thus contextualize Junot Díaz's *The Brief Wondrous Life of Oscar Wao* within an emerging corpus of Latino/a dictatorship novels such as Francisco Goldman's *The Long Night of White Chickens* (1992), Graciela Limón's *In Search of Bernabé* (1993), Julia Alvarez's *In the Time of the Butterflies* (1994), Demetria Martínez's *Mother Tongue* (1994), Héctor Tobar's *The Tattooed Solider* (1998), Loida Maritza Pérez's *Geographies of Home* (1999), Sandra Benítez's *The Weight of All Things* (2001), Angie Cruz's *Let it Rain Coffee* (2005), Daniel Alarcón's *Lost City Radio* (2007), Sylvia Sellers-García's *When the Ground Turns in Its Sleep* (2007), Carolina De Robertis's *The Invisible Mountain* (2009), and Cristina García's *King of Cuba* (2013). While these Latino/a dictatorship novels grapple with differing local and national histories—moving between New Jersey and the Dominican Republic, Massachusetts and Guatemala, Miami and Cuba, New Mexico and El Salvador, New York and Peru, among other sites—they are all haunted by the specter of authoritarian regimes.[65] Often the children of those who lived under and fled repressive regimes, many of the novels' characters (like Oscar and Lola) and indeed the writers themselves (like Junot Díaz) have not directly experienced dictatorship. The novels give narrative space to second-generation perspectives as they grapple with dictatorships and the afterlives of these regimes in Latin America and the United States. The residues of authoritarian pasts are thus marking Latino/a fiction across national origin groups, generating a pan-Latino/a and trans-American dictatorship novel tradition.[66]

The Brief Wondrous Life of Oscar Wao and its counterpart Latino/a dictatorship novels collectively reconceptualize dictatorial power by constructing intersectional analyses of authoritarianism, imperialism, heteropatriarchy, and racism in the hemisphere. Connecting and contesting various forms of power that dictate marginalization in the Americas, these novels construct what I term a Latino/a counter-dictatorial imaginary. The trans-American imaginary, as articulated by Paula M. L. Moya and Ramón Saldívar, is an experiential field through which authors imagine and forge transnational symbolic representations that serve as important forms of meaning-making. The novel is one expressive mode through which Latinos/as imagine transnational identities and experiences marked by dictatorship, for writers use fiction and its world-making possibilities to understand and even reconfigure political and discursive hierarchies of power in the Americas. By examining the politics of narrative strategies in *The Brief Wondrous Life of Oscar Wao*, such as the demotion of Trujillo and elevation of Oscar in the character-system and the imitation of underground storytelling modes, I have traced some of the formal contours of Díaz's counter-dictatorial imaginary and how it formally functions as a counter-dictatorial zafa.

As socially symbolic acts, Latino/a dictatorship novels like *The Brief Wondrous Life of Oscar Wao* interrogate transnational modes of domination and attempt to imagine an ending to authoritarian power in its myriad configurations and manifestations. Junot Díaz and his Latino/a counterparts are continuing the long tradition of dictatorship novels that fan the spark of hope for an end to authoritarianism, for the appearance of the disappeared in the archives of fiction and history, and for justice for the oppressed.[67] In a Gramscian moment marked by pessimism of the intellect and optimism of the will and of the imagination, Díaz concludes his remarks on apocalypses and ruin-reading by declaring, "Truth be told, I'm not very optimistic. I mean, just look at us. No, I'm not optimistic—but that doesn't mean I don't have hope. . . . Yes, I have hope."[68]

In thematizing and formalizing the process of decolonizing relations of domination through the fukú-zafa dialectic, *The Brief Wondrous Life of Oscar Wao* opens up a dialogue about how to rebuild, on both an individual and a communal level, in a postdictatorship future haunted by past trauma and mired in persistent present inequalities. *The Brief Wondrous Life of Oscar Wao* dictates a story against dictatorship without dictating the successful ends of its critique. In this sense, the story must remain unfinished. For decolonial ruin-reading is a continual and necessary process as long as the coloniality of power, and the dictatorial structures and norms it perpetuates, remain. *The Brief Wondrous Life of Oscar Wao*, then, is not just a zafa. It is a zafaing.

Notes

1. Junot Díaz, "Apocalypse: What Disasters Reveal," *Boston Review*, May 1, 2011, accessed April 22, 2015, http://www.bostonreview.net/junot-diaz-apocalypse-haiti-earthquake.

2. Miguel Ángel Asturias, "El señor presidente como mito," *El señor presidente: Edición crítica*, ed. Gerald Martin (Barcelona: Galaxia Gutenberg, 2000), 470. This and all subsequent translations are mine.

3. Junot Díaz, *The Brief Wondrous Life of Oscar Wao* (New York: Riverhead Books, 2007), 97.

4. Latin American novelists have frequently explored the relationship between narrative creation and dictatorial control by figuring the dictator as a writer. The Chicano author Salvador Plascencia, in contrast, makes the writer a dictator in his novel *The People of Paper* (2005). The novel figures the writer as a dictator who omnipotently rules over his characters' life stories, omnisciently reads their thoughts, and materially profits off his novelistic representations of them. In rebellion, his fictional creations stage a coup against the very author of the novel in which they appear, waging "one of the greatest wars against tyranny . . . a war against the future of this story." The novel displaces political conflict onto symbolic terrain as the characters attempt to topple the author and dictator of their world. Salvador Plascencia, *The People of Paper* (San Francisco: McSweeney's, 2005), 46.

5. Díaz, *Oscar Wao*, 43.

6. Díaz, *Oscar Wao*, 233, 235, 251, 11, 279. Also of note is the novel's hurricane trope, which both signals and uncovers disaster. Anacanoa, the Taino warrior-woman, tells the Spaniards to "kiss my hurricane ass"; the Trujillato disappears political prisoners "as victims of the hurricane"; Beli falls in love with a wealthy boy who has a "hurricane whorl" in his crew-cut hair; Lola survives the "urikán" of rape and has premonitions that "hit with the force of a hurricane"; and a hurricane-like wind blasts away the stalks of cane to reveal a nearly dead Oscar so that Clives can rescue him.

7. Díaz, *Oscar Wao*, 1–2.

8. Díaz, *Oscar Wao*, 2.

9. Díaz, *Oscar Wao*, 2.

10. See José David Saldívar, "Conjectures on 'Americanity' and Junot Díaz's 'Fukú Americanus' in *The Brief Wondrous Life of Oscar Wao*," *Global South* 5, no. 1 (spring 2011): 120–36. According to scholars such as José David Saldívar, Aníbal Quijano, Walter Mignolo, and Maria Lugones, "modernity/coloniality" is a world-system that came into being in the sixteenth century during the colonization of the Americas. Coloniality, they argue, is constitutive of modernity, its dark underside; Americanity is the form coloniality takes in the Americas. The coloniality of power enacts domination and

exploitation through the creation and imposition of hierarchical classifications of race, labor, and capitalist modes of production, as well as gender relations.

11. Díaz, *Oscar Wao*, 5, 143.

12. Díaz, *Oscar Wao*, 6–7.

13. Mabel Moraña, Enrique Dussel, and Carlos A. Jáuregui, "Colonialism and Its Replicants," in Mabel Moraña, Enrique Dussel, and Carlos A. Jáuregui, eds., *Coloniality at Large: Latin America and the Postcolonial Debate* (Durham, NC: Duke University Press, 2008), 19.

14. Alex Woloch, *The One vs. The Many: Minor Characters and the Space of the Protagonist in the Novel* (Princeton, NJ: Princeton University Press, 2003), 13.

15. Woloch, *The One vs. The Many*, 31.

16. See Derby and López-Calvo for insightful analyses of Trujillo's titles and the "vernacular politics" the regime used to justify its reign (Derby, 7). Ignacio López-Calvo, *God and Trujillo: Literacy and Cultural Representations of the Dominican Dictator* (Gainesville: University Press of Florida, 2005), and Lauren Derby, *The Dictator's Seduction: Politics and the Popular Imagination in the Era of Trujillo* (Durham, NC: Duke University Press, 2009).

17. Díaz, *Oscar Wao*, 2, 214, 217, 155, 216, 225, 80.

18. Díaz, *Oscar Wao*, 3.

19. Díaz, *Oscar Wao*, 217. *Culo* means "ass" and the suffixes *-cracy* and *-crat* denote a form of government and a member of government respectively, so the humorous bilingual neologisms *culocracy* and *culocrat* (or "asscracy" and "asscrat") indicate a regime ruled by hypermasculine sexuality.

20. Díaz, *Oscar Wao*, 154, 217.

21. Díaz, *Oscar Wao*, 12.

22. Juan Carlos García, *El dictador en la literatura hispanoamericana* (Chile: Mosquito Comunicaciones, 2000), 27.

23. To put it in Monica Hanna's vivid terms, the novel stages a "historiographic battle royal" between Yunior's and Trujillo's different "historiographic models" (504).

24. Trujillo's loss of power on a symbolic level is not equated with a total loss of political power since Trujillo's presence is ever palpable and his regime permanently fractures the de Léon and Cabral family. Rather, the novel takes away Trujillo's power as the supreme narrative maker.

25. Díaz, *Oscar Wao*, 324.

26. Díaz, *Oscar Wao*, 146, 147.

27. Díaz, *Oscar Wao*, 148.

28. Díaz, *Oscar Wao*, 51.

29. Díaz, *Oscar Wao*, 298.

30. Raymond Williams, *Marxism and Literature* (New York: Oxford University Press, 1977), 122.

31. Karl Marx, "The Eighteenth Brumaire of Louis Bonaparte," in Robert C. Tucker, ed., *The Marx-Engels Reader* (New York: W. W. Norton, 1978), 595.

32. Díaz, *Oscar Wao*, 194.

33. Díaz, *Oscar Wao*, 194.

34. Díaz, *Oscar Wao*, 194.

35. Díaz, *Oscar Wao*, 11.

36. In fact, Lola's narrative initiates both chapters that take place under the Trujillato. As La Inca begins to reveal to Lola what happened to her mother and grandfather, Lola remarks, "She was about to say something and I was waiting for whatever she was going to tell me. I was waiting to begin." Díaz, *Oscar Wao*, 75. With these words Lola's narrative ends and the chapter about Beli's life under the Trujillato begins. Lola's choice of words is important. She does not say, "I was waiting for *her* to begin" but "I was waiting *to* begin" as if she herself will only begin as a subject with the story of her family history. Lola comes into a being as a subject transgenerationally through connecting to her family's past and, like Oscar, she is moored to that past.

37. Díaz, *Oscar Wao*, 11.

38. Díaz, *Oscar Wao*, 21.

39. Rosemary Garland-Thomson, *Extraordinary Bodies* (New York: Columbia University Press, 1997), 7.

40. Elena Machado Sáez argues that Yunior is a dictator in the text because he narrates "a foundational fiction about Oscar's progression from inauthentic diasporic male to an assimilated, unsentimental un-virgin" (538) and thereby silences "Oscar's points of queer Otherness" and suppresses hints of a "homosocial romance" between Yunior and Oscar (524). Elena Machado Sáez, "Dictating Desire, Dictating Diaspora: Junot Díaz's *The Brief Wondrous Life of Oscar Wao* as Foundational Romance," *Contemporary Literature* 52, no. 3 (2011): 522–55. Yunior the character certainly exhibits authoritarian tendencies as he criticizes and seeks to discipline Oscar into the prototypical Dominican male, but an additional reading arises when we foreground the formal features of the novel. I highlight Trujillo's demoted and Oscar's elevated positions within the novel's character-system, and I contend that parody and exaggeration are key critical modes in the novel, whether they are used to deflate and denigrate Trujillo or subtly criticize Oscar's social marginalization.

41. Díaz, *Oscar Wao*, 19.

42. Díaz, *Oscar Wao*, 5, 1.

43. See several of the varying uses of *to say* (1, 107, 120, 141, 241, 154, 251), *to believe* (3, 17, 83, 111, 125, 151, 243, 226), *to claim* (139, 248), *rumors* (78, 91, 106, 110, 120, 121, 145, 255, 266), *legends* (97, 155, 212), *whispers* (80, 245, 226), *secrets* (99, 217, 227, 245), etc.

44. James C. Scott, *Domination and the Arts of Resistance: Hidden Transcripts* (New Haven, CT: Yale University Press, 1990), xii.

45. Díaz, *Oscar Wao*, 225–26 (emphasis mine).

46. This is a significant number if we think of Oscar as a martyr figure who died young. It is additionally compelling if we consider the number's signification of truth and the triumph of good, which resonates with Yunior's declaration to craft a zafa against the fukú and my argument that the zafa occurs through the form in which in the story is told.

47. This includes the prologue, which deals heavily with the Trujillato; thus, only three footnotes are found in the sections dealing with Oscar's life.

48. Kevin Jackson, *Invisible Forms: A Guide to Literary Curiosities* (New York: St. Martin's, 2000), xvii; Shari Benstock, "At the Margin of Discourse: Footnotes in the Fictional Text," PMLA 98, no. 2 (1983): 204.

49. Benstock, "At the Margin of Discourse," 204.

50. Scott, *Domination and the Arts of Resistance*, xii.

51. Jackson, *Invisible Forms*, 140.

52. Benstock, "At the Margin of Discourse," 204.

53. Díaz, *Oscar Wao*, 2–3.

54. Díaz, *Oscar Wao*, 2–3.

55. Díaz, *Oscar Wao*, 229.

56. Díaz, *Oscar Wao*, 149.

57. Díaz, *Oscar Wao*, 119.

58. Díaz, *Oscar Wao*, 243 (emphasis mine).

59. Díaz, *Oscar Wao*, 119.

60. Díaz, *Oscar Wao*, 234.

61. Díaz, *Oscar Wao*, 243, 132.

62. Díaz, *Oscar Wao*, 22, 139, 243.

63. Díaz, *Oscar Wao*, 335, 331.

64. Latin Americanists consistently begin their genealogies of the tradition with Domingo Faustino Sarmiento's deeply influential work of creative nonfiction *Facundo: Civilización y barbarie* (1845), while early works such as José Mármol's *Amalia* (1851), Ramón del Valle-Inclán's *El tirano banderas* (1926), Miguel Ángel Asturias's *El señor presidente* (1946), and Enrique Lafourcade's *La fiesta del rey Acab* (1959) helped shape the tradition until the mid-1970s, when the so-called Boom generation of writers produced an iconic group of novels: Augusto Roa Bastos's *Yo el supremo* (1974), Alejo Carpentier's *El recurso del método* (1974), and Gabriel García Márquez's *El otoño del patriarca* (1975). The tradition has flourished in subsequent decades, in particular due to the creative production of writers such as Luisa Valenzuela, Diamela Eltit, Cristina Peri Rossi, Ariel Dorfman, and Roberto Bolaño.

65. I use the term *dictatorship novel* instead of *dictator novel* to categorize these Latino/a texts because doing so moves the focus away from a single figure of power toward the various regimes of domination running through the fiction. There is no terminological consensus among Latin Americanists, but most critics use *la novela del dictador* ("the dictator novel") or *la novela de la dictadura* ("the dictatorship novel"), though Carlos Pacheco prefers *la narrativa de la dictadura* ("the dictatorship narrative") and Julio Calviño Iglesias employs *la novela del dictador y del poder personal* ("the dictator and personal power novel"). Of the critics publishing in English, Ignacio López-Calvo uses *the novel of the dictator*, Roberto González Echevarría *the dictator-book* and *the dictator-novel*, and Raymond Leslie Williams *the dictator novel* and *the novel of dictatorship*.

66. Latin American scholarship on dictatorship and postdictatorship aesthetic production has focused predominantly on a single nation or a particular region, in

particular the Southern Cone, Hispaniola, and Central America. For example, Idelber Avelar, Macarena Gómez-Barris, Sophia McClennen, Diana Taylor, and editors Nelly Richard and Alberto Moreiras all focus on the Southern Cone (in particular on Chile and Argentina). Caribbean scholars such as Lauren Derby, Ignacio López-Calvo, and editors Marta Caminero-Santangelo and Roy Boland Osegueda focus on the Dominican Republic and Haiti. Scholars such as Laura J. Craft, Ana Patricia Rodríguez, Ileana Rodríguez, and María Josefina Saldaña-Portillo focus on Central America (in particular on Nicaragua, El Salvador, and Guatemala). I contend that reading Latino/a novels across different national and regional traditions reveals a broader Latino/a dictatorship novel tradition.

67. As Ramón Saldívar eloquently puts it with regard to what he terms its mode of "historical fantasy" ("Historical Fantasy," 585), *The Brief Wondrous Life of Oscar Wao* "indicates desires for forms of social belonging that link the realm of public political life to the mysterious workings of the heart's fantastical aspirations for substantive justice, social, racial, poetic, or otherwise" (596).

68. Díaz, "Apocalypse."

Part III

Doing Race in Spanglish

9. Dismantling the Master's House
The Decolonial Literary Imaginations of Audre Lorde and Junot Díaz
Paula M. L. Moya

> I urge each one of us here to reach down into that deep place of knowledge inside herself and touch that terror and loathing of any difference that lives there. See whose face it wears.
>
> —Audre Lorde, "Master's Tools"

In this essay, I read the Pulitzer Prize–winning Dominican American author Junot Díaz alongside the black, lesbian, feminist poet and essayist Audre Lorde to highlight his indebtedness to a feminist tradition of decolonial thinking about identity. This tradition is shaped by the theorizing that took place in the 1980s and 1990s under the conceptual framework of "women of color feminism," and that developed a historically unprecedented understanding of race, class, gender, and sexuality as mutually constituting and consequential aspects of identity. To many, reading Diaz with Lorde might seem like an odd move. Currently, Díaz is as mainstream as Lorde is marginal. Díaz's literary star is in ascendance with his receipt in October 2012 of a MacArthur Genius Fellowship, the nomination of his collection *This Is How You Lose Her* (October 2012) for the National Book Award, and the publication of a tantalizing excerpt from his latest novel in progress, *Monstro*, in the special Science Fiction issue of *The New Yorker* (June 2012). Erudite in the ways of the literary intelligentsia (but also street smart), hip (but unabashedly nerdy), and well versed in genre-blending twenty-first-century eclecticism, Díaz would seem, on the surface, to have little in common with the kind of protest feminism associated with women of color such as Lorde. Lorde's theoretical insights, by contrast, have lately been neglected within literary criticism, consigned by many literary scholars to the dustbin of recent history as an exemplar of the kind of "identity politics" they are grateful to move beyond.[1]

Yet there is a cost, I contend, to turning away from the insights about identity given to us by women of color writers.[2] It is a cost paid with a pervasive sense of anxiety about the relevance of our discipline and a loss of methodological focus. Turning away from identity has meant turning away from an acknowledgment of what literature does best—which is to provide us access to the thoughts, feelings, experiences, and stories of implied persons, those "others" whose fictional lives challenge, provoke, amuse, and inform our own. Literature and its interpretation have always pointed back around to ourselves, and to the meaning humans make out of our situatedness in the world. Incorporating into one's critical methodology a nuanced and trained awareness of the epistemic consequences of identity, I argue, is a necessary aspect of interpreting *all* works of literature—and especially those works written by an author whose perspective is substantially different from, or challenging to, one's own. This is why tracing Diaz's indebtedness to this tradition of thinking about identity functions as a dual intervention, allowing us to contextualize Díaz as a writer and thinker while also recognizing the ongoing relevance, scope, and reach of the writings of women of color.

In what follows, I trace the continuity between Diaz's fiction and the writings of late twentieth-century women of color writers to claim him as a writer who is thinking in a complex, materialist way about the dynamics of racial identity. I focus on Díaz's short story "How to Date a Browngirl, Blackgirl, Whitegirl, or Halfie" because the story has a tight focus on the character of Yunior, and especially on Yunior's attitudes about racialized gender. I begin by laying out key features of women of color feminist theory—with Lorde as the exemplary figure—in order to limn Díaz's indebtedness to the set of schemas they developed collectively during the 1980s and early 1990s. I then highlight, through a close reading of "How to Date," the corrosive effects of the racial self-hatred that remains a notable legacy of European co-lonialism for people of color in the Americas. My readings of both Díaz and Lorde account for the epistemic consequences of identity and the shaping power of the multiple cultural and historical contexts in which they write. My point is to show that—for all their temporal, generic, stylistic, gender, and sexual differences—Díaz and Lorde are engaged in complementary critical and imaginative projects. Such a decolonial recalibration of intellectual and literary history allows us to appreciate the continuing relevance of women of color theory and to recognize Diaz's contribution to the ongoing theorizations of race and intersectionality in our contemporary, so-called postrace moment.[3]

Bearing Witness to Ourselves

Audre Lorde was one of a group of nonwhite women writers (many of whom identified as lesbian) who came of age in the United States during a time of intense political activism around three issues that most activists saw as separate political concerns: race, gender, and sexuality. What distinguishes these women from the activists who advocated on behalf of a single issue is that the former came to understand—as a result of their daily lived experience and their political involvement with feminist, lesbian and gay, antiwar, antipoverty, and antiracist social movements—that such purportedly separate vectors of oppression were in fact mutually constituted. Over time, they found that male-run nationalist movements, white-run feminist organizations, and lesbian separatist groups of whatever race or ethnicity were not conducive either to their personal liberation or to significant social change. As a result, in the late 1970s, women such as Gloria Anzaldúa, Maxine Baca Zinn, Toni Cade Bambara, Joy Harjo, bell hooks, Cherríe Moraga, Aurora Levins Morales, Rosario Morales, Maria Lugones, Barbara Smith, Juanita Ramos, Bernice Johnson Reagon, Nellie Wong, Merle Woo, Mitsuye Yamada, and Lorde (among others) began to share ideas about what it meant to be nonwhite women living, loving, and working in late twentieth-century America. In the process, they developed—alongside specific group identities such as "Chicana feminist," or "black feminist" or "Asian American feminist"—the political identity of "women of color," as well as a distinct theoretical framework and practice associated with the same.[4] Not only did women of color forever alter the trajectory of critical thinking about the dynamics of social inequality, they also remain at the forefront of thinking about how the mutual constitution of race, gender, class, and sexuality affects a person's experience of his or her most intimate self.

Although the women of color who were writing from the late 1970s through the mid-1990s only occasionally set out in academic fashion the features of what others and I recognize as "women of color theory," those features are nevertheless remarkably consistent across a wide range of writers. At its heart is a conviction regarding the knowledge-generating significance of identity. Beyond that are three fundamental features: a central thesis regarding the multiplicity of identity, a specific conception of the human self as embodied and embedded, and a guiding ethos regarding the necessity of sustained and brutally honest self-examination.

First, the central thesis is what, following the literary critic Michael Hames-García, I call the multiplicity thesis.[5] The basic idea is that human identity is multiple—it is raced, gendered, sexed, and classed, all at once. It follows from this that any analysis of a person's relation to society must take into account all of these aspects as intermeshing, constitutive aspects of her self.

Second, women of color forged a conception of the human self as embodied and as embedded within a complex web of overlapping systems of social relations. The human self as figured by women of color signals a rejection of the Western, neoliberal, individual subject that first splits and then privileges mind over body, the spiritual over the material, white over black, and male over female. It is a self that moves through the world as a thinking body with weight, shape, color, and texture; it is a creative entity that cognizes abstract concepts and feels pain and pleasure, while also loving, hungering, eating, and excreting.[6] And while an understanding of the self as an embodied, thinking, feeling being may no longer be revelatory in light of recent neurological studies asserting the same, it is worth noting that women of color figured the self as such in the decades *preceding* the scientific studies that made this idea consecrated knowledge (e.g., Damasio). Finally, the woman-of-color self does not come into being as an autonomous, agential, individual bearer of personal attributes; she is highly interdependent and constituted through her interactions with other selves and with institutionalized ideologies of race, gender, and sexuality.[7]

Third, women of color share a guiding ethos that is readily apparent in the performative nature of their writings. This ethos involves the imperative to undertake difficult and sustained self-examination in the service of personal and social change. At the core of the impulse women of color have toward brutal self-examination is a trenchant understanding of the way their self-concepts have been negatively shaped by the social structures in which they live. As persons who were multiply positioned as "outsiders" to a putative and idealized "norm" (commonly understood in U.S. society to be a propertied, able-bodied, heterosexual European man), women of color comprehended that a close examination of their personal experiences with, and intimate feelings about, those aspects of themselves that caused them to be positioned as outsiders could provide important information about the complex way our society is organized.[8] Accordingly, in their essays, stories, and novels, women of color frequently perform the ceremonies required for their own healing. Sometimes that healing is thematized, as in Leslie Marmon Silko's novel *Ceremony*, Joy Harjo's poem, "I Give You Back," or Toni Cade Bambara's novel *The Salt Eaters*. Other times it emerges over the course of the story or essay as the author simultaneously describes and performs the actions required for healing the wounds inflicted by the racism, classism, sexism, and homophobia to which they are subjected. This is the case with Lorde's, "Eye to Eye: Black Women, Hatred, and Anger," to which I turn as an illustrative example.[9] The essay discovers, describes, and analyzes the anger that is manifest in relationships between black women, but it is also a painful working-through of the destructive effects that racism and sexism had on Lorde's self-concept. Finally, it is an instructive narrative example of an intentional journey toward self-acceptance and self-love.

Lorde begins "Eye to Eye" by acknowledging the power of the "Black woman's anger" that is unleashed "most tellingly against another Black woman at the least excuse."[10] According to Lorde, this anger has its "root cause" in "hatred, that societal death wish," that she faces as a result of having been "born Black and female in America."[11] She notes that black women are not the source of her anger, merely its most frequent recipients. Having made this observation, she then asks two questions, the answers to which require the kind of self-examination implied by the guiding ethos of women of color: "Why do I judge [another Black woman] in a more critical light than any other, becoming enraged when she does not measure up? And if behind the object of my attack should lie the face of my own self, unaccepted, then what could possibly quench a fire fueled by such reciprocating passions?"[12] Answering these two questions required Lorde to scrutinize her "own expectations of other Black women, by following the threads of [her] own rage at Blackwomanness back into the hatred and despisal that embroidered [her] own life with fire long before [she] knew where that hatred came from, or why it was being heaped upon [her]."[13] Only by examining and dismantling the barrier created by "America's measurement" of her "piece by painful piece" would she be able to use her "energies fully and creatively." Only by accepting as beautiful and worthy and undiminished that about her which others find contemptible—her Blackwomanness—could Lorde effectively "remove the source of that pain" from her "enemies arsenals" and lessen their power over her.[14]

Lorde begins her narrative examination by recounting some of her most painful childhood encounters with racism—on the subway train, at the eye doctor's office, at school, and even in her lighter-skinned mother's preferential evaluation of Lorde's lighter-skinned siblings: "Did bad mean Black? The endless scrubbing with lemon juice in the cracks and crevices of my ripening, darkening, body."[15] She notes that because childhood experiences of racist hatred are absorbed without being understood, the anger they generate can be corrosive: Lorde's own anger is "like a pool of acid deep inside [her]."[16] Echoes of that hatred subsequently return as anger and cruelty in black women's dealings with each other, because they see themselves reflected in each other's visage: "For each of us bears the face that hatred seeks, and we have each learned to be at home with cruelty because we have survived so much of it within our own lives."[17] Getting over "America's measurement" of her is thus a necessary step in Lorde's difficult journey toward self-acceptance and a decolonial love.

To move past the pain and suffering caused by that measurement, Lorde turns to the "Black woman's anger [that] is a molten pond at the core of [her]."[18] Like any powerful force, anger has uses and effects that are both constructive and destructive. In this chapter, as in "The Uses of Anger: Women Responding to Racism," Lorde evokes anger's redemptive potential; she does so by recounting a wide variety of incidents and experiences to which she and other black woman throughout the world and over time have been privy. They range from the banal (the casual rudeness of a black woman clerk at the public library toward another black woman) to the truly horrific (the spectacle of a black woman in labor, whose legs have been tied together by white doctors "out of a curiosity masquerading as science" so that her baby dies in the course of trying to be born).[19] As Lorde conjures anger for herself and for us through the fearless lyricism of her prose, she urges us to pay attention to and learn from that anger, to harness its power in the service of personal and institutional transformation. She does this even as she acknowledges that anger is "an incomplete form of human knowledge."[20] She explains: "My anger has meant pain to me but it has also meant survival, and before I give it up I'm going to be sure that there is something at least as powerful to replace it on the road to clarity."[21]

Recognizing Lorde's narrative trajectory in "Eye to Eye" involves appreciating the distinction she makes in the essay between suffering and pain. Suffering, she explains, "is the nightmare reliving of unscrutinized and unmetabolized pain." By contrast, "pain is an event, an experience that must be recognized, named, and then used in some way in order for the experience to change, to be transformed into something else, strength or knowledge or action."[22] Of the two, only pain can generate the anger that might lead to clarity and positive action. Thus, Lorde's reimmersion into the pain and anger generated by past (and present) hatred is done deliberately and with the intent of moving her own personal story beyond suffering, pain, and anger to the self-love and other-love that may be found on the other side. What Lorde seeks to demonstrate through the course of her narrative is that, as difficult as it is to come away undiminished from the experience of looking full face into the eyes of someone who despises you for something that is not in itself despicable, the cost of not doing so is much greater. The cost for black women, Lorde suggests, is nothing less than a diminution of their profound worth and genuine possibility, as well as the loss of their ability to fully love themselves and those in whom they see themselves.[23] Speaking directly to black women, Lorde writes: "I have to learn to love myself before I can love you or accept your loving. You have to learn to love yourself before you can love me or accept my loving. Know we are worthy of touch before we can reach out for each other."[24]

"Eye to Eye" is thus performative in the following way: Lorde confronts the hatred, which caused the suffering, experiencing it anew as pain, and transforming it into anger. She then uses that anger to gain clarity about her situation for the sake of gaining knowledge about herself and the world she lives in. All this is prior to taking some kind of positive action toward changing her sense of self and the world she lives in. By learning to love herself, she can, without fear, reach out and love the other who is most like her. And while "Eye to Eye" is a particularly powerful example of its genre, it is not unique. In conception and execution it is of a piece with similar writings by other—black and nonblack—women of color who also had to confront their internalized racism, sexism, and homophobia in order to learn to love themselves and others like them. Notable examples include Nellie Wong's poem, "When I Was Growing Up," Merle Woo's epistolary essay, "Letter to Ma," Moraga's essays "La Güera" and "A Long Line of Vendidas," and Gloria

Anzaldúa's several essays in *Borderlands/La Frontera: The New Mestiza*, especially "How to Tame a Wild Tongue" and "*La conciencia de la mestiza*: Towards a New Consciousness."

Díaz was a student in the 1980s and 1990s, during the time when the writings of women of color were being published and taught in the academy. Their influence on him has been significant. In an interview in the *Boston Review*, Díaz acknowledges that women of color were "producing in knowledge . . . something that [he] needed to hear in order to understand [himself] in the world." Key to the "genius" of women of color, he notes, was the fact that this knowledge had been "cultivated *out of* their raced, gendered, sexualized subjectivities":

> To me these women were not only forging in the smithies of their body-logos radical emancipatory epistemologies—the source code of our future liberation—but also they were fundamentally rewriting Fanon's final call in *Black Skin, White Masks*, transforming it [from: "O my body, make me always a man who questions!"] into "O my body, make me always a woman who questions . . . my body" (both its oppressions and interpellations *and* its liberatory counter-strategies).[25]

Here we see Díaz's characteristic and deft interweaving of scholarly, literary, and popular culture references: Frantz Fanon, *Black Skin, White Masks*; James Joyce, *Portrait of the Artist as a Young Man*; and Duncan Jones's movie *Source Code*. We also witness how he transmutes into his own richly allusive language all three features of women of color theory: first, he acknowledges the mutual constitution of race, class, gender, and sexuality in the shaping of subjectivity (see the multiplicity thesis); second, he figures the embodied self as constituted by, and embedded within, a web of relations; and, third, he pays tribute to the importance of examining one's own embodied self as a locus of oppression and a source for radical emancipatory epistemology and practice.

I turn now to one of Lorde's most quoted (and misunderstood) passages in her celebrated essay "The Master's Tools Will Never Dismantle the Master's House" as a way of highlighting what was at stake for Díaz as he embarked on his career as a writer of African descent growing up on "the sharp end of the stick" of racial meaning in America ("Dark America"). Lorde writes:

> Those of us who have been forged in the crucibles of difference—those of us who are poor, who are lesbians, who are Black, who are older—know that *survival is not an academic skill*. It is learning how to stand alone,

unpopular and sometimes reviled, and how to make common cause with those others identified as outside the structures in order to define and seek a world in which we can all flourish. It is learning how to take our differences and make them strengths. *For the master's tools will never dismantle the master's house.* They may temporarily beat him at his own game, but they will never enable us to bring about genuine change.[26]

We should be clear about what Lorde is saying here. First, she is not saying, let me make a world where black lesbians who are poor and older get to wield power over the white former master. Nor is she asking for those who live comfortably within current structures of power to open up the door and let her in. Rather, she is hoping to define and build "a world in which we can all flourish." Hers would be a world where differences can be generative rather than something to be feared, avoided, denigrated, and rendered shameful. It would be a world in which black does not mean "bad," and being lighter skinned is not better just because those who were lighter at a certain point in history had the military power to create the institutional structures and ideological systems that continue, even today, to make those ideas into a commonly accepted "truth" of our social reality.

But what exactly are the tools that won't dismantle the master's house? Hames-García, drawing on the work of the Latina feminist philosopher Maria Lugones, has answered this question by arguing that the master's tools are the tools of purity and separation: the impulse to split subject from object; mind from body; sex from gender; and race from class, gender, sexuality, and ability.[27] All aspects of the self, Hames-García reminds us, are mutually constituted: "They blend, constantly and differently, like the colors of a photograph," and how any one aspect manifests in a given case will depend on how it is constituted in combination with all the other aspects.[28] Díaz adds to this by pointing to a lesson he learned from women of color regarding what he describes as the "true source of the power" of the regimes that imprison people of color as neocolonial subjects in the twenty-first century—namely, "our consent, our participation." He explains: "Why these sisters struck me as the most dangerous of artists was because in the work of, say, Morrison, or Octavia Butler, we are shown the awful radiant truth of how profoundly constituted we are of our oppressions . . . These sisters not only describe the grim labyrinth of power that we are in as neocolonial subjects, but they also point out that we play both Theseus and the Minotaur in this nightmare drama."[29]

Díaz here suggests that the necessity of finding one's way out of the racial labyrinth, or of dismantling the master's house, has not diminished in our contemporary moment. He understands, moreover, that the pain and work involved remains significant. In his Kieve Address at Stanford University, Díaz responded to a young Caribbean American woman's question about the difficulties of psychic and emotional decolonization by asking the audience to consider the agonizing emotional work involved in "bearing witness to ourselves":

> For me to actually say: You know what? My mother did like me a lot less because she preferred my racially lighter siblings. Who the hell wants to say that about their parent? And who the hell wants to not just think that that's a delusion, that's just because I think I wasn't loved enough. Who wants to actually plant that? And who wants to say that, like, I've always like super-envied my older brother who passes for white because I've envied his privilege and because I wanted the attention he had. Who wants to *really* embrace that, and integrate that in? And who wants to say that I felt fucked-up and poor and weak and ugly and stupid for most of my fucking life? Who wants to integrate that? And that I made as many people around me pay for that as I could, except the people who should've paid, and the structure that should've paid. Who wants to integrate that? Who wants to integrate that? Or say this: I date who I date because I was told that people who look lighter are better.[30]

For an aware person of color living in post–civil rights America, the difficulty of admitting that one has integrated into one's self-concept Eurocentric racial values involves multiple layers of complexity. First is admitting that one does not see oneself as beautiful. In an American culture that values self-affirmation above all else, it is a shameful thing in itself to admit to feeling ugly. Second is the discomfort involved in recognizing a disjunction between the decolonizing imperative to perceive nonwhite people as beautiful and the truth that one might prefer people with European-origin features. Third is the shame generated by the fact of having learned those preferences from one's own parents. And finally, there is the resistance to giving up whatever privilege one might have accrued as a result of incorporating into one's life prevailing mainstream values and practices.[31] Indeed, given the implications for changes to his practice that such a witness would call for, Díaz went on to say that it took "more courage and more work for [him] to bear witness to [himself] as a Caribbean person," than to face the violence of the crack epidemic that so terrified him when he was growing up in the 1980s and 1990s as a poor young immigrant boy in New Jersey.[32]

It is in "How to Date a Browngirl, Blackgirl, Whitegirl, or Halfie" that Díaz undertakes the project of bearing witness to himself in order to confront his own racial self-loathing. It is there that he heeds Lorde's call to reach "down into that deep place of knowledge inside [himself]," touch the "terror and loathing of any difference that lives there," and "see whose face it wears." In my reading of the story, I show that critics and readers who seize on the sexism and racism encoded in lines in the story—like "If she's a white girl, you know you'll at least get a hand job," for instance—and who then subsequently marshal such lines as evidence that the story itself endorses sexism and racism, fail to consider these sentiments in the context of the story and of Díaz's oeuvre as a whole. Such statements are admittedly upsetting. But a perceptive reader will ask: Why is that statement there? Why does this young Dominican American character think that about white girls? And, more crucially, does the story as a whole endorse that statement? Moving too fast to condemn a representation in a work of fiction can obscure an understanding of how a fictional work might be structured to bring to light the dynamics around difficult issues like race, class, gender, and sexuality without necessarily either endorsing or resolving the logic behind those dynamics.

The Search for Decolonial Love

As intimated by its title, the story "How to Date a Browngirl, Blackgirl, Whitegirl, or Halfie" takes the form of a set of guidelines for how to date. Crucially, the girl in question is not just any girl. Rather, she will be a type— a racial type. Even before the story begins, the title rejects the idea that there might be a generic (nonracialized) ideal called "girl" that one could imagine dating, while invoking the commonly accepted—but less openly acknowledged—practice of treating people differently according to the race, class, and gender with which they are associated. A second noteworthy feature of the title is its address to the reader as the recipient of the proffered advice. Like Althusser's policeman who, by hailing the passing pedestrian ("Hey, you there!"), subjects him to the authority of the state, so does the title of the story hail the reader as learner, interpellating her into its system of racial understanding.

But who is the intended addressee of the story? As we begin reading the story, we notice that the "you" of the story is incredibly specific. "You" turns out to be someone whose mother and brother have gone for a visit to Union City, who has an aunt who likes to "squeeze your nuts," whose family keeps government cheese in the refrigerator, and whose mother displays a picture of him with an Afro. What becomes increasingly apparent—a fact confirmed when "your nemesis, Howie" addresses him directly—is that "you" is none other than Díaz's fictional alter-ego and most frequently recurring character, Yunior. With the exception of two stories in Drown ("Aurora," and "No Face"), and one in This Is How You Lose Her ("Otravida, Otravez"), Yunior appears as the protagonist or narrator (or both) of every narrative in each of Díaz's first three books, including his Pulitzer Prize–winning novel The Brief Wondrous Life of Oscar Wao.[33] It is for this reason that a perceptive understanding of Yunior's identity is crucial to an understanding of Díaz's oeuvre as a whole.

Briefly, the story presents a scenario in which a thirteen-year-old Yunior, having finally succeeded in getting the family's apartment to himself for the night, talks himself through a hypothetical date with one of several female classmates. Yunior narrates in the imperative mode, as he instructs himself through the process of preparing for, waiting for, entertaining, manipulating, taking leave of, and then regretting his interaction with the girl who is his date. The second-person narration of "How to Date a Browngirl, Blackgirl, Whitegirl, or Halfie" makes it anomalous within the context of Drown, while giving it a superficial resemblance to three stories in This Is How You Lose Her.[34] The difference between "How to Date a Browngirl, Blackgirl, Whitegirl, or Halfie" and the stories in Lose Her is that the latter function as retrospective, diaristic dispatches from the front lines of a war between the sexes that Yunior is so far losing badly; they do so by probing the "outrageous sinvergüencería" he evinces in his devastatingly failed romantic relationships.[35] Their primary focus is thus on the roots and consequences of Yunior's gender politics—particularly as it relates to his inability to control his compulsive promiscuity. "How to Date a Browngirl, Blackgirl, Whitegirl, or Halfie," by contrast, uses Yunior's present-tense second-person narration to self-reflexively examine his painful implication in the Eurocentric racial logic at work in the Dominican diaspora. What makes the story especially pertinent to an exploration of the constitutive power of race as a system of social distinction interactive with gender and class is that, rather than focusing on a specific romantic relationship, the story presents an ever-shifting scenario in which Yunior's attitude and behavior changes according to the racial type of the girl he ends up dating. Recall that the question implied by the title is not *if* Yunior should date these different girls but *how* he is to interact with them. How, given a girl's race and class status, is she likely to regard him? What will she want from him? How should he treat her to maximize his chances of getting what he wants from her? Is what he wants the same if she is a browngirl or a blackgirl, as if she is a whitegirl or halfie? Given all the possible identity contingencies Yunior is likely to face, what is a poor boy supposed to do?[36]

To make the story work at a narrative level, Díaz employs an unusual syntax, one that combines present-tense conditional sentences with the imperative mode. The resulting sentence structure takes the form of "If she is X, do Y" as in: "If the girl's from the Terrace stack the boxes behind the milk" or "If she's a halfie don't be surprised that her mother is white."[37] When the issue under consideration is the girl's (rather than Yunior's) behavior and attitude, Díaz alters the syntax slightly. In that case, he drops the imperative mode and the sentence structure becomes a true conditional in the form of "If she is X, then she will do Y," as in: "If the girl's an outsider she will hiss now and say, What a fucking asshole."[38] The overall effect is to place the reader inside the narrative, allowing him or her to explore the possible outcomes of the hypothetical date alongside Yunior as it progresses.

What becomes evident as we move with Yunior through the story is that he lives in a world whose values are not of his choosing and the mechanisms of which are largely out of his control. Even so, he angles to position himself most advantageously—given his available resources—to influence those mechanisms in his favor. Yunior is acutely aware that his ability to get what he wants depends on who the girl is—what a girl of "her type" might want from a boy of "his type." He is further cognizant of the fact that the girl's perception of him will differ according to *her* positioning within the socioeconomic and racial order, as well as how she understands that positioning—even in those cases where *his* behavior remains constant. So, for example, while at dinner at El Cibao, Yunior commands himself to "order everything in your busted-up Spanish," reminding himself to "let her correct you if she's Latina and amaze her if she's black."[39] In the way that light passing through a prism produces a dazzlingly full spectrum of colors, so does perception refracted through identity produce a wide and varied range of interactional dynamics. What Díaz's odd syntactical sentences make clear is that, as the specific factors involved in setting the scene proliferate, the identity contingencies multiply correspondingly. Du Boisian double consciousness here opens up into Díazian multiple consciousness.

Part of Yunior's difficulty is figuring out which combination of type of girl and sort of behavior will bring him the satisfaction he seeks. Possessing little money or status other than what being young and male give him, and burdened by a shaming sense of racial inferiority, Yunior's resources amount to intelligence, charm, and a watchful sense of behavioral restraint.[40] Demonstrating the sensitivity to relational dynamics that will make him such a successful seducer in subsequent Díazian narratives, Yunior is careful to take his cues from his date; he rightly intuits that, when resources are limited, not missing or thwarting an opportunity might be the best way to succeed. Escaping Yunior's control entirely, however, are the basic contours of his sexual and aesthetic desire—formed as they have been by the coloniality of power: "She might kiss you and then go, or she might, if she's reckless, give it up, but that's rare. Kissing will suffice. A whitegirl might just give it up right then. Don't stop her. She'll take her gum out of her mouth, stick it to the plastic sofa covers and then will move close to you. You have nice eyes, she might say. Tell her that you love her hair, that you love her skin, her lips, because, in truth, you love them more than you love your own."[41] Statements like this last one amount to what Díaz refers to as a "speaking of Voldemort's name" in fictional form.[42] For Díaz, as for the women of color who came before him, saying the shameful thing out loud is the first step to escaping its power. Making a belief manifest renders it available to be confronted, examined, contextualized, and evaluated, in order that it may be rejected, destroyed, or altered through a transformation of the underlying ideas and practices that give it vitality. Having Yunior admit his preference for European-origin features over his own African-origin features is thus Díaz's fictional way of pushing Yunior (and the reader) forward in the journey toward epistemic and emotional decolonization. He is thus doing in fictional form what Lorde did so well in the form of the personal essay.

A distinctive feature of Díaz's fiction is an emphasis on the embodiment of his characters—their skin color, hair texture, height, body shape, and abundance or lack of flesh. At a basic narrative level, this serves to characterize the fictional individuals who inhabit his stories. But it is also Díaz's way of representing his characters as beings whose habitus has been formed by the particular structures of race, class, and gender through which they come into being. It also recalls the second feature of women of color theory, which is a conception of the human self as embodied and embedded within a complex web of overlapping systems of relations. For Díaz, attending to the embodiment of his characters is preliminary to interrogating the meanings physical features like hair texture and skin color have been made to bear.

When Díaz includes lines such as "Hide the pictures of yourself with an Afro" or "Run a hand through your hair like the whiteboys do even though the only thing that runs easily through your hair is Africa," he is referencing and commenting on a peculiarly Dominican attitude about the relationship between hair texture and race.[43] In *Black behind the Ears: Dominican Racial Identity from Museums to Beauty Shops*, the sociologist Ginetta Candelario describes the importance of beauty culture and hair texture to Dominican attitudes about their ancestry and relationship to whiteness. For historical reasons having to do as much with the fact that the Dominican Republic shares the island of Hispaniola with Haiti (whose citizens, in the Dominican imagination, are indisputably "black" and of African descent), as with the fact that the country was ruled for decades by a dictator whose interests were aligned with the military, political, and economic interests of the United States, Dominicans tend to identify themselves in ways that do not acknowledge their African ancestry.[44] They distance themselves from the legacy of slavery and antiblack racism through a variety of linguistic, behavioral, and ideological practices. One such practice involves describing themselves with language that "affirms their 'Indian' heritage—Indio, Indio oscuro, Indio claro, Trigueño," thus facilitating the construction of a nonblack Indo-Hispanic Dominican identity.[45] Another involves focusing on those aspects of their physical beings that are in crucial ways "alterable" and so subject to the long-term process of encoding whiteness on the body referred to as *blanqueamiento*.[46] For Dominicans, whiteness is less a matter of skin color than an "explicitly achieved (and achievable) status with connotations of social, political, and economic privilege."[47]

According to Candelario, a central aspect of Dominican beauty culture turns on the racial meanings assigned to what is referred to as *pelo malo* (bad hair) and what is considered *pelo bueno* (good hair): "*Pelo malo* is hair that is perceived to be tightly curled, coarse, and kinky. *Pelo bueno* is hair that is soft and silky, straight, wavy, or loosely curled. There are clearly racial connotations to each category: the notion of *pelo malo* implies an outright denigration of African-origin hair textures, while *pelo bueno* exalts European, Asian, and indigenous hair textures. Moreover, those with good hair are, by definition, 'not black,' skin color notwithstanding. What is instructive about the Dominican case is the seeming possibility of racial transformation through hair care."[48]

Given Dominicans' historically derived habit of distancing themselves from blackness, discounting dark skin color as a signifier of African ancestry and equating African-origin hair with blackness, the setting, curling, drying, and taming of hair becomes the focus of considerable time and attention of Dominican women. For Dominicans, Candelario explains, hair serves as an "alterable sign" that is the "principal bodily signifier of race."[49]

Note that I am not making a negative judgment regarding Dominicans' "mystified" understanding about their "true" racial identity. Race has no being outside a specific community of meaning; its bodily and behavioral signifiers are historically determined and variable rather than natural and unchanging. For instance, there is no reason why skin color, rather than hair texture, should be the primary (although not sole) determinant of racial identity in the United States—other than this is the way racial distinction has evolved here. One possible explanation may be that hair texture alone is insufficient to distinguish between people of European descent and the wide variety of peoples of non-European descent (including people indigenous to the Americas) whose presence has been foundational to the development of this country's racial imaginary. Over the course of the United States' history, people from many different ethnic and religious backgrounds with varying phenotypes have been in continuous contact with each other. In such a context, skin color and facial physiognomy taken together are more consistently reliable as racial markers than hair texture alone would be. My point is that race—as a system of social distinction parasitic upon perceived physical and behavioral bodily characteristics—is both opportunistic and somewhat arbitrary. Consequently, individuals and institutions that "do race" will seize on and make much of whatever physical or behavioral differences allow them to most effectively distinguish between putatively "superior" and supposedly "inferior" groups in any given social context. If in the Dominican Republic what gets seized on is hair texture, then in the United States it is skin color and facial physiognomy. It is a difference without a distinction.

I am, however, less sanguine about Dominicans' attitudes about their putatively non-African Indo-Hispanic biogeographical ancestry, or about the association some might assume between non-African ancestry and human beauty. In itself, a person's biogeographical ancestry is an empirical matter devoid of aesthetic, intellectual, or cultural significance. It is only because race works as the interpretive framework through which Dominicans and U.S. Americans alike apprehend biogeographical ancestry, that being of European descent is believed by many people in both the United States and the Dominican Republic to be more desirable than being of African, Asian, or Indigenous American descent. Given the legacy of European colonialism, rejecting one's African (or Asian or indigenous) ancestry is tantamount to actively participating in and reproducing the racialized logic that sustains white supremacy. This doing of race is precisely what Díaz works against in his remarkable short story.

"How to Date a Browngirl, Blackgirl, Whitegirl, or Halfie," with its references to Africa and Afros, thus performatively claims for Yunior his African ancestry even as it stages a critical consideration of the way Dominican attitudes about hair as a racial signifier affect Dominican men and boys. The most salient difference between Dominican and U.S. American attitudes about the relationship between African ancestry and race derives from the fact that the United States has undergone a civil rights movement, a crucial part of which was the Black Pride movement. As a result, African Americans as an ethnoracial group in the United States have done important decolonizing work through their sustained efforts to delink African ancestry from notions of biological inferiority. Díaz, as a Dominican American of African descent, has benefitted from this delinking, and my effort in this chapter is to demonstrate how it shows up, both thematically and formally, in his fiction.

Consider, in this sociocultural and political context, Yunior's use of the term *Afro* to describe his younger self's pictured hairstyle. Although the term has become naturalized for us today as a neutral descriptor of a particular hairstyle featuring long, thick, tightly curled hair combed away from the scalp into a large, rounded shape, it crucially references the Black Power political movement of the 1960s. Despite the fact that variations of the style have been worn in other times and places, the hairstyle's designation in the mid-1960s as an Afro (a name that derives from "Afro-American") was an intentionally political act.[50] And even though the Afro's political significance has been obscured by its commodification as "revolutionary glamour" in the 1990s, most of the young people who chose to wear Afros during the 1960s were making antiestablishment, antiauthoritarian, antiwar, and often antiwhite political statements.[51] As the most iconic symbol of the "Black Is Beautiful" movement, the Afro hairstyle connoted—especially for the young black men and women who wore it—pride in one's African heritage and resistance to a bodily aesthetic that privileges a European somatic norm.[52] Díaz's decision to have Yunior describe the pictured hairstyle as an Afro activates at the level of the story's political unconscious the ideology of black pride and enacts a rejection of Yunior's rejection of his own Africanness. The fact that the narrator does so at the same time as he instructs his younger self to hide the picture away creates a boomerang movement— simultaneously pointing a way out of the "grim labyrinth of power" in which Yunior remains imprisoned, while also acknowledging the arduousness of escaping the encircling bonds of shame that racial self-hatred can forge.

It is noteworthy that the most troubling and difficult interactions Yunior has during his hypothetical date are with the "halfie," presumably a girl of mixed European and African ancestry whose parents are associated with different races. The "whitegirl" appears untroubled by her own sexual desire; she openly expresses a liking for "Spanish guys" and hums along with the radio as she washes up after her sexual encounter with Yunior.[53] By contrast, the "local" or "homegirl" (read Latina or black) "won't be quick about letting you touch [her]" because she "has to live in the same neighborhood" and "has to deal with you being all up in her business."[54] The halfie, though, is represented as being uncomfortable with her racial identity and ambivalent about her sexuality. She expresses a dislike for black people, who, she says, "treat me real bad," and she breaks away from Yunior in the midst of intimate touching by crossing her arms and saying "I hate my tits." She pulls away again when he strokes her hair and says, "I don't like anybody touching my hair." And finally, she complains about the fact that Yunior is "the only kind of guy" who asks her out—him and "the blackboys."[55] The point to be made here is not that this is how halfies are. Rather, this is how Díaz represents Yunior as perceiving them to be. The discomfort evinced by the halfie is thus indicative of how Yunior sees himself in relation to another person who, like him, is existentially neither-nor. In the halfie's case, it is neither black nor white; in Yunior's, it is neither black nor white, neither American nor Dominican, neither Spanish-speaking nor English-speaking. The epigraph for *Drown*, taken from a poem by the Cuban American poet and scholar Gustavo Pérez Firmat, generalizes this sense of an existential neither-nor to the project of the book as a whole: "My subject: how to explain to you that I / don't belong to English / though I belong nowhere else." The halfie in "How to Date a Browngirl, Blackgirl, Whitegirl, or Halfie" functions as the paradigmatic representational mirror for Yunior's developing self. As such, she reflects back to him his as-yet-unconsummated desire for a decolonial love—a love that might emerge only in the wake of the radical acceptance and welcoming home of the formerly racially and sexually denigrated non-European self.

Junot Díaz as Audre Lorde's "Man Child"

I close with a meditation by Audre Lorde about the challenges of raising her then-teenage son as a way of figuring Díaz's relationship to her theoretical insights. Lorde writes: "I wish to raise a Black man who will not be destroyed by nor settle for those corruptions called *power* by the white fathers who mean his destruction as surely as they mean mine. I wish to raise a Black man who will recognize that the legitimate objects of his hostility are not women but the particulars of a structure that programs him to fear and despise women as well as his own Black self. For me, that task begins with teaching my son that I do not exist to do his feeling for him."[56]

Díaz, I suggest, is Lorde's political, spiritual, and emotional man child. Having learned the lessons of women of color, he takes responsibility for his own feelings, and advances the project of "forging in the smith[y] of his body-logos" a "radical emancipatory epistemolog[y]." By routing the critique of white supremacy through the body of his fictional alter-ego, Yunior, Díaz takes up the "set of strategies and warrior-grammars" mapped out by women of color in the 1980s and 1990s.[57] In so doing, he responds to Moraga's call to come to terms with our own suffering in order to challenge and, if necessary, "change ourselves, even sometimes our most cherished block-hard convictions."[58] He responds to Mitsuye Yamada's call to reject as inevitable the "unnatural disaster" of racism and sexism that results in an inability to see women of color as fully human.[59] He responds no less to Gloria Anzaldúa's call to put "history through a sieve" in order to winnow out the lies we have inherited about non-European people's supposed racial and cultural inferiority.[60] He responds to Joy Harjo's call to "release" the "fear to be loved" that is the legacy of European colonialism for native peoples.[61] And he responds to Audre Lorde's call "to reach down into that deep place of knowledge inside [ourselves] and touch that terror and loathing of any difference that lives there" in order to "see whose face it wears."[62] And while Yunior has not yet (and might never) succeed in doing so, Díaz enables himself (and invites us, through his fiction) to reach for "the oldest cry," the "deeply personal cry for one's own pain."[63] It is this cry that the character of Nel in Toni Morrison's *Sula* needs to cry in order to understand that the one whose love she really desired was not Jude, but Sula, Nel's own mirror-self. The great tragedy of that novel, of course, is that Nel is only able to cry that cry years after she has lost Sula, first to a misunderstanding bred by the racist and sexist structures that imprisoned her, and then to death.

By holding up a representational mirror to his own broken-by-the-coloniality-of-power self in a story that compellingly invites our emotional and psychic engagement, Díaz reminds us what is at stake for people with subordinated identities who must choose among different epistemological, scholarly, and political alignments as they fashion their critical and artistic practices. He shows us that recognizing the epistemic consequences of identity does not entail reifying present identity categories or elevating them beyond critique.[64] Nor does it prevent the possible reimagining and refiguring of a different kind of present or future. Instead, it makes us more alive to the multifarious insights and perceptions of those whose perspectives are different from ours—insights and perceptions that will affect our present lives and imaginative futures whether or not we want them to. In choosing to confront his own participation in the structures of power that imprison him, Díaz thus joins women of color in writing the "source code of our future liberation."[65] But Díaz, like the women of color who precede him, cannot write it by himself—Pulitzer Prize, MacArthur Award, and a prodigious intellect notwithstanding. This code is open source, and it is up to us as his readers and interpreters to help him write it. Writing this open-source code involves, among other things, understanding what intersectional feminist approaches to race look like in the contemporary moment, particularly in the hands of writers like Díaz. It involves recognizing the men as well as the women who have spent time engaging the work of women of color feminists as a step toward, and as an ongoing practice of, epistemic decolonization, and who dare to represent the complex lives they lead in our contemporary "postrace" moment. As much as we need to map the new in Díaz's fiction, we also need to rethink what has been cast out as the old and ask ourselves why it has been discarded. Finally, we need to identify writings (like those of Díaz) that work as decolonial "worm holes" between worlds—allowing unexpected, time-delayed but necessary cross-fertilizations of creativity between artists and groups often seen as separate or unrelated. This chapter, then, is a kind of time-travel companion piece, if you will, reminding us that Diaz's new literary geographies come etched in tlilli tlapalli, in a kind of Anzaldúan red and black ink, the symbolic colors of ancient writing and wisdom, as passed down and reinterpreted by women of color.

Notes

1. The critiques of identity politics are almost too manifold to mention, since criticizing identity politics has become a shibboleth for many humanities scholars anxious to distance themselves from naïve forms of essentialism. For a useful review (and rebuttal), see Hames-García, *Identity Complex*; Alcoff, *Visible Identities*; Alcoff, "Who's Afraid of Identity Politics?"; Alcoff and Mohanty, "Reconsidering Identity Politics." Of course some scholars, especially women and queers of color, continue to draw on Lorde's insights. See, e.g., Hames-García, *Fugitive Thought*; Hames-García, *Identity Complex*; Martínez, *On Making Sense*; J. Muñoz, *Disidentifications*; Holland, *Raising the Dead*; Holland, *The Erotic Life of Racism*; Ferguson, *Aberrations in Black*.

2. I use the term *women of color* throughout the essay to refer to a particular intellectual formation that emerges in the early 1980s. It is an identity term rather than an essentialist descriptor of female human beings who have been racialized by society as nonwhite. By "identity," I mean the complex and mediated way that situated, embodied human beings look out onto and interpret the world they live in. Insofar as identities track social relations, they are highly contextual and subject to change in response to the transformation of social relations; they come into being through the kinds of experiences we have, and they inform the way we interpret the world around us. Under this conception, identities are not reducible to social categories (i.e., woman, black, Chicana, gay, etc.), nor do they refer exclusively to people's subjective (raceless, genderless, bodiless) "senses of self." Rather, they are socially significant and context-specific ideological constructs that refer in nonarbitrary (if partial) ways to verifiable aspects of the social world. See Moya, *Learning from Experience*; Moya and Hames-García, *Reclaiming Identity*.

3. Rather than the expression of a biological or cultural essence located inside the culture or the body of the racialized person (as most people believe it to be), race is a system of social distinction that emerges as a result of the ongoing interactions of individuals who are associated, by themselves or others, with a multiplicity of competing ancestral, ethnic, and religious groups. Because race is one of the fundamental organizing features of capitalism, it shares that economic system's prodigious flexibility, morphing in appearance and expression according to the demands of capital, labor, raw materials, manufacturing capacity, and market demand. What distinguishes race as such in its various guises over time and across space is that it involves creating and maintaining ethnoracial groups based on perceived physical and behavioral characteristics usually linked to an individual's biogeographical ancestry, associating differential power and privilege with these characteristics, and then justifying the resulting group inequalities (Markus and Moya). Against those scholars who suggest that we have lately moved into a new "postrace" era (see, e.g., R. Saldívar), I contend that this dynamic process—this *doing* of race—has not abated or changed in a fundamental way over the past several decades.

4. My knowledge of women of color theory has been acquired through years of reading and teaching a large volume of their writings—fictional, essayistic, and scholarly.

Scholars interested in consulting some key sources might begin with Alexander and C. Mohanty, *Feminist Genealogies, Colonial Legacies, Democratic Futures*; Anzaldúa, *Borderlands/La Frontera*; Anzaldúa, *Making Face, Making Soul—Haciendo Caras*; Baca Zinn and Dill, *Women of Color in U.S. Society*; Bambara, *The Black Woman*; Chow, "The Development of Feminist Consciousness among Asian American Women"; hooks, *Feminist Theory*; Hurtado, "Relating to Privilege"; Lorde, *Sister Outsider*; Mohanty, Russo, and Torres, *Third World Women and the Politics of Feminism*; Moraga, *Loving in the War Years*; Moraga and Anzaldúa, *This Bridge Called My Back*; Moya, *Learning From Experience*; Ramos, *Compañeras*; Smith, *Home Girls*; Wong, Woo, and Yamada, *3 Asian American Writers Speak Out on Feminism*. For a helpful account of the historical development of and relationships between Chicana, black, and white feminisms, see Roth, *Separate Roads to Feminism*. This is just a sampling; there are many other works as well.

5. Michael R. Hames-García, *Identity Complex: Making the Case for Multiplicity* (Minneapolis: University of Minnesota Press, 2011), 4–7.

6. Perspiration, spilled breast milk, and menstrual blood figure prominently in the writings of women of color. Representative fictional examples include Milkman's extended nursing in Toni Morrison's *Song of Soloman*, Sethe's stolen milk in Toni Morrison's *Beloved*, the sweat that trickles down between Estrella's breasts in Helena María Viramontes's *Under the Feet of Jesus*, and the menstrual blood that so bedevils Velma in Toni Cade Bambara's *The Salt Eaters*.

7. The self as figured by women of color thus anticipates as well the interdependent self described in the groundbreaking studies about different cultural models of the self done by the social psychologists Hazel Markus and Shinobu Kitayama. Although their early work focused on the different types of selves associated with middle-class Japanese college students (interdependent) compared to middle-class European American college students (independent), subsequent work in cultural psychology demonstrates that factors of class and race affect the extent to which an American is likely to be an independent as opposed to an interdependent self.

8. See Moya, *Learning from Experience*, 23–101. In 1968, the sociologist Erving Goffman helpfully catalogued the features associated with American normativity when he wrote: "In an important sense there is only one complete unblushing male in America: a young, married, white, urban, northern, heterosexual Protestant father of college education, fully employed, of good complexion, weight and height and a recent record in sports," in *Stigma: Notes on the Management* (Englewood Cliffs, NJ: Prentice-Hall, 1963), 128. Compare this to the list of attributes Audre Lorde associates with herself in a 1984 essay entitled "Age, Race, Class, and Sex: Women Redefining Difference"; it becomes clear why she understands herself to be a paradigmatic outsider: "As a forty-nine-year-old Black lesbian feminist socialist mother of two, including one boy, and the member of an inter-racial couple, I usually find myself a part of some group defined as other, deviant, inferior, or just plain wrong," in "Age, Race, Class, and Sex: Women Redefining Difference," *Sister Outsider: Essays and Speeches* (Freedom, CA: Crossing, 1984), 114.

9. An abbreviated version of the essay was published in *Essence* 14, no. 6 (October 1983). This and all essays by Lorde referred to in this chapter are collected in her book *Sister Outsider*.

10. Audre Lorde, "Eye to Eye: Black Women, Hatred, and Anger," *Sister Outsider: Essays and Speeches* (Freedom, CA: Crossing, 1984), 145.

11. Lorde, "Eye to Eye," 145, 146.

12. Lorde, "Eye to Eye," 145–46.

13. Lorde, "Eye to Eye," 146.

14. Lorde, "Eye to Eye," 146–47.

15. Lorde, "Eye to Eye," 147–49.

16. Lorde, "Eye to Eye," 150.

17. Lorde, "Eye to Eye," 146. Compare Anzaldúa's observation that internalized oppression negatively affects Chicanas' relationships with each other: "To be close to another Chicana is like looking in the mirror. We are afraid of what we'll see there. *Pena.* Shame. Low estimation of self." Gloria Anzaldúa, *Borderlands/La Frontera: The New Mestiza* (San Francisco: Spinsters/Aunt Lute, 1987), 58.

18. Lorde, "Eye to Eye," 145.

19. Lorde, "Eye to Eye," 150.

20. Lorde, "Eye to Eye," 152.

21. Lorde, "Eye to Eye," 132.

22. Lorde, "Eye to Eye," 171.

23. Lorde, "Eye to Eye," 169–74.

24. Lorde, "Eye to Eye," 174–75.

25. Junot Díaz, interview by Paula M. L. Moya, "The Search for Decolonial Love, Parts I & II," *Boston Review*, June 26–27, 2012, accessed August 14, 2012, http://www.bostonreview.net/BR37.4/junot_diaz_paula_moya_drown_race.php.

26. Audre Lorde, "The Master's Tools Will Never Dismantle the Master's House," *Sister Outsider: Essays and Speeches* (Freedom, CA: Crossing, 1984), 112.

27. Hames-Garcia, *Identity Complex*, 1–37.

28. Hames-Garcia, *Identity Complex*, 6.

29. Díaz, "Search for Decolonial Love."

30. Junot Díaz, "Dark America," Anne and Loren Kieve Distinguished Lecture, Stanford University, May 18, 2012, M4A file.

31. As Moraga notes, the hardest part of remembering what it "feels like to be a victim" in a way that would preclude our victimization of others is that "it may mean giving up whatever privileges we have managed to squeeze out of this society by virtue of our gender, race, class, or sexuality." Cherríe Moraga, *Loving in the War Years: Lo Que Nunca Pasó Por Sus Labios* (Boston: South End, 1983), 53.

32. Díaz, "Dark America."

33. Elena Machado Sáez's suggestion that there are multiple Yuniors who appear across Díaz's oeuvre is provocative, but unconvincing. Elena Machado Sáez, "Dictating Desire, Dictating Diaspora: Junot Díaz's *The Brief Wondrous Life of Oscar Wao* as Foundational

Romance," *Contemporary Literature* 52, no. 3 (fall 2011): 529–33. There is too much continuity in the character, and Díaz himself speaks about Yunior as a recurring character. Díaz, "Search for Decolonial Love."

34. "Alma," "Miss Lora," and "The Cheater's Guide to Love." Yunior, who narrates all four stories, is presumably talking to himself in each. A fourth story in *This Is How You Lose Her*, "Flaca," is also written using second-person narration with Yunior as the narrator, but in that story Yunior is talking not to himself but to a former girlfriend with that nickname.

35. Junot Díaz, *This Is How You Lose Her* (New York: Riverhead Books, 2012), 48.

36. The social psychologist Claude Steele defines an identity contingency as the specific set of responses that a person with a given identity has to cope with in a specific setting.

37. Junot Díaz, *Drown* (New York: Riverhead Books, 1996), 143, 145.

38. Junot Díaz, *Drown*, 146.

39. Junot Díaz, *Drown*, 145.

40. It is worth noting that the word *don't* appears seventeen times in this story of approximately sixteen hundred words, eleven of which represent a direct order from Yunior to himself toward the end of the story

41. Díaz, *Drown*, 147.

42. In my interview with him, Díaz emphasized the need for people of color to confront their own participation in the perpetuation of white supremacist ideas and practices:

> How can you change something if you won't even acknowledge its existence, or if you downplay its significance? . . . The silence around white supremacy is like the silence around Sauron in *The Lord of the Rings*, or the Voldemort name which must never be uttered in the Harry Potter novels. And yet here's the rub: if a critique of white supremacy doesn't first flow through you . . . you have, in fact, almost guaranteed its survival and reproduction. There's that old saying: the devil's greatest trick is that he convinced people that he doesn't exist. Well, white supremacy's greatest trick is that it has convinced people that, if it exists at all, it exists always in other people, never in us.

43. Díaz, *Drown*, 143, 145. While not unrelated, Dominicans' attitudes regarding the relationship between hair texture and race differs somewhat from that of African Americans' understanding in the relative priority Dominicans put on hair texture (as opposed to skin color) as the primary marker of race.

44. Candelario lists a series of regionally anomalous events that further account for Dominicans' distinctive racial formation and relation to whiteness: the relatively short duration and limited importance of plantation slavery; the massive depopulations caused by white emigration; the impoverishment of the remaining white and creole colonials during the seventeenth century; and the heavy reliance on blacks and mulattos in the armed forces and religious infrastructure (3). What seems clear is that people in the Dominican Republic with visible African ancestry—who might have faced re-

sistance had they been living in a society with more people with European ancestry in positions of power—had the economic, political, and social power to construct themselves as "white." Ginetta E. B. Candelario, *Black behind the Ears: Dominican Racial Identity from Museums to Beauty Shops* (Durham, NC: Duke University Press, 2007), 224. See also Frank Moya Pons, *The Dominican Republic: A National History* (New Rochelle, NY: Hispaniola Books, 1995), 206–7.

45. Candelario, *Black behind the Ears*, 5.

46. Ginetta E. B. Candelario, "Hair Race-Ing: Dominican Beauty Culture and Identity Production," *Meridians* 1, no. 1 (2000): 138.

47. Candelario, "Hair Race-Ing," 131.

48. Candelario, "Hair Race-Ing," 182.

49. Candelario, "Hair Race-Ing," 252, 223.

50. Kobena Mercer, "Black Hair/Style Politics," in *Welcome to the Jungle: New Positions in Black Cultural Studies* (New York: Routledge, 1994), 97–130; Robin D. G. Kelley, "Nap Time: Historicizing the Afro," *Fashion Theory* 1, no. 4 (1997): 339–52.

51. Davis, "Afro Images."

52. Kelley, "Nap Time: Historicizing the Afro," 348–49.

53. Díaz, *Drown*, 148.

54. Díaz, *Drown*, 147.

55. Díaz, *Drown*, 148.

56. Audre Lorde, "Man Child: A Black Lesbian Feminist's Response," in *Sister Outsider: Essays and Speeches* (Freedom, CA: Crossing, 1984), 74.

57. Díaz, "Search for Decolonial Love."

58. Cherríe Moraga and Gloria Anzaldúa, eds., *This Bridge Called My Back: Writings by Radical Women of Color*, 2nd ed. (New York: Kitchen Table/Women of Color Press, 1983), i.

59. Mitsuye Yamada, "Invisibility Is an Unnatural Disaster: Reflections of an Asian American Woman," *Bridge: An Asian American Perspective* 7, no. 1 (1979).

60. Anzaldúa, *Borderlands*, 82.

61. Joy Harjo, "I Give You Back," *She Had Some Horses* (New York: Thunder's Mouth Press, 1983).

62. Lorde, "Master's Tools," 113.

63. Morrison, *Sula*, 108.

64. Díaz, "Search for Decolonial Love."

65. Díaz, "Search for Decolonial Love."

10. Now Check It
Junot Díaz's Wondrous Spanglish
Glenda R. Carpio

The terms Latino and Hispanic are provisional at best because they only loosely suggest a complex set of experiences—at once multinational and uniquely American—shared by a great many and diverse number of immigrants and descendants of immigrants in the contemporary U.S. landscape.[1] While, on the whole, people of Latin American descent living in the United States prefer to describe themselves according to specific geographical places of origin (Dominican, Venezuelan, etc.) or to hyphenate their identities if they are American born (as in Cuban-American, Mexican-American, and so on), they use either Hispanic or Latino to designate the social and political bonds that, in one way or another, tie them together across differences. Those who use the term Hispanic, a term introduced by the U.S. Census Bureau in 1973, generally privilege language as a medium that connects them not only to each other in the United States, but also to people living in Latin America and in the countries of the Iberian peninsula. Others, especially younger generations, reject the term Hispanic in favor of Latino, despite the latter's own problematic nature, because Hispanic carries, in its phonetic sound alone, a legacy of colonialism that obfuscates the complex cultural heritage of Latin Americans, including the histories of indigenous Americans and Africans who were brought forcefully to the Americas.[2]

Paula Moya, like the late Juan Flores and other prominent critics, has come to see the need for a strategic use of the term *Latino*. According to Moya, *Latino* articulates an affiliation, "a kind of 'imaginary community,' that is based partly on the common experience of being interpellated as a particular kind of 'minority' person in the United States." Moya argues that "this minority experience is one that Latina/os do not share with people living outside this country"; it is an experience that "Latin American and Spanish scholars who immigrate to [the US] (especially those who are from the elite classes in their own countries)" find it hard "to appreciate and understand."[3] *Latino* also describes the intercultural connections that people from different parts of Latin America make as they live, interact, and intermarry in the United States and suggests the related term *latinidad*, which, since José Martí's seminal essay "Nuestra America" (1891), and Simón Bolívar's nineteenth-century dream of a unified Latin America, invokes a panethnic category through which Latin Americans have defined themselves against both Spanish colonialism and U.S. imperialism.

Ironically, in the United States, the term *Latino* has come to signal current and past Latin American migration as a function of American political and economic domination. Such domination, and older forms of colonialism, has produced a set of experiences that many Latin Americans share across national differences, experiences that they bring to the United States when they emigrate. But it is the "experience of analogous inequalities" in the United States that has had the most impact in producing a "shared sense of 'connectedness' among Latinos."[4] For second-generation and third-generation Latinos, those further removed from the migration experience, and even those who may be immigrants themselves but who no longer have strong ties with their culture of origin, the term has also come to serve as a way of asserting a particular kind of American citizenship while signaling affiliation with a group of people living in the United States whose ancestors have come to the country from the different regions of Latin America.[5]

Consequently, the question of how the fastest growing minority in the United States, a group whose numbers have exceeded that of African Americans, defines itself and is defined from the outside is complex. Yet, in American popular media, the term *Latino* has been almost entirely stripped of its complexity. In particular, popular representations have tended to erase the racial diversity of Latinos. Juan Flores rightly argued that the consumer version of Latino ethnicity—which for a while made white-looking figures such as Ricky Martin the Latino poster boy—not only elides big differences among Latinos but obscures what they do have in common: the fact that many Latinos are black (especially according to the codes operative in the United States) or Native American (from the great diversity of indigenous cultures in the Americas). But one thing is for sure: while we in the academy have gotten very fancy in our theorizing about the malleability of race as a social fiction, the fact remains that the darker in shade Latinos look the more they are bound to be subject to rampant racial profiling, police brutality, massive incarceration, and other manifestations of racial violence that African Americans suffer in disproportionate measures. "On the streets and in the dominant social institutions," writes Flores, "'brown' is close enough to black to be suspect."[6]

While this situation is clearly problematic and reminds us, once again, of how much "the problem of the color line" persists, it also highlights the problems of thinking within the old black-white binary, which has rarely, if ever, designated absolute categories except that it has certainly been conceptualized and acted upon as if it did. But obsession about the black-white binary (from either side) also obscures the alliances, albeit sometimes ambivalent, between sectors of the African American and Latino populations. These alliances, I should stress, are more prevalent in the realm of literature, music, and art, in a clear case in which the arts imagine a better world than the one in which we live. In the sociopolitical terrain, many commentators have highlighted the sharp distinctions between black and Latino communities. And it is true, as Mark Sawyer and others have noted, that conflicts among black Americans and Latinos have been nurtured by the unresolved racism within Latino communities, "a racism that has its origins in their respective countries of origin." But the tensions are also due to "the frequently parochial way in which African Americans privilege the U.S. born black experience and fail to recognize the struggles of immigrants of all colors." As Sawyer notes, "these narrow definitions of social, cultural, and political identity prevent interethnic alliances and issue grave concerns."[7]

Afro-Latinos, however, have been representing both the possibilities and limits of black and Latino alliances for generations. Juan Flores urges us to turn "to the contributions of Puerto Rican collector and bibliophile Arturo Schomburg during the Harlem Renaissance," to "music history . . . with the beginnings of Latin Jazz" in the 1940s, and, in more recent times, to the involvement of Latino youth in the "forging of hip-hop and other expressive styles." Finally, Flores urges us to turn to literature, in the "writings of Jesús Colón in the 1950s and Piri Thomas in his 1967 novel *Down These Mean Streets*."[8]

Since his literary debut in 1996, the Dominican American writer Junot Díaz has been advancing the Afro-Latino heritage to which Juan Flores alludes, giving sharp-witted eloquence to the complexities of being Afro-Latino and immigrant in the United States. In his collection of short stories *Drown* (1996) and in his first novel, *The Brief Wondrous Life of Oscar Wao* (2007), Díaz breaks away from the conventions set in place by earlier immigrant classics such as Mary Antin's *The Promised Land* (1912), while also producing an Afro-Latino literature that does not obsess over questions of race. Instead, the focus of the novel is on craft and the art of showing, in language, what it means to be black, Latino, and immigrant in the United States. This is not to say that Díaz dispenses with historical context. To the contrary, Díaz is a novelist who is firmly rooted in the specificities of Dominican history. Yet, far from focusing myopically on the topic, he expertly shows the ways the African diaspora, U.S. imperialism, and the exodus of Dominicans to the United States, caused largely by the U.S.-backed Trujillo dictatorship, are interrelated. The many footnotes that accompany his novel serve as the principal lens into Dominican history, but (and one can see this typographically) they also allow Díaz to let history serve as the base for his fiction, and in many ways comment upon that fiction, without subsuming his craft. In fact, he develops an intricate relationship between history and fiction through his footnotes, since they comment upon the fiction, largely from a historical perspective, but are also clearly fictional constructs written in the same aesthetic tone and style as the main text.

Díaz has directly recognized Piri Thomas as a seminal influence. In *Down These Mean Streets*, which is, more properly speaking, a fictionalized memoir, Thomas offers a portrait of a young man, born of a black Cuban father and a white Puerto Rican mother, who wrestles with what he calls being "hung up between two sticks." This phrase comes to figure both the biracial identity that he gets from his parents and his desire to identify, on the one hand, with his African American friends—boys with whom he rolls in the tough streets of Spanish Harlem in the 1940s—and, on the other, to stress his Puerto Rican identity as a way of distinguishing himself from the African American experience, given the repeated acts of degradation that he both witnesses and experiences as a black Puerto Rican boy in the United States.

Thomas renders his ambivalent position between the two sticks—the black and white binary of his family and of American race relations—through a language that resembles that of the streets in which he grew up. In one scene, he sits on a stoop listening to the sounds of his neighborhood: "I began listening for real," he writes, "I heard the roar of multicolored kids, a street blend of Spanish and English with a strong tone of Negro American."[9] While Thomas and other Nuyorican writers have experimented formally so as to give the blend and tones of a black and Latino street language textual form, such experimentation has been most successful in poetry, especially in the work of Nuyorican poets. Like Afro-Latin jazz, this poetry has incorporated the accents and rhythms of a black-brown sound. An excerpt from Tato Laviera's poem "the salsa of bethesda fountain" can give you a sense of how that sound has been invoked through poetry via allusions to music:

> and permit me to say these words in afro-spanish:
> la bomba y la plena puro són
> de puerto rico que ismael es el rey y el juez
> meaning the same as marvin gaye singing spiritual social songs
> to black awareness
> a blackness in spanish
> a blackness in english
> mixtures met on jam sessions in central park,
> there were no differences in
> the sounds emerging from the inside
> soul-salsa is universal
> meaning a rhythm of mixtures
> with world-wide bases
>
> did you say you want it stronger? well, ok, it is a root called africa in all
> of us.[10]

The poem invokes an Afro-Latino and African American alliance based upon a mutual recognition of African retentions as a unifying core. As is the case in many early invocations of this alliance, the base is figured as sound and movement. It is in music and dance, in the sounds and rhythms of the bomba and the plena, that one can hear and see the culture born first out of the displacement of Africans in the Caribbean and their interactions with European and indigenous cultures, and it is in music, in the sound of salsa, that one can hear the result of a second displacement, that of

Latinos of African descent in the United States. During jam sessions in Central Park, around its Bethesda Fountain, the sound of these displacements mixes freely with soul music (personified here by Marvin Gaye), the result of another related displacement, that of Africans in the United States and their own interactions with Europeans and indigenous peoples. The succinct alliteration of "soul-salsa" alone suggests the layers of displacement and transculturation of the African diaspora while the "rhythm of mixtures / with world-wide bases" names them in terms of sound and movement.

Whereas Laviera and other Nuyorican poets have given formal shape to the "rhythm of mixtures" of the African Diaspora in Latino and black American cultures, Thomas and, to a greater extent, Díaz embrace the challenge of doing so in the realm of narrative. What sound do the many dislocations invoked by Laviera's poem have in the casual language of the streets? And what is significant about moving away from the formalized language of poetry and the allusions to music and dance upon which Nuyorican poets relied? While such poets tended to celebrate connections across cultures, or to claim a specific Nuyorican soul, Thomas, and later Díaz, opened up the possibility of exploring both the promises and tensions of an Afro-Latino and black American alliance. And, in doing so in the "Spanish and English with a strong tone of Negro American" of the streets, both Thomas and Díaz have tapped into the capacity that narrative fiction has to represent what statistics and ideological debates about terms (*Latino* versus *Hispanic*) and the possibility or impossibility of a black-brown alliance leave out or obfuscate.

Down These Mean Streets reveals how Piri Thomas gets caught up in gangs and petty thievery, partly as a result of his family's inability to deal with its mixed-race identity. This fact alone marks Thomas's narrative as pioneering since, as early as 1967, it explores the intricacies of life between the "two poles," not only in a bilingual, transnational context, but also beyond the conventions of the tragic mulatto theme established in African American literature. Thomas does associate his mixed-race identity with a kind of pathology. But, in the middle of the narrative, he attempts to resolve Piri's predicament by exploring his affiliation with African American culture.[11] We can see this best through Piri's relationship with Brew, an African American young man from the South living in Spanish Harlem. A tense conversation between the two friends exemplifies the ambivalent alliance between black and brown cultures to which I have been alluding. Frightened by the specter of racial violence, figured through allusions to lynching, Piri rejects the repeated gestures of camaraderie that his African American friend offers. He is also nearly consumed by a racial self-hatred that he inherits from his father, thus he also consistently tries to deny the fact that he is, like his friend, black. But Brew challenges him at every turn such that Piri is forced to reflect: "Was I trying to tell Brew that I'm better than he is 'cause he's only black and I'm a Puerto Rican dark-skin?" He then adds, "Like his people copped trees on a white man's whim, and who ever heard of Puerto Ricans getting hung like that?"[12] The rhythm of this sentence, unlike the rhythms to which Laviera's poem alludes, serves to succinctly express the racial violence against African Americans that prevents Piri from embracing his blackness. Ironically, that same rhythm is inflected by the "strong tone of Negro American" with which Piri speaks English. The phrase then serves both to distance and embrace life not between the poles of a black and white divide, but between black and brown worlds.

Piri's insistence that he is a Puerto Rican might suggest that he is embracing an immigrant identity over and against that of African Americans as a way to resolve his racial conflict. Yet, like many other Nuyoricans, he has never been to Puerto Rico. And, given the status of Puerto Rico as a commonwealth of the United States (since 1952), Piri would not be, strictly speaking, an immigrant even if he had been born on the island. Still, because according to the United States Supreme Court, Puerto Rico is an "unincorporated territory" of the United States, "a territory appurtenant and belonging to the United States, but not a part of the United States," Piri's matrilineage marks him as an outsider who is not a full citizen of the United States while his patrilineal racial status pushes him further into statelessness.[13] However, Piri clings to the difference that his Puerto Rican background purportedly gives him in the United States, his country of birth, almost as a matter of survival. His conversation with Brew, however, constitutes the beginning of a significant change in consciousness. Brew consistently challenges Piri's assumptions while Piri begins to see that his statelessness is not significantly different from that of African Americans in pre–civil rights movement America. On his end, Brew better understands what it means to be a black Puerto Rican in the United States. The conversation ends as the two friends bond: "Brew shoved his big hand at me. I grabbed it and shook it, adding a slap of skin to bind it. I looked at our different shades of skin and thought, *He's a lot darker than I am, but one thing is for sure, neither of us is white.*"[14]

The memoir fetishizes racial difference even as it strives to critique the black and white binary that has been so intrinsic to U.S. racial politics. But it also shows how Piri and Brew put into action the revelations that they gain during their conversation. They take a trip down South, a trip that Piri initiates as a result of his new gained consciousness and that Brew accepts partly because he would like to go back home but also because he would like to help his black Puerto Rican brother understand an important aspect of the African American experience. The trip from the North to the South recalls those taken by W. E. B. Du Bois in *The Souls of Black Folk* (1903) and by the protagonist of James Weldon Johnson's *The Autobiography of an Ex-Colored Man* (1912), especially because it serves to educate a young black man in the racial formation of his country.

Brew and Piri enlist in the Merchant Marine and, while in the South, they encounter not only outright bigotry but also more subtle forms of racism and discrimination. The narrative focus, however, remains on two friends trying to be men in a society that ritually humiliates them.[15] But suddenly, Brew disappears somewhere in the South and, while Piri continues to travel for some time, Piri eventually returns to Harlem just as conflicted as before. He returns to a life of gangs, drugs, and crime, in which the only sustaining belief is that he cannot let his street reputation falter; it is the only thing that defines him. Sadly, this lands him in jail at the young age of twenty-two where he spends seven years. The ending is thus decidedly unsentimental. *Down These Mean Streets* is so poignant in spite of, or perhaps because of, this lack of sentimentality. To so many young men like Piri, today and in 1967, the memoir validates experiences that are rarely represented without distortion or at all. For Junot Díaz, the memoir would become a template for his own fictional renditions of Afro-Latino life in the United States.

If *Down These Mean Streets* explores the peculiar statelessness of Puerto Rican Afro-Latinidad, Díaz's short story collection *Drown* takes a slightly different direction since it addresses issues of immigration that are not immediately pertinent to Piri. Díaz's stories shuttle between the Dominican Republic and the United States (New Jersey), and revolve around many of the subjects found in Thomas's memoir: family dramas intensified by the losses of immigrant uprooting (as in the case of Piri's parents), poverty in American ghettoes, the drugs that infest them, and the lack of opportunity and depression suffered by its inhabitants. Like Thomas, Díaz renders these experiences through an Afro-Latino consciousness and in a language that clearly shows an affinity for African American expressive culture. Even James Wood who, in a review, argues that Díaz "shows very little interest in doing something new with the [English] language," notes the stories' "non-literary vernacular, compounded by African American slang, loosened Spanish and standard American short storytelling (a la Raymond Carver)."[16]

But, unlike Thomas's memoir, Drown does not take as one of its main topics the wrestling and confusion of a black Latino "hung between [the] two sticks" of black and white America. Instead it *assumes* an Afro-Latino identity and focuses much more on language rather than on issues of identity as impacted by racial tensions.

Díaz's choice of epigraph is telling in this respect. He quotes Gustavo Pérez Firmat's poem "Dedication":

> The fact that I
> am writing to you
> in English
> already falsifies what I
> wanted to tell you.
> My subject:
> how to explain to you that I
> don't belong to English
> though I belong nowhere else.[17]

The shift to the terrain of language does not mean a relinquishing of racial concerns. Rather, in Drown and in his first novel, Díaz shows not only how Spanish sounds "tropicalize" Standard English, but also how African American slang intertwines with an Afro-Latino immigrant language, thereby expressing the possibilities of a brown-black alliance in the aesthetic realm. Focusing on "Latino/a fiction and poetry written entirely or almost entirely in English," Frances Aparicio defines "tropicalization" as a process of "rewriting and transforming 'American' culture" from a Latino perspective, a process that includes exploring "new possibilities for metaphors, imagery, syntax, and rhythms that Spanish subtexts provide literary English."[18] But this tropicalization also includes a mixing with African American rhythms, akin to the sound of "soul-salsa."

Díaz's inclusion of African American rhythms in his mixture of Spanish and English is not a simple matter of appropriation or mimicry. Nor is it a matter of exoticizing linguistic difference or of romanticizing affinities as Aparacio's term *tropicalization* and Laviera's poetic *soul-salsa* suggest. Instead, as Evelyn Nien-Ming Ch'ien notes, Díaz "explores the possibilities for linguistic disjuncture and compatibility in his work by including a variety of communities . . . To read their interactions is to experience the ways in which communities grow proximate and distant from one another through language."[19] African American slang becomes part of Díaz's work in part because his characters exist in worlds in which Latino and black communities come in constant contact with one another. But Díaz's language also shows the tensions that exist in that contact. "The Black community," he said in an interview, "loves Dominicans and Puerto Ricans only as long as we support them and erase ourselves."[20] At the same time, as Díaz states, "Dominicans also have much work to do. Some of us have embraced a white racist view of African Americans we must vehemently reject."[21] Díaz shows how black Americans and Latinos grow "approximate and distant" from one another in language, by both embracing African American slang and refusing to translate and italicize Spanish in his texts. For him, both would be tantamount to marking Spanish as a minority language and erasing a seminal aspect of what distinguishes Afro-Latino culture. "Spanish is not a minority language," he has said, "Not in this hemisphere, not in the United States, not in the world inside my head. So why treat it like one?"[22] In fact, as Ch'ien argues, Díaz "reforms the idea of what constitutes American language by asserting that his Dominican and homogenized Spanish [the Spanish spoken by all the different kinds of Latinos] is American . . . to embrace Spanish as an American language is to resist the urge to translate it or appropriate it."[23]

In moving toward the realm of language, Díaz also approaches the subject of statelessness, so suggestively figured in Thomas's memoir, from a linguistic rather than a narrowly nationalistic perspective. A great deal of the potency in Pérez Firmat's "Dedication" comes from the fact that its main gesture—to embrace English reluctantly as a home that is not really a home—resonates with so many people living lives shaped by British and American imperialism and its related shifts in immigration worldwide, as well as by homegrown forms of colonization and slavery such as South African apartheid and U.S. slavery and racism. In invoking this kind of linguistic statelessness as the opening of *Drown*, Díaz positions his exploration of Dominican immigration to the United States in a broad framework that moves away from the fetishization of racial difference that we find in Thomas, as well as from a focus on national boundaries, and toward one within which it is also possible to see African American slang as a product of the linguistic statelessness invoked by Pérez Firmat. Díaz, writing in an English comingled with Spanish, with a "strong tone of Negro American,"

explores the cross-cultural alliances that illuminate not only the African retentions shared across the diaspora but also the linguistic homelessness
and creativity that are part of not belonging to English and yet belonging
nowhere else.

Thus James Wood errs in underestimating just how much Díaz is interested in doing something new with the English language. More so than
Drown, *The Brief Wondrous Life of Oscar Wao* best exemplifies what Wood somewhat pejoratively calls "the mongrel brilliance of [Díaz's] language."[24] From
the title alone, one gets the sense of literary play at work in Díaz's novel,
since it evokes the Bildungsroman tradition in general and titles such as
Ernest Hemingway's "The Short Happy Life of Francis Macomber." More
specifically, the title includes a play on the name Oscar Wilde, since Oscar
Wao is actually the nickname of the main protagonist, a sweet but overweight Dominican nerd growing up in a New Jersey ghetto, who on one fateful Halloween dons a costume that absurdly reminds everyone of the king
of dandyism, Oscar Wilde. The name invokes the Dominican play on Wilde,
its transformation through Spanish into Wao (perhaps a joke on Díaz's part
on the seeming disconnect between Wilde and Wao as cultural referents),
but also underscores Oscar's persecution because he is "different."

Told from the perspective of Yunior (his name also puns on the typical
"j" and "y" confusion of Spanish and English speakers), Oscar's sister's one-
time boyfriend, the novel ranges across an impressive number of genres,
styles, and referent points. As A. O. Scott puts it, the novel, including its
numerous footnotes, encompasses a "multigenerational immigrant family
chronicle that dabbles in tropical magic realism, punk-rock feminism, hip-
hop machismo, post-postmodern pyrotechnics and enough polymorphous
multiculturalism to fill up an Introduction to Cultural Studies syllabus."[25]
Connecting these various strands is Oscar's story, his dreams of becoming
the Dominican J. R. R. Tolkien and of finding love.

But Oscar is a misfit among misfits. A Dominican who, unlike most of
his peers, is not concerned with pretending he is not black, Oscar sports
an Afro and wears his love for fantasy genres like a badge: "Dude wore his
nerdiness like a Jedi wore his light saber or a Lensman her lens. Couldn't
have passed for Normal if he wanted to."[26] The fact that he is a "ghetto
nerd" makes things much more complicated. As Yunior writes in one of
his footnotes, "You really want to know what being an X-man feels like?
Just be a smart bookish boy of color in a contemporary US ghetto . . . [It's]
like having bat wings or a pair of tentacles growing out of your chest."[27]

Oscar's nerdiness is not the only problem: Oscar does not fit in either black or white America. When Oscar arrives at Rutgers for college, for instance, he has high hopes of achieving escape velocity. But, alas, this does not happen. Yunior describes Oscar's predicament: "The White kids looked at his Black skin and his afro and treated him with inhuman cheeriness. The kids of color, upon hearing him speak and seeing him move his body shook their head. You're not Dominican. And he said, over and over again. But I am. Soy Dominicano. Dominicano soy."[28]

Oscar's nerdiness excludes him from the ultra machismo of his Dominican peers and the coolness of his African American brothers. In imagining a character so outside the common stereotypes of brownness and blackness, Díaz takes up themes that are often overshadowed by ghetto fiction and immigrant narratives aimed at largely white audiences, tourist-like investigations of "how the other half lives," to invoke Jacob Riis's photojournalistic take on the squalid conditions of immigrants in downtown Manhattan at the end of the nineteenth century (which incidentally also invokes the subtitle of Harriet Beecher Stowe's Uncle Tom's Cabin, or Life among the Lowly). The novel is also partially told from the perspective of Oscar's sister, Lola, another character who defies the stereotypical expectations of Latina characters. Tired of the force with which communities impose stereotypes on their own members, Lola rejects the injunction to be a señorita, becoming instead a punk chick with a Goth look. Lola describes the results as such: Puerto Rican kids "on the block couldn't stop laughing when they saw my hair, they called me Blacula, and the morenos, they didn't know what to say: they just called me devil-bitch. Yo, devil-bitch, yo, yo! My tia Rubelka thought it was some kind of mental illness."[29] Like Oscar, Lola lives in the ambivalence of being black and white but not quite either. When she runs away with her white boyfriend and lives with him and his father on the Jersey shore, she knows it is over when the boyfriend casually remarks: "Do you know what Pontiac stands for? Poor Old Nigger Thinks It's a Cadillac," looking straight at her when he delivers the punch line.[30]

Lola and, mainly, Yunior relate the story of Oscar's quest for love and the three heartbreaks of their mother Hypatía Belicia Cabral, about which they learn after she succumbs to breast cancer. Significantly, that narrative is not what one might expect: the saga of how an immigrant family deals with the tragedy of breast cancer (although, of course, that has its place too). Instead what we get is the story of what Díaz humorously calls the "Fukú americanus," or the curse that afflicts Oscar's family and all of us in the Americas, given the massacre and devastation that the birth of the New World entailed. "They say it came first from Africa, carried in the screams of the enslaved," writes Díaz in the opening line of the novel, "that it was the death bane of the Tainos, uttered just as one world perished and another began."[31] This invocation of the African diaspora and death of the Native American people haunts the lives of all those living in the Americas and frames Oscar's brief and wondrous life. In less able hands this set up might seem preposterous: What does the story of a forlorn ghetto nerd have to do with massive historical dramas? Díaz offers the proposition with a healthy dose of humor, but he also seriously proposes that history is not only the grand dramas of dictators and the theater of war and repression that they orchestrate but also the lives of the common people whose lives they shape. In framing his novel with this evocation, he also readily assumes an Afro-Latino consciousness.

The second wide-angle frame for Oscar's tale is located in his mother's past in the Dominican Republic. "Before there was an American Story," writes Díaz, "before Paterson spread before Oscar and Lola like a dream, or the trumpets from the Island of our eviction had even sounded, there was their mother, Hypatía Belicia Cabral . . . a girl so tall your leg bones ached just looking at her . . . so dark it was if the Creatrix had, in her making, blinked."[32] This black mother has a figurative mother, an aunt who is known as La Inca, a name that obviously suggests the native peoples of the Americas. These two women are the sources of life for Oscar and Lola, our Latinos living in America. Díaz invokes the complicated cultural heritage that Latinos bring to the United States. This cultural heritage involves the devaluation and persecution of blackness. Halfway through the novel we learn that Belicia survives a brutal beating in a cane field, orchestrated by Trujillo's sister. Part personal revenge, the beating also recalls the massacre of Haitians and Haitian Dominicans carried out by Trujillo in 1934. The Dominican Republic, Díaz shows, is a country where blackness is and continues to be despised despite the heavy African aspect of Dominican culture. Belicia thus becomes the symbol of what is considered abject in her own country. But the heritage she bequeaths to her children is not only one of pain and suffering. It is also one of obstinate survival despite huge odds. It is one of intense love. And Díaz renders her legacy with a language that swings to the rhythms of a narrativized soul-salsa.

"She Stood Like She Was Her Own Best Thing"

Ishmael Reed calls it "Jes Grew." Derek Walcott calls it "a grace born from subtraction."[33] Junot Díaz calls it the "zafa" against the "the Fukú." What all three authors are invoking is the legacy of survival that La Inca and Hypatía Belicia Cabral bequeath to future generations. "She stood like she was her own best thing."[34] This is Lola's description of La Inca, as the older woman waits for her upon the young one's arrival in Santo Domingo. Díaz's allusion to Toni Morrison's Beloved (1987) is one of the more subtle ways he connects this legacy of survival to the history of slavery and genocide.[35] As we have seen, he frames the entire novel with explicit references to this history and, throughout the text, suggests that it is this history that still shapes the "white supremacy and people-of-color self-hate" that surround Oscar, Lola, and Yunior.[36] But how does one represent the legacy of slavery and genocide without romanticizing survival or espousing static notions of history or of power? Whereas Walcott's medium is elegiac poetry, Reed's and Díaz's is postmodern humor. Both authors strike a balance between playful invocations of a struggle to survive against great odds and pointedly specific cases of this struggle in the context of the enslavement and persecution of black people in the Americas. The balance renders fluid notions of freedom and survival while not granting history a totalizing power. In their work, the immense impact of the history of slavery and genocide in the New World is unquestionable. In fact, both Reed and Díaz invoke the structures—for instance, multinational corporations and dictatorships—that perpetuate the ideologies born out of that history. Yet, individual choices, chance, circumstance, all have their place within the struggles that both authors represent.

In Mumbo Jumbo (1972), Reed sets "the Wallflower Order," an international conspiracy obsessed with power and profit against "Jes Grew," a fluid, hybrid, collaborative, decentralized, infectious phenomenon with no true definition, a sort of "anti-plague" that moves people to free forms of expression. The infection starts in colored ghettoes, and has its source in black culture (but even this is rendered in loose terms for, like Topsy, the virus "jes grew") but soon moves across racial divides and threatens to dismantle a world order forged upon the backs of the poor, the dispossessed, the dark. One cannot explain or give textual form to Jes Grew without destroying its carefree feeling. Yet without a text, it cannot survive for too long before it is rendered dormant by the power of the Order, which is loosely racialized as white. Jes Grew springs back and prospers eventually but cannot sustain its power. It is Reed's challenge to give Jes Grew textual expression and in *Mumbo Jumbo* he does so without killing its free nature.

Similarly, Díaz conjures the battle between the fukú, the curse that plays phonetically with a mundane curse ("fuck you," as Oscar absentmindedly discovers when he rolls "the word experimentally") and the zafa, defined as a "surefire counterspell," a simple word that for some is part of everyday superstition but for others can take the shape of an entire novel.[37] "It used to be more popular in the old days," writes Yunior, "bigger, so to speak, in Macondo than in McOndo," but there are still people, like his uncle "Miguel in the Bronx who still zafa everything." "He's old school like that," he tells us, "If the Yanks commit an error in the late innings it's zafa; if somebody brings shells in from the beach it's zafa; if you serve a man parcha it's zafa." But then, Yunior also suggests that the very book we are reading is "a zafa of sorts," his "very own counterspell."[38] Both spell and counterspell are playfully concocted oral and written words, fictional and yet connected clearly to historical events. After all, the "high priest" of the fukú is none other than Rafael Leónidas Trujillo Molina, the "pig-eyed mulato who bleached his skin" (sic) and who ruled the Dominican Republic in a dictatorship that lasted between 1930 and 1961."[39] Trujillo treated the Dominican Republic "like it was a plantation and he was the master," Yunior tells us, and waged a "genocide against the Haitian and Haitian-Dominican community," thus giving free rein to his and his country's hatred for black people. Díaz, like Thomas, is keen to the machinations of racial hatred, to the fact that it can be ingested and deployed by the very same people against which that hatred is directed. Thus, while he uses similes that clearly invoke the history of slavery to suggest the scope of Trujillo's tyranny, he also locates the legacy of that history in Trujillo's hatred of blackness, from his bleached skin to his genocidal acts. "No one knows whether Trujillo was the Curse's servant or its master, its agent or its principal," Yunior writes, and then, casually using African American slang, concludes, "but it was clear he and it had an understanding, that them too was tight."[40] Díaz thus leaves a certain amount of indeterminacy around the Curse and its agents, never negating their intimacy or effect, but nevertheless refusing to reify them.

For all of the indeterminacy surrounding the Curse, Trujillo's tyranny assumes extraordinary proportions and Díaz uses the fantastical language of science fiction and the hyperbolic verbal gestures of black barbershops and barrio corners to represent it. Alluding to major villains in fantasy genres and comic books, Yunior writes that for Dominicans Trujillo "was our Sauron, our Arawn, our Darkseid, our Once and Future Dictator, a personaje so outlandish, so perverse, so dreadful that not even a sci-fi writer could have made his ass up."[41] Díaz interweaves the different modes of expression that Yunior uses seamlessly. Again, Spanish is never italicized or translated, nor are the fantasy genre and comic book references explained. Fact is indeed stranger than fiction as Trujillo supersedes even the most fantastical characters in Yunior's hyperbolic comparisons, which also include his use of the casual language of the streets. Yet the informality of Yunior's modes of expression does not detract from the seriousness of his topic. The Curse, as William Deresiewicz notes, is a "kind of colonial Original Sin" that shapes the histories and contemporary cultures of all of the Americas.[42] (Puerto Rico, Peru, Mexico, Cuba are among the many other countries in the continent that become frequent points of reference throughout the novel.) Díaz challenges the reader to stay balanced between the two poles that he constructs: between the obviously fictional modes he employs to render a story that is stranger than the most outlandish fiction and the irresolute materiality of the history of which the fiction makes use.

While the Curse descends upon the poor, the dark, the disenfranchised, it also destroys those who might seem to be shielded from it by power and fame. In fact, Yunior suggests that the curse that seems to afflict the Kennedy family might in fact be connected to the Curse itself. John F. Kennedy was the one who "green-lighted the assassination of Trujillo in 1961, who ordered the CIA to deliver arms to the Island."[43] And what happened to him and his family? Keeping the mixture of humor and seriousness that he maintains throughout his discussion of the Curse, Yunior argues that Kennedy was killed by the fukú: "For what Kennedy's intelligence experts failed to tell him was what every single Dominican, from the richest jibao in Mao to the poorest güey in El Buey, from the oldest anciano sanmacorisano to the littlest carajito in San Francisco, knew: that whoever killed Trujillo, their family would suffer a fukú so dreadful it would make the one that attached itself to the Admiral jojote in comparison."[44] William Deresiewicz rightly highlights this passage as exemplary of the "audacity, bounce and brio" of Díaz's "bilingualism," which aggressively shifts the power balance away from monolingual readers.[45] This shifting also informs Díaz's challenge to hackneyed ideas regarding immigrants. In this passage, for instance, he locates Dominicans in San Francisco, expanding the scope of the Dominican diaspora well beyond New York and the North in general, and identifies more power in common peoples' knowledge than in that of intelligence experts. The pleasure of language is evident to all, however, in Díaz's rhymes ("jibao in Mao") and especially evident for those able to fully appreciate how seamlessly Díaz intertwines English and Spanish.

While Díaz challenges his readers' assumptions and linguistic knowledge in humorously teasing ways, what propels him to do so has a much more serious component. When asked to identify an author who has influenced his work, Díaz chose Toni Morrison because she "writes specifically for an African Diasporic community. Anyone who can read and can get a hold of her books is welcomed, but . . . we people of African descent are her privileged audience." Díaz adds, "Morrison is not attempting to translate black American culture for a white audience, she is no guide, no native informant. That is in itself revolutionary."[46] Díaz has also spoken about the pariah-like relationship that "many Latinos and black writers who are writing to white audiences, who are not writing to their own people," have in relationship to the communities from which they draw upon to make their art; they "loot them of ideas, and words, and images," Díaz argues, in order to "coon them to the dominant group."[47]

In his novel, by contrast, Díaz takes Morrison's cue and expands it, highlighting the specific qualities of Dominican Spanish and the distinctiveness of African American slang in order to create a sense of linguistic communities and inclusiveness. His privileged audience are those who recognize the "blunt, irreverent cant of the pueblo," coming both from the Dominican Republic and "142nd and Broadway," as well as those who, for instance, can and know how to use the controversial words "nigger" or "negro" as terms of endearment and affiliation.[48] Elaborating his theory that it was the fukú that killed Kennedy, Yunior asks, "How about Vietnam? Why do you think the greatest power in the world lost its first war to a Third World country like Vietnam? I mean, Negro, please."[49] His discussion of the machinations of the fukú mixes the exaggerations, founded and unfounded assertions, and paranoia of barbershop talks (in both Harlem and Spanish Harlem) with the surprising connections and pleasurable verbal flourishes that give those talks their distinctiveness. Yunior exemplifies the point he makes explicitly, mainly that common folk may know better and more than intelligence experts. Thus Yunior can just as easily switch into the language of an informant, though not a native informant, who can disclose information that his more general readership may not know about itself:

It might interest you that just as the U.S. was ramping up its involvement in Vietnam, LBJ launched an illegal invasion of the Dominican Republic (April 28, 1965). (Santo Domingo was Iraq before Iraq was Iraq). A smashing military success for the US, and many of the same units and intelligence teams that took part of the "democratization" of Santo Domingo were immediately shipped off to Saigon. What do you think these soldiers, technicians, and spooks carried with them, in their rucks, in their suitcases, in their shirt pockets, on the hair inside their nostrils, caked up around their shoes? . . . That's right, folks, Fukú.[50]

The switch in Yunior's tone, from the playfully lyrical use of Spanglish, to a more formal voice that provides historical facts (April 28, 1965), and connects parts of history not normally associated with one another (Vietnam, Santo Domingo, Iraq) and then back to a more teasing tone reveals a key aspect of Yunior as the novel's main narrator: he may be playful but he is always guided by serious concerns. The pleasure he takes in storytelling does not take away from one of his main subjects, which is the rendering in narrative how Oscar and Lola's mother survives and the legacy that she bequeaths to them. The story of that survival is at the center of the novel and storytelling is a key element of that story.

Indeed, storytelling is key in survival at different registers. For instance, Oscar survives his life as an ostracized nerd by taking refuge both in the fantasy genres that he loves and by writing profusely. He leaves behind copious notes, letters, and a manuscript for a four-book "never-to-be-completed-opus," which Yunior keeps after Oscar is killed in the Dominican Republic.[51] More important, he leaves behind his story, which haunts Yunior for ten years, demanding that it be told. Or, rather, the story of how Oscar came to be haunts Yunior, for Oscar's own story is not at the center of the novel. Oscar risks and ultimately loses his life for a chance to know real love but he remains something of a mystery. As William Deresiewicz notes, "We ultimately see much less of his inner life, and even of his outer life, than those of a handful of other characters," while he remains "something of a blank, perhaps deliberately" so.[52] What moves Yunior is the story of how and why Oscar, an unlikely hero, comes to have so much faith in love, so much so that he tries to defy death for it. And part of the answer lies in the story of his mother's survival.

We first meet Belicia through the eyes of her children, who see her only as a cantankerous workaholic, but Yunior allows us to see her in her youth, in a city of the Dominican Republic that is "famed for its resistance to blackness." Alas, it was here, writes Yunior, "that the darkest character of our story resided."[53] Belicia, to whom Yunior also refers as "our girl," or "our Beli," with the same kind of tender possessiveness that he refers to the narrative he is constructing ("our story"), is the last remaining survivor of a family killed by Trujillo. While the family's persecution has much more to do with Trujillo's sexual avarice than anything connected to race and racism, Beli's struggle to survive in the aftermath of her family's destruction is always associated with the fact of her blackness. As Yunior puts it, there was no escaping the tyranny of Trujillo since he made the Dominican Republic into the "Alcatraz of the Antilles." Options for anyone were "as rare as Tainos," but for those like Beli, "darkskinned flacas of modest means they were rarer still."[54] Díaz is intent upon marking "our girl" black not because he wants to cling to essentialist notions of race, but because he wants to recover and highlight part of the culture of the Dominican Republic that is vehemently denied.

Belicia's story comes to us mediated through Yunior's piecing together of her story, mainly from stories that he hears from Lola (who hears stories from Belicia herself when Belicia is dying), from Oscar's writing, and from family legends and tales, which Yunior collects and intertwines with his own historiographic forays into Dominican history and then recounts against the background of a metanarrative commentary. Yunior places a great deal of emphasis on the constructed nature of the story, but this never detracts from the story's force. Rather, it highlights the zafa aspect of storytelling. Its constructed nature is part of what makes storytelling a strong counterspell against such life-denying forces as the Curse, since through it one can give meaning to one's existence despite the chaos, the violence, and senselessness of persecution and destruction. In the case of Belicia, the Curse and its counterspell are both intimately connected to race and racism.

Yet, at one level, the story of Beli's coming of age is simply that: the story of a boy-crazy, stubborn, and beautiful girl who falls for the wrong guy, a character known only as the Gangster, who turns out to be married to Trujillo's sister. Díaz sustains the simplicity of this tale, letting the reader savor a common story told in a style that is fresh within American letters. But he also places that story in the context of racial hatred in the Dominican Republic, a racial hatred that he subtly identifies as a consequence of the enslavement of African peoples in the Americas and of its perpetuation by agents like Trujillo and his U.S. backers. Born sickly and quickly orphaned, Beli is sold by her own family to people who basically abuse her as they would a slave. She is so badly treated by her owners that she is burnt horribly and bears a terrible scar on her back, one reminiscent of the scar on Sethe's back in *Beloved* and on the back of the anonymous slave whose image was widely used by abolitionist press (taken April 2, 1863, in Baton Rouge, Louisiana).[55] "A monsterglove of festering ruination," is how Yunior describes the scar, which extends "from the back of her neck to the base of her spine."[56] Beli's scar, like Sethe's, comes to symbolize her status as orphaned, dark, and enslaved, for she comes to be known as "La Prieta Quemada or La Fea Quemada."[57]

Significantly, Beli is the last surviving member of a family that was not only light-skinned enough to be considered white but that was also wealthy and well respected. As La Inca never tires of reminding Beli, her father, Abelard Luis Cabral, was a famous doctor who came from a family that was "practically royalty."[58] However, his beautiful wife Socorro was darker than he was. Thus, while the first two daughters, Jacquelyn and Astrid, were only prone to suffering what Yunior teasingly calls "Mulatto Pigment Degradation Disorder, a.k.a. tans," Beli was born unquestionably black and "not just any kind of black. But *black* black—kongoblack, shangoblack, kaliblack, zapotecblack, rekhablack—and no amount of fancy Dominican racial legerdemain was going to obscure the fact."[59] Beli, by the very fact of her birth, exposes her country's open secret, its fierce denial of African roots, even among families that can pass for white. Díaz takes pleasure in exposing the secret through his composite words, the sound and typography of which evidence his delight in playing with form. Yet his play here, as elsewhere, is also pointed. The first two words clearly invoke Africa but the next three extend the allusion beyond it, including a reference to Kali, or the Dark Mother of Hindu mythology, who is a ferocious form of the mother goddess but whose jet black body is also meant to symbolize her all-embracing and transcendental nature. With his reference to Rekha, a Bollywood diva and Indian sex symbol in the 1980s, Díaz invokes an incarnation of Kali and associates Beli's darkness with both. By combining two references to powerful, dark Indian female figures with a reference to the "Zapotec," a pre-Columbian indigenous people from Oaxaca, in Central Mexico, a region noted for its African retentions, Díaz playful invokes another "Indian" people whose dark skin is rarely attributed to the African presence in Mexican culture. The three references also suggest the mixture of cultures that make up the Caribbean, including people from Southeast Asia (brought to the area through indentured servitude) and native peoples (like the Zapotec) who mixed with African captives. Of course, these associations are so embedded in Díaz's rhythmical language that it is also possible to read the lines without their references and appreciate the playfulness with which Díaz describes Beli's darkness.

Again, that playfulness does not obscure a sobering context. When La Inca, after having rescued her, wins Beli a scholarship at a wealthy, white school, Beli is ostracized. Even the only Chinese girl in the school, herself the object of racial hatred, has some "choice words for Beli": "You black, she said, fingering Beli's thin forearm. Black- black."[60] Later, when Beli falls for a boy who could not be whiter (Yunior jokingly calls him "albino"), richer, and more powerful, she hunts him like "Ahab after you-know-who." Given all the things the boy "was a symbol of," Yunior asks in parenthesis, "Wonder ye at the fiery hunt?"[61] Through the allusion to Melville, Díaz begins to link the perversity of miscegenation in the Dominican Republic and in the United States, extending the implied connection as Yunior relates the scandal that erupts when, after becoming lovers, Beli and her albino are caught in the act. "The fucking of poor prietas was considered standard operating procedure for elites," writes Yunior, using a curse word to bring into language the violence to which he is referring and then casually but poignantly adding, "Just as long as it was kept on the do-lo, what is elsewhere called the Strom Thurmond Maneuver."[62] The casual references to the fiery hunts and secrets of race and sexuality "elsewhere" reinforce the connections Díaz makes between the cultural heritage that the Latino characters in the novel inherit and the racial dynamics already in place (since before Melville through Strom Thurmond) in the United States, the country of their birth.

Distantly echoing the recuperative strategy implicit in the mantra "black is beautiful," Díaz balances the victimization of Beli by exalting her physical beauty—already suggested by his allusion to Rekha—and sense of integrity. Shortly before her first sexual conquest, Beli blooms into womanhood, and this is how Yunior describes the transformation:

> For the record, that summer our girl caught a cuerpazo so berserk that only a pornographer or a comic-book author could have designed it with a clear conscience. Every neighborhood has its tetúa, but Beli could have put them all to shame, she was La Tetúa Suprema: her tetas were globes so implausibly titanic they made generous souls pity their bearer and

drove every straight male in the vicinity to reevaluate his sorry life. She had the breasts of Luba (35DDD). And what about that supersonic culo that could tear the words right out of niggers' mouths, pull windows from out their motherfucking frames?[63]

Because Díaz repeatedly calls attention to Yunior's particular perspective, the description of Beli pulls the reader out into the frame of the story and back to the United States, where Yunior has learned the particular mix of verbal flourishes and street language that characterize his rendition of young Beli. The subject in question then becomes not only Beli and her beauty but also the language with which Yunior describes her, a language that embraces the particularities of the speaker and provides a version of the "street blend of Spanish and English with a strong tone of Negro American" that Piri hears on his stoop. The sexual brio that drives the passage is telling of Yunior's masculinist perspective, even of his machismo, but the passage is also driven by the exhilarating improvisational freedom with which Díaz combines Dominican Spanish and African American English. As William Deresiewicz puts it, the energy that drives Yunior's language is the "energy of the youth, of the streets, of desire—but it is also the energy of two languages meeting in secret hot, illicit sex."[64] The fact that Díaz relishes the slang of the languages he uses also adds to the illicit pleasure evident in the description. He is making art out of what is normally associated with the abject and the recovery is full of pleasure.

But while Yunior's Beli is a constructed fantasy—part pornographic dream, part comic book exaggeration (Luba is a reference to a busty and sexy character in the comic book series *Love and Rockets*)—he also combines his physical depiction of Beli with nuanced insights into her character. We know that she does not embrace her blackness. Despite the obvious, people around her do not dare call her "morena," but "india" instead, because she takes offense and is liable to beat people for it.[65] Yet she is also developing into a "hardnose no-nonsense femme-matador" and thus, after her rich white boy tosses her to the side when scandal erupts, she vows never to make herself subject to anyone else's will ever again.[66] In fact, she makes a vow that would "follow her into adulthood, to the States, and beyond." She declares, "I will not serve," a vow that comes to resonate with the history of slavery that, despite her own refusals, informs her identity.[67]

Her resolve is tested, however, when she falls in love with the Gangster. Unlike her earlier love affair, this one with the Gangster is "the real deal:

pure uncut unadulterated love, the Holy Grail that would so bedevil her children throughout their lives."[68] Significantly, Yunior connects the intensity of her desire "to be in love and to be loved back" to her abject position as a morena who was orphaned and sold as a slave by her own family. "As expected," he writes, "she, the daughter of the Fall, recipient of its heaviest radiations, loved atomically."[69] As expected? One might indeed expect the opposite. Morrison's *Beloved* and Gayl Jones's *Corregidora* (1975), among other novels that take up the sexual legacy of slavery, expose the near impossibility of romantic love in the aftermath of "the Fall" (which in Díaz's work is loosely connected to the Curse and its origins in colonialism and slavery). Díaz, however, challenges his readers to imagine the possibility that a survivor of the Fall may actually long for love, may believe in love precisely because it has been denied her. Perhaps because love is often dismissed as a feminine emotion, devoid of any political value, it is hardly ever considered in the literature that examines the legacy of slavery except as either an impossible emotion or as a source of tragedy. In Díaz, the desire for love is produced in part by its fierce denial. The same logic arguably informs the Ellisonian notion that African Americans believe fervently in American democracy precisely because they have been denied the freedom and dignity it can ideally afford.

But this is not to say that Díaz presents an unproblematic vision of love as transcendence. Beli pays dearly for loving. Since everything in the Dominican Republic is somehow filtered and controlled through Trujillo, it is not surprising that Beli's love should cross none other than the despot's sister, the Gangster's wife, who sends Beli to a beating in a cane field that ought to ensure her death. Díaz's choice of place as well as his deliberate descriptions of Beli as she is being beaten evoke a violent history in which blackness symbolizes utter abjection. "They beat her like she was a slave," he writes simply but forcefully. They beat her "like she was a dog."[70] Significantly, Díaz dispenses with details about the beating itself, noting only the hurt Beli feels in her nearly destroyed body after her aggressors leave her for dead. He notes each part of her broken body ("her clavicle, chicken-boned; her right humerus, a triple facture . . . five ribs, broken . . .") but never makes a spectacle of the violence inflicted upon it.[71] Instead, he notes the utter loneliness that enwraps her afterward: "It was into that loneliness that she was sliding, and it was here that she would dwell forever, alone, black, fea, scratching at the dust with a stick, pretending that the scribble was letters, words, names."[72] The fact that there are no witnesses to the violence and that she, having barely survived, seeks futilely to scribble evidence for it again points to Díaz's layered narrative: he is both telling Beli's story and reflecting on the role of writing in the construction of that story. Here, Beli's pretend writing, her scratching, compounds the already explicit description of her as abject—"alone, black, fea." Writing, like love, is far from romanticized. If it can give meaning to an existence under violent attack, it can also, through its perceived absence, measure the depth of one's subjection, of one's pain.

But Díaz expands his focus on love beyond romance. Yunior's act of recuperation, his piecing together of Beli's story and his placing it in the context of Oscar's, Lola's, and his own life, is an act of reclaiming a mother figure who is part Kali, part Rekha, part Indian; it is itself an act of love. We see this through Yunior's style but also through the parts of Beli's story that move him the most, which are those having to do with her obstinate will to survive. "Here she is," he writes, describing Beli when La Inca first rescues her, "Hypatía Belicia Cabral, the Third and Final daughter. Suspicious, angry, scowling, uncommunicative, a wounded hungering campesina, but with an expression and posture that shouted in bold, gothic letters: DEFIANT."[73] Strikingly, Yunior gives us a sense of Beli's defiance through the very rhythm and typography of his sentences. *Defiant*, in bold, is the last and reigning word in a sentence made of negative adjectives. (It stands out even in this very paragraph.) Again, however, Beli's survival is neither sugar-coated nor presented merely as a product of her character. We know that she survives in part by forgetting the past entirely. Echoing Derek Walcott, Yunior writes that Beli embraced "the amnesia that was so common throughout the Islands, five parts denial, five parts negative hallucination," and from this forgetting, she "forged herself anew."[74] Beli's survival is also absolutely predicated upon the help of others. La Inca is, of course, a central character in this respect. But there are also other forces Díaz explores that are less specific.

In a passage in which Díaz plainly plays with the conventions of magical realism, a genre that is all too easily associated with Latin American fiction because of its marketability, he gives us a vision of Beli's survival in the cane field. Beli survives the brutal beating only because "a creature that would have been an amiable mongoose if not for its golden lion eyes and the absolutely black of its pelt" appears out of nowhere to give her strength and guide her out of the maze made by the cane.[75] The would-be mongoose seems to have magical powers: it speaks and sings to Beli, filling her with strength, hope, and a vision of the children (Lola and Oscar) she will have in the future if she fights to survive. It flashes its "chabine eyes" to guide her and sings in an accent, "maybe Venezuelan, maybe Colombian," and with a "woman's tilt."[76] Díaz is clearly intent upon highlighting the fictional lens through which Yunior portrays Beli's survival. In fact, Yunior, in one of his many footnotes, has this to say about the small animal that saves Beli:

> The Mongoose, one of the great unstable particles of the Universe and also one of its greatest travelers. Accompanied humanity out of Africa and after a long furlough in India jumped ship to the other India, a.k.a. the Caribbean. Since its earliest appearance in the written record—675 B.C.E., in a nameless scribe's letter to Ashurbanipal's father, Esarhaddon—the Mongoose has proven itself to be an enemy of kingly chariots, chains, and hierarchies. Believed to be an ally of Man. Many Watchers suspect that the Mongoose arrived to our world from another, but to date no evidence of such migration has been unearthed.[77]

A nameless scribe writing to Ashurbanipal's father first refers to this mysterious being that appears more than once in the novel as an unknown but saving force. Through him, Díaz seems to ask, What is survival? How does someone like Beli, or the countless other dark-skinned victims of brutal beatings in the cane fields of slave societies, ever survive? Rather than answer the question by staging a period scene that makes an attempt at historical realism, or by employing a style rendered innocuous through its commercialization (magical realism), he emphasizes the imaginative act of fictive play. The mock footnote clearly works toward this goal. Díaz thus maintains a certain strategic mystery to the act of survival—not in order to mystify it, but in order to highlight its origins in the brutality of oppression. How can survival, a force so life affirming, come forth from its opposite, death and destruction? Díaz asks a version of this question when he opens the scene with the creature. "And now we arrive at the strangest part of our tale," he writes, whether "what follows is a figment of Beli's wracked imagination or something else altogether, I cannot say . . . But no matter the truth, remember: Dominicans are Caribbean and therefore have an extraordinary tolerance for extreme phenomena. How else could we have survived what we survived?"[78] Fiction, especially outlandish fiction, has served as a means of organizing the utter chaos created by the historical events that Díaz cites with the first sentence of his novel and which, as we see in the Latino characters in the novel, continue to resonate in the lives of those living in the aftermath. Fiction, especially the kind that Yunior produces in the process of reclaiming both the black (Beli) and native (La Inca) mothers of the New World, is one of the few means we may have to make palpable how survival is possible under conditions that obliterate reason and purpose.

The spirit of survival in Díaz's novel takes physical shape in a small furry black animal that, according to Yunior's humorous footnote, has a long history of serving humanity. Again, Yunior's playfulness is also historically connected. Díaz's nod in the footnote to Ashurbanipal, who is known both as the last great king of the Neo-Assyrian Empire and for his extensive royal library, subtly underscores both endings and legacies while calling attention to Yunior's role as the writer and preserver of a narrative of survival. At the same time, his play leaves open the mystery of survival without reducing it to sentimental renderings of heroism or limiting its power, by defining it in much the same way that Ishmael Reed invokes but does not defuse the power of Jes Grew. Of course, survival takes forms other than the mongoose in Díaz's novel, yet each form is rendered through obviously fictive means. Apart from Beli's defiance, there is also La Inca's love, which becomes communal when Beli is dragged to the cane fields. Like Beli's, La Inca's ability to hope is tested when she sees Beli disappear with Trujillo's agents. "Standing on the edge of the neighborhood, rigid as a post," writes Yunior, La Inca stared "hopelessly into the night," and "felt herself borne upon a cold tide of despair, bottomless as our needs . . . [she] let herself be lifted from her moorings . . . beyond the bright reef of her faith and into the dark reaches."[79] It is then that the ghost of her beloved dead husband speaks to her saying, "*You must save her . . . or no one else will.*"[80] And she does. She does so by praying intensely. Anticipating cynical responses, Yunior writes: "We postmodern plátanos tend to dismiss the Catholic devotion of our viejas as atavistic, an embarrassing throwback to the olden days, but it's exactly at these moments, when all hope is vanished, when the end draws near, that prayer has dominion."[81] La Inca's fierce praying attracts all of the women in the neighborhood so that "young and old, fierce and mansa, serious and alegre" gather to pray for Beli.[82]

A mongoose-like creature, a ghost, and a crowd of praying women are the means through which Yunior invokes the spirit of survival that ultimately gives birth to Lola and Oscar. Yunior's fictive playfulness might seem to mock the intensity and importance of the spirit that he invokes. Yet, by seemingly giving up the posture of authorship over his subject, he in fact highlights its enormity. It is only by gesturing playfully toward it that he can begin to hint at the mystery of what allows for survival when all hope seems to be gone. At the same time, Díaz also includes just enough realism to make his efforts effective. Anger, courage, and chance play a definite part in Beli's survival. Despite the mongoose, Beli almost succumbs to despair until she remembers her vow not to serve. It is then that her ire assumes cosmic levels, for she realizes that, in her need to love and be loved, she became blind to the callousness and cruelty of those who would easily use her (the Gangster) and dispose of her (Trujillo's system).[83] Yunior fittingly employs the hyperbolism of comic books, especially since the genre often depicts great battles between good and evil, to render the power of Beli's anger: "Like Superman in *Dark Knight Returns*, who drained from an entire jungle the photonic energy he needed to survive Coldbringer, so did our Beli resolve out of her anger her own survival."[84] Beli's recollection of her vow, in the middle of the cane fields, subtly reframes the battle she finally wins within the historical context with which the novel begins. Beli, daughter of the Fall, survives because she refuses to serve.

As an artist, Díaz also refuses to serve. Rather than act as a native informant or cultural translator, he maintains the brio of his hybrid language, finding a way of paying homage to the ancestral spirit of survival that he locates in Beli's plight without romanticizing it. Again, a touch of realism goes a long way. Once led out of the cane by the mongoose-like creature, Beli is almost flattened to the ground by a truck speeding by her. Yunior writes, "Now check it: the truck held a perico ripiao conjunto, fresh from playing a wedding in Ocoa. Took all the courage they had not to pop the truck in reverse and peel out of there. Cries of, It's a baká, a ciguapa, no, a hatiano! silenced by the lead singer, who shouted, It's a girl!"[85] The humorous replay of "it's a bird, it's a plane" with cultural signifiers that raise but mock Dominican jokes about Haitians and their black otherness, introduces the unlikely heroes of Beli's deliverance, lowly musicians with thinning hair who nevertheless play the *perico ripiao*, a type of merengue with strong African sounds that inspires sensual dances. Despite their utter fright when they learn that Beli has been subjected to a Trujillo beating, they take her to La Inca (it helps that Beli's eyes, described as the "golden eyes of a chabine," shine on the lead singer) and thus our Beli survives.[86]

Beli's legacy to her children is complicated. From her they inherit the great desire and need for love, but like her, they suffer because of it. Oscar, after all, is pulled back to the Dominican Republic by the force of love and dies in a cane field because of it. This "world seemed strangely familiar to him," Yunior writes, recounting Oscar's entry into the field. "He had the overwhelming feeling that he'd been in this very place, a long time ago."[87] In showing how the great drama of Beli's survival does not render future generations safe, Díaz suggests that each generation must contend with the violence of the past. At the same time, Yunior, in his self-consciously fictive account of the legacy that Beli bequeaths to her son, celebrates the stubborn desire for love even when it means facing death. The desire to live and love to the fullest despite the past's violent pull is what Oscar inherits from Belicia, and it is the legacy that Yunior is intent on preserving.

In the novel's last pages, we learn that Yunior has kept all of Oscar's writings to safeguard them for the youngest member of the family, Lola's daughter, Isis, for whom, in part, Yunior writes the novel that we are reading. Maybe "if she's as smart and as brave as I'm expecting she'll be," writes Yunior, "she'll take all we've done and all we've learned and add her own insights and she'll put an end to it."[88] He is referring, of course, to the Curse, which Yunior suspects will never be eradicated. But he is also referring to the cultural heritage that he has recovered and embraced through the vigor of his fiction. That heritage includes the valorization of the African roots of Dominican culture, which Díaz embodies in Beli. Yet, while Díaz centers the historical conditions that threaten and nearly kill Beli and what she embodies, through Yunior he also creates what Walter Mosley calls a "rousing hymn about the struggle to defy bone-cracking history with ordinary, and extraordinary love."[89] Love is at the center of the novel in all of its varieties—there is Lola's love for her nerdy brother, Yunior's lasting love for Lola despite their break-up, La Inca's love for her daughter figure Beli, Beli's love for her Gangster, Oscar's love for Ybon, Beli's love for life, Oscar's love for fiction, and finally Yunior's, and by extension Díaz's, love of language.

Díaz's choice to celebrate love, in a novel that addresses large historical events and their repercussions in the present, reflects his overall desire to challenge limiting conceptions of what writers of color should address and how. Too often simple but powerful human stories—such as those of the love between the various characters in *Oscar Wao*—are drowned out by more overtly political concerns. Díaz balances his resolve to be a responsible, conscientious writer and his firm desire not to compromise his fiction in the name of fitting into some prefabricated notion of what a writer of color ought to write about and how. His mixing of languages in his work highlights not only the "possibilities of linguistic disjuncture and compatibility" in the various communities he draws from, especially the Latino and black communities, but also his desire to break an implicit taboo. "Groups of color rarely write to each other," he said in an interview. "They write for themselves or white people. Rarely do you see Asian American writers writing for themselves and for the African American or Latino community, or African American writers writing for themselves and the Latino community." Instead, they "encounter each other at the level of appropriation [and 'kitsch'] but not on a historical level."[90] Díaz, by contrast, couches his experiments with Dominican Spanish, Latino Spanish, and African American slang in a historical framework that anchors his work without weighing it down.

Díaz's formal experimentation allows him to highlight one of the most persistent means by which the oppressed have survived. Language, Díaz claims in an interview, "is in some ways a catalog or a pantheon of our survival, because in all languages—inside their lexicons, inside their syllabaries—in there are all these survivors from past catechisms."[91] As Díaz explains, if, due to Spanish colonialism, the Taino language of the natives of what is now the Dominican Republic was stamped out, vestiges of that language remain imprinted in the Spanish spoken in the Dominican Republic. Similarly, if English were to override the Spanish of a person like Díaz, who came to the United States as a child and learned English as a second language, Spanish would stubbornly remain a part of his creative process even as he writes primarily in English. What survives, as in the case of Taino language in Spanish, may only be "tiny relics," "small, little fragments," against "huge waves" of another language that swallows up the language of the conquered. But Díaz sees his role as a novelist as entailing the carrying forward of the fragments, big or small, because it is in those fragments that we can find a "testament of what happened" not only to those that were conquered but also to those that conquered. "All of our history," Díaz concludes, "all of our crimes, all of the good things we've done are embedded in that fluid thing we call language."[92]

Notes

1. See, for instance, Juan Flores, "Nueva York, Diaspora City," in Bilingual Games, ed. Doris Sommer (Cambridge, MA: Harvard University Press, 2003); Paula M. L. Moya, "Why I Am Not Hispanic: An Argument with Jorge Gracia," Newsletter on Hispanic/Latino Issues in Philosophy 1, no. 1, 17 paragraphs; Paula M.L. Moya, "With US or Without Us: The Development of a Latino Public Sphere," Nepantla: Views from South 4, no. 2 (2003): 245–52; Marta Caminero-Santangelo, On Latinidad: U.S. Latino Literature and the Construction of Ethnicity (Gainesville: University Press of Florida, 2007).

2. The Puerto Rican-Colombian actor John Leguizamo has humorously rejected the identity label *Hispanic* on the grounds that he does not want to be associated with a term that includes the word *panic*. See also Ivonne García, who writes:

> Under Hispanic, the OED proposes as its main definition: "Pertaining to Spain or its people; esp. pertaining to ancient Spain," and notes that the first use of "Hispanicall" is found in 1584, as in the "Hispanicall inquisition." Later, in the nineteenth century, the OED notes usages of "Hispanicisms" and "Hispanisms" in several sources. The second meaning accepted by the OED for Hispanic refers to "Spanish-speaking, esp. applied to someone of Latin-American descent living in the United States." The first reference to that secondary definition that the OED found is from 1974. For Latino, the OED states: "A Latin-American inhabitant of the United States," and finds its first usage in 1946. For the OED, then, Hispanic is directly related to Spain, while Latino refers only to Latin Americans. I think there are many of us who would take issue with those definitions, especially the latter one.
>
> The OED has its own culturally specific view, as we all do. But if I have learned one thing about names it is that while they do matter, they should not become a source of disunity among us. Whether we call ourselves Latin@, Puerto Rican, Boricua, Nuyorican, Chican@, Mexican-American, Mexican, Salvadoran, Guatemalan, Ecuadorean, or Hispanic, we're all, in many ways, in the same politically disenfranchised, economically deprived and struggle-ridden boat. (Ivonne García, "Latin@ or Hispanic: Does It Make a Difference?," accessed November 29, 2008, http://quepasa.osu.edu/issues /spo5/article14.htm.

3. Moya, "Why I Am Not Hispanic," paragraph 17.

4. Caminero-Santangelo, *On Latinidad*, 21.

5. As Paula Moya argues, "How a person identifies herself has profound consequences for how she understands the world and, consequently, for how she chooses to act within it." A Mexican American, she refers to herself as Latina when she "wants to signal an experiential, and to a lesser degree political and cultural affiliation with a larger group of people living in the US who themselves or whose ancestors have come to this country" from the various countries of Latin America. The term refers to "basically the same group of people" designated by the term *Hispanic*, "with one crucial difference." When Moya refers to Latinos/as, she is "not referring to people living in Latin America or Spain." This is not because she is "a nationalist, or because [she] is biased against Latin Americans and Spaniards." In fact, she acknowledges "the important connections (economic, political, intellectual, familial, and cultural) that exist between Latina/os in the United States and Latin America and residents of the Iberian peninsula." Yet, she rightly believes that "when it comes to assigning and describing social identities . . . it is important to recognize the specificity of geopolitical space, and the experiential significance of being an ethnic minority citizen or resident of a country like the United States." ("Why I Am Not Hispanic," paragraphs 2 and 6.) Elsewhere Moya

has written about the role of the "US government, corporate advertisers, television ex-ecutives, print media, and the entertainment industry" in producing the ethnic group called Hispanic, or Latino. But, she is also open to the possibility of using the identity ef-fectively "for progressive political or social change" ("With US or Without Us," 245–52.)

6. Flores, "Nueva York," 73.

7. Mark Sawyer, "Racial Politics in Multiethnic America: Black and Latina/o Identi-ties and Coalitions," in Anani Dzidzienyo and Suzanne Oboler, eds., *Neither Enemies Nor Friends: Latino/as, Blacks, Afro Latinos* (New York: Palgrave, 2005), 265.

8. Flores, "Nueva York," 73.

9. Piri Thomas, *Down These Mean Streets* [1967] (New York: Vintage Books, 1997), 121.

10. Tato Laviera, "The Salsa of Bethesda Fountain," in *La Carreta Made a U-Turn* [1979] (Houston: Arte Público, 1992), 67.

11. Here and throughout I distinguish between Thomas, the author of the memoir, and Piri, its protagonist.

12. Thomas, *Down These Mean Streets*, 122.

13. Downes v. Bidwell 182 US244, 287 (1901); Balzac v. Porto Rico, 258 US 298 (1922). The United States federal law is applicable to Puerto Rico, even though Puerto Rico is not a state of the American Union and has no voting representative in the United States Congress.

14. Thomas, *Down These Mean Streets*, 125.

15. Some critics have noted that the homosocial bond between Brew and Piri comes at the expense of women. See, for instance, Marta E. Sánchez, "La Malinche at the In-tersection: Race and Gender in *Down These Mean Streets*," PMLA: *Publications of the Modern Language Association of America* 113, no. 1 (January 1998): 117–29. In an interview Thomas states that Brew is a composite character that he created by splicing his memories of the real Brew and another person named Isaac Nasario. See Dorotee von Huene Green-berg, "Piri Thomas: An Interview," MELUS: *The Society for the Study of the Multi-Ethnic Lit-erature of the United States* 26, no. 3 (fall 2001): 82–84.

16. James Wood, "Call It Sleep," *The New Republic*, December 16, 1996, 41, 39.

17. Junot Díaz, *Drown* (New York: Riverhead Books, 1996). See also Gustavo Pérez Firmat, "Dedication," in Virginia Seeley, ed., *Latino Caribbean Literature* (Los Angeles: Paramount, 1994), 10.

18. Frances Aparicio, "On Sub-versive Signifiers: US Latino/a Writers Tropicalize English," *American Literature* 66, no. 4 (December 1994): 796–97.

19. Evelyn Nien-Ming Ch'ien, *Weird English* (Cambridge, MA: Harvard University Press, 2004), 202.

20. Quoted in Ch'ien, *Weird English*, 208.

21. Milca Esdaille, "Same Trip, Different Ships," *Black Issues Book Review* 3, no. 2 (March/April 2001): paragraph 18, accessed via Academic Search Premier.

22. Junot Díaz, interview with Silvio Torres-Saillant and Diogenes Cespedes, "Fic-tion Is the Poor Man's Cinema," *Callaloo* 23, no. 3 (summer 2000): 904.

23. Ch'ien, *Weird English*, 204.

24. Wood, "Call It Sleep," 39.

25. A. O. Scott, "Dreaming in Spanglish," review of *The Brief Wondrous Life of Oscar Wao*, by Junot Díaz, paragraph 4, accessed April 22, 2015, http://www.nytimes.com/2007/09/30/books/review/Scott-t.htm.

26. Junot Díaz, *The Brief Wondrous Life of Oscar Wao* (New York: Riverhead Books, 2007), 21.

27. Díaz, *Oscar Wao*, 22.

28. Díaz, *Oscar Wao*, 49.

29. Díaz, *Oscar Wao*, 54.

30. Díaz, *Oscar Wao*, 66–67.

31. Díaz, *Oscar Wao*, 1.

32. Díaz, *Oscar Wao*, 77.

33. Ishmael Reed, *Mumbo Jumbo* (Garden City, NY: Doubleday, 1972). See also Derek Walcott, *Omeros* (New York: Farrar, Straus and Giroux, 1990), 149–50. A 325-page epic poem with rolling hexameters in *terza rima*, *Omeros* imaginatively excavates sites of memory—the floor of the Atlantic, precolonial Africa—to memorialize the victims of the slave trade. A "grace born of subtraction" is the phrase the poet uses to imagine the act of survival in the context of a brutal history. Díaz chose a section from Walcott's "The Schooner's Flight," in *The Star-Apple Kingdom* (1979), another poem that memorializes the victims of the slave trade, as the epigraph for *The Brief Wondrous Life of Oscar Wao*.

34. Díaz, *Oscar Wao*, 74.

35. "You your own best thing," Paul D tells a heartbroken Sethe at the end of *Beloved*. Díaz has identified both *Down These Mean Streets* and *Beloved* as powerful influences on his work. "They just opened my mind to the power of words." See Junot Díaz, interview with Silvio Torres-Saillant and Diogenes Cespedes, 900. "Morrison fundamentally altered my entire vision of writing," Díaz told Milca Esdaille. Esdaille, "Same Trip, Different Ships," paragraph 7.

36. Díaz, *Oscar Wao*, 264.

37. Díaz, *Oscar Wao*, 304, 7.

38. Díaz, *Oscar Wao*, 7.

39. Díaz, *Oscar Wao*, 2.

40. Díaz, *Oscar Wao*, 2–3.

41. Díaz, *Oscar Wao*, 2.

42. William Deresiewicz, "Fukú Americanus," *The Nation*, November 2007, 37–38.

43. Díaz, *Oscar Wao*, 3.

44. Díaz, *Oscar Wao*, 3.

45. Deresiewicz, "Fukú Americanus," 39–40.

46. Esdaille, "Same Trip, Different Ships," paragraph 7.

47. Díaz, interview with Silvio Torres-Saillant and Diogenes Cespedes, 900.

48. Díaz, *Oscar Wao*, 108.

49. Díaz, *Oscar Wao*, 4.

50. Díaz, *Oscar Wao*, 4.

51. Díaz, *Oscar Wao*, 333.

52. Deresiewicz, "Fukú Americanus," 41.

53. Díaz, *Oscar Wao*, 78.

54. Díaz, *Oscar Wao*, 80.

55. See http://research.archives.gov/description/533232, accessed April 22, 2015. The image is accompanied by the following description: "Overseer Artayou Carrier whipped me. I was two months in bed sore from the whipping. My master come after I was whipped; he discharged the overseer. The very words of poor Peter, taken as he sat for his picture."

56. Díaz, *Oscar Wao*, 257. Díaz's choice of the word *ruination* signifies on Michelle Cliff's novel *No Telephone to Heaven* (1987), in which the word figures prominently. A novel about a mixed-race Jamaican family that immigrates to the United States, *No Telephone to Heaven* also focuses on Jamaica and the image of ruination, a Jamaican term used to describe lands which were once cleared for agricultural purposes by ruling classes but have now lapsed back into their original wild states, into "bush." Ruination consumes the land and makes it unusable for the poor, but it also overthrows the colonial and commercial order. The word and concept come to have ambiguous meaning in Cliff's novel, balancing between images of ruin and those of victorious reappropriation. Díaz's use of the word to describe Beli's scar gestures toward a novel that, like *The Brief Wondrous Life of Oscar Wao*, explores the intersection of immigration and race in the United States in the context of Caribbean history. It also suggests a symbolic connection between Beli's body and that of her native island as literarily branded by the violence of racism although, as in Cliff, that branding does not mean utter subjugation.

57. Díaz, *Oscar Wao*, 261.

58. Díaz, *Oscar Wao*, 212.

59. Díaz, *Oscar Wao*, 213, 248.

60. Díaz, *Oscar Wao*, 84.

61. Díaz, *Oscar Wao*, 95.

62. Díaz, *Oscar Wao*, 100.

63. Díaz, *Oscar Wao*, 92.

64. Deresiewicz, "Fukú Americanus," 41.

65. Díaz, *Oscar Wao*, 115.

66. Díaz, *Oscar Wao*, 101. Díaz's use of the phrase *femme-matador* is a nod to Patrick Chamoiseau's great novel *Texaco* (1998), a work that is central to his formal experimentation, particularly his use of footnotes (which critics, as Díaz has clarified in readings of his novel, have erroneously compared to those in the works of David Foster Wallace). Like *Oscar Wao*, *Texaco* focuses on the plight of a female character, Marie-Sophie Laborieux, an indomitable and profanely wise "femme-matador," whose intense desire, for real love, for a country, for a home, Chamoiseau intertwines with the birth of his native Martinique and the often violent struggles between the French and the African peoples that gave it birth.

67. Díaz, *Oscar Wao*, 103.

68. Díaz, *Oscar Wao*, 125–26.

69. Díaz, *Oscar Wao*, 126.

70. Díaz, *Oscar Wao*, 147.

71. Díaz, *Oscar Wao*, 147.

72. Díaz, *Oscar Wao*, 148.

73. Díaz, *Oscar Wao*, 258.

74. Díaz, *Oscar Wao*, 258–59. See Derek Walcott's poem "Laventille," from *The Castaway and Other Poems* (1965) included in *Collected Poems 1948–1984* (New York: Farrar, Straus and Giroux, 1986), 85–88. Here the poet explores the "amnesiac blow" that the survivors of the slave trade suffered (88).

75. Díaz, *Oscar Wao*, 149.

76. Díaz, *Oscar Wao*, 150. "Chabine," is another nod to Walcott who, in "The Star-Apple Kingdom," the poem that Díaz quotes in the epigraph of his novel, names his protagonist Chabine. This character is of mixed cultural background: "I'm just a nigger who loved the sea, / I had a sound colonial education, / I have Dutch, nigger, and English in me, / and either I'm nobody or I am a nation."

77. Díaz, *Oscar Wao*, 151.

78. Díaz, *Oscar Wao*, 149.

79. Díaz, *Oscar Wao*, 144.

80. Díaz, *Oscar Wao*, 144.

81. Díaz, *Oscar Wao*, 144.

82. Díaz, *Oscar Wao*, 144.

83. We know that the Gangster wants Beli in great part only as a diversion from his troubled, violent life (124–25). As Yunior writes, there is "a pretty solid argument to be made that La Inca was right; the Gangster was simply an old chulo preying on Beli's naïveté" (126).

84. Díaz, *Oscar Wao*, 148.

85. Díaz, *Oscar Wao*, 150–51.

86. Díaz, *Oscar Wao*, 151.

87. Díaz, *Oscar Wao*, 298.

88. Díaz, *Oscar Wao*, 330–31.

89. Walter Mosley, blurb for *The Brief Wondrous Life of Oscar Wao*.

90. Junot Díaz, interview with Evelyn Ch'ien, July 26, 2002. Printed in Ch'ien, *Weird English*, 218.

91. Armando Celayo and David Shook, "In Darkness We Meet: A Conversation with Junot Díaz," *World Literature Today* 82, no. 2 (March–April 2008): 17.

92. Díaz, in Celayo and Shook, "In Darkness We Meet: A Conversation with Junot Díaz," 17.

11. A Planetary Warning?

The Multilayered Caribbean Zombie in "Monstro"

Sarah Quesada

> Apocalypse is a darkness that gives us light.
> —Junot Díaz, "Apocalypse"

The ubiquitous nature of the zombie figure is symptomatic of socioenvironmental decomposure. Born from slavery, these creatures unconsciously emerge as a "comment on the disruption of an economy" that signals unprecedented global changes.[1] If they are traditionally found at the intersection of doom and hope, of pandemonium and adaptation, zombie monsters surface textually as signifiers recasting the past to illuminate present circumstances that portend future chaos. Underneath their supposed misunderstood appearance, these "othered" beings function as symbols for social commentary. Junot Díaz's short story "Monstro" (2012) possesses, at the base of its criticism, an eerie quintessential globalization model that foretells the end results of neoliberal capitalism. This Caribbean sci-fi journey is, in essence, a futuristic account of an unimaginably prosperous sugar island, turned darkly decadent, whose only hope is found in an allegorical signifier—that is, the legend of the living dead. This being will most likely become the epicenter of his humorous satire, one which Díaz is developing, he says, into his next novel.

In the Afro-futurist Antillean setting of "Monstro," the narrator, an unnamed ivy league Dominican student, "chas[es] after a girl."[2] While he agonizes over her, he tells in analepsis that a cataclysm erupted with the appearance in Haiti of a disease. At the root of the story is Díaz's critical dialectic on race, with the illness appearing as a "negrura" ("blackness") that "makes Haitians darker."[3] As this infection progresses, it morphs the "viktims" into zombie-like creatures in a predicted future where the precariat live amid a naturally degraded, socially unjust society.[4] The infected soon become lethal, termed "The Possessed."[5] In order to contain the violence, a presumably futuristic nuclear warhead is dropped by a Western "Joint Chief of Staff," rendering the world "white."[6] The blast only serves to further reveal the ultimate transformation of the monsters into Caribbean-cannibalistic-Caliban creatures that will forever threaten the delicate thread of human existence.

The apocalypse of "Monstro" is a literary subversion that enables the evolution of the zombie figure from a plantational to racialized subject, to a victim of neoliberal policies, and ultimately a signifier of decolonial resistance. This chapter analyzes the development of the zombie while uncovering the variegated symbolic levels of Díaz's zombies. Although apocalypse manias are commonplace in our day and age, what is less evident to readers is the appearance of a giant monster leading to earth's extinction. Indeed, we must only look to the title, "Monstro" (phonetic for *monstruo* in Spanish), to reflect on its Latin root *monere*, which, according to the *Oxford English Dictionary*, means *to warn* and *to instruct*. It will be crucial then to question what specifically Díaz is warning us about with a Caribbean-incepted zombie and its developing transformations. The claim I make is that their evolution mirrors the historical progression of capital-based societies, insofar as they inherit westernized structures of power and have now entered an unsustainable era of production. On the one hand, I analyze how these monster-creatures can be read as symbols that underscore a commentary on past transatlantic economies (and ever-present racism) and current neoliberalization. On the other hand, drawing from the theoretical "monster" posited by Michel Foucault, I read how these paradigms, reused in the literary imaginary, culminate in a decolonial reading, which conveys that the zombie may be a mere illusion meant to be morally and futuristically cautionary. As a result, not only does "Monstro" prompt a meditation on a vodou-animated creature coated in raciology, but science fiction as a genre facilitates a social critique that translates the persistent and transcendental effects of the colonial apparatus.

In light of Díaz's renderings of an impossible yet impossibly real tale is the consideration of the Latin American postmodern and Caribbean poetics influencing the story. In terms of a strictly Latin American paradigm, the textual techniques of realism used in the 1960s that preceded his writing were crucially formative. To communicate catastrophes or incredible spectacles, the Cuban writer Alejo Carpentier resorted to what he termed lo real maravilloso, which the Colombian Nobel laureate Gabriel García Márquez also used stylistically. The postmodern critical frameworks emerging in the second half of the twentieth century resulted in an alternative to journalism or modern realism. These tools adopted a position somewhere between fiction and reality, in which playful yet stern societal criticism was implicit— an elemental tool for Díaz, who now raises narrative up a level with science fiction. With regard to the Caribbean black aesthetic, it is vital to consider the Cuban poet Nicolás Guillén and his conception of "blackness" prior to the 1940s Négritude movement. Guillén's poetics inform the early notion of blackness in Díaz's Antillean racial critique and thus empower his ideological, decolonial project. Díaz's predecessors contextualize the hermeneutics of his uprooting of race and space codifications embodied in a transformational zombie.

A final point before I turn to analysis is the following claim: Díaz's trans-American but also transatlantic story uses former and current impasses of the African diaspora, including the jarring misery of Haiti's past and present state. Therefore, to ground "Monstro" as a moralizing tale, placed within an Afro-futuristic aesthetic, we must look at how Haiti became for Díaz a devotional space to reflect on anthropogenic catastrophes. Díaz's journalistic career and intimate experience with the Dominican-Haitian racial conflict compelled him to write his philosophical meditation "Apocalypse" (2010) following the devastation of the earthquake in Haiti in 2010. Within this essay, Díaz identified Haiti as a country oppressed by the coloniality of power and never freed from the curse of having been the archetypal plantocracy. Díaz therefore sees in Haiti a microcosm that causes the reader to reevaluate the fundamental historiography of early and late capital production and its global effects. Emphatic and confrontational, "Apocalypse" becomes a realist prequel to "Monstro" and furnishes us with crucial tools for understanding the futuristic accounts that his short story seeks to foretell.

The Racialized (Plantational) Zombie

The opening lines of "Monstro" offer a dialectic on race as an infectious disease spreads in Haiti: "They called it la negrura, blackness."[7] The disruption and de-centering of Eurocentric racial concepts in "Monstro" is set in the crucial former plantation realm of the Caribbean. Crucial, due first to Díaz's personal and emotional investment toward identity relations between the Dominican Republic and Haiti, and second, because the preferred and oft-repeated Caribbean backdrop of Díaz's fiction is an obvious choice to express the stories of impossibly real colonial effects on theories of race discourse. Alejo Carpentier, in his prologue to El reino de este mundo (1949), stated that in fact it was while he was in Haiti that he came "in contact with the quotidian [of] the marvelous real."[8] The liberationist exploits of Mackandal, Toussaint Louverture, and Henri Christophe not only drew Cuban authors such as Carpentier to Haiti's history, they intrigued an entire continent.[9] The marvelous real (lo real maravilloso), as coined by Carpentier, conceived of the Caribbean as a locale where the incidences of colonial contact merge with the fantastic, and the famous line "who is more sci-fi than us [the Caribbean]?" from his prior work The Brief Wondrous Life of Oscar Wao points to Díaz's corroboration of Carpentier's claim.[10] As if echoing Carpentier, in "Monstro," the narrator's friend Alex, upon picking him up from the airport, calls out "welcome to the country of las maravillas," alluding to a palimpsest of meanings surrounding the fantastic conditions of the island shared by two nations.[11] Revolutionizing the narrative with humor, Díaz's active syncretization of genre and colonialism—literature and history—works congruently to reveal the bestiality of empire (old and new). Even though Díaz regrets that science fiction is a genre that "nobody takes seriously," he explains that it is "best suited to explaining the events of colonialism and its extreme cultural violence."[12] Not available to Carpentier as a genre in his lifetime per se, Díaz takes full advantage of science fiction to weave a narration that is racially charged, arising from the Caribbean plantocracy.

"Monstro" is located in Haiti specifically, as exemplary of lo real maravilloso, for two main reasons. First, if the strange disease is rooted in colonialism, then placing the story in Haiti—as one of the first ports of the European arrival of slavery—would be telling of the story's decolonial argument against racial hierarchies initiated in the Caribbean. Second, it is in Haiti where, during the slave trade and the formation of the Atlantic world, the realization of the zombie conception fully emerges. The historical arrival of zombification to the New World dislocated Western concepts of order in the colonies. In narrative discourse, this subversion was relayed as a "curse" in *The Brief Wondrous Life of Oscar Wao*. In "Monstro," however, Díaz's zombie makes its appearance in the form of a disease that is both racially selective and racial in and of itself.

In Díaz's story, recognizable signs in the diseased point to the fact that they are not only developing into another species but, more specifically, zombies. These various symptoms include "low body temperature" fluctuating to "radiant blue" (code for stone dead), "lingering on and on," "roaming about the camp at odd hours," "never sleeping," unintelligibly "shriek[ing] together," and being described as "bewitched."[13] Eventually the dogged strength of "the Possessed" leads to bloodshed. They are "so relentless that they clung onto" escaping victims, having to be "shot off."[14] In contrast to their popular depiction as relentless, murderous creatures of evil origins, the zombies of "Monstro" are the inevitable products of capitalism. They come into existence when an individual is "transformed purely into alienated labour power . . . and made to serve as someone else's privatized means of production."[15] The most ancient form of industrialization's means of production in the Americas is slavery, and zombies are a byproduct of slave-trade commerce. Zombies therefore are conceived of as an Atlantic world, trans-American phenomenon.

During the plantocracy in the Caribbean, the success of the large-scale transatlantic slave trade was due to the acquisition of inexpensive labor to produce a desired commodity. If the Caribbean was the empire of sugar production, Haiti—then Saint-Domingue—was its capital. In the seventeenth century and the eighteenth, this "pearl of the Antilles" also became the principal receptor of African slaves. Imported into the New World market, the slaves also introduced their cultural artifacts, reacting to the despicable treatment of the French plantations. Their spiritual practices generated a syncretic resistance in the form of *voudism* (vodun, or voodoo), once practiced in Dahomey (today the Republic of Benin). This spiritual buttress found its home in Haiti, as did the conception of the zombie as a derivative element of vodun. A zombie, as it was conceived in Benin, was an individual arrested while crossing from life to death. On the plantation, to commit suicide was to risk being kidnapped by a spiritual presence and turned into a walking automaton without agency. This was a deep source of anguish for slaves seeking to escape a life of bondage—even if it meant through death. The underlying hindrance was that to become a zombie, one would continue being a slave even after death.[16] Since that time, the living dead have evolved into a mainstay of popular culture, but the zombie's original source in the Americas was the plantation.

Unbeknownst to mainstream culture, the zombie "arose from the mixture of old African religious beliefs and the pain of slavery."[17] Since zombies are connected to New World slavery and the transatlantic slave trade, they are also racialized symbols of plantational labor. In fact, the literary critic Saidiya Hartman metaphorically argued that "the human pulse stops at the gate of the barracoon," referencing how a zombie was code for a slave who upon being "uprooted" became an "earmark of the dead man."[18] In other words, perceptions of nonwhite identity in the colonial era became synonymous with a person's "unnatural death."[19] Slaves were not participating citizens in society; they were the opposite, and as subjects without agency their skin color signaled their status. For Díaz, then, if the living dead are a politicized statement on the interruption of an ill-functioning system, they may also be the archetype for a discourse on race. Analyzed from a certain vantage point, Díaz's indelible sarcasm recognizes New World plantation history.

Transporting the reader to the locale of slavery with the zombie figure, "Monstro" meditates on the "coloniality of power," a term chiefly advanced by Aníbal Quijano.[20] The power exerted over the Caribbean, as a laboratory for empire, presumes in Quijano's words a "codification of the differences between conquerors"—those who would exert such power—"and the conquered in the idea of 'race.'"[21] In these specified spaces, the idea of race supposed innate differences justifying a natural "inferiority."[22] As if to illustrate the historical discourse on racial hierarchy constructions, "Monstro" comments on slavery's indelible mark, which "hardened into" a "color line."[23] In Díaz's Bildungsroman, the opening lines, "They say it came from Africa screaming in the voices of the enslaved," refer to both the transAtlantic slave trade and a colonial curse that eventually lead to the crystallization of racism.[24] Díaz's choice to focus on Haiti reels in the history of the island as both the birthplace of voudism and that of the plantocracy, which led to the internalization of race differences. This "color complex" produced the acceptance of terms such as blanqueamiento ("racial whitening") that would enable the achievement, or preservation, of a higher-class status.[25] The term is visibly one of those products of colonialism "Monstro" localizes and dislodges.

Juxtaposed with the internalization of blanqueamiento, then, is *negrura*. Evidently aware of his predecessors in the so-called *negrista* movement, Díaz construes in his zombie story a concept of "darkness" the way the Cuban poet Nicolás Guillén reimagined blackness.[26] By harnessing *blackness*, a term that endured a negative connotation before and during Guillén's lifetime, Guillén destabilized its meaning at the beginning of the twentieth century. He employed the vernacular Cuban *chotismo* to underscore the repressive culture toward the black Cuban, all while introducing colloquial black speech into modernity's poetics. In what is arguably his most famous poem, "Negro bembón," the poetic voice asks, "Why do you get angry when they call you black *bembón* / if your mouth is holy?"[27] The word *bembón* ("thick-lipped") was a racial slur used in an intentionally deprecating way but in his poem, Guillén materializes the term *bembón* and, with it, the race complex by pointing to the effects of slavery on the very idea of blackness.

Far from eliminating Caribbean racial intolerance as Guillén would have hoped, discriminatory attitudes have persisted.[28] In Díaz's context, this is particularly true when it comes to relations between Haiti and Díaz's native Dominican Republic.[29] With almost caustic humor at its disposal, "Monstro" takes negrura—the opposite of blanqueamiento—a bold step further. Díaz's convocation of negrura can be described as audacious because of the way it mocks blackness as a disease: "At first Negroes thought it *funny*. A disease that could make a Haitian blacker? It was the joke of the year. Everybody in our sector accusing everybody else of having it. You couldn't display a blemish or catch some sun on the street because then the jokes would start."[30] The comment on epidemic (and epidermal) blackness here is analogous with Guillén's "black condition" in "Negro bembón." Like the normalizing effect on blackness that Guillén championed for *modernismo*, the narrator's playful raciological assertion should be read as a condemnation of the internalized logic of finding blackness to be conceived of as a "condition" in the first place.

When Frantz Fanon published *Black Skin, White Masks* (1952) as an outcry against the lamentable, internalized black complex, he pinpointed the existence of an apparent "state of being a negro."[31] This for Fanon was prototypical to the black man and was a "disaster," he says, due to "the fact that he was once enslaved."[32] At the core of Díaz's usually sarcastic humor while taking on important, sensitive issues such as race is a wishful hope to end that state and to see blackness as one would whiteness: not as a complex or condition at all. Playing off the idea of blanqueamiento is that of blackness. This condition, while rooted in colonialism, is still prevalent in the Dominican Republic, where "European and indigenous heritages have been celebrated at the expense of an African past."[33] The state's policies that still affect the black population, which Díaz follows, are cemented in colonialism's ideology of blanqueamiento and negrura. Assertive and ironic, the mockery compels the reader to confront racism frontally. A decolonial reading of the negrura in "Monstro" would aim at erasing the color line as if this would dilute with it the lateral divisions between Díaz's homeland and its famed resilient neighbor.

Blackness as a condition, however, is inextricably tied to modern-era economics, a factor crucial to Díaz's short story. Not only is the racialized disease making an individual "blacker," it is also a selective one: it chooses "the poorest of the poor."[34] Inevitably, what surfaces in the narration is a comment on the paradigms of race and class merging. As the British cultural critic Paul Gilroy explains, blackness and its unoccupied place in modernity are tied to the paradigm of economic exclusion. The rigorous and systematic intellectual in Díaz then wedges the root causes of African American (in the continental sense) marginalization into the neoliberal apparatus—a system from which the new zombie emerges.

The Neoliberal Apparatus and Its New Zombie

In his essay "Apocalypse," Díaz points to the origins of the devastating earthquake in Haiti as forces that were just as much political and economic as they were natural. Starting with the plantation system, he explains, this economic frame would foretell our present "zombie stage of capitalism," prototypically displayed in Haiti. Within this modified economic system, a new signifier of the living dead surfaces. Díaz's new zombie then becomes a reflection of how slave-based economic structures developed into a neoliberal notion of the free market. According to Immanuel Wallerstein and Pierre Bourdieu, neoliberalism emerged in 1989, on the basis of deregulation and privatization leading to a significant decrease of government participation in the state's economy.[35] The only way of ratifying the system would be to pursue modifications for a new social order in a collective manner. However, far from being ratified, these policies are globally affecting the proletariat disproportionately and creating what Díaz terms "the new zombie."[36]

The consequences of a flawed economic system, which create this new being, are thus adapted into "Monstro." Since instances of free-market consequences are vast in the story, I delineate the four main elements as follows: the disappearance of social benefits such as employment and health care, class disparity and immigration, ecological disaster, and untreatable diseases. These instances seem realistic while reading them in fiction, due to Díaz's narratological technique of incorporating the future within the present. In other words, while "Monstro" is set fifty to eighty years from now, it is simultaneously reining in present and real concerns affecting the reader's actuality.

When the narrator explains that he is joining his mother in the Dominican Republic, it is due to the dearth of summer employment in what is presumably the United States: "I wouldn't have come to the Island that summer if I'd been able to nab a job or a summer internship, but the droughts that year and the General Economic Collapse meant nobody was nabbing shit."[37] The use of upper case, a play of words that echoes the Great Depression, patently conveys that an economic stagnation period, while treated with humor, is a very menacing and realistic prospect. The actual fears of disappearing social benefits are another one of the reader's realistic and actual concerns conveyed in the story (projected into the distant future) and in our current reality. When the narrator's mother is consumed with an unprecedentedly treatable disease, she flees the North due to unaffordable health-care costs:

> No chance she was going to be taken care of back North. Not with what you had to pay for medicines, or what the cheapest nurses charged . . . Say what you want, but family on the Island was still more reliable for heavy shit, like, say, dying than in the North. . . . Medicine was cheaper, too, with the flying territory in Haina, its Chinese factories pumping out pharma like it was romo, growing organ sheets by the mile, and for somebody as sick as my mother with only rental income to live off, that was what made sense.[38]

A journalist, Díaz is clearly drawing from the reader's real situation in this passage. So when Díaz re-creates a setting in his story similar to that of "medical tourism" to perform otherwise costly surgeries abroad, he is leveraging real press stories with fiction.[39]

"Monstro" is also a comment on the neoliberal policies that enable the corporate domain to benefit, resulting in a face-to-face collision of class differences. Without a doubt, racial issues in the Dominican Republic derive from deep roots, as I have established. And yet, class differences exacerbate the already racially charged atmosphere. In "Monstro," the truly destitute are Haitians: "Only poor Haitian types getting fucked up," "our poor east-coast neighbors, those who are also getting sick," "viktims who had nine kinds of ill already in them."[40] But the characters within the Dominican Republic are not often racialized. The narrator, in fact, never identifies himself racially or ethnically. Rather, the descriptions of the characters fall on categories of class status.

Contrasted with the narrator's unfortunate economic status is his wealthy Brown University classmate Alex. They may both be "ivy leaguers" but Alex, the narrator insists, is "a prince": "Alex was more than just a rico, he was royalty; a fucking V—, son of the wealthiest, most priv'ed up family on the Island."[41] As the narrator sees the stark difference between himself and Alex ("him prince, me prole") in telling about an attempt at ransom when Alex got kidnapped in Mexico, it is revealed that his father had an obviously profitable business overseas: "He used to live in Mexico, where the old man had a company."[42] The peripheral comment on Alex's father could be read as an allusion to NAFTA's aftermath. Since Mexico, after the free-trade agreements, became a receptor of U.S. companies seeking inexpensive labor and the reduction of tariffs, it would be logical to assume that these policies made Alex's father wealthy. The kidnapping of Alex in Mexico would point not only to his extreme affluence but also to the well-known corruption that ensured the signing of NAFTA laws.

Even less acknowledged perhaps is the sense that Alex lives a trans-American reality due to immigration. A Dominican, Alex has lived in three regions within the Americas (the Caribbean, the United States, and Mexico). Adding to the trans-American dimension is that his mother flies to "Miami every week just to shop and fuck this Senegalese lawyer."[43] Here, Díaz inserts not only Caribbean contemporary diaspora movements, he is also disorientating the common threshold of perception of immigration. This time, the immigration of the Senegalese lawyer points to a different hemispheric Americanness and trans-Americanness: it is also transatlantic, much like the plantation zombie discussed earlier. Thus, the relations of trans-Americans on the Western hemisphere are affected by a new kind of African diaspora, one that is of a new economic status. It is only in this world where Alex's mother's relationship takes place. With these examples of geographic mobility that dislocate categories of identity, Díaz has indeed become a "new kind of US/Latino writer," projecting an entirely different notion of "American."[44]

While immigration may be part of globalization trends, degradation of the environment is another common concern of Caribbean intellectuals. In this respect, ecocriticism seeded in Caribbean literature emerged under the notion that in order to fill in the voids of the human record, natural history had to be considered. Nature, as an undeniable presence, not only witnessed extermination, destruction, and subjugation but suffered it as well. Veritably, the Caribbean as a whole has not been offered any relief in its past, much less in its present, as multibillion-dollar corporations have further left their mark on the ecosystem. In this regard, the Martinican thinker Édouard Glissant, whose works represented a new ecoliterary concern, lamented that the Caribbean is an "abused earth, where blood breaks through as a cry."[45] While Díaz never claimed to be part of the ecocritical movement, the setting in "Monstro" noticeably evokes environmental concerns. Keeping with Díaz's ironic tone when faced with grave matters, the narrator expresses delight when he excitedly announces he will "take in some of that ole-time climate change."[46] Not only does the narrator comment sarcastically about the heat produced by global warming, the parallel story about the developing epidemics afflicting "the infected" also claims marine life: "Coral reefs might have been adios in the ocean floor but they were alive and well on the arms and backs and heads of the infected."[47] It is as if, within the space of "Monstro," natural resources are being substituted for strange morphological diseases.

The disappearance of the coral reefs and extreme warming producing "zoonotics by the pound" will nevertheless give way to the development of Díaz's new zombie. When insatiable heat generates erosion and alters the vegetation ("Everybody blamed the heat. Blamed the Calentazo. Shit, a hundred straight days over 105°"), a disease emerges.[48] Díaz's shrewd humor reveals itself ever more pointedly when this outbreak morphs the racialized zombie into a new being, although the disease itself is unquestionably bizarre: "A black mold-fungus-blast that came on like a splotch and then slowly just started taking you over, tunneling right through you—though as it turned out it wasn't a mold-fungus-blast at all. It was something else. Something new."[49] This ailment, like the narrator's mother's "rupture virus," points to a world so infected it cannot contain its epidemics.[50] And mother earth, "Monstro" seems to imply, can no longer heal its natural surroundings.

Inevitably, the diseased will turn into zombies within a world not too far removed from our present circumstances. Turning again to his revelations in "Apocalypse," Díaz's futuristic stage here ceaselessly points to neoliberal policies that form the context in the narration: "In order to power the explosion of the super-rich and the ultra-rich, middle classes are being forced to fail, working classes are being re-proletarianized, and the poorest are being pushed beyond the grim limits of subsistence, into a kind of sepulchral half-life, perfect targets for any 'natural disaster' that just happens to wander by."[51] Díaz succinctly summarizes the elemental features that compose neoliberalism. Diagnosing disasters as natural insofar as they are weather-related, Díaz postulates that the devastation of precarious nations is rather the "explosion of the super-rich." This means that a hurricane-prone state's poorest, such as the ones in Haiti, become significantly vulnerable where the working class turns infrahuman. In "Monstro," Díaz's "poorest," or those who begin living a "sepulchral half-life," become the new zombie and continue being disregarded like the plantation slave in the colonial era.

In "Monstro," the disease marks a stark socioeconomic imbalance when the outbreak does not alarm authorities, because they discern that it selectively affects the downtrodden: "In the end this one didn't cause too much panic because it seemed to hit only the sickest of the sick . . . You literally had to be falling to pieces for it to grab you."[52] Here we are reminded of Díaz's typically unsympathetic dark humor, used to effectively pinpoint instances of society's cruelest stances on race and class in the face of disaster. In the story, when it is evident the disease only afflicts poor Haitians, the narrator reports that there is "no real margin in that," as if recalling the unfortunate after-effect of Hurricane Katrina that Díaz reminded us of in "Apocalypse."

Haiti has traditionally been a standing beacon of black resistance, but the island is also considered to be the poorest country in the western hemisphere.[53] Affected by the neoliberal policies set into motion within our last century, as "Apocalypse" explains, foreign investments fueling dictatorships have altered the self-sustenance of the citizenry, a sector that has visibly veered into oblivion in Haiti's ill-fated democracy.[54] In "Monstro," Henri Casimir, one of the infected patients who was once a minister, has been reduced to "carting sewage."[55] In the case of the narrator, his unemployment causes him to meaninglessly wander about the Dominican Republic—his class status and nationality being the only means by which he differs from the jobless Haitians across the national border. In the context of the story, "Monstro" seems to suggest that if the zombie prior to the industrial revolution was a metaphor for unending labor as a slave, in the twenty-first century it is a victim of the opposite. In "Apocalypse," Díaz writes, "In the old days, a zombie was a figure whose life and work had been captured by magical means. Old zombies were expected to work around the clock with no relief. The new zombie cannot expect work of any kind—the new zombie just waits around to die."[56] In Díaz's words, this new, subjugated other becomes symptomatic with mechanisms of power that disfavor the precariat. With a 40.4 percent unemployment rate and 78 percent of the population under the poverty line in Haiti, the emergence of the new zombie in "Monstro"'s fictitious plot is congruent with these facts.[57]

Both examples in the story point to governing entities' overlooking the proletariat. Therefore if "zombie tales dramatize the strangeness of what has become real," for Díaz, an admitted fan of William Gibson, the use of zombification—for both the economy and the victim it produces— becomes an effective testament to a failed democratic system.[58] The jobless and the poor, some now sickened by disease, are the new zombies, without any hope of sustenance available to them amid a decaying world. Nevertheless, the disease these subverted neoliberal subjects possess in "Monstro" will ultimately make them subversive. The ultimate goal here, as it were, is to connect the genre of the fantastic to theories of decoloniality. The new zombies in "Monstro" become the operating principle for reading resistance within Díaz's decolonial project. In Díaz's fabricated narrative, the coloniality of the subaltern zombies is first understood in reference to their blackness and later their socioeconomic status. A new point of referentiality will be drawn in terms of their behavior within the context of their signification (as a "signifier," that is). Ultimately, we will be led to question their etymological (and epistemological) significance, and thus existence in "Monstro," especially considering the zombie's context within the Caribbean.

The Decolonial Zombie

In "Monstro," the connections between disease and poverty are emphasized in the behaviors that start shaping what the infected person will become. Later in the story, after the diseased display zombie-like qualities, they "abruptly stopped communicating."[59] Recalling the postcolonial debates in which subalterns may possess neither a voice nor a worldview that would position them within traditional Western frameworks, "Monstro" borrows threads from this logic.

When the victims become speechless, they are not only othered (for they were already), they literally refuse to speak. While speechlessness adds to their subaltern position, the phase in which the zombies stop speaking is deemed "the Silence" period: "And stranger shit was in the offing: eight months into the epidemic all infected viktims, even the healthiest, abruptly stopped communicating. Just went silent. Nothing abnormal in their bloodwork or in the balance of the infection. They just stopped speaking—friends, family, doctors, strangers, it didn't matter. No stimuli of any form could get them to speak, either. Watched everything and everyone, clearly understood commands and information—but they refused to say anything."[60] Their cognizance of everyone participating as part of a civilization clashes with their "refusal" to speak, a factor that is resonant with a subversive resistance. Added to the unnerving effect of the zombies' apparent muteness is the signifier of their silence itself: these are othered subjects that, for no apparent reason, stop communicating. This silence nevertheless is what places them in a position of unprecedented authority. However, it is a moment feared by society's uninfected: it is a cataclysmic moment—the calm before the storm. The case of epidemic insomnia that threatens the social order of civilization in Gabriel García Márquez's *Cien años de soledad* [One Hundred Years of Solitude] (1967) is an appropriate comparison for understanding the subalternity of Díaz's zombies' silence and the significance of their resistance in the context of Latin American colonization.

In García Márquez's fabricated town of Macondo, an apocalyptic amnesia plague threatens to erase civilization's language. The townspeople start inscribing names onto things so as to not forget their use. The loss of civilization's artifact, a normative sense of spoken or written discourse, may lead to silence. The zombies in "Monstro," like the Macondians, are also faced with breaking from this "human" element.[61] From the point of view of the uninfected, however, the zombie's reticence to speak, like Macondo's loss of memory, also implies a threat—even if it is a silent one. In our global day and age, the threat of planetary obliteration—biological weapons, nuclear wars, and the like—are menacing fears vis-à-vis our distrustful economy and certainly add to the paranoia about earth's end. But if all were to fall silent, the paranoia would be exponentially worse. Díaz's futuristic neoliberal-ridden planet contains zombies who were initially just a strange nuisance congregated in an avoided quarantine zone. Yet, the fear they effect when their silence interrupts the quotidian alter their former position as subalterns.

The period of silence in "Monstro" and townspeople's dementia in *Cien años de soledad* are thus apocalyptic moments in which civilization might lose its "social composure."[62] Yet in both texts, these changes are instigated by an outside agent. In the novel, it is the character of Rebecca who reaches the Buendía clan moments before the amnesia outbreak takes place. Rebecca is continually referred to as an "other" ("did not ascribe to a Buendía name," "ate dirt," "only reacted to the sounds of a clock").[63] And whether coincidental or not, the oddity of her presence as an other leads to both the knowledge of the outside world and the menacing elimination of Macondo's memory.[64] Similarly, in "Monstro," it is the arrival of a disease whose symptoms change over time. Because in "Monstro" the disease was initially racialized, leading then to silence, the disease points to the presence of creatures resisting the structure of a Macondo-like civilization (like Rebecca refusing a Buendía name).

The threat of these new diseases—outside agents—can be read similarly to the threat of European epidemics wiping out an entire Carib population. Yet Díaz's zombies and García Márquez's Rebecca are not the power structure agents themselves that are destructive. Rather, they are the result of an act of resistance. When they confront colonial and neocolonial structures of power, they create an effect. In the case of Macondo, it is widespread amnesia and eventually Macondo's disappearance. In Díaz's "Monstro," it is the displaying of outright zombie behavior. Where García Márquez's Macondo and Díaz's Haiti differ in terms of their resistant agent is that, while Rebecca embraces solitude and confinement until old age, the zombies in "Monstro" do the complete opposite.

The effects of solitude (and solidarity) thus vary in both texts. In *Cien años de soledad*, solitude is crystalized upon the arrival of an adolescent slave in Macondo; the onset of dementia immediately follows. The *mulata* child is indebted to her grandmother for burning down her house and is forced into prostitution to pay off her debt. Adapted later in 1978 into a novella, the story of the mulata gestures toward the effects of solitude and slavery that García Márquez weaves into *Cien años de soledad*. The understanding of racialized slavery in Latin America that we take from this passage makes the brief comparison between this novel and Díaz's "Monstro" a compelling one: solitude remains a consequence of slavery's tragedy in both García Márquez's and Díaz's texts. Yet, the way these narratives assess solitude varies.

In *Cien años de soledad*, when young Aureliano enters the mulata's shed, "63 men had been through the room."[65] Their presence is felt in sheets "weigh[ing] like a canvas," and upon turning the mattress, "sweat came out of it from the other side."[66] The magical realist exaggeration sternly criticizes the tragedy of child prostitution, but what is crucial is Aureliano's inability to affect the girl's misfortune. Upon leaving the room, he feels "terribly alone."[67] Unable to liberate her, he throws himself into solitude, agonizing over his incompetence. While slavery's imprint is a common heritage shared among those in the Caribbean region, the inability to abolish modern (and old) forms of slavery, as observed in Aureliano's character, abound in Díaz's Haiti. It is as if "Monstro"'s unruly and unequal world owes its misfortune—indirectly but assuredly—to the slave trade. In "Monstro," the narrator's impossible love pursuit, Misty, has also been sexually abused by a family member. A victim of incest, the narrator comments, "she was as much of a loner as I was."[68] Interesting to the legacy of slavery, solitude in these stories is tolerated in the same spaces where, historically, the plantation precluded solidarity among slaves.

One of the driving forces behind Latin American narratives of the mid-twentieth century was precisely a call for unity against solitude. In *Cien años de soledad*, the critique underlined in the novel is that of an unattainable solidarity among the Buendía clan that leads to their inevitable extinction. In the case of "Monstro," solitude lingers around the narrator and his human equals, but not among the zombies. Historical theories of Latin American solitude function as a subtext in "Monstro" where Díaz places it at the center of narration, as the infected deconstruct it to reveal an ultimate moral lesson right before total chaos erupts.

After the period of devastating silence, the infected gather silently in a church-like community. The chants that ensue are more horrifying than the preceding quietness: "The entire infected population simultaneously le[t] out a bizarre shriek—two, three times a day. Starting together, ending together."[69] Neither the narrator nor the doctors possess any explanation as to how, without apparent prior communication, the infected chant in unison. The shrieking is so unbearable that "no uninfected could stand to hear it."[70] In other words, the subaltern, while initially not speaking and then emitting an unendurable unified chant, is once again marking its difference. In this vein, rather than seeing these contemporary zombies as a form of escapism, "Monstro" privileges them as decolonial signifiers and attempts to draw an example of solidarity.

Similar to the eerie solitude conjured in Macondo, "Monstro"'s zombies develop a stance on isolation vis-à-vis the "un-infected." This isolation from the healthy creates within the group of infected a kind of family. The claim here is that the behaviors that isolate the diseased from the general public but unite them within their own sphere can also be read within a decolonial thread if we consider the following passage: "Doctors began reporting a curious change in the behavior of infected patients—they wanted to be together, in close proximity, all the time. They no longer tolerated being separated from other infected, started coming together in the main quarantine zone just outside Champ de Mars. All the viktims seemed to succumb to the ingathering compulsion."[71] Indeed, what do we make of the fact that the infected—poor, suffering, diseased—cannot stand to be without each other? If we consider the idea that these beings are joining together against adversity, we might concede that what is at work here is a decolonial clan in the making.

The clan has formed a new community, but to contextualize this solidarity further we should again consider Haiti as "Monstro"'s stage. In Haiti, not only did the population's ancestors suffer as slaves, they are also enduring a faulty economy and a plethora of disease.[72] In "Monstro," the infected merely tolerated pain, which is characterized by bearing "nine kinds of ill already."[73] In this respect, the clan's "compulsion to stay together" becomes similar to that of the gathering of slaves in *palenques* during the plantation era.

The kinship development between different ethnic populations of slaves on certain plantations, and the subsequent escape of some into marooned societies, are well documented.[74] The formation of these communities was essential for slaves, and planters sought to undo them to preclude revolts. Separated from their families or linguistic and ethnic groups, some found a home in these palenques, *quilombos*, or clans.[75] The solitude these slaves could not endure is similar to the kind the zombies find dreadful in "Monstro." In fact, the zombies cannot stand this solitude physically: when attempting to separate the infected from each other, the narrator reports that "they went batshit, trying everything they could to break free, to *return*."[76] I stress return here because it takes us to the beginning of this chapter, in which we recall that the slaves' anguish in becoming zombies was the inability to return to the African west coast. In the case of "Monstro," instead of seeking a homeland, the infected pursue their developed family, similar to that of the slaves forming a new community in the New World.

Also reminiscent of colonial slavery are the in-unison shrieks of the zombies. In "Monstro," "the phenomenon that became known as the Chorus" recalls the cases of vodun bewitchment of the plantation era.[77] Indeed, the unintelligible chants the zombies produce are the same ones Casimir starts emitting, for which his wife claims he is "bewitched."[78] The narrator of "Monstro" further discloses the "widespread rumors that the infected were devils" and that there had been "reports" indicating that even "relatives attempt[ed] to set their infected family members on fire."[79] Such accounts, however, are rooted in history, since during the plantocracy, witchcraft trials (and consequentially the burning or lynching of those "bewitched") were accounted for in the Inquisition records in the Americas, dating back to the sixteenth century and the seventeenth.[80] During these times, "devil acts" were synonymous with slaves' spiritual practices, including vodun, safeguarded by palenques and quilombos but deeply feared by planters. A result of this fear was the outlawing of spiritual practices.[81]

In the case of "Monstro," the rumored zombie-turned-devil conjures up the plantational zombie to reflect on voudism as a feared product of the plantation system. Díaz's fiction relies on this history, since witchcraft was believed to have originated in zombie black magic. Casimir's "bewitchment" is articulated as his "tramping about without destination" and as his being drawn to the chants.[82] Nevertheless, his aversion to Dr. De-Graff's attempt to remove him from the other infected, resulting in the patient's "exploding" and "bounding" himself "out the car," make apparent his need for proximity to the other infected.[83] For the outside world, Casimir is bewitched; yet, like the others within the quarantine zone, he is also part of a new palenque-like clan that cannot (and will not) stand to be apart. Díaz therefore seems to be playing with the allusion to, and illusion of, the decolonial nature of the Caribbean, as the zombies remain racialized via the trope of slavery.

The idealized imagery of a harmonious zombie clan, alas, cannot last forever. The story ends with a sense of urgency, when the innocent infected-turned-lethal are violently attacked. While the narrator recounts his unconsummated desire and ill-fated love attempt amid destruction, Haiti is leveled as foreign governments attempt to contain the aggressive diseased: "The Detonation Event—no one knows what else to call it—turned the entire world white. Three full seconds. Triggered a quake that was felt all across the Island."[84] While I will come back to the use of word *white* here, I want to point out first that Díaz's positioning of a world seized by fright is reminiscent of Haiti's real, historical earthquake. It would be a superficial reading to readily dismiss the story's outcome as evidence of merely mischievous satire at the expense of an impoverished nation. Instead, it may be more fruitful to consider this imagery in the context of the story in particular and of Díaz's stance on racial geopolitics in general. In this context, what might this new apocalypse in "Monstro" actually reveal, as the etymology of the word implies?

Instead of ending "Monstro" with the real apocalypse he so masterfully covered in his essay published in 2010, Díaz turns to science fiction when the zenith of tension is that of the infected fully morphing into man-eating zombies. When the narrator describes a Polaroid that is found amid the debris, it shows that the possessed are now "forty-foot-tall cannibal motherfuckers running loose on the Island."[85] The anthropophagic nature of the infected is coated in biblical meaning. On the back of the same rescued photograph, scripture is quoted: "Numbers 11:18. *Who shall give us flesh to eat?*"[86] The apparition of the cannibal seems foretold in his essay "Apocalypse," where Díaz presages that we will be "picked off by the hundreds of thousands by 'natural disasters' justified as 'acts of god.'"[87]

The passage regarding cannibalism cited in the story is one of many accounts contained in the Bible. While cannibalism was witnessed during European wars, religiously it was also conceived as a biblical sign of the coming of Armageddon. Obviously when it comes to colonialism, evangelization played a role in empire; thus, in Christianity, cannibalism was deemed barbaric. Anthropophagy, like race, was a means by which colonization was justified in the Americas. But the Caribbean was named after "cannibalism." The term was associated with the Antillean islands when, lost in translation, the first explorers inferred that the "carib" (referring to the inhabitants of Cuba and Saint-Domingue) were societies that ate human flesh.[88] Cannibalistic accounts in the Americas may have been refuted back in the sixteenth century but the difference between a "cannibal" and a "carib" was not distinguished until 1796, after the Caribbean had already been named.[89] The Caribbean region was therefore conceived on account of refracted European fears.

Similar to the fukú curse in *The Brief Wondrous Life of Oscar Wao* that ceaselessly resurfaces, in "Monstro" the fear of anthropophagy does so exponentially. Within Díaz's context of globalization, "Monstro"'s man-eating creatures make a comeback in a globalized McOndo super-size manner. In this regard, though the caribs were wiped out during colonization, they seem to reappear as colonialists' worst nightmare. Dangerous creatures, they are not deterred by "point[ing] a gauss-gun at them" and are "only stopped when they [are] killed."[90] When these born-again caribs re-surface—as if coming back from the dead, or claiming their land—Díaz's short story comes full circle. It is as if "Monstro" is ending a chapter of Antillean colonialism with the return of the *new* carib. But if "Monstro" achieves closure, it does so only to start over again: in the story, the "a soon-to-be-iconic Polaroid" marks the return of the Carib-Cannibal as the emergence of what the narrator calls a "Class 2" creature.[91] The Caribbean region might have been taken over by a new transculturated phenomenon, but the reader hopes it does not lead to forms of futuristic colonization. Considering Díaz's tendency toward playful irony, however, this may well be his intention.

If moralizing apocalyptic tales focusing on power struggle require a monster, the use of a symbolic monster in this decolonial context is not new. In Latin America, the critical interpretation of the foundational *Ariel* (1900), written by the Uruguayan essayist José Enrique Rodó—taken from Shakespeare's revered *The Tempest* (1611)—was that the monster Caliban represented an invasive nineteenth-century imperialistic nation. Later, the groundbreaking essay "Calibán" (1971), by the Cuban intellectual Roberto Fernández Retamar, also based on *The Tempest*, rejects Rodó's fundamental premise, and instead utilizes the subjugated islander of Caliban to embody Latin America as the subaltern other.

Just as Caliban was for Rodó and Fernández Retamar a transatlantic, cross-cultural reconfiguration of Shakespeare's character, Shakespeare's Caliban came to life at the intersection of the halting Renaissance and the colonization of the Americas. Therefore Shakespeare's Caliban projected a Europe attempting to figure out the limits of its colonial power. Caliban as a decolonial subject, however, calls attention to the act of resistance. In the colonial imaginary, conflict arose when resistance was "only in the pres-ence of, or at a close remove from, absolute power."[92] Within a decolonial sphere, for Fernández Retamar as for Díaz, a monster-like figure such as Caliban or a carib-turned-cannibal-turned-Caliban is emblematic of this resistance, and points to the limits of hegemonic dominance. More impor-tant, the symbol of Caliban as a monster effectively reveals the origin of that confrontation. Like *The Tempest*, "Monstro" causes us to reevaluate our hereditary spaces of power while testing their limits. While neoliberalism is a failing system in "Monstro," the story also suggests through the trope of the monster that the Americas are interconnected, which is why Haiti's lessons are not exclusively for its own sake. As Díaz postulates in "Apocalypse," Haiti's devastation was part of the "larger trend of *global inequality*" that will lead to "the transformation of our planet into a Haiti."[93] In other words, "Monstro" teaches us that, if Caliban was Latin America, today Haiti is all of us.

While the monster (Caliban) signals warning, as its etymology implies, for Foucault, it further reveals "the emergence of difference."[94] Far from a Rabelaisian, carnivalesque freak, and more in the sense of "out of normalcy," a monster is a development of something beyond our comprehension.[95] Earlier I established that the zombie monster first conveyed its difference when becoming silent and then shrieking out in a choral fashion. Now, the monster's development leads to its transforming into a symbolic prototype of (and necessary element to) narratives of catastrophe, in order to, in effect, reveal a deeper message. The narrative Díaz weaves in "Monstro" is that of his reality: Haiti—Prospero's laboratory—and the neoliberal policies weighed down on a nation turned calamity. In "Monstro," the instructional quality of the monster symbol is that it may uncover deep societal problems, as Díaz admits to staging: "I wanted the story-world to be on the cusp of a catastrophic ecological collapse, a year or so before things really go down the chute for humanity. A world more messed up than ours but equally stubbornly delusional. So caught up in the vampire logic of late capital that it can't stop eating itself alive."[96] The punishment for not possessing better economic discernment, and as if conforming to a sense of universal justice, are the cannibalistic zombies that will literally "eat" the world "alive," the reason being that their planetary reality does not function as it should and therefore must cease to exist, if only to restart anew.

If human life expires, "Monstro"'s cannibalistic monster will be resilient. This resilience is another quality innate to the monster. Foucault recalls that monsters characteristically wish to "remain in existence" and adjust to the changes of the environment.[97] After all, the monster emerges "when a natural revolution occurs" such as the global warming of the planet that Díaz stages in "Monstro."[98] In this case, as though they are in a process of Darwinian natural selection, Díaz's zombies evolve and adapt to the natural and unnatural climate of "Monstro"'s inhabitable settings: "A world more messed up than ours."[99] While they are feared for their "knotting together" and "coming together," according to Foucault, a monster is just that: a "solid expanse" or "merely the fragmentary result of a much more tightly knit, much finer continuity."[100] In other words, they are an evolved species, a prototype of the human, but their ability to form kin makes them a perfected and naturally developed species habilitated to survive. Far from abnormal, fearsome creatures, they are the ideal artifact to teach humanity a lesson: just as memory is necessary to avoid the calamities endured in our past, in a sense, monsters are also essential as a warning for the future. In a moralizing tale such as "Monstro," meant to urge a "stubbornly delusional" society from further damaging the planet, monsters signal caution.[101]

If the monsters that develop in Díaz's short story appear impossibly un-realistic (if we were to forget for an instant that we are immersed in science fiction), it would be helpful to read the zombies as imaginary. The zombies might therefore act as a Brechtian illusion: the fictional dangers tied into the story reverberate in the reader's reality, so we might not readily identify with the zombies, but instead acknowledge the degeneracy of our ways. As readers, we discover that the monster's existence, much like that of Caliban, signals why we are entering a stage of decadence and extinction in the first place. If, in Foucault's terms, "the monster provides an account, as though in caricature, of the genesis of differences," these differences are tied to the colonial machine that gave genesis to the fictional chaotic end that "Monstro" proposes.[102] Díaz's monsters can be read as fictional caricatures, but they indeed reveal a social malaise that can be traced back to the formation of the Americas.

In the story, therefore, if the zombies may be conceived as science fiction caricatures, we may symbolically consider them to be reflections of objects similar to those of the allegory of the cave. The zombies might not be real, but they function as an illusion of the actual real reflected onto walls. This is due to the fact that the representation of reality through the image of a monster is more manageable than reality itself. Otherwise, we would be blinded by the immensity of truth if we walked out of Plato's cave, which "Monstro" alludes to when DeGraff "burn[s] out the optic nerve [of her] right eye," at-tempting to see reality unfolding as the zombies are bombed.[103] Humor and caricature, after all, while critical here, are much more palatable than the tragic accounts of human life. Since society is reticent to accept the real while "star[ing] into the ruins—bravely, resolutely" as Díaz hopes in "Apocalypse," science fiction, Díaz concludes, is the next available alternative.

When the nuclear bomb is dropped on the previously "blackened" Haiti, the assault "turned the entire world white."[104] Similar to the beginning of the story, when Díaz's narrator dialogizes with race, the ending comes back to the dialectic of black-white opposites. In this case, whiteness as the coun-terpoint of its binary other is produced by such intense illumination that it does not reveal clarity. Rather, its brightness is blinding, both literally (for it blinds DeGraff's eye) and figuratively, as it occludes the distinction of reality. The reinscription of the universal in light, like the dichotomy of blanqueamiento and negrura, is thus reversed in "Monstro." Díaz had conferred that negrura was an opportunity to see clearly, when in his essay published in 2010 he stated, "Apocalypse is a darkness that gives us light." Calling attention to the apocalypse as a means to reveal truths, for "Monstro," the traditional categories of light and white emphasize occlusion and blindness, whereas darkness and blackness are revelation and truth. The usual understanding of the binary terms, once defined by normative Eurocentric logic, is dislodged, and within the story a new conception of both race and color are veiled. As both the etymological and epistemological meanings of "Monstro" suggest, we are warned against adopting traditional references for the colonially rooted construction of identity.

In the end, however, Díaz's ambiguity—Who is the narrator? Will the world really come to an end? Where does this strange disease, la negrura, come from?—makes "Monstro" aporetic in that there are many unknowns. What we are presented with, then, is a story with multiple layers of meaning and an added component of playfulness typical of Díaz's genius. In other words, "Monstro" is a fluid ambiguity whose monsters can be read from various angles and vantage points, as this chapter has demonstrated. We may determine that the science fiction narrative mode is, in effect, just as challenging to analytically entertain as genres like realism or modernist prose.

Final Words

When Díaz wrote his post-Haiti earthquake piece, there were residues of hope flickering through his contemplation of the ghastly effects of natural destruction: "Apocalypses," Díaz wrote, "like the Haitian earthquake are not only catastrophes; they are also opportunities: chances for us to see ourselves, to take responsibility for what we see, to change."[105] While his meditative essay was indeed hopeful, "Monstro" ends with an analogy of the human race's neglecting this urgent message. While there might still be hope in the story's development into a novel, in its short story form the human experience's extinction is self-caused. The misery the zombie has endured was tolerable no longer. In the story, as in any ideological literary piece, monsters are a "necessity" for making poignant claims about history and therefore are "introduce[ed] into a scheme."[106] "Monstro" places at our reach the results of a warning far too clear, yet ignored for far too long. The final point I will make about this story is a certainty: Díaz's zombie represents a resilient being that is ending unjust humanity, figuratively or literally, just as scripture prophesied. Zombies are created by the world and will destroy the world that created them. Affecting the Caribbean initially, the monsters will become a true planetary concern, suggesting the interconnectivity of world history from the crusades, to colonialism, to neoliberalism.

Writing "Monstro" was an earnest, soul-searching revelation for Díaz. It revealed that even after slavery and colonialism ended in our Americas, "the coloniality of power did not."[107] Haiti was for Díaz a window into the future. From "Apocalypse" to "Monstro," with a fearful eye toward the future, Díaz turned from journalistic commentary to science fictionalization. What we make of this outcome can be understood as a fictional tale intended to save the nonfictitious reality. We may cause the destruction of our ways, Díaz infers, but catastrophe stories, whether metaphorical or not, are meant to inspire people to action. While a multivalent symbol, in the end, the zombie monstro is an activist signal of hope. The zombie, then, is not only a Byronic antihero of a moralizing tale. Díaz's monstro is, in this case, both a haunting reminder of our past and a steadfast warning for our future.

Notes

1. Jean Comaroff and John Comaroff, "Alien-Nation: Zombies, Immigrants, and the Millennial Capitalism," *South Atlantic Quarterly* 101, no. 4 (2002): 23.

2. Typical of the Afro-futuristic aesthetic is the presence of the concerns of the African diaspora that look at both the causes and origins of diaspora, their effects in present times, and the imagined place of peoples of African extraction in the future. Therefore, it uses three temporalities, which "Monstro" interweaves in the following manner: Díaz recalls the past in its implied provocations of the zombie origin, it is anchored in current times as it takes on neoliberalization of the Americas, and it is contemplative of futuristic reimaginings of a world too obstinate to amend itself, resulting in its own possible annihilation. In a further developed version of this essay, I would like to detail the use of science fiction and Afro-futurism Díaz employs in his stories. Junot Díaz, "Monstro," *The New Yorker*, June 2012.

3. Díaz, "Monstro."

4. Díaz, "Monstro."

5. Díaz, "Monstro."

6. Díaz, "Monstro." While Díaz might not be referring to a particular type of bomb, he might be joining imagery from popular representations of weapons of mass de-

struction. The Joint Chiefs of Staff is assumed to be "Western," since the weapon is carried out of the termed "Southern Command" within Puerto Rico, an island which is still an unincorporated territory of the United States.

7. Díaz, "Monstro."

8. Alejo Carpentier, El reino de este mundo (New York: HarperCollins, 2009), 5 (this and all subsequent references to this text are my translation).

9. Consider William Faulkner (1936), Derek Walcott (1949), Ralph Ellison (1941), Pablo Neruda (1950), Aimé Césaire (1961, 1963), and Édouard Glissant (1997), who incorporate the Haitian revolution into their work.

10. Junot Díaz, The Brief Wondrous Life of Oscar Wao (New York: Riverhead Books, 2007), 21.

11. Díaz, "Monstro."

12. Junot Díaz, interview by "American Voices," Johns Hopkins University, August 2013.

13. Díaz, "Monstro."

14. Díaz, "Monstro."

15. Comaroff and Comaroff, "Alien-Nation," 23.

16. Amy Wilentz, "A Zombie Is a Slave Forever," New York Times, October 30, 2012.

17. Wilentz, "A Zombie Is a Slave Forever."

18. Saidiya V. Hartman, Lose Your Mother: A Journey along the Atlantic Slave Route (New York: Farrar, Straus and Giroux, 2007), 157.

19. Hartman, Lose Your Mother, 157.

20. Aníbal Quijano, "Coloniality of Power, Eurocentrism, and Latin America," Nepantla: Views from the South 1 no. 3 (2000): 533.

21. Quijano, "Coloniality of Power, Eurocentrism, and Latin America," 533.

22. Quijano, "Coloniality of Power, Eurocentrism, and Latin America," 533.

23. Hartman, Lose Your Mother, 5.

24. Díaz, Oscar Wao, 1.

25. Frantz Fanon, Peau noire, masques blancs (Paris: Éditions du Seuil, 1971), 72. This and all subsequent references to this text are my translation. Frantz Fanon calls this color complex a névrose d'abandon, or an internalized acceptance of one's inferiority vis-à-vis the color line.

26. A movement that started in the Hispanic Caribbean inspired the Harlem Renaissance in the United States at the beginning of the twentieth century. Though erroneously attributed to white writers, like Luís Palés Matos (a negrista poet), from Puerto Rico, it eventually became known as a movement spearheaded by Nicolás Guillén.

27. Nicolás Guillén, Sóngoro cosongo, Motivos de son, West Indies LTD., España: Poema en cuatro angustias y una esperanza (Buenos Aires: Losada, 1952), 39 (my translation).

28. Hartman, Lose Your Mother, 157.

29. In one of Díaz's recent concerns on his social media, he shares an article pointing to Dominican citizenry revoked to children of Haitians born after 1929; accessed April 22, 2014, http://www.bbc.co.uk/news/world-latin-america-24445661. Díaz covers these cases carefully and periodically posts cases referring to these issues, such as

the story of Dominican officials welcoming the building of a border wall between the neighboring states, as another example.

30. Díaz, "Monstro."

31. Fanon, *Peau noire, masques blancs*, 13.

32. Fanon, *Peau noire, masques blancs*, 231.

33. David John Howard, *Coloring the Nation: Race and Ethnicity in the Dominican Republic* (Oxford: Signal Books, 2001), 1.

34. Díaz, "Monstro."

35. Ljubiša Mitrovic, "Bourdieu's Criticism of the Neoliberal Philosophy of Development, the Myth of Mondialization and the New Europe," *Philosophy, Sociology and Psychology Review* 4, no. 1 (2005): 40.

36. Junot Díaz, "Apocalypse," *Boston Review*, May 2011, accessed April 22, 2014, http://www.bostonreview.net/junot-diaz-apocalypse-haiti-earthquake.

37. Díaz, "Monstro."

38. Díaz, "Monstro."

39. Elisabeth Rosenthal, "The Growing Popularity of Having Surgery Overseas," *New York Times*, August 6, 2013; Walecia Konrad, "Going Abroad to Find Affordable Health Care," *New York Times*, March 20, 2009.

40. Díaz, "Monstro."

41. Díaz, "Monstro."

42. Díaz, "Monstro."

43. Díaz, "Monstro."

44. José David Saldívar, *Trans-Americanity: Subaltern Modernities, Global Coloniality, and the Cultures of Greater Mexico* (Durham, NC: Duke University Press, 2012), 3.

45. Édouard Glissant, *Les Indes* (Paris: Editios du Seuil, 1965), 26 (my translation).

46. Díaz, "Monstro."

47. Díaz, "Monstro."

48. Díaz, "Monstro."

49. Díaz, "Monstro."

50. Díaz, "Monstro."

51. Díaz, "Apocalypse."

52. Díaz, "Apocalypse."

53. This resistance is immortalized in Carpentier's *El reino de este mundo*, as I have stated, but also in Victor Hugo's *Bug Jargal* (1826), Pablo Neruda's *Canto general* (1950), Aimé Césaire's *Toussaint Louverture* (1960), and C. L. R. James's *The Black Jacobins* (1963), to name a few.

54. The Haitian anthropologist Michel-Rolph Trouillot held at the core of his critique that the peasantry, while crucial for Haiti's development, were virtually ignored by the government. Michel-Rolph Trouillot, *Haiti: State against Nation* (New York: Monthly Review, 1990), 116.

55. Díaz, "Monstro."

56. Díaz, "Apocalypse."

57. World Bank, "Haiti," accessed September 2013, data.worldbank.org/country/Haiti.

58. Comaroff and Comaroff, "Alien-Nation," 23.

59. Díaz, "Monstro."

60. Díaz, "Monstro."

61. Díaz, "Monstro."

62. I take the expression *social composure* from Homi Bhabha, who conveys the signifier of silence in the following way: when "the social event encounters the silence of the word," this instance is when the written word, civilization, "may lose its historical composure." Homi Bhabha, *The Location of Culture* (London: Routledge, 2004), 26.

63. Gabriel García Márquez, *Cien años de soledad* (Buenos Aires: Editorial Sudamericana, 1967), 56–62 (this and all subsequent references to this text are my translation).

64. See Brett Levinson's analysis of Rebecca in "Anatomy of the Latin American 'Boom' Novel," *Literary Cultures of Latin America: A Comparative History*, ed. Mario J. Valdés and Djelal Kadir (Oxford: Oxford University Press, 2004), 345–52.

65. García Márquez, *Cien años de soledad*, 69.

66. García Márquez, *Cien años de soledad*, 70.

67. García Márquez, *Cien años de soledad*, 70.

68. Díaz, "Monstro."

69. Díaz, "Monstro."

70. Díaz, "Monstro."

71. Díaz, "Monstro."

72. World Bank, "Haiti."

73. Díaz, "Monstro."

74. Sidney Wilfred Mintz and Richard Price, *The Birth of African-American Culture: An Anthropological Perspective* (Boston: Beacon, 1992), viii.

75. Mintz and Price, *The Birth of African-American Culture*, 26.

76. Díaz, "Monstro" (emphasis added).

77. Díaz, "Monstro."

78. Díaz, "Monstro."

79. Díaz, "Monstro."

80. James H. Sweet, *Domingos Álvares, African Healing, and the Intellectual History of the Atlantic World* (Chapel Hill: University of North Carolina Press, 2011), 51.

81. In Jamaica, for instance, Obeah had been criminalized as a "counter-insurgency measure" for fear of slaves' rebellion; accessed April 22, 2014, http://www.stabroeknews.com/2013/features/in-the-diaspora/03/18/a-legacy-of-emancipation/.

82. http://www.stabroeknews.com/2013/features/in-the-diaspora/03/18/a-legacy-of-emancipation/.

83. http://www.stabroeknews.com/2013/features/in-the-diaspora/03/18/a-legacy-of-emancipation/.

84. Díaz, "Monstro."

85. Díaz, "Monstro."

86. Díaz, "Monstro."

87. Díaz, "Apocalypse."

88. Peter Hulme, *Colonial Encounters: Europe and the Native Caribbean, 1492–1797* (London: Routledge, 1992), 15.

89. Hulme, *Colonial Encounters*, 15.

90. Díaz, "Monstro."

91. Díaz, "Monstro."

92. Roland Greene, "Colonial Becomes Postcolonial," MLQ: *Modern Language Quarterly* 65 no. 3 (2004): 429.

93. Díaz, "Apocalypse."

94. Michel Foucault, *The Order of Things: An Archaeology of the Human Sciences* (New York: Pantheon Books, 1971), 156–59.

95. In his famous *Essais*, Michel de Montaigne explains in "Des cannibales" (1580) that the term *barbarian* meant rather, vis-à-vis Greek society, "outside of normalcy"; Michel de Montaigne, *Des Essais* (London: Nouvelles Editions, 1771), 107.

96. Junot Díaz, interview by Cressida Leyshon, "This Week in Fiction: Junot Díaz," *The New Yorker*, July 16, 2012, accessed September 10, 2013, http://www.newyorker.com /online/blogs/books/2012/07/this-week-in-fiction-junot-diaz-1.html.

97. Foucault, *The Order of Things*, 159.

98. Foucault, *The Order of Things*, 153, 155.

99. Díaz, "This Week," 2012.

100. Díaz, "Monstro"; Foucault, *The Order of Things*, 154.

101. Díaz, "Apocalypse."

102. Foucault, *The Order of Things*, 157.

103. Díaz, "Monstro."

104. Díaz, "Monstro."

105. Díaz, "Apocalypse."

106. Foucault, *The Order of Things*, 153.

107. José David Saldívar, *Trans-Americanity: Subaltern Modernities, Global Coloniality, and the Cultures of Greater Mexico* (Durham, NC: Duke University Press, 2012), xi.

Part IV

Desiring Decolonization

12. Junot Díaz's Search for Decolonial Aesthetics and Love

José David Saldívar

Decolonial aesthetics refers to ongoing artistic projects responding and delinking from the darker side of imperial globalization. Decolonial aesthetics seeks to recognize and open options for liberating the senses. This is the terrain where artists around the world are contesting the legacies of modernity and its re-incarnations in postmodern and altermodern aesthetics.
—Decolonial Aesthetics Working Group's "Manifesto"

In Oscar Wao we have a family that has fled, half-destroyed, from one of the rape incubators of the New World, and they are trying to find love. But not just any love. How can there be "just any love" given the history of rape and sexual violence that created the Caribbean—that Trujillo uses in the novel? The kind of love that I was interested in, that my characters long for intuitively, is the only kind of love that could liberate them from that horrible legacy of colonial vio-lence. I am speaking about decolonial love.
—Junot Díaz, "The Search for Decolonial Love"

Junot Díaz is the first Latino writer working in the United States in the twenty-first century to be put forward as a major figure in the world-system of letters.[1] He received a Guggenheim Fellowship in 1999, and following the publication of Drown (1996) and The Brief Wondrous Life of Oscar Wao (2007), which was awarded the Pulitzer Prize for Fiction, he became one of the most famous young writers in the world. In 2012, he published This Is How You Lose Her, a finalist for the National Book Award, and almost simultaneously that year he was awarded the prestigious MacArthur Award. The Brief Wondrous Life of Oscar Wao, which has been translated into French, Spanish, Portuguese, Chinese, Dutch, and other major languages, brought the experiences of racial and gender coloniality in the United States and the Greater Antilles to a mass readership inside and outside the global Americas. These achievements are all the more noteworthy because they took place in a period when the injustices of white supremacy in U.S. culture and society, explored so rigorously in his work, are so rarely commented on in the hegemonic and "postrace" public sphere of the United States.[2]

Díaz's success can also be used to measure significant changes in the cultural politics and the political economy of publishing Latino/a writers in the United States. On the one hand, his ongoing relationship with the mainline New Yorker magazine—which under Tina Brown's editorial regime and acumen had published his first major short story, "How to Date a Brown Girl," when he was completing his MFA degree at Cornell University, and later in 2012 published "Monstro," an excerpt of his new science fiction novel, in progress, set in an apocalyptic future Dominican Republic and Haiti where aliens, viruses, and zombies invade and eat the island—is an entirely new phenomenon for a Latino writer approaching the distinctive cultural dominance of our mainline literary society.[3] On the other hand, his imaginative writing occupies a central place in the hemispheric political culture of postcontemporary Latin American literature, for in 2007 Bogotá's Department of Culture and the Hay Festival named Díaz one of the most important thirty-nine authors under thirty-nine in América Latina. Forces in both the United States and in Latin America are responsible for introducing Díaz to the rest of the reading planet.[4]

Junot Díaz is, in a sense, a new kind of Latino writer, one whose fearless projection of a dark America releases creative possibilities and changes the terms of the cultural conversation in which the dissident racial and gender politics of literary expression are articulated. Díaz's work provides an opportunity to extend our consideration of issues arising from the relationship of Latinos to coloniality and the coalitional projects of decolonial aesthetics and decolonial feminisms, formulations on the coloniality of gender and decolonial (sucio/a) love by the philosopher María Lugones and the sociologist Deb Vargas.[5] Through his fiction, we can explore, in the memorable phrase of the historian and novelist Emma Pérez, "the decolonial imaginary."[6] Díaz's writing itself, his career as a public figure in the Global South and the Global North, his political critique of white supremacy, and the debates his imaginative literature are beginning to generate raise a number of the themes of writers of color from the United States and the Greater Antilles: the possibility of dissident ethnic, gender, and racial identity within the scales of Americanity; the development of a robust decolonial aesthetics; and the philosophical character of the cultural politics of a migratory Latinidad and Afro-Latinidad.

Bearing in mind Paula M. L. Moya's endorsement of Junot Díaz's search for "decolonial love" in his three supreme books of fiction as well as her revelation that Díaz had informed her that his central consciousness, Yunior, had "ideas about women and the actions of these ideas [about them] always [left] him more alone, more thwarted, more disconnected from his community and himself,"[7] I want to make some claims in this chapter for the value of searching for decolonial aesthetics and love in his work. I will begin first by analyzing a paratextual passage (a footnote) from Díaz's The Brief Wondrous Life of Oscar Wao, in which Yunior de las Casas critically reflects on his friend's spectacularly closeted reading of science fiction and fantasy books and the effects Oscar's reading in the closet has on Oscar's mother, community friends, and on Yunior as the text's "faithful watcher."[8] Indeed the whole point of Yunior's observation and the incomparable allegory of Oscar's reading in the closet, I suggest, is for us to start thinking about what happens to Latino and Latina "immigrant rising" barrio kids (like Oscar, Yunior, and Lola) when they read imaginative literature, and, more important, what goes on in their complex inner lives. While Yunior, throughout the course of his narrating Oscar's brief and wondrous life, engages in highlighting Oscar's developing identity politics (who he really is), Yunior is also interested in championing Oscar's and his own changing politics of subjectivity (how they feel) as humans, their evolving dialectics of negative aesthetics, and their ethics of convivencia and coexistence. Yunior's negative aesthetics—including his text's intentional gaps, paginas en blanco, and blanks—expose the limitations of his own systems of thought and entice readers to articulate thoughts that are absent.[9] I will conclude by focusing in the chapter's last section on Yunior's forty-something, fulsome search for decolonial love in "The Cheater's Guide to Love," the concluding story of *This Is How You Lose Her* (2012). Here Díaz's Yunior de las Casas, now a fully professionalized assistant professor of creative writing within what the literary historian Mark McGurl calls U.S. academia's "program era" of creative writing, offers us much more than a low-brow guide to his series of thwarted attempts to make human intimacy for himself and his series of lovers.[10] I want to view both of Díaz's linked texts as extended exercises in dissident antihomophobic inquiry and racial hermeneutics that have had important effects on the author's provocative theories about the coloniality of power, and gender, identity, sexuality, and their interrelation.

In the case of his best-selling novel *The Brief Wondrous Life of Oscar Wao*, Díaz paints a deliberate and critical understanding of a pair of "black, Latino, migrant Dominican Jersey, smart boys" through the lenses and projects of decolonial love. In "The Cheater's Guide to Love," Díaz changes gears by working through Yunior's philosophical praise of decolonial love, and the writer's critical self-analysis, resembling psychoanalysis, which is his hyperaware (writerly) way of expressing a decolonial love for himself and for others in his fiction. Like his favorite U.S. feminist writers, Toni Morrison and Sandra Cisneros, Díaz uses his central character, Yunior de las Casas (a kind of Paul D or Celaya Reyes), to bear witness to what really happens to young Latino men of color who have been traumatized by economic migration, racial oppression, sexual abuse, and rape. Grappling with this culture of sexual violence and abuse is what Díaz sees as his characters' doomed search for love. In "Ysrael," for example, the lead story of Díaz's *Drown*, set in Santo Domingo and its campo, nine-year-old Yunior is instructed by his older brother Rafa to sit at the back of the bus while on one of their ordinary summer travels of boyish mischief, violence, and havoc. Yunior obeys Rafa and sits next to an older Dominican man: "I lowered myself stiffly into my seat but the pastelito [I was eating] had already put a grease stain on my pants. . . . You have to watch out for stains like that, the man said to me. He had big teeth and wore a clean fedora. . . . These things are too greasy, I said. Let me help. He spit on his fingers and started to rub at the stain but then he was pinching at the tip of my pinga through the fabric of my shorts. You pato, I said."[11] This scene of sexual molestation wherein a wolflike man with "big teeth" gropes the preadolescent Yunior ends with his testifying: "The man squeezed my biceps, quickly, hard, the way my friends smack me in church. I whimpered."[12] In "Drown," the titular story of the collection set in New Jersey, the college-bound Beto, Yunior's best barrio bud, performs a hand job (and more) on him: "We had just come back from the pool and were watching a porn at his parents' apartment. . . . We were an hour into the new movie . . . when he reached into my pants. What the fuck are you doing? I asked, but he didn't stop. His hand was dry. I came right away, smearing the plastic covers."[13] As this scene powerfully suggests, part of Yunior de las Casas's charm, vulnerability, and contradictions as a developing character in Díaz's fictional matrix is not that he is a dishonest chronicler of his erotic and sexual intimacies but that Díaz often paints Yunior as being too incredibly honest and fantastically observant about what he sees as his grim reality.

Still later, in Díaz's *London Times* award-winning story "Miss Lora," from the linked collection of stories that make up *This Is How You Lose Her*, Yunior's *profesora*, a high school teacher named Miss Lora, frequently invites him over to her flat to have sex with him. Among other things, Díaz's "Miss Lora" investigates Yunior's teenage "ambivalences" about having sex with an older woman (who has power over him). Though we often think of adolescent teenage boys of color as already hypersexualized, Díaz suggests that Yunior is not yet capable of seeing his couplings with Miss Lora as criminal and abusive. Many years later, it is only after Yunior recounts his travails with Miss Lora to his Rutgers University girlfriend, Lola, that he begins to see how abusive this doomed coupling with the high school profesora had been.

Díaz's Yunior de las Casas is a complex contradictory, and "kooky" persona that Díaz uses in his linked fictional work to create complex narratological character-spaces and an evolving character-system in which he weighs the sexual abuses, race crazinessness, and transgressions Yunior experiences growing up in Santo Domingo and in New Jersey and how this abuse has centrally shaped who he is and how he feels as a subject.[14] As Díaz has noted in the *New Yorker*, "Yunior's been with [him] a long time" and he's "watched this frustrating fool grow up" and as a result has a "pretty good sense of his kinks and contradiction." Moreover, Yunior's particular blindness and insights allow us to see how his culture's heteronormativity and his masculinist ideas about women so often leave him feeling utterly disconnected or alienated from his lovers, family, and community. If Yunior senses how he constructs his own oppressive chains and he often rages against them and himself, he is unable to break free from them. As Díaz suggests to Moya, "Yunior's desire for communion with self and with other" is often "tragic," since he's continually "undermined" by his own "unwillingness to see women in his life as fully human."[15] If Yunior fails to recognize "the women parts of his identity as human," as Díaz describes, then how in the world can Yunior begin to "recognize himself as fully human?"[16]

Díaz's painting of Yunior de las Casa's developing and fraught character is important to the overall argument in this chapter because, as I have broadly outlined above, his early adolescent life in Santo Domingo and his teenage years in New Jersey constitute a fragmentary history in which he searches for decolonial hope, love, and compassion. But there is no real understanding of Yunior's full development as a character "without viewing him," Díaz suggests to the writer Greg Barrios, "through the lens of these [sexual scenes of abuse and rape]," lenses carefully thematized in Díaz's linked stories "Ysrael," "Drown," and "Miss Lora," and fully examined in the extended predatory rape culture of the dictator Trujillo's Dominican Republic in *The Brief Wondrous Life of Oscar Wao*.[17] In Díaz's fiction, Yunior de las Casas learns how to work through his own wounded traumas of economic migration and criminal sexual abuse, and through this process of working through his past experiences he learns how to become a more compassionate writer, who "suffers with" those around him. Yunior "will not need lots of talent," Díaz suggests, "to succeed." What Díaz's central consciousness, Yunior, needs "is more humanity. Yunior becomes very aware that part of what he lacks both in a relationship as a lover and perhaps even as an artist, what he lacks is not training, not will, but humanity, or what we would call sympathy or compassion."[18]

Oscar Wao's Spectacular Barrio Closet

[Oscar] wanted to blame the books, the sci-fi, but he couldn't—he loved them too much.
—Junot Díaz, *The Brief Wondrous Life of Oscar Wao*, 50

What does Yunior de las Casas in *The Brief Wondrous Life of Oscar Wao* tell us about Oscar de León's reading? I approach the question not in the current fashionable flourishing that intellectual historians of the book use to turn up a great deal of information about what Robert Darnton calls "the external history of reading," or what the literary theorist of the novel Franco Moretti and his Digital Humanities team of researchers at Stanford University call "quantitative formalism," but in the most literal (imaginative) way by reading a terrific footnote by Junot Díaz, one that shows us the hero Oscar engaged in the act of reading the "speculative genres," that is, science fiction novels.[19] This procedure may raise the question, Does Oscar's brain, so saturated on J. R. R. Tolkien and other fantasy books' storylands, arrest his development, like Quixote's reading of chivalrous literature or romances that fry his brain? Does Oscar's reading in the barrio closet thematize for Yunior an antihomophobic and dissident way of receiving, interpreting, and recoding science fiction's alien cultures otherwise? Oscar, Díaz tells us, "wanted to blame the books, the sci-fi, but he couldn't . . . he loved them too much."[20] I will not argue below that Oscar de León's "closeted" identification suggests a transparent meaning of Oscar's erotic and sexual orientations; instead, I want to demonstrate that Yunior's allegory of Oscar's reading in the closet helps him initiate a dissident way of understanding Oscar's gendered feelings and how they relate to their heteronormative and racist worlds in New Jersey and the Dominican Republic. Queer meaning, as David Halperin says, is a characteristic "recoding" of hegemonic (straight), heteronormative "meanings already encoded in that culture."[21] Thus Yunior observes that unlike other teenage boys on the mean streets of Paterson who, say, "pitched quarters," "played wall balls" or "drove their older brothers'" fast cars, Oscar de León preferred to "gorge himself [in the closet] on a steady stream of Lovecraft, Wells, Burroughs, Howard, Alexander, Asimov, Bova, and Heinlein, and even the old ones who were already beginning to fade—E. E. Doc Smith, Stapledon, and the guy who wrote all the Doc Savage books."[22]

In Oscar's reading this vast quantity of science fiction and speculative realist texts—Yunior estimates that by the time Oscar was in middle school he had read Tolkien's modernist *The Lord of the Rings* hundreds of times, "one of his greatest loves and comforts of his life he'd first discovered"— his Dominican grandmother, La Inca, insists proudly that he "showed the genius" that "was part of the [De León-Cabral] family's patrimony."[23] But not everyone in the De León family agreed with La Inca's sense of Oscar's "genius." Yunior, in one of the novel's thirty-three remarkable footnotes, rushing upward from the novel's marginal lower frequencies at the bottom of the page to his main text, suggests that Oscar's thick love for the "speculative genres" might have been a sociological consequence of Oscar's deep diasporic and oceanic feelings—that is, the hero's "being Antillean (who more SF than us?)."[24] Alternatively, Yunior speculates that Oscar's love of reading "jumped off" for Oscar when, having lived "the first couple of years of his life" in the Global South (the Dominican Republic), he "abruptly" and "wrenchingly" many years later had to relocate to the Global North (the Greater Jersey environs)—"a single green card," Yunior notes, "shifting not only worlds" geoculturally from the Global South to the Global North but also spatiotemporally "centuries (from almost no TV or electricity to plenty of both)."[25]

In *The Brief Wondrous Life of Oscar Wao*, Yunior sets this extraordinary scene of reading within a "spacy" epistemology of the closet and within the hidden and secret spaces and encoded meanings in their Paterson barrio house. In the paratextual passage, Yunior attempts to explain to his readers why Oscar loves to read so much and, as a "smart bookish" Dominicano boy of color, what "the [sociocultural] consequences" of too much reading are for Oscar's decolonial "aesthetic education" and his emergent queered, dissident gender formation.[26] Yunior suggests that for those *muchachos* of color living on the mean and hard streets of Paterson—where "the pure products of America go crazy," as the great Latino poet laureate of New Jersey William Carlos Williams put it in his modernist poem "To Elsie"—Oscar's bookishness is as if he had enormous "bat wings or a pair of tentacles growing out of [his] chest."[27] In other words, Yunior testifies to how Oscar's bookishness and dissident queerness led to his always being victimized by Paterson's ill-read barrio street toughs. They would kick, punch, belittle him and, worse, they would tear violently his "new Scholastic books" in half: "You like books, [Oscar,] the urchins asked him?" They would then rip his books "in half before his very eyes. Now you got two."[28] So here in this passage Díaz's Yunior demonstrates how Oscar's immersive reading in the closet can help us to understand Oscar's Dominican American queerness not as something that he is, but as something that he does.[29]

Díaz's Yunior stages and investigates how Oscar's bookishness and his reading (and writing) are performative activities loaded with survivance and imaginative regeneration. On the one hand, Oscar's carrying his books on the streets of Paterson makes "him stick out even more than he already did" as a nerdy, overly book-smart Dominican barrio boy. Oscar's mother, Belicia, also finds his bookish reading preoccupations "nutty" and she often belittles him so.[30] But Díaz's Yunior poses one of the novel's central questions, about why Oscar de León prefers the secret and safe spaces of his Paterson home's upstairs closet. There are a consistent series of attractive attributes that Oscar associates with the well-being of safety from the street cats on the mean streets of Paterson: inside his house, with his older sister Lola and his mother Belicia, Oscar secludes himself, Yunior writes, "in the upstairs closet."[31] By homing in on the realities of Oscar's closet, Yunior begins calling our attention to one of the most powerful and catalyzing aspects of queer theory's emergent "antihomophobic inquiry," which we know through Eve Kosofsky Sedgwick's work on the epistemology of the closet.[32] Like Sedgwick's fight against heterosexism's dominance, Díaz's Yunior, too, uses the insights of antihomophobic queer inquiry to help him dissect the regime of Oscar de León's closetedness and what Belicia calls her muchacho Oscar's "nuttiness," especially through the closet's structuring of power and knowing and not knowing (heteronormativity's willful ignorance) and the experiences and possibilities of queer dissidence. Yunior, moreover, asks what it is possible to know or say about Oscar's nuttiness in the closet. Are Oscar's racial and gendered identities inherent or socially hardwired? Why are his inner feelings and desires for others so unpredictable and powerful for Yunior?

I want to suggest that Yunior seizes on this opportunity early in the paratextual lower frequencies of The Brief Wondrous Life of Oscar Wao to explore Oscar's inner life, and this also helps him to strategically explore his own evolving, fraught, male subjectivity. Oscar's closet does not operate to conceal his queered subjectivity, but it stands in for Yunior as a way of highlighting Oscar's masculine sensibility, affect, pleasure, and identifications as a reader of speculative realist fantasy books (who is in love with fantasy). Is there a relation here of desire to the decolonial aesthetics of science fiction and of dissident queerness and culture for Oscar de León and Yunior de las Casas? Yunior is determined at the beginning of the novel to crack open Oscar's love and shame for the solitary pleasures of reading and in the process wants us to understand all of Oscar's feelings for aesthetics and culture that are assiduously closeted in the barrio. Yunior proceeds to let the light in the closet by means of a distant social and literary analysis—an allegory of barrio reading—revealing Oscar's hopes of light and darkness in Paterson as a bookish young boy of color, demonstrating that it may be possible to approach his friend's subjectivity without recourse to ego psychology. He is also able to begin painting the pathogenic consequences of Oscar de León's living in a racist and homophobic world.

This safe and secret space is itself linked metaphorically by Yunior to the restorative "slat of light" where Oscar reads science fiction books, tranquilly bathing him in a "razored" sublime light that rushes in "from the cracked door of the closet." Yunior sees Oscar reading in solitude and wonders what joyous opportunities for imaginative contemplation exist for Oscar in his acts of reading. Can the strengthening of the power-knowledge couplet brought on by reading aid in shaping the thick love Oscar has for the "speculative genres"—genres that have traditionally helped readers challenge their culture's hegemonic social, sexual, and ethnoracial codes of conduct? Yunior suggests that by closeting himself in his home and reading by the chiaroscuro crack of "razored light," Oscar's soaring imagination finds access to other worlds and galaxies free from the real razors and the brutal and "normalized" gendered identifications of the Paterson world outside. Rather than dismissing Yunior's nuanced and antihomophobic conjuring of his allegory of Oscar's reading in the closet as outrageous, I want to try to understand what Yunior thinks Oscar's reading in the closet means for the Cabral-De León family, for his neighborhood childhood friends, and for him. What exactly is at stake for Yunior? What are the larger implications of Oscar's reading in the closet?

Yunior gets at these questions by first highlighting how Belicia's reaction to Oscar's reading in the upstairs closet sets off other metaphorical and figural chains of signifying connotations: "Pa' 'fuera! [Oscar's] mother roared. And out he would go, like a *condemned* boy, to spend a few hours being tormented by the other boys—Please I want to stay; he would beg his mother but she shoved him out—You ain't a woman to be staying in the house."[33] Against the (symbolic) interiorized pleasure of Oscar's secret hiding space, where the rising immigrant hero is free to feel, fantasize, and love, the imaginative mind as the closet, or the house of science fiction's utopian epistemology, Belicia bodily "shoves" Oscar out of the closet and "roars" at him to go "Pa fuera." Yunior, the novel's central "humble watcher" as he dubs himself, observes all of this and highlights Oscar's coming out as a performative staging of what the philosopher María Lugones terms "the coloniality of gender," for he obeys his mother and goes out, he says, "like a condemned [and damned] boy" (Oscar as a Fanonian *damné de la terre?*).[34] With his beautifully wrought Proustian flourish, Yunior brilliantly plays the "inside" secret space of Oscar's closet's recuperative powers, where his reading of the speculative genres helps him attain his aesthetic education against the harsh, male-centered, and violent urban space's "outside" ("Pa' 'Fuera") on the Paterson streets, where a multitude of hypermasculinized and homophobic boys torment the hero, Oscar.[35] If we have not yet felt the full weight of Belicia's rigid and normalizing structures of feeling—a conservative mindset of a popular barriocentric and heteronormative *tíguere latinidad* formed both in the Dominican Republic and in New Jersey, where she equates Oscar's love of reading with a gendered domesticity—this scene dramatizes for Yunior the harsh heteronormative ideology implicit in Belicia's comments, which imply that every human being must be assigned "a binarized identity," to use Sedgwick's terms, based on the gender of object choice.[36] Yunior de las Casas then goes on to quote Belicia's bilanguaging and stigmatizing interpellation of her closeted son: "Pórtate como un muchacho normal," for "You ain't a woman to be staying the house."[37] Belicia not only prohibits Oscar's reading (and his spontaneous fantasizing) in the closet, Yunior emphasizes this prohibition by using Michel Foucault's iconic discourse, suggesting that Oscar's family and culture want to "normalize" and discipline him as a "straight" subject within their gender regime.[38] Alas, only Oscar's sister Lola, a serious and capacious book-reader herself and a *loca* in decolonial love to boot, consoles her brother by bringing him more "books from her school library, which had a better library."[39]

Although Díaz's Yunior role as a "watcher" offers his readers no explanation for the emergence of Belicia's normalized gendered categorization and language—"un muchacho normal," to shame Oscar into straight normalization—he expertly traces its impact on Oscar's development both in New Jersey and the Dominican Republic and on the aesthetic figural and tropological ways we can really know those cultures. Oscar's secrecy and disclosure in the closet, Oscar's imaginative wholeness and fragmentariness inside his secret space, and Oscar's mental health and suicidal anxieties come to mean what they mean in *The Brief Wondrous Life of Oscar Wao* through their figural relationship to the matrix of the "muchacho normal" and the dissident queered boy's reading in the closet. What Yunior's complex meditation does here in *The Brief Wondrous Life of Oscar Wao* is allegorically illuminated, like the "razored" light rushing in through "the cracked [upstairs closet] door," the dizzying contradictory significance of the secret signified by Oscar's barrio closet.[40] Yunior thus enlarges Oscar's identification as a bookish, alienated, "bloated," and "dyspeptic" Dominicano "nerd" growing up on the mean streets of Paterson by problematizing the complex and overlapping varieties of oppression—ethnic, sexual, racial, and gendered—he seeks to liberate himself from in his quest for decolonial love and compassion and the liberation from his world's hegemonic, binarized identifications, which he discovers in his books.[41] Yunior's incomparable reading of Oscar's closeted reading in the footnoted passage is in large agreement with Sedgwick's focus on the intersectionality of oppression, as Sedgwick insisted persuasively that "all oppressions . . . are differently structured and so must intersect in complex embodiments."[42]

If we now turn from the domestic, gendered economy of the barrio closet to the commercial and heteronormative economy Oscar's mother Belicia condemns him to, Oscar's being shoved out his closet forces him to come face to face with the contours of his prescribed normalization on the brutish, gendered, urban streets of Paterson. Oscar "morphs" right in front of Yunior's eyes from a "nutty" and "smart bookish" young boy of color ("who ain't a woman") into a young, queered, dissident, and "oppressed" muchacho who appears to the straight boys on Paterson's mean streets as if he had "bat wings . . . growing out of his chest." Alas, "no one," Yunior concludes in his allegory of reading, was "more oppressive than the oppressed."[43] In Oscar's being pushed by his mother "Pa fuera," he experiences other ways his iconic gendered Latinidad is defined, constrained, and designed in Yunior's cognitive mapping by the patriarchal culture and society around him and then plotted metonymically through the circuits of the contiguous Paterson streets that determine his social horizons. The chronotope of Oscar's spectacular closet and of the domestic De León *oikos* that Yunior so rigorously links through the aesthetic, metonymic circuits of the street refer less to a poetics of the closet and the house than to the mutually overdetermining spheres of the private spaces and what the historian Mike Davis calls the "magical urbanism" of the social barrioscape in the Global North.[44] Here the spatialized temporalities of Oscar's everyday barrio life—figured by Yunior as the closet and the house—stand out against the institutionalization of the subject into the heteronormativity of his culture and society. Yunior stages Oscar's reading science fiction texts in the sheltered and secret spaces of the closet (a cradle and a retreat) that protects him against the invasion of the outside world but also borrows from this outside world some of its qualities—that is, the fragile but razored light that comes from the sun. Yunior valorizes Oscar's rich inner world (where he is able to feel freely) as vastly preferable to the violent, outside, urban world of the streets.

This primal paratextual scene—footnoted in the novel—is pivotal because it powerfully gives us one of the text's first tropologically rigorous indications of how the inner and the outer national and outer planetary aesthetic worlds operate for Oscar and Yunior in *The Brief Wondrous Life of Oscar Wao*. For Díaz's Yunior, this is the importance of being Oscar Wao!

In Praise of Yunior de las Casas's Search for Decolonial (Sucio/a) Love

In this last section on Yunior de las Casas's searching for decolonial love, I will conclude by analyzing the last story, "The Cheater's Guide to Love," from Díaz's *This Is How You Lose Her*. What kind of "love event" is Yunior de las Casas working through in this "guide"? Are there any new philosophical "truth procedures" that Yunior is grappling with? Why is the radioactive "half-life of (decolonial) love" that his story leaves us with a philosophical "event" for him?[45]

"The Cheater's Guide to Love" is the central story from which all of the other stories showcasing Yunior's verbal and idiolectical virtuosity and narratological energy in *This Is How You Lose Her* are derived, but this does not mean that the other linked stories in the book are pretexts or wonderful fictional shards of "The Cheater's Guide to Love." In stories such as "Nilda," for instance, Díaz not only paints a fourteen-year-old Yunior yearning for sucio/a love, but also portrays him (nine years later) working through a deep and soulful mourning for his older brother, Rafa, who dies not only from the destructive effects of leukemia but also from the radioactive treatments he receives to stop this destruction. Yunior recounts his mother Virta's and his own reactions to Rafa—once a terrific "overmuscled" boxer and "papi chulo"—as he lies dying in their forlorn London Terrace apartment in Parlin, New Jersey. At night, Rafa, "the hardest dude in the nabe" and the cruelest, most *chiflado*, abusive, and monstrous older brother to Yunior, regularly sneaks the Dominicana Nilda and other barrio girls "orbiting around him" into the apartment's basement bedroom, which he shares with Yunior, and has sex with them.[46] Fourteen-year-old Yunior endures all of this embarrassment because his mother does not allow her boys to sleep upstairs on the living room couch. But "Nilda" begins years later, when twenty-three-year-old Yunior runs into Rafa's former girlfriend Nilda in a laundromat years after his brother's death and thinks that anything in his London Terrace multiverse—even escape from their downtrodden world—is still possible. This moment, however, closes quickly.

Nilda once had super-long black hair and "world-class looks."[47] Some nights she and Yunior would sit on the couch while Rafa was off at his job at the carpet factory or working out at the gym. But as soon as Rafa showed up, Nilda jumped into his arms. Díaz's teenage Yunior has an "I.Q. that would have broken you in two" but he would have traded his smarts in for a halfway decent face in a second.[48] The story then loops back to earlier times when Nilda had been visiting Yunior and first met Rafa. Rafa noticed Nilda because she was wearing a tank top that "couldn't have blocked a sneeze."[49] They went out that whole summer, and Rafa was tired all the time and pale, and some mornings, Yunior remembers, Rafa's "leg bones hurt so much he couldn't get of bed."[50] There is nothing heartbroken Yunior can do to help to "soothe Rafa's pain," not even "massag[ing] Rafa's shins."[51] Rafa eventually quits high school, works manual-labor jobs, and dreams of going to California. One night, at the end of summer, Yunior overhears Nilda's telling Rafa about her plans for the future: she wants to get away from her mom and their downtrodden world and open up a group home for runaway kids. "Listening to her imagining herself," Yunior writes, "was about the saddest thing you ever heard."[52] Rafa didn't even say "wow."[53] An hour later she gets up and leaves. A week later Rafa is seeing some other London Terrace "nabe" girl.

But why was Nilda so doomed, Yunior asks? Why did an older man scoop her up, when she had just gotten back from the group home? And why had Nilda gotten tossed out when the older barrio cat "bounced" and then been handed around from man to man?[54] Two years later, Yunior's brother Rafa dies and the friendless Yunior is out of school most of the time and smoking *mota* at the toxic Global Landfill next to the London Terrace Apartments and chronicling in his mind everything about Rafa's and Nilda's woes, incapable of effecting any change for them. Yunior's sad story records Nilda's downward spiral: how she fell in with more "stupid" street cats, got a "Brick city beat down," and lost some of her teeth.[55] She continues to be in and out of school until she finally drops out completely. She loses her world-class looks, and she "cuts her hair down to nothing."[56]

The story concludes when Yunior (now twenty-three) is washing his clothes up at the mini mall and he happens to run into Nilda. She tells him that she misses his brother, Rafa. "He treated me the best."[57] What else can they really say about their London Terrace multiverse, Yunior muses? They then walk back through the old New Jersey neighborhood, and Yunior, "his heart beating fast" has an epiphany: Could they do anything?[58] Even marry and drive off together to the West Coast, as Rafa once desired, and start off in a better California world? But this moment in "Nilda" closes quickly and they are back in the downtrodden London Terrace world they have always known. "Remember the day we met?" Nilda asks.[59] Nilda had been wearing a tank top, and Yunior, who wanted to play baseball, made her put on a shirt before he would let her be on his team. "I remember," Yunior the chronicler says.[60] They never speak again. Many years later, Yunior goes away to Rutgers, and he discovers "he didn't know where the fuck she went."[61] "Nilda" is one of saddest and most well-wrought stories Yunior de las Casas writes about the brutalizing inequality of wealth for those like Nilda living in Parlin's London Terrace Apartments, and it is sadder still because in "Nilda" Yunior ingeniously chronicles how Rafa was mourned for. It "broke my heart," he writes.[62]

Like Nilda and the multitude of other young, doomed women painted in *This Is How You Lose Her*, Díaz's Yunior yearns for a better multiverse: it "was the summer when everything we would become was hovering just over our heads." "In another universe," he philosophizes, he might have "come out OK, ended up with mad novias and jobs and a sea of love in which to swim, but in this world I had a brother dying of cancer and a long dark patch of life like a mile of black ice waiting for me up ahead."[63] Yunior's captivating "dark patches of life," sucio/a love and loss—like the miles of black ice waiting ahead for him—are at the very heart of Díaz's prodigious book, but there is a deeper feeling still that Yunior stitches together in "Nilda": Yunior madly loves his dying brother, Rafa, and Nilda's love for the "papi chulo" Rafa makes Yunior fall madly in love with her. As he agonizes over his mourning for Rafa, he cannot suppress his memories about the doomed Dominicana Nilda. Every time he runs into her in their London Terrace nabe, she acts as a painful reminder to him of everything he has lost in his multiverse. At the funeral his mother and he arrange for Rafa, a broken down and toothless Nilda spectrally appears: "What a short skirt she'd worn," Yunior writes, "like maybe she could still convince" the dead Rafa "of something."[64] While Virta cannot easily place this forlorn Nilda, all she can remember about her she says to Yunior that "she was the one who smelled good . . . It wasn't until Mami said it that I realized it was true."[65] The story ends with an older but still foolish Yunior's remembering his London Terrace world and attempting to make sense of his dark and icy patch of kinks and contradictions—and to chronicle Rafa's loss: "He's gone; he's gone, he's gone."[66] In stories such as "Nilda" Yunior cannot offer us an epic or grand anatomy of decolonial love. But in Díaz's perfectly crafted and linked stories such as "Nilda" and "The Cheater's Guide to Love," Díaz's Yunior opens up a small window on the subject of his searching for decolonial love.

Díaz's "The Cheater's Guide to Love" is the most philosophically and aesthetically nuanced of his imaginative work, centering on the forty-something

Yunior's throwing down some thoughts on decolonial (sucio/a) love's risks and instabilities. It is also Díaz's most unstinting analysis of Yunior's culpability for a relationship that he did not want to see collapse. Does sucio/a love disrupt? Or does sucio/a love refashion the self in love with the other? I am also interested in thinking about why "The Cheater's Guide to Love" may be Díaz's most legible story at this stage in his writing career in praise of (doubting) love, where Yunior's lost love is never usefully described or represented. Indeed, Yunior's fiancée is irrevocably lost to him and he has to figure out in his "cheater's guide" how to paint this irrevocable loss, which he ingeniously does by literally making his fiancée invisible throughout the story to the reader.

Here is the long and short of Yunior's cheater's guide to love: the story is divided by Yunior into the last six "years" of his life in praise of (doubting) sucio love, where he works on his lost and shattered love on his own terms and wants to chronicle those heartbreaks that never leave him. The longitudinal scope of the guide allows Yunior to both measure this wounding, absent, lost love and to simultaneously open up a question about decolonial (sucio/a) love that his imaginative cheater's guide cannot possibly answer through his hypermasculinist, self-centered focalizations. In other words, if Yunior's serial cheating has carved up such a gaping hole in his forty-something immigrant heart, what ugly feelings and pain had his cheating opened up for his fiancée?

Yunior's "The Cheater's Guide to Love" blasts off with "Year 0," a kind of ground zero of love where Yunior's knowledge about love has been hidden in the transparency and worldliness of the "0." Six numbered years in Yunior's midlife crisis in love and loss follow. "Year 0" chronicles the collapse of Yunior's adult life as a professor of writing in Cambridge, Massachusetts, where he has never wanted to live, where he feels himself "exiled" from New Jersey and Harlem's conviviality and racial diversity. His fiancée, a successful Latina lawyer working in New York, called off their engagement for his rampant "cheating" on her.[67] Yunior the writer and chronicler has forgotten to empty the emails on his computer's desktop trashcan, and his fiancée finds an archive fever of trashed but not erased emails that document his love "affairs" with some fifty women. In order to begin the real gathering of all of the broken pieces of his pain, Yunior tells his fiancée that he will change his cheating ways, and he begins his rehabilitation by not only closing his Facebook account (a social networking service initially conjured by some Harvard nerds to hook up with college women), but also by giving his intended all of his email passwords, and taking her to Salsa dance classes so that they can begin living a life from the lovers' perspective of twoness. Yunior's intended is "immensely sad[dened]" by Yunior's reckless infidelities, but he tries to apologize for his cheating by blaming it on the patriarchy, his having been groomed for cheating by the serial peccadilloes of his father, an officer in the Dominican military police, and by the pressures of his life as an assistant professor, for he is struggling to move up in the university's ranks from an assistant professor to an associate professor with tenure.[68] "It was the book," he confesses—the great American novel he is in the process of completing in Cambridge—on which he blames all of his amorous troubles. Wearied by Yunior's prevarications the fiancée says, "Ya," as in the EZLN's Zapatismo's "Ya Basta."[69] This may be for Yunior a critical scene of ruptured difference. "Ya" suggests that he must stop showing up at his fiancée's New York City apartment "at odd hours"—and "stop the phoning and emails," or, his fiancée's sister tells him, his intended will put "a restraining order on you."[70]

The next sections—one through five—in "The Cheater's Guide to Love" document Yunior's attempts to reconstruct how he has ended up as a cheating serial shagger. Yunior's cheating life implodes, and he tries to pull himself together by addressing his foolish immigrant cheating, kinks, and contradictions. Does Yunior's search for decolonial love end up any better at the end of his story? Or is his life one huge doomed mess? Why has he always cheated on all of his girlfriends and why does he continue thriving on his infidelities? Lola de León? Magda? Veronica? Cassandra? Alma? Paloma? His fiancée? The list is a partial one. And why have Yunior's betrayals continued so blatantly even in the face of his fiancée's threat that she would take "a machete" to him if he "ever cheated?"[71]

The first eight linked stories of This Is How You Lose Her are Yunior's attempt to fill in the glorious gaps of ephemerality in "The Cheater's Guide to Love" (and Yunior dutifully and lyrically documents all of his failed commitments and his major infidelities). In his "cheater's guide" he wants to leave it all out in the open, writing that he "needs to finish" his guide in order to show "[the reader] what kind of fool I was."[72] Throughout this linked book of stories, forty-something Yunior self-critically begins to see himself and his life's relational longue durée as "weak" and "full of mistakes."[73] He even sees himself as others truly see him—as the many ex-novias in the book end up seeing him—as a "typical Dominican man," as Magda says, in the book's opening, linked story, "The Sun, the Moon, the Stars." Not only is he a typical Dominicano male, he is also a "sucio" and an "asshole," as his novia calls him. If Yunior is a "totally batshit cuero" who does not have the discipline to commit himself to his fiancée, by the time the forty-something writing-professor Yunior chronicles the trauma of his younger, high school, criminal affair he experienced with the high school teacher Miss Lora, he wants to avoid the whole thing.[74]

But Díaz's Yunior can do no such thing. In the story "Miss Lora," for example, an analytic Yunior looks back on his life and asks himself: "Are you your father's son and your brother's brother?" Are all of the de las Casas men "genetically" "batshit" "sucios," he asks?[75] And perhaps it is only in this tale where the heartbroken and still mourning Yunior wonders about the criminalized love affair he had with the high school teacher: "You wonder if she feels like you do. Like it might be love."[76] While the hypersexualized, sixteen-year-old Yunior does not yet have any real understanding about human erotic love, the forty-something writing-professor Yunior recalls the ugly feelings of "panic" he felt as a result of his couplings with Miss Lola: "Now it's official."[77] Yunior writes about himself in the third person; "he's the worst of sucios"—just like his abusive and corrupt father Ramón (who used to take him with him "on his pussy runs") and his monstrous brother Rafa (who "banged girls in the bed next to his").[78] In listening to all of Yunior's fulsome confessions and revelations about his sexual peccadilloes and pain, another friend, Paloma, grows weary and tells him to stop, for she does not have the time to listen to all of his loco "craziness."[79] So Yunior's "The Cheater's Guide to Love" tries to address both the large flow of the dark patches of black ice that constituted his downtrodden, immigrant life, and to salvage his shattered and broken love.

One can therefore read Yunior de las Casas's linked stories from *Drown* and *This Is How You Lose Her*—as I have attempted to do in this chapter—not only as linked stories that work perfectly well on their own terms, but also as collective historias that chronicle and work with and against one another, producing an arresting "surplus of feeling" and affect that go beyond the ordinary sum of the parts. This is the wonderful patch of liminality that Díaz's Yunior (in his own Dominican island Odyssey) spins out for us both in his linked story collections of a son abandoned on his island by his father and in the novel *The Brief Wondrous Life of Oscar Wao*, texts in which he chronicles the historia of Oscar and his own journeys through heartbreak and as he emerges possessing something approximating what I am calling human, decolonial love.

Yunior documents in "Year 1" how he has gone through the various stages of mourning following the shattered love and break up with his intended, and in "Year 2" Yunior chronicles how after the worst of his grieving is over, he begins to date Naomi, a nurse. But he screws this budding relationship up too when one day he "classlessly" and clumsily asks Naomi if "she is planning to give him some ass anytime soon."[80] In "Year 3," Yunior recounts how he wishes to take better care of himself: he takes up yoga, starts running along the paths next to the Charles River, and he rededicates himself to completing a new novel he is writing. He begins dating again and this time dates a young woman half his age who is attending Harvard Law School. Yunior says that she is one of those "super geniuses who finished undergrad when she was nineteen."[81] But, alas, she dumps him when she decides to take up with a law school classmate who is more her age. The year ends with yet another doomed love affair Yunior has with a married and upper-class woman from the Dominican Republic who is studying at the Harvard Graduate School of Business. In "Year 4," Yunior's off-and-on law school girlfriend returns to his life and tells him that she is pregnant and that he is the father, which adds to what he describes as his life's "berserkería."[82] She moves in with Yunior, takes over his bedroom, and exiles him to the living room couch.

It is hard for me not to pull a Pierre Menard and simply write out the entire section of events that make up "Year 5" of "The Cheater's Guide to Love" because they are so important to the central philosophical point Yunior's guide is making about what he terms the radioactive half-life of his (doubting) decolonial love.[83] Near the story's end, Yunior decides to read what he calls "The Doomsday Book," a book he has hidden in a folder under his bed. The "Doomsday Book," in fact, consists of "copies of all the emails and fotos" from Yunior's cheating life we have been reading about— the dumped and trashed emails his fiancée" found in his computer's trash, printed out, and then "compiled, [bound], and mailed to [him] a month after she ended it."[84] "Dear Yunior," the ex (intended) explains, "for your next book."[85]

Yunior sits and reads "the whole thing cover to cover." "You are surprised," he later writes, "at what a fucking chickenshit coward you are. It kills you to admit it but it's true. You are astounded by the depth of your mendacity."[86] Many days later, after Yunior and Elvis (his AfroDominicano sidekick) are pulled over by the Boston police for driving while brown, Elvis encourages Yunior to think seriously about writing "The Cheater's Guide to

Love," that is, the doomsday book of e-mails and photographs his intended sent him.[87] In the months that follow, Yunior writes, "you bend to the work, because it feels like hope, like grace—and because you know in your lying cheater's heart that sometimes a start is all we ever get."[88]

But why does Díaz's "The Cheater's Guide to Love" underscore the philosophical conclusion in praise of the radioactive "half-life of love" that forty-something Yunior ends his book with? Why does Yunior believe that the "half-life of love is forever?"[89] Does this revelation mark the central turning point of Yunior's redemption, a passionate redemption that he fills in through the stories he has composed in *This Is How You Lose Her*? When we finish reading Yunior's book of linked stories do we comprehend that, in addition to creating a greater and cooler distance between himself and his readers, his many second-person stories are not simply focalized stories directed to his readers but are in fact stories he has been writing to his "sucio," cheating, prevaricating self? Díaz calls this strategy his "writer's trick," which he uses through his character Yunior, to play on the reader: "It's that the book we are reading is not directly from me. It's Yunior de las Casas's book. He, at the end of the book, is seen writing the book that now we realize we have been reading."[90]

Before offering a few answers to some of these key questions, allow me to spell out some of the philosophical frames of reference to the case I am making about Yunior's "The Cheater's Guide to Love" as his search for a (doubting) decolonial love. Much of what I have been arguing about Yunior de las Casas's search for decolonial love in the chronicle he is writing has been framed not only by the critical work of decolonial feminists such as the historian and novelist Emma Pérez, the philosopher María Lugones, and the sociologist Deborah R. Vargas but also by the work of two thinkers who have diametrically opposed views on human love—the French postexistentialist philosopher Alain Badiou, who writes in praise of love as a kind of "communism," and the modernist founder of psychoanalysis, Sigmund Freud. In one of his iconic case histories, Freud philosophized about one of his patient's obsessional neurosis about love that paralyzed him with doubts, writing the following prodigious sentence to get at the limits of masculine human love: "A man who doubts his own love, may, or indeed, must doubt every lesser thing."[91] I will also conclude by circling back to Junot Díaz's definition of decolonial love as a kind of revolutionary Fanonian hope and love. Does Yunior's doubting (sucio/a) love incite or foreclose love? Can we frame Yunior's search for decolonial love in his guide as his becoming philosophical about his quotidian intimacies and passions? If Yunior does not kill his passions in "The Cheater's Guide to Love" by thinking them into the ground, through writing about his passions he seeks to think deeply about them, posing his question about why "the half-life of love lasts forever" into the practice of decolonial love.[92]

In Badiou's In Praise of Love, he uses the Western philosophical concepts he developed in Theory of the Subject (1982) and Being and Event (1988) to give us a comprehensive theory of love by arguing that love in our late capitalist epoch threatens to destroy love's passions, risks, and buoyant unpredictability. His book (a long interview with Peter Truong in 2009) praising love—like Yunior's guide to the half-life of love—interests me for what he says about the praising of love in the face of the "cozi[ness]" of a globalized love market and its "consumerist permissiveness."[93] Some of the themes Badiou covers are the relationships between love and politics, love and aesthetics, and love in the face of risk-free, on-line, commodified dating agencies.

One of the main features of (heteronormative) love for Badiou is its incitation of risk, for love is an "event" and events contain volatility, instability, and risk. Put more precisely, an event is a radical break with the existing state of affairs. "It's something that doesn't enter into the immediate order of things."[94] Events are totally new, Badiou suggests. Badiou then looks at the structure of what he calls the "love event" and its transformation into a "truth procedure." With respect to the love event, the site is not to be found in our risk-free on-line dating services but rather in our everyday relations with others at schools, work, meetings, and political rallies. For Badiou, love is an encounter based entirely on chance (like a Mallarmé poem), a totally random encounter. One cannot plan on love events because they are often impossible to imagine.

Further, the French philosopher defines love by the difference between the two lovers who by chance meet and fall in love. Their different standpoint locations and epistemologies of the world demand what we might call their pluritopical perspectives. "Love," Badiou writes, "is a decision to live a life . . . no longer from the perspective of One but from the perspective of Two," for "you have two. Love involves two."[95] And it is precisely this critical difference between the two lovers that makes love so risky for Badiou and this riskiness is what gives love its possibilities for creating "a different way of living in life" and a "desire for an unknown duration."[96]

Put briefly, for Badiou, it is through the chance encounter that the lovers transform the love event into a "truth procedure": by declaring their love and fidelity to the other. This performative declaration "seals the act of the encounter" and constitutes a "commitment" to one another.[97] By naming the void through language that structures the encounter, one makes oneself vulnerable to the other and risks losing everything. Love is thus "the proof of two."[98] If love has the same structure as "minimal communism," for Badiou it is because both love and politics concern becoming collective rather than the individual.[99] "People in love," he concludes, "put their trust in difference rather than being suspicious of it."[100] "To love" is thus "to struggle, beyond solitude, with everything in the world that can animate existence."[101]

Are Yunior's love encounters in *This Is How You Lose Her* in general and "The Cheater's Guide to Love" in particular what constitute his truth procedures as a writer? Does it follow that the radioactive half-life of Yunior's search for (decolonial) love is a love shattered and destroyed by his cheating? Can Freud's prodigious dictum I quoted above or Deborah R. Vargas's incisive feminist reading of sucio/a love serve as our partial guides to men's doubting love and help us make some initial sense of Yunior's manifesto on love? While Yunior makes a statement about the possibility of decolonial love, he also gives us a warning and an admonition. Yunior ends "The Cheater's Guide to Love" by doubting the possibility of (decolonial) love, but does he—as Freud suggests all men who doubt love must do—also doubt himself? Does Díaz's Yunior here lose his epistemological anchor of certainty about decolonial love? Does he, like Freud, hesitate that men who doubt their own love "may" or rather "must" doubt "every lesser thing"? Is every lesser love the same as the other thing—love?

I want to suggest that Yunior dramatizes in "The Cheater's Guide to Love" a questioning man grappling both with the foreclosure and the incitation of what he calls the radioactive half-life of love. What good is it, for the forty-something Yunior, to question love? Is Yunior's love a problem of his manhood? Does he love when he thinks that he does? Or when he says he does? Can U.S. men of color like Yunior be wise in the moment of love? Or is part of the point of Yunior's "The Cheater's Guide to Love" to make the claim that love is unreliable under systems of the coloniality of power and gender?

All things considered, it should come as no surprise that Díaz's Yunior de las Casas cannot tell us that love is wise or that it furnishes the grounds on which we might have a certain knowledge of love. That is just the way Junot Díaz's thinking about Yunior's "kinks and contradictions" work in his linked, supreme texts. But Díaz's decolonial readers can also glean that when

Yunior begins to explore his sucio love and his masculinist self-formation and enters a critical self-analysis, he might also be entering a scene of de-colonial love. So Yunior's forty-something self-analysis is a kind of decolonial (sucio) love, and Yunior's "guide" and linked historias in *Drown*, *The Brief Wondrous Life of Oscar Wao*, and *This Is How You Lose Her* might be too. While Yunior's critical self-analyses are not exactly models or schemas of love, they are relationships that resemble dreams, fantasies, drives, and fields of affective structures of feeling. When desire comes to speech in Yunior's linked texts, desire and meaning consort amicably together, though they also continually displace one another aesthetically and figurally.

This is why it is crucial to ground Junot Díaz's search for decolonial love in his fiction in both aesthetic (sublime) and bodily terms that emerge, he emphasizes, out of the poetics of the Greater Antilles and the feminism written by women of color in the United States, which he carefully read as a student at Rutgers and Cornell University. In his *Boston Review* interview with Paula M. L. Moya, Díaz recounts the genesis of his search for decolonial love by first quoting from the insights of the "prayer" with which the Martinican Frantz Fanon famously ended his classic *Black Skin, White Masks* (1952): "O my body, always make me a man who questions."[102] He then updates Fanon's prayer by explaining how women of color writers in the United States have supplemented Fanon's work on love. Can Fanon's transcultural (revolutionary) psychiatry—like Freud's psychoanalysis—help us define decolonial love as a doubting or questioning human enterprise? Like Fanon and the Chicana feminists Gloria Anzaldúa and Cherríe Moraga that Díaz cites often in his interviews, his imaginative writings like theirs touch his readers affectively, bodily, and sensually. Words and writing have a charge and they powerfully have the color of "quivering flesh" and what Moraga and Anzaldúa called a "theory in the flesh."[103] Fanon, Moraga, Anzaldúa, and Díaz all critically diagnose societies whose pathological, heteronormative, and raciological cultures have created alienated peoples (black, brown, mixed, and white).

Whether or not everyone today shares either in Fanon's phenomenological, existentialist hope or in Anzaldúa's and Moraga's bodily theory of the flesh and *conocimientos*, Díaz suggests that by acknowledging and supplementing Fanon's rich psychiatry of questioning from the body and by turning to the ways Latina feminists have, in their theorizing in the flesh "wield[ed] a genius that had been cultivated of their raced, gendered, sexualized subjectivities," we can better understand his linked collection of stories and his novel as a searching for decolonial love.[104] Like Anzaldúa and Moraga, Díaz attempts to forge in his characters' very bodies what he envisions as "a source code" for their own "future liberation." Thus envisaged, decolonial love for Díaz involves a radical questioning from the body, a radical decolonial (doubting) love, with all of its "oppressions," "interpellations," and its contrapuntal "liberatory counter-strategies."[105] This is the "quantum leap" that Latina feminists have made since Fanon's decolonial questioning from the body in 1952, and this is the astonishing leap that Junot Díaz himself wishes to elaborate on and join in with his own supreme fiction. It is the epistemological and aesthetic ground or "basis" of his art: "The kind of love that I [am] interested in, that my characters long for intuitively, is the only kind of love that [can] liberate them from that horrible legacy of colonial violence."[106]

Notes

1. Instead of using Pascale Casanova's Eurocentered World Republic of Letters (Cambridge, MA: Harvard University Press, 2007), where consecration through Paris was a crucial stage in the world reception of non-French writers, I propose that Junot Díaz's work belongs to a rather different planetary framework marked by the Global South's narratological voices and poetics from, say, William Faulkner, Edouard Glissant, Derek Walcott, Fernando Ortiz, Aimé Césaire, Frantz Fanon, Gabriel García Márquez, Toni Morrison, Gustavo Pérez Firmat, and Sandra Cisneros, among others. This trans-American imaginative writing has been promoted and translated into a genuinely planetary genre, outside the confines of U.S.-centric creative writing programs. In other words, I think it is possible to glimpse in Díaz's fiction the outlines of some wholly different world-coloniality system of letters coming into being.

2. See George M. Fredrickson, White Supremacy: A Comparative Study in American and South African History (New York: Oxford University Press, 1987). As Fredrickson puts it, "The phrase 'white supremacy' applies with particular force to the historical experience of two nations—South Africa and the United States. As generally understood, white supremacy refers to the attitudes, ideologies, and policies associated with the rise of blatant forms of white or European dominance over 'nonwhite' populations. In other words, it involves making invidious distinctions of a socially crucial kind that are based primarily, if not exclusively, on physical characterizations and ancestry" (ix).

3. Under Tina Brown's editorial leadership at The New Yorker, circulation increased steadily, from just under 659,000 at the end of 1992 to a little over 830,000 two years later. At Vanity Fair, where she worked before she arrived at The New Yorker, Brown is said to have broken the magazine industry's $2-a-word barrier. Vanity Fair and The New Yorker made magazine writing lucrative enough that writers didn't have to flee to Hollywood

to do well. See Joanne Weintraub, "Tina Brown's New Yorker," AJR, April 1995, accessed March, 20, 2013, http://www.ajr.org/article.asp?id=1692.

4. Selected by a jury comprising the Colombian novelists Piedad Bonnett, Héctor Abad Faciolince, and Oscar Callazos, all of the other recipients of the "39 under 39" Best Latin American authors award, with the exception of the Peruvian American Daniel Alarcón, write strictly in Spanish and hail from Latin American countries.

5. According to Walter Mignolo's *The Darker Side of Western Modernity: Global Futures, Decolonial Options* (Durham, NC: Duke University Press, 2011), a transmodern planet has emerged, reconfiguring the past five hundred years of coloniality and its aftermath, modernity, postmodernity, and transmodernity. A significant feature of this transformation is the creativity and aesthetic production in and from the non-Western world and its political consequences—independent thoughts and decolonial freedoms in all spheres of life. The decoloniality of knowledge and María Lugones's the "coloniality of gender," two philosophical concepts that have been introduced by the Modernity-Coloniality Working Group with which I have been affiliated, are two of the key concepts that grapple with the decoloniality of aesthetics and gender in order to join different gendered genealogies of reexistence in artistic practices all over the world. In this chapter I stitch together Mignolo's and Lugones's work in decolonial aesthetics and decolonial feminism in order to grasp the liberation of sensing, bodily feelings, affects, and sensibilities trapped by modernity and its darker side: coloniality. (See María Lugones, "Toward a Decolonial Feminism," *Hypatia* 25, no. 4 [fall 2010]: 742–59.) Last but not least, I have benefited in my work from the sociologist Deb Vargas's acute focus (in her chapter in this collection) on the racialized, classed politics of "lo sucio and la sucia": the unclean, the filthy, the imperfect. In her analysis of Díaz's fiction, lo sucio and la sucia operate as an analytic for explaining the constructions of racialized, classed masculinities and femininities. Moreover, she examines the various ways lo sucio and la sucia operate in Díaz's texts as a structural metonymy for nonnormative constructions of intimacy, sexual desire, and kinship. In other words, the sucias and sucios in Díaz's *This Is How You Lose Her* inhabit racialized genders and sexualities that represent the "deficit citizenry" of institutional regimes of normative love and intimacy, including marriage, monogamy, biological reproduction, fidelity, and commitment. Vargas considers how the multitude of female characters in Díaz's texts love aggressively and decolonially without any commitments to a life promised by the "American dream."

6. See Emma Pérez's *The Decolonial Imaginary: Writing Chicanas into History* (Bloomington: Indiana University Press, 1999). Throughout this chapter, I use the idea of decolonial love put forward by the Chicana feminist theorist and novelist Pérez, what she describes as a "theoretical tool for uncovering the hidden voices of the past that have been relegated to silences, passivity, [and] to a third space where agency is enacted through third space feminism" (xvi). In Pérez's search "for another site of remembrance," her aim is to remake and reclaim other stories—stories of love, compassion, and hope.

7. Junot Díaz, interview by Paula M. L. Moya, "The Search for Decolonial Love, Parts I & II," *Boston Review*, June 26–27, 2012, accessed August 14, 2012, http://www.bostonreview .net/BR37.4/junot_diaz_paula_moya_drown_race.php.

8. According to Díaz, "the footnotes are there for a number of reasons; primarily, to create a double narrative. The footnotes, which are in the lower frequencies, challenge the main text, which is the higher narrative. The footnotes are like the voice of the jester, contesting the proclamations of the king. In a book that's all about the dangers of dictatorship, the dangers of the single voice—this felt like a smart move to me." See Junot Díaz, interview by Meghan O'Rourke, "Questions for Junot Díaz: An Interview with the Pulitzer Prize-winning Author," *Slate*, April 8, 2008, accessed April 22, 2015, http://www.slate.com/id/218849//. Díaz, *Oscar Wao*, 92.

9. For more on negative aesthetics, see Winfried Fluck, "The Role of the Reader and the Changing function of Literature: Reception Aesthetics, Literary Anthropology, Funktionsgeschichte," *European Journal of Literary Studies* 6, no. 3 (2002): 253–71.

10. See Mark McGurl's *The Program Era* (Cambridge, MA: Harvard University Press, 2010). Pointing to the proliferation of degree-granting "creative writing programs" in U.S. universities during the postwar era of the twentieth century, McGurl requires us to take into account the institution of the university and the processes of the democratization of higher education in the United States to fully understand the nature of postcontemporary literature in the postwar period.

11. Junot Díaz, *Drown* (New York: Riverhead, 1996), 11–12.

12. Junot Díaz, *Drown*, 12.

13. Junot Díaz, *Drown*, 103–4.

14. See Alex Woloch, *The One vs. the Many: Minor Characters and the Space of the Protagonist in the Novel* (Princeton, NJ: Princeton University Press, 2003). Here Woloch develops a powerful new theory of the novel and imaginative fiction by demonstrating that the representation of any character takes place within a shifting field of narrative attention and obscurity. Each character—whether or not the central character or a subordinated one—emerges as a character only through his or her contingent space within the narrative as a whole. Because character-spaces mark the dramatic interaction between a character and his or her delimited position within a narrative, the totality of the organization and clashes between many character-spaces constitutes the text's character system.

15. Díaz, interview by Moya.

16. Díaz, interview by Moya.

17. Junot Díaz, "Greg Barrios Interviews Junot Díaz," *Los Angeles Review of Books*, October 7, 2012. For an exploration of the rape culture of the Trujillato thematized in Díaz's work, see my essay, "Conjectures on 'Americanity' and Junot Díaz's 'Fukú Americanus' in *The Brief Wondrous Life of Oscar Wao*," *Global South* 5, no. 1 (spring 2011): 101–20.

18. Junot Díaz, interview by Sue Fassler, "The Baseline Is, You Suck: Junot Díaz on Men Who Write about Women," *The Atlantic*, September 12, 2012.

19. Robert Darnton, "First Steps Toward a History of Reading," *The Kiss of Lamourette: Reflections in Cultural History* (New York: W. W. Norton, 1990), 157. See Sarah Allison, Ryan Heuser, Matthew Jockers, Franco Moretti, and Michael Witmore's "Quantitative Formalism: An Experiment," *Literary Lab, Pamphlet 1*, Stanford University, January 15, 2011. They define quantitative formalism as "formalism, because all of us, in one way

or another, were interested in the formal conventions of genre; and quantitative, because we were looking for more precise—ideally, measurable—ways to establish generic differences." Díaz, *Oscar Wao*, footnote 6, 20–21.

20. Díaz, *Oscar Wao*, 50.

21. David Halperin, *How to Be Gay* (Cambridge, MA: Belknap Press, 2012), 12.

22. Díaz, *Oscar Wao*, footnote 6, 20–21.

23. Díaz, *Oscar Wao*, footnote 6, 20–21; 307.

24. Díaz, *Oscar Wao*, footnote 6, 20–21; 307.

25. Díaz, *Oscar Wao*, footnote 6, 20–21.

26. In addition to the decolonial work on aesthetics by Mignolo, Pérez, and Fanon I have discussed above, let me mention just a few more texts that take up the issues of aesthetics and aesthetic education in substantial ways: Immanuel Kant, *Critique of the Power of Judgment*, trans. Paul Geyer and Eric Mathews (Cambridge: Cambridge University Press, 2000); Friedrich Schiller, *On the Aesthetic Education of Man* (New York: Dover, 2004); Gayatri Chakravorty Spivak, *An Aesthetic Education in the Era of Globalization* (Cambridge, MA: Harvard University Press, 2012); and Sianne Ngai, *Our Aesthetic Categories: Zany, Cute, Interesting* (Cambridge, MA: Harvard University Press, 2012). An aesthetic education—from Kant and Schiller to Spivak and Ngai—seems to be most easily defined by what it is not. It is not the teaching of logical form or matters of fact. Generally, aesthetics seems to be the defining characteristic of the humanities and the arts, with which it is usually identified. Kant and Schiller saw the central task of aesthetic education as the improvement of taste, claiming that this required the development of two tendencies: the capacity to produce aesthetic gratification from complex objects that are characterized by various Aristotelian forms of unity, and a dependence on beautiful and sublime objects as sources of aesthetic satisfaction.

27. William Carlos Williams, "To Elsie," *Collected Poems, Volume 1: 1909–1939*, ed. Walton Litz and Christopher MacGowan (New York: New Directions, 1991), 221. Díaz, *Oscar Wao*, footnote 6, 21.

28. Díaz, *Oscar Wao*, footnote 6, 22.

29. Junot Díaz may also be addressing another more complex educational issue of why boys in our U.S. schools are in academic trouble. Unlike Oscar and Yunior, boys are lagging behind girls from early primary to secondary school. Why are boys doing poorly in reading in early grades, and why do they fail to complete their higher education programs at a higher rate than their female counterparts? Are boys' brains somehow hardwired differently than girls' brains? Are there no role models for the boys? In all of his work his central characters—Yunior, Oscar, Lola—all champion reading and writing skills, for our world has become increasingly verbal. For an overview of why boys are failing, see Richard Whitmore's *Why Boys Fail: Saving Our Sons from an Educational System That's Leaving Them Behind* (New York: AMACON, 2010).

30. Díaz, *Oscar Wao*, 22.

31. Díaz, *Oscar Wao*, footnote 6, 21.

32. See Eve Kosofsky Sedgwick's *The Epistemology of the Closet* (Berkeley: University of California Press, 1990).

33. Díaz, *Oscar Wao*, footnote 6, 22 (my emphasis).

34. Díaz, *Oscar Wao*, 92. See María Lugones's "Toward a Decolonial Feminism," *Hypatia* 25, no. 4 (fall 2010): 742–59. For Lugones, the coloniality of gender involves the process of how "the colonized became subjects" in the first modernity, that is, "the tensions created by the brutal imposition of the modern, colonial gender system" (743).

35. Later, Yunior rewrites the Madeleine allegorical experience in Proust's *Recherche* by contrasting young Marcel's dipping a piece of the French cake in tea and tasting it and undergoing a vision of inner gardens and alleys that marvelously grow out of the teacup like Japanese paper flowers by depicting Oscar's experiences of resurrecting his Caribbean past through a different geocultural dynamic. Once Belicia and Oscar arrive in Santo Domingo to visit their island family, Oscar breathes in the island's "fecund tropical smell that he had never forgotten, that to him was more evocative than any madeleine . . . like a whole new country was materializing atop the ruins of old ones" (273). In this Antillean island setting, the planet's exteriority does not lose its privileged position but helps release the impulse through smell and sight for Oscar's imaginative production of a completely internal world which is that of his own past that is reborn and transfigured. Can whole historical periods and other worlds, as Yunior suggests, be hidden in the "dilapidated" tropicalized streets of the Dominican Republic and the Global South? Is Santo Domingo the ontological site of unfolded remembered time for Oscar? As Yunior brilliantly suggests, Oscar's dynamic of the involuntary memory is tropologically metonymical: the whole of the Dominican Republic emerges from the Caribbean heat and smell of Santo Domingo's "pollution and the thousands of motos and cars" on the city's roads (273). Oscar thus compares his inner world, which is largely shaped by his reading of the speculative genres, with his Caribbean island's spatialized urban smells and sounds. But we also discover, as I argued above, that Yunior's tropological model of allegory in a wider range of varieties organizing Oscar's world of reading the speculative fictive genres: in footnote six, Yunior models Oscar's interiority as a hiding-place of secret and ideality, of dense aesthetic atmosphere.

36. In her study of the popular Dominican masculine imagination in the age and afterlife of the Trujillato, the anthropologist Lauren Denby incisively defines the *tíguere* as "the figure of the popular hero from the barrio—the quintessential Dominican underdog who gains power, prestige, and social status through a combination of extra-institutional wits, force of will, sartorial style and cojones. The *tíguere* seduces. . . . A man of the street, the *tíguere* operates through cunning, frequently via illicit means" (114). See Denby's *The Dictator's Seduction: Politics and the Popular Imagination in the Era of Trujillo* (Durham, NC: Duke University Press, 2009).

37. Díaz, *Oscar Wao*, footnote 6, 22.

38. Junot Díaz's Yunior de las Casas (like Díaz himself) is well versed in queer theory and decolonial feminism's theorization of power and gender. Here he is conjuncturally uniting Michel Foucault's iconic work on power and gender—that far from enslaving its objects it constructs them as subjective agents—with his rewriting of Marcel Proust. Foucault's idea of power does not only indirectly terrorize its subjects, it also directly

"normalizes," "responsibilizes," and disciplines. See Michel Foucault's *The History of Sexuality: Volume 1: An Introduction*, trans. Robert Hurley (New York: Vintage, 1980).

39. Díaz, *Oscar Wao*, 22.

40. Díaz, *Oscar Wao*, 22.

41. Díaz, *Oscar Wao*, 28.

42. Sedgwick, *The Epistemology of the Closet*, 33.

43. Díaz, *Oscar Wao*, footnote 6, 22.

44. See Mike Davis, *Magical Urbanism: Latinos Reinvest the U.S. Big City* (New York: Verso, 2000).

45. Junot Díaz, *This Is How You Lose Her* (New York: Riverhead, 2012), 213.

46. Díaz, *This Is How You Lose Her*, 34.

47. Díaz, *This Is How You Lose Her*, 30.

48. Díaz, *This Is How You Lose Her*, 31.

49. Díaz, *This Is How You Lose Her*, 33.

50. Díaz, *This Is How You Lose Her*, 37.

51. Díaz, *This Is How You Lose Her*, 37.

52. Díaz, *This Is How You Lose Her*, 38.

53. Díaz, *This Is How You Lose Her*, 38.

54. Díaz, *This Is How You Lose Her*, 32.

55. Díaz, *This Is How You Lose Her*, 40.

56. Díaz, *This Is How You Lose Her*, 40.

57. Díaz, *This Is How You Lose Her*, 42.

58. Díaz, *This Is How You Lose Her*, 42.

59. Díaz, *This Is How You Lose Her*, 42.

60. Díaz, *This Is How You Lose Her*, 43.

61. Díaz, *This Is How You Lose Her*, 43.

62. Díaz, *This Is How You Lose Her*, 40.

63. Díaz, *This Is How You Lose Her*, 38.

64. Díaz, *This Is How You Lose Her*, 40.

65. Díaz, *This Is How You Lose Her*, 41.

66. Díaz, *This Is How You Lose Her*, 41.

67. Díaz, *This Is How You Lose Her*, 175.

68. Díaz, *This Is How You Lose Her*, 175.

69. Díaz, *This Is How You Lose Her*, 177.

70. Díaz, *This Is How You Lose Her*, 177.

71. Díaz, *This Is How You Lose Her*, 175.

72. Díaz, *This Is How You Lose Her*, 25.

73. Díaz, *This Is How You Lose Her*, 3.

74. Díaz, *This Is How You Lose Her*, 175.

75. Díaz, *This Is How You Lose Her*, 163.

76. Díaz, *This Is How You Lose Her*, 163.

77. Díaz, *This Is How You Lose Her*, 165.

78. Díaz, *This Is How You Lose Her*, 165.

79. Díaz, *This Is How You Lose Her*, 165.

80. Díaz, *This Is How You Lose Her*, 185.

81. Díaz, *This Is How You Lose Her*, 189.

82. Díaz, *This Is How You Lose Her*, 193.

83. See Jorge Luis Borges's "Pierre Menard, Author of the Quixote," *Labyrinths: Selected Stories and Other Writings*, ed. Donald A. Yates and James E. Irby (New York: New Directions Books, 1962), 36–44. In the form of a scholarly article, Borges's iconic short story tells of the writer Pierre Menard, who has undertaken the task of rewriting Cervantes's *Don Quixote* as a literal translation of his own creativity. Menard wants his text to "coincide with" the original—word for word. Because of Borges's erudite reputation, the publication of this ficción sent readers to discover the author Pierre Menard. They unearthed a minor writer.

84. Díaz, *This Is How You Lose Her*, 212.

85. Díaz, *This Is How You Lose Her*, 212.

86. Díaz, *This Is How You Lose Her*, 212.

87. Díaz, *This Is How You Lose Her*, 212.

88. Díaz, *This Is How You Lose Her*, 213.

89. Díaz, *This Is How You Lose Her*, 213.

90. Junot Díaz, interview by Richard Wolinsky, "Growing the Hell Up: From Middle Earth to NJ," *Guernica*, November 1, 2012, 13.

91. Sigmund Freud, *Three Case Histories: The "Wolf Man," the "Rat Man," and the Psychotic Doctor Schreber* (New York, Collier Books, 1963), 95–96.

92. Díaz, *This Is How You Lose Her*, 213.

93. Alain Badiou, *In Praise of Love*, with Nicolas Truong (London: Serpent's Tail, 2012), 7.

94. Badiou, *In Praise of Love*, 28.

95. Badiou, *In Praise of Love*, 29.

96. Badiou, *In Praise of Love*, 32, 33.

97. Badiou, *In Praise of Love*, 36.

98. Badiou, *In Praise of Love*, 49.

99. Badiou, *In Praise of Love*, 90.

100. Badiou, *In Praise of Love*, 98.

101. Badiou, *In Praise of Love*, 104.

102. Frantz Fanon, *Black Skin, White Masks*, trans. Richard Philcox (New York: Grove, 2008), 206.

103. Cherríe Moraga and Gloria Anzaldúa, *This Bridge Called My Back: Writings by Radical Women of Color* (New York: Kitchen Table, 1983), 22.

104. Díaz, interview by Paula Moya.

105. Díaz, interview by Paula Moya.

106. Díaz, interview by Paula Moya.

13. Sucia Love
Losing, Lying, and Leaving in
This Is How You Lose Her
Deborah R. Vargas

Junot Díaz's collection of stories *This Is How You Lose Her* (2012) follows the protagonist Yunior de la Casas's life from age six, when he immigrates with his mother and brother Rafa from the barrios of Santo Domingo to the inner city of New Jersey, through his adult years as a successful writer and college professor. *This Is How You Lose Her* chronicles the loser's side of love. Yunior is a big loser. Yunior is lost. Yunior's love interests consistently lose out. In Yunior's world love is accumulated through deficit. Yunior's mundane experiences of foreclosed intimacies with lovers—most of whom he deems *sucias*, or dirty and nasty—construct love's underbelly through fraught affections, deception, and infidelity.[1] Yunior's immigrant life experiences run counter to the triumphant immigrant narrative. The stories, mostly titled by the lovers that frame Yunior's life (Nilda, Alma, Flaca, and Miss Lora) narrate the wandering sexual exploits of Yunior and Rafa and even their father's extramarital affairs. And because Yunior's losing is contemplated through "how," to question the conditions and means of a result, rather than "why," to question one's reason or judgment, means that losing (love, intimacy, hope) must also take into account Yunior's world, based on the structural residues of immigrant class experience, racialized poverty, and shifting geographies of race in the Dominican diaspora. Although peppered with what can be recognized as educational and economic accomplishments, Yunior's love life remains committed to the down and dirty sexual play of lo sucio.

This chapter is less intrigued with Yunior's promiscuity and performances of his masculinity and more fascinated with the women who surround him. I find more captivating the sucias in Yunior's life and what a focus on their orbits of grimy love may offer our critical engagement with Latina femininities. The term sucias is understood in this collection of stories as a Latino vernacular for those racialized feminine genders and sexualities deemed literally, often due to associations with economically disenfranchised places, and figuratively unclean, as racially sexualized others, as filthy and nasty. In This Is How You Lose Her, sucias represent the obscene manner in which Yunior goes about losing love as well as the wasted matter cumulatively marking his lost loves. My analysis of lo sucio, and more precisely the sucias in Yunior's world, intends to argue for the ways that class-disenfranchised and immigrant communities of color, especially feminine genders, reconfigure losing (out on love as well as their bodies as disposable objects) as a means of sustaining endless strategies for the accumulation of material traces, unconventional joys, and forbidden desires. The sucias in Díaz's novel predictably encourage the reader to comprehend them as loss in Yunior's life according to normative terms—as exploited victims, through unfulfilled desires, and failures at class mobility. Following Michel de Certeau's theorization of tactics, I propose a reappraisal of these sucias and their navigations and reconfigurations of loss and losing, or their tactics for opting out of heteronormativity's structural violence.[2]

In this focus on This Is How You Lose Her, lo sucio is the social structural context from which constructions of racialized classed masculinities and femininities, referred to as sucios and sucias respectively, emerge. By extension, I consider the ways lo sucio operates as a structural metonym for nonnormative constructions of intimacy, sexual desire, sociality, and kinship. Specifically, the sucias and sucios of Díaz's book embody racialized genders and sexualities that designate what I refer to as the "deficit citizenry" of institutional regimes of normative love and intimacy, including marriage, family, monogamy, biological reproduction, fidelity, and commitment. For example, the racialized femininities of characters such as Magdalena, Pura, and Yasmin love aggressively and cynically with no commitments to a life promised by the fictions of an "American dream." Drawing on the notion of "face," posited by the queer Chicana feminist Gloria Anzaldúa, as that embodied display of structural inequalities, I argue that these sucias are "faces" of brown, diasporic, working-class, Spanglish-speaking, racialized genders who are persistently the feminine-gendered projects constantly the targets to be "cleaned up" by neoliberal capitalism and white middle-class feminism.[3] This chapter's focus on las sucias thus aims to consider nonnormative and delinquent modes of intimacy in This Is How You Lose Her that are tactically impure or nonredeemable within the logics of capitalism's constructions of love. In other words, I propose a reading of This Is How You Lose Her as a tale of lo sucio, or enactments of what I call the "filthy love" of sucias, as a way to reconsider the loss or losing (her) that constructs their subjectivities. Instead, I propose that sucias offer us much to contend with through tactics of residual love achieved within heteronormative constraints of intimacy and affection.

Sucias are weary of the heteronormative temporality of love as defined by guarantees, for-sures, and forevers.[4] Sucias—unlike women whose feminine gender garners privilege through whiteness or economic class advantage—I contend, consistently cultivate clever tactics to avoid dispossession and disappearance. In order to avoid being the loser or being the loss (of structural systems that normalize gender and sexuality), they learn to lag behind, opt out, and move around the promises they know too well were never intended for them. Sucias have configured a different calculus for love that is not reliant on economic security, reproduction, and safety. Sucias know to leave before being left and how to linger when left.

Surplus Love and Sucias

Lo sucio—generally translated into English as that which is dirty or filthy—and by extension the gendered terms sucia and sucio (women and men, respectively)—is theorized in this chapter as composed of three racialized, ideological discourses: genders and sexualities of color as lewd, obscene, offensive hypersexually undisciplined bodies; darkened, suspect citizens perpetually untrustworthy, impure, and disloyal to the state; diseased subjects of "cultures of poverty," overdetermined at failing to arrive at normative womanhood and manhood.

The discourse of sucias and sucios often involves genders that are racialized and classed through phenotypic characteristics such as darker skin color, non-European speaking accent, hair texture, large body size, aesthetic stylizations including speaking loudly or dressing in excessively larger jewelry or bright colors, in addition to working-class or welfare-class cultural sensibilities, and associations with residential spatialities referred to as el barrio or the ghetto.[5] The term *white trash* also designates a working-class or welfare-class racialization of subjects generally characterized by their associations to rural geographic areas and trailer parks. For example, the term *white trash* is a common referential cousin to the lesser-used *country* or *hillbilly*. Such terms mark whiteness as "trash," or dirty, based on characterizations of poverty, low educational attainment, cultural unsophistication, and backwardness in relation to normative white constructions of family and gender.[6]

Various scholarly fields ranging from sociological to literary and historical studies have produced and analyzed the ways a myriad of ideologies and representations are cast upon Latinas, and other women of color, as dirty and diseased.[7] Arguably, the most outstanding examples of how social science has produced and perpetuated such racist ideologies are the countless urban and rural ethnographies conducted throughout the twentieth century. A quintessential example here is Oscar Lewis's ethnographic study, *Five Families: Mexican Case Studies in the Culture of Poverty* (1959), that went on to influence the Moynihan Report's application of Lewis's "culture of poverty."[8] Oscar Lewis proposed a similar thesis about Puerto Rican families in *La Vida: A Puerto Rican Family in the Culture of Poverty* in 1966.[9] As early as 1929—as the United States was having to adjust to an unprecedented influx of poor Mexicans escaping the Mexican Revolution—the concern over repairing the indecency of Mexican girl's womanhood was the objective of projects such as *Americanization through Homemaking* that asserted "sanitary, hygienic, and dietic measures are not easily learned by the Mexican. Teach Mexican girls the importance of durable and clean underwear. They are apt to be lax in this respect. Impress it upon the girl's mind that a clean body and a clean mind are the attributes of a good citizen."[10] In 1955 a *Science Newsletter* issue warned of the public health threat posed by Mexicans with the study's title "Wetbacks Bring Insects." It is common knowledge that throughout the first half of the twentieth century it was normal protocol for U.S. government agencies to forcibly impose DDT fumigation and other hydrocyanic sanitary baths on Mexicans crossing the U.S.-Mexico border to work in the United States.

U.S. media, especially cinema and television, have always initiated the appearance of brown bodies as Latino characters who are dirty and suspect.

The most obvious example is Hollywood's genre of "greaser films."[11] In fact, Hollywood's first major motion picture that addressed interracial marriage between Anglos and Mexican Americans was the movie *Giant*, released in 1956, starring Elizabeth Taylor as Leslie Benedict, who, during an early pivotal scene, expresses disgust at the ways Mexican ranch hands are living in squalor, without indoor plumbing, and suffering illness. In the pilot episode of *Chico and the Man* (the first television comedy with a Latino protagonist), the earliest interaction the cranky white car mechanic Ed (played by Jack Albertson) has with the Chicano Chico (played by Puerto Rican comedian actor Freddie Prinze), who stops by his garage looking for a job, is to tell him: "Get out and take your flies with you." Frances Negrón-Muntaner reminds us that dirty and conniving characterizations of Latinos remained even as the twentieth century transitioned to the twenty-first. Negrón-Muntaner's *Boricua Pop* opens with a description by the columnist Taki Theodoracopulos, of the London-based *Spectator*: "There has never been—nor will there ever be—a single positive contribution by a Puerto Rican outside of receiving American welfare and beating the system." Theodoracopulos continues by expressing that he is deeply disgusted by the "fat, squat, ugly, dusky, dirty and unbelievably loud" Puerto Rican people.[12]

Yunior, in fact, often sees such pathologically undisciplined, gendered characteristics in himself and the other Dominican men in his neighborhood. Most families, according to Yunior, kept their Dominican daughters on "serious lockdown" because of such beliefs. He would see the young women "on the bus and at school and maybe at the Pathmark, but since most families knew exactly what kind of tigueres were roaming the neighborhood these girls weren't allowed to hang out."[13] Ultimately though, there is always a potential for strategies of sexual agency that exist across the range between those who remain within lockdown and those who escape its disciplinary confines.

Such structural and pathologically discursive mechanisms of disinfection and disciplinarity contextualize the racialized construction of sucias as those subaltern-class, female, feminine-presenting Latina genders who have always done the dirty work of U.S. empire as perpetual domestics, servants in the service industry, and agricultural laborers. Simultaneously, the sexuality of sucias is persistently one represented by the filthy, nasty, and dirty sexual acts prohibited as risky and unspeakable and yet extremely desirable. A powerfully disturbing example of the ways sucias encompass the simultaneous racist ideologies of hypersexuality and service labor occurs by simply conducting a Google search with the words "dirty" (sucia) and "Latina." The top sites that emerge are pornographic sites advertising "dirty hot Latina maids" or "dirty Latina maids." Examples such as these are precisely why television dramas such as "Devious Maids," which attempts to make Latina domestics sexy through the characters of young, thin, brown women, have very little discursive space to counter the hegemonic ideologies of Latinas as dirty, devious, and domestic.[14] Yet, there are competing logics that I believe the characters Yunior refers to as sucias encourage us to seriously consider, especially in our current context of neoliberal pressures for Latinas to fulfill normative citizenship.

Drawing from Roderick Ferguson's theory of "surplus populations," I theorize sucia as an analytic metonym for surplus love.[15] While the dominant ideology of love is expressed through the currency of capital, I define surplus love—the residue of heteronormative constructions of love as dual-partnered, monogamous, reproductive, and always aspiring to remain on normative time—as a system of sexual intimacy produced through U.S. capital that surplus populations negotiate, reimagine, repurpose, and at times willfully fail to abide by. Surplus love is often actively disinvested in the sustainability of prolonged intimacy as assumed to reap benefits and potential resources guaranteeing comfort, sexual gratification, and inheritance. Accordingly, sucias demonstrate how capital sometimes disrupts hierarchies that "account for the polymorphous perversions that arise out of the production of labor," and "as capital disrupts social hierarchies in the production of surplus labor, it disrupts gender ideals and sexual norms that are indices of racial difference."[16] In *This Is How You Lose Her*, the sucias emerge as "nonheteronormative racial formations" that create surplus love.[17] Such is the case of Pura, whose goal in caring for Rafa until his death from cancer was not to fulfill her devotion to love or loyalty as a wife who remains until death ("do you part"), but actually to hang around long enough to eventually run off with Yunior's family car, the TV, their beds, and "the X amount of dollars Rafa had stolen for her."[18]

Sucias hardly ever own anything but they never lack in possessions: material goods, lovers, dreams, futures, homes, children. Sucias, I assert, recognize the deception of U.S. capital's construction of citizenship and belonging, which is why they are continually creating new modes of transactions that refuse self-disciplining. Sucias want it all and they want to be wanted in ways that do not always align with wanting to be declared (through state regulations). Kara Keeling's theorizations of surplus popu-

lations assert that "simultaneous to the constitution of these nonheteronormative, racialized social formations is the proliferation of racialized
discourses of gender and sexuality and attempts by the state to produce and
regulate heteronormativity as a universal category of citizenship."[19] Sucias
are surplus subjectivities of heteronormative reproductivity. In the sucias'
orbit we can recognize how universalized notions of love operate as a currency of the state. Love as a fastening force of normative sociality is a way
capital valorizes itself.

Reducing This Is How You Lose Her's sucias to mere victims of Yunior's and
Rafa's sexist misogyny, or as pure radical transgressors of nonnormativity,
does not allow for the ways that their actions are simultaneously troublesome
and yet potentially dissentingly queer. I propose that Yunior's orbit, configured through the varied characters in This Is How You Lose Her, is the context
created by the sucia's surplus love. Stated another way, sucias create Yunior's
orbit as nonheteronormative racial formations of queer, unsustainable love,
always anticipating to be lost, and prepared to find their way back.[20] Sucias
love themselves through lovers that will be a testimony to their past. Past
lovers create a practice to trace themselves in a world desirous of their disappearance, as symbolized in the following poem by Gloria Anzaldúa:

> She has this fear   that she has no names   that she
> Has many names   that she doesn't know her names   She has
> this fear   that she's an image   that comes and goes
> clearing and darkening   the fear that she's the dreamwork
> inside someone else's skull   She has this fear   that if
> she takes off her clothes   shoves her brain aside
> peels off her skin   that if she drains   the blood
> vessels   strips the flesh from the bone   flushes out
> the marrow   She has this fear   that when she does
> reach herself   turns around to embrace herself   a
> lion's or witch's or serpent's head   will turn around
> swallow her and grin   She has this fear that if she digs
> into herself   she won't find anyone   that when she gets
> "there"   she won't find her notches on the trees   the
> birds will have eaten all the crumbs   She has this fear
> that she won't find her way back[21]

In Borderlands/La Frontera, Gloria Anzaldúa theorizes the violence of
shame and the public gaze on those she refers to as the "abnormal," which

I understand to be the queer or nonnormative. In "El secreto terrible y la rajadura" (or the terrible secret and the crack, or fissure, or split), Anzaldúa discusses—through her now well-known theory of the Coatlicue state—the way "abnormality" or nonnormativity operates through public shame, in particular, how shame as a structural disciplining device on female bodies reproduces normative gender and community.[22] Likewise, the sucia is quite aware of her aberrance. They are the public imperfections of communities who deem them as collateral genders to a social world invested in the capital benefits of normative love. As such, the sucia develops a strategy of remaining one step ahead of fulfilling her fear of disappearance. In the following passage from *Borderlands*, the abnormal subject reflects on the exposure of her failed gender. Moreover, Anzaldúa sensually indicates the ways feelings of intimacy are actually what create powerlessness and a bind to those who continually weigh down their femininity and sexuality from the ability to move outside of normativity: "Her soft belly exposed to the sharp eyes of everyone; they see, they see. Their eyes penetrate her; they slit her from head to belly. *Rajada* [cowardly, timid]. She is at their mercy, she can do nothing to defend herself. And she is ashamed that they see her so exposed, so vulnerable. She has to learn to push their eyes away. She has to still her eyes from looking at their feelings—feelings that can catch her in their gaze, bind her to them."[23]

To be sure, the structurally racist representation of a sucia also operates as a system of internalized racism often deployed to distance oneself from a disparaged class or a despicable performance of gender and sexuality. This is precisely what is occurring in the novel when Yunior critiques himself and his brother's sexual behavior, as well as the behaviors of most sexual partners they interact with. In fact, our first introduction to a sucia that Yunior actually refers to as "brown trash" is Nilda. The first description that Yunior offers about Nilda is that she is his brother's girlfriend because "this is how all these stories begin." Rafa represents a love for Yunior that he despises. Rafa is the embodiment of lo sucio that Yunior does not want to become but cannot ever quite overcome. In actuality, most of Yunior's sexually intimate relationships appear and disappear through the ebbs and flows of his violent yet adoring relationship with Rafa. The only exception in this orbit of surplus love is the unnamed fiancée, who, after all, is the loss that Yunior is never able to recuperate.

Sucia Love

This Is How You Lose Her opens with "The Sun, the Moon, the Stars" and introduces us to Magdalena. Magda, as Yunior refers to her, is a teacher in New Jersey, self-possessed, and unforgiving of Yunior's discretions. Magda is arguably the one lover in Yunior's orbit who is distinctly not sucia. Yunior claims, "you couldn't think of anybody worse to screw than Magda," and yet Yunior does.[24] Whereas "The Sun, the Moon, the Stars" reveals the cause of the breakup to be Yunior's indiscretion with Cassandra, the closing chapter, "The Cheater's Guide to Love," reveals that Yunior's unnamed fiancée learns that he has been with fifty sucias over their six-year relationship.

While one assessment of Magda is to view her as the "good" woman amid the sucias, it is also worth considering Cassandra's actions, not in relation to Yunior but in relation to Magda. Yunior spends a good amount of energy laying blame on Magda's girlfriends, who treat him like he "ate somebody's favorite kid."[25] "I blamed all that shit on her girls, who I knew for a fact were still feeding her a bad line about me." Yunior describes Magda's friends as "the sorest losers on the planet," who advise her to take the trip to the Dominican Republic, which he believes is about reconciliation, and then never speak to him again.[26] Yunior blames Cassandra for his breakup with Magda, because she sent the incriminating letter to Magda detailing all that Yunior has shared with her about Magda's being less than stellar as a sexual partner. The letter is scathing in its details, revealing the kind of things "you wouldn't even tell your boys drunk."[27]

While we may understand Cassandra's objective in writing the scandalous letter to Magda as being about Yunior—to spite him or maybe in hopes of winning him away from Magda—we may also understand Cassandra's tactic as an attempt to allow Magda to persevere. As disenfranchised-class and racial-gendered subjects, sucias learn to experience the social world through endurance rather than bank on the acquisition of material goods, comfort, and unconditional loyalty from lovers as well as by the state. Cassandra's letter not only allows her to sustain her agency as Yunior's marginal love interest but also attempts to prevent Magda from simply being a loss that occupies the space of the leftover. In this story, space, in fact, becomes a metaphor for loss or the space of void and absence. As Catherine Ramírez reminds us in her analysis of women pachucas/zoot suiters during World War II, the gendered politics of space is key for comprehending what she refers to as "aberrant forms of femininities" and the ways working-class women of color refashion themselves to disidentify with normative gender.[28] Loss, in this story, is symbolized through the spatiality of water that separates Dominican diasporic subjects from the island they leave behind. Similarly, Magda's and Yunior's trip to the island is an attempt to put space between the before and now of Magda's pain, as demonstrated when Yunior drops his arms around Magda after she informs him that she needs her space. If there is one thing sucias like Cassandra learn in persevering within the social realities of structural loss and normative love, it is the act of recalculating loss's deficit into a resource for something else. In the end, Yunior never gets over losing Magda. In fact, Yunior becomes that typical Dominican man he always sees in Rafa and in others. Yunior becomes the sucio who, according to the sucia standard, is the real loser, for realz.

If sucias, as I argue, are the subjects of perpetual debt—as deficiencies to the state that must be repressed if capital's normativity is to be sustained—then one signifier in their persistence to "find their way back" from being embodiments of loss is through modes of overabundance. In "Nilda," Yunior describes Nilda as "brown trash," citing the typical characteristics of her undisciplined feminine sexuality. Nilda has a "mean-ass drunk" for a mother, is in and out of group homes for runaways, and is "always out in the world, always cars rolling up beside her."[29] "She'd already slept with Toño and Nestor and Little Anthony from Parkwood. She crashed over at our apartment a lot because she hated her moms, who was the neighborhood borracha. In the morning she slipped out before my mother woke up and found her. Waited for heads at the bus stop, fronted like she'd come from her own place, same clothes as the day before and greasy hair so everybody thought her a skank."[30] Yunior's description of Nilda is a compilation of her deficits, no mother, no home, no control over her body. Nilda's suciedad is a performance of abundance, a weighty burden for all to recall.

Yunior seems like a hopeless romantic around Nilda, continually yearning for her uncontainability, having witnessed her transformation from a quiet introvert to a physically overdeveloped young woman, a *cuero*, or piece of skin, as Yunior describes her. Yunior seems lost in the ways Nilda loses herself to the men, like Rafa, around her. When Yunior asks her about her experience in the group home, Nilda's memories come out through the surplus of her body, "It was pretty cool up there, she said . . . pulling on the front of her halter top, trying to air her chest out. The food was bad but there were a lot of cute guys in the house with me. They all wanted me."[31] Nilda's sucianess is defined by enactments of sexual exchange value. For example, Yunior perceives that Nilda is seeing the "three hundred year old" Vietnam veteran from the back apartments "because he had a car and a record collection and foto albums from his Vietnam days and because he bought her clothes to replace the old shit she was wearing."[32] In Yunior's world of surplus love, Nilda is always waiting, waiting for the next guy who would become her "man." Yunior says, "Sometimes I could grab her and pull her back on the couch, and we'd stay there a long time, me waiting for her to fall in love with me, her waiting for whatever."[33] Yet, when it comes to Rafa, Nilda easily succumbs to him, letting him fondle her on the bus ride to school. It does not take long for Nilda to become another of Rafa's lovers, dating him for an entire summer. For Nilda, though, Rafa represents something other than merely the "whatever" she has been waiting for.

Rafa is Nilda's way of maintaining a forward progress to a something else she can only imagine. Her nasty sexual dynamic with Rafa constructs—drawing from José Esteban Muñoz—a queerness to her futurity, a utopia "not yet here."[34] Yunior speaks about the ways Nilda yearns to escape the here and now. For example, when Rafa declares he is not going back for his senior year of high school, he tells Yunior and Nilda, "I'd like to take a long fucking trip. See California before it slides into the ocean." Nilda desires to be a part of this futurity: "I'd like to go there, too, but Rafa didn't answer."[35] Sucias must contemplate what is yet to come so that they do not get too left behind. One day Yunior overhears a conversation between her and Rafa expressing how she wants to get away from her mother and open up a group home for runaway kids. Nilda explains, "But this one would be real cool . . . It would be for normal kids who just got problems," thereby distinguishing "problems" from the nonnormative behavior often associated with sucias.[36] Nilda's sexuality is constructed with less regard for stability and more for a life of impermanence. This is poignantly expressed when Yunior is confused by Nilda's early departure after she and Rafa have sex. "Why'd she leave?" asks Yunior. Rafa replies, "She had to go."[37] Rafa's recognition that Nilda had to "go" instead of "leave" signifies a movement toward something, somewhere unknown, unpredictable. Whereas, leaving stabilizes a place, a person, a state one may return to, to go draws focus on movement and flight and the traces of presence to be charted.

In Yunior's terms, Nilda does in fact never leave. "Nilda didn't fare so well . . . A lot of the things that happened to her, though, had nothing to do with me or my brother. She fell in love a couple more times."[38] Yet Yunior's observations do not mean that Nilda failed to go. There is never a place to leave from in the sphere of surplus love. Going, on the other hand, leaves an opening and a dedication to be continually weary of the stability and security of normativity. This weariness is worn on the "face" of Nilda whose once attractive figure is now lost to weight gain and by the smiles carved out through the two bottom teeth she got knocked out. Sucias like Nilda are constantly being worn out and wasted away, by structural institutions and by racial logics that deem them as disposable. Nilda had to go because it may have been the only way to trace herself forward, out in the there of not here with Rafa.

In the three-page story "Alma," we are introduced to Yunior's girlfriend Alma through a very detailed discussion about her ass, one that, according to Yunior, "seems to exist in a fourth dimension."[39] Alma is street-wise Dominican *alternatina*, or alternative Latina, who grew up in Hoboken in the 1980s, listening to Sonic Youth music and reading comic books. She is a painting student at Mason Gross School of the Arts at Rutgers, and she attempts to reclaim her Dominican heritage by learning Spanish. Alma is only the third Latina Yunior has ever dated, up to this point in his young life. Alma is pure lewdness and sexual excess. She tells Yunior "terrible white-girl things" during sex like asking him if he wants to orgasm on her breast or talking "while she's being dirty."

As symbolized through the brevity of the chapter, Alma is too much, too abundant to be legible within the normative confines of Yunior's life, as either sexual exploit or sexless. "It's a great-sex sort of thing, it's a no-thinking sort of thing. It's wonderful! Wonderful! Until the day Alma discovers that you are also fucking this beautiful freshman girl name Laxmi."[40] Alma's discovery is partly due to Yunior's journaling of his indiscretions. One may read Yunior's practice of journaling his affairs with other women as conceited. Yet, I believe the containment of Yunior's sexual excess within a journal—similar to the little space given to Alma in this brief story—also signals an attempt at protecting his own sexual feats that may otherwise be lost within Alma's "wonderful" excess. When it becomes obvious to Yunior that Alma finds his journal, Yunior is not angry or fearful; he is sad and pathetic. Yunior becomes the "punk motherfucker," "fake-ass Dominican," with a "little penis" in Alma's wonderful sucia love. The most clever response by Yunior is to express to Alma, "baby, this is part of my novel."[41] To be sure, Alma is not swayed as the last sentence in this story makes clear, "This is how you lose her." And yet, in the spirit of journaling as a practice of self-editing one's life, we might also consider that, for Alma, "lose her" is not a far stretch from "loser," the designated "h" and "e" or "he" edited out of Alma's life.

In "Otravida, Otravez" the narrator is Yasmin, twenty-eight and the "other woman" to a married Dominican man whose wife still lives in the Dominican Republic, and Yasmin's world occupies very little space. Her entire life takes place between her small apartment and the basement of the hospital where she works. Yet, space seems to be extended by the slow motion of her quotidian life, watching her lover Ramón wake up, sleep, and get dressed to leave for work. Yasmin and Ramón live with Ana Iris, Yasmin's best friend, whom she considers her sister. Yasmin's place in Ramón's life is transient, as symbolized by the rusty razor and the countless inquiries about Ramón by her neighbors.

Yasmin works at one of the filthiest jobs one might imagine, washing the soiled, blood-stained sheets at St. Peter's Hospital, emblematic of the increasing reliance on surplus labor as hospitals shift to for-profit systems. "Never leave the laundry room. Never leave the heat. I load washers, I load dryers, peel the lint skin from the traps, measure out heaping scoops of crystal detergent. I'm in charge of four other workers, I make an American wage, but it's a donkey job."[42] Yasmin's job is typical of what Roderick Ferguson describes as "both superfluous and indispensable [as] surplus populations fulfill and exceed the demands of capital."[43] Yasmin recalls having arrived in the states, sent here by her parents. Yasmin is a disposable immigrant body doing indispensable labor on bodily waste.

Yasmin's entire world pivots on what is unsure, unanswerable, insecure. Her life is not about gratification or dreams; it is about survival and sustenance. "We are not here for fun, Ana Iris told me the day we met, and I said Yes, you're right, even though I did not want to admit it."[44] Yasmin's job and her relationship with Ramón is really a coexistence with the literal and symbolic filth that is the life of surplus populations in the United States, there nothing gets easier, life never improves, and promises are never fulfilled. This is her relationship with the states, and it is her relationship with Ramón.

Yasmin's relationship with Ramón seems to be of less significance than the relationship she has with the life he has left behind. Yasmin is fascinated by what will come of Ramón's relationship with his wife, Virta, which is similar to her curiosity about the characters on her telenovela. Virta's life with Ramón is a story Yasmin has witnessed unfolding through the eight years of letters held together with a fat, brown rubber band. "Always reading her letters I always feel better. I don't think this says good things about me," thinks Yasmin.[45] Ramón's wife and their deceased son grow increasingly intimate to Yasmin's life, in comparison to her relationship with Ramón. She has low expectations for men like Ramón—she recalls when they first met that at least he had not tried to rape her like many of her other bosses. We learn so much more about Yasmin's relationships with her job, with her coworkers, with Ramón's other life. For Yasmin, there's a heretofore constructed through a connection to Ramón's other life, more so than with a past she has lived with Ramón himself. She even imagines what Ramón's wife looks like: "When I think of Ramón's wife I see her, in heels, flashing yards of brown leg, a woman warmer than the air around her . . . I do not imagine Ramón's wife as uneducated. She watches telenovelas simply to pass the time."[46]

Throughout the chapter we learn that Ramón's main goal is to buy a house, a powerful symbol of normative family and American citizenship, especially for immigrants and working-class populations. According to feminist critiques, the home and the goal of buying a home become a gendered project of U.S. heteropatriarchy and gender, or what Richard Rodríguez refers to as the "normatively domesticating effect" of gender.[47] The potential home purchase becomes a source of tension for Yasmin and Ramón because it represents the broader dilemma of where Yasmin fits into a future with Ramón. Yasmin reflects, "Here there are calamities without end— but sometimes I can clearly see us in the future, and it is good."[48] At other times, she expresses to Ramón that she is "not one for change . . . I see only what's wrong with the places he wants, and later, in the car, he accuses me of sabotaging his dream, of being dura."[49]

Yasmin's characterization of Ramón's house-hunting is suspect and represents a mode of vulnerability marginal subjects often have in relation to financial institutions that so often—as recent statistics in foreclosure among the U.S. working class attest to—result in their disposability. Yasmin perpetually has one foot inside and another outside of Ramón's dream home. At times, Yasmin's defense mechanism results in a patronizing attitude: "He makes an event of [house hunting], dressing like he's interviewing for a visa."[50] Yasmin is Ramón's proxy for citizenship, the surrogate wife, the placeholder for Ramón's normative legitimation of American masculinity as homeowner and patriarch. And yet, Yasmin knows better than to make those goals her own. Every opportunity Yasmin has to be in Ramón's future is met with apprehension. During a conversation that Yasmin has with

Ramón he talks to her about a coworker who has just been killed at work, asking, "What would you have done?" Yasmin has an internal conversation that symbolizes the power dynamic in their relationship and her awareness that her presence in his life is a loss always potentially filled by Virta. "I set my face against him; he has known the wrong women if he expects more. I want to say, Exactly what your wife's doing in Santo Domingo."[51]

From her friend Ana Iris, Yasmin learns that the best strategy to keep from losing (one's mind) is to "not think on these things . . . keep them out of your mind . . . this is how Ana Iris survives here, how in part we all survive here."[52] On the final day spent with Ana Iris—after learning that the letters from Virta, which had once stopped, have now begun again—she is invited for a walk. They both are at a crossroads with Ana Iris having to decide if she should stay or go back to the Dominican Republic to be with her children and Yasmin, not knowing what to do with a letter she has intercepted for Ramón from Virta. Both are on the verge of losing and being lost. "We embrace at the front door for what feels like an hour."[53] In the end, Yasmin decides to give Ramón Virta's letter. Virta is no longer lost to Ramón. Yasmin's actions divert the possibility of Ramón losing her and instead redirects her own loss of Ramón as intimacy to be constructed anew.

In "Flaca," the sucia is an evanescent lover. Yunior recalls his fleeting two-year relationship with Veronica Hardrada, whom he nicknames Flaca. Veronica, or Flaca, raised outside of Paterson, New Jersey, is described by Yunior as "white trash" based on her "no-fashion sense" and the fact that she had dating experience with numerous Dominican men. Veronica is a teacher whom Yunior initially meets while both are taking a college course on James Joyce. Flaca is a kind of sucia that is hard to lose because love is perpetually fleeting to her. "It wasn't supposed to get serious between us. I can't see us getting married or nothing and you nodded your head and said you understood."[54]

Flaca appears and disappears in the dailiness of Yunior's life. She is his sexual partner of last resort on late nights out, drops in and out of his apartment with meals, and even when she stays over and "the boys would find you in the kitchen the next morning . . . [and] they didn't complain, because they guessed you would just go away."[55] Ironically, although never claimed by Yunior as a girlfriend, it is one of the most equitable relationships Yunior has throughout the novel. They have similar temperaments, interests in reading, and noninvestment in a long-term monogamous relationship.

There is no losing Flaca. Their relationship—they decide through contemplations of when in the past they might have met—is misplaced, out of time. Even as Flaca persists at lingering in Yunior's life, it is as if she is referring to a relationship already lost. "Maybe we were together some other time," Flaca says, "I can't think of when," says Yunior. "You tried not to look at me. Maybe five million years ago," replies Flaca.[56] Yunior struggles with how to define Flaca's existence in his life—as "*loss* or *love* or some other words that we say when it's too fucking late"[57]—because Flaca is too impermanent to fully lose. "I remember how the next morning you were gone, and nothing in my bed or the house could have proven otherwise."[58]

In "The Pura Principle," Rafa loses his battle with cancer, and Yunior and Mami lose their material possessions to Pura. Rafa meets Pura Adames while working at the Yarn Barn, a job he takes after recovering from his latest hospital stay. "Dude was figuerando *hard*. Had always been a papi chulo, so of course he dove right back into the grip of his old sucias, snuck them down into the basement whether my mother was home or not."[59] According to Yunior, Pura is a provincial Dominican—symbolized by the English translation of her name, "pure" or "authentic"—"a *Dominican* Dominican . . . a fresh-off-the-boat-didn't-have-no-papers-Dominican."[60] We learn that Pura's father died when she was very young and her mother sold her as a teenage bride to a fifty year old, resulting in the birth of her first son Nestor.

Yunior's mother's friends provide a list of what I would argue are sucia credentials: "Ella es prieta. Ella es fea. Ella dejó un hijo en Santo Domingo. Ella tiene otro aquí. No tiene hombre. No tiene dinero. No tieno papeles. [¿]Qué tú crees que ella busca por aquí?"[61] And yet, Pura and Mami seem quite familiar to one another and seem to have an unspoken agreement when it comes to Pura's role in Rafa's life. Based on the structural systems that have shaped her gender and sexuality, especially as a teenage bride sold and as someone who lacks formal U.S. citizenship, Pura develops what I argue is a trickster way of being. L. H. Stallings theorizes the trickster's sexuality as a deceiving, trick-player, shape-shifter, and as a situation inverter. Extending Stallings's analysis of Black women's gender and sexuality through the trickster trope, I argue that Pura's trickster sexuality is counter to normative femininity as loyal, subservient, and nurturing. In fact, argues Stallings, the trickster's "primary agenda is to resist the act of rescuing so that individuals or societies at large may learn from the chaos."[62]

Pura and Mami seem to share similarities in their lives prior to coming to the United States. Mami is similarly disinvested in an intimate relationship with her husband. Pura's actions seem to be familiar to Mami. The relationship dynamic between Mami and Pura often plays itself out through the possession of material goods, rather than through normative registers of love such as fidelity, loyalty, or commitment. In fact, there seem to be several trickster strategies both Pura and Mami use when it comes to Rafa. For example, unbeknownst to Yunior, Mami and Rafa agree that Mami will continue to leave money for Rafa in her tin box, "secretly" hidden away in her bedroom where supposedly no one can find it. Rafa similarly has a marriage agreement with Pura, defying his mother's wishes not to marry Pura. Moreover, this twisted dynamic also results in Rafa's stealing money from Mami to give to Pura. It becomes obvious that Mami likely knows her money is being stolen and that ultimately this transaction between Pura and Mami is about stealing time for Rafa.

Pura's goal is to never return to the Dominican Republic. For Pura, marriage is a transaction of lag time, a credential that allows her to not become a a new deficit in someone else's life as a fresh bride, but a way to remain, to persist from being stolen goods again. When Rafa nears his passing, Pura visits Mami to ask for money, claiming that it is money Rafa owes her. Mami goes into her bedroom and returns with a hundred dollar bill, nowhere near the two thousand dollars Pura tells Mami Rafa owes her. What occurs during this interaction symbolizes the struggle over love (for and by Rafa) between Mami and Pura, of letting go, loss, and of losing out. Love here is characterized through the tug of war over surplus currency. "She gave the bill to Pura but didn't let go of her end. For a minute they stared at each other, and then Mami let the bill go, the force between them so strong the paper popped."[63] Mami loses Rafa just as Pura loses out. Both struggle—holding on to the dollar bill—to stay ahead of losing to the other.

In "Invierno" we are introduced to the early experiences that shape Mami and her relationship with Rafa. "Invierno" depicts Yunior's immigrant childhood, arriving in Westminster, New Jersey, after his father finally brings the entire family over from the Dominican Republic, having waited for five years for their travel. Yunior's memories are narrativized through their first snowy winter, which becomes a metaphor for the containment and frigidity enacted by Yunior's father, Papi. Papi is cold, not intimate, and distant. He often leaves the family for days at a time while not allowing the family to leave the house. All Rafa and Yunior have during their sequestering is time—time to watch television, time to imagine what outside feels like, time that seems to drag on in every mundane activity they find to pass the day.

Mami had been the authority with all the power when it was just the three of them in the Dominican Republic. By week three in the United States, she was becoming depressed, disconnected from this place and from what she knew was home. "She was depressed and sad and missed her father and her friends, our neighbors. Everyone had warned her that the US was a difficult place where even the Devil got his ass beat, but no one had told her that she would have to spend the rest of her natural life snowbound with her children. She wrote letter after letter home, begging her sisters to come as soon as possible. The neighborhood is empty and friendless. And she begged my father to bring his friends over. She wanted to talk about unimportant matters, to speak to someone who wasn't her child or her spouse."[64] What becomes exciting for Mami is the outside world, so, as Yunior recalls, she begs Papi to bring over a guest for dinner and is delighted when he finally does, for two Fridays in a row. "She started out each night natural and unreserved . . . but as the men loosened their belts and aired out their toes and talked their talk, she withdrew; her expressions narrowed until all that remained was a tight, guarded smile that seemed to drift across the room the way a shadow drifts slowly across a wall."[65]

Toward the end of the chapter, Mami leaves the house after having cooked and cleaned for dinner guests and after Papi tells her he has to go to work. Rafa and Yunior think that perhaps she is leaving them. "We heard her in the closet, pulling on her coat and her boots . . . when we heard the front door open, we let ourselves out of our room and found the apartment empty."[66] Yunior says he thinks she is losing it and Rafa tells him she is just lonely. The chapter ends with Mami's leaving the apartment again. All three of them end up finally breaking out of the apartment during their first big snowstorm, when Papi is unable to make it home from work. Mami is figuratively on the edge as she stands at the boundary of their neighborhood. Together they make their way back to the apartment, finally having experienced the outside they've missed out on. It is here when, having arrived back home, the frigidity is finally broken through Mami's tears. It is not clear whether her tears are those of joy or of sadness in them having found their way home. What is more unmistakable, I believe, is that being lost—in Papi's world as symbolized by being lost in the snow—will come to shape Mami's life with Rafa and Yunior, where Papi melts away as a presence.

The chapter "Miss Lora" represents Yunior's life after he loses his brother, Rafa, to cancer. Here we find Yunior in a relationship with one of the few women whose gender and sexuality is the antithesis to the sucias in his orbit of surplus love. Paloma is hard-working and a very cautious girlfriend to Yunior. She is mature and self-assured, focused on getting out of the life she's lived—represented by the one-bedroom apartment she shares with four younger siblings—through the promise of doing well in school. Paloma is so focused on her schooling that Yunior describes her as the "only Puerto Rican girl on the earth who wouldn't give up the ass for any reason."[67] In fact, Paloma equates having sex with Yunior as her permanent sentencing to a life with her family. "Imagine if I don't get in anywhere, she said. You'd still have me, you tried to reassure her, but Paloma looked at you like the apocalypse would be preferable."[68] It is 1985 and Yunior is at the primal age of sixteen and thus in a constant stage of being an *enamorado*, capable of "falling in love with a girl over an expression, over a gesture."[69] Yunior predictably cheats on Paloma with Miss Lora, the single, childless, forty-something neighbor, even though Paloma sternly warns Yunior, "You better not fuck her."[70] Clearly Paloma does not want to have sex with Yunior, but she also requires devotion to their intimate relationship. Paloma will go as far as letting Yunior place his tongue on her clitoris but no further.

The emphasized salutation of "Miss" in front of "Lora" is intended to symbolize both the designation as unmarried as well as respectful reference for elder women or, in this case, Lora's profession as Yunior's teacher. Yunior spends a good amount of time focused on how skinny Miss Lora is, describing her physique as having no breasts or ass and so thin she even made Iggy Pop "look chub."[71] Miss Lora and Yunior's mother share the same birthplace of La Vega, in the Dominican Republic, Miss Lora having arrived in the United States with her parents and siblings. Miss Lora's mother abandoned them for an Italian waiter, moving to Rome with him. Lora spent the following years relocating with her father, eventually moving in with a widow who despised her. Miss Lora described her young life in high school as not having many friends and sleeping with her high school history teacher. One day Yunior runs into Miss Lora while carrying a four-piece meal from Chicken Holiday with a chicken leg in his mouth, a sexual metaphor for Miss Lora's thin physique and as a trace of their pasts on an island of scarce resources. Miss Lora's apartment represents all she has left behind, covered in images of family and friends.

The apocalypse metaphorically frames this chapter, with the thinness of Miss Lora's body reflecting disappearance. In fact, Yunior is what Miss Lora needs as a witness to her presence; she goes from not requesting that Yunior stay the night to finally allowing him to stay with her. Paloma does not have time for Yunior, either. The day after his first sexual encounter with Miss Lora, Yunior reveals his indiscretion to Paloma in a confessional blaming of his sucio genealogy that includes his father and brother, that purportedly explains his being destined to break his promise to Paloma. In fact, Yunior's fear of being caught is somewhat self-created. No one actually cares if he is having sex, yet he is continually anxious about it, as when his mother leaves for the Dominican Republic to care for her father. Yunior keeps imagining his mother or sister catching him having sex with Miss Lora, describing himself in a moment of self-reflection: "Sucios of the worst kind and now it's official: you are one too."[72] Paloma, however, does not provide Yunior with the dramatic reaction expected of someone beholden to his actions to represent her worth. Half asleep on their way to school, "Yunior, she stirs from her doze, I don't have time for your craziness, OK?"[73] Miss Lora doesn't want Yunior, either; instead, she is always pushing college admissions on him as a way for him to leave. Eventually, Miss Lora leaves London Terrace, too, just like Paloma.

When Juno Diaz's closes *This Is How You Lose Her* with "The Cheater's Guide to Love," Yunior has not only gone to college, he is nearing forty, working as a writing professor at MIT, and living in a racist Boston. The story takes us on Yunior's five-year journey to get over his breakup with his unnamed fiancée, who will never return to him. This story is the bookend to the beginning of the novel, when we find out what Yunior did to cause this monumental breakup that haunts his everyday.

I suggest that the sucias and the sucia love imagined in *This Is How You Lose Her* have much more to offer our critical engagement with modes of love, intimacy, and commitment than does a reduction of them as merely lessons for judging the sexist performances of Dominican, working-class, immigrant masculinities. Loving nasty, filthy, and dirty as sucias do prompts us to reconsider joy and self-gratification based on surplus love. In other words, surplus love—exemplified by the sucia's always being left for the "good woman" and her performances of perverse sexual acts—should be understood not as what one strives to survive and heal from but more accurately as "the half life of love that is forever,"[74] as Yunior states. I contend that modes of sexual pleasure disconnected from intimacy and cohabitation disconnected from biological family imagine forevers outside the institutional violence of heteronormative constructs of the state. Sucia love sharply signals for us to be highly suspect of such constructs. The sucias in Yunior's life should ring familiar to many of us. We know them, we may at times in our life be them, and we cannot afford to forget them. Flaca, Pura, and the other filthy women in these stories are the faces of a constant crisis that nonnormative feminine genders represent within the neoliberal era of institutions that uphold heteronormative modes of joy, desire, and love.

The sucias in *This Is How You Lose Her*, as well as those we encounter in our own socia (friend/kin/community) orbits, activate love in surplus, that is, forms of love initiated by surplus populations. Sucias love, following Carlos Decena's theorizations, as "tacit subjects" who live through partiality, polyvalence, and contestation.[75] Their actions do not make sense when assessed through neoliberal constructs of heteronormative love. Commitment, loyalty, and pleasure become the filthy residue of capital embodied by sucias whom, too often, we would rather redeem than appreciate. Sucias insist that we bend questions over and flip our attention to embrace the supposed crises of dirty love anew. Here I am reminded of La Monda Horton Stallings's response during the question and answer portion of a panel on Black women and pornography when most questions represented a concern over how much agency Black women had in sex-worker industries. "If we are so concerned about Black women, violence, and agency," challenged Stallings, "then why don't we ever talk about the institution of marriage? Marriage is one of the most violent structural institutions Black women have always had to survive."[76] Stallings's response captures the spirit of what I argue sucia love requires of us in the ways we ask questions about sexuality, violence, and racism with regard to nonnormative gender and sexuality.

The sucias in *This Is How You Lose Her* never evolve into content and healthy citizen-subjects. Yunior, on the other hand, grows, makes mistakes, and transforms—from immigrant boy to hypersexual teenage nerd to elite university professor—through all of the relationships he and Rafa have with sucias in their lives. Thus, in some respect, there may be a tendency to comprehend sucias as subjects of damaged and deficient genders and sexualities because their temporalities seem truncated and stifled. Yet, I argue, these sucias, as well as Magda and Mami and the unnamed fiancée, are never truly lost by not remaining as permanent heteronormative partners of Yunior, Rafa, Papi, and Ramón. Rather, their impermanence allows them to stay ahead, get over, and get by. To invoke Anzaldúa again, these sucias know how to "create notches on the trees" and names for themselves; in so doing, they charge us to more critically and tenaciously ponder how and why they oftentimes actually do find their way back.[77]

Notes

1. Throughout this chapter the terms *sucia* and *sucio* are not merely reduced to their English translations of "dirty" or "filthy" but rather operate throughout the chapter as queer analytics of nonnormative genders and sexualities. The term *sucia* thus draws attention to structural systems of power that construct Latina queer genders and sexualities as disposable and loathsome others. The terms *sucia, sucio, lo sucio* are italicized in their initial appearance and thereafter in the chapter no longer italicized. See Juana Maria Rodriguez, *Queer Latinidad: Identity Practices, Discursive Spaces* (New York: New York University Press, 2003); Richard Rodriguez, *Next of Kin: The Family in Chicano/a Cultural Politics* (Durham, NC: Duke University Press, 2009); Carla Trujillo, *Chicana Lesbians: The Girls Our Mothers Warned Us About* (Berkeley: Third Woman Press, 1991).

2. De Certeau refers to tactics as those clever tricks and turnings of the tables that "the weak" take up against "the strong." See Michel de Certeau, *The Practice of Everyday Life*, trans. Timothy J. Tomasik (Minneapolis: University of Minnesota Press, 1998).

3. For more analysis of the body as a geography of raced and gendered meanings and modes of differentiation, see Linda McDowell, *Gender, Identity and Place* (New York: Blackwell, 1999).

4. See Carolyn Dinshaw et al., "Theorizing Queer Temporalities: A Roundtable Discussion," GLQ 13, nos. 2–3 (2007); Elizabeth Freeman, *Time Binds: Queer Temporalities, Queer Histories* (Durham, NC: Duke University Press, 2010); Judith Halberstam, *In a Queer Time and Place: Transgender Bodies, Subcultural Lives* (New York: New York University Press, 2005).

5. The field of Latino media studies offers critical analysis of the politics of darker skin color and lower social class status. See, for example, Arlene Dávila, *Latinos Inc.: The Marketing and Making of a People* (Berkeley: University of California Press, 2001); Ana Rodríguez, *Making Latino News: Race, Language, Class* (Thousand Oaks, CA: Sage, 1999).

6. Matt Wray and Annalee Newitz, *White Trash: Race and Class in America* (New York: Routledge, 1997); Matt Wray, *Not Quite White: White Trash and the Boundaries of Whiteness* (Durham, NC: Duke University Press, 2006); John Hartigan, "Unpopular Culture: The Case of 'White Trash,'" *Cultural Studies* 11, no. 2 (1997): 316–43.

7. Examples of these works include Steven Bender, *Greasers and Gringos: Latinos, Law, and the American Imagination* (New York: New York University Press, 2003); and John Mckiernan-González, *Fevered Measures: Public Health and Race at the Texas-Mexican Border, 1848–1942* (Durham, NC: Duke University Press, 2012).

8. Daniel Patrick Moynihan, *The Negro Family: The Case for National Action* (Washington, DC: Office of Planning and Research, U.S. Department of Labor, 1965).

9. Oscar Lewis, *La Vida: A Puerto Rican Family in the Culture of Poverty* (San Juan: Random House, 1966).

10. Pearl Idelia Eillis, *Americanization through Homemaking* (Los Angeles: Wetzel, 1929), 26.

11. Charles Ramirez Berg, *Latino Images in Film: Stereotypes, Subversion, Resistance* (Austin: University of Texas Press, 2002); Clara Rodríguez, *Latin Looks: Images of Latinas and Latinos in the U.S. Media* (Boulder, CO: Westview Press, 1997).

12. Frances Negrón-Muntaner, *Boricua Pop: Puerto Ricans and the Latinization of American Culture* (New York: New York University Press, 2004), xi; Taki Theodoracopulos, "Why Should We Pay?" *Spectator*, June 14, 1997, 62–63.

13. Junot Díaz, *This Is How You Lose Her* (New York: Riverhead, 2012), 32.

14. Another attempt in reappropriating the term *sucia* is found in *The Dirty Girls Social Club*, by Alisa Valdes-Rodriguez; the character Lauren explains that the Buena Sucia Social Club defines sucia as "dirty girl." "Buena sucia is actually pretty offensive to most Spanish-speaking people, akin to being smelly 'ho.' So Buena Sucia Social club is, how do you say irreverent. Right? And obnoxious." Alisa Valdes-Rodriguez, *The Dirty Girls Social Club: A Novel* (New York: St. Martin's, 2003), 5.

15. Roderick A. Ferguson, *Aberrations in Black: Toward a Queer of Color Critique* (Minneapolis: University of Minnesota Press, 2004), 15.

16. Ferguson, *Aberrations*, 14–17.

17. Ferguson, *Aberrations*, 15.

18. Díaz, *This Is How You Lose Her* (New York: Riverhead Books, 2012), 117.

19. Kara Keeling, *The Witch's Flight: The Cinematic Black Femme and the Image of Common Sense* (Durham, NC: Duke University Press, 2007), 104.

20. Ferguson, *Aberrations*, 15.

21. Gloria Anzaldúa, *Borderlands/La Frontera: The New Mestiza* (San Francisco: Aunt Lute Books, 1987), 43.

22. Anzaldúa, *Borderlands/La Frontera*, 64–65.

23. Anzaldúa, *Borderlands/La Frontera*, 65.

24. Díaz, *This Is How You Lose Her*, 5.

25. Díaz, *This Is How You Lose Her*, 4.

26. Díaz, *This Is How You Lose Her*, 7.

27. Díaz, *This Is How You Lose Her*, 3.

28. Catherine S. Ramírez, *The Woman in the Zoot Suit: Gender, Nationalism, and the Cultural Politics of Memory* (Durham, NC: Duke University Press, 2009), 56, 81, 124; José Esteban Muñoz, *Disidentifications: Queers of Color and the Performance of Politics* (Minneapolis: University of Minnesota Press, 1999).

29. Díaz, *This Is How You Lose Her*, 32.

30. Díaz, *This Is How You Lose Her*, 30.

31. Díaz, *This Is How You Lose Her*, 31.

32. Díaz, *This Is How You Lose Her*, 32.

33. Díaz, *This Is How You Lose Her*, 33.

34. José Esteban Muñoz, *Cruising Utopia: The Then and There of Queer Futurity* (New York: New York University Press, 2009), 22.

35. Díaz, *This Is How You Lose Her*, 36.

36. Díaz, *This Is How You Lose Her*, 38.

37. Díaz, *This Is How You Lose Her*, 39.

38. Díaz, *This Is How You Lose Her*, 39.

39. Díaz, *This Is How You Lose Her*, 45.

40. Díaz, *This Is How You Lose Her*, 47.

41. Díaz, *This Is How You Lose Her*, 50.

42. Díaz, *This Is How You Lose Her*, 54.

43. Ferguson, *Aberrations*, 15.

44. Díaz, *This Is How You Lose Her*, 59.

45. Díaz, *This Is How You Lose Her*, 59.

46. Díaz, *This Is How You Lose Her*, 68.

47. Richard T. Rodríguez, *Next of Kin*, 3–4. For other feminist critiques of family, private, and public space, see also Marie "Keta" Miranda, *Homegirls in the Public Sphere* (Austin: University of Texas Press, 2003); Rosa Linda Fregoso, "Familia Matters," in *MeXicana Encounters: The Making of Social Identities on the Borderlands* (Berkeley: University of California Press, 2003).

48. Díaz, *This Is How You Lose Her*, 68.

49. Díaz, *This Is How You Lose Her*, 57.

50. Díaz, *This Is How You Lose Her*, 57.

51. Díaz, *This Is How You Lose Her*, 52.

52. Díaz, *This Is How You Lose Her*, 67.

53. Díaz, *This Is How You Lose Her*, 76.

54. Díaz, *This Is How You Lose Her*, 81.

55. Díaz, *This Is How You Lose Her*, 81.

56. Díaz, *This Is How You Lose Her*, 85.

57. Díaz, *This Is How You Lose Her*, 86.

58. Díaz, *This Is How You Lose Her*, 87.

59. Díaz, *This Is How You Lose Her*, 94.

60. Díaz, *This Is How You Lose Her*, 104. "She is dark, she is ugly, she left a son in Santo Domingo, she has another child here, she doesn't have a man, she doesn't have money, she doesn't have citizenship papers. What do you think she is looking for here?" (translation by author).

61. Díaz, *This Is How You Lose Her*, 100.

62. L. H. Stallings, *Mutha' Is Half a word: Intersections of Folklore, Vernacular, Myth, and Queerness in Black Female Culture* (Columbus: Ohio State University Press, 2007), 16.

63. Díaz, *This Is How You Lose Her*, 116.

64. Díaz, *This Is How You Lose Her*, 138–39.

65. Díaz, *This Is How You Lose Her*, 140.

66. Díaz, *This Is How You Lose Her*, 141.

67. Díaz, *This Is How You Lose Her*, 151.

68. Díaz, *This Is How You Lose Her*, 152.

69. Díaz, *This Is How You Lose Her*, 150.

70. Díaz, *This Is How You Lose Her*, 157.

71. Díaz, *This Is How You Lose Her*, 154.

72. Díaz, *This Is How You Lose Her*, 161.

73. Díaz, *This Is How You Lose Her*, 161.

74. Carlos Decena, *Tacit Subjects: Belonging and Same-Sex Desire among Dominican Immigrant Men* (Durham, NC: Duke University Press, 2011), 8, 19–20.

75. "Race, Sex, Power: New Movements in Black and Latina/o Sexualities" Conference, University of Illinois, Chicago, April 11–12, 2008. "Currently, Black feminism and womanism prohibits several dialogues necessary for producing a politically effective Black women's movement for the twenty-first century: strategic separatism, economic empowerment, pro-sex politics (not simply reproductive rights or arguments over the representation of black female sexuality), critique of nuclear family and traditional marriage, armed offense in the defense of black female bodies, community-based education programs where black women can study black women, a critique of black religious institutions for their sexism, heterosexism, and homophobia, and the founding of new spiritual institutions if so needed." L. H. Stallings, "Eulogy for Black Women's Studies" in Kim Vaz and Gary Lemons, eds., *Feminist Solidarity at the Crossroads* (New York: Routledge, 2013), 144.

76. Díaz, *This Is How You Lose Her*, 213.

77. Anzaldúa, *Borderlands/La Frontera*, 43.

14. "Chiste Apocalyptus"
Prospero in the Caribbean and the Art of Power
Ramón Saldívar

In part II, chapter 5, "Poor Abelard 1944–46," we hear three jokes that go a long way toward explaining why so much of the middle portions of Junot Díaz's *The Brief Wondrous Life of Oscar Wao* is taken up with the sad history of the Dominican Republic. From the perspective of narrative form, it is not surprising that by this point in the narrative Díaz should continue to compound the numerous narrative shifts that the reader has already experienced by turning to a comedic mode that the narrator, Yunior, calls "Chiste Apocalyptus."[1] Still, of all possible narrative forms appropriate for the telling of the history of injustice, torture, and death that characterizes Dominican history generally and the history of Abelard Cabral's family particularly, why jokes and comedy? What do jokes and comedy have to do with history?[2]

Shortly after the fateful party at which Abelard fails to produce his wife and daughter for Trujillo's certain abuse, Abelard is "buttonholed by some 'buddies' on the street and invited for a few drinks at Club Santiago."[3] Trying "to shake off his sense of imminent doom by talking vigorously about history, medicine, Aristophanes, by getting very very drunk," Abelard asks the "boys" for help in relocating a bureau he had bought for his wife that afternoon (a pretense to seeing his mistress, really). Fumbling for the keys to open the trunk of his car, Abelard may or may not have uttered the following words of the first joke: "I hope there aren't any bodies in here."[4] Innocent enough, really, even if the car of our concern was a Packard, the very kind of car that cast a shadow on Dominican history, by being the kind of car "in which Trujillo had, in his early years, terrorized his first two elections away from the pueblo."[5]

This mild first "trunk joke" leads to a second one: "During the Hurricane of 1931 the Jefe's henchmen often drove their Packards to the bonfires where the volunteers were burning the dead, and out of their trunks they would pull out 'victims of the hurricane.' All of whom looked strangely dry and were often clutching opposition party materials." The punch line to joke number two: "The wind, the henchmen would joke, drove a bullet straight through the head of this one. Har-har."[6] With joke number two, the narrative is clearly edging toward more dangerous ground than the first joke.

Whether the third joke was actually uttered is even much less certain than the possibilities of Abelard's having told joke number one or that Trujillo's henchmen really uttered joke number two. In fact, part of the horror of the subsequent torture, humiliation, and final destruction of Abelard at the hands of the secret police is that it is not at all certain, in fact is highly unlikely, that Abelard actually spoke joke number three. The occasion of joke number three claims that "when Dr. Abelard Luis Cabral opened the trunk of the Packard, he [is purported to have said], 'Nope, no bodies here, *Trujillo must have cleaned them out for me.*'"[7] In this narrative sequence, a joke uttered or not determines the course of one man's, one family's doom.

Two weeks after the events in question, "two atomic eyes opened over civilian centers in Japan and, even though no one knew it yet, the world was remade. Not two days after the atomic bombs scarred Japan forever . . . three Secret Police officers in their shiny Chevrolet" wind up the road to Abelard's house and "Already it's the Fall."[8] Apocalypse and the Fall, simultaneously, on a personal level as well as on the level of world history. In the history of the Abelard family, for the next nine years one apocalyptic shock follows upon another, leaving Abelard, at the end, a mindless remnant of the elegant human specimen he had once been. "Poor Abelard," indeed.

In order to round out the reader's justified sense of rational explanation, Yunior poses the question that instrumental understandings of the course of history require: Did Abelard say the jokes or not? "Did he have a hand in his own destruction?"[9] Was his tragic demise "an accident, a conspiracy, or a fukú?"[10] In response, Yunior claims, "The only answer I can give you is the least satisfying: you'll have to decide for yourself."[11] The fukú does not leave memoirs; the Trujillato "didn't share their German contemporaries' lust for documentation," so no documentary evidence will surface to endorse an answer.[12] And yet, and here is perhaps the best part of these miserable jokes, Yunior surmises: perhaps Abelard "didn't get in trouble because of his daughter's culo or because of an imprudent joke."[13]

An alternate explanation "contends that he got in trouble because of a book."[14] In this alternate version,

> Sometime in 1944 . . . while Abelard was still worried about whether he was in trouble with Trujillo, he started writing a book about—what else— Trujillo . . . an exposé of the supernatural roots of the Trujillo regime! A book about the Dark Powers of the President, a book in which Abelard argued that the tales the common people told about the president—may in some ways have been true. That it was possible that Trujillo was, if not in fact, then in principle, a creature from another world! . . . Alas, the grimoire in question (so the story goes) was conveniently destroyed after Abelard was arrested.[15]

The grimoire in question is Abelard's lost book on Trujillo, "conveniently destroyed." Let us dwell on the word *grimoire*. The word *grimoire* is commonly held to be derived from the Old French word *grammaire*, which had initially been used to refer to books written in Latin (that is, for all practical purposes during the early modern period, all books).[16] By the end of the eighteenth century, however, the term had gained its now more common usage and had begun to be used to refer purely to books of magic. However, the term *grimoire* also developed into a figure of speech used to indicate something that was difficult or even impossible to understand.[17] It was only in the nineteenth century, with the increasing interest in occultism in England following the publication of Frances Barrett's *The Magus* (1801) that the term entered the English language in reference to the specific mystery occasioned by books of magic.[18]

From ancient Mesopotamia in cuneiform tablets, through the early modern period in Jewish and Islamic texts, and then into the Caribbean in the fifteenth century and early sixteenth, grimoires inscribing magical incantations and spells, divinatory texts, and mystical philosophy left Europe and were imported to those parts of the Americas controlled by the Spanish, Portuguese, British, and French empires. In the Americas, grimoires came into contact with the natural philosophies and mystical beliefs of countless indigenous peoples and thus intersected with structures of knowledge of other new populations brought to America from Africa. From descriptions of a set of symbols and how to combine them to create well-formed sentences in Latin, and then, by extension and metonymy, to books of magic, a grimoire thus becomes the grammar of magic, the rhetoric of magic spells, the syntax of charms and divinations, as well as the form of books on how to summon or invoke supernatural entities such as angels, spirits, or demons, conveying the protocols of belief systems outside the pale of accepted patterns of belief. In time, the very books themselves, as mystical book objects, come to be imbued with magical powers.

Into this history of the grimoire enters the history of Abelard. As José David Saldívar has pointed out, Abelard was nothing if not a bookish bookman.[19] In the novel, Yunior describes him as "widely read in Spanish, English, French, Latin and Greek; a collector of rare books, an advocate of outlandish abstractions, a contributor to the *Journal of Tropical Medicine*, and an amateur ethnographer in the Fernando Ortiz mode" and, moreover, as "the author of four books."[20] None of these books, neither the "Lost Final Book of Dr. Abelard Luis Cabral"—the grimoire naming Trujillo as "a supernatural, or perhaps alien, dictator who had installed himself on the First Island of the New World"—nor the "hundreds he owned," survived his fall and destruction at the hands of the torturous police.[21] "All of them lost or destroyed," "confiscated and reportedly burned," including "every paper he had in his house," and leaving "not one single example of his handwriting."[22] An eerie replay of Caliban's advice to "destroy Prospero's books."

In *The Tempest*, Caliban is represented as a less than human monster. Yet, Prospero has given him the tools to understand the fact that he has been made less than human:

You taught me language, and my profit on't
Is, I know how to curse you. The red plague rid you
For learning me your language![23]

Too dim-witted to organize his own rebellion, Caliban finds wandering the island the greedy, drunken, shipwrecked sailor Stephano and urges him on as an ally against Prospero. And sensing that Prospero's power comes from the force of his language, his words, and most importantly, his books, Caliban understands that to take Prospero's power he needs "first to possess his books."[24]

Precisely because of moments such as this in the play, it is not surprising to find that Caliban has been the focus of some of the best critical discussions of *The Tempest* by postcolonial scholars. A notable case is an essay entitled "Caliban" by the Cuban critic and theoretician Roberto Fernández Retamar.[25] Retamar sees the plight of Shakespeare's half-man, half-monster as an allegory for the status of the inhabitants of the colonized world: Prospero invaded our lands, killed our ancestors, enslaved us, and taught us his language to make himself understood. He has possessed us with his books. "What is our history, what is our culture, if not the history and culture of Caliban?" asks Retamar.[26]

There are many links, then, between Shakespeare's monster Caliban and Abelard's story in *The Brief Wondrous Life of Oscar Wao*: ideas concerning human monsters, education, language, political power, and the magical agency of books. Of these various possibilities of similarity of purpose between *The Brief Wondrous Life of Oscar Wao* and *The Tempest*, perhaps the most important one concerns the relationship between political power and aesthetics, especially the aesthetic form of knowledge in books. The examples I have given from *The Brief Wondrous Life of Oscar Wao* and *The Tempest* demonstrate that politics is itself an aesthetic practice. It is a human endeavor that is rooted in individuals' desire to impose their imprint upon particular situations and things. This is as true of progressive democracies as it is of right-wing, neoliberal dictatorships. In order to shape their world, individuals must use means to represent ideas, sometimes misrepresent motives, carefully imitate past deeds and actors, and mobilize people through the rhetorical manipulation of emotional reactions. All this for the grand aim of giving lasting form to a particular state, political struggle, or to shape the course of a movement.

On Monsters and Postcolonial Subjects

As odd a connection as it might seem, Junot Díaz's take on *The Tempest* is not unlike Kingsley Amis's. In *The New Maps of Hell* (1960), Amis had noted of *The Tempest*: "Even if one resists the temptation to designate Caliban as an early mutant—'a freckled whelp,' you remember, 'not gifted with a human shape,' but human in most other ways . . . Prospero's attitude . . . and indeed his entire role as an adept, seems to some degree experimental as well as simply thaumaturgical."[27] Whether magician or adept, Prospero in his relation to Caliban reinforces the connection between science and magic, human and monster, that vectors the force of power and knowledge in a colonial context.[28] Certainly in Junot Díaz's most recent fiction, particularly in the short story "Monstro," this connection is at the core of the critique of racism and colonialism.[29] What distinguishes Díaz's monsters from Caliban is that they narrate their own history, unhinged from the framework of Prospero's design and the romantic account of the victory of culture over monstrosity.

In the past, some theorists, philosophers, and social critics have recognized aesthetic aspects to politics. Yet the rubric in which they have worked has always been that of ethically based thinking about politics. Certainly, there is an important link between ethics and politics, but this link is neither necessary nor sufficient to understand political life.[30] What *The Brief Wondrous Life of Oscar Wao* continuously shows is that there is a wide chasm between ethics and politics. As a result, political theory guided by impulses of right, justice, or rectitude—all laudably desired ends of political action—often turns out to fall short of what occurs in the lived experience of any particular set of individuals. *The Brief Wondrous Life of Oscar Wao* asks us to do something incredibly different than to bet on a functional relationship between ethics and politics. It asks whether we can think of examples of how other forms of political theory might be useful to comprehending actual experience.

In particular, can we think of how aesthetic theory might be a useful tool for comprehending actual experience in a realistic manner? The notion of imagination, especially as codified in Prospero's books—the master's tools, emblems and avatars of power—is the nexus between aesthetic theory and political theory. That political theory and aesthetics share the key concept of the imagination must force us to think whether the connection is merely contingent, semantic, or holds a deeper meaning. In *The Brief Wondrous Life of Oscar Wao*, it turns out that when we press the question of the role of the imagination in both political and aesthetic terms we see that the imagination is fundamental to the way that we experience political belonging in a nation-state of any kind.

The experiences Yunior narrates are not weird or fantastic, exotic or based in a third world divided exotically from the metropolitan United States, Macondo unrelated to McOndo, as it were. In the world of *The Brief Wondrous Life of Oscar Wao*, the simultaneity of modernization and dependency, indeed, the interdependence between the modern, postmodern, and never modern has become the new norm, even the paradigm of the new norm in the Americas. The great achievement of *The Brief Wondrous Life of Oscar Wao*, then, is Díaz's ability to balance a coming-of-age story and a meditation on the history of horrors in the Americas since the first days of discovery with the sci-fi, role playing, comic book fantasy-life in the imaginary of one of the least heroic of disappearing fantasy heroes one could imagine through the power of art and the book as grimoire. This is a case where the Bildungsroman leads us inexorably to the realm of the transnational imaginary.

If we conceive of the syntax of codes, images, and icons, as well as the tacit assumptions, convictions, and beliefs that seek to bind together the varieties of national discourses as forming a social, imaginary structure, then a transnational imaginary is the attempt to describe imaginary structures emerging from the social, cultural, and political intersections of multinational populations and polycultural meanings across nation states. While I am in accord with views emphasizing the persistence of national power, I maintain that the transnational spaces we see developing around the globe today also emphasize the limits of national power. They do so by exceeding the bounds of nationally prescribed versions of culture, economics, and politics. Current debates on the meaning of citizenship as a right of national polities have often ignored the ways processes of decolonization and migration, as well as social identities based on ethnicity, race, and gender, point to the existence of identities other than national identities as the basis for defining citizenship.

In understanding the power of the visualization of a transnational world beyond restrictive nationalisms, literary works exploring the nature of the transnational experience and the art of power are laying the groundwork for an understanding of a contemporary staging of new versions of the self, activating the new forms of identity, and imagining the new cultural and political worlds that we see today emerging at the intersections of the Global South and North.[31]

At the very least, this representation of a transnational reality that does not yet exist in fully realized form serves to enable the postethnic and post-race visions emerging since the turn of the millennium, and especially since 9/11, from a whole new generation of writers, born for the most part in the post–civil rights era. The works of these writers represent the post-magical realism, post-postmodern, postborderlands and neofantasy transnational turn in what one could call the search for a new racial imaginary in the contemporary era of American literature. *The Brief Wondrous Life of Oscar Wao* requires us to consider the nature of the formation of nation and community, the ethos of justice, and the crossing of symbolic borders and inhabiting the transnational imaginary, but all in the mode of multicultural fantasy and romance.

In my own work of the past few years, I use a particular battery of terms to get at some of these issues having to do with the intersections, overlaps, and contact points between the Global North and South: chief among them being the idea of alternative modernities to describe the knowledge that exists in the borders between Global North and South.[32] The writings of intellectuals from this domain of overlap draw their power from subjection and, in turn, help to give form to the condition. This is what I term vernacular poetics—an imagination of borderland experience in which exclusion from the domain of rationality and history rules. If, as Winfried Fluck has argued, "Fictional texts represent made-up worlds, even when they claim to be 'realistic,'" then how is it possible for fiction and its "made-up worlds" to reveal something meaningful about history?[33] In his discussion of Wolfgang Iser's reception aesthetics, Fluck uses the term *negative aesthetics* to refer to one way fantasy and the imaginary intersect with history. Negative aesthetics refers to the potential of literature to "expose the limitations and unacknowledged deficiencies of accepted systems of thought."[34]

In the case of contemporary ethnic fiction, negative aesthetics allows us to conceive how fantasy functions in relation to history to create an imaginary vision that goes beyond the formulations of realism, modernism, magical realism, and postmodern metafiction to articulate precisely what is absent in realism, magical realism, and metafiction. Formally, the role of the imaginary is thus crucial to the functioning of contemporary ethnic fiction, for in allowing the experience of something not literally represented, it compels readers to "provide links" across the "blanks" created by the intentional "suspension of relations" between meaningful segments of the text.[35] But beyond literary modernism's defamiliarizing function of compelling "the reader to become active in making sense of what often appears incomplete or incomprehensible," the literary works I refer to here as examples of a search for a new racial imaginary do something more in linking fantasy, history, and the imaginary.[36]

If it is justice we seek in love, in life, and in the world, then justice, poetic or otherwise, is precisely what we do *not* get at the end of *The Brief Wondrous Life of Oscar Wao*. Murdered cruelly, mercilessly, Oscar is not redeemed by romance; the history of the Dominican Republic, forged in both imported and home-grown tyranny, is not atoned by utopian desire.[37] And if we think we might be able to bracket the tyranny by seeing it as a product of distant Third World perversities, it turns out that Ybón's jealous boyfriend has full "First World" credentials, as an "American citizen," "naturalized in the city of Buffalo, in the state of New York."[38] Given the magnitude of the crimes assembled in the chronicle of Oscar's family's story, itself a synecdoche of trans-American hemispheric history, none of the novel's three endings can even hope to account for, let alone blunt, the apocalyptic, world destroying evil "that not even postmodernism can explain away."

While romanticism gives us fantasy coalescing with reality, and literary modernism gives us the defamiliarization of reality, and postmodernism gives us the ludic play of metafiction, The Brief Wondrous Life of Oscar Wao gives us something else, namely, the mimetic representation of fantasy. Not fantasy, as such, but its imitation, at double and sometimes triple remove. Why? And where does the mimesis of fantasy, the staging of fantasy, rather than the representation of fantasy itself, leave us within the realms of the imaginary? Without the ending of a comic book, sci-fi, or fantasy, Oscar Wao requires us to read the story of the history of conquest, colonization, diaspora, and social injustice in the Americas by forging links between the fantasy of the imaginary and the real of history.

This connection between fantasy and history, bewildering in the continual oscillation of the narrative's multiple referentiality to both the real and the imaginary, cannot be formulated by the text but forms the unwritten base that conditions and transcends the literal meanings of both history and fantasy, in the process creating something new, something we might call imaginary history or historical fantasy. It is the aesthetic equivalent of what I have identified as the rhetorical function of parabasis and irony in other related contexts of contemporary American ethnic fiction. It is a way of describing the "something more" that the literary works I refer to as postrace fictions do in linking fantasy, history, and the imaginary—the imaginary history—in order to remain true to ethnic literature's utopian allegiance to social justice.[39]

In the end, true to the forms of fantasy that the narrative uses to tell his story, Oscar remains invisible, absent, and pieced together only tenuously from fragments and absences, all in the mode of fantasy, science fiction, gothic, and horror—that is to say, in the form of all the "genres" in the service of history gone awry.[40] As a sexual being manqué, racialized, classed, and colonized by the long historical legacies of coloniality and modernity, at the novel's end Oscar does not so much disappear as he continues to perform his disappearance as a subject of history from the story of his own emergence. In contrast to the fantasy of heroic individual sexual desire, figured by Yunior's compulsive and destructive hypermasculine sexuality, a sexuality for which Oscar always longs and by which he is finally destroyed, Oscar's historical fantasy leads elsewhere. It binds him more closely to Beli, Lola, Ybón, Abelard, and all of the women and men caught in the total terror of real dictatorial regimes such as the historical Trujillato, even if narrated in the form of "the more speculative genres," as Oscar describes them. The terror created by really bad men masks "The beauty!" which is but another name for life.[41]

How could one possibly conceive of a narrativity to still this chaos? How create romance from consciousness colonized by self-hate and self-doubt? What kind of beauty could we even imagine to counter the horror before and after the beauty? And to what end? What would a literature of political and racial romance, sensation, fantasy, gothic, marvels, and absolute otherness appropriate to transport us to the margins of the Imaginary and the Real that earlier forms of U.S. ethnic literature have not? What would its referential world look like?

It is the nature of romantic literature to pose these kinds of questions. But when fantasy and metafiction come into contact with history and the racialized imagination, vernacular cultures, and the stories of figures from the American Global South, they become something else again. And now we are back to the role of history. Being a Latino/a writer in the United States, appropriating history and the concerns of the distinctively modern experience of the borderlands with the Global South does not require orthodox narrative structures and realist codes of representation. Sharing the goal of most ethnic writers to imagine a state of achieved social justice, Díaz certainly employs all of the classical forms and themes available to ethnic writers to make his point. Díaz draws from the traditions of vernacular narrative, popular culture, and the literary avant-garde, however, not simply to reiterate them, but precisely to show the constant and complete rupture between the redemptive course of American history and its origins in conquest.[42]

Going beyond the defamiliarizing strategies of avant-garde literature, works like Díaz's *The Brief Wondrous Life of Oscar Wao* attempt to articulate an imaginary fantasy to the second and third degrees that might, paradoxically, serve as the real basis for understanding our bewilderingly complex postcontemporary history. Far from mere parody or a sign of the exhaustion of the avant-garde, Díaz's use of the comedic "Chiste Apocalyptus," the joke at the end of the world, is a formal attempt to counter the reduction of the reality of horror under the sheer weight of the commonplace. That is why, with the cruel murder of our hero, Díaz returns us pitilessly, as does Oscar at the moment of his brutal beating, "back to the Real," with a capital R.[43] He compels us to see that in the age of free markets and globalization the world has diminished and constricted so that we "Americans" now share with others around the globe a synthetic fantasy culture of television shows, animated films, space operas, graphic novels, and digital media, a synchrony of intersecting fantasies worthy of being considered "magical." The reality of this new world is not gratuitous, or virtual; but in its longing for a new world yet to be it might well be postmagical, and postracial. It takes us into the heart of Prospero's power, and the functioning of the art of power.

Notes

1. Junot Díaz, *The Brief Wondrous Life of Oscar Wao* (New York: Riverhead, 2007), 233.

2. This essay is an elaboration of a reading of Junot Díaz I first offered in "Historical Fantasy, Speculative Realism and Postrace Aesthetics in American Fiction," *American Literary History* 23, no. 3 (2011): 574–99.

3. Díaz, *Oscar Wao*, 233.

4. Díaz, *Oscar Wao*, 234.

5. Díaz, *Oscar Wao*, 234.

6. Díaz, *Oscar Wao*, 234.

7. Díaz, *Oscar Wao*, 235.

8. Díaz, *Oscar Wao*, 237.

9. Díaz, *Oscar Wao*, 243.

10. Díaz, *Oscar Wao*, 243.

11. Díaz, *Oscar Wao*, 243.

12. Díaz, *Oscar Wao*, 243.

13. Díaz, *Oscar Wao*, 245.

14. Díaz, *Oscar Wao*, 245.

15. Díaz, *Oscar Wao*, 245.

16. Owen Davies, *Grimoires: A History of Magic Books* (Oxford: Oxford University Press, 2009), 1–2.

17. Davies, *Grimoires*, 1.

18. Davies, *Grimoires*, 135–36.

19. José David Saldívar, "Conjectures on 'Americanity' and Junot Díaz's 'Fukú Americanus' in *The Brief Wondrous Life of Oscar Wao*," *Global South* 5, no. 1 (spring 2011): 120–36.

20. Saldívar, "Conjectures," 213.

21. Saldívar, "Conjectures," 246.

22. Saldívar, "Conjectures," 246.

23. Shakespeare, *The Tempest*, act 1, scene 2.

24. Shakespeare, *The Tempest*, act 3, scene 2.

25. Roberto Fernández Retamar, *Caliban and Other Essays* (Minneapolis: University of Minnesota Press, 1989).

26. Fernández Retamar, *Caliban and Other Essays*, 24.

27. Kingsley Amis, *New Maps of Hell: A Survey of Science Fiction* (New York: Harcourt, Brace, 1960), 30.

28. See Michele Braun, "Science Fiction as Experimental Ground for Issues of the Postcolonial Novel," in Masood A. Raja, Jason W. Ellis, and Swaralipi Nandi, *The Postnational Fantasy: Essays on Postcolonialism, Cosmopolitics and Science Fiction* (Jefferson, NC: McFarland, 2011), 17–29.

29. Junot Díaz, "Monstro," *The New Yorker*, June 4, 2012, 106.

30. See Diego A. von Vacano, *The Art of Power: Machiavelli, Nietzsche, and the Making of Aesthetic Political Theory* (Lanham, MD: Lexington Books, 2007), 1–8, for an excellent discussion of the relationship among art, power, and knowledge.

31. See Brook Thomas, "The Fictive and the Imaginary: Charting Literary Anthropology, or, What's Literature Have to Do with It?" *American Literary History* 20, no. 3 (2008): 622–31. Thomas's discussion of Iser's "reception aesthetics" and Fluck's notion of "the cultural imaginary" are immensely useful articulations of the functioning of literary texts to compel readers to imagine not an "existing reality" but to "realize something that does not yet exist" (625).

32. See especially "Historical Fantasy, Speculative Realism and Postrace Aesthetics in American Fiction," 574–99.

33. Winfried Fluck, "The Role of the Reader and the Changing Functions of Literature: Reception Aesthetics, Literary Anthropology, *Funktionsgeschichte*," *European Journal of English Studies* 6, no. 3 (2002): 255. See also Winfried Fluck, "The Search for Distance: Negation and Negativity in Wolfgang Iser's Literary Theory," *New Literary History* 31, no. 1 (2000): 175–210. Here, concerning Iser's notion of "negativity," as "an unlimited negating potential" in a text, Fluck argues that as an integral and foundational quality of a text, negativity "dislocates all norms, meanings, and forms of organization, not just those we would like to negate. This continuous invalidation is . . . the precondition for activating literature's special potential," allowing it to serve as a permanent and ongoing "negation of the negation" (186).

34. Fluck, "The Role of the Reader," 256.

35. Fluck, "The Role of the Reader," 258. Fluck puts it this way: "Every text consists of segments that are determinate, and of blanks between them that are indeterminate. In order to establish consistency between these segments, the reader has to become active in providing links for that which is missing. A blank is thus not a mere gap, or

an ideologically instructive omission. It is an intentional, often carefully crafted, suspension of relations in order to make us provide links for what is disconnected. The
difference is significant: A mere gap allows readers to indulge in their own projections,
a blank compels them to set up relations between their own imaginary constructs and
the text" (258).

36. Fluck, "The Role of the Reader," 256.

37. On the relationship between "justice" and "literature," see Winfried Fluck, "Fiction and Justice," *New Literary History* 34, no. 1 (2003): 19–42. See also Martha Nussbaum, *Poetic Justice: The Literary Imagination and Public Life* (Boston: Beacon, 1995). The
relationship between justice and aesthetics is the core of my argument in "Historical
Fantasy, Speculative Realism and Postrace Aesthetics in American Fiction," 574–99.

38. Díaz, *Oscar Wao*, 295.

39. On the representation of social justice, see Fluck, "Fiction and Justice," 20–21.

40. See Caroline Roberts, "Bostonist Interview: Junot Díaz, Author," *Bostonist*, September 10, 2007, accessed April 22, 2015, http://bostonist.com/2007/09/10/bostonist
_inter_1.php.

41. Díaz, *Oscar Wao*, 335.

42. Paul Gilroy, *The Black Atlantic: Modernity and Double Consciousness* (Cambridge, MA:
Harvard University Press, 1993), 222.

43. Díaz, *Oscar Wao*, 298.

Photo by Nina Sabin. © Junot Diaz.

15. The Search for Decolonial Love
A Conversation Between Junot Díaz and
Paula M. L. Moya

While Paula Moya and Junot Díaz were at Stanford University attending our "Junot Diaz: A Symposium," they met for a breakfast during which they discussed race, gender, and decolonial aesthetics. Their conversation, originally printed in the *Boston Review*, is reproduced below.

Prefatory Note by Moya: On May 19, 2012, I met over breakfast with Junot Díaz; we were both attending a two-day symposium about his work at Stanford University. The resulting conversation touched on Díaz's concern with race, his debt to the writings of women of color, and his fictional explorations of psychic and emotional decolonization. It also provided us the happy opportunity to renew our friendship, which began when we were graduate students at Cornell University in the early 1990s.

> Paula: I was so pleased when, during your Kieve lecture yesterday, you stated—clearly and unapologetically—that you write about race. I have always been struck by the fact that, in all the interviews you have given that I have read, no one ever asks you about race. If it does come up, it is because *you* bring it up. Yet it has long been apparent to

me that race is one of your central concerns. This is why, for my contribution to the symposium, I decided to focus on your story, "How to Date a Browngirl, Blackgirl, Whitegirl, or Halfie." And because the story is about the way race, class, and gender are mutually constituted vectors of oppression, I decided to read it using the theoretical framework developed by the women of color who were writing in the 1980s and 1990s. Honestly, though, I feel like I am swimming against the current—lately, I have seen a forgetting and dismissal, in academia, of their work; it is as if their insights are somehow passé. But it seems right to me to read your work through the lens of women of color theory. Does this make sense to you?

Junot: Absolutely. In this we are in sync, Paula. Much of the early genesis of my work arose from the 1980s and specifically from the weird gender wars that flared up in that era between writers of color. I know you remember them: the very public fulminations of Stanley Crouch versus Toni Morrison, Ishmael Reed versus Alice Walker, Frank Chin versus Maxine Hong Kingston. Talk about passé—my students know nothing about these exchanges but for those of us present at the time they were both dismaying and formative. This was part of a whole backlash against the growing success and importance of women-of-color writers—*but from men of color.* Qué irony. The brothers criticizing the sisters for being inauthentic, for being anti-male, for airing the community's dirty laundry, all from a dreary nationalist point of view. Every time I heard these Chin-Reed-Crouch attacks, even I as a male would feel the weight of oppression on me, on my physical body, increased. And for me, what was fascinating was that the maps these women were creating in their fictions—the social, critical, cognitive maps, these matrixes that they were plotting—were far more dangerous to the structures that had me pinioned than any of the criticisms that men of color were throwing down. What began to be clear to me as I read these women of color: Leslie Marmon Silko, Sandra Cisneros, Anjana Appachana—throw in Octavia Butler and the great [Cherríe] Moraga of course—was that what these sisters were doing in their art was powerfully important for the community, for subaltern folks, for women writers of color, for male writers of color, for me. They were heeding [Audre] Lorde's exhortation by forging the tools that could actually take down the master's house. To read these sisters in the 1980s as a young college student was not only intoxicating, it was soul-changing. It was metanoia.

Paula: Can you say more about why the maps plotted by women of color seemed to you more dangerous than the critiques that were made by the men of color who were attacking them?

Junot: Think about that final line in [Frantz] Fanon's *Black Skin, White Masks*: "O my body, make me always a man who questions!" I remember reading these sisters and suddenly realizing (perhaps incorrectly but it felt right to me at the time) that women-of-color writers were raising questions about the world, about power, about philosophy, about politics, about history, about white supremacy, *because* of their raced, gendered, sexualized bodies; they were wielding a genius that had been cultivated *out of* their raced, gendered, sexualized subjectivities. And what they were producing in knowledge was something that the world needed to hear in order to understand itself, that I needed to hear in order to understand myself in the world, and that no one—least of all male writers of color—should be trying to silence. To me these women were not only forging in the smithies of their body-logos radical emancipatory epistemologies—the source code of our future liberation—but also they were fundamentally rewriting Fanon's final call in *Black Skin, White Masks*, transforming it into "O my body, make me always a woman who questions . . . my body" (both its oppressions and interpellations *and* its liberatory counterstrategies). To me (and many other young artists and readers) the fiction of these foundational sisters represented a quantum leap in what is called the post-colonial-slash-subaltern-slash-neocolonial; their work completed, extended, complicated the work of the earlier generation (Fanon) in profound ways and also created for this young writer a set of strategies and warrior-grammars that would become the basis of my art. That these women are being forgotten, and their historical importance elided, says a lot about our particular moment and how real a threat these foundational sisters posed to the order of things.

Paula: What do you think was the most important advance that women of color made on the work of those earlier male thinkers?

Junot: Well, first of all these sisters were pretty clear that redemption was not going to be found in the typical masculine nostrums of nationalism or armed revolution or even that great favorite of a certain class of writerly brother: transracial intimacy. Por favor! If transracial intimacy was all we needed to be free, then a joint like the Dominican Republic would be the great cradle of freedom—which, I assure you, it is not. Why these sisters struck me as the most dangerous of artists was because in the work of, say, Morrison, or Octavia Butler, we are shown the awful radiant truth of how profoundly constituted we are of our oppressions. Or said differently: how indissolubly our identities are bound to the regimes that imprison us. These sisters not only describe the grim labyrinth of power that we are in as neocolonial subjects, but they also point out that we play both Theseus and the Minotaur in this nightmare drama. Most importantly these sisters offered strategies of hope, spinning the threads that will make escape from this labyrinth possible. It wasn't an easy thread to seize—this movement toward liberation required the kind of internal bearing-witness of our own role in the social hell of our world that most people would rather not engage in. It was a tough praxis, but a potentially earthshaking one too. Because rather than strike at this issue or that issue, this internal bearing of witness raised the possibility of denying our oppressive regimes the true source of their powers—which is, of course, our consent, our participation. This kind of praxis doesn't attack the head of the beast, which will only grow back; it strikes directly at the beast's heart, which we nurture and keep safe in our own. Heady stuff for a young writer. Theirs was the project I wanted to be part of. And they gave me the map that I, a poor Dominican immigrant boy of African descent from New Jersey, could follow.

Paula: This reminds me of a point you made in the question and answer session following your lecture yesterday. You said that people of color fuel white supremacy as much as white people do; that it is something we are all implicated in. You went on to suggest that only by first recognizing the social and material realities we live in—by naming and examining the effects of white supremacy—can we hope to transform our practices.

Junot: How can you change something if you won't even acknowledge its existence, or if you downplay its significance? White supremacy is the great silence of our world, and in it is embedded much of what ails us as a planet. The silence around white supremacy is like the silence around Sauron in *The Lord of the Rings*, or the Voldemort name which must never be uttered in the Harry Potter novels. And yet here's the rub: if a critique of white supremacy doesn't first flow through you, doesn't first implicate you, then you have missed the mark; you have, in fact, almost guaranteed its survival and reproduction. There's that old saying: the devil's greatest trick is that he convinced people that he doesn't exist. Well, white supremacy's greatest trick is that it has convinced people that if it exists at all it exists always in other people, never in us.

Paula: I wanted to ask you about something else you said in the lecture yesterday. You said you wanted to, and thought you could, "figure out a way to represent most honestly—represent in the language, and represent in the way people talk, and represent in the discourse—what [you], just one person, thought was a racial reality," but without endorsing that reality. You indicated that you aim to realistically represent "our entire insane racial logic" but in a way that "the actual material does not endorse that reality" *at the level of structure*. This is certainly what I would argue your work succeeds in doing. But I would like to hear more about how you go about creating, at the level of structure, a disjuncture between the realistic representation of race and an endorsement of the racial logic on which the representation is based.

Junot: The things I say. [*Laughs*] OK let me see if I can make sense of my own damn self. Let's see if I can speak to the actual texts. Well, at its most simplistic in, say, *Drown*, we have a book where racist shit happens—but it's not like at a thematic level the book is saying: Right on, racist shit! I was hoping that the book would expose my characters' race craziness and that this craziness would strike readers, at the very minimum, as authentic. But exposing our racisms, etc., accurately has never seemed to be enough; the problem with faithful representations is that they run the risk of being mere titillation or sensationalism. In my books, I try to show how these oppressive paradigms work together with the social reality of the characters to undermine the very dreams the characters have for themselves. So, Yunior thinks X and Y about people and that logic is, in part, what fucks him up. Now if the redounding is too blunt and obvious, then what you get is a moralistic parable and not literature. But, if it's done well, then you get both the ugliness that comes out of showing how people really are around issues like race and gender, but also a hidden, underlying countercurrent that puts in front of you the very real, very personal, consequences of these orientations.

Yunior, for example, uses the "n word" all the time and yet he is haunted by antiblack racism within and without his community. Haunted and wounded. In "How to Date," for instance, we see explicitly how he is victimized by a powerful antiblack self-hate of the Fanon variety. That for me would be a concrete example of how the deeper narrative of *Drown* offers a complicated counterpoint to Yunior's often-toxic racial utterances, the kind of call-response I'm trying to achieve in the work.

In *Drown* as a whole, the million-dollar question is this: Are Yunior's gender politics, his generalizations and misogyny, rewarded in the book's "reality?" Do they get him anything in the end? Well, if we chart the progress of the stories in *Drown* it appears to me that Yunior's ideas about women, and the actions that arise out of these ideas, always leave him more alone, more thwarted, more disconnected from his community and from himself. Yunior cannot even hope to bear witness to what happened between his mother and his father—which is to say he can't bear witness to what really happened to him—without first confronting the role he plays and continues to play in that kind of male behavior that made his family's original separation and later dissolution inevitable. Yunior's desire for communion with self and with other is finally undermined by his inability, his unwillingness, to see the women in his life as fully human. (Which is kinda tragic, since without being able to recognize the women parts of his identity as human, he cannot in turn recognize himself as fully human.) The reason why the character of Yunior is at all interesting to me is because he senses this. He senses how he makes his own chains and he rages against the chains and against himself, and yet he continues to forge them, link by link by link.

Paula: This makes so much sense to me in terms of the way you create that disjuncture in *Drown*. Can you say more about how this all plays out in *The Brief Wondrous Life of Oscar Wao?*

Junot: In *Oscar Wao* we have a family that has fled, half-destroyed, from one of the rape incubators of the New World and they are trying to find love. But not just any love. How can there be "just any love," given the history of rape and sexual violence that created the Caribbean—that Trujillo uses in the novel? The kind of love that I was interested in, that my characters long for intuitively, is the only kind of love that could liberate them from that horrible legacy of colonial violence. I am speaking about decolonial love.

One of the arguments that the book makes about Oscar is that he ain't getting laid because he's fat and nerdy. That might be part of it, but that is also a way of hiding other possibilities. Perhaps one of the reasons Oscar ain't getting laid is because he is the son of a survivor of horrific sexual violence. In the same way that there is intergenerational transfer of trauma from mothers who are rape victims to their daughters, there is also intergenerational transfer of rape trauma between mothers and their sons. But most readers don't notice how Oscar embodies some of the standard reactions of young rape victims to their violations. Many women in the aftermath of sexual violence put on weight—in some cases as an attempt to make themselves as unattractive as possible. Oscar isn't fat just to be fat—at least not in my head. His fatness was partially a product of what's going on in the family in regards to their bodies, in regards to the rape trauma.

For me, the family *fukú* is rape. The rape culture of the European colonization of the New World—which becomes the rape culture of the Trujillato (Trujillo just took that very old record and remixed it)— is the rape culture that stops the family from achieving decolonial intimacy, from achieving decolonial love.

Yunior, in this context, is a curious figure. He's clearly the book's most salient proponent of the masculine derangements that are tied up to the rape culture . . . he is its biggest proponent and its biggest "beneficiary." He's most clearly one of Trujillo's children—yet he, too, is a victim of this culture. A victim in the lowercase sense because his failure to disavow his privileged position in that rape culture, to disavow the masculine discourse and behaviors that support and extend that culture, end up costing him the love of his life, his one best chance at decolonial love and, through that love, a decolonial self. But Yunior's a victim in a larger second sense: I always wrote Yunior as being a survivor of sexual abuse. He has been raped too. The hint of this sexual abuse is something that's present in *Drown* and it is one of the great silences in *Oscar Wao*. This is what Yunior can't admit, his very own *página en blanco*. So, when he has that line in the novel: "I'd finally try to say the words that could have saved us. / _____ _____ _____," what he couldn't say to Lola was that "I too have been molested." He could bear witness to everyone else's deep pains but, in the end, he couldn't bear witness to his own sexual abuse. He couldn't tell the story that would have tied him in a human way to Lola, that indeed could have saved him.

Paula: Right. Now, am I just a bad reader? Or . . .

Junot: No.

Paula: . . . is it that silenced?

Junot: It's that silenced; that elliptical. Perhaps it's too great a silence, which is to say, it's probably too small a trace to be read. Only visible, if visible at all, by inference. By asking: what is really bothering Yunior? Why is Yunior such a dog? Just because? Or is there something deeper? Think about it: isn't promiscuity another typical reaction to sexual abuse? Compulsive promiscuity is certainly Yunior's problem. A compulsive promiscuity that is a national masculine ideal in some ways and whose roots I see in the trauma of our raped pasts. Like I said: it's probably not there at all—too subtle. But the fact of Yunior's rape certainly helped me design the thematic economy of the book.

Paula: Well, let's go back to Oscar for a minute. You suggested that, for Oscar, putting on so much weight was a way of protecting himself.

Junot: That unconscious manifestation of fear of molestation, yeah, I think that is what is . . .

Paula: So, Oscar and Yunior are both reacting to the rape culture of the Dominican Republic, but they are doing so in different ways. Moreover, they are reacting to their different experiences of that same culture: Yunior is reacting to his own violation by becoming hyperpromiscuous, whereas Oscar has absorbed some sense of violation from his mother and so responds by making himself—certainly not as a matter of conscious will—sexually unavailable.

Junot: Yes, ma'am. In the novel you see the way the horror of rape closes in on them all. The whole family is in this circuit of rape. And, you know, the point the book keeps making again and again and again is that, in the Dominican Republic, which is to say, in the world that the DR built, if you are a Beli, a Lola, a Yunior—if you are anybody—rape is never going to be far.

Paula: This is so interesting because, thinking back to your story "Ysrael," the description of what happens to Ysrael when his mask is torn away—just the whole way that happens—is completely reminiscent of a rape.

Junot: Sure, and it's preluded by Yunior being sexually assaulted.

Paula: Exactly! And between Yunior and Ysrael there's a kind of mirroring, a doubling that you see structured into the story and, then—it's just devastating.

Junot: [Nods quietly] One has to understand that all the comments, all the things that Yunior does in Oscar Wao, move him inexorably away from the thing that he most needs: real intimacy which must have vulnerability, forgiveness, acceptance as its prerequisites. So that even though Yunior is sexist, even though he's misogynist, even though he's racist, even though he mischaracterizes Oscar's life, even though he's narcissistic—at the end he's left with no true love, doesn't find himself, doesn't find that decolonial love that he needs to be an authentic self. In fact, he ends up—like the work that he assembles and stores in the refrigerator—incomplete.

You know how he assembles this work on Oscar, how he says it needed someone else to complete, a someone he fantasizes as Lola's daughter, Isis? Isis's name, of course, is a bit of an inside joke, but an important one. Because, what does Isis do, what is she known for mythologically? In the Egyptian legends I grew up on, Isis assembles her lover-brother Osiris, she assembles the pieces of Osiris that have been chopped up and scattered by Set. That's one of the great mythical tasks of Isis, except—What does she leave out? In the legends it says that Isis doesn't find Osiris's penis, but I like to believe she just leaves it out. Osiris comes back to the world alive but penisless. Which for some is a horror but for others a marked improvement. In keeping with the Isis metaphor, I've always thought the thing with Yunior is that he couldn't reassemble himself in a way that would leave out the metaphoric penis, that would leave out all his attachments to his masculine, patriarchal, phallocratic privileges. Which is what he needed to do to finally "get" Lola. In the end, Yunior is left . . . with not much. No Lola, no Isis, no Oscar.

Thinking about Yunior as having been raped made (in my mind at least) his fucked-up utterances in the novel have a different resonance. And while he wasn't yet ready to bear witness to his own rape, it gave him a certain point of view around sexual violence that I don't think would have been possible otherwise. It helped me produce a novel with a feminist alignment. A novel whose central question is, Is it possible to overcome the horror legacy of slavery and find decolonial love? Is it possible to love one's broken-by-the-coloniality-of-power self in another broken-by-the-coloniality-of-power person?

Paula: Your new collection of short stories, *This Is How You Lose Her*, just appeared in print. And you are also at work on a new novel, a portion of which you had intended to read from yesterday before you decided instead to give that amazing and insightful CCSRE Kieve lecture. Will you tell me a bit about *Monstro*?

Junot: Of course. *Monstro* is an apocalyptic story. An end of the world story set in the DR of the near future. It's a zombie story. (On that island, how could it not be?) It's an alien invasion story. It's a giant monster story. It's about the Great Powers (China, the United States) attempting to contain the growing infestation by reinvading the island for, what, the twelfth time? I always say if people on my island know about anything they know about the end of the world. We are after all the eschaton that divided the Old World from the New. The whole reason I started writing this book is because of this image I have of this fourteen-year-old girl, a poor, black, Dominican girl, half-Haitian—one of the Island's *damnés*—saving the world. It's a book about this girl's search for—yes—love in a world that has made it its solemn duty to guarantee that poor, raced, "conventionally unattract-ive" girls like her are never loved.

Paula: That's so interesting because just a couple of days ago I went to a talk by the Stanford sociologist Corey Fields; he is doing some pilot studies about the impact of race on black women's love lives. During his talk, Fields mentioned a book by Averil Clarke called *Inequalities of Love*. The thing about this book is that it talks about the fact that college-educated black women, in particular, date less, marry less, and have fewer romantic relationships than their college-educated white and Latina counterparts, *and* than non-college-educated black women. But the important intervention that Clarke makes is that she points out that everyone talks about this fact as a kind of difference. Well, sure, it is a difference, but it is not just a difference—it's an in-equality. So she frames the situation in terms of an inequality and describes it as a "romantic deprivation" that black women suffer.

Junot: Love this!

Paula: And this romantic deprivation has all manner of cascading impli-cations for everything else in their lives.

Junot: Oh man.

Paula: Anyway, Clarke's book sounds like it is getting at something that you are getting at in your fiction.

Junot: Without a doubt. The inequality of love.

Paula: So how far along are you on *Monstro*?

Junot: Not far enough. You know, it sounds ridiculous, but the amount of deep structural work that I have to wrestle with before the first chapters start to roll . . . it's the same thing that happened with *Oscar Wao*. I had to get all this stuff that I'm talking about to you now *in place* in my head. And so I have to wrestle with all this weirdness, have to wrestle with the voice, have to wrestle with the characters. I've written about two hundred pages now and they're actually not bad. But all of it was to set up the book and, in fact, none of these pages are going to go in.

Paula: Oh—that's one of those mature realizations you come to over time. You write and write and write, and it does not end up in the book, but it was *still necessary*. It was all part of the process.

Junot: Totally true. I used to hate it. Now I'm more tolerant. Ever since my life exploded five years ago, I've learned a bunch of things and now, with the body failing, it makes you a little bit more humble. But it was great to get through that work. I feel like the first big part is done. And now I just started writing the novel, and I finished the first fifty pages, a part of which is what is coming out in *The New Yorker*.

Bibliography

Abrams, Dennis. "Junot Díaz Wrote a Short Story Worth a New Mercedes." *Publishing Perspectives*, March 26, 2013. Accessed April 22, 2015. http://publishingperspectives.com/2013/03/junot-diaz-takes-30000-story-prize-from-the-brits/.

Alcoff, Linda Martín. *Visible Identities: Race, Gender, and the Self*. New York: Oxford University Press, 2006.

Alcoff, Linda Martín. "Who's Afraid of Identity Politics?" In *Reclaiming Identity: Realist Theory and the Predicament of Postmodernism*, edited by Paula M. L. Moya and Michael Hames-García, 312–44. Berkeley: University of California Press, 2000.

Alcoff, Linda Martín, and Satya P. Mohanty. "Reconsidering Identity Politics: An Introduction." In *Identity Politics Reconsidered*, edited Linda Martin Alcoff, Satya P. Mohanty, Michael Hames-García, and Paula M. L. Moya, 1–9. New York: Palgrave Macmillan, 2006.

Alcoff, Linda Martín, Satya P. Mohanty, Michael Hames-García, and Paula M. L. Moya, eds. *Identity Politics Reconsidered*. New York: Palgrave Macmillan, 2006.

Alemán, Jesse. "Barbarous Tongues: Immigrant and Ethnic Voices in Contemporary American Literature." *Modern Fiction Studies* 54, no. 2 (2008): 398–404.

Alexander, M. Jacqui, and Chandra Talpade Mohanty, eds. *Feminist Genealogies, Colonial Legacies, Democratic Futures*. New York: Routledge, 1997.

Alfaguara. "Premio Alfaguara de Novela." Alfaguara.com. N.d. Accessed March 20, 2013. http://www.alfaguara.com/es/premio-alfaguara-de-novela/.

Almagüer, Tomás. "Chicano Men: A Cartography of Homosexual Identity and Behavior." In *The Lesbian and Gay Studies Reader*, edited by Henry Abelove, Michele Aina Barale, and David M. Halperin, 255–73. New York: Routledge, 1993.

Althusser, Louis. "Ideology and Ideological State Apparatuses (Notes Towards an Investigation)." In *Lenin and Philosophy*, 127–86. New York: Monthly Review, 1971.

Alvarez, Julia. *In the Time of the Butterflies*. New York: Algonquin Books, 2010.

Amis, Kingsley. *New Maps of Hell: A Survey of Science Fiction*. New York: Harcourt, Brace, 1960.

Amis, Martin. *The Moronic Inferno and Other Visits to America*. New York: Viking, 1987.

Andrade, Oswald de. "Cannibalist Manifesto." Translated by Leslie Bary. *Latin American Literary Review* 19, no. 38 (July–December 1991): 38–47.

Anjaria, Ulka. "Staging Realism and the Ambivalence of Nationalism in the Colonial Novel." *Novel: A Forum on Fiction* 44, no. 2 (2011): 186–207.

Antebi, Susan. *Carnal Enscriptions: Spanish American Narratives of Corporeal Difference and Disability*. New York: Palgrave Macmillan, 2009.

Anzaldúa, Gloria. *Borderlands/La Frontera: The New Mestiza*. San Francisco: Spinsters/Aunt Lute, 1987.

Anzaldúa, Gloria, ed. *Making Face, Making Soul—Haciendo Caras: Creative and Critical Perspectives by Women of Color*. San Francisco: Aunt Lute Books, 1990.

Aparicio, Frances R. "On Sub-Versive Signifiers: U.S. Latina/o Writers Tropicalize English." *American Literature* 66, no. 4 (December 1994): 795–801.

Appadurai, Arjun. *Modernity at Large: Cultural Dimensions of Globalization*. Minneapolis: University of Minnesota Press, 1996.

Apple, R. W., Jr. "Death of a First Lady: The Overview; Jacqueline Kennedy Onassis Is Buried." *New York Times*, May 24, 1994.

Arreola, Daniel David. *Hispanic Spaces, Latino Places: Community and Cultural Diversity in Contemporary America*. Austin: University of Texas Press, 2004.

Asturias, Miguel Ángel. "El señor presidente como mito." In *El señor presidente: Edición crítica*, edited by Gerald Martin, 468–78. Barcelona: Galaxia Gutenberg, 2000.

Avelar, Idelber. *The Untimely Present: Postdictatorial Latin American Fiction and the Task of Mourning*. Durham, NC: Duke University Press, 1999.

Baca Zinn, Maxine, and Bonnie Thornton Dill, eds. *Women of Color in U. S. Society*. Philadelphia: Temple University Press, 1994.

Badiou, Alain. *In Praise of Love*. With Nicolas Truong. Translated by Peter Bush. London: Serpent's Tail, 2012.

Bakhtin, M. M. "The Bildungsroman and Its Significance in the History of Realism (Toward a Historical Typology of the Novel)." In *Speech Genres and Other Late Essays*, translated by Vern W. McGee, edited by Caryl Emerson and Michael Holquist, 10–59. Austin: University of Texas Press, 1986.

Bambara, Toni Cade. *The Black Woman: An Anthology*. New York: New American Library, 1970.

Bambara, Toni Cade. *The Salt Eaters*. New York: Vintage, 1981.

Barradas, Efrain. "El realism comico de Junot Díaz: Notas sobre *The Brief Wondrous Life of Oscar Wao*." SECOLAS 53, no. 1 (2009): 99–111.

Bautista, Daniel. "Comic Book Realism and Genre in Junot Díaz's *The Brief Wondrous Life of Oscar Wao*." *Journal of the Fantastic Arts* 21, no. 1 (2010): 41–53.

Bender, Steven. *Greasers and Gringos: Latinos, Law, and the American Imagination*. New York: New York University Press, 2003.

Benstock, Shari. "At the Margin of Discourse: Footnotes in the Fictional Text." PMLA 98, no. 2 (1983): 204–25.

Borges, Jorge Luis. *Collected Fictions*. Translated by Andrew Hurley. New York: Penguin Books, 1998.

Borges, Jorge Luis. "Pierre Menard, Author of Don Quixote." In *Labyrinths: Selected Stories and Other Writings*, edited by Donald A. Yates and James E. Irby, 36–44. New York: New Directions Books, 1962.

Bosque-Pérez, Ramón, and José Javier Colón Morera. *Las carpetas: Persecucion política y derechos civiles en Puerto Rico*. San Juan: Centro para la Investigación y Promoción de los Derechos Civiles, 1997.

Boyden, Michael, and Patrick Goethals. "Translating the Watcher's Voice: Junot Díaz's *The Brief Wondrous Life of Oscar Wao* into Spanish." *Meta: Journal des traducteurs* 56, no. 1 (2011): 20–41.

Braun, Michele. "Science Fiction as Experimental Ground for Issues of the Postcolonial Novel." In *The Postnational Fantasy: Essays on Postcolonialism, Cosmopolitics and Science Fiction*, edited by Masood A. Raja, Jason W. Ellis, and Swaralipi Nandi, 17–29. Jefferson, NC: McFarland, 2011.

Braziel, Jana Evans, and Anita Mannur, eds. *Theorizing Diaspora: A Reader*. Hoboken, NJ: Wiley-Blackwell, 2003.

Buford, Bill. "Reading Ahead." *The New Yorker*, June 21 and 28, 1999.

Bussie, Jacqueline. *The Laughter of the Oppressed: Ethical and Theological Resistance in Wiesel, Morrison, and Endo*. New York: T and T Clark, 2007.

Calviño Iglesias, Julio. *La novela del dictador en hispanoamérica*. Madrid: Cultura Hispánica, 1985.

Caminero-Santangelo, Marta. *On Latinidad: U.S. Latino Literature and the Construction of Ethnicity*. Gainesville: University Press of Florida, 2007.

Candelario, Ginetta, E. B. *Black behind the Ears: Dominican Racial Identity from Museums to Beauty Shops*. Durham, NC: Duke University Press, 2007.

Candelario, Ginetta E. B. "Hair Race-Ing: Dominican Beauty Culture and Identity Production." *Meridians* 1, no. 1 (2000): 128–56.

Carballal, Ana Isabel. Review of *Global Matters: The Transnational Turn in Literary Studies*, by Paul Jay. *Rocky Mountain Review* 65, no. 2 (2011): 242–44.

Carpentier, Alejo. *El reino de este mundo*. New York: HarperCollins, 2009.

Carpentier, Alejo. *The Kingdom of This World*. 1949. Translated by Harriet de Onís. New York: Farrar, Straus and Giroux, 1957.

Casanova, Pascale. *World Republic of Letters*. Translated by M. D. DeBevoise. Cambridge, MA: Harvard University Press, 2004.

Celayo, Armando, and David Shook. "In Darkness We Meet: A Conversation with Junot Díaz." *World Literature Today* 82, no. 2 (2008): 12–17.

Céspedes, Diógenes, and Silvio Torres-Saillant. "Fiction Is the Poor Man's Cinema: An Interview with Junot Díaz." *Callaloo* 23, no. 3 (2000): 892–907.

Chabram-Dernersesian, Angie. "And . . . Yes the Earth Did Part." In *Building with Our Hands*, edited by Adela de la Bore and Beatriz Pesquera, 34–56. Berkeley: University of California Press, 1993.

Chávez-Silverman, Susana, Librada Hernández, and Robert Richmond Ellis. *Reading and Writing the Ambiente: Queer Sexualities in Latino, Latin American, and Spanish Culture*. Madison: University of Wisconsin Press, 2000.

Ch'ien, Evelyn Nien-Ming. *Weird English*. Cambridge, MA: Harvard University Press, 2004.

Chow, Esther Ngan-Ling. "The Development of Feminist Consciousness among Asian American Women." *Gender and Society* 1, no. 3 (1987): 284–99.

Cisneros, Sandra. *Caramelo: A Novel*. New York: Vintage, 2002.

Cisneros, Sandra. *The House on Mango Street*. New York: Vintage, 1984.

Clifford, James. "Diasporas." *Cultural Anthropology* 9, no. 3 (1994): 302–38.

Clifford, James. *Routes: Travel and Translation in the Late Twentieth Century*. Cambridge, MA: Harvard University Press, 1997.

Cohen, Leah Hager. "Love Stories: Review of *This Is How You Lose Her* by Junot Díaz." *New York Times Book Review*, September 23, 2012.

Colás, Santiago. "Of Creole Symptoms, Cuban Fantasies, and Other Latin American Postcolonial Ideologies." *PMLA* 110, no. 3 (1995): 382–96.

Comaroff, Jean, and John L. Comaroff. "Alien-Nation: Zombies, Immigrants, and the Millennial Capitalism." *South Atlantic Quarterly* 101, no. 4 (2002): 779–805.

Comaroff, Jean, and John L. Comaroff. *Theory from the South: Or, How Euro-America Is Evolving toward Africa*. Boulder, CO: Paradigm, 2012.

Connor, Anne. "Desenmascarando a Ysrael: The Disfigured Face as Symbol of Identity in Three Latino Texts." *Cincinnati Romance Review* 21 (2002): 148–62.

Costello, Brannon. "Randall Kenan beyond the Final Frontier: Science Fiction, Superheroes, and the South in *A Visitation of Spirits*." *Southern Literary Journal* 43, no. 1 (2010): 125–50.

Craft, Linda J. *Novels of Testimony and Resistance from Central America*. Gainesville: University Press of Florida, 1997.

Critchley, Simon. *On Humour*. London: Routledge, 2002.

Cruz, Nilo. *Anna in the Tropics*. New York: Theater Communications Group, 2005.

Dalleo, Raphael, and Elena Machado Sáez. *The Latino/a Canon and the Emergence of Post-Sixties Literature*. New York: Palgrave Macmillan, 2007.

Damasio, Antonio R. *Descartes' Error: Emotion, Reason, and the Human Brain*. New York: Putnam, 1994.

Danta, Chris. "Sarah's Laughter: Kafka's Abraham." *Modernism/modernity* 15, no. 2 (2008): 343–59.

Darder, Antonia. "The Politics of Language: An Introduction." *Latino Studies* 2 (2004): 231–36.

Darnton, Robert. "First Steps toward a History of Reading." In *The Kiss of Lamourette: Reflections in Cultural History*, 154–87. New York: W. W. Norton, 1990.

Dávila, Arlene. *Culture Works: Space, Value, and Mobility across the Neoliberal Americas*. New York: New York University Press, 2012.

Dávila, Arlene. "A Fix for Ignorance and Exclusion." *New York Times*, April 27, 2011.

Dávila, Arlene. *Latinos, Inc.: The Marketing and Making of a People*. Berkeley: University of California Press, 2001.

Davis, Angela Y. "Afro Images: Politics, Fashion, and Nostalgia." *Critical Inquiry* 21, no. 1 (1994): 37–45.

Davis, Mike. *Magical Urbanism: Latinos Reinvent the U.S. Big City*. New York: Verso, 2000.

Decena, Carlos. *Tacit Subjects: Belonging and Same-Sex Desire among Dominican Immigrant Men*. Durham, NC: Duke University Press, 2011.

de Certeau, Michel. *The Practice of Everyday Life*. Translated by Timothy J. Tomasik. Minneapolis: University of Minnesota Press, 1998.

Decolonial Aesthetics Working Group. "Manifesto." 2011.

de las Casas, Bartolomé. *Apologética historia sumaria*. Edited by Edmundo O'Gorman. Mexico City: Instituto de Investigaciones hisóricas, 1967.

de las Casas, Bartolomé. *Brevísima relación de la destrucción de las Indias*. Mexico City: Fontamara, 1984.

de las Casas, Bartolomé. *Historia de las Indias*. Mexico City: Fondo de Cultural Económica, 1965.

Deleuze, Gilles, and Félix Guattari. *Kafka: Toward a Minor Literature*. 1975. Minneapolis: University of Minnesota Press, 1986.

De Maeseneer, Rita. *Encuentros con la narrativa dominicana contemporánea*. Madrid: Iberoamericana/Vervuert, 2006.

De Maeseneer, Rita. *Seis ensayos sobre narrativa dominicana contemporánea*. Santo Domingo: Colección del Banco Central de la República Dominicana, 2011.

Derby, Lauren. *The Dictator's Seduction: Politics and the Popular Imagination in the Era of Trujillo*. Durham, NC: Duke University Press, 2009.

Deresiewicz, William. "Fukú Americanus." *The Nation* (November 2007): 36–41.

Díaz, Carmen Graciela. "La rebeldía de leer." *El Nuevo Día*, July 24, 2011, 16–18.

Díaz, Junot. "Apocalypse: What Disasters Reveal." *Boston Review*, May 1, 2011. Accessed April 22, 2015. http://www.bostonreview.net/junot-diaz-apocalypse-haiti-earthquake.

Díaz, Junot. "Becoming a Writer." *O, The Oprah Magazine*, November 2009. Accessed April 22, 2015. http://www.oprah.com/spirit/Junot-Diaz-Talks-About-What-Made-Him-Become-a-Writer/2.

Díaz, Junot. "The Brief Wondrous Life of Oscar Wao." *The New Yorker*, December 25, 2000.

Díaz, Junot. *The Brief Wondrous Life of Oscar Wao*. New York: Riverhead, 2007.

Díaz, Junot. Conversation with Toni Morrison. New York Public Library, December 13, 2013. Accessed April 22, 2015. http://www.nypl.org/events/programs/2013/12/12/toni-morrison-junot-diaz.

Díaz, Junot. "Dark America." Anne and Loren Kieve Distinguished Lecture. Stanford University. May 18, 2012. M4A file.

Díaz, Junot. *Drown*. New York: Riverhead, 1996.

Díaz, Junot. "How (In a Time of Trouble) I Discovered My Mom and Learned to Live." In *Las Mamis: Favorite Latino Authors Remember Their Mothers*, edited by Esmeralda Santiago, 157–68. New York: Vintage, 2000.

Díaz, Junot. Interview by "American Voices." Johns Hopkins University. August 2013.

Díaz, Junot. Interview by Armando Celayo and David Shook. "In Darkness We Meet: A Conversation with Junot Díaz." *World Literature Today* 82, no. 2 (2008): 13–17.

Díaz, Junot. Interview by Bill Moyers. "Junot Díaz on Rewriting the Story of America." *Moyers and Company*, December 28, 2012. Accessed April 22, 2015. http://billmoyers.com/episode/full-show-rewriting-the-story-of-america/.

Díaz, Junot. Interview by Channing Kennedy. "Junot Díaz on Decolonial Love, Revolution, and More." YouTube, December 4, 2012. Accessed March 20, 2013.

Díaz, Junot. Interview by Cressida Leyshon. "This Week in Fiction: Junot Díaz." *The New Yorker*, July 16, 2012. Accessed April 22, 2015. http://www.newyorker.com /online/blogs/books/2012/07/this-week-in-fiction-junot-diaz-1.html.

Díaz, Junot. Interview by Greg Barrios. "Greg Barrios Interviews Junot Díaz." *Los Angeles Review of Books*, October 7, 2012. Accessed April 22, 2015. http:www.lareviewofbooks .org/article.phd?id=979&fulltext=1.

Díaz, Junot. Interview by Matt Okie. "Mil Máscaras: An Interview with Pulitzer-Winner Junot Díaz (*The Brief Wondrous Life of Oscar Wao*)." *Identity Theory*, September 2, 2008. Accessed April 22, 2015. http://www.identitytheory.com/interview-pulitzer -winner-junot-diaz-wondrous-life-oscar-wao/.

Díaz, Junot. Interview by Maya Jaggi. "Junot Díaz, a Truly All-American Writer." *The Independent*, February 29, 2008. Accessed April 22, 2015. http://www.independent.co .uk/arts-entertainment/books/features/junot diaz-a-truly-allamerican-writer-789382. hmtl.

Díaz, Junot. Interview by Meghan O'Rourke. "Questions for Junot Díaz: An Interview with the Pulitzer Prize-winning Author." *Slate*, April 8, 2008. Accessed April 22, 2015. http://www.slate.com/articles/news_and_politics/recycled/2008/04/questions_for _junot_daz.single.html.

Díaz, Junot. Interview by Michel Martin. *Tell Me More*. National Public Radio. June 10, 2009. Accessed April 22, 2015. http://www.npr.org/templates/story/story.php ?storyId=105193110.

Díaz, Junot. Interview by Richard Wolinsky. "Growing the Hell Up: From Middle Earth to NJ." *Guernica*, November 1, 2012. Accessed April 22, 2015. http://www.guernicamag .com/interviews/growing-the-hell-up-from-middle-earth-to-nj/.

Díaz, Junot. Interview by Stephen Colbert. *The Colbert Report*, March 25, 2013. Accessed April 22, 2015. http://thecolbertreport.cc.com/videos/bwz16t/junot-diaz.

Díaz, Junot. Interview by Sue Fassler. "The Baseline Is, You Suck: Junot Díaz on Men who Write about Women." *The Atlantic*, September 12, 2012.

Díaz, Junot. Introduction to *The Beacon Best of 2001: Great Writing by Women and Men of All Colors and Cultures*. Edited by Junot Díaz, vii–xi. Boston: Beacon, 2001.

Díaz, Junot. Introduction to *Dismantle: An Anthology of Writing from the VONA/Voices Writing Workshop*. Edited by Marissa Johnson-Valenzuela, 1–8. Philadelphia: Thread Makes Blanket, 2014.

Díaz, Junot. "Junot Díaz, Diaspora, and Redemption: Creating Progressive Imaginaries. Interview. Conducted by Katherine Miranda." *Sargasso* 2 (2008–9): 23–40.

Díaz, Junot. "Language, Violence, and Resistance." In *Voice-Overs: Translation and Latin American Literature*, edited by Daniel Balderston and Marcy E. Schwartz, 42–44. Albany: State University of New York Press, 2002.

Díaz, Junot. "Loving Ray Bradbury." *The New Yorker*, June 6, 2012. Accessed April 22, 2015. http://www.newyorker.com/online/blogs/books/2012/06/loving-ray-bradbury .html.

Díaz, Junot. "MFA v. POC." *The New Yorker*, April 30, 2014. Accessed April 22, 2015. http://www.newyorker.com/online/blogs/books/2014/04/mfa-vs-poc.html.

Díaz, Junot. "Monstro." *The New Yorker*, June 2012. Accessed April 22, 2015. http://www .newyorker.com/fiction/features/2012/06/04/120604fi_fiction_diaz.

Díaz, Junot. *Negocios*. Translated by Eduardo Lago. New York: Vintage Books, 1997.

Díaz, Junot. "New York: Science Fiction." In *Empire City: New York through the Centuries*, edited by David S. Dunbar and Kenneth T. Jackson, 962–64. New York: Columbia University Press, 2002.

Díaz, Junot. "One Year: Storyteller-in-Chief." *The New Yorker*, January 20, 2010. Accessed April 22, 2015. http://www.newyorker.com/online/blogs/newdesk/2010/01/one-year -storyteller-in-chief.html.

Díaz, Junot. "Q&A." Penguin. Accessed April 22, 2015. http://www.penguin.com/author /junot-diaz/1000039301.

Díaz, Junot. *This Is How You Lose Her*. New York: Riverhead, 2012.

Díaz, Junot. "This Week in Fiction: Junot Díaz." *The New Yorker*, July 2012. Accessed April 22, 2015. http://www.newyorker.com/online/blogs/2012/07/this-week-in-fiction -junot-diaz-1.html.

Digital Humanities at the University of Iowa. "Iowa Literaria." n.d. Accessed March 26, 2013. http://dsph.uiowa.edu/dhatiowa/node/56.

Di Iorio, Lyn. *Killing Spanish: Literary Essays on Ambivalent U.S. Latino/a Identity*. New York: Palgrave Macmillan, 2004, 2009.

Di Iorio, Lyn. "The Latino Scapegoat: Knowledge through Death in Short Stories by Joyce Carol Oates and Junot Díaz." In *U.S. Latino/a Literary Criticism*, edited by Lyn Di Iorio Sandín and Richard Perez, 15–33. New York: Palgrave Macmillan, 2007.

Dinshaw, Carolyn, Lee Edelman, Roderick Ferguson, Carla Freccero, Elizabeth Freeman, Judith Halberstam, Annamarie Jagose, Christopher Nealon, and Nguyen Tan Hoang. "Theorizing Queer Temporalities: A Roundtable Discussion." *GLQ* 13, nos. 2–3 (2007): 2–3.

DiTrapano, Giancarlo. "A Brief History of Junot Díaz." *Playboy Magazine*, September 2013, 100–102 and 130.

Dorfman, Ariel. "9/11: The Day Everything Changed, in Chile." *New York Times*, September 7, 2013.

Duany, Jorge. *Blurred Borders: Transnational Migration between the Hispanic Caribbean and the United States*. Chapel Hill: University of North Carolina Press, 2011.

Duany, Jorge. "Reconstructing Racial Identity: Ethnicity, Color, and Class among Dominicans in the United States and Puerto Rico." *Latin American Perspectives* 25, no. 3 (1998): 147–72.

Duany, Jorge. "Transnational Migration from the Dominican Republic: The Cultural Redefinition of Racial Identity." *Caribbean Studies* 29, no. 2 (1996): 253–82.

Eillis, Pearl Idelia. *Americanization through Homemaking.* Los Angeles: Wetzel, 1929.

Eliot, T. S. *Selected Essays.* New York: Harcourt, Brace, and World, 1950.

English, James F. *The Economy of Prestige: Prizes, Awards, and the Circulation of Cultural Value.* Cambridge, MA: Harvard University Press, 2005.

Erickson, Kai. "Notes on Trauma and Community." In *Trauma: Explorations in Memory,* edited by Cathy Caruth, 183–99. Baltimore: Johns Hopkins University Press, 1995.

Esdaille, Milca. "Same Trip, Different Ships." *Black Issues Book Review* 3, no. 2 (March/April 2001): paragraph 7. Accessed via Academic Search Premier.

Fanon, Frantz. *Black Skin, White Masks.* 1952. Translated by Richard Philcox. New York: Grove, 2008.

Fanon, Frantz. *Les damnés de la terre.* Paris: Editions La Decouverte, 2002.

Fanon, Frantz. *Peau noire, masques blancs.* Paris: Éditions du Seuil, 1971.

Ferguson, Roderick A. *Aberrations in Black: Toward a Queer of Color Critique.* Minneapolis: University of Minnesota Press, 2003.

Fernández Retamar, Roberto. *Caliban and Other Essays.* Translated by Edward Baker. Minneapolis: University of Minnesota Press, 1989.

Fiol-Matta, Licia. "Pop Latinidad: Puerto Ricans in the Latin Explosion, 1999." *Centro Journal* 14, no. 1 (spring 2002): 26–51.

Flood, Alison. "Junot Díaz Wins World's Richest Story Prize." *Guardian,* March 22, 2013.

Flores, Juan. *The Diaspora Strikes Back: Caribeño Tales of Learning and Turning.* New York: Routledge, 2009.

Flores, Juan. *From Bomba to Hip-Hop: Puerto Rican Culture and Latino Identity.* New York: Columbia University Press, 2000.

Flores, Juan. "Nueva York, Diaspora City." In *Bilingual Games,* edited by Doris Sommer, 69–77. Cambridge, MA: Harvard University Press, 2003.

Flores, Juan. "Pan-Latino/Trans-Latino: Puerto Ricans in the 'New Nueva York.'" In *From Bomba to Hip Hop: Puerto Rican Culture and Latino Identity,* 141–65. New York: Columbia University Press, 2000.

Flores-Rodíguez, Daynalí. "Addressing the Fukú in the US: Junot Díaz and the New Novel of Dictatorship." *Antípodas: A Journal of Hispanic and Galician Studies* 20 (2009): 91–106.

Fluck, Winfried. "Fiction and Justice." *New Literary History* 34, no. 1 (2003): 19–42.

Fluck, Winfried. "The Role of the Reader and the Changing Functions of Literature: Reception Aesthetics, Literary Anthropology, Funktionsgeschichte." *European Journal of English Studies* 6, no. 3 (2002): 253–71.

Fluck, Winfried. "The Search for Distance: Negation and Negativity in Wolfgang Iser's Literary Theory." *New Literary History* 31, no. 1 (2000): 175–210.

Foucault, Michel. *The History of Sexuality, Volume 1: An Introduction.* Translated by Robert Hurley. New York: Vintage, 1980.

Foucault, Michel. *The Order of Things: An Archaeology of the Human Sciences.* New York: Pantheon, 1971.

Franco, Jean. *The Modern Culture of Latin America: Society and the Artist*. New York: Penguin, 1970.

Fredrickson, George M. *White Supremacy: A Comparative Study in American and South African History*. Oxford: Oxford University Press, 1987.

Freeman, Elizabeth. *Time Binds: Queer Temporalities, Queer Histories*. Durham, NC: Duke University Press, 2010.

Fregoso, Rosa Linda. "Familia Matters." In *MeXicana Encounters: The Making of Social Identities on the Borderlands*. Berkeley: University of California Press, 2003.

Freud, Sigmund. "Humour." Translated by Joan Riviere. *International Journal of Psychoanalysis* 9, no. 1 (1927): 1–6. Accessed April 22, 2015. http://www.scribd.com/doc /34515345/Sigmund-Freud-Humor-1927.

Freud, Sigmund. *Jokes and Their Relation to the Unconscious*. 1905. Translated by James Strachey. New York: W. W. Norton, 1990.

Freud, Sigmund. *Three Case Histories: The "Wolf Man," the "Rat Man," and the Psychotic Doctor Schreber*. New York: Collier Books, 1963.

Frydman, Jason. "Violence, Masculinity, and Upward Mobility in the Dominican Diaspora: Junot Díaz, the Media, and *Drown*." In *Bloom's Modern Critical Views: Hispanic American Writers*, edited by Harold Bloom, 133–44. New York: Infobase, 2009.

Fuguet, Alberto, and Sergio Gómez. "Presentación del país McOndo." In *McOndo*, edited by Alberto Fuguet and Sergio Gómez, 9–18. Barcelona: Mondadori, 1996.

García, Juan Carlos. *El dictador en la literatura hispanoamericana*. Chile: Mosquito Comunicaciones, 2000.

García Canclini, Néstor. *Latinoamericanos buscando lugar en este siglo*. Buenos Aires: Editorial Paidós, 2002.

García Márquez, Gabriel. *Cien años de soledad*. Buenos Aires: Editorial Sudamericana, 1967.

Garland Mahler, Anne. "The Writer as Superhero: Fighting the Colonial Curse in Junot Díaz's *The Brief Wondrous Life of Oscar Wao*." *Journal of Latin American Cultural Studies: Travesía* 19, no. 2 (2010): 119–40.

Garland-Thomson, Rosemarie. *Extraordinary Bodies: Figuring Physical Disability in American Culture and Literature*. New York: Columbia University Press, 1997.

Garland-Thomson, Rosemarie. *Staring: How We Look*. Oxford: Oxford University Press, 2009.

Gates, David. "English Lessons." Review of *Drown* by Junot Díaz. *New York Times*, September 29, 1996.

Geek's Guide to the Galaxy. "Junot Díaz Aims to Fulfill His Dream of Publishing Sci-Fi Novel with Monstro." Wired.com. Geek's Guide to the Galaxy, episode 70. October 3, 2012. Accessed April 22, 2015. http://www.wired.com/2012/10/geeks-guide-junot -diaz/.

Gilroy, Paul. *The Black Atlantic: Modernity and Double Consciousness*. Cambridge, MA: Harvard University Press, 1993.

Girard, René. *Deceit, Desire, and the Novel: Self and Other in Literary Structure*. Baltimore: Johns Hopkins University Press, 1976.

Glissant, Édouard. *Les Indes*. Paris: Editions du Seuil, 1965.

Goffman, Erving. *Stigma: Notes on the Management.* Englewood Cliffs, NJ: Prentice-Hall, 1963.

Gómez-Barris, Macarena. *Where Memory Dwells: Culture and State Violence in Chile.* Berkeley: University of California Press, 2009.

González, Aníbal. *Killer Books: Writing, Violence, and Ethics in Modern Spanish American Narrative.* Austin: University of Texas Press, 2001.

González Echevarría, Roberto. *The Voice of the Masters: Writing and Authority in Modern Latin American Literature.* Austin: University of Texas Press, 1985.

Gosztold, Brygida. "A Dominican American Experience of Not Quite Successful Assimilation." In *Crossroads in Literature and Culture: Second Language Learning and Teaching,* edited by Jacek Fabiszak, Ewa Urbaniak-Rybicka, and Bartosaz Wolski, 209–20. Berlin: Springer, 2012.

Greene, Julie. *The Canal Builders: Making America's Empire and the Panama Canal.* New York: Penguin Books, 2009.

Grosfoguel, Ramón, Nelson Maldonado-Torres, and José David Saldívar, eds. *Latino/as in the World-System: Decolonization Struggles in the 21st Century U.S. Empire.* Boulder, CO: Paradigm, 2006.

Gruesz, Kirsten Silva. "Alien Speech, Incorporated: On the Cultural History of Spanish in the US." *American Literary History* 25, no. 1 (spring 2013): 18–32.

Gruesz, Kirsten Silva. "What Was Latino Literature?" PMLA 127, no. 2 (March 2012): 335–41.

Guillén, Nicolás. *Sóngoro Cosongo, motivos de son, West Indies LTD., España: Poema en cuatro angustias y una esperanza.* Buenos Aires: Losada, 1952.

Gutiérrez, Ramon A. "Hispanic Diaspora and Chicano Identity in the United States." *South Atlantic Quarterly* 98, nos. 1–2 (1999): 203–15.

Halberstam, Judith. *In a Queer Time and Place: Transgender Bodies, Subcultural Lives.* New York: New York University Press, 2005.

Hall, Stuart. "Cultural Identity and Diaspora," In *Contemporary Postcolonial Theory: A Reader,* edited by Jonathon Rutherford and Padmini Mongia, 110–21. London: Arnold, 1996.

Hall, Stuart. "Ethnicity: Identity and Difference." *Radical America* 23, no. 4 (1991): 9–20.

Halperin, David. *How to Be Gay.* Cambridge, MA: Belknap Press, 2012.

Hames-García, Michael. *Fugitive Thought: Prison Movements, Race, and the Meaning of Justice.* Minneapolis: University of Minnesota Press, 2004.

Hames-García, Michael. *Identity Complex: Making the Case for Multiplicity.* Minneapolis: University of Minnesota Press, 2011.

Hames-García, Michael. "Which America Is Ours?: Martí's 'Truth' and the Foundations of 'American Literature.'" *Modern Fiction Studies* 49, no. 1 (spring 2003): 19–53.

Hanna, Monica. "'Reassembling the Fragments': Battling Historiographies, Caribbean Discourse, and Nerd Genres in Junot Díaz's *The Brief Wondrous Life of Oscar Wao.*" *Callaloo* 33, no. 2 (2010): 498–520.

Harford Vargas, Jennifer. "Dictating a Zafa: The Power of Narrative Form in Junot Díaz's *The Brief Wondrous Life of Oscar Wao.*" MELUS 39, no. 3 (fall 2014): 8–30.

Harjo, Joy. "I Give You Back." In *She Had Some Horses.* New York: Thunder's Mouth, 1983.

Hartigan, John. "Unpopular Culture: The Case of 'White Trash.'" *Cultural Studies* 11, no. 2 (1997): 316–43.

Hartman, Saidiya V. *Lose Your Mother: A Journey along the Atlantic Slave Route.* New York: Farrar, Straus and Giroux, 2007.

Heredia, Juanita. "The Dominican Diaspora Strikes Back: Cultural Archive and Race in Junot Díaz's *The Brief Wondrous Life of Oscar Wao.*" In *Hispanic Caribbean Literature of Migration: Narratives of Displacement,* edited by Vanessa Pérez Rosario, 207–21. New York: Palgrave Macmillan, 2010.

Hijuelos, Oscar. *The Mambo Kings Play Songs of Love.* New York: Hyperion, 1989.

"Hispanic Students at Cornell University Protest Vandalism of Art Work." *New York Times,* November 20, 1993. Accessed April 22, 2015. http://www.nytimes.com/1993/11/20/nyregion/hispanic-students-at-cornell-u-protest-vandalism-of-artwork.html?emc=eta1.

Hobbes, Thomas. *The Leviathan.* 1651. Buffalo, NY: Broadview Books, 2011.

Holland, Sharon Patricia. *The Erotic Life of Racism.* Durham, NC: Duke University Press, 2012.

Holland, Sharon Patricia. *Raising the Dead: Readings of Death and (Black) Subjectivity.* Durham, NC: Duke University Press, 2000.

hooks, bell. *Feminist Theory: From Margin to Center.* Boston: South End, 1984.

Horyn, Cathy. "Jacqueline Kennedy's Smart Pink Suit, Preserved in Memory and Kept Out of View." *New York Times,* November 14, 2013.

Howard, David John. *Coloring the Nation: Race and Ethnicity in the Dominican Republic.* Oxford: Signal Books, 2001.

Howard, David John. "Development, Racism, and Discrimination in the Dominican Republic." *Development in Practice* 17, no. 6 (2007): 725–38.

Howard, David John. "When Art Remembers: Museum Exhibits as Testimonio Del Trujillato." Special Issue. "Trujillo, Trauma, Testimony: Mario Vargas Llosa, Julia Alvarez, Edwidge Danticat, Junot Díaz and Other Writers on Hispaniola." *Antípodas* 20 (2009): 235–51.

Howe, Irving. "Black Boys and Native Sons." In *A World More Attractive: A View of Modern Literature and Politics.* New York: Horizon, 1963.

Hulme, Peter. *Colonial Encounters: Europe and the Native Caribbean, 1492–1797.* London: Routledge, 1992.

Hurtado, Aida. "Relating to Privilege: Seduction and Rejection in the Subordination of White Women and Women of Color." *Signs: Journal of Women in Culture and Society* 14, no. 4 (1989): 833–55.

"Iowa School to Offer Masters Degree in Creative Writing in Spanish." *Hispanically Speaking News,* November 9, 2011. Accessed April 24, 2012. http://www.hispanicallyspeakingnews.com/notitas-de-noticias/details/iowa-school-to-offer-masters-degree-in-creative-writing-in-spanish/11573.

Irizarry, Ylce. "Making It Home: A New Ethics of Immigration in Dominican Literature." In *Hispanic Caribbean Literature of Migration: Narratives of Displacement,* edited by Vanessa Pérez Rosario, 89–103. New York: Palgrave Macmillan, 2010.

Jackson, Kevin. *Invisible Forms: A Guide to Literary Curiosities.* New York: St. Martin's, 2000.

Jay, Paul. *Global Matters: The Transnational Turn in Literary Studies.* Ithaca, NY: Cornell University Press, 2011.

Jiménez Román, Miriam, and Juan Flores, eds. *The Afro-Latin@ Reader: History and Culture in the United States.* Durham, NC: Duke University Press, 2010.

Joyce, James. *A Portrait of the Artist as a Young Man.* New York: Penguin, 2003.

Kanellos, Nicolás. *Hispanic Immigrant Literature: El Sueño del Retorno.* Austin: University of Texas Press, 2011.

Kant, Immanuel. *Critique of Judgement.* 1790. New York: Cosimo Classics, 2007.

Kant, Immanuel. *Critique of the Power of Judgment.* Translated by Paul Geyer and Eric Mathews. Cambridge: Cambridge University Press, 2000.

Kaufman, Walter, ed. *The Portable Nietzsche.* New York: Penguin, 1959.

Keeling, Kara. *The Witch's Flight: The Cinematic Black Femme and the Image of Common Sense.* Durham, NC: Duke University Press, 2007.

Kelley, Robin D. G. "Nap Time: Historicizing the Afro." *Fashion Theory* 1, no. 4 (1997): 339–52.

Khaldûn, Ibn. *The Muqaddimah: An Introduction to History.* Translated by Franz Rosenthal. Abridged and edited by N. J. Dawood. Princeton, NJ: Princeton University Press, 1967.

Konrad, Walecia. "Going Abroad to Find Affordable Health Care." *New York Times,* March 20, 2009. Accessed April 22, 2015. http://www.nytimes.com/2009/03/21/health /21patient.html?_r=0.

Kunsa, Ashley. "History, Hair, and Reimagining Racial Categories in Junot Díaz's *The Brief Wondrous Life of Oscar Wao.*" *Critique: Studies in Contemporary Fiction* 54, no. 2 (2013): 211–24.

Kurlansky, Mark, Julia Alvarez, Edwidge Danticat, and Junot Díaz. "In the Dominican Republic, Suddenly Stateless." *Los Angeles Times,* November 10, 2013. Accessed April 22, 2015. http://articles.latimes.com/2013/nov/10/opinion/la-oe-kurlansky -haiti-dominican-republic-citizensh-20131110.

Lago, Eduardo. "'EE.UU. tiene pesadillas en español.'" *El País,* May 1, 2008. Accessed April 19, 2012. http://elpais.com/diario/2008/05/01/cultura/1209592801_850215.html.

Lanzendörfer, Tim. "The Marvelous History of the Dominican Republic in Junot Díaz's *The Brief Wondrous Life of Oscar Wao.*" MELUS 38, no. 2 (2013): 127–42.

Laviera, Tato. *La Carreta Made a U-Turn.* 1979. Houston: Arte Público, 1992.

Lee, Li-Young. "The Cleaving." In *The City in Which I Love You,* 77–87. Rochester, NY: BOA Editions, 1990.

Lee, Stan, and Jack Kirby. *Fantastic Four* 1, no. 13 (April 1963).

Levins Morales, Aurora, and Rosario Morales. *Getting Home Alive.* Ithaca, NY: Firebrand Books, 1986.

Lewis, Oscar. *La Vida: A Puerto Rican Family in the Culture of Poverty.* San Juan: Random House, 1966.

Li, Stephanie. *Signifying without Specifying: Racial Discourse in the Age of Obama.* New Brunswick, NJ: Rutgers University Press, 2011.

Lipsitz, George. *The Possessive Investment in Whiteness: How White People Profit from Identity Politics.* Rev. ed. Philadelphia: Temple University Press, 2006.

Llorente, Elizabeth. "John F. Kennedy's Legacy through the Eyes of the First Lady's Top Assistant." Fox News Latino, November 22, 2013.

López-Calvo, Ignacio. God and Trujillo: Literacy and Cultural Representations of the Dominican Dictator. Gainesville: University Press of Florida, 2005.

Lorde, Audre. Sister Outsider. Freedom, CA: Crossing, 1984.

Loss, Jacqueline. "Junot Díaz." In Latino and Latina Writers, vol. 2, edited by Alan West-Duran, 803–16. New York: Scribner, 2004.

Louie, Vivian. Keeping the Immigrant Bargain: The Costs and Rewards of Success in America. New York: Russell Sage Foundation, 2012.

Lugones, Maria. "Heterosexualism and the Modern / Colonial Gender System." Hypatia 22, no. 1 (2007): 186–219.

Lugones, Maria. Pilgrimages/Peregrinajes: Theorizing Coalition against Multiple Oppressions. Lanham, MD: Rowman and Littlefield, 2003.

Lugones, Maria. "Toward a Decolonial Feminism." Hypatia 25, no. 4 (fall 2010): 742–59.

Machado Sáez, Elena. "Dictating Desire, Dictating Diaspora: Junot Díaz's The Brief Wondrous Life of Oscar Wao as Foundational Romance." Contemporary Literature 52, no. 3 (2011): 522–55.

Madureira, Luís. Cannibal Modernities: Postcoloniality and the Avant-Garde in Caribbean and Brazilian Literature. Charlottesville: University of Virginia Press, 2005.

Maldonado Torres, Nelson. Against War: Views from the Underside of Modernity. Durham, NC: Duke University Press, 2008.

Manrique Sabogal, Winston. "El alma hispana del inglés." El País, June 7, 2008. Accessed April 19, 2012. http://elpais.com/diario/2008/06/07/babelia/1212796211_850215.html.

Manzanas-Calvo, Ana María. "Teaching Junot Díaz's 'Aurora.'" Salzburg Seminar 2010: American Literary History in a New Key. Salzburg, Austria, 2010.

Maria Hinojosa: One on One. WGBH, October 6, 2010.

Markus, Hazel Rose, and Shinobu Kitayama. "Culture and the Self: Implications for Cognition, Emotion, Motivation." Psychological Review 98, no. 2 (1991): 224–53.

Markus, Hazel Rose, Shinobu Kitayama, and Rachel J. Heiman. "Culture and 'Basic' Psychological Principles." Social Psychology: Handbook of Basic Principles, edited by Edward Tory Higgins and Arie W. Kruglanski, 857–913. New York: Guilford, 1996.

Markus, Hazel Rose, and Paula M. L. Moya, eds. Doing Race: 21 Essays for the 21st Century. New York: W. W. Norton, 2010.

Martínez, Ernesto Javier. On Making Sense: Queer Race Narratives of Intelligibility. Stanford, CA: Stanford University Press, 2013.

Martinez, Victor. Parrot in the Oven: Mi Vida. New York: Joanna Cotler Books, 1996.

Marx, Karl. "The Eighteenth Brumaire of Louis Bonaparte." In The Marx-Engels Reader, edited by Robert C. Tucker, 594–617. New York: W. W. Norton, 1978.

McClennen, Sophia A. The Dialectics of Exile: Nation, Time, Language, and Space in Hispanic Literatures. West Lafayette, IN: Purdue University Press, 2004.

McDowell, Linda. Gender, Identity and Place. New York: Blackwell, 1999.

McGurl, Mark. The Program Era: Postwar Fiction and the Rise of Creative Writing. Cambridge, MA: Harvard University Press, 2009.

Mckiernan-González, John. *Fevered Measures: Public Health and Race at the Texas-Mexico Border, 1848–1942.* Durham, NC: Duke University Press, 2012.

Méndez, Danny. *Narratives of Migration and Displacement in Dominican Literature.* New York: Routledge, 2012.

Mercer, Kobena. "Black Hair/Style Politics." In *Welcome to the Jungle: New Positions in Black Cultural Studies,* 97–130. New York: Routledge, 1994.

Mermann-Jozwiak, Elizabeth Maria. "Beyond Multiculturalism: Ethnic Studies, Transnationalism, and Junot Díaz's Oscar Wao." *Ariel: A Review of International English Literature* 43, no. 2 (2013): 1–24.

Mignolo, Walter. "Coloniality at Large: The Western Hemisphere in the Colonial Horizon of Modernity." Translated by Michael Ennis. CR: *The New Centennial Review* 1, no. 2 (2003): 19–54.

Mignolo, Walter. *The Darker Side of Western Modernity: Global Futures, Decolonial Options.* Durham, NC: Duke University Press, 2011.

Miller, T. S. "Preternatural Narration and the Lens of Genre Fiction in Junot Díaz's The Brief Wondrous Life of Oscar Wao." *Science Fiction Studies* 38, no. 1 (2011): 92–114.

Mintz, Sidney Wilfred, and Richard Price. *The Birth of African-American Culture: An Anthropological Perspective.* Boston: Beacon, 1992.

Miranda, Katherine. "Junot Díaz, Diaspora and Redemption: Creating Progressive Imaginaries." *Sargasso* 2 (2008–9): 23–39.

Miranda, Marie "Keta." *Homegirls in the Public Sphere.* Austin: University of Texas Press, 2003.

Mitchell, David, and Sharon Snyder. *Narrative Prosthesis: Disability and the Dependencies of Discourse.* Ann Arbor: University of Michigan Press, 2000.

Mitrovic, Ljubiša. "Bourdieu's Criticism of the Neoliberal Philosophy of Development, the Myth of Mondialization and the New Europe." *Philosophy, Sociology and Psychology Review* 4, no. 1 (2005): 37–49.

Mohanty, Chandra Talpade, Ann Russo, and Lourdes Torres, eds. *Third World Women and the Politics of Feminism.* Bloomington: Indiana University Press, 1991.

Moore, Alan. *Watchmen.* Illustrated by Dave Gibbons. New York: DC Comics, 2005.

Moraga, Cherríe L. *Loving in the War Years: Lo que nunca pasó por sus labios.* 2nd ed. Cambridge, MA: South End, 2000.

Moraga, Cherríe, and Gloria Anzaldúa, eds. *This Bridge Called My Back: Writings by Radical Women of Color.* 2nd ed. New York: Kitchen Table/Women of Color Press, 1983.

Morales, Ed. "Junot What?" *Village Voice,* September 10, 1996.

Morales, Ed. *The Latin Beat: The Rhythms and Roots of Latin Music from Bossa Nova to Salsa and Beyond.* New York: Da Capo, 2003.

Moraña, Mabel, Enrique Dussel, and Carlos A. Jáuregui. "Colonialism and Its Replicants." In *Coloniality at Large: Latin America and the Postcolonial Debate,* edited by Mabel Moraña, Enrique Dussel, and Carlos A. Jáuregui, 1–22. Durham, NC: Duke University Press, 2008.

Moreno, Carolina. "Marc Anthony Addresses 'God Bless America' Performance's Racist Remarks after MLB All-Star Game." *Huffington Post,* July 18, 2013. Accessed

April 22, 2015. huffingtonpost.com/2013/07/18/marc-anthony-god-bless-america
_n_3618420.html.

Moreno, Marisel. "'All the Important Things Hide in Plain Sight': A Conversation with Junot Díaz." *Latino Studies* 8, no. 4 (2010): 532–42.

Moreno, Marisel. "Debunking Myths, Destabilizing Identities: A Reading of Junot Díaz's 'How to Date a Browngirl, Blackgirl, Whitegirl, or Halfie.'" *Afro-Hispanic Review* 26, no. 2 (2007): 103–17.

Moretti, Franco. *The Way of the World: The Bildungsroman in European Literature.* London: Verso, 1986.

Moretti, Franco, Sarah Allison, Ryan Heuser, Matthew Jockers, and Michael Witmore. "Quantitative Formalism: An Experiment." *Literary Lab: Pamphlet 1*, Stanford University, January 15, 2011.

Morreall, John, ed. *The Philosophy of Laughter and Humor.* Albany: State University of New York Press, 1987.

Morrison, Toni. *Beloved: A Novel.* New York: Knopf, 1987.

Morrison, Toni. *Song of Solomon.* New York: Knopf, 1977.

Morrison, Toni. *Sula.* 1973. New York: Plume, 1982.

Moya, Paula M. L. "Another Way to Be: Women of Color, Literature, and Myth." In *Doing Race: 21 Essays for the 21st Century*, edited by Hazel Rose Markus and Paula M. L. Moya, 483–508. New York: W. W. Norton, 2010.

Moya, Paula M. L. *Learning from Experience: Minority Identities, Multicultural Struggles.* Berkeley: University of California Press, 2002.

Moya, Paula M. L. "The Search for Decolonial Love, Part I: An Interview with Junot Díaz." *Boston Review*, June 26, 2012. Accessed October 6, 2012. http://www.boston review.net/BR37.4/junot_diaz_paula_moya_drown_race.php.

Moya, Paula M. L. "The Search for Decolonial Love, Part II: An Interview with Junot Díaz." *Boston Review*, June 27, 2012. Accessed October 6, 2012. http://www.boston review.net/BR37.4/junot_diaz_paula_moya_2_oscar_wao_monstro_race.php.

Moya, Paula M. L. "Who We Are and from Where We Speak." *Transmodernity* 1, no. 2 (fall 2011): 79–94.

Moya, Paula M. L. "Why I Am Not Hispanic: An Argument with Jorge Gracia." *Newsletter on Hispanic/Latino Issues in Philosophy* 00, no. 2 (2001): 17 paragraphs. Accessed April 22, 2015. http://www.apa.udel.edu/apa/publications/newsletters/v00n2/his panic/02.asp.

Moya, Paula M. L. "With US or Without Us: The Development of a Latino Public Sphere." *Nepantla: Views from the South* 4, no. 2 (2003): 245–52.

Moya, Paula M. L., and Michael R. Hames-García, eds. *Reclaiming Identity: Realist Theory and the Predicament of Postmodernism.* Berkeley: University of California Press, 2000.

Moya, Paula M. L., and Hazel Markus. "Doing Race: An Introduction." In *Doing Race: 21 Essays for the 21st Century*, edited by Hazel Rose Markus and Paula M. L. Moya, 1–102. New York: W. W. Norton, 2010.

Moya, Paula M. L., and Ramón Saldívar. "Fictions of the Trans-American Imaginary." *Modern Fiction Studies* 49, no. 1 (spring 2003): 1–18.

Moya Pons, Frank. *The Dominican Republic: A National History*. New Rochelle, NY: Hispaniola Books, 1995.

Moyers and Company. "Rewriting the Story of America." American Public Television, December 28, 2012.

Moynihan, Daniel Patrick. *The Negro Family: The Case for National Action*. Washington, DC: Office of Planning and Research, U.S. Department of Labor, 1965.

Muñoz, José Esteban. *Cruising Utopia: The Then and There of Queer Futurity*. New York: New York University Press, 2009.

Muñoz, José Esteban. *Disidentifications: Queers of Color and the Performance of Politics*. Minneapolis: University of Minnesota Press, 1999.

Nabokov, Vladimir. *Pale Fire*. New York: Vintage, 1989.

Negrón-Muntaner, Frances. *Boricua Pop: Puerto Ricans and the Latinization of American Culture*. New York: New York University Press, 2004.

Nelson, Victoria. *The Secret Life of Puppets*. Cambridge, MA: Harvard University Press, 2003.

Ngai, Sianne. *Our Aesthetic Categories: Zany, Cute, Interesting*. Cambridge, MA: Harvard University Press, 2012.

NPR Staff. "Fidelity in Fiction: Junot Díaz Deconstructs a Cheater." NPR Books, September 11, 2012. Accessed October 6, 2012. http://www.npr.org/2012/09/11/160252399/fidelity-in-fiction-junot-diaz-deconstructs-a-cheater.

Nussbaum, Martha. *Poetic Justice: The Literary Imagination and Public Life*. Boston: Beacon, 1995.

Oates, Joyce Carol, ed. *The Oxford Book of American Short Stories*. 2nd ed. New York: Oxford University Press, 2013.

Obejas, Achy. "A Conversation with Junot Díaz." *Review: Literature and Arts of the Americas* 42, no. 1 (2009): 43–47.

Obejas, Achy. "Translating Junot: 'This Is How You Lose Her' by Junot Díaz." *Chicago Tribune*, September 14, 2012. Accessed March 17, 2013. http://articles.chicagotribune.com/2012–09-14/features/ct-prj-0916-book-of-the-month-20120914_1_dominican-republic-oscar-wao-spanglish.

Oboler, Suzanne. *Latinos and Citizenship: The Dilemma of Belonging*. New York: Palgrave Macmillan, 2006.

Okie, Matt. "Mil Máscaras: An Interview with Pulitzer-Winner Junot Díaz (*The Brief Wondrous Life of Oscar Wao*)." *Identity Theory*, 2008. Accessed April 22, 2015. http://www.identitytheory.com/interviews/okie_Díaz.php.

Olesiuk, Sarah. "Taking Over Day Hall." *Cornell Daily Sun*, November 19, 2007. Accessed April 22, 2015. http://cornellsun.com/2629.

O'Rourke, Meghan. "Questions for Junot Díaz: An Interview with the Pulitzer Prize-winning Author." *Slate*, 2008. Accessed April 22, 2015. http://www.slate.com/id/2188494/.

Pacheco, Carlos. *Narrativa de la dictadura y crítica literaria*. Caracas: Fundación Centro de Estudios Latinoamericanos Rómulo Gallegos, 1987.

Paravisini-Gebert, Lizabeth. "Junot Díaz's *Drown* Revisiting 'Those Mean Streets.'" In *US Latino Literature: A Critical Guide for Students and Teachers*, edited by Harold Augenbraum and Margarite Fernández Olmos, 167–73. Westport, CT: Greenwood, 2000.

Parikh, Crystal. *An Ethics of Betrayal: The Politics of Otherness in Emergent U.S. Literatures and Culture.* New York: Fordham University Press, 2009.

Parkes, Nii Ayikwei. "What to Read Now: Migration Narratives." *World Literature Today* 86, no. 4 (2012): 7.

Partridge, Jeffrey F. L. "The Politics of Ethnic Authorship: Li-Young Lee, Emerson, and Whitman at the Banquet Table." *Studies in the Literary Imagination* 37, no. 1 (spring 2004): 103–26.

Patterson, Orlando. *Slavery and Social Death: A Comparative Study.* Cambridge, MA: Harvard University Press, 1982.

Patteson, Richard. "Textual Territory and Narrative Power in Junot Díaz's *The Brief Wondrous Life of Oscar Wao.*" *Ariel: A Review of International English Literature* 42, nos. 3–4 (2012): 5–20.

Pérez, Emma. *The Decolonial Imaginary: Writing Chicanas into History.* Bloomington: Indiana University Press, 1999.

Perez, Richard. "Racial Spills and Disfigured Faces in Piri Thomas's *Down These Mean Streets* and Junot Díaz's 'Ysrael.'" In *Contemporary U.S. Latino/a Literary Criticism*, edited by Lyn Di Iorio Sandín and Richard Perez, 93–112. New York: Palgrave Macmillan, 2007.

Pérez Firmat, Gustavo. *Bilingual Blues.* Tempe, AZ: Bilingual P/Editorial Bilingüe, 1995.

Pérez Firmat, Gustavo, and José David Saldívar, eds. *Toward a Theory of Latino Literature.* Special ed. Dispositio 16, no. 41 (1991).

Pinzón, Dulce. "The Real Story of Superheroes." Accessed April 22, 2015. http://www.dulcepinzon.com/en_projects_superhero.htm.

Plascencia, Salvador. *The People of Paper.* San Francisco: McSweeney's Books, 2005.

Plato. *The Republic.* Translated by Desmond Lee. 2nd ed. New York: Penguin Books, 2003.

Preziuso, Marika. "Mapping the Lived-Imagined Caribbean: Postcolonial Geographies in the Literature of the 'Diasporic' Caribbean." *Journal of Intercultural Studies* 31, no. 2 (2010): 145–60.

Proust, Marcel. *A la recherche du temps perdu.* Paris: Gallimard, 2002.

Quayson, Ato. *Aesthetic Nervousness: Disability and the Crisis of Representation.* New York: Columbia University Press, 2007.

Quijano, Aníbal. "Colonialidad y modernidad/racionalidad." In *Los conquistadores: 1492 y la población indígena de América*, edited by Heraclio Bonilla, 437–47. Bogotá: Tercer Mundo/FLASCO, 1992.

Quijano, Aníbal. "Coloniality of Power, Eurocentrism, and Latin America." *Nepantla: Views from the South* 1, no. 3 (2000): 533–80.

Quijano, Aníbal. "The Coloniality of Power and Eurocentrism in Latin America." *International Sociology* 15, no. 2 (2000): 215–32.

Quijano, Aníbal, and Immanuel Wallerstein. "Americanity as a Concept, or the Americas in the Modern World-System." *International Social Science Journal* 29 (1992): 549–97.

Raboteau, Albert Jordy. "Conversation with Junot Díaz: (To the Woman in the Mountain Cabin)." *Callaloo* 31, no. 3 (2008): 919–22.

Railton, Ben. "Novelist-Narrators of the American Dream: The (Meta-) Realistic Chronicles of Cather, Fitzgerald, Roth, and Díaz." *American Literary Realism* 43, no. 2 (2011): 133–53.

Ramazami, Jahan. "A Transnational Poetics." *American Literary History* 18, no. 2 (2006): 332–59.

Ramírez, Catherine S. *The Woman in the Zoot Suit: Gender, Nationalism, and the Cultural Politics of Memory*. Durham, NC: Duke University Press, 2009.

Ramírez, Sergio. "La nueva novela latinoamericana." *La Insignia*, October 16, 2008. Accessed April 19, 2012. http://www.lainsignia.org/2008/octubre/cul_002.htm.

Ramos, Juanita, ed. *Compañeras: Latina Lesbians*. 1987. New York: Routledge, 1994.

Ramos, Julio. *Divergent Modernities: Culture and Politics in Nineteenth-Century Latin America*. Translated by Jodi Blanco. Durham, NC: Duke University Press, 2001.

Reed, Ishmael. *Mumbo Jumbo*. Garden City, NY: Doubleday, 1972.

Remeseira, Claudio Iván. "Authors Junot Díaz, Francisco Goldman Showcase Radio Program of Human Stories from Latin America." *NBC Latino*, February 4, 2013. Accessed March 16, 2013. http://nbclatino.com/2013/02/04/authors-junot-diaz-francisco -goldman-showcase-a-radio-program-featuring-human-stories-from-latin-america/.

Richard, Nelly, and Alberto Moreiras. *Pensar en/la postdictadura*. Santiago: Editorial Cuarto Propio, 2001.

Riofrio, John. "Situating Latin American Masculinity: Immigration, Empathy and Emasculation in Junot Díaz's *Drown*." *Atenea* 28, no. 1 (June 2008): 23–36.

Rivera, Tomás. *. . . And the Earth Did Not Devour Him*. Houston: Arte Público, 1987.

Robbins, Jill. "Neocolonialism, Neoliberalism, and National Identities: The Spanish Publishing Crisis and the Marketing of Central America." *Istmo* 8 (January–June 2004). Accessed April 22, 2015. http://istmo.denison.edu/n08/articulos/neocolonialism.html.

Roberts, Caroline. "Bostonist Interview: Junot Díaz, Author." *Bostonist*, September 10, 2007. Accessed April 22, 2015. http://bostonist.com/2007/09/10/bostonist_inter_1 .php.

Rodríguez, Ana. *Making Latino News: Race, Language, Class*. Thousand Oaks, CA: Sage, 1999.

Rodríguez, Ana Patricia. *Dividing the Isthmus: Central American Transnational Histories, Literatures, and Cultures*. Austin: University of Texas Press, 2009.

Rodríguez, Ileana. *Women, Guerrillas, and Love: Understanding War in Central America*. Translated by Ileana Rodríguez and Robert Carr. Minneapolis: University of Minnesota Press, 1996.

Rodriguez, Richard T. *Next of Kin: The Family in Chicano/a Cultural Politics*. Durham, NC: Duke University Press, 2009.

Romero, Lora. "Nationalism and Internationalism: Domestic Differences in a Postcolonial World." *American Literature: A Journal of Literary History, Criticism, and Bibliography* 67, no. 4 (1995): 795–800.

Rosenthal, Elisabeth. "The Growing Popularity of Having Surgery Overseas." *New York Times*, August 6, 2013.

Roth, Benita. *Separate Roads to Feminism: Black, Chicana, and White Feminist Movements in America's Second Wave*. New York: Cambridge University Press, 2004.

Sáez, Elena Machado. "Dictating Desire, Dictating Diaspora: Junot Díaz's *The Brief Wondrous Life of Oscar Wao* as Foundational Romance." *Contemporary Literature* 53, no 2 (2011): 522–55.

Said, Edward W. *Reflections on Exile and Other Essays*. Cambridge, MA: Harvard University Press, 2000.

Saldaña-Portillo, María Josefina. *The Revolutionary Imagination in the Americas and the Age of Development*. Durham, NC: Duke University Press, 2003.

Saldívar, José David. "Conjectures on 'Americanity' and Junot Díaz's 'Fukú Americanus' in *The Brief Wondrous Life of Oscar Wao*." *Global South* 5, no. 1 (2011): 120–36.

Saldívar, José David. *Trans-Americanity: Subaltern Modernities, Global Coloniality, and the Cultures of Greater Mexico*. Durham, NC: Duke University Press, 2012.

Saldívar, Ramón. "Historical Fantasy, Speculative Realism, and Postrace Aesthetics in Contemporary American Fiction." *American Literary History* 23, no. 3 (2011): 574–99.

Sánchez, Marta E. "La Malinche at the Intersection: Race and Gender in *Down These Mean Streets*." *PMLA* 113, no. 1 (January 1998): 117–29.

Sandoval, Chela. *Methodology of the Oppressed*. Minneapolis: University of Minnesota Press, 2000.

San Juan, E., Jr. "The Poverty of Postcolonialism." *Pretexts: Literary and Cultural Studies* 11, no. 1 (2002): 57–74.

Santiago, Roberto. Review of *Drown*, by Junot Díaz. *Hispanic* 9, no. 12 (1996): 70.

Sarlo, Beatriz. *Jorge Luis Borges: A Writer on the Edge*. London: Verso, 1993.

Sawyer, Mark. "Racial Politics in Multiethnic America: Black and Latina/o Identities and Coalitions." In *Neither Enemies nor Friends: Latino/as, Blacks, Afro Latinos*, edited by Anani Dzidzienyo and Suzanne Oboler, 265–79. New York: Palgrave, 2005.

Schiller, Friedrich. *On the Aesthetic Education of Man*. New York: Dover, 2004.

Schindler, Max. "Students Gather, Recount Latino Day Hall Takeover." *Cornell Daily Sun*, November 23, 2010.

Schopenhauer, Arthur. *The World as Will and Idea*. 1818. Vol. 2. Translated by E. F. J. Payne. Mineola, NY: Dover, 1966.

Scott, A. O. "Dreaming in Spanglish." Review of *The Brief Wondrous Life of Oscar Wao*, by Junot Díaz. *New York Times*, September 30, 2007. Accessed April 22, 2015. http://www.nytimes.com/2007/09/30/books/review/Scott-t.html.

Scott, James C. *Domination and the Arts of Resistance: Hidden Transcripts*. New Haven, CT: Yale University Press, 1990.

Sears, David O., and Donald R. Kinder. "Racial Tensions and Voting in Los Angeles." In *Los Angeles: Viability and Prospects for Metropolitan Leadership*, edited by Werner Z. Hirsch. New York: Praeger, 1971.

Sedgwick, Eve Kosofsky. *The Epistemology of the Closet*. Berkeley: University of California Press, 1990.

Shakespeare, William. *The Tempest*. New York: Signet Classics, 1998.

Sheffer, Gabriel, ed. Introduction to *Modern Diasporas in International Politics*, 1–15. London: Croom Helm, 1986.

Siebers, Tobin. *Disability Aesthetics*. Ann Arbor: University of Michigan Press, 2010.

Silko, Leslie. *Ceremony*. New York: Viking, 1977.

Smith, Barbara, ed. *Home Girls: A Black Feminist Anthology*. New York: Kitchen Table/ Women of Color, 1983.

Smiths, The. *The Queen Is Dead*. 1986. Warner Bros/Wea, B00000oL9J, 1990. Compact disc.

Socolovsky, Maya. *Troubling Nationhood in U.S. Latina Literature: Explorations of Place and Belonging*. New Brunswick, NJ: Rutgers University Press, 2013.

Sollors, Werner. *Beyond Ethnicity: Consent and Descent in American Culture*. New York: Oxford University Press, 1986.

Sparrow, Thomas. "La dominicana que conoció los secretos de los Kennedy." BBC Mundo, November 22, 2013.

Spivak, Gayatri Chakravorty. *An Aesthetic Education in the Era of Globalization*. Cambridge, MA: Harvard University Press, 2012.

Stallings, L. H. "Eulogy for Black Women's Studies." In *Feminist Solidarity at the Crossroads*, edited by Kim Vaz and Gary Lemons, 132–48. New York: Routledge, 2013.

Stallings, L. H. *Mutha' Is Half a Word: Intersections of Folklore, Vernacular, Myth, and Queerness in Black Female Culture*. Columbus: Ohio State University Press, 2007.

Steele, Claude M. "Not Just a Test." *The Nation* 278, no. 17 (2004): 38–40.

Stern, Daniel. "One Who Got Away." Review of *Down These Mean Streets*, by Piri Thomas. *New York Times Book Review*, May 21, 1967.

Stewart, Barbara. "Outsider with a Voice." *New York Times*, December 8, 1996.

Stoler, Ann Laura, ed. *Haunted by Empire: Geographies of Intimacy in North American History*. Durham, NC: Duke University Press, 2006.

Stringer, Dorothy. "Passing and the State in Junot Díaz's 'Drown.'" MELUS: Multi-Ethnic Literature of the United States 38, no. 2 (2013): 111–26.

Sweet, James H. *Domingos Álvares, African Healing, and the Intellectual History of the Atlantic World*. Chapel Hill: University of North Carolina Press, 2011.

Taylor, Diana. *Disappearing Acts: Spectacles of Gender and Nationalism in Argentina's "Dirty War."* Durham, NC: Duke University Press, 1997.

Thomas, Brook. "The Fictive and the Imaginary: Charting Literary Anthropology, or, What's Literature Have to Do with It?" *American Literary History* 20, no. 3 (2008): 622–31.

Thomas, Piri. *Down These Mean Streets*. 1967. New York: Vintage Books, 1997.

Tolkien, J. R. R. *The Fellowship of the Ring: Being the First Part of The Lord of the Rings*. New York: Houghton Mifflin, 1954.

Tolkien, J. R. R. *The Return of the King: Being the Third Part of The Lord of the Rings*. New York: Houghton Mifflin, 1954.

Tolkien, J. R. R. *The Two Towers: Being the Second Part of Lord of the Rings*. New York: Houghton Mifflin, 1954.

Torres-Saillant, Silvio. *Diasporic Disquisitions: Dominicanists, Transnationalism, and the Community.* Dominican Studies Working Papers 1. New York: CUNY Dominican Studies Institute/City College of New York, 2000.

Torres-Saillant, Silvio. *An Intellectual History of the Caribbean.* New York: Palgrave Macmillan, 2006.

Torres-Saillant, Silvio. "The Tribulations of Blackness: Stages in Dominican Racial Identity." *Latin American Perspectives* 25, no. 3 (1998): 126–46.

Torres-Saillant, Silvio, and Ramona Hernandez. "Dominicans: Community, Culture, and Collective Identity." In *One out of Three: Immigrant New York in the Twenty-First Century,* edited by Nancy Foner, 223–45. New York: Columbia University Press, 2013.

Valdes-Rodriguez, Alisa. *The Dirty Girls Social Club.* New York: St. Martin's, 2003.

Vasconcelos, José. *The Cosmic Race/La raza cósmica.* Los Angeles: Centro de Publicaciones, Dept. of Chicano Studies, California State University, Los Angeles, 1979.

Veeser, Cyrus. "Inventing Dollar Diplomacy: The Gilded-Age Origins of the Roosevelt Corollary to the Monroe Doctrine." *Diplomatic History* 27, no. 3 (2003): 301–26.

Viramontes, Helena Maria. *Under the Feet of Jesus.* New York: Dutton, 1995.

Volpi, Jorge. *El insomnio de Bolívar: Cuatro consideraciones intempestivas sobre América Latina en el siglo XXI.* Mexico City: Debate, 2009.

Walcott, Derek. *Omeros.* New York: Farrar, Straus and Giroux, 1990.

"Weddings: Gustavo Paredes, Elizabeth Alexander." *New York Times,* September 19, 1993.

Weintraub, Joanne. "Tina Brown's New Yorker." *AJR,* April 1995. Accessed March 20, 2013. http://www.ajr.org/article.asp?id=1692.

Whitmore, Richard. *Why Boys Fail: Saving Our Sons from an Educational System That's Leaving Them Behind.* New York: AMACON, 2010.

Wilde, Oscar. *De Profundis.* New York: Dover, 2011.

Wilentz, Amy. "A Zombie Is a Slave Forever." *New York Times,* October 30, 2012. Accessed April 22, 2015. http://www.nytimes.com/2012/10/31/opinion/a-zombie-is-a-slave -forever.html.

Williams, Raymond. *Marxism and Literature.* New York: Oxford University Press, 1977.

Williams, Raymond Leslie. *The Twentieth-Century Spanish American Novel.* Austin: University of Texas Press, 2003.

Williams, William Carlos. "To Elsie." In *Collected Poems, Volume 1: 1909–1939,* edited by Walton Litz and Christopher MacGowan, 217–19. New York: New Directions, 1991.

Williamson, Edwin. *Borges: A Life.* New York: Viking, 2004.

Woloch, Alex. *The One vs. The Many: Minor Characters and the Space of the Protagonist in the Novel.* Princeton, NJ: Princeton University Press, 2003.

Wong, Nellie. "When I Was Growing Up." In *This Bridge Called My Back: Writings by Radical Women of Color,* edited by Cherríe Moraga and Gloria Anzaldúa, 7–8. 2nd ed. New York: Kitchen Table/Women of Color Press, 1983.

Wong, Nellie, Merle Woo, and Mitsuye Yamada. *3 Asian American Writers Speak Out on Feminism.* San Francisco: SF Radical Women, 1979.

Woo, Merle. "Letter to Ma." In *This Bridge Called My Back: Writings by Radical Women of Color*, edited by Cherríe Moraga and Gloria Anzaldúa, 140–47. 2nd ed. New York: Kitchen Table/Women of Color Press, 1983.

Wood, James. "Call It Sleep." *The New Republic*, December 16, 1996, 39–42.

World Bank. "Haiti." Accessed September 2013. data.worldbank.org/country/Haiti.

Wray, Matt. *Not Quite White: White Trash and the Boundaries of Whiteness*. Durham, NC: Duke University Press, 2006.

Wray, Matt, and Annalee Newitz. *White Trash: Race and Class in America*. New York: Routledge, 1997.

Wucker, Michelle. *Why the Cocks Fight: Dominicans, Haitians, and the Struggle for Hispaniola*. New York: Macmillan, 2000.

Yamada, Mitsuye. "Invisibility Is an Unnatural Disaster: Reflections of an Asian American Woman." *Bridge: An Asian American Perspective* 7, no. 1 (1979): 11–13.

Zentella, Ana Celia. "'Dime con quién hablas, y te dire quién eres': Linguistic (In)security and Latina/o Unity." In *A Companion to Latina/o Studies*, edited by Juan Flores and Renato Rosaldo, 25–38. Malden, MA: Blackwell, 2007.

Contributors

Glenda R. Carpio is professor of African and African American studies and English at Harvard University. Her research focuses on African American cultural production, history, and culture of New World Slavery, and Anglophone Caribbean literatures. She is the author of *Laughing Fit to Kill: Black Humor in the Fictions of Slavery* (2008) and the coeditor of *African American Literary Studies: New Texts, New Approaches, New Challenges* (2011) with Werner Sollors. Her work has appeared in journals including *American Literature*, PMLA, and *American Literary History*. She is currently working on a book on recent immigrant fiction in American culture.

Arlene Dávila is professor of Anthropology and Social and Cultural Analysis at New York University. Her research focuses on urban and ethnic studies, the political economy of culture, and media and consumption studies. She is the author of *Culture Works: Space, Value, and Mobility across the Neoliberal Americas* (2012); *Latino Spin: Public Image and the Whitewashing of Race* (2008); *Barrio Dreams: Puerto Ricans, Latinos, and the Neoliberal City* (2004); *Latinos, Inc.: Marketing and the Making of a People* (2001); and *Sponsored Identities: Cultural Politics in Puerto Rico* (1997); as well as the coeditor of *Mambo Montage: The Latinization of New York* (2001).

Lyn Di Iorio is professor of English at the City College of New York and the Graduate Center of the City University of New York. Her short novel,

Outside the Bones, won ForeWord Review's 2011 Silver Book of the Year Award, was Best Debut Novel on the 2011 Latinidad List, and a finalist for the 2012 John Gardner Fiction Prize, among others. She was also #2 on LatinoStories.com's 2012 Top Ten Latino Authors to Watch (and Read) list. Her most recent short fiction appeared in *Review: Literature and Arts of the Americas: The Americas in New York* (2014). She is currently on the shortlist for the 2015 William Faulkner–William Wisdom Novel-in-Progress award. She is also the author of *Killing Spanish: Literary Essays on Ambivalent U.S. Latino/a Identity* (2004), and coeditor of *Contemporary U.S. Latino/a Literary Criticism* (2007) and *Moments of Magical Realism in U.S. Ethnic Literatures* (2012). She is currently at work on a full-length novel, *The Sound of Falling Darkness*, an excerpt of which was a runner-up for the 2011 Pirate's Alley Faulkner Society Novel-in-Progress Award. She received her bachelor's degree from Harvard University, her master's from Stanford University's Creative Writing Program, where she was a Patricia Harris fellow, and her PhD from the University of California, Berkeley.

Junot Díaz is professor of Writing at MIT. He is the author of *This Is How You Lose Her* (2012), *The Brief Wondrous Life of Oscar Wao* (2007), *Drown* (1997), and a number of short stories and articles. His fiction has appeared in the *New Yorker*, the *Paris Review*, *African Voices*, *The Best American Short Stories*, *Pushcart Prize XXII*, and the *O'Henry Prize Stories*. *The Brief Wondrous Life of Oscar Wao* won numerous awards, including the Pulitzer Prize for Fiction and the National Book Critics Circle Award, and *This Is How You Lose Her* was a finalist for the National Book Award. Among many awards and fellowships, he has received a MacArthur "Genius" grant, a Guggenheim fellowship, a PEN/Malamud Award, a Creative Artist Fellowship from the National Endowment for the Arts, and a fellowship at the Radcliffe Institute for Advanced Study at Harvard University. He is also currently the fiction editor at *The Boston Review*.

Monica Hanna is an assistant professor of Chicana and Chicano studies at California State University, Fullerton. She holds a PhD in comparative literature from the Graduate Center of the City University of New York. Her research focuses on literatures of the Americas, genres including historical fiction and literary journalism, and nationalisms. Her work has appeared in *Callaloo*, *Metamorphoses*, *Label Me Latina/o*, and *Latina/o Literature in the Classroom: 21st Century Approaches to Teaching*.

Jennifer Harford Vargas is an assistant professor of English at Bryn Mawr College. Her research interests include Latino/a cultural production, hemispheric American studies, theories of the novel, and *testimonio* forms in the Americas. She is currently completing a book manuscript tentatively titled *Forms of Dictatorship: Power, Narrative, and Authoritarianism in the Latina/o Novel*. Her work has appeared in MELUS; *Callaloo; Colonialism, Modernity, and the Study of Literature: A View from India*; and *Latina/o Literature in the Classroom: 21st Century Approaches to Teaching*.

Ylce Irizarry is an associate professor of English at the University of South Florida. Her research is centered on U.S. Latino/a and Chicano/a narrative, Hispanic transnational cultural production, Caribbean historical fiction, testimonio, and visual rhetorics. She is the author of *Chicano/a and Latino/a Fiction: The New Memory of Latinidad* (2016). Her research has appeared in journals including *Centro, Antípodas, Contemporary Literature, Comparative American Studies*, and *Literature, Interpretation, and Theory*.

Claudia Milian is an associate professor in the Department of Romance Studies and Director of the Program in Latino/a Studies in the Global South at Duke University. Her research interests include citizenship, climate change and environmental degradation, southern studies, twentieth-century Latin American, Latino/a, and African American literature. She is the author of *Latining America: Black-Brown Passages and the Coloring of Latino/a Studies* (2013) and the coeditor of two special journal issues: the fall 2012 edition of *The Global South* on "Interoceanic Diasporas and The Panama Canal's Centennial" and the summer 2013 volume of *Latino Studies* on "U.S. Central Americans: Representations, Agency, and Communities."

Julie Avril Minich is assistant professor of English and Mexican American and Latina/o Studies at the University of Texas, Austin. Her research interests include Chicano/a and Latino/a cultural studies, feminist theory, queer theory, and disability studies. She is the author of *Accessible Citizenships: Disability, Nation, and the Cultural Politics of Greater Mexico* (2014). Her articles have appeared in *Modern Fiction Studies*, MELUS, *Comparative Literature, Arizona Journal of Hispanic Cultural Studies*, and *Journal of Literary and Cultural Disability Studies*.

Paula M. L. Moya is professor of English at Stanford University. Her research focuses on narrative and narrative theory, race and ethnicity, feminist theory, multicultural pedagogy, and Latino/a and Chicano/a as well as decolonial literature and identity. She is the author of *The Social Imperative: Race, Close Reading, and Contemporary Literary Criticism* (2015) and *Learning from Experience: Minority Identities, Multicultural Struggles* (2002). She is the coeditor of *Doing Race: 21 Essays for the 21st Century* (2010), *Identity Politics Reconsidered* (2006), and *Reclaiming Identity: Realist Theory and the Predicament of Postmodernism* (2000).

Sarah Quesada is a PhD candidate in the Department of Iberian and Latin American Cultures at Stanford University and an ACLS Mellon Fellow. Her research interests focus on the African Diaspora in Caribbean and Latino/a literature. Her articles and interviews have appeared in *Afro-Hispanic Review*, *The Journal of Haitian Studies*, *Latin American and Caribbean Ethnic Studies* (LACES), and *Postcolonial Text*.

José David Saldívar is professor of comparative literature and director of the Center for Comparative Studies in Race and Ethnicity at Stanford University. His research focuses on late postcontemporary culture, especially the literatures of the trans-American hemisphere, and of border narratives and poetics from the sixteenth century to the present. He is the author of *Trans-Americanity: Subaltern Modernities, Global Coloniality, and the Cultures of Greater Mexico* (2012), *Border Matters: Remapping American Cultural Studies* (1997), *The Dialectics of Our America: Genealogy, Cultural Critique, and Literary History* (1991); coeditor (with Héctor Calderón) of *Criticism in the Borderlands* (1991); and editor of *The Rolando Hinojosa Reader* (1985). He is currently working on a new book project provisionally entitled "Junot Díaz: The Early Wondrous Years."

Ramón Saldívar is the Hoagland Family Professor in Humanities and Sciences and professor of English and comparative literature at Stanford University. His research centers on cultural studies, literary theory, modernism, Chicano narrative, and comparative American studies. He is the author of *The Borderlands of Culture: Américo Paredes and the Transnational Imaginary* (2006), *Chicano Narrative: The Dialectics of Difference* (1990), and *Figural Language in the Novel: The Flowers of Speech from Cervantes to Joyce* (1984). In 2011, he was awarded the National Humanities Medal by President Barack Obama. He is currently working on a new project, tentatively titled "The Racial Imaginary: Speculative Realism and Historical Fantasy in Contemporary American Fiction."

Silvio Torres-Saillant is professor of English at Syracuse University, where he has headed the Latino-Latin American Studies Program, held the William P. Tolley Distinguished Teaching Professor in the Humanities, and directed the Humanities Council. His research centers on the racial regimes spawned by the colonial transaction, intellectual history, Latino discourse, ethnic American literatures, and comparative poetics. He has authored *Caribbean Poetics* (1997; 2nd ed. 2013), *El tigueraje intelectual* (2002; 2nd ed. 2011), *Introduction to Dominican Blackness* (1999; 2nd ed. 2010), *An Intellectual History of the Caribbean* (2006), *Diasporic Disquisitions: Dominicanists, Transnationalism, and the Community* (2000), and *El retorno de las yolas: Ensayos sobre diaspora, democracia y dominicanidad* (1999), in addition to coauthoring *The Once and Future Muse: The Poetry and Poetics of Rhina P. Espaillat* (forthcoming) with literary scholar Nancy Kang and *The Dominican-Americans* (1998) with sociologist Ramona Hernandez. He has coedited *The Challenges of Higher Education in the Hispanic Caribbean* (2004), *Desde la orilla: Hacia una nacionalidad sin desalojos* (2004), and *Recovering the U.S. Hispanic Literary Heritage*, vol. 4 (2002). He is currently completing "The Advent of Blackness," a study that seeks to tell the story of how we became racial beings.

Deborah R. Vargas is associate professor in the Department of Ethnic Studies at the University of California, Riverside. Her areas of research and teaching expertise include Chicano and Latino cultural studies, critical race feminisms, queer of color critique, feminist ethnography, borderlands theory, and oral histories. She is the author of *Dissonant Divas in Chicana Music: The Limits of La Onda* (2012), and her publications have appeared in *Feminist Studies*, *Women and Performance: A Journal of Feminist Theory*, *Aztlán: A Journal of Chicano Studies*, and the edited collection *Latina/o Sexualities: Probing Powers, Passions, Practices, and Policies*.

Index

Fanon, Frantz, 49–51, 54–56, 343

fantasy, as influence, 4, 13–15, 24, 42, 122–24, 127–30, 271–72; in *Brief Wondrous Life of Oscar Wao*, 267

feminism, 232, 343–44. *See also* women of color theory and feminism

"Fiesta, 1980" (short story, Díaz), 52, 132. *See also Drown*

"Flaca" (short story, Díaz), 365–66. *See also This Is How You Lose Her*

footnotes, in novels of Díaz, 24, 93–94, 124–25, 187–88, 202, 209, 214–18, 260

Foucault, Michel, 311

Freedom University, 5, 11

Freud, Sigmund, 72, 75, 79, 82, 340; "Humour" essay of, 81–82

fukú (Dominican magic spell), 7, 73–76, 189, 203–4, 207, 271–73

García Márquez, Gabriel, 304–6

Garland-Thomson, Rosemarie, 49–50, 54–55

Gates, David, 134

gender: nonnormative, 345, 352–53, 357–58, 361, 371

Glissant, Édouard, 187

global Latino literary modes, 175

Global South and North, 57, 186; disability and, 52

grimoires, 126, 379–80

Guillén, Nicolás, 293

hair texture, 118, 244–47

Haiti, 34, 269, 314; Díaz on Haitian earthquake, 201, 293. *See also* "Monstro"

Hall, Stuart, 150–51

Hames-García, Michael, 10

Hanna, Monica, 138

healing: writing as, 91, 235

Hernandez, Jaime, 26

heteronormativity, 155–56, 325, 327, 331–32, 343

Hispanic, as term, 257–58

homophobia, 157, 330

homosexuality, 155–61

"How to Date a Browngirl, Blackgirl, Whitegirl, or Halfie" (short story, Díaz), 23, 134, 232; Dominican internalized racism in, 162–63; immigration and, 151–52; racialized gender and sexuality in, 241–45, 247–48. *See also Drown*; race and racism

humanity, recognition of, 62–63, 131, 326

humor, 69, 269–70, 272, 283, 387; Abelard and Dominican history and, 377–78; in *Brief Wondrous Life of Oscar Wao*, 138; in "Monstro," 292. *See also* laughter

"Humour" (essay, Freud), 81–82

immigration literature, 116–17, 148–51; Dominican immigration and, 151–60; familial separation in, 161–62

In Praise of Love (Badiou), 341

"Invierno" (short story, Díaz), 367–68. *See also This Is How You Lose Her*

"Junot Díaz: A Symposium" at Stanford University, 13, 15–16; conversation between Junot Díaz and Paula Moya at, 391–401

Kennedy curse, 125

Kieve Address at Stanford University, 15, 240

King, Stephen, 2, 41, 122, 138

künstlerroman (artist's novel), 20, 89–90, 100–101

La Casa Azul Bookstore, 38

language, 2–3, 23, 141, 272–73, 278, 284–85; Afro-Latino vernaculars, 3, 265–66; in *Brief Wondrous Life of Oscar Wao*, 126, 189–90; in *Drown*, 133–34, 265–67; linguistic statelessness and,